1966

CAMBRIDGE EDITION

Under the General Editorship of

Gordon N. Ray

THE COMPLETE

POETICAL WORKS OF

John

Milton

EDITED BY

Douglas Bush

HARVARD UNIVERSITY

HOUGHTON MIFFLIN COMPANY · BOSTON

To the Memory of

ARTHUR WOODHOUSE

PREFACE

This volume contains all of Milton's poetry, English, Latin, Greek, and Italian, including scraps of verse in the prose works which he did not include in his collected editions. The poems are printed in chronological order, so far as that is known; sometimes only guesses are possible. All translations of the Latin, Greek, and Italian verse are by the editor.

Since the present edition is designed for readers, not scholars, the text is modernized in spelling and sufficiently in punctuation to facilitate understanding. *Paradise Regained* and *Samson Agonistes* had only one edition (1671) in Milton's lifetime. The text of the minor poems is based on both the first and the second editions (1645, 1673); that of *Paradise Lost* on the second (1674), with some corrections from the first (1667). Some of Milton's preferred forms are retained: e.g., he usually has "highth" for "height." No editor can make a text of *Paradise Lost* that certainly embodies the poet's intention in all particulars because, along with some apparent errors uncaught or added, there are too many inconsistencies both in and between the first two editions. Thus in his normal concern for the decasyllabic line and the avoiding of a supernumerary syllable he commonly elided the "e" of "the" before a vowel, but often he — or the printer — did not; "heaven" and "evening" are commonly spelled as a monosyllable and disyllable respectively, but there are many exceptions; and so on. Since Milton had both to compose and to read proof with the aid of amanuenses, we often cannot be sure whether such inconsistencies are accidental or deliberate; it seems safer to take them as they stand in the early editions than to iron them all out by turning Milton's general practices into inflexible rules. Some textual variants and emendations are recorded (in modernized form) in the notes. Milton's supposed system of emphatic spelling ("wee" for "we," etc.), even if the evidence for it were much stronger than it is, would obviously not affect a modernized text. The meter is usually a guide to the pronunciation of words whose accent has shifted in modern English, but in this edition the stress, in a number of possibly puzzling words, is indicated by an acute accent (´). When a final "ed" has a syllabic value not now current, it is given a grave accent (`).

If a one-volume edition is not to become unwieldy, apparatus must be largely limited to bare bones. It is therefore impossible — however ungracious such silence is — to cite innumerable books and articles, especially of course the annotated editions, that have contributed ideas and information to introductions and notes. For the same reason the notes can hardly begin to suggest the

wide-ranging knowledge available to Milton's imagination, and such samples
as are given, chiefly from the Bible and the Latin and Greek classics, must
normally be confined to references without quotation. References to Spenser,
Shakespeare, and other English writers are a much smaller sampling; whether
or not Milton echoed them, such items are reminders of his native inheritance
(the few quotations are usually modernized). Explanatory notes and comments are also kept close to a minimum and do not in general try to anticipate
a reader's perceptions and reactions, though sometimes this rule is broken
for what seem good reasons. Notes on the Latin and Italian poems are numbered according to the lines of the original texts but are attached to the corresponding words and phrases of the English versions. Recurrent words and
allusions are normally omitted in the notes and assembled in the Glossary
(which does not include seventeenth-century meanings that are still alive).
In his English as well as his Latin poems Milton, like other Renaissance poets,
commonly used the Roman names of Greek mythological figures, and this
practice is commonly followed in the notes and Glossary. No bibliography is
given of modern editions and scholarly and critical writings because the Miltonic library is so huge, because bibliographies go so rapidly out of date, and
because there are full or selected lists in many books and annual lists in current bibliographies.

I am obliged to the Viking Press for permission to make use of translations
of several of the Latin poems included in my *Portable Milton;* to Dr. Herbert
Davis of Oxford for looking up some variant readings in early editions of
Horace; and for grants of money from the Harvard Foundation for Advanced
Study and Research. I am very grateful also to Dr. Henry Thoma and Miss
Eleanor Wiles of Houghton Mifflin Company for their interest and editorial
skill and care.

D.B.

CONTENTS

LIST OF PLATES

(*between pages xvi–xvii*)

PLATE I. MILTON AT THE AGE OF 10, 1618

Oil painting by an unknown artist (formerly attributed to Cornelius Johnson or Janssen). Now in The Pierpont Morgan Library, New York.

PLATE II. MILTON AT THE AGE OF 20–21, 1629

Acquired in 1961 by the National Portrait Gallery, London. After cleaning, it appeared to be probably the "Onslow portrait," which was once owned by Arthur Onslow (1691–1768), Speaker of the House of Commons, but disappeared after being sold at auction in 1827.

PLATE III. MILTON AT THE AGE OF 36–37

Frontispiece engraved by William Marshall for Milton's *Poems*, 1645. For Milton's opinion of the likeness see *In Effigiei Eius Sculptorem*, page 172 below.

PLATE IV. MILTON AT ABOUT 52

A clay bust, 11 inches high, probably done by Edward Pierce about 1660. In Christ's College, Cambridge. (Photograph, courtesy of the National Portrait Gallery, London)

PLATE V. MILTON AT THE AGE OF 62

Frontispiece engraved from life by William Faithorne for Milton's *History of Britain*, 1670. The most widely familiar portrait. (Courtesy of the National Portrait Gallery, London)

PLATE VI.   THE PRINCETON PORTRAIT, DONE ABOUT 1670

A crayon drawing, 10⅝ × 8⅛ inches, attributed to William Faithorne; acquired in 1959 by the Princeton University Library. For its history and authentication see *The Portrait of John Milton at Princeton and its place in Milton Iconography* by John Rupert Martin (Princeton: Princeton University Library, 1961).

Information about many portraits is given by Martin. For fuller accounts and references see J. Milton French, *Life Records of John Milton*, 5 vols. (New Brunswick: Rutgers University Press, 1949–58), and, on Plate II, David Piper, *Catalogue of Seventeenth-Century Portraits in the National Portrait Gallery 1625–1714* (Cambridge: At the University Press, 1963).

INTRODUCTION*

Milton was born on December 9, 1608, in London — the London in which Shakespeare was still living and writing — at his father's house (and place of business) in Bread Street, Cheapside. The poet's grandfather, an Oxfordshire yeoman, had held out as a Roman Catholic recusant and was said to have disinherited his son John for turning Protestant. This son, John Milton senior, went to London and became a prosperous scrivener (or notary and conveyancer) and money-lender. Thus the poet may be said to have inherited a strain of religious nonconformity. His father was also a composer, not one of the brightest galaxy of that great age of English music, but talented enough to be a contributor to Thomas Morley's famous anthology, *The Triumphs of Oriana* (1601) and Thomas Ravenscroft's *Whole Book of Psalms* (1621). The boy grew up in an atmosphere of music as well as piety, and music was to be the theme of many glowing allusions in his verse and prose and one of his resources through the years of blindness.

Some time between 1615 and 1620 Milton entered St. Paul's School, which John Colet had founded a century earlier. Its head, Alexander Gill, was one of the notable schoolmasters in England, a classical scholar like all his tribe, but also the author of a book on the English language and of an exposition of liberal theology. His son and namesake, a teacher in the school and a Latin poet, became a literary friend of Milton's. A much closer friendship formed at St. Paul's was with an Italian physician's son, Charles Diodati, to whom Milton addressed his first and sixth Elegies (1626, 1629) and whose early death he lamented in the *Epitaphium Damonis* (1639–40). Milton seems to have found St. Paul's highly congenial, and in his free time he was an ardent reader. From the age of twelve, he said in the *Second Defence* (1654), he hardly ever went to bed before midnight; such assiduous reading, much of it by candle-light of course, had its effect on naturally weak eyes (inherited from his mother, not his father, who read without spectacles in his old age). Because of his intellectual zeal the boy's school work was supplemented by tutoring at home, partly in the classics, partly, it would appear, in such other things as modern languages. One of his tutors was Thomas Young, to whom he later addressed Elegy 4 and letters in prose. While at school Milton began to write verse; we have several certain items and others that may date from his schooldays.

Milton went into residence at Christ's College, Cambridge, for the spring term of 1625, and from 1626 onward we have much fuller knowledge of his

---

* Since individual poems are discussed in headnotes, this introduction is limited to biography, with some account of the prose works.

mind, personality, and poetic development, thanks to his output of mainly Latin verse, his seven Prolusions (Latin speeches on assigned topics delivered before a college or university audience), and some private letters. In his first Latin Elegy, written from London in the spring of 1626 to Diodati, Milton spoke briefly of having been rusticated or suspended because of a clash with his college tutor; but this episode was apparently not held against him, since he graduated in the usual time (B.A., March 26, 1629). He remained three years longer at Cambridge, enjoying no doubt the relative freedom allowed candidates for the M.A.; he received that degree on July 3, 1632. Along with much Latin verse, through which he had learned much of his craft, Milton had, soon after his twenty-first birthday, written his first great English poem, *On the Morning of Christ's Nativity* (Christmas, 1629). *L'Allegro* and *Il Penseroso* belong probably to his last long vacation, the summer of 1631. Milton's scholarly ardor and literary tastes had early marked him out, in his elders' eyes and his own, for the church, but during his Cambridge years — we do not know just when — the idea of a clerical career, if not wholly rejected, at least grew dim. The reason he later gave was his antagonism toward Anglican prelacy; we may assume also a mounting conviction that he was committed to poetry. In that age there were of course many poets among the clergy, and some good ones, like George Herbert, but they were far from sharing Milton's nonconformity.

Whatever uneasiness the generous but prudent father felt about his son's not taking up a gainful profession (witness *Ad Patrem*, written perhaps in 1631–32), he evidently acquiesced in Milton's spending nearly six years, from July, 1632, until the spring of 1638, in private reading at home. (In 1632 the family were living, it seems, in suburban Hammersmith; in or about 1635 they moved to a country estate at Horton, not far from Windsor.) Milton pursued a voluntary course of humane study in literature, history, religious and philosophic thought, the kind of nourishment Cambridge had not provided; and, he says, he made occasional visits to London to get books in mathematics and music. It was in these years that he laid the foundation of his liberal thinking. His Latin and English verse would not have told a reader much about his view of the worlds of thought and affairs, but in his seventh Prolusion (1631–32?) the traditional ideals of Renaissance humanism were kindled into flame by an individual vision, Christian, Platonic, and Baconian, of a new era to be created by the godlike mind of man. If Milton saw himself as one of those creative spirits, he was very humble in the sonnet "How soon hath Time," written probably on his twenty-fourth birthday, December 9, 1632, when he had for half a year been in studious seclusion at home; whatever the uncertainties of his future, he will live "As ever in my great Task-Master's eye." This was the most direct of Milton's early dedications of his talents to God's service (the *Nativity* and Elegy 6 had been indirect); if he could not be a priest, he could be a poet-priest.

Of the two chief poetic products of these years, the first, the masque we know under the eighteenth-century title *Comus*, was performed on September 29, 1634, at Ludlow Castle in Shropshire, as part of the inaugural festivities

PLATE I. *Milton at the age of 10, 1618*

PLATE II. *Milton at the age of 20–21, 1629*

PLATE III. *Milton at the age of 36–37*

PLATE IV. *Milton at about 52*

Gul. Faithorne ad Vivum.   Delin. et sculpsit.

Joannis Miltoni Effigies Ætat: 62.
1670.

PLATE V. *Milton at the age of 62*

PLATE VI. *The Princeton portrait, done about 1670*

in honor of the Earl of Bridgewater, Lord President of Wales. Milton had been introduced to the aristocratic world through the miniature masque *Arcades*, which celebrated the Earl's stepmother and had presumably been commissioned by Henry Lawes, the court musician and musical tutor to the Egerton family. *Comus* was a larger commission. Lawes directed it, composed the music, acted the role of Thyrsis, and in 1637 published the text. Milton must have consented to publication, though he withheld his name; a Virgilian epigraph implied a perfectionist's reluctance to appear in public. If the masque was on one level the most elaborate display of the young Milton's courtly, pastoral, and lyrical art, on another it was a private expression of his Christian-Platonic idealism, a first and relatively serene version of the theme of temptation, the conflict between good and evil. So far Milton's English poems, however notable for artistry, might be called songs of innocence. *Lycidas*, written in November, 1637, was a first and reverberating song of experience, a deeply troubled effort to reconcile the apparent wrongness of things with faith in God's providence. While almost wholly impersonal, *Lycidas* owed something of its theme and tone to its coming at the end of five years of arduous and outwardly unprofitable toil, the period that had begun with a poem of less acute anxiety and less difficult resolution, the sonnet "How soon hath Time."

Milton's mother had died in April, 1637. In the spring of 1638 he was able to fulfill his desire for foreign travel, and set off, with a servant, for Italy. He had a letter of advice from the ex-ambassador, Sir Henry Wotton, now Provost of Eton, and was furnished with letters of introduction by the English ambassador in Paris. There he met Hugo Grotius, the diplomat and jurist (and author of Latin verse which Milton had probably read). Nearly all of his fifteen months abroad were spent in Italy, and chiefly in Florence, Rome, and Naples; he was always strongly attached to the country's language and literature, and he had written, perhaps about 1630, a group of love-poems in Italian. The *Epitaphium Damonis,* letters to Italian friends, and the sketch of his travels in the *Second Defence* (1654) show how much it meant to him to see Italy and especially to associate with its literary men (most of whom are now remembered only because they met him). Although Milton had written a number of more or less great poems, some of them were unpublished, *Comus* had been anonymous, and *Lycidas*, by "J. M.," was almost lost in an unattractive Cambridge anthology. Thus he was unknown at home outside a small circle, and Italian acceptance of him as a poet must have happily confirmed his choice of a vocation. And he enjoyed cultivated social life. While his dislike of Catholicism was not altogether quiescent — and somewhat disturbed his Neapolitan host, the elderly Marquis of Villa, to whom he addressed *Mansus,* one of his best Latin poems — the young Protestant could relax enough to like his Italian acquaintances, to celebrate the famous singer, Leonora Baroni, in extravagant religious terms, and to partake of the musical hospitality of Cardinal Barberini. The one great man he saw in Italy was Galileo, whose situation he recalled in *Areopagitica* and whose observations he referred to in

Paradise Lost. News of growing political and religious friction in England led Milton to give up the idea of visiting Sicily and Greece, although, as he says in his candid account, he spent some months longer in saying farewell to Italy. He got back to England in July or August, 1639.

While in Italy Milton had learned of the death, in August, 1638, of his one close friend, Charles Diodati, but it was not until he was at home, among the scenes of their companionship, that he felt able to write the elaborate pastoral elegy, *Epitaphium Damonis.*

Milton was now faced with the need of making a livelihood. He rented a house in London and began to take in pupils, first of all the sons of his sister Anne, Edward and John Phillips. But the private schoolmaster was the young man who had refused to take orders and who in *Lycidas* had put into St. Peter's mouth a strident attack on the hireling shepherds of the church, and if he had one eye on his young charges, he had the other on public affairs. In *Mansus* and *Epitaphium Damonis* he had told of his plans for an Arthurian epic (an heroic poem was the serious Renaissance poet's goal), and around 1640 he set down nearly a hundred subjects for dramas from biblical and British history (he may have made a similar list of epic subjects). But now his religious and humanistic sense of civic responsibility compelled Milton to put aside poetic ambition and devote himself to the cause of liberty. He did not know when he began that the crusade would cost him his twenty best years and his eyesight as well, but, even if he had known, he could not have failed to heed the sound of God's trumpet.

Milton's first five pamphlets of 1641–42 were his share in the general agitation against prelacy being led by a group of Presbyterian divines whose initials formed the collective name "Smectymnuus" (the "ty" was Milton's old tutor, Thomas Young). His first pamphlet, *Of Reformation in England* (1641), included all the aims and principles that had animated Puritanism since it began in the 1560's. The Church of England, as established at the commencement of Elizabeth's reign (after several official changes of faith during the previous generation), was a deliberate compromise. It retained the traditional hierarchy and the traditional liturgy (now in the English of the *Book of Common Prayer*), while the Articles embodied Protestant doctrine. Those members of both the clergy and the laity who were soon called Puritans — some of them with Genevan experience and inspiration — had a vision of the apostolic simplicity of the primitive church; they abhorred the Anglican compromise and were determined to complete the Reformation by abolishing all vestiges of Romanism. Until well on in the seventeenth century there was no doctrinal split, since both the church and Puritans inside or outside the church were Calvinistic.

Thus Milton attacks traditionalism, formalism, worldliness, and all things prelatical, and exalts the religion of the spirit that makes every man his own interpreter of the Bible. Also, at this stage in his thinking he is a good monarchist, and, whereas King James had summed up Stuart policy in the phrase "No bishop, no king," Milton sees prelacy as a danger to monarchy. (We may remember that the alliance of church and crown solidified the alliance between Puritanism and the champions of parliamentary rights.) Milton rejoices that England, in the person of Wycliffe, had been the standard-bearer of the European Reformation; and he ends with a magnificent prayer for its fulfilment before the second coming of the "shortly expected King." The last paragraph consigns the bishops to the lowest depths of hell.

Of these five tracts the most important are this first one and the more sober fourth, *The Reason of Church Government* (1642), but the personal passage in the latter is of special value in regard to Milton the poet. Taking his non-literary readers into his confidence, with a very Miltonic naiveté, he explains why he must postpone the heroic poem he has in mind, and sets forth with very Miltonic fervor the Renaissance conception of poetry as the teacher of religion and virtue. The personal passage in *An Apology for Smectymnuus* (1642) is the best introduction to *Comus* and other early poetry.* Replying to controversial opponents' charges of immorality, Milton tells of his ideal of chastity and of reading that nourished it, of his moving upward from the delightful but sensual art of Ovid and his fellows to the Christian idealism of Dante and Petrarch, to romances of chivalry, to "the divine volumes of Plato" and Platonic love of the Good, and, above all these, the teachings of Christianity.

About the end of May, 1642, Milton married. The seventeen-year-old bride, Mary Powell, was the daughter of an Oxfordshire squire who was in debt to the poet's father; she came from a large, easy-going, quite unintellectual family to live with a deeply committed scholar, writer, and teacher of 33, and anyone but Milton could have predicted the result. After a few weeks she went back to her family for a visit and declined repeatedly to return to her husband. The Civil War, which had begun on August 22, was at first going in the king's favor and — as Edward Phillips said later — Mary's royalist family may have repented of the match. As for the personal rift, we can readily imagine faults on both sides. We can imagine also the many-sided shock marital failure was for a man who had dedicated himself to God's service, who had led an exemplary life, had approached marriage with high expectations and prayers, and now discovered that he had made an irreparable mistake, one that poisoned life at the root.

In August, 1643, Milton published *The Doctrine and Discipline of Divorce* (enlarged early in 1644). His main thesis was that adultery, the canonical ground for divorce, is a less heinous cause than mental incompatibility, that an enforced union without mutual love and companionship is a continuous torment and a barbarous crime against human dignity. Milton's plea grew out of a high ideal of marriage, but it was as a libertine that he now gained his first fame or notoriety; he was publicly attacked by his former Presbyterian allies as well as others. While the note of personal anguish is intermittently heard in the tract, experience adds emotion to abstract principle. Milton was treating a subject he had thought about before, as his Commonplace Book shows, a subject which had been discussed by Reformation divines. His second tract,

---

* Both passages are printed at the end of this introduction.

The Judgment of Martin Bucer concerning Divorce (August, 1644), was indeed a summary and paraphrase from the work of one famous divine whose views, Milton had found, anticipated his own. His third and fourth tracts, *Tetrachordon* and *Colasterion*, were published in March, 1645. It was in the former that he made the much-quoted declaration that "no ordinance, human or from heaven, can bind against the good of man."

The tracts on divorce, or the first and third of them, mark a stage in the general growth of Milton's liberalism. In wrestling, as he was bound to do, with biblical passages on the subject, he took up an idea touched in the *Reason of Church Government* and moved further toward what was to be his grand principle of "Christian liberty." In brief, this Pauline doctrine, stressed by Luther and Calvin and developed by their successors, in its extreme form involved the abrogation of the whole Mosaic law (except those parts sanctioned by universal "right reason"), and set up instead the self-governing freedom of the individual regenerate Christian. Thus "Christian liberty," the superseding of the covenant of works by the covenant of grace, could be revolutionary, even anarchical, in freeing individual man from all outward allegiance and authority.

In 1644 appeared the two Miltonic tracts most generally familiar nowadays, the short *Of Education* (June) and *Areopagitica* (November). The former, written at the request of Samuel Hartlib, could not have been altogether pleasing to that follower of Comenius, since Milton, while emphasizing all branches of science, kept in the center the classical and liberal tradition of Renaissance humanism. Reacting strongly against the scholastic logic that still dominated university curricula, he proposed academies that would cover both secondary and preprofessional university education, and a program inspired by ancient examples, his memories of St. Paul's, and his own practice in teaching. The tract has its place in his general campaign for liberty; and some of his remarks illuminate his poetic theory — his stress on "decorum" (that is, harmony among all the elements of a composition) and on poetry as "more simple, sensuous, and passionate" than logic and rhetoric. Most important of all, perhaps, in regard to his late major poems is the idea of man's fall and recovery in the first of his two definitions of education (the religious one, which is much less often quoted than the secular):

> The end then of learning is to repair the ruins of our first parents by regaining to know God aright, and out of that knowledge to love him, to imitate him, to be like him, as we may the nearest by possessing our souls of true virtue, which, being united to the heavenly grace of faith, makes up the highest perfection.

Traditional censorship of the press had broken down with the Long Parliament's abolition of the Star Chamber in 1641, and among the flood of unlicensed pamphlets were all of Milton's except *Of Education*. But censorship was revived by parliamentary ordinance in 1643. *Areopagitica* was not a plea for complete freedom of speech; as a liberal of the seventeenth century,

Milton did not object to censorship after publication, if books were found to be subversive of Protestantism and morality. But he brought all the eloquence of a scholar and poet (and satirical raciness also) to the denunciation of censorship before publication; that meant the strangling of all free inquiry, the maintenance of starched conformity. Nowhere does Milton display more invincible confidence in the English mind and character, in the success of the Revolution, and in the power of truth to prevail against error. In this fallen world man must face both good and evil, he must have the freedom to choose. Everyone knows the most beautiful and most Miltonic sentence in all his prose: "I cannot praise a fugitive and cloistered virtue, unexercised and unbreathed, that never sallies out and sees her adversary, but slinks out of the race where that immortal garland is to be run for, not without dust and heat." *Areopagitica,* now the best-known of the countless pamphlets of its age, and one of the classic possessions of the free world, had in its own time almost no discernible effect. One reason was that during 1644–45 the main theme of pamphlet controversy was what had become the first full-scale debate on religious toleration: the English (and Scottish) Presbyterians wanted rigid Presbyterian uniformity; for the emerging Independents toleration was a necessity for survival. Milton only glanced at this debate, in a plea for mutual charity, but he showed throughout his disillusionment with the Presbyterians whose ally he had been in 1641–42. Now, Presbyterian tyranny is no better than episcopal; as he said in a sonnet, "New Presbyter is but old Priest writ large."

Perhaps in 1644–45 Milton, who never lacked the courage of his convictions (and who in his *De Doctrina Christiana* found biblical sanction for polygamy), began to pay court to a Miss Davis, but she, according to Edward Phillips, was "averse . . . to this motion." Possibly rumors of this, along with the Powells' financial reverses caused by the war, moved them to action. Friends of both Milton and his wife arranged to have her surprise him in London, and reconciliation followed; how fully successful the renewed marriage was we do not know. At any rate Milton took into his house for about a year a troop of Powells, whose talkative presence was torture to a writer in need of quiet. Four children were born to the Miltons: Anne (July, 1646), who was crippled and had an impediment in speech; Mary (October, 1648); John (March, 1651), who died in infancy; and Deborah, whose birth in May, 1652, was followed in a few days by the death of her mother.

In January, 1646, Milton's *Poems,* containing almost all that he had done in English, Latin, Greek, and Italian, were published (dated 1645, Old Style); in a laudatory preface Humphrey Moseley, the most literary of publishers, linked the new poet with Spenser. In the later 1640's Milton was working chiefly on a history of Britain. On January 30, 1649, King Charles was executed. Two weeks later appeared Milton's first political tract, *The Tenure of Kings and Magistrates,* which he had written with the aim of reconciling the public mind to the event. His main thesis, buttressed with many authorities, was that sovereign power resides always with the people, who may recall it and depose or even execute a monarch if he abuses his trust. This view of "the social contract" was the opposite of that set forth in *Leviathan* (1651) by the absolutist Hobbes, who argued that the people surrender all their rights and may not resist established sovereignty.

In March Milton was invited to become Secretary for Foreign Tongues to Cromwell's Council of State. Though he would be reluctant to leave his private studies, he would welcome the opportunity to be on the inside of political action. The post gave Milton no voice in the making of policy; his work was to translate diplomatic documents into Latin and also to defend the new Commonwealth government against royalist attacks. The first assignment of the latter kind was beyond even Milton's powers — an answer to *Eikon Basilike*, perhaps the most effective piece of propaganda ever issued in England. This book, put together by Dr. John Gauden from King Charles's papers and with his help, had been published at the time of the King's execution, and the picture of the royal saint and martyr made a deep impression on all who were shocked by the manner of his trial and of his death. Milton's *Eikonoklastes* (October, 1649), with its recital of the King's double-dealing, could not push back the wave of emotion.

His next opponent was the French Claudius Salmasius, perhaps the chief classical scholar in Europe, who was employed by the exiled Charles II to attack the English regicides. Milton's long *Pro Populo Anglicano Defensio* (February, 1651), written in Latin since it was addressed to learned Europe, demolished Salmasius' historical arguments and pilloried Salmasius himself in such ignominious roles as that of hen-pecked husband. Milton's controversial manner, here and sometimes elsewhere, is not what we like to associate with him, but in a sacred cause no holds were barred; and in all the Christian centuries up through Milton's, churchmen as well as laymen could be violent. The consciousness of having routed the great Salmasius remained for Milton a source of patriotic and personal pride.

Since about 1644 Milton's sight had been weakening and by 1650 he had almost lost the use of one eye; he was warned of the probable result of continued labor on the *Defensio*, but he persevered. His blindness became complete in the winter of 1651–52, when he was only 43 and the great poem had not yet been written. The best-known of his sonnets must surely have recorded his first reactions to a blow that it needed all his religious fortitude to bear. Milton was necessarily relieved of some of his secretarial duties, but he carried on others up to 1659.

Another royalist attack evoked the *Defensio Secunda* (May, 1654), which, with all its drubbing of the supposed author, Alexander More, was a nobler testimony than the first to Milton's much-tried but unconquerable faith in the achievements of the Revolution and the Commonwealth. Yet the resolute republican, even while praising Cromwell, warned him against the dangers of autocracy. Cromwell died on September 3, 1658, the anniversary of his victories of Dunbar and Worcester, and at the state funeral in November Milton walked as one of a humble group of secretaries — Andrew Marvell, Samuel Hartlib, and young John Dryden — more important than the bigwigs.

Early in that year Milton had suffered a deep personal loss. In November, 1656 he had married Katherine Woodcock, who gave birth to a child a year later and died, some weeks before the child, in February, 1658. She was commemorated in Milton's last sonnet, a tender and poignant expression of devoted love. During the years of prose and public affairs, 1642–58, Milton composed seventeen occasional sonnets: three of them satirical, the others addressed mainly to Commonwealth leaders or to personal friends. The latter sonnets are both dignified and genial and, biographically, go along with other evidence to show Milton's capacity for friendship with old and young.

About 1657–58 Milton began to compose *Paradise Lost* and during 1658–60 he finished the large Latin treatise *De Doctrina Christiana*. The latter he regarded as his richest possession; he evidently hoped that it might provide a basis for Protestant unity, though it did not reach print until 1825. Milton had read commentators, but he grounded his body of doctrine, including his heresies, strictly on what he found in the Bible. The work is a very useful theological gloss on *Paradise Lost*. The most important thing in it is Milton's repudiation of the grim Calvinistic doctrine of election and reprobation in favor of the liberal Arminian view and his own central principle of Christian liberty; he had regarded himself as a Calvinist at least as late as 1644–45. In *A Treatise of Civil Power in Ecclesiastical Causes* (February, 1659) he pleaded again for freedom of conscience.

Milton's last major pamphlet, *The Ready and Easy Way to Establish a Free Commonwealth*, gave proof of both principle and reckless courage. From mid-February of 1660 onward the Restoration was more and more clearly in sight, but Milton's tract — the chief of several anti-monarchical protests he made at this time — appeared in February and in an enlarged edition in April. Charles II made his triumphal entry into London on May 29. The tract, though it proposed a new republican constitution, was really a cry of despair. The republican idealist, who in *Areopagitica* had seen a noble and puissant nation renewing her mighty youth, can hardly believe that his countrymen have become a nation of slaves eager to run their heads under the yoke, "choosing them a captain back for Egypt."

Abuse of Milton reached its peak in 1660, and the author of *Eikonoklastes*, the two *Defences*, and the *Ready and Easy Way* was in real danger from the punitive measures of the new government. Some Commonwealth leaders escaped abroad, some were imprisoned, some executed (Sir Henry Vane, Milton's friend, not until 1662). On January 30, 1661, the anniversary of Charles I's execution, the exhumed bodies of Cromwell, Henry Ireton, and John Bradshaw were dragged to Tyburn and decapitated, and their heads were stuck on poles outside Westminster Hall. Milton's friends concealed him during the summer of 1660, so that the proclamation for his arrest could not be carried out. But his offending books were burned and in parliament his name was proposed for exclusion from the list of men to be pardoned. However, friends, certainly Marvell (now an M.P.) and presumably others of greater influence, worked on his behalf, and he was not excluded from the Act of Pardon

(August 29). But, perhaps through a misunderstanding somewhere, he was arrested and held in custody until December 17. It was clearly at some time after the Restoration that Milton composed the great lines in the invocation to book 7 of *Paradise Lost:*

> Standing on earth, not rapt above the pole,
> More safe I sing with mortal voice, unchanged
> To hoarse or mute, though fall'n on evil days,
> On evil days though fall'n, and evil tongues;
> In darkness, and with dangers compassed round,
> And solitude. . . .

The body of prose that constitutes four fifths of Milton's works had been his main occupation during the years 1641–60. Two pieces are widely known, half a dozen others (and parts of the *Christian Doctrine*) are read in college courses, and the rest are left to specialists. If in its own day Milton's prose had little visible influence on the public mind and none on the course of events (his fame as a spokesman for liberty began to grow at the time of the Revolution of 1689), it remains important for several reasons. Milton himself saw prose as the work of his left hand, and a sacrifice of poetry, yet it came to be in his mind a reassuring substitute for the unwritten heroic poem. Then the prose works are a many-sided contemporary interpretation of the Puritan Revolution, and Milton has his place in histories of political thought. As a revelation of his experience in the public arena, of his development into a political and religious radical, of his hopes and visions and disillusionments and final defeat, the prose is the indispensable prelude to the themes of his last three poetical works, to his stress upon individual regeneration and fortitude and faith in God's grace and providence. Finally, Milton's always individual eloquence gives him a high rank in an age of masters. While it has been said that the most disciplined of English poets wrote the most undisciplined prose, a closer look suggests that prolonged exercise of the arts of persuasion contributed much to the tough fibre, the cumulative periods, the forceful compression of syntax, the mingled elevation and "prosaic" plainness of diction, the variety and vitality of "unpoetical" as well as "poetical" images, that mark the later poetry. Such qualities had begun to appear in the sonnets, especially the public ones.

Along with his share of the paternal inheritance — Milton had an older sister and a younger brother, the lawyer (and royalist) Christopher — he had as Secretary received a salary of £288, which in 1655 was reduced to £200. But heavy losses of savings at the time of the Restoration necessitated frugality; at his death Milton left somewhat less than £1000. In 1663 he married a young Elizabeth Minshull, a niece of one of his friends. Except in the short time of his second marriage his three daughters had been without a mother since May, 1652. The payment of readers and amanuenses was doubtless, after 1660, an item in the budget; friends and friends' children, callers, and nephews were happy to serve on occasion, but they could not replace regular help.

Milton's teaching his two younger daughters to read languages they did not understand caused friction — we do not know the precise facts about their services — and all three were sent out, presumably at some expense, to learn the arts of embroidery. Deborah at least looked back on her father with strong affection. She and other persons testified to Milton's lively and agreeable (and often satirical) conversation.

Milton told one caller that his blindness would be tolerable if it were not for the pains of gout (arthritis), which would grow more and more acute as the disease progressed. But, says John Aubrey, "he would be cheerful even in his gout fits and sing." A small household organ was one consolation. Milton's day began at 4:30, when a man came to read aloud from the Hebrew Bible; there followed meditation, composition, more reading, walking in the garden (he always had a garden where he lived, says Aubrey), and talking with friends and visitors. These last were both a pleasure and a plague. Most of them, especially the foreigners, came to see the conqueror of Salmasius, but in his last years others came as admirers of *Paradise Lost*. One was Dryden, who asked Milton's leave to turn the epic into a rhymed opera; Milton's consent is not the smallest evidence of his magnanimity. The day ended at 9, with a glass of water and a pipe. Much composition of poetry was done at night, in bed. On Sundays reading was wholly religious (Milton did not attend any church); he considered the Psalms the greatest poetry in the world.

Milton's later years were busily productive, in spite of all his handicaps. *Paradise Lost* was finished by 1665, published in 1667, and somewhat revised for the second edition of 1674. A second and enlarged edition of the early *Poems* appeared in 1673. *Paradise Regained* and *Samson Agonistes,* published together in 1671 or 1670, had presumably been composed some time in the preceding decade. There were a number of miscellaneous works in prose which remind us that Milton was still a Renaissance humanist. The *History of Britain,* which had been interrupted by his Secretaryship and which he found himself unable to complete, was published as a large fragment in 1670. Textbooks of grammar and logic appeared in 1669 and 1672; a collection of familiar letters and the Cambridge Prolusions in 1674; a *Brief History of Moscovia,* written before he became blind, in 1682. Apart from the publication of books, the chief event of Milton's later life was his moving with his family to Chalfont St. Giles in Buckinghamshire during the Great Plague of 1665–66; the small house, now a shrine, is the only one of his dozen places of residence that still stands. Resettled in London, the Miltons witnessed the Great Fire of September, 1666, which destroyed the old family house in Bread Street, Milton's only property other than his last residence in Bunhill Fields.

Milton died on or about November 9, 1674, a month before he would have reached 66. He was buried with his father in the Church of St. Giles, Cripplegate; burial of the anti-monarchist in Westminster Abbey would hardly have been considered by the authorities. The funeral, says a contemporary, was attended by both high and low.

The fame of the libertarian and the poet continued to grow, as multiplying editions and eulogies make plain; and the writing of five biographies within twenty-five years of Milton's death was remarkable recognition of a private citizen and author. In 1695 Patrick Hume edited *Paradise Lost* with the kind of annotation hitherto reserved for the Latin and Greek poets. *Paradise Lost* was well established as a great classic before its status was confirmed in different ways by Addison's eighteen papers in *The Spectator* (1712) and Pope's parodying of Milton along with Homer and Virgil. Eighteenth-century poets paid Milton the heavy tribute of more or less uninspired imitation; but some editors and commentators had more knowledge and insight than many of their successors. The poets and critics of the romantic age established two views of Milton — that is, of *Paradise Lost* — which have persisted up into the twentieth century. From Blake and Shelley came the notion that Milton was the great rebel against authority whose Satan was a projection of his real self. Others, recoiling from the ideas or supposed ideas of the grim Puritan, listened only to the organ-voice of the artist. Some modern anti-Miltonists went on to attack Milton the artist as well. About 1917 American scholarship began to re-create a true image of the Christian humanist, the thinker, and the poet, and in recent years books on *Paradise Lost* — not to mention countless articles on it and other works — have been appearing at a quite unprecedented rate. Such sophisticated criticism, philosophic and aesthetic, has revealed qualities of Milton's thought and art that earlier generations for the most part did not see or saw very dimly, so that nowadays readers can come closer to full understanding and appreciation than was ever possible before. If our world does not at present offer many things to contemplate with satisfaction, that is one.

PERSONAL PASSAGES

FROM

The Reason of Church Government

AND

An Apology for Smectymnuus

The Reason of Church Government
Urged Against Prelaty

(1642)

The Second Book

. . . Concerning therefore this wayward subject against prelaty, the touching whereof is so distasteful and disquietous to a number of men, as by what hath been said I may deserve of charitable readers to be credited that neither envy nor gall hath entered me upon this controversy, but the enforcement of conscience only and a preventive fear lest the omitting of this duty should be against me when I would store up to myself the good provision of peaceful hours: so, lest it should be still imputed to me, as I have found it hath been, that some self-pleasing humor of vain-glory hath incited me to contest with men of high estimation, now while green years are upon my head; from this needless surmisal I shall hope to dissuade the intelligent and equal auditor, if I can but say successfully that which in this exigent behoves me; although I would be heard only, if it might be, by the elegant and learned reader, to whom principally for a while I shall beg leave I may address myself. To him it will be no new thing though I tell him that if I hunted after praise by the ostentation of wit and learning, I should not write thus out of mine own season, when I have neither yet completed to my mind the full circle of my private studies (although I complain not of any insufficiency to the matter in hand); or, were I ready to my wishes, it were a folly to commit anything elaborately composed to the careless and interrupted listening of these tumultuous times. Next, if I were wise only to mine own ends, I would certainly take such a subject as of itself might catch applause, whereas this hath all the disadvantages on the contrary, and such a subject as the publishing whereof might be delayed at pleasure, and time enough to pencil it over with all the curious touches of art, even to the perfection of a faultless picture; whenas in this argument the not deferring is of great moment to the good speeding, that if solidity have leisure to do her office, art cannot have much. Lastly, I should not choose this manner of writing, wherein, knowing myself inferior to myself, led by the genial power of nature to another task, I have the use, as I may account it, but of my left hand. And though I shall be foolish in saying more to this purpose, yet, since it will be such a folly as wisest men going about to commit have only confessed and so committed, I may trust with more reason, because with more folly, to have courteous pardon. For although a poet, soaring in the high region of his fancies with his garland and singing robes about him, might without apology speak more of himself than I mean to do, yet for me, sitting here below in the cool element of prose, a mortal thing among many readers of no empyreal conceit, to venture and divulge unusual things of myself, I shall petition to the gentler sort, it may not be envy to me.

I must say, therefore, that after I had from my first years, by the ceaseless diligence and care of my father (whom God recompense), been exercised to the tongues and some sciences, as my age would suffer, by sundry masters and teachers both at home and at the schools, it was found that whether aught was imposed me by them that had the overlooking, or betaken to of mine own choice in English or other tongue, prosing or versing, but chiefly this latter, the style, by certain vital signs it had, was likely to live. But much latelier, in the private academies of Italy, whither I was favored to resort — perceiving that some trifles which I had in memory, composed at under twenty or thereabout (for the manner is that everyone must give some proof of his wit[1] and reading there), met with acceptance above what was looked for, and other things which I had shifted in scarcity of books and conveniences to patch up amongst them, were received with written encomiums, which the Italian is not forward to bestow on men of this side the Alps — I began thus far to assent both to them and divers of my friends here at home, and not less to an inward prompting which now grew daily upon me, that by labor and intent study (which I take to be my portion in this life) joined with the strong propensity of nature, I might perhaps leave something so written to aftertimes as they should not willingly let it die. These thoughts at once possessed me, and these other: that if I were certain to write as men buy leases, for three lives and downward, there ought no regard be sooner had than to God's glory by the honor and instruction of my country. For which cause, and not only for that I knew it would be hard to arrive at the second rank among the Latins,[2] I applied myself to that resolution which Ariosto followed against the persuasions of Bembo,[3] to fix all the industry and art I could unite to the adorning of my native tongue; not to make verbal curiosities the end (that were a toilsome vanity), but to be an interpreter and relater of the best and sagest things among mine own citizens throughout this island in the mother dialect. That what the greatest and choicest wits of Athens, Rome, or modern Italy, and those Hebrews of old did for their country, I, in my proportion, with this over and above of being a Christian, might do for mine; not caring to be once named abroad, though perhaps I could attain to that, but content with these British islands as my world; whose fortune hath hitherto been that, if the Athenians, as some say, made their small deeds great and renowned by their eloquent writers, England hath had her noble achievements made small by the unskillful handling of monks and mechanics.

Time serves not now, and perhaps I might seem too profuse to give any certain account of what the mind at home, in the spacious circuits of her musing, hath liberty to propose to herself, though of highest hope and hardest attempting: whether that epic form whereof the two poems of Homer and those other two of Virgil and Tasso are a diffuse, and the book of Job a brief, model; or whether the rules of Aristotle herein are strictly to be kept, or nature to be followed, which, in them

---

[1] wit: talent.   [2] Latins: probably modern writers of Latin verse.   [3] Ludovico Ariosto (1474–1533), author of the romance *Orlando Furioso*, was urged by Cardinal Bembo (1470–1547), the arbiter of taste, to write in Latin.

that know art and use judgment, is no transgression but an enriching of art; and lastly, what king or knight before the conquest might be chosen in whom to lay the pattern of a Christian hero. And as Tasso gave to a prince of Italy his choice whether he would command him to write of Godfrey's expedition against the infidels, or Belisarius against the Goths, or Charlemagne against the Lombards; if to the instinct of nature and the emboldening of art aught may be trusted, and that there be nothing adverse in our climate or the fate of this age, it haply would be no rashness, from an equal diligence and inclination, to present the like offer in our own ancient stories; or whether those dramatic constitutions, wherein Sophocles and Euripides reign, shall be found more doctrinal and exemplary to a nation. The Scripture also affords us a divine pastoral drama in the Song of Solomon, consisting of two persons and a double chorus, as Origen rightly judges. And the Apocalypse of St. John is the majestic image of a high and stately tragedy, shutting up and in-termingling her solemn scenes and acts with a sevenfold chorus of halleluiahs and harping symphonies: and this my opinion the grave authority of Pareus, commenting that book, is sufficient to confirm. Or if occasion shall lead, to imitate those magnific odes and hymns, wherein Pindarus and Callimachus are in most things worthy, some others in their frame judicious, in their matter most an end[4] faulty. But those fre-quent songs throughout the law and prophets beyond all these, not in their divine argument alone, but in the very critical art of composition, may be easily made appear over all the kinds of lyric poesy to be incomparable. These abilities, where-soever they be found, are the inspired gift of God, rarely bestowed, but yet to some (though most abuse) in every nation; and are of power, beside the office of a pulpit, to inbreed and cherish in a great people the seeds of virtue and public civility, to allay the perturbations of the mind, and set the affections in right tune; to celebrate in glorious and lofty hymns the throne and equipage of God's almightiness, and what he works and what he suffers to be wrought with high providence in his church; to sing the victorious agonies of martyrs and saints, the deeds and triumphs of just and pious nations doing valiantly through faith against the enemies of Christ; to deplore the general relapses of kingdoms and states from justice and God's true worship. Lastly, whatsoever in religion is holy and sublime, in virtue amiable or grave, whatsoever hath passion or admiration in all the changes of that which is called fortune from without, or the wily subtleties and refluxes of man's thoughts from within, all these things with a solid and treatable smoothness to paint out and describe. Teaching over the whole book of sanctity and virtue through all the in-stances of example, with such delight to those especially of soft and delicious temper, who will not so much as look upon truth herself unless they see her elegantly dressed, that whereas the paths of honesty and good life appear now rugged and difficult, though they be indeed easy and pleasant, they would then appear to all men both easy and pleasant, though they were rugged and difficult indeed. And what a benefit this would be to our youth and gentry may be soon guessed by what we know of the corruption and bane which they suck in daily from the writings and interludes of libidinous and ignorant poetasters, who, having scarce ever heard of that which is the main consistence of a true poem, the choice of such persons as they ought to introduce, and what is moral and decent to each one, do for the most part lap up vicious principles in sweet pills to be swallowed down, and make the taste of virtuous documents harsh and sour.

But because the spirit of man cannot demean[5] itself lively in this body without some recreating intermission of labor and serious things, it were happy for the com-

---

[4] most an end: for the most part.   [5] demean: conduct.

monwealth if our magistrates, as in those famous governments of old, would take into their care not only the deciding of our contentious law-cases and brawls, but the managing of our public sports and festival pastimes; that they might be, not such as were authorized a while since,[6] the provocations of drunkenness and lust, but such as may inure and harden our bodies by martial exercises to all warlike skill and performance; and may civilize, adorn, and make discreet our minds by the learned and affable meeting of frequent academies, and the procurement of wise and artful recitations sweetened with eloquent and graceful enticements to the love and practice of justice, temperance, and fortitude, instructing and bettering the nation at all opportunities, that the call of wisdom and virtue may be heard everywhere, as Solomon saith: "She crieth without, she uttereth her voice in the streets, in the top of high places, in the chief concourse, and in the openings of the gates."[7] Whether this may not be, not only in pulpits but after another persuasive method, at set and solemn panegyries,[8] in theatres, porches, or what other place or way may win most upon the people to receive at once both recreation and instruction, let them in authority consult.

The thing which I had to say, and those intentions which have lived within me ever since I could conceive myself anything worth to my country, I return to crave excuse that urgent reason hath plucked from me by an abortive and foredated discovery. And the accomplishment of them lies not but in a power above man's to promise; but that none hath by more studious ways endeavored, and with more unwearied spirit that none shall, that I dare almost aver of myself, as far as life and free leisure will extend; and that the land had once enfranchised herself from this impertinent yoke of prelaty, under whose inquisitorious and tyrannical duncery no free and splendid wit can flourish. Neither do I think it shame to covenant with any knowing reader, that for some few years yet I may go on trust with him toward the payment of what I am now indebted, as being a work not to be raised from the heat of youth or the vapors of wine, like that which flows at waste from the pen of some vulgar amorist or the trencher fury of a rhyming parasite; nor to be obtained by the invocation of Dame Memory and her siren daughters;[9] but by devout prayer to that eternal Spirit who can enrich with all utterance and knowledge, and sends out his Seraphim with the hallowed fire of his altar to touch and purify the lips of whom he pleases:[10] to this must be added industrious and select reading, steady observation, insight into all seemly and generous arts and affairs; till which in some measure be compassed, at mine own peril and cost I refuse not to sustain this expectation from as many as are not loth to hazard so much credulity upon the best pledges that I can give them.

Although it nothing content me to have disclosed thus much beforehand, but that I trust hereby to make it manifest with what small willingness I endure to interrupt the pursuit of no less hopes than these, and leave a calm and pleasing solitariness, fed with cheerful and confident thoughts, to embark in a troubled sea of noises and hoarse disputes, put from beholding the bright countenance of truth in the quiet and still air of delightful studies, to come into the dim reflection of hollow antiquities sold by the seeming bulk, and there be fain to club quotations with men whose learning and belief lies in marginal stuffings, who, when they have like good sumpters laid ye down their horse-load of citations and fathers[11] at your door, with a rhapsody

---

[6] The so-called *Book of Sports,* issued by King James and reissued by King Charles, which authorized dancing and games on Sunday.   [7] Prov. 1.20–21.   [8] panegyries: assemblies.   [9] Classical poets' invocations of the Muses.   [10] Isa. 6.6–7. Cf. Milton, *Nativity* 28.   [11] fathers: the early church fathers, often cited by defenders of prelacy.

of who and who were bishops here or there, ye may take off their packsaddles, their day's work is done, and episcopacy, as they think, stoutly vindicated. Let any gentle apprehension, that can distinguish learned pains from unlearned drudgery, imagine what pleasure or profoundness can be in this, or what honor to deal against such adversaries. But were it the meanest under-service, if God by his secretary conscience enjoin it, it were sad for me if I should draw back; for me especially, now when all men offer their aid to help ease and lighten the difficult labors of the church, to whose service, by the intentions of my parents and friends, I was destined of a child, and in mine own resolutions: till coming to some maturity of years, and perceiving what tyranny had invaded the church — that he who would take orders must subscribe slave and take an oath withal, which, unless he took with a conscience that would retch, he must either straight perjure or split his faith — I thought it better to prefer a blameless silence before the sacred office of speaking, bought and begun with servitude and forswearing. Howsoever thus church-outed by the prelates, hence may appear the right I have to meddle in these matters, as before the necessity and constraint appeared.

An Apology for Smectymnuus[1]

(1642)

. . . I had my time, readers, as others have who have good learning bestowed upon them, to be sent to those places where, the opinion was, it might be soonest attained; and, as the manner is, was not unstudied in those authors which are most commended. Whereof some were grave orators and historians, whose matter methought I loved indeed, but as my age then was, so I understood them; others were the smooth elegiac poets,[2] whereof the schools are not scarce, whom both for the pleasing sound of their numerous[3] writing, which in imitation I found most easy and most agreeable to nature's part in me, and for their matter, which what it is, there be few who know not, I was so allured to read that no recreation came to me better welcome. For that it was then those years with me which are excused, though they be least severe, I may be saved the labor to remember ye. Whence having observed them to account it the chief glory of their wit, in that they were ablest to judge, to praise, and by that could esteem themselves worthiest to love those high perfections which under one or other name they took to celebrate, I thought with myself by every instinct and presage of nature, which is not wont to be false, that what emboldened them to this task might, with such diligence as they used, embolden me; and that what judgment, wit, or elegance was my share, would herein best appear, and best value itself, by how much more wisely and with more love of virtue I should choose (let rude ears be absent) the object of not unlike praises. For albeit these thoughts to some will seem virtuous and commendable, to others only pardonable, to a third sort perhaps idle, yet the mentioning of them now will end in serious.

---

[1] The name is explained in the Introduction, p. xviii.
[2] Ovid, Propertius, and Tibullus, whose love-poems were written in the elegiac meter.
[3] numerous: metrical, rhythmical.

Nor blame it, readers, in those years to propose to themselves such a reward as the noblest dispositions above other things in this life have sometimes preferred: whereof not to be sensible when good and fair in one person meet, argues both a gross and shallow judgment and withal an ungentle and swainish breast. For by the firm settling of these persuasions I became, to my best memory, so much a proficient that, if I found those authors[4] anywhere speaking unworthy things of themselves, or unchaste of those names which before they had extolled, this effect it wrought with me: from that time forward their art I still applauded, but the men I deplored, and above them all preferred the two famous renowners of Beatrice and Laura,[5] who never write but honor of them to whom they devote their verse, displaying sublime and pure thoughts, without transgression. And long it was not after when I was confirmed in this opinion, that he who would not be frustrate of his hope to write well hereafter in laudable things, ought himself to be a true poem, that is, a composition and pattern of the best and honorablest things[6]; not presuming to sing high praises of heroic men or famous cities unless he have in himself the experience and the practice of all that which is praiseworthy. These reasonings, together with a certain niceness[7] of nature, an honest haughtiness, and self-esteem either of what I was or what I might be (which let envy call pride), and lastly that modesty, whereof, though not in the title-page, yet here I may be excused to make some beseeming profession; all these, uniting the supply of their natural aid together, kept me still above those low descents of mind beneath which he must deject and plunge himself that can agree to saleable and unlawful prostitutions.

Next (for hear me out now, readers) that I may tell ye whither my younger feet wandered, I betook me among those lofty fables and romances which recount in solemn cantos the deeds of knighthood founded by our victorious kings, and from hence had in renown over all Christendom. There I read it in the oath of every knight, that he should defend to the expense of his best blood, or of his life if it so befell him, the honor and chastity of virgin or matron; from whence even then I learned what a noble virtue chastity sure must be, to the defense of which so many worthies, by such a dear adventure of themselves, had sworn. And if I found in the story afterward, any of them, by word or deed, breaking that oath, I judged it the same fault of the poet as that which is attributed to Homer, to have written indecent things of the gods. Only this my mind gave me, that every free and gentle spirit, without that oath, ought to be born a knight, nor needed to expect the gilt spur, or the laying of a sword upon his shoulder, to stir him up both by his counsel and his arm to secure and protect the weakness of any attempted[8] chastity. So that even those books which to many others have been the fuel of wantonness and loose living, I cannot think how, unless by divine indulgence, proved to me so many incitements, as you have heard, to the love and steadfast observation of that virtue which abhors the society of bordellos.

Thus, from the laureate fraternity of poets, riper years and the ceaseless round of study and reading led me to the shady spaces of philosophy, but chiefly to the divine volumes of Plato and his equal,[9] Xenophon: where, if I should tell ye what I learnt of chastity and love, I mean that which is truly so, whose charming cup is only virtue, which she bears in her hand to those who are worthy (the rest are cheated with a thick intoxicating potion which a certain sorceresss,[10] the abuser of

---

[4] authors: Ovid and other love-poets.   [5] The women celebrated by Dante and Petrarch.   [6] A classical ideal revived by Renaissance poets; cf. Jonson's dedication of *Volpone*.   [7] niceness: fastidiousness.   [8] attempted: attacked.   [9] equal: contemporary.   [10] sorceress: Circe.

love's name, carries about), and how the first and chiefest office of love begins and ends in the soul, producing those happy twins of her divine generation, knowledge and virtue — with such abstracted sublimities as these, it might be worth your listening, readers, as I may one day hope to have ye in a still time, when there shall be no chiding; not in these noises, the adversary, as ye know, barking at the door, or searching for me at the bordellos, where it may be he has lost himself, and raps up without pity the sage and rheumatic old prelatess, with all her young Corinthian laity,[11] to inquire for such a one.

Last of all, not in time, but as perfection is last, that care was ever had of me, with my earliest capacity, not to be negligently trained in the precepts of Christian religion: this that I have hitherto related hath been to show that, though Christianity had been but slightly taught me, yet a certain reservedness of natural disposition, and moral discipline learnt out of the noblest philosophy, was enough to keep me in disdain of far less incontinences than this of the bordello. But having had the doctrine of Holy Scripture, unfolding those chaste and high mysteries, with timeliest care infused, that "the body is for the Lord, and the Lord for the body,"[12] thus also I argued to myself: that if unchastity in a woman, whom St. Paul terms the glory of man,[13] be such a scandal and dishonor, then certainly in a man, who is both the image and glory of God, it must, though commonly not so thought, be much more deflowering and dishonorable; in that he sins both against his own body, which is the perfecter sex, and his own glory, which is in the woman, and, that which is worst, against the image and glory of God, which is in himself. Nor did I slumber over that place[14] expressing such high rewards of ever accompanying the Lamb with those celestial songs to others inapprehensible, but not to those who were not defiled with women, which doubtless means fornication; for marriage must not be called a defilement.

Thus large I have purposely been, that if I have been justly taxed with this crime, it may come upon me, after all this my confession, with a tenfold shame.

[11] laity: prostitutes.　　[12] 1 Cor. 6.13.　　[13] Ibid., 11.7.　　[14] place: passage (Rev. 14.3–4).

ABBREVIATIONS USED IN THE NOTES

Aen.: see Virgil.

Ariosto, *O.F.: Orlando Furioso.*

Bible: the standard abbreviations.

Cicero, *Rep.: De Re Publica.*

Dante, *Inf., Purg., Par.: Inferno, Purgatorio, Paradiso.*

Hesiod, *Theog.: Theogony.*

Hooker, Richard, *Eccles. Pol.: Of the Laws of Ecclesiastical Polity.*

Horace, *Od.: Odes; Epod.: Epodes.*

Lactantius, *Div. Inst.: Divine Institutes.*

Lucretius: *De Rerum Natura.*

Milton, *C.D.: Christian Doctrine (De Doctrina Christiana).*

     Nativity: On the Morning of Christ's Nativity.

     Naturam: Naturam non pati senium.

     P.L.: Paradise Lost.

     P.R.: Paradise Regained.

     S.A.: Samson Agonistes.

     Works: Columbia edition (20 volumes, 1931–40).

     C.P.W.: Complete Prose Works (in progress, Yale University Press, 1953 f.).

Ovid, *Met.: Metamorphoses.*

Plato, *Rep.: Republic.*

Pliny, *Nat. Hist.: Natural History.*

Sandys, George, *Ovid: Ovid's Metamorphosis Englished, Mythologized, and Represented in Figures* (Oxford, 1632).

———, *Relation: A Relation of a Journey begun An. Dom. 1610* (London, 1615).

Spenser, Edmund, *F.Q.: The Faerie Queene.*

Sylvester: Josuah Sylvester, *Divine Weeks and Works,* tr. Du Bartas, in *Complete Works of Joshuah Sylvester,* ed. A. B. Grosart (2 vols., 1880).

Tasso, *G.L.: Gerusalemme Liberata.*

Theocritus, *Id.: Idyls.*

Virgil, *Aen.: Aeneid.*

     Ecl.: Eclogues.

     Georg.: Georgics.

THE COMPLETE

POETICAL WORKS OF

John Milton

POEMS

OF

Mr. *John Milton*,

BOTH

ENGLISH and LATIN,

Compos'd at several times.

Printed by his true Copies.

The SONGS were set in Musick by
Mr. HENRY LAWES Gentleman of
the KINGS Chappel, and one
of His MAIESTIES
Private Musick.

———*Baccare frontem*
Cingite, ne vati noceat mala lingua futuro,
Virgil, Eclog. 7.

Printed and publish'd according to
ORDER.

LONDON,
Printed by *Ruth Raworth* for *Humphrey Moseley,*
and are to be sold at the signe of the Princes
Arms in S. *Pauls* Church-yard. 1645.

THE STATIONER TO THE READER

IT IS NOT any private respect of gain, gentle reader, for the slightest pamphlet is nowadays more vendible than the works of learnedest men, but it is the love I have to our own language that hath made me diligent to collect and set forth such pieces both in prose and verse as may renew the wonted honor and esteem of our English tongue; and it's the worth of these both English and Latin poems, not the flourish of any prefixed encomions that can invite thee to buy them, though these are not without the highest commendations and applause of the learnedest academics, both domestic and foreign; and amongst those of our own country, the unparalleled attestation of that renowned Provost of Eton, Sir Henry Wotton.[1] I know not thy palate how it relishes such dainties, nor how harmonious thy soul is; perhaps more trivial airs may please thee better. But howsoever thy opinion is spent upon these, that encouragement I have already received from the most ingenious men in their clear and courteous entertainment of Mr. Waller's late choice pieces, hath once more made me adventure into the world, presenting it with these evergreen and not to be blasted laurels. The author's more peculiar excellency in these studies was too well known to conceal his papers, or to keep me from attempting to solicit them from him. Let the event guide itself which way it will, I shall deserve of the age by bringing into the light as true a birth as the Muses have brought forth since our famous Spenser wrote, whose poems in these English ones are as rarely imitated as sweetly excelled. Reader, if thou art eagle-eyed to censure[2] their worth, I am not fearful to expose them to thy exactest perusal.

Thine to command
Humph. Moseley.[3]

---

1 Sir Henry's eulogy of *Comus* is quoted in the headnote to that work.   2 censure: judge.   3 This preface was omitted in the 1673 edition. The tributes of Milton's Italian friends, prefixed to his Latin poems in 1645, are not included in the present volume.

POEMS, &c.

UPON

Several Occasions.

BY

Mr. *JOHN MILTON:*

Both ENGLISH and LATIN, &c.
Compofed at feveral times.

With a fmall Tractate of

EDUCATION

To Mr. HARTLIB

LONDON,
Printed for *Tho. Dring* at the *Blew Anchor*
next *Mitre Court* over againft *Fetter*
Lane in *Fleet-ftreet.* 1673.

THE VERSIFYING of the Psalms, a practice established in the mid-sixteenth century by the pedestrian Sternhold and Hopkins, was carried on still more actively in the earlier seventeenth century, by religious and even by quite worldly poets. One main motive was the production of simple metrical versions for congregational singing. Milton's father had contributed some tunes to Thomas Ravenscroft's *Whole Book of Psalms* (1621), and his own early efforts were both poetical exercises and natural results of the common impulse; he versified two groups of Psalms as late as 1648 and 1653. The juvenile paraphrases display vigor and some (not unusual) freedom; the young Milton is already stirred in celebrating the power of the God who watches over his own. The influence of Josuah Sylvester's very popular translation of Du Bartas' epic of creation appears in such words and phrases as "froth-becurlèd," "Erythraean," and "walls of glass"; and there seem to be some echoes of George Buchanan's Latin versions of the Psalms.

A Paraphrase on Psalm 114

This and the following Psalm were done by the author at fifteen years old. [Milton's note]

When the blest seed of Terah's faithful son
After long toil their liberty had won,
And passed from Pharian fields to Canaan land,
Led by the strength of the Almighty's hand,
Jehovah's wonders were in Israel shown,   5
His praise and glory was in Israel known.
That saw the troubled sea, and shivering fled,
And sought to hide his froth-becurlèd head
Low in the earth; Jordan's clear streams recoil,
As a faint host that hath received the foil.   10
The high, huge-bellied mountains skip like rams
Amongst their ewes, the little hills like lambs.
Why fled the ocean? And why skipped the mountains?
Why turnèd Jordan toward his crystal fountains?
Shake, earth, and at the presence be aghast   15
Of him that ever was, and aye shall last,
That glassy floods from rugged rocks can crush,
And make soft rills from fiery flint-stones gush.

(1624)

1. Terah's . . . son: Abraham (Gen. 11.27; Heb. 11.8); in the Bible, "the house of Jacob." Cf. *P.L.* 12.151–52.
3. Pharian: Egyptian, from the island and tower of Pharos off Alexandria. Cf. the "high Pharian tower" in Sylvester, 1.1.500, and George Buchanan's *arva Phari* ("fields of Pharus") in his translation of Ps. 114.

5

Psalm 136

Let us with a gladsome mind
Praise the Lord, for he is kind;
   For his mercies aye endure,
   Ever faithful, ever sure.

Let us blaze his name abroad,   5
For of gods he is the God;
   For his, &c.

O let us his praises tell,
Who doth the wrathful tyrants quell;   10
   For his, &c.

Who with his miracles doth make
Amazèd heav'n and earth to shake;
   For his, &c.   15

Who by his wisdom did create
The painted heav'ns so full of state;
   For his, &c.   19

Who did the solid earth ordain
To rise above the wat'ry plain;
   For his, &c.

Who by his all-commanding might   25
Did fill the new-made world with light;
   For his, &c.

And caused the golden-tressèd sun
All the day long his course to run;   30
   For his, &c.

The hornèd moon to shine by night,
Amongst her spangled sisters bright;
   For his, &c.   35

He with his thunder-clasping hand
Smote the first-born of Egypt land;
   For his, &c.   39

And in despite of Pharaoh fell,
He brought from thence his Israel;
   For, &c.

10–25. Ed. 2, Who; ed. 1, That.

The ruddy waves he cleft in twain 45
Of the Erythraean main;
   For, &c.

The floods stood still like walls of glass,
While the Hebrew bands did pass; 50
   For, &c.

But full soon they did devour
The tawny king with all his power;
   For, &c. 55

His chosen people he did bless
In the wasteful wilderness;
   For, &c. 59

In bloody battle he brought down
Kings of prowess and renown;
   For, &c.

He foiled bold Seon and his host, 65
That ruled the Amorrean coast;
   For, &c.

And large-limbed Og he did subdue,
With all his over-hardy crew; 70
   For, &c.

And to his servant Israel
He gave their land therein to dwell;
   For, &c. 75

He hath with a piteous eye
Beheld us in our misery;
   For, &c. 79

And freed us from the slavery
Of the invading enemy;
   For, &c.

All living creatures he doth feed, 85
And with full hand supplies their need;
   For, &c.

Let us therefore warble forth
His mighty majesty and worth; 90
   For, &c.

---

46. Erythraean main: Red Sea.   73. Israel: Jacob (Gen. 32.28; 35.10–12).
66. Amorrean: of the Amorites.

That his mansion hath on high
Above the reach of mortal eye;
For his mercies aye endure,   95
Ever faithful, ever sure.

(1624)

ELEGIAC VERSES AND ASCLEPIADS

THESE TWO SETS of verses have only an illegitimate place among Milton's poems, since he himself did not print them. An autograph copy was discovered in 1874, along with Milton's Commonplace Book; the somewhat damaged sheet of paper had also a short Latin essay on the same standard inspirational theme of early rising. All three pieces were evidently exercises done during Milton's last year or two at St. Paul's School. The longer poem contains many of the stock phrases found in the manuals for Latin verse-making, yet it has freshness of feeling. The second piece, in the lesser Asclepiad meter, illustrates the same theme with a brief summary of the episode narrated in the *Aeneid*, 9.176–449.

Carmina Elegiaca

Surge, age, surge, leves, iam convenit, excute somnos,
    Lux oritur, tepidi fulcra relinque tori.
Iam canit excubitor gallus, praenuncius ales
    Solis, et invigilans ad sua quemque vocat.
Flammiger Eois Titan caput exerit undis   5
    Et spargit nitidum laeta per arva iubar.
Daulias argutum modulatur ab ilice carmen
    Edit et excultos mitis alauda modos.
Iam rosa fragrantes spirat silvestris odores,
    Iam redolent violae luxuriatque seges.   10
Ecce novo campos Zephyritis gramine vestit
    Fertilis, et vitreo rore madescit humus.
Segnes invenias molli vix talia lecto
    Cum premat imbellis lumina fessa sopor.
Illic languentes abrumpunt somnia somnos   15
    Et turbant animum tristia multa tuum;
Illic tabifici generantur semina morbi.
    Qui pote torpentem posse valere virum?
Surge, age, surge, leves, iam convenit, excute somnos,
    Lux oritur, tepidi fulcra relinque tori.   20

(1624–25?)

ELEGIAC VERSES

Come, get up, get up! now it is time, shake off light sleep. The dawn is rising; leave the posts of your warm bed. Now crows the sentinel cock, the bird that heralds the sun and, keeping close watch, rouses everyone to his work. Flaming Titan[5] lifts his head from the eastern waves and scatters radiant light over the fruitful fields. From the oak-tree the Daulian bird[7] trills her clear song and the gentle lark sends forth her polished notes. Now the wild rose breathes out sweet odors, the violets diffuse their fragrance, and the grain flourishes. See, the fertile wife of Zephyr[11] clothes the fields with fresh grass and the ground is wet with glassy dew. Lazy fellow, you would hardly find such delights in your soft bed, when ignoble sleep weighs upon your tired eyes. There dreams break off languid slumber and many cares trouble your mind. There the seeds of wasting disease are bred. What strength can there be in a sluggish man? Come, get up, get up! now it is time, shake off light sleep. The dawn is rising; leave the posts of your warm bed.

5. Titan: the sun.
7. Daulis in central Greece was the scene of the story of Tereus, Procne, and Philomela, all of whom were changed into birds, Procne (the Daulian bird: Ovid, *Heroides* 15.154), into a swallow, Philomela into a nightingale (Ovid, *Met.* 6.668–74).
11. Glossary.

[Asclepiads]

Ignavus satrapam dedecet inclytum
Somnus qui populo multifido praeest.
Dum Dauni veteris filius armiger
Stratus purpureo procubuit [toro].
Audax Eurialus, Nisus et impiger   5
Invasere cati nocte sub horrida
Torpentes Rutilos castraque Volscia;
Hinc caedes oritur clamor et absonus.
                    (1624–25?)

Slothful sleep is a disgrace to a renowned governor who rules over multitudes of people. While the warrior son of old Daunus[3] lay stretched on his purple bed,[4] bold Euryalus and active Nisus in the fearful night made a cunning attack on the sleeping Rutilians and the Volscian camp. Hence arose slaughter and hideous clamor.

3. son . . . Daunus: Turnus, leader of the Italian tribes against Aeneas.
4. A conjectural restoration by editors, since the manuscript is damaged.

Apologus de Rustico et Hero

Rusticus ex malo sapidissima poma quotannis
Legit, et urbano lecta dedit domino:
Hic incredibili fructus dulcedine captus
Malum ipsam in proprias transtulit areolas.

Hactenus illa ferax, sed longo debilis aevo,   5
  Mota solo assueto, protinus aret iners.
Quod tandem ut patuit domino, spe lusus inani,
  Damnavit celeres in sua damna manus.
Atque ait, "Heu quanto satius fuit illa coloni
  (Parva licet) grato dona tulisse animo!   10
Possem ego avaritiam frenare, gulamque voracem:
  Nunc periere mihi et foetus et ipsa parens."
                                          (1624–25?)

A FABLE OF A PEASANT AND HIS LANDLORD

THIS PIECE, though first printed in the second edition (1673) of Milton's *Poems*, was probably a schoolboy exercise in imitative verse-making. The original — which had had other imitations before Milton's — was by the famous Neo-Latin poet Baptista Spagnuoli, commonly called Mantuanus (the "good old Mantuan" of *Love's Labor's Lost*, 4.2.97).

A peasant yearly gathered the most savory apples from his tree and gave what he had picked to his landlord in the city. The latter, delighted by the amazing sweetness of the fruit, transplanted the tree into his own gardens. Hitherto it had been productive, but it was now weakened by old age, and, moved from its accustomed soil, it quickly withered into barrenness. When at length the landlord saw this, mocked by vain hope he cursed the swift hands that had caused his own loss. "Alas," said he, "how much better it was to accept gratefully those gifts of my tenant, small though they were! I could have restrained my covetousness and greedy gullet! But now I have lost both fruit and parent tree."

Philosophus ad Regem

Philosophus ad regem quendam qui eum ignotum et insontem inter reos forte captum inscius damnaverat, τὴν ἐπὶ θανάτῳ πορευόμενος, haec subito misit.

’Ω ἄνα εἰ ὀλέσῃς με τὸν ἔννομον, οὐδέ τιν’ ἀνδρῶν
Δεινὸν ὅλως δράσαντα, σοφώτατον ἴσθι κάρηνον
Ρηϊδίως ἀφέλοιο, τὸδ’ ὕστερον αὖθι νοήσεις,
Μαψιδίως δ’ ἄρ’ ἔπειτα τεὸν πρὸς θυμὸν ὀδύρῃ,*
Τοιόνδ’ ἐκ πόλεως περιώνυμον ἄλκαρ ὀλέσσας·   5
                                          (1624–25?)

* Line 4 is the altered reading of 1673.

A PHILOSOPHER TO A KING

THIS SMALL fable, printed in the *Poems* of 1645, was probably, like the *Apologus*, a school exercise. The first Greek Milton composed after leaving school was, he said, Psalm 114 (*c.* December 1, 1634). It has been suggested that, if the fable was written soon after that, it might have referred to Milton's friend Alexander Gill, whose spoken approval of the Duke of Buckingham's assassination (August, 1628) got him into trouble with the Star Chamber (and who was pardoned in 1630). But such a reference would seem both tenuous and belated.

This appeal was suddenly sent to a certain king by a philosopher who was being taken to execution because he happened to be arrested along with some criminals and the king in ignorance had condemned him, unrecognized and innocent.

King, if you execute me, a man who abides by the law and has done no injury to any man, know that you can easily destroy a very wise head; but later you will see this, and you will lament vainly to your soul because you have destroyed so renowned a safeguard of the city.

Elegia prima ad Carolum Diodatum

Tandem, care, tuae mihi pervenere tabellae,
    Pertulit et voces nuntia charta tuas;
Pertulit occidua Devae Cestrensis ab ora
    Vergivium prono qua petit amne salum.
Multum, crede, iuvat terras aluisse remotas   5
    Pectus amans nostri, tamque fidele caput,
Quodque mihi lepidum tellus longinqua sodalem
    Debet, at unde brevi reddere iussa velit.
Me tenet urbs reflua quam Thamesis alluit unda,
    Meque nec invitum patria dulcis habet.   10
Iam nec arundiferum mihi cura revisere Camum,
    Nec dudum vetiti me laris angit amor.
Nuda nec arva placent, umbrasque negantia molles;
    Quam male Phoebicolis convenit ille locus!
Nec duri libet usque minas perferre magistri   15
    Ceteraque ingenio non subeunda meo.
Si sit hoc exilium, patrios adiisse penates,
    Et vacuum curis otia grata sequi,
Non ego vel profugi nomen sortemve recuso,
    Laetus et exilii conditione fruor.   20
O utinam vates nunquam graviora tulisset
    Ille Tomitano flebilis exul agro;
Non tunc Ionio quicquam cessisset Homero,
    Neve foret victo laus tibi prima, Maro.
Tempora nam licet hic placidis dare libera Musis,   25

Et totum rapiunt me, mea vita, libri.
Excipit hinc fessum sinuosi pompa theatri,
    Et vocat ad plausus garrula scena suos.
Seu catus auditur senior, seu prodigus haeres,
    Seu procus, aut posita casside miles adest,   30
Sive decennali fecundus lite patronus
    Detonat inculto barbara verba foro;
Saepe vafer gnato succurrit servus amanti,
    Et nasum rigidi fallit ubique patris;
Saepe novos illic virgo mirata calores   35
    Quid sit amor nescit, dum quoque nescit, amat:
Sive cruentatum furiosa Tragoedia sceptrum
    Quassat, et effusis crinibus ora rotat;
Et dolet, et specto, iuvat et spectasse dolendo;
    Interdum et lacrimis dulcis amaror inest;   40
Seu puer infelix indelibata reliquit
    Gaudia, et abrupto flendus amore cadit;
Seu ferus e tenebris iterat Styga criminis ultor,
    Conscia funereo pectora torre movens;
Seu maeret Pelopeia domus, seu nobilis Ili,   45
    Aut luit incestos aula Creontis avos.
Sed neque sub tecto semper nec in urbe latemus,
    Irrita nec nobis tempora veris eunt.
Nos quoque lucus habet vicina consitus ulmo
    Atque suburbani nobilis umbra loci.   50
Saepius hic blandas spirantia sidera flammas,
    Virgineos videas praeteriisse choros.
Ah quoties dignae stupui miracula formae
    Quae possit senium vel reparare Iovis!
Ah quoties vidi superantia lumina gemmas,   55
    Atque faces quotquot volvit uterque polus;
Collaque bis vivi Pelopis quae brachia vincant,
    Quaeque fluit puro nectare tincta via,
Et decus eximium frontis, tremulosque capillos,
    Aurea quae fallax retia tendit Amor;   60
Pellacesque genas, ad quas hyacinthina sordet
    Purpura, et ipse tui floris, Adoni, rubor!
Cedite laudatae toties heroides olim,
    Et quaecunque vagum cepit amica Iovem;
Cedite Achaemeniae turrita fronte puellae,   65
    Et quot Susa colunt, Memnoniamque Ninon;
Vos etiam Danaae fasces submittite nymphae,
    Et vos Iliacae, Romuleaeque nurus;
Nec Pompeianas Tarpeia Musa columnas
    Iactet, et Ausoniis plena theatra stolis.   70
Gloria virginibus debetur prima Britannis;
    Extera sat tibi sit femina posse sequi.
Tuque urbs Dardaniis, Londinum, structa colonis,
    Turrigerum late conspicienda caput,
Tu nimium felix intra tua moenia claudis   75

Quicquid formosi pendulus orbis habet.
Non tibi tot caelo scintillant astra sereno,
 Endymioneae turba ministra deae,
Quot tibi conspicuae formaque auroque puellae
 Per medias radiant turba videnda vias.   80
Creditur huc geminis venisse invecta columbis
 Alma pharetrigero milite cincta Venus,
Huic Cnidon, et riguas Simoentis flumine valles,
 Huic Paphon, et roseam posthabitura Cypron.
Ast ego, dum pueri sinit indulgentia caeci,   85
 Moenia quam subito linquere fausta paro;
Et vitare procul malefidae infamia Circes
 Atria, divini molyos usus ope.
Stat quoque iuncosas Cami remeare paludes,
 Atque iterum raucae murmur adire scholae.   90
Interea fidi parvum cape munus amici,
 Paucaque in alternos verba coacta modos.

(1626)

ELEGY I

To Charles Diodati

CHARLES DIODATI (1609–38), the son of a prominent physician of Italian origin, entered St. Paul's School probably in 1617–18, went up to Oxford in February, 1623, received his B.A. in December, 1625, and stayed on as a candidate for the M.A. He was Milton's one close friend, and his cultivated charm and wit were mournfully recalled in the *Epitaphium Damonis*. Milton was admitted to Christ's College, Cambridge, on February 12, 1625, matriculated on April 9, and began residence in that Easter term. Near the end of his first year, in the Lent term of 1626, he was apparently rusticated or suspended because of friction, temperamental or intellectual or both, with his tutor, William Chappell. At home, Milton writes this epistle to Diodati, who is visiting near Chester. It may be a reply to the second of Diodati's two extant letters in Greek (in Milton's *Works*, 12, 292–95;

C.P.W. 1, 337). Milton passes rapidly over his injured dignity to link his exile with that of his favorite model, Ovid, who had written so many doleful laments from barbarous Tomis on the Black Sea; Cambridge and Tomis are both uncongenial to poets. But mainly he tells of his freedom to enjoy books ("the books that are my life"), plays, and the sight of lovely girls in the parks. This last theme inspires extravagantly allusive and perhaps half-playful rhetoric, but behind it there is a sensuous intensity none the less real because his moral temper brings in a concluding reference to the divine aid of moly. The suspension was not held against Milton; on his return to Cambridge for the Easter term he was, in spite of college rules, assigned to another tutor (so Milton's brother Christopher told the biographer John Aubrey), and he graduated in the usual time.

At last, my dear friend, your letter has reached me and the paper messenger has brought your words, brought them from the western bank of Chester's river Dee,[3] where with downward rush it seeks the Vergivian Sea.[4] I am delighted, believe me,

3. Chester is actually on the east bank of the Dee.

4. Vergivian: Irish.

that a remote district nourishes a heart that loves me and such a faithful soul, and that a distant region is in debt[7] to me for a charming companion yet is ready when asked to give him back soon. I am now in the city washed by the changing tidal waves of the Thames, and not against my will do I stay in my sweet birthplace. I am not anxious to return to the reedy Cam, no love for my long-forbidden abode afflicts me; I have no pleasure in bare fields that afford no pleasant shade. How uncongenial that place is to votaries of Phoebus! Nor am I disposed to go on enduring the threats of a harsh tutor and other indignities my spirit will not bear. If this be exile, to be again in the paternal home and, free from cares, to follow pleasant diversions, then I do not refuse either the name or the fate of an outlaw and happily enjoy my state of banishment. O would that no heavier stroke had fallen upon the poet, that pitiful exile in the land of Tomis![22] Then he would not have yielded a jot to Ionian Homer, and you, Virgil, would have been vanquished and would have failed of first place.

For here I am free to give my time to the quiet Muses, and the books that are my life possess me wholly. If I grow tired, the splendor of the curved theatre welcomes me and the flood of speech on the stage invites applause.[29] Sometimes I listen to a shrewd old man or a spendthrift heir, or a lover appears, or a soldier without his helmet, or a lawyer, grown rich on a ten-year case, thunders forth his barbarous jargon to an uncouth court. Often a clever slave comes to the help of an enamored son and at every turn outwits the straitlaced father under his very nose. There often a girl, wondering at the new fire within her, does not know what love is, and, not knowing, is in love. Or frenzied Tragedy, with disheveled hair, shakes her blood-stained scepter and rolls her eyes.[38] I suffer, and look, and it is a pleasure to look and suffer. Sometimes there is a sweet bitterness even in tears: as when a hapless young man leaves his joys untasted and is torn from his love by lamentable death; or when a grim avenger of crime returns from the dark underworld across the Styx and with his fatal torch strikes fear into guilty souls;[44] or when grief comes upon the house of Pelops or noble Ilus,[45] or Creon's court atones for incestuous forebears.[46]

But I am not always confined under a roof or within the city; I do not let springtime pass by me in vain. I visit too a grove of close-set elms and a famous place of shade near the city. There you may often see groups of girls stroll by, stars that breathe out tempting flames. Ah, how many times have I stood transfixed by the marvelous beauty of a form that could restore youth even to old Jove! Ah, how many times have I seen eyes brighter than jewels and all the stars that both poles turn about, necks that surpass the arms of the twice-living Pelops and the [Milky] Way that flows with pure nectar; and a glorious brow and waving hair, golden snares set by deceitful Love; alluring cheeks that make pallid the crimson of the hyacinth

7. in debt: an echo of Horace's farewell to Virgil (*Od.* 1.3.5–8).

22. In 8 A.D. Ovid was banished by Augustus to the shore of the Black Sea. The reasons are uncertain, though *Ars Amatoria* (*The Art of Love*) was apparently one of them. Milton's comparisons show his youthful and extreme admiration.

29. Most of the references in 29–36 fit the stock characters and plots of Roman rather than English comedy, so that, although he speaks as a spectator, Milton seems to be describing plays he has been reading. The lawyer perhaps comes from Latin satire, ancient and modern.

38. Cf. Ovid, *Amores* 3.1.11–13 (and the sober image of Tragedy in *Il Penseroso* 97–98).

44. Lines 41–44 have been related to *Romeo and Juliet* and to *Richard III, Hamlet,* and *Macbeth,* but they hardly fit. As lines 45–46 imply, Milton is thinking of Greek and Senecan tragedies.

45. Ilus: a mythical founder of Troy (Ilium).

46. Creon: brother-in-law of Oedipus.

and the glow of even your flower, Adonis! Give way, you heroines[63] so often praised of old, and every woman who captivated fickle Jove. Give way, you Achaemenian[65] girls with turreted head-dress, and all those who dwell in Susa and Memnonian Nineveh; you too, Danaid nymphs,[67] and you women of Troy and the race of Romulus, surrender; let not the Tarpeian Muse[69] boast of Pompey's colonnade[69] and theatres filled with Ausonian robes. The prime glory belongs to British maidens; let it be enough for you, foreign women, to have second place. And you, London, the city built by Dardanian settlers, widely conspicuous with your towered head,[74] you, too happy, enclose within your walls whatever beauty the pendant world[76] contains. The stars that sparkle upon you from the clear sky, the host that ministers to Endymion's goddess,[78] are not so many as the crowd to be seen shining through your streets, girls of golden grace. Kindly Venus is believed to have come hither, borne by her twin doves and attended by her quiver-bearing troops, and would prefer this place to Cnidus and the valleys watered by the river Simois, and to Paphos and rosy Cyprus.[84]

As for me, while the indulgence of the blind boy permits, I am preparing to depart with all speed from this fortunate city and, with the help of divine moly,[88] to keep far from the infamous halls of the treacherous Circe. It is settled also that I go back to the rushy fens of the Cam, back to the hoarse murmur of the classroom. Meanwhile, accept the small gift of a loyal friend, these few words molded into alternate measures.[92]

63. heroines: women of ancient myth and history and Ovid's *Heroides* in particular.

65. Achaemenian: Persian (from Achaemenes, founder of the Persian dynasty).

67. Danaid: Greek (from Danaus, mythical founder of Argos and father of fifty daughters, the Danaides).

69. Tarpeian Muse: Ovid, whose house in Rome was near the Capitoline hill, on the side of which was the Tarpeian rock.   Pompey's colonnade: a fashionable Roman promenade in the Campus Martius.

74. Cf. *L'Allegro* 117.

76. Cf. Ovid, *Met.* 1.12–13; Shakespeare, *Measure for Measure* 3.1.126; *P.L.* 2.1052 and 4.1000.

78. The mortal Endymion was loved by Diana, goddess of the moon.

84. Cnidus in Asia Minor and Paphos in Cyprus had temples of Venus. The river Simois at Troy recalls Mount Ida, where Paris gave her the prize of beauty.

88. See the note on *Comus* 636.

92. The elegiac meter, composed of alternating hexameters and pentameters (hence the "limp" of Elegy 6.8), is the meter especially identified with the love poems of Ovid, Propertius, and Tibullus, "the smooth elegiac poets" whom the young Milton greatly liked and imitated.

Elegia secunda, Anno aetatis 17

In obitum Praeconis Academici Cantabrigiensis

Te, qui conspicuus baculo fulgente solebas
  Palladium toties ore ciere gregem,
Ultima praeconum praeconem te quoque saeva
  Mors rapit, officio nec favet ipsa suo.
Candidiora licet fuerint tibi tempora plumis   5
  Sub quibus accipimus delituisse Iovem,
O dignus tamen Haemonio iuvenescere succo,
  Dignus in Aesonios vivere posse dies,
Dignus quem Stygiis medica revocaret ab undis
  Arte Coronides, saepe rogante dea.   10

Tu si iussus eras acies accire togatas,
　Et celer a Phoebo nuntius ire tuo,
Talis in Iliaca stabat Cyllenius aula
　Alipes, aetherea missus ab arce Patris;
Talis et Eurybates ante ora furentis Achillei　　　　　　　15
　Rettulit Atridae iussa severa ducis.
Magna sepulcrorum regina, satelles Averni
　Saeva nimis Musis, Palladi saeva nimis,
Quin illos rapias qui pondus inutile terrae?
　Turba quidem est telis ista petenda tuis.　　　　　　　20
Vestibus hunc igitur pullis, Academia, luge,
　Et madeant lacrimis nigra feretra tuis.
Fundat et ipsa modos querebunda Elegeia tristes,
　Personet et totis naenia moesta scholis.

(1626)

ELEGY II

At the Age of 17

On the Death of the Beadle of Cambridge University

RICHARD RIDDING, Senior Esquire Bedell (Beadle) of the University, resigned on September 16, 1626 the ceremonial office he had held for thirty years, and died well before November 28, when his will was probated. Milton no doubt was somewhat touched by the death of a patriarchal and picturesque figure, but the poem is mainly an exercise, a tissue of mythological allusions.

You who, conspicuous with your shining mace, were wont so many times to call together the Palladian throng,[2] even you, the Beadle, remorseless Death, the last of beadles, has carried off, showing no favor to her own office. Although your temples were whiter than the plumage in which, we are told, Jove was disguised,[6] yet you were worthy to have your youth renewed by Haemonian drugs, worthy to have your strength prolonged to Aeson's age, worthy to be recalled from Stygian waves, at the persistent urging of the goddess, by the medical art of Coronis' son.[10] You, if commanded by your Phoebus[12] to go, a swift messenger, to assemble the gowned ranks, were like wing-footed Cyllenius when, sent from his father's celestial citadel, he stood in the Trojan palace;[14] or like Eurybates when in the face of angry Achilles he reported the stern orders of the chief, Atrides.[16] Great queen of sepulchres, servant of Avernus, too cruel to the Muses, too cruel to Pallas, why do you not take away those who are a useless burden to the earth? That is the crowd you should attack with your darts. Mourn therefore for this man, Academe, in your black robes, and let his dark bier be wet with your tears. Let wailing Elegy herself pour forth sad measures and sound a funeral dirge through all the schools.

2. Votaries of Pallas Athene, i.e. members of the University.

6. Jove visited Leda in the form of a swan whose whiteness was proverbial.

10. Aesculapius, son of Apollo and Coronis, and the mythical archetype of the physician, restored Hippolytus to life at the urgency of Diana.

12. The Vice-Chancellor of the University.

14. Cyllenius (Hermes, Mercury) met Priam on the Trojan plain, not in the palace (*Iliad* 24.334–57).

16. Eurybates was one of the squires sent by Agamemnon (Atrides, son of Atreus) to demand from Achilles the surrender of his prize, Briseis (*Iliad* 1.320–33; Ovid, *Heroides* 3.9–10).

Elegia tertia, Anno aetatis 17

In obitum Praesulis Wintoniensis

Moestus eram, et tacitus nullo comitante sedebam,
  Haerebantque animo tristia plura meo:
Protinus en subiit funestae cladis imago
  Fecit in Angliaco quam Libitina solo;
Dum procerum ingressa est splendentes marmore turres   5
  Dira sepulcrali mors metuenda face;
Pulsavitque auro gravidos et iaspide muros,
  Nec metuit satrapum sternere falce greges.
Tunc memini clarique ducis, fratrisque verendi
  Intempestivis ossa cremata rogis.   10
Et memini heroum quos vidit ad aethera raptos,
  Flevit et amissos Belgia tota duces.
At te praecipue luxi, dignissime praesul,
  Wintoniaeque olim gloria magna tuae;
Delicui fletu, et tristi sic ore querebar: 15
  "Mors fera, Tartareo diva secunda Iovi,
Nonne satis quod silva tuas persentiat iras,
  Et quod in herbosos ius tibi detur agros,
Quodque afflata tuo marcescant lilia tabo,
  Et crocus, et pulchrae Cypridi sacra rosa?   20
Nec sinis ut semper fluvio contermina quercus
  Miretus lapsus praetereuntis aquae.
Et tibi succumbit liquido quae plurima coelo
  Evehitur pennis quamlibet augur avis,
Et quae mille nigris errant animalia silvis,   25
  Et quod alunt mutum Proteos antra pecus.
Invida, tanta tibi cum sit concessa potestas,
  Quid iuvat humana tingere caede manus?
Nobileque in pectus certas acuisse sagittas,
  Semideamque animam sede fugasse sua?"   30
Talia dum lacrimans alto sub pectore volvo,
  Roscidus occiduis Hesperus exit aquis,
Et Tartessiaco submerserat aequore currum
  Phoebus, ab eoo litore mensus iter.
Nec mora, membra cavo posui refovenda cubili,   35
  Condiderant oculos noxque soporque meos,
Cum mihi visus eram lato spatiarier agro;
  Heu nequit ingenium visa referre meum.
Illic punicea radiabant omnia luce,
  Ut matutino cum iuga sole rubent.   40
Ac veluti cum pandit opes Thaumantia proles,
  Vestitu nituit multicolore solum.
Non dea tam variis ornavit floribus hortos
  Alcinoi, Zephyro Chloris amata levi.
Flumina vernantes lambunt argentea campos,   45
  Ditior Hesperio flavet arena Tago.

Serpit odoriferas per opes levis aura Favoni,
  Aura sub innumeris humida nata rosis.
Talis in extremis terrae Gangetidis oris
  Luciferi regis fingitur esse domus.   50
Ipse racemiferis dum densas vitibus umbras
  Et pellucentes miror ubique locos,
Ecce mihi subito praesul Wintonius astat,
  Sidereum nitido fulsit in ore iubar;
Vestis ad auratos defluxit candida talos,   55
  Infula divinum cinxerat alba caput.
Dumque senex tali incedit venerandus amictu,
  Intremuit laeto florea terra sono.
Agmina gemmatis plaudunt caelestia pennis,
  Pura triumphali personat aethra tuba.   60
Quisque novum amplexu comitem cantuque salutat,
  Hosque aliquis placido misit ab ore sonos:
"Nate, veni, et patrii felix cape gaudia regni;
  Semper abhinc duro, nate, labore vaca."
Dixit, et aligerae tetigerunt nablia turmae;   65
  At mihi cum tenebris aurea pulsa quies.
Flebam turbatos Cephaleia pellice somnos.
  Talia contingant somnia saepe mihi!

(1626)

ELEGY III

At the Age of 17
On the Death of the Bishop of Winchester

LANCELOT ANDREWES was probably the most eminent churchman of his age, a notable figure and famous preacher at court, a major champion of the Anglo-Catholic position against continental polemicists; and he was one of the translators of the King James Bible. He was held in deservedly high repute for both learning and sanctity, although he was not entirely immune from the weaknesses of Jacobean bishops. He had been Master of Pembroke Hall in Cambridge during 1589–1605.

Andrewes (b. 1555) died September 25, 1626, and Milton must have written his poem soon after that date (see the headnote on the elegy on the Bishop of Ely). Here, as in his other early obituary pieces, the young academic craftsman is seizing the usual kind of subject, but, though the poem has much of the conventional, it is also the young Christian's first challenge to death and ends with the first of his many radiant visions of heaven.

I was sorrowful and sitting in silence, with no companion. Many griefs were afflicting my mind, when, lo, there came a vision of the calamitous mortality that Libitina wrought on English soil,[4] while grim Death, fearful with her sepulchral torch, entered great men's palaces of gleaming marble, knocked on walls heavy with gold and jasper, and did not shrink from cutting down troops of nobles with her scythe. Then I remembered the illustrious leader and his revered brother,[9] whose bones were consumed on untimely pyres; and I remembered the heroes whom

4. The ancient Italian goddess of corpses, equivalent to Death. In London during 1625 the plague cost over 35,000 lives.

9. The great leader and his brother (i.e. comrade) are usually taken to be Duke Christian of Brunswick (1599–June 6, 1626) and

Belgia saw carried to the skies, the lost chieftains[12] whom the whole country mourned. But you chiefly I lamented, honored bishop, in years past the signal glory of Winchester. I melted in tears, and thus in sad speech I complained: "Cruel Death, goddess second to Tartarean Jove,[16] is it not enough that the forest feels your fury, that you are given sway over the growth of the fields, and that the lilies and the crocus and the rose, sacred to beautiful Cypris, wither under your pestilent breath? Nor do you allow the oak on the river bank to watch for ever the flow of the passing water. And all the birds that are borne on their wings through the clear sky, despite their gift of augury, fall victims to you, and the countless animals that roam the dark woods, and the dumb herd the caves of Proteus harbor. Envious goddess, since all this power has been granted you, why do you take pleasure in staining your hands with human blood, in sharpening your unerring shafts against a noble breast, and in driving a half-divine soul from its abode?"

While in tears I brooded deeply on such thoughts, dewy Hesperus rose out of the western waters and Phoebus, having measured his journey from the eastern shore, had sunk his chariot in the Tartessian sea. Forthwith I laid myself down to rest in my hollow bed, and night and sleep had closed my eyes, when I seemed to be walking in a broad field. Alas, I have not the power to relate what I saw. There all things were bathed in rosy light, as when mountain heights are flushed by the morning sun: the earth was bright with many-colored attire, as when the daughter[41] of Thaumas spreads out her wealth; Chloris, the goddess beloved by mild Zephyr, did not adorn the gardens of Alcinous with such variety of flowers. Silver streams washed fields of springtime green; their yellow sand was richer than that of Hesperian Tagus.[46] The gentle breath of Favonius stole through this place of sweet-smelling luxuriance, a moist breath born under myriads of roses. Such is said to be the home of the sovereign Light-bearer,[50] on the farthest shores of the land of the Ganges. While I gazed in wonder at the deep shades under the grape-laden vines and at the sunlit spaces all about, lo, suddenly the Bishop of Winchester stood before me. A starry light beamed in his glowing face;[54] a shining white robe flowed down to his golden sandals; a white fillet encircled his divine head. And as the venerable old man, thus garbed, came forward, the flowery earth trembled with a joyful sound. The celestial hosts applaud with their jeweled wings, and the pure air of heaven resounds with triumphal notes of the trumpet. All greet their new comrade with an embrace and song, and one spoke these words with serene face: "Come, my son, and enjoy the felicity of your Father's kingdom; henceforth, my son, rest for ever from your hard labors."[64] He spoke, and the winged squadrons touched their harps.[65] But for me golden rest was banished along with darkness, and I grieved for the sleep broken by Cephalus' love. May dreams like these often fall to my lot![68]

Count Ernest of Mansfeld (*c.* 1580–*c.* November 29, 1626), who fought on the Protestant side in the Thirty Years' War. The date of Mansfeld's death is one difficulty in regard to a poem written apparently in early October. Also, it seems inconceivable that Milton, writing about illustrious deaths of the last year or two, would omit that of King James (1566–March 27, 1625). A royal "brother" would be Prince Maurice of Orange (1567–April 23, 1625), the leader of Protestant Holland.

12. Among leaders who died during service in the Low Countries were the Earl of Southampton (1624), the 18th Earl of Oxford (1625), and Duke Christian (mentioned above).

16. Pluto.

41. Iris.

46. The golden sand of the river Tagus in Portugal and Spain was a poetic commonplace in antiquity and later.

50. Light-bearer: Lucifer, the sun (cf. Ovid, *Met.* 1.778–79).

54. Cf. Moses (Exod. 34.29–35).

64. Matt. 25.21, Rev. 14.13.

65. Rev. 14.2.

68. Apparently an echo of the prayers of Ovid (*Amores* 1.5.26) and Tibullus (1.1.49) in a very different situation.

Anno aetatis 17. In obitum Praesulis Eliensis

Adhuc madentes rore squalebant genae,
  Et sicca nondum lumina;
Adhuc liquentis imbre turgebant salis
  Quem nuper effudi pius,
Dum maesta caro iusta persolvi rogo   5
  Wintoniensis praesulis,
Cum centilinguis Fama (proh semper mali
  Cladisque vera nuntia)
Spargit per urbes divitis Britanniae
  Populosque Neptuno satos,   10
Cessisse morti, et ferreis sororibus
  Te, generis humani decus,
Qui rex sacrorum illa fuisti in insula
  Quae nomen Anguillae tenet.
Tunc inquietum pectus ira protinus   15
  Ebulliebat fervida,
Tumulis potentem saepe devovens deam:
  Nec vota Naso in Ibida
Concepit alto diriora pectore,
  Graiusque vates parcius   20
Turpem Lycambis execratus est dolum,
  Sponsamque Neobolen suam.
At ecce diras ipse dum fundo graves,
  Et imprecor neci necem,
Audisse tales videor attonitus sonos   25
  Leni, sub aura, flamine:
"Caecos furores pone, pone vitream
  Bilemque et irritas minas.
Quid temere violas non nocenda numina,
  Subitoque ad iras percita?   30
Non est, ut arbitraris elusus miser,
  Mors atra Noctis fllia,
Erebove patre creta, sive Erinnye,
  Vastove nata sub Chao:
Ast illa caelo missa stellato, Dei   35
  Messes ubique colligit;
Animasque mole carnea reconditas
  In lucem et auras evocat,
Ut cum fugaces excitant Horae diem
  Themidos Iovisque filiae;   40
Et sempiterni ducit ad vultus patris;
  At iusta raptat impios
Sub regna furvi luctuosa Tartari
  Sedesque subterraneas.
Hanc ut vocantem laetus audivi, cito   45
  Foedum reliqui carcerem,
Volatilesque faustus inter milites

Ad astra sublimis feror,
Vates ut olim raptus ad coelum senex
  Auriga currus ignei.   50
Non me Bootis terruere lucidi
  Sarraca tarda frigore, aut
Formidolosi Scorpionis brachia,
  Non ensis, Orion, tuus.
Praetervolavi fulgidi solis globum,   55
  Longeque sub pedibus deam
Vidi triformem, dum coercebat suos
  Frenis dracones aureis.
Erraticorum siderum per ordines,
  Per lacteas vehor plagas,   60
Velocitatem saepe miratus novam,
  Donec nitentes ad fores
Ventum est Olympi, et regiam crystallinam, et
  Stratum smaragdis atrium.
Sed hic tacebo, nam quis effari queat   65
  Oriundus humano patre
Amoenitates illius loci? mihi
  Sat est in aeternum frui."

(1626)

ON THE DEATH OF THE BISHOP OF ELY

At the Age of 17

NICHOLAS FELTON (1556–October 5, 1626) had been Master of Pembroke Hall, Cambridge, in 1617–19 and followed Andrewes as Bishop of Ely, 1619–26. Though much less illustrious than Andrewes, Felton was a good and scholarly man and a noted preacher. He died ten days after Andrewes, and Milton begins by saying that he had barely paid his tribute to the latter when news came of Felton's death. The poem is similar in pattern to Elegy 3, but the poet's picture of heaven is replaced by Felton's account of his journey thither; the flight through space has many precedents, from Cicero (*Rep.* 6.15 f.), Ovid (*Met.* 2.167 f.), Dante (*Par.* 1 f.), and Chaucer (*House of Fame* 529 f., *Parliament of Fowls* 29 f.) to Donne's *Second Anniversary* (185–210).

My cheeks were still wet and stained with tears, and my eyes, not yet dry, were still swollen with the salty rain that in reverence I lately poured forth as I paid my sorrowful tribute to the precious bier of the Bishop of Winchester, when hundred-tongued Rumor — always, alas, a true messenger of evil and calamity — spread through the cities of rich Britain and the people sprung from Neptune the news that death and the cruel sisters[11] had claimed you, an ornament of the human race, who were the head of the church[13] in the island that bears the name of Ely.[14] Then forthwith my troubled breast boiled up with hot anger and many curses against the goddess[17] who holds sway over tombs. No fiercer imprecations did Ovid conceive

11. The Fates.
13. The phrase renders *rex sacrorum* ("king of the sacrifices"), a priestly title in ancient Rome; most translators give "king of holy men" or a similar phrase.

14. According to Bede, "Ely" meant "eel-island," because the fens harbored many snakes (*anguilla*, eel).
17. Libitina (cf. Elegy 3.4), Death (ibid., 3.6), or Proserpine.

in the depths of his heart when he attacked Ibis;[18] and more restrained was the Greek bard who denounced the base duplicity of Lycambes and Neobule, his promised bride.[22] But lo, while I poured out my bitter curses and demanded that death must die, I seemed to hear, with wonder, these words in the gently moving air:

"Put away your blind rage; put away your gleaming bile[28] and vain threats. Why do you rashly assail deities that cannot be injured and are quickly roused to wrath? Death is not, as you in your wretched delusion think, the black daughter of Night, nor of Erebus, nor of Erinys,[33] nor was she born of vast Chaos.[34] But, sent from starry heaven, she everywhere gathers in the harvests of God. Souls hidden within a mass of flesh[37] she calls forth into the light and air, as when the flying Hours, the daughters of Themis and Jove, awaken the day; and she leads them into the presence of the eternal Father. But the wicked she justly carries down to the baleful realms of dark Tartarus, the infernal habitation. When with joy I heard her calling, I quickly left my foul prison[46] and, happy among the winged warriors,[47] I was carried aloft to the stars, as once the old prophet,[49] driver of the fiery chariot, was swept up to heaven. I was not terrified by bright Bootes with his Wain, sluggish in the cold, or the claws of the terrible Scorpion, nor by your sword, Orion. I flew past the globe of the fiery sun and far below my feet I saw the triform goddess[56] checking her dragons with golden reins. Through the ranks of the wandering stars,[59] through the Milky Way, I was borne, often marveling at my strange speed, until I reached the shining doors of Olympus and the crystalline palace, the court paved with emeralds.[64] But I will say no more, for who that is son of a mortal father can describe the beauties of that place?[67] For me it is enough to enjoy them forever."

18. The exiled Ovid's *Ibis* (*The Crane*) was an invective against a probably fictitious enemy.

22. Lycambes, whose daughter Neobule was betrothed to the Greek poet Archilochus, refused to allow the marriage and was attacked in such savage verse that he was said to have hanged himself.

28. Greek medical writers attributed madness to a condition of the black bile which gave it a peculiar glitter.

33. One of the Furies.

34. With 32–34 cf. Cicero, *De Natura Deorum* 3.17.44.

37. The idea of the soul's release from its bodily prison, starting from Plato and Cicero, became a part of Christianity, especially of the Platonic tradition.

46. Of the flesh and earthly life (see preceding note).

47. Cf. *Upon the Circumcision* 1.

49. Elijah (2 Kings 2.11).

56. Glossary, "Diana"; see *Il Penseroso* 59–60 and note.

59. The planets.

64. Rev. 21.11, 19, 21.

67. 1 Cor. 2.9.

Anno aetatis 16. In obitum Procancellarii medici

Parere fati discite legibus,
Manusque Parcae iam date supplices,
    Qui pendulum telluris orbem
        Iapeti colitis nepotes.
Vos si relicto mors vaga Taenaro
Semel vocarit flebilis, heu morae
    Tentantur incassum dolique;
        Per tenebras Stygis ire certum est.
Si destinatam pellere dextera

Mortem valeret, non ferus Hercules   10
  Nessi venenatus cruore
    Aemathia iacuisset Oeta.
Nec fraude turpi Palladis invidae
Vidisset occisum Ilion Hectora, aut
  Quem larva Pelidis peremit   15
    Ense Locro, Iove lacrimante.
Si triste fatum verba Hecateia
Fugare possint, Telegoni parens
  Vixisset infamis, potentique
    Aegiali soror usa virga.   20
Numenque trinum fallere si queant
Artes medentum, ignotaque gramina,
  Non gnarus herbarum Machaon
    Eurypyli cecidisset hasta.
Laesisset et nec te, Philyreie,   25
Sagitta echidnae perlita sanguine;
  Nec tela te fulmenque avitum,
    Caese, puer, genetricis alvo.
Tuque, O alumno maior Apolline,
Gentis togatae cui regimen datum,   30
  Frondosa quem nunc Cirrha luget,
    Et mediis Helicon in undis,
Iam praefuisses Palladio gregi
Laetus, superstes, nec sine gloria;
  Nec puppe lustrasses Charontis   35
    Horribiles barathri recessus.
At fila rupit Persephone tua
Irata, cum te viderit artibus
  Succoque pollenti tot atris
    Faucibus eripuisse mortis.   40
Colende praeses, membra precor tua
Molli quiescant cespite, et ex tuo
  Crescant rosae calthaeque busto,
    Purpureoque hyacinthus ore.
Sit mite de te iudicium Aeaci,   45
Subrideatque Aetnaea Proserpina,
  Interque felices perennis
    Elysio spatiere campo.

      (1626)

ON THE DEATH OF THE VICE-CHANCELLOR,
A PHYSICIAN

At the Age of 16

DR. JOHN GOSTLIN, Master of Caius College, Professor of Physic (Medicine) and Vice-Chancellor of the University, died on October 21, 1626, when Milton was seventeen, so that his dating of the poem was a slip of memory. As the elegies on the two bishops are similar in length and pattern, so are those on the Beadle and the Vice-Chancellor. In contrast with the religious visions of the former pair, in writing of laymen Milton embroiders their official or professional functions with mythology and, in this poem, with strained periphrasis. But these Horatian Alcaics end with a clear, grave dignity.

Learn to obey the laws of destiny and now raise suppliant hands to the goddess of Fate,[2] you descendants of Iapetus who inhabit the pendulous globe of the earth. If, leaving Taenarus, roving Death has once called you with woeful voice, alas, it is vain to attempt delays and stratagems; your journey through Stygian darkness is fixed. If man's right arm had the strength to ward off appointed death, fierce Hercules would not have been laid low on Emathian Oeta by Nessus' poisonous blood;[12] nor would Ilium have seen Hector killed through the base deceit of envious Pallas,[13] or him[15] whom the phantom of Achilles slew with Locrian sword, while Jove wept. If Hecateian spells could banish melancholy doom, the mother[18] of Telegonus would have continued her infamous life, and the sister[20] of Aegialeus the use of her potent wand. If medical arts and rare herbs could deceive the triple deity,[21] Machaon,[23] with his knowledge of plants, would not have fallen to the spear of Eurypylus; nor would the arrow smeared with serpent's blood have afflicted you, son[25] of Philyra; nor would the bolts of your grandsire's thunder have struck you, boy[28] cut from your mother's womb.

And you, greater than your pupil Apollo, you to whom was given rule over the gowned tribe, whom now leafy Cirrha[31] mourns, and Helicon amid its fountains, you would still, happily alive and not without glory, be presiding over the Palladian flock, and would not have traversed in Charon's[35] boat the horrible depths of the abyss. But Persephone broke your thread of life, angry when she saw that by your arts and powerful drugs you had snatched so many from the black jaws of death.[37] Reverend Chancellor, may your limbs, I pray, rest in the soft turf, and from your grave may roses and marigolds grow, and the purple-lipped hyacinth. May Aeacus[45] pronounce a mild judgment upon you, and Etnaean[46] Proserpine smile, and may you walk forever among the blessed in the Elysian field.[48]

2. Three Fates are more usual than Milton's one.

12. See the note on *P.L.* 2.542–46.

13. Pallas Athene caused Hector's death by appearing to him in the form of his brother Deiphobus and urging him to fight with Achilles (*Iliad* 22.226–404).

15. Sarpedon, son of Zeus, was killed by the Locrian Patroclus, who was wearing Achilles' armor (*Iliad* 16.458–506).

18. In non-Homeric tradition Telegonus was the son of Circe and Odysseus.

20. Medea, fleeing with Jason, killed her brother and scattered fragments of his body on the sea to delay her father's pursuit.

21. The Fates (cf. 2 above).

23. Son of Aesculapius; a physician in the Greek army at Troy.

25. Chiron the centaur.

28. Because Aesculapius (cf. Elegy 2.10) revived even the dead, his grandfather Zeus killed him with a thunderbolt.

31. Cirrha: the port of Delphi, hence a symbol of Apollo; here, Cambridge and the learned world.

35. Charon: ferryman of the dead over the Styx.

37. Persephone (Proserpine), queen of the dead, was jealous of Gostlin the healer as Zeus was of Aesculapius (cf. 28 above).

45. A judge of the dead in Hades.

46. Sicilian (from Mount Etna).

48. Here the Christian heaven.

The Fifth Ode of Horace, Lib. I

Quis multa gracilis te puer in rosa, rendered almost word for word without rhyme, according to the Latin measure, as near as the language will permit.

THERE IS no real clue to the date of this experiment. Its being first printed in the 1673 edition does not necessarily mean composition after 1645, since two poems of 1628 were first printed in 1673. Nor does its being placed after the sonnets provide any firm ground for conjecture. It is hard to imagine Milton in the 1640's or later being diverted by Pyrrha from more urgent and exalted concerns. Possibly the piece was an offshoot of Milton's practice with Horatian meters in his elegies on the bishop of Ely and the Vice-Chancellor of Cambridge (although the autumn of 1626 is overloaded with longer poems, and in style the ode is unlike the youthful Milton). The translation has received some high praise, but it may be thought that Milton only partly overcame the combined difficulties of extreme literalness and the original meter (fourth Asclepiadean). Some good phrases stand out from the prevailing stiffness — which in lines 9–11 becomes ambiguous awkwardness.

What slender youth, bedewed with liquid odors,
Courts thee on roses in some pleasant cave,
    Pyrrha? For whom bind'st thou
    In wreaths thy golden hair,
Plain in thy neatness? O how oft shall he   5
On faith and changed gods complain, and seas
    Rough with black winds and storms
    Unwonted shall admire,
Who now enjoys thee credulous, all gold;
Who always vacant, always amiable,   10
    Hopes thee, of flattering gales
    Unmindful. Hapless they
To whom thou untried seem'st fair. Me, in my vowed
Picture, the sacred wall declares t' have hung
    My dank and dropping weeds   15
    To the stern god of sea.

                     (*c.* 1626–28?)

AD PYRRHAM. ODE V

Horatius ex Pyrrhae illecebris tanquam e naufragio enataverat, cuius amore irretitos, affirmat esse miseros.

    Quis multa gracilis te puer in rosa
    Perfusus liquidis urget odoribus,
        Grato, Pyrrha, sub antro?
        Cui flavam religas comam
    Simplex munditie? heu quoties fidem
    Mutatosque deos flebit, et aspera
        Nigris aequora ventis
        Emirabitur insolens,
    Qui nunc te fruitur credulus aurea:

Qui semper vacuam, semper amabilem   10
    Sperat, nescius aurae
    Fallacis. miseri quibus
Intentata nites. me tabula sacer
Votiva paries indicat uvida
    Suspendisse potenti   15
    Vestimenta maris Deo.

THE HORATIAN text, as Milton printed it along with his English, has several variants from modern orthodoxy: the singular *munditie* instead of the plural and *quoties* instead of *quotiens* (line 5), and *Intentata* instead of *Intemptata* (13). Milton's text of the poem and also the Latin headnote are verbally identical with those in the editions of Horace edited by John Bond in 1620 and 1630; the differences in Milton — *v* in place of *u* and commas around

Pyrrha — are trifles within the compositor's scope. While two of the cited variants appear in other men's editions of these and earlier years (so far as I have explored), Bond alone seems to have *munditie* (and his 1614 edition has *munditiis*). Apparently, then, the text Milton used was available from at least 1620 onward (I have not seen Bond's earliest editions, but in this case they do not matter).

EPIGRAMS ON THE GUNPOWDER PLOT

THE EPIGRAM, a form widely cultivated in the Renaissance in both Latin and the vernaculars, was a short, terse poem of almost any kind — satirical, amatory, obituary, complimentary, or what not — which had an ingenious or sententious climax. The great classical models were the poems of the Greek Anthology and Martial. Milton's five

epigrams on the Gunpowder Plot, which are of the popular satirical type, link themselves with his long poem on the subject (1626). They may have been written at various times, or, since the first four are variations on one idea, possibly at the same time. The second obviously came after King James's death (March 27, 1625).

In Proditionem Bombardicam

Cum simul in regem nuper satrapasque Britannos
    Ausus es infandum, perfide Fauxe, nefas,
Fallor? an et mitis voluisti ex parte videri,
    Et pensare mala cum pietate scelus?
Scilicet hos alti missurus ad atria caeli,   5
    Sulphureo curru flammivolisque rotis,
Qualiter ille, feris caput inviolabile Parcis,
    Liquit Iordanios turbine raptus agros.
                                            (*c.* 1626?)

ON THE GUNPOWDER PLOT

When lately, treacherous Fawkes, you dared an unspeakable crime against the king and British peers, did you — or am I mistaken? — wish to show a sort of kindness and make up for your evil deed with evil piety? Clearly you were going to send them to the courts of high heaven, in a sulphurous chariot with wheels of flame, like him[7] — a head the cruel Fates could not touch — who, swept up in a whirlwind, left the fields of the Jordan.

7. Elijah. Cf. the elegy on the Bishop of Ely, lines 49–50.

In eandem

Siccine tentasti caelo donasse Iacobum
    Quae septemgemino Belua monte lates?
Ni meliora tuum poterit dare munera numen,
    Parce, precor, donis insidiosa tuis.
Ille quidem sine te consortia serus adivit   5
    Astra, nec inferni pulveris usus ope.
Sic potius foedos in caelum pelle cucullos,
    Et quot habet brutos Roma profana deos,
Namque hac aut alia nisi quemque adiuveris arte,
    Crede mihi, caeli vix bene scandet iter.   10

(*c.* 1626?)

ON THE SAME

Was it thus you attempted to give James admission to heaven, you Beast[2] who lurk among the seven hills? Unless your divinity is able to bestow better presents, forbear, I beg, your insidious gifts. He at a late age joined his kindred stars without your help and without the use of hellish gunpowder. So rather send your dirty friars to the skies, and all the dumb idols of profane Rome; for, if you do not aid them in this way or another, believe me, they will hardly succeed in climbing the road to heaven.

2. The papacy in Rome, the city of the seven hills, was identified by zealous Protestants with the Beast of Rev. 13 and 17.

In eandem

Purgatorem animae derisit Iacobus ignem,
    Et sine quo superum non adeunda domus.
Frenduit hoc trina monstrum Latiale corona
    Movit et horrificum cornua dena minax.
Et "Nec inultus" ait "temnes mea sacra, Britanne,   5
    Supplicium spreta religione dabis.
Et si stelligeras unquam penetraveris arces,
    Non nisi per flammas triste patebit iter."
O quam funesto cecinisti proxima vero,
    Verbaque ponderibus vix caritura suis!   10
Nam prope Tartareo sublime rotatus ab igni
    Ibat ad aethereas umbra perusta plagas.

(*c.* 1626?)

ON THE SAME

King James scoffed at the idea of purgatorial fire without which the soul cannot attain its heavenly home. At this the Roman monster with the triple crown[3] gnashed its teeth and shook its ten horns[4] with horrid threats. "Briton," it declares, "you shall not scorn my sacred tenets with impunity. You shall pay the penalty for insulting religion, and, if you ever reach the starry citadels, only a painful way through flames will be open." How close was your prophecy to the grim truth, and how little your words fell short of fulfilment! For he did, almost, ascend to the celestial realms, a burnt-up shade, whirled aloft by Tartarean fire.

3. Cf. *In quintum Novembris* 55.   4. Rev. 13.1, 17.3,7.

In eandem

Quem modo Roma suis devoverat impia diris,
    Et Styge damnarat Taenarioque sinu,
Hunc vice mutata iam tollere gestit ad astra,
    Et cupit ad superos evehere usque Deos.
                                                          (*c.* 1626?)

ON THE SAME

Him[1] whom impious Rome had recently laid under her dire anathema and condemned to the Styx and the Taenarian abyss, him she now, reversing her aims, is eager to raise to the stars and wishes to send up even to the celestial gods.

1. King James, baptized a Roman Catholic but reared a Protestant, would be, in the Romanist view, excommunicate.

In inventorem Bombardae

Iapetionidem laudavit caeca vetustas,
    Qui tulit aetheream solis ab axe facem;
At mihi maior erit qui lurida creditur arma
    Et trifidum fulmen surripuisse Iovi.
                                                          (*c.* 1626?)

ON THE INVENTOR OF GUNPOWDER

Blind antiquity praised the son[1] of Iapetus who brought celestial fire from the sun's chariot; but to me he will be a greater man who is thought to have stolen from Jove his lurid arms and three-forked thunderbolt.

1. Prometheus.

In quintum Novembris, Anno aetatis 17

Iam pius extrema veniens Iacobus ab arcto
Teucrigenas populos, lateque patentia regna
Albionum tenuit, iamque inviolabile foedus
Sceptra Caledoniis coniunxerat Anglica Scotis:
Pacificusque novo felix divesque sedebat   5
In solio, occultique doli securus et hostis:
Cum ferus ignifluo regnans Acheronte tyrannus,
Eumenidum pater, aethereo vagus exul Olympo,
Forte per immensum terrarum erraverat orbem,
Dinumerans sceleris socios, vernasque fideles,   10
Participes regni post funera moesta futuros.
Hic tempestates medio ciet aere diras,
Illic unanimes odium struit inter amicos,
Armat et invictas in mutua viscera gentes;
Regnaque olivifera vertit florentia pace,   15
Et quoscunque videt purae virtutis amantes,
Hos cupit adiicere imperio, fraudumque magister
Tentat inaccessum sceleri corrumpere pectus;
Insidiasque locat tacitas, cassesque latentes
Tendit, ut incautos rapiat, ceu Caspia tigris   20
Insequitur trepidam deserta per avia praedam
Nocte sub illuni, et somno nictantibus astris.
Talibus infestat populos Summanus et urbes
Cinctus caeruleae fumanti turbine flammae.
Iamque fluentisonis albentia rupibus arva   25
Apparent, et terra deo dilecta marino,
Cui nomen dederat quondam Neptunia proles
Amphitryoniaden qui non dubitavit atrocem
Aequore tranato furiali poscere bello,
Ante expugnatae crudelia saecula Troiae.   30
   At simul hanc opibusque et festa pace beatam
Aspicit, et pingues donis Cerealibus agros,
Quodque magis doluit, venerantem numina veri
Sancta Dei populum, tandem suspiria rupit
Tartareos ignes et luridum olentia sulphur,   35
Qualia Trinacria trux ab Iove clausus in Aetna
Efflat tabifico monstrosus ab ore Typhoeus.
Ignescunt oculi, stridetque adamantinus ordo
Dentis, ut armorum fragor, ictaque cuspide cuspis.
Atque "Pererrato solum hoc lacrimabile mundo   40
Inveni," dixit, "gens haec mihi sola rebellis,
Contemtrixque iugi, nostraque potentior arte.
Illa tamen, mea si quicquam tentamina possunt,
Non feret hoc impune diu, non ibit inulta."
Hactenus; et piceis liquido natat aere pennis;   45
Qua volat, adversi praecursant agmine venti,
Densantur nubes, et crebra tonitrua fulgent.
   Iamque pruinosas velox superaverat Alpes,

Et tenet Ausoniae fines. A parte sinistra
Nimbifer Appenninus erat, priscique Sabini;   50
Dextra veneficiis infamis Hetruria, nec non
Te furtiva, Tibris, Thetidi videt oscula dantem;
Hinc Mavortigenae consistit in arce Quirini.
Reddiderant dubiam iam sera crepuscula lucem,
Cum circumgreditur totam Tricoronifer urbem,   55
Panificosque deos portat, scapulisque virorum
Evehitur; praeeunt summisso poplite reges,
Et mendicantum series longissima fratrum;
Cereaque in manibus gestant funalia caeci,
Cimmeriis nati in tenebris vitamque trahentes.   60
Templa dein multis subeunt lucentia taedis
(Vesper erat sacer iste Petro), fremitusque canentum
Saepe tholos implet vacuos, et inane locorum:
Qualiter exululat Bromius, Bromiique caterva,
Orgia cantantes in Echionio Aracyntho,   65
Dum tremit attonitus vitreis Asopus in undis,
Et procul ipse cava responsat rupe Cithaeron.
   His igitur tandem solenni more peractis,
Nox senis amplexus Erebi taciturna reliquit,
Praecipitesque impellit equos stimulante flagello,   70
Captum oculis Typhlonta, Melanchaetemque ferocem,
Atque Acherontaeo prognatam patre Siopen
Torpidam, et hirsutis horrentem Phrica capillis.
   Interea regum domitor, Phlegetontius haeres,
Ingreditur thalamos (neque enim secretus adulter   75
Producit steriles molli sine pellice noctes);
At vix compositos somnus claudebat ocellos,
Cum niger umbrarum dominus, rectorque silentum,
Praedatorque hominum, falsa sub imagine tectus
Astitit; assumptis micuerunt tempora canis,   80
Barba sinus promissa tegit, cineracea longo
Syrmate verrit humum vestis, pendetque cucullus
Vertice de raso, et ne quicquam desit ad artes,
Cannabeo lumbos constrinxit fune salaces,
Tarda fenestratis figens vestigia calceis.   85
Talis, uti fama est, vasta Franciscus eremo
Tetra vagabatur solus per lustra ferarum,
Silvestrique tulit genti pia verba salutis
Impius, atque lupos domuit, Libycosque leones.
   Subdolus at tali Serpens velatus amictu   90
Solvit in has fallax ora execrantia voces:
"Dormis, nate? Etiamne tuos sopor opprimit artus?
Immemor O fidei, pecorumque oblite tuorum,
Dum cathedram, venerande, tuam, diademaque triplex
Ridet Hyperboreo gens barbara nata sub axe,   95
Dumque pharetrati spernunt tua iura Britanni;
Surge, age, surge piger, Latius quem Caesar adorat,
Cui reserata patet convexi ianua caeli,
Turgentes animos, et fastus frange procaces,

Sacrilegique sciant tua quid maledictio possit,   100
Et quid Apostolicae possit custodia clavis;
Et memor Hesperiae disiectam ulciscere classem,
Mersaque Iberorum lato vexilla profundo,
Sanctorumque cruci tot corpora fixa probrosae,
Thermodoontea nuper regnante puella.   105
At tu si tenero mavis torpescere lecto,
Crescentesque negas hosti contundere vires,
Tyrrhenum implebit numeroso milite pontum,
Signaque Aventino ponet fulgentia colle:
Reliquias veterum franget, flammisque cremabit,   110
Sacraque calcabit pedibus tua colla profanis,
Cuius gaudebant soleis dare basia reges.
Nec tamen hunc bellis et aperto Marte lacesses;
Irritus ille labor; tu callidus utere fraude;
Quaelibet haereticis disponere retia fas est.   115
Iamque ad consilium extremis rex magnus ab oris
Patricios vocat, et procerum de stirpe creatos,
Grandaevosque patres trabea canisque verendos;
Hos tu membratim poteris conspergere in auras,
Atque dare in cineres, nitrati pulveris igne   120
Aedibus iniecto, qua convenere, sub imis.
Protinus ipse igitur quoscumque habet Anglia fidos
Propositi factique mone; quisquamne tuorum
Audebit summi non iussa facessere Papae?
Perculsosque metu subito, casumque stupentes   125
Invadat vel Gallus atrox, vel saevus Iberus.
Saecula sic illic tandem Mariana redibunt,
Tuque in belligeros iterum dominaberis Anglos.
Et nequid timeas, divos divasque secundas
Accipe, quotque tuis celebrantur numina fastis."   130
Dixit et adscitos ponens malefidus amictus
Fugit ad infandam, regnum illaetabile, Lethen.
    Iam rosea Eoas pandens Tithonia portas
Vestit inauratas redeunti lumine terras;
Maestaque adhuc nigri deplorans funera nati   135
Irrigat ambrosiis montana cacumina guttis;
Cum somnos pepulit stellatae ianitor aulae,
Nocturnos visus et somnia grata revolvens.
    Est locus aeterna septus caligine noctis,
Vasta ruinosi quondam fundamina tecti,   140
Nunc torvi spelunca Phoni, Prodotaeque bilinguis
Effera quos uno peperit Discordia partu.
Hic inter caementa iacent praeruptaque saxa,
Ossa inhumata virum, et traiecta cadavera ferro;
Hic Dolus intortis semper sedet ater ocellis,   145
Iurgiaque, et stimulis armata Calumnia fauces,
Et Furor, atque viae moriendi mille videntur,
Et Timor; exanguisque locum circumvolat Horror,
Perpetuoque leves per muta silentia Manes,
Exululat tellus et sanguine conscia stagnat.   150

Ipsi etiam pavidi latitant penetralibus antri
Et Phonos et Prodotes, nulloque sequente per antrum,
Antrum horrens, scopulosum, atrum feralibus umbris,
Diffugiunt sontes, et retro lumina vortunt.
Hos pugiles Romae per saecula longa fideles   155
Evocat antistes Babylonius, atque ita fatur:
"Finibus occiduis circumfusum incolit aequor
Gens exosa mihi; prudens Natura negavit
Indignam penitus nostro coniungere mundo:
Illuc, sic iubeo, celeri contendite gressu,   160
Tartareoque leves difflentur pulvere in auras
Et rex et pariter satrapae, scelerata propago;
Et quotquot fidei caluere cupidine verae
Consilii socios adhibete, operisque ministros."
Finierat: rigidi cupide paruere gemelli.   165
    Interea longo flectens curvamine coelos
Despicit aetherea Dominus qui fulgurat arce,
Vanaque perversae ridet conamina turbae,
Atque sui causam populi volet ipse tueri.
    Esse ferunt spatium qua distat ab Aside terra   170
Fertilis Europe, et spectat Mareotidas undas;
Hic turris posita est Titanidos ardua Famae,
Aerea, lata, sonans, rutilis vicinior astris
Quam superimpositum vel Athos vel Pelion Ossae.
Mille fores aditusque patent, totidemque fenestrae,   175
Amplaque per tenues translucent atria muros;
Excitat hic varios plebs agglomerata susurros;
Qualiter instrepitant circum mulctralia bombis
Agmina muscarum, aut texto per ovilia iunco,
Dum Canis aestivum coeli petit ardua culmen.   180
Ipsa quidem summa sedet ultrix matris in arce,
Auribus innumeris cinctum caput eminet olli,
Queis sonitum exiguum trahit, atque levissima captat
Murmura, ab extremis patuli confinibus orbis.
Nec tot, Aristoride, servator inique iuvencae   185
Isidos, immiti volvebas lumina vultu,
Lumina non unquam tacito nutantia somno,
Lumina subiectas late spectantia terras.
Istis illa solet loca luce carentia saepe
Perlustrare, etiam radianti impervia soli.   190
Millenisque loquax auditaque visaque linguis
Cuilibet effundit temeraria; veraque mendax
Nunc minuit, modo confictis sermonibus auget.
Sed tamen a nostro meruisti carmine laudes,
Fama, bonum quo non aliud veracius ullum,   195
Nobis digna cani, nec te memorasse pigebit
Carmine tam longo; servati scilicet Angli
Officiis, vaga diva, tuis tibi reddimus aequa.
Te Deus, aeternos motu qui temperat ignes,
Fulmine praemisso alloquitur, terraque tremente: 200
"Fama, siles? an te latet impia Papistarum

Coniurata cohors in meque meosque Britannos,
Et nova sceptrigero caedes meditata Iacobo?"
Nec plura: illa statim sensit mandata Tonantis,
Et, satis ante fugax, stridentes induit alas,   205
Induit et variis exilia corpora plumis;
Dextra tubam gestat Temesaeo ex aere sonoram.
Nec mora: iam pennis cedentes remigat auras,
Atque parum est cursu celeres praevertere nubes;
Iam ventos, iam solis equos post terga reliquit: 210
Et primo Angliacas solito de more per urbes
Ambiguas voces incertaque murmura spargit;
Mox arguta dolos et detestabile vulgat
Proditionis opus, nec non facta horrida dictu,
Authoresque addit sceleris, nec garrula caecis   215
Insidiis loca structa silet. Stupuere relatis,
Et pariter iuvenes, pariter tremuere puellae,
Effetique senes pariter, tantaeque ruinae
Sensus ad aetatem subito penetraverat omnem.
Attamen interea populi miserescit ab alto   220
Aethereus Pater, et crudelibus obstitit ausis
Papicolum. Capti poenas raptantur ad acres;
At pia thura Deo, et grati solvuntur honores;
Compita laeta focis genialibus omnia fumant;
Turba choros iuvenilis agit: Quintoque Novembris   225
Nulla dies toto occurrit celebratior anno.

(1626)

ON THE FIFTH OF NOVEMBER
At the Age of 17

CATHOLIC plots for the assassination of Elizabeth caused public reactions far less violent and lasting than the Gunpowder Plot of 1605 which was to exterminate both king and parliament. The day of its exposure, November 5, has been celebrated down to our own time. Milton's small epic presumably had some connection with the celebration at Cambridge in 1626. Since the day was sure to come around, and since obituaries were keeping him busy that autumn, he may have written the poem in the summer. Phineas Fletcher had composed but did not publish until 1627 a partly similar piece, *Locustae* (*The Apollyonists* in its English version), which Milton may have seen in manuscript; but patriotic and vehemently anti-Catholic things of this kind were bound to have a family likeness, and the young Milton was as capable of invention as Phineas Fletcher. Although the ending is huddled up, perhaps because he was tired of the subject, the work is at least a remarkable display of sustained energy for a boy of seventeen. But we read it, if we do read it, rather as a document than as a poem. There is some interest in Milton's first picture of Pluto-Satan, who is rather less crude than the similar figures of the mature Tasso and Marino. Also, Milton evidently and naturally had in mind both structural features and details of the *Aeneid*.

Now the pious James, coming from the far north, ruled the people of Trojan descent[2] and the widespread realms of Albion's sons, and now an inviolable league

2. See the note on *Comus* 923.

had joined the scepters of the English and the Caledonian Scots. Peace-loving, fortunate, and rich, he occupied his new throne, fearing no secret plot or open enemies. But the fierce tyrant of Acheron's fiery stream,[7] the father of the Furies, the wandering exile from ethereal Olympus, had by chance roamed over the vast globe of the earth, counting his associates in crime and his faithful slaves, destined after their miserable deaths to be partakers of his kingdom.[11] Here he stirs up wild storms in the middle air;[12] there he engenders hatred between loving friends. He arms unconquered peoples for bitter war against one another, and overturns nations flourishing under the olive of peace. And wherever he sees lovers of pure virtue, he is eager to bring them under his sway, and the master of fraud seeks to corrupt the heart that is not open to crime. He lays silent snares, spreads invisible nets to catch the unwary, as the Caspian tigress through pathless wastes pursues its frightened victim in the moonless night when the stars are sleepily glimmering. With such ways of destruction does Summanus,[23] girt with blue flame and eddying smoke, attack peoples and cities. And now Satan comes in sight of the land with white, wave-beaten cliffs,[25] the land dear to the sea-god and named long ago from Neptune's son,[27] who did not fear to cross the sea and engage Amphitryon's fierce son[28] in furious battle, before the cruel times of the sack of Troy.

But as soon as he saw this land, happy in its wealth and hallowed peace, and its acres rich in Ceres' gifts, and — what stung him more — this people worshiping the sacred divinity of the true God, then at length he gave vent to sighs that reeked of Tartarean fires and lurid sulphur, such as the savage monster Typhoeus, confined by Jove in Trinacrian Etna, pours from his baneful jaws. His eyes blaze, the grinding of his set of adamantine teeth is like the din of arms and the clash of spear on spear.[39] "I have traversed the whole world," he exclaims, "and have found only this one cause of grief: this nation alone is rebellious against me, scornful of my yoke and stronger than my art. Yet, if my efforts are of any avail, it shall not long persist in this course with impunity, it shall not go unpunished." Thus he spoke, and swam through the liquid air on his pitch-black wings. Wherever he flies, a band of warring winds rush before him, clouds thicken, and there is incessant thunder and lightning.

And now he had swiftly crossed over the snowy Alps and entered Ausonian country. On his left side were the cloud-capped Apennines and the region of the old Sabines; on his right, Etruria, notorious for its sorceries, and you, Tiber, he sees giving furtive kisses to Thetis.[52] Then he alights on the citadel of Quirinus,[53] the son of Mars. Now, when late evening has brought dim twilight, the wearer[55] of the triple crown makes a circuit of the whole city, bearing his gods made of bread, and is himself borne on men's shoulders. Kings go before him with obsequious gait, and a long line of mendicant friars carrying wax candles in their hands — men blind of soul, who are born and lead their lives in Cimmerian darkness. Then they enter temples shining with many torches (it was the eve[62] sacred to St. Peter), and the sound of chanting often fills the airy domes and empty spaces. Such are the cries and songs of Bromius[64] and the Bromian throng in their orgies on Echionian

---

7. Satan as the equivalent of Pluto. The infernal river usually called fiery was Phlegethon.

11. An ironic echo of Heb. 3.14, etc.

12. Glossary, "mid-air."

23. An obscure nocturnal deity who caused lightning.

25. Of Dover.

27. Glossary, "Albion."

28. Hercules.

39. Cf. Tasso, *G.L.* 4.6–8.

52. That is, the Tiber joins the sea.

53. Romulus.

55. The pope.

62. June 28.

64. Dionysus (Bacchus).

Aracynthus,[65] while astonished Asopus[66] trembles in his glassy waves and far-off Cithaeron[67] itself reverberates from its hollow cliff.

When at length these rites had been performed according to custom, Night silently left the embraces of old Erebus and drove with urgent whip her galloping horses, blind Typhlon, vicious Melanchaetes, sluggish Siope of Acherontean birth, and Phrix bristling with shaggy hair.

Meanwhile the tamer of kings,[74] the heir of Phlegethon, entered his bridal chamber (for the secret libertine spends no barren nights without a pleasant concubine). But his eyes were hardly closed in settled sleep when the dark lord of the shades, the ruler of the silent dead, who preys upon men, stood beside him, wearing a false disguise. His temples shone under the white hair he had assumed; a long beard covers his chest; his ash-colored robe sweeps the ground with a long train; a cowl hangs from his shaven head; and, to complete his wiles, he had girded his lustful loins with a hempen cord, and he planted his latticed sandals with slow steps.[85] In such garb, the story has it, Francis used to wander in the great desert, alone amid the horrid haunts of wild beasts, and, though impious himself, he carried the pious gospel of salvation to the woodland race, and tamed wolves and Libyan lions.[89]

Clothed in such attire, the subtle Serpent uttered these deceitful words from his odious lips:

"Are you asleep, my son? Does slumber weigh down your limbs? O, unmindful of the faith and forgetful of your flock, while a barbarous race, born under the Hyperborean sky, scoffs at your throne, venerable father, and at your triple diadem, while the quiver-bearing Britons spurn your authority. Come, rise up, rise, slothful pontiff, you to whom the Roman Caesar[97] bows down, to whom the gate of vaulted heaven lies wide open. Break their swelling spirit and insolent pride; let the profane know the power of your anathema, the power of the apostolic key[101] that you hold. Remember vengeance for the scattered Hesperian armada,[102] the Iberian standards sunk in the wide deep, and all the bodies of saints fixed on the infamous cross in the late reign of the Thermodontean[105] virgin. But if you prefer to lie torpid in your soft bed, and refuse to destroy the growing strength of the foe, he will fill the Tyrrhenian Sea with his armed host and plant his gleaming ensigns on the Aventine hill.[109] He will break and burn in flames the relics of the ancients,[110] and with sacrilegious feet tread on your sacred neck, the neck of him whose shoes kings have rejoiced to kiss. But do not attack this enemy with arms and open war; that would be a vain effort. Use cunning and deceit. It is right to spread any kind of net for heretics. Even now the great king is summoning to council, from the farthest corners of his land, the gentry and nobles of high descent,[117] and old fathers, ven-

---

65. Echionian: Theban (from Echion, father of Pentheus).   Aracynthus: a mountain commonly placed between Boeotia and Attica.

66. A Boeotian river and river-god.

67. A range of hills between Boeotia and Attica associated with Dionysian orgies.

74. The pope.

85. The picture of Satan in Franciscan garb is indebted to passages in George Buchanan's Latin poems.

89. The St. Francis of Catholic legend and anti-Catholic feeling.

97. Emperors of the Holy Roman Empire.

101. Matt. 16.19.

102. The Spanish Armada, scattered by the English navy and storms in 1588.

105. Amazonian (from the river Thermodon in the Amazon country of Pontus). After the pope's bull of 1570 deposing Elizabeth and the discovery of Catholic plots to assassinate her, conspirators and Jesuit missionaries were executed on charges of treason. Satan of course omits the many Protestants burned in Mary's reign.

109. One of the seven hills of Rome.

110. Many Catholic shrines and relics were destroyed in Henry VIII's reign and later.

117. Members of the House of Commons and House of Lords.

erable with their robes and gray hair.[118] These you will be able to scatter limb from limb into the air and consume to ashes, with a charge of nitrous powder stored under the building where they have assembled. At once therefore warn all the faithful in England of the plan of action, and will any one of your followers dare to disregard the commands of the sovereign pope? While the people are panic-stricken and stunned by the catastrophe, let either the fierce Gaul or the cruel Iberian[126] invade their country. So at last it will see the Marian age[127] return, and you will again hold sway over the warlike English. And, that you may have no fear, know that you have the favor of the gods and goddesses, all the divinities who are honored in your calendar."[130]

So the deceiver spoke, and putting off his disguise fled to the joyless realm of accursed Lethe.

And now the rosy wife[133] of Tithonus, opening the eastern gates, with her returning light gives the earth a golden vesture; and, still mourning the sorrowful death of her black son, she waters the mountain tops with ambrosial drops.[136] And now the keeper of the starry court[137] drives away sleep, recalling his nocturnal visions and pleasant dreams.

There is a place enclosed in the eternal darkness of night, once the huge foundation of a ruined building, now the den of brutal Murder and double-tongued Treason,[141] whom savage Discord brought forth in one birth. Here amid rubble and broken rocks lie unburied bones of men and dead bodies pierced by iron. Here for ever sits black Guile with twisted eyes, and Quarrels, and Calumny, her jaws armed with fangs, and Fury, and a thousand ways of dying are seen, and Fear, and pale Horror flutters about the place, and in the dead silence bodiless ghosts perpetually fly around; the conscious earth howls and overflows with blood.[150] Murder and Treason themselves tremble and lurk in the depths of the cave; and, though no one follows them through the cave, horrible, craggy, and black with grisly shades, the guilty pair flee with backward glances. These defenders of Rome, faithful through long ages,[155] the Babylonian[156] priest summons and thus speaks:

"In the west, surrounded by the sea, dwells a people I hate. Wise nature cut off that unworthy country from our continent. My command is that you hasten thither with all speed. Let the king and his nobles together, the whole abominable race, be blown into thin air by Tartarean powder. And gather as partners in the plot and doers of the deed all who are on fire with love for the true faith." He ended, and the pitiless twins eagerly obeyed.

Meanwhile the Lord who turns the skies in their large orbit and sends the lightning from his heavenly citadel looks down and laughs[168] at the vain attempts of the wicked crew and himself undertakes to defend the cause of his people.

---

118. Bishops, as members of the House of Lords, and Privy Councillors.

126. The French and Spanish.

127. The speaker means the reign of the Catholic Mary as a returning golden age, but in ancient Latin usage *Mariana* meant the bloody period of Marius and Sulla. Milton's friend Gill had used the grim pun in an anti-Catholic poem of 1623.

130. The Catholic saints.

133. Aurora.

136. Aurora's tears for the death of her Ethiopian son Memnon were the morning dew.

137. The pope, as keeper of the keys of heaven.

141 f. The most famous list of such personifications is in *Aen.* 6.274 f.

150. The Latin text of 149–50 is that directed in the Errata of the 1673 edition and carried out in the 1695 edition, since it would seem to have been Milton's own alteration.

155. Milton would have in mind such things as the Inquisition and the massacre of St. Bartholomew.

156. Some Catholics — such as Petrarch, in his Sonnet 108, which Milton later translated in part — and many Protestants identified Rome with the Babylon of Rev. 14.8, 17.5.

168. Cf. Ps. 2.4 (and *P.L.* 2.731, 5.736–37, 8.78).

Men say there is a place that divides fertile Europe from Asia and looks toward the waters of Mareotis.[171] Here Fame[172] the Titaness has her lofty tower, brazen, broad, full of sounds, nearer to the ruddy stars than Athos or Pelion heaped upon Ossa.[174] A thousand doors and approaches lie open, and as many windows, and spacious courts within shine through the thin walls. Here a dense crowd of people start various whisperings, as swarms of flies hum and buzz about the milk-pails or in the wattled sheepfolds, when in summer the Dog Star seeks the highest point of the sky. Fame herself, the avenger of her mother,[181] sits in the top of her tower and holds up her head, encircled with countless ears, with which she catches the slightest sound and seizes the faintest murmur from the farthest limits of the wide world. You, son of Arestor,[185] harsh guardian of the heifer Isis, did not turn so many eyes in your cruel face, eyes that never droop in quiet sleep, eyes that look out over the far-stretched lands below. With these she is wont to peer into places void of light and impervious even to the sun's rays. With a thousand tongues babbling Fame pours out recklessly to anyone what she has heard and seen; now she falsely diminishes the truth, now she enlarges it with made-up tales.

But yet, Fame, you have deserved praise in my song, for one good report than which nothing was ever more true; you are worthy to be sung by me, and I shall not be sorry for having celebrated you at such length. For certainly it was through your offices, inconstant goddess, that we English were saved, and we return you just thanks. God, who governs the eternal fires in their motion, first hurled his thunderbolt and, while the earth trembled, he spoke to you:

"Fame, do you keep silent? Does it escape you that an impious band of papists have conspired against me and my Britons, and that a new kind of murder is planned for scepter-bearing James?"

He said no more. She at once understood the Thunderer's[204] command and, swift as she was before, she now puts whistling wings and varied plumage on her slender body; in her right hand she carries a resounding trumpet made of Temesan[207] brass. And with no delay she plies her wings through the yielding air, and she not merely outstrips the swift clouds in her flight; she leaves behind her now the winds, then the horses of the sun. And first, in her usual way, she scatters through the English cities ambiguous words and vague rumors. Soon with a clear voice she makes known the plots and the horrible work of treason, and to the unutterable deed she adds the names of the authors; nor does her busy tongue conceal the place prepared for secret treachery. Hearers are dumbfounded by the news; young men and women and feeble elders, all alike tremble; the thought of such a calamity quickly struck deep into persons of every age. But in the meantime the heavenly Father from on high feels pity for his people and frustrates the papists' murderous attempt. They are captured and dragged away to severe punishments. Pious incense and grateful prayers are offered to God; the festive squares all smoke with joyful bonfires; and crowds of young people dance. In the whole year no day that comes round is more famous than the fifth of November.

171. A lake west of the Nile, near Alexandria, standing for Africa.

172 f. The account of Fame (i.e. Rumor) combines details from Ovid, *Met.* 12.43–63 and Virgil, *Aen.* 4.173–97.

174. The Giants attacked the gods by piling mountains on top of one another; the Giants and Titans were confused in antiquity and later.

181. Fame was the daughter of Terra (Earth), who produced her in revenge for the Giants' defeat by the gods.

185. Glossary, "Argus."

204. A common epithet for Jupiter, here used of God.

207. Temesa: a city in the toe of Italy noted for its copper mines.

Elegia quarta. Anno aetatis 18

Ad Thomam Iunium praeceptorem suum, apud mercatores Anglicos
Hamburgae agentes, Pastoris munere fungentem

Curre per immensum subito, mea littera, pontum;
　　I, pete Teutonicos laeve per aequor agros;
Segnes rumpe moras, et nil, precor, obstet eunti,
　　Et festinantis nil remoretur iter.
Ipse ego Sicanio frenantem carcere ventos　　　　　　　　　　　5
　　Aeolon, et virides sollicitabo deos,
Caeruleamque suis comitatam Dorida nymphis,
　　Ut tibi dent placidam per sua regna viam.
At tu, si poteris, celeres tibi sume iugales,
　　Vecta quibus Colchis fugit ab ore viri;　　　　　　　　　　10
Aut queis Triptolemus Scythicas devenit in oras,
　　Gratus Eleusina missus ab urbe puer.
Atque ubi Germanas flavere videbis arenas,
　　Ditis ad Hamburgae moenia flecte gradum,
Dicitur occiso quae ducere nomen ab Hama,　　　　　　　　　15
　　Cimbrica quem fertur clava dedisse neci.
Vivit ibi antiquae clarus pietatis honore
　　Praesul Christicolas pascere doctus oves;
Ille quidem est animae plusquam pars altera nostrae;
　　Dimidio vitae vivere cogor ego.　　　　　　　　　　　　20
Hei mihi, quot pelagi, quot montes interiecti
　　Me faciunt alia parte carere mei!
Carior ille mihi quam tu, doctissime Graium,
　　Cliniadi, pronepos qui Telamonis erat;
Quamque Stagirites generoso magnus alumno,　　　　　　　　25
　　Quem peperit Libyco Chaonis alma Iovi.
Qualis Amyntorides, qualis Philyreius heros
　　Myrmidonum regi, talis et ille mihi.
Primus ego Aonios illo praeeunte recessus
　　Lustrabam, et bifidi sacra vireta iugi,　　　　　　　　　30
Pieriosque hausi latices, Clioque favente,
　　Castalio sparsi laeta ter ora mero.
Flammeus at signum ter viderat arietis Aethon
　　Induxitque auro lanea terga novo,
Bisque novo terram sparsisti, Chlori, senilem　　　　　　　　35
　　Gramine, bisque tuas abstulit Auster opes;
Necdum eius licuit mihi lumina pascere vultu,
　　Aut linguae dulces aure bibisse sonos.
Vade igitur, cursuque Eurum praeverte sonorum;
　　Quam sit opus monitis res docet, ipsa vides.　　　　　　40
Invenies dulci cum coniuge forte sedentem,
　　Mulcentem gremio pignora cara suo;
Forsitan aut veterum praelarga volumina patrum
　　Versantem, aut veri biblia sacra Dei,

Caelestive animas saturantem rore tenellas, 45
    Grande salutiferae religionis opus.
Utque solet, multam sit dicere cura salutem,
    Dicere quam decuit, si modo adesset, herum.
Haec quoque paulum oculos in humum defixa modestos,
    Verba verecundo sis memor ore loqui: 50
"Haec tibi, si teneris vacat inter praelia Musis,
    Mittit ab Angliaco litore fida manus.
Accipe sinceram, quamvis sit sera, salutem;
    Fiat et hoc ipso gratior illa tibi.
Sera quidem, sed vera fuit, quam casta recepit 55
    Icaris a lento Penelopeia viro.
Ast ego quid volui manifestum tollere crimen,
    Ipse quod ex omni parte levare nequit?
Arguitur tardus merito, noxamque fatetur,
    Et pudet officium deseruisse suum. 60
Tu modo da veniam fasso, veniamque roganti,
    Crimina diminui, quae patuere, solent.
Non ferus in pavidos rictus diducit hiantes,
    Vulnifico pronos nec rapit ungue leo.
Saepe sarissiferi crudelia pectora Thracis 65
    Supplicis ad moestas delicuere preces.
Extensaeque manus avertunt fulminis ictus,
    Placat et iratos hostia parva deos.
Iamque diu scripsisse tibi fuit impetus illi,
    Neve moras ultra ducere passus Amor. 70
Nam vaga Fama refert, heu nuntia vera malorum!
    In tibi finitimis bella tumere locis,
Teque tuamque urbem truculento milite cingi,
    Et iam Saxonicos arma parasse duces.
Te circum late campos populatur Enyo, 75
    Et sata carne virum iam cruor arva rigat.
Germanisque suum concessit Thracia Martem;
    Illuc Odrysios Mars pater egit equos.
Perpetuoque comans iam deflorescit oliva,
    Fugit et aerisonam diva perosa tubam, 80
Fugit io terris, et iam non ultima virgo
    Creditur ad superas iusta volasse domos.
Te tamen interea belli circumsonat horror,
    Vivis et ignoto solus inopsque solo;
Et, tibi quam patrii non exhibuere penates, 85
    Sede peregrina quaeris egenus opem.
Patria, dura parens et saxis saevior albis
    Spumea quae pulsat litoris unda tui,
Siccine te decet innocuos exponere fetus;
    Siccine in externam ferrea cogis humum, 90
Et sinis ut terris quaerant alimenta remotis
    Quos tibi prospiciens miserat ipse Deus,
Et qui laeta ferunt de caelo nuntia, quique
    Quae via post cineres ducat ad astra, docent?

Digna quidem Stygiis quae vivas clausa tenebris,   95
    Aeternaque animae digna perire fame!
Haud aliter vates terrae Thesbitidis olim
    Pressit inassueto devia tesqua pede,
Desertasque Arabum salebras, dum regis Achabi
    Effugit atque tuas, Sidoni dira, manus.   100
Talis et horrisono laceratus membra flagello,
    Paulus ab Aemathia pellitur urbe Cilix.
Piscosaeque ipsum Gergessae civis Iesum
    Finibus ingratus iussit abire suis.
At tu sume animos, nec spes cadat anxia curis,   105
    Nec tua concutiat decolor ossa metus.
Sis etenim quamvis fulgentibus obsitus armis,
    Intententque tibi millia tela necem,
At nullis vel inerme latus violabitur armis,
    Deque tuo cuspis nulla cruore bibet.   110
Namque eris ipse Dei radiante sub aegide tutus;
    Ille tibi custos, et pugil ille tibi;
Ille Sionaeae qui tot sub moenibus arcis
    Assyrios fudit nocte silente viros;
Inque fugam vertit quos in Samaritidas oras   115
    Misit ab antiquis prisca Damascus agris,
Terruit et densas pavido cum rege cohortes,
    Aere dum vacuo buccina clara sonat,
Cornea pulvereum dum verberat ungula campum,
    Currus arenosam dum quatit actus humum,   120
Auditurque hinnitus equorum ad bella ruentum,
    Et strepitus ferri, murmuraque alta virum.
Et tu (quod superest miseris) sperare memento,
    Et tua magnanimo pectore vince mala.
Nec dubites quandoque frui melioribus annis,   125
    Atque iterum patrios posse videre lares."

(1627)

ELEGY IV

At the Age of 18

To Thomas Young, His Tutor, Performing the Duties of Pastor to the English Merchants Living in Hamburg

THE SCOTTISH Thomas Young (1587–1655) was in 1618–20 one of the private tutors Milton had in addition to his school work (because of his zeal for learning, not backwardness.) Young lived in Hamburg from 1620 to 1628 and, returning to England, held a vicarage in Suffolk. Later he was one of the group of Presbyterian opponents of prelacy with whom Milton allied himself in his pamphlets of 1641–42; after that their views diverged.

Milton's dating (and lines 33–38) put this poem in March or April of 1627. Young had apparently visited England in 1625 and Milton, who has not seen him since, is embarrassed over not having written. He is now stirred by news that the Thirty Years' War is about to engulf Hamburg. The epistle, on the Ovidian model, has its share of rhetorical padding, but also much genuine emotion. Milton is grateful to the tutor who had introduced him to Latin poetry; and, whatever Young's reasons for going abroad, his admirer celebrates him as a religious exile and martyr cast out by a harsh country (as in Elegy 1 Milton had linked his own exile with Ovid's). In Elegy 4 an incipient Puritan feeling about Young may have been heightened by Milton's unwillingness to take holy orders, though we do not know when that decision was made. The same kind of feeling animates the resonant lines 113–22, where he rejoices in the rout of Israel's enemies by the Lord of Hosts.

Quickly, my letter, run over the wide waters; go, seek Teutonic lands across a propitious sea. Shake off lazy slackness and let nothing, I beg, impede your going, let nothing hold up your speedy journey. I myself will pray to Aeolus, who curbs the winds in his Sicanian prison, and the sea-green gods, and dark-hued Doris[7] and her attendant nymphs, that they may grant you a smooth way through their realms. But, if you can, possess yourself of the swift team that carried the Colchian[10] when she fled from the face of her husband, or that Triptolemus[11] drove to the Scythian land when he was sent, a welcome envoy, from the Eleusinian city. And, when you see the yellow sands of Germany, turn your course to the walls of wealthy Hamburg, which is said to take its name from the slaying of Hama,[15] done to death, they say, by a Cimbrian club. There lives, in the lustre of his primitive piety, a pastor well fitted to feed his Christian flock. He is indeed more than half of my soul; without him I am forced to live but half a life. Alas, how many seas, how many mountains cut me off from that other part of myself! He is dearer to me than you, wisest[23] of the Greeks, were to Cliniades,[24] who was a descendant of Telamon; dearer than the great Stagirite[25] to his royal pupil, whom the gracious woman[26] of Chaonia bore to Libyan Jove. What the son of Amyntor, what Philyra's heroic son was to the king of the Myrmidons,[28] such is he to me. Under his tutelage I first visited the retreats of Aonia and the hallowed glades of the twin-peaked mountain,[30] and drained Pierian waters, and by Clio's favor I thrice[32] wet my happy lips with Castalian wine. But three times has fiery Aethon[33] seen the sign of the Ram and covered his fleecy back with new gold, and twice, Chloris,[35] have you spread new grass over the aged earth, and twice has Auster[36] swept away your riches; and not yet have my eyes been able to feast on his face or my ears to drink in the sweet sounds of his voice.

Go, then, and in your flight outstrip whistling Eurus; how much need there is for such urging the situation makes clear and you yourself see. You will find him sitting perhaps with his sweet wife, fondling on his lap the dear pledges of their

7. Wife of Nereus (glossary) and mother of the Nereids.

10. Medea fled in her dragon-chariot after killing her and Jason's children and his new wife.

11. Sent by Ceres (Demeter) from Eleusis in a dragon-chariot to plant grain in uncultivated regions.

15. A Saxon champion killed by a Danish (Cimbrian) giant.

23. Socrates.

24. Alcibiades, son of Clinias. Telamon was father of Ajax, the Greek warrior at Troy.

25. Aristotle, tutor of Alexander the Great.

26. See note on *P.L.* 9.508–10.

28. Achilles, king of the Myrmidons, was tutored by both Phoenix, son of Amyntor, and Chiron the centaur, son of Philyra.

30. Parnassus.

32. Perhaps a reference to poems written, or only the number common in charms.

33. One of the four horses of the sun. He has three times seen the zodiacal sign of the Ram, i.e., three vernal equinoxes have gone by.

35. Chloris' festival at Rome began on April 28.

36. The south wind, in the harvest season.

love; or perhaps turning over the massive volumes of the old fathers,[43] or the sacred Scriptures of the true God, or nourishing tender souls with heavenly dew, religion's great work of salvation. As the custom is, be sure to salute him with warmth, to say what your master would fittingly say if only he were there. And, for a space bending your eyes modestly upon the ground, remember to say this also with reverent lips:[50]

"These lines a loyal hand sends to you from English shores, if there is time for the delicate Muses in the midst of battles. Accept this sincere greeting, late though it is, and let it be the more welcome to you for that reason. Late indeed but heart-felt was the greeting that chaste Penelope, daughter of Icarius, received from her tardy husband.[56] But why should I wish to blot out a manifest fault, which the culprit himself can in no way diminish? He is justly accused of delay, and he avows his guilt, and is ashamed to have neglected his duty. Only grant pardon to one who confesses and asks for pardon; offenses candidly acknowledged are wont to be lessened. The wild beast does not open its wide jaws against trembling victims; the lion does not strike the prostrate with its vicious claws; often the cruel heart of the Thracian spearman is softened by the woeful pleas of the suppliant; uplifted hands ward off the stroke of the thunderbolt, and a small sacrifice appeases angry gods.

For a long time he has had it in mind to write to you, and now Love permitted no further delays. For wandering Rumor — a true reporter, alas, of calamities — says that the tide of war is rising in places near you, that you and your city are surrounded by brutal soldiers, and that now the Saxon leaders have got ready their arms. All around you Enyo[75] is ravaging the country, and blood waters ground sown with men's flesh. Thrace has given up her Mars to the Germans; thither the father of war has driven his Odrysian[78] horses. The ever-flowering olive now with-ers, and the goddess[80] who abhors the brazen trumpet has fled, lo, she has fled from the earth, and the maid of justice,[81] it is thought, was not the last to take flight to the mansions above. But you, meanwhile, are encompassed by the horrible sounds of war, and live alone and without resources in a foreign land; and want sends you abroad to seek the livelihood your native country denied you. Native country, harsh parent, more cruel than the white rocks[87] that are beaten by the foaming waves of your coast, is it right for you thus to expose your innocent children? Do you thus without pity force them away to an alien soil, do you allow them to go to far lands in quest of subsistence, men whom God's providence has sent to you, who bear the joyful tidings from heaven, and who teach the way that after death leads to the stars? You deserve, indeed, to live immured in Stygian darkness and to perish in eternal hunger of soul! In like case the prophet[97] of the Tishbite land with un-accustomed foot once trod remote wastes, the rough deserts of Arabia, when he fled from King Ahab and your hands, dread woman of Sidon. So too Cilician Paul[102] was driven from the Emathian city, his flesh torn by the hissing lash; and the un-grateful people of fishy Gergessa ordered Christ himself to depart from their borders.[104]

---

43. The church fathers.
50. So far Milton has been speaking to his own letter; now he tells it what to say to Young.
56. Odysseus.
75. Goddess of war.
78. Thrace (Odrysia) was Mars' traditional home.
80. Eirene (Latin *Pax*), goddess of peace and one of the Hours (glossary).

81. Astraea (glossary).
87. The cliffs of Dover.
97. Elijah fled when threatened by Jezebel, wife of King Ahab and daughter of the king of Sidon (1 Kings 16.31, 19.1–4).
102. Paul, of Tarsus in Cilicia, was scourged at Philippi in Macedonia (Acts 16.22–40, 21.39).
104. Matt. 8.34.

Yet take heart and do not let anxious hope succumb to cares, nor pale fear shake your frame. For although you are beset by flashing arms and countless weapons threaten you with death, yet none shall wound your defenseless side, no spear shall drink your blood. For you shall be secure under the bright shield of God; He will be your guardian, He your defender — He who in the silent night destroyed the Assyrian host under the walls of Zion's citadel;[114] who put to rout the army sent by old Damascus from its ancient land against the Samaritans, and terrified the massed troops and their trembling king, when the clear trumpet sounded in empty air, the horny hoof thudded on the dusty plain, and the racing chariot shook the sandy earth, and there was heard the neighing of horses rushing to battle, and the din of arms, and the loud cries of men.[122] And you, remember to hope — the last resource of those in trouble — and overcome evils by heroic fortitude. And do not doubt that some time you will enjoy better years and be able again to see your native home."

114. When Sennacherib attacked Jerusalem the angel of the Lord destroyed the Assyrian army (2 Kings 19.35–36).
122. The king of Damascus and his troops, besieging Samaria, took flight when God made them hear the noises of a great host (2 Kings 7.6–7).

Elegia septima, Anno aetatis undevigesimo

Nondum blanda tuas leges, Amathusia, noram,
    Et Paphio vacuum pectus ab igne fuit.
Saepe Cupidineas, puerilia tela, sagittas,
    Atque tuum sprevi maxime numen, Amor.
"Tu puer imbelles," dixi, "transfige columbas;   5
    Conveniunt tenero mollia bella duci:
Aut de passeribus tumidos age, parve, triumphos;
    Haec sunt militiae digna trophaea tuae.
In genus humanum quid inania dirigis arma?
    Non valet in fortes ista pharetra viros."   10
Non tulit hoc Cyprius (neque enim deus ullus ad iras
    Promptior), et duplici iam ferus igne calet.
Ver erat, et summae radians per culmina villae
    Attulerat primam lux tibi, Maie, diem;
At mihi adhuc refugam quaerebant lumina noctem,   15
    Nec matutinum sustinuere iubar.
Astat Amor lecto, pictis Amor impiger alis;
    Prodidit astantem mota pharetra deum;
Prodidit et facies, et dulce minantis ocelli,
    Et quicquid puero dignum et Amore fuit.   20
Talis in aeterno iuvenis Sigeius Olympo
    Miscet amatori pocula plena Iovi;
Aut qui formosas pellexit ad oscula nymphas,
    Thiodamantaeus naiade raptus Hylas;
Addideratque iras, sed et has decuisse putares,   25
    Addideratque truces, nec sine felle, minas.

Et "Miser exemplo sapuisses tutius," inquit;
  "Nunc mea quid possit dextera testis eris.
Inter et expertos vires numerabere nostras,
  Et faciam vero per tua damna fidem.   30
Ipse ego, si nescis, strato Pythone superbum
  Edomui Phoebum, cessit et ille mihi;
Et, quoties meminit Peneidos, ipse fatetur
  Certius et gravius tela nocere mea.
Me nequit adductum curvare peritius arcum,   35
  Qui post terga solet vincere, Parthus eques:
Cydoniusque mihi cedit venator, et ille
  Inscius uxori qui necis auctor erat.
Est etiam nobis ingens quoque victus Orion,
  Herculeaeque manus, Herculeusque comes.   40
Iupiter ipse licet sua fulmina torqueat in me,
  Haerebunt lateri spicula nostra Iovis.
Cetera quae dubitas melius mea tela docebunt,
  Et tua non leviter corda petenda mihi.
Nec te, stulte, tuae poterunt defendere Musae; 45
  Nec tibi Phoebaeus porriget anguis opem."
Dixit, et, aurato quatiens mucrone sagittam,
  Evolat in tepidos Cypridos ille sinus.
At mihi risuro tonuit ferus ore minaci,
  Et mihi de puero non metus ullus erat.   50
Et modo qua nostri spatiantur in urbe Quirites,
  Et modo villarum proxima rura placent.
Turba frequens, facieque simillima turba dearum,
  Splendida per medias itque reditque vias;
Auctaque luce dies gemino fulgore coruscat.   55
  Fallor? an et radios hinc quoque Phoebus habet?
Haec ego non fugi spectacula grata severus,
  Impetus et quo me fert iuvenilis agor;
Lumina luminibus male providus obvia misi,
  Neve oculos potui continuisse meos.   60
Unam forte aliis supereminuisse notabam;
  Principium nostri lux erat illa mali.
Sic Venus optaret mortalibus ipsa videri,
  Sic regina deum conspicienda fuit.
Hanc memor obiecit nobis malus ille Cupido   65
  Solus et hos nobis texuit ante dolos.
Nec procul ipse vafer latuit, multaeque sagittae,
  Et facis a tergo grande pependit onus.
Nec mora; nunc ciliis haesit, nunc virginis ori,
  Insilit hinc labiis, insidet inde genis;   70
Et quascunque agilis partes iaculator oberrat,
  Hei mihi, mille locis pectus inerme ferit.
Protinus insoliti subierunt corda furores;
  Uror amans intus, flammaque totus eram.
Interea misero quae iam mihi sola placebat   75
  Ablata est, oculis non reditura meis;

Ast ego progredior tacite querebundus, et excors,
    Et dubius volui saepe referre pedem.
Findor, et haec remanet, sequitur pars altera votum;
    Raptaque tam subito gaudia flere iuvat.   80
Sic dolet amissum proles Iunonia coelum,
    Inter Lemniacos praecipitata focos;
Talis et abreptum solem respexit, ad Orcum
    Vectus ab attonitis Amphiaraus equis.
Quid faciam infelix, et luctu victus? Amores   85
    Nec licet inceptos ponere, neve sequi.
O utinam spectare semel mihi detur amatos
    Vultus, et coram tristia verba loqui!
Forsitan et duro non est adamante creata,
    Forte nec ad nostras surdeat illa preces.   90
Crede mihi, nullus sic infeliciter arsit;
    Ponar in exemplo primus et unus ego.
Parce, precor, teneri cum sis deus ales amoris;
    Pugnent officio nec tua facta tuo.
Iam tuus O certe est mihi formidabilis arcus,   95
    Nate dea, iaculis nec minus igne potens:
Et tua fumabunt nostris altaria donis,
    Solus et in superis tu mihi summus eris.
Deme meos tandem, verum nec deme, furores;
    Nescio cur, miser est suaviter omnis amans: 100
Tu modo da facilis, posthaec mea siqua futura est,
    Cuspis amaturos figat ut una duos.

                    (1627–28?)

ELEGY VII

At the Age of 18 [19?]

THIS POEM Milton associates with May Day, presumably that of 1627 or 1628, when he was eighteen or nineteen (the phrase with which he dated it was a unique departure from his usual practice and remains puzzling). The theme has precedents in Roman and Neo-Latin love poetry. The poet's contempt for Cupid brings its nemesis; while the incident described is the most innocent of amorous encounters, the intensity of the response is clear.

I was not yet, seductive goddess of Amathus,[1] acquainted with your laws and my heart was untouched by Paphian fire. Often I scorned Cupid's arrows as childish weapons and scoffed greatly at your divine power, Love. "Boy," I said, "shoot the timid doves; soft battles befit a tender warrior. Or, little one, win swelling triumphs over the sparrows. These are trophies worthy of your prowess. Why aim your feeble shafts at human beings? That quiver of yours has no force against strong men." The Cyprian god[11] could not bear this taunt — for no deity is quicker to anger — and now the cruel boy is inflamed with double heat.

1. One of Venus' temples was at Amathus   11. Cupid.
in Cyprus.

It was spring and the sun, shining over the house-tops of the town, had brought in May Day. But my eyes still sought retreating night and could not endure the brightness of dawn. Beside my bed appeared Love, busy Love with his colored wings; the movement of his quiver betrayed the god as he stood. His face betrayed him too, and his sweetly menacing eyes, and whatever else belonged to the boyish god of love. He looked like Sigeian[21] Ganymede when on eternal Olympus he mixes full cups for amorous Jove, or like Hylas, the son of Thiodamas, who drew to his kisses the beautiful nymphs and whom a naiad carried into the depths. But Cupid was angry besides, though you would say his anger was becoming, and he uttered threats, fierce and bitter.

"Wretch," he exclaimed, "you would have learned wisdom more safely from the fate of others; now you shall find out what my right hand can do. You shall be numbered among those who have felt my power, and assuredly through your pangs I will confirm men's belief in me. It was I — in case you do not know — who subdued Phoebus, while he gloried in his slaying of the Python; even that great god yielded to me. And, as often as he remembers Daphne, he admits that my arrows cause surer and keener wounds than his own. The Parthian horseman, who conquers as he retreats,[36] cannot wield the bow more skilfully than I. The Cydonian[37] hunter is inferior to me, and he who unwittingly killed his wife.[38] I have other victims too — huge Orion and mighty Hercules and Hercules' comrade.[40] Jove himself may turn his thunderbolts upon me, but my darts will stick in the side of Jove. For the rest of your doubts, you will be better taught by my arrows and by your own heart, at which I must aim no gentle shaft. Fool! your Muses will not be able to defend you, nor will the serpent-son[46] of Phoebus help you with his healing art." Thus he spoke and, shaking an arrow with a golden point,[47] he flew away to the warm bosom of his Cyprian mother.[48] But I was ready to laugh at his loud, rough threats, and had no fear at all of the boy.

Sometimes parts of the town where people stroll and sometimes the neighboring fields attract me, and there many radiant girls, lovely as a throng of goddesses, come and go along the walks. They double the bright glory of the day. Is it a fancy, or does Phoebus derive his rays from them? These charming sights I did not austerely shun; instead I followed where youthful impulse led. With no thought beyond the moment, I sent my eyes to meet their eyes; I could not control my gaze. By chance I observed one who surpassed the others; that bright vision was the beginning of my pain. She looked as Venus herself might wish to appear to mortals; such to behold must the queen[64] of the gods have been. It was that vengeful and wicked Cupid who thrust her upon my sight; he alone wove this snare for me. Not far off the rascal himself was hiding, with his full quiver and his great torch hanging on his back. He did not delay. He clung now to the girl's eyelids, now to her face; then he alighted on her lips, then settled on her cheeks. And wherever the nimble archer fluttered, he wounded my defenseless breast — alas for me! — in a thousand places. All at once strange passions attacked my heart; I burned inwardly with love, I was all one flame.

---

21. Trojan.
36. See note on *P.R.* 3.322–24.
37. Cretan.
38. Cephalus.
40. Many men were called comrades of Hercules; the reference might be to Hylas (24 above) or Theseus, the lover of Ariadne and others.

46. Aesculapius, the son of Phoebus, went to Rome in the form of a serpent and ended a pestilence.
47. Cupid's gold-tipped arrows inspired love.
48. Venus.
64. Juno, sister and wife of Jupiter.

Meanwhile she who alone charmed me had disappeared and left me dark, never again to return to my sight. And now I go on my way, complaining to myself in my distress, and in doubt I often long to retrace my steps. I am split in two; one part of me stands still, the other follows my desire. I feel a sort of pleasure in grieving for joy thus suddenly snatched away. So Juno's son,[81] when he was thrown down among the hearths of Lemnos, mourned for his lost heaven. So Amphiaraus[84] took his last glance at the vanishing sun as he was carried down to hell by his thunder-frightened horses. Miserable and overcome by sorrow, what shall I do? This new passion I can neither put aside nor obey. O that it may be granted me to look once more on those features that I love, and tell her face to face how I suffer! Perhaps she is not made of flinty adamant, perhaps she would not be deaf to my prayers. No one, surely, ever burned with such an ill-fated love; I shall be cited as the first and only example. Since you are the winged god of tender love, be merciful, I beg. Let not your deeds war with your duty. Child of Venus, whose darts have no less power than fire, now indeed I acknowledge the terror of your bow. Henceforth your altars shall smoke with my offerings; for me you shall be among the gods alone and supreme. Take away my madness then — yet do not take it away; somehow it happens that every lover cherishes his pain. Only, if hereafter any maiden is to be mine, be gracious and grant that a single shaft may transfix us both and make us one.

81. Vulcan: glossary.
84. Amphiaraus, the Greek prince and seer, had, against his will, to join in the war of the seven against Thebes, and fled after the defeat; Zeus, in kindness, opened the earth and sent him down to Hades.

On the Death of a Fair Infant
Dying of a Cough
Anno aetatis 17 [19]

Apart from the Psalms (and Horatian ode?), this is Milton's earliest extant poem in English; it was first printed in the second edition of the *Poems* (1673). The year of his age was apparently a printer's mistake or his own. The infant was his sister Anne Phillips', and the first known death in her family was that of the daughter who was born in January, 1626, and died in January, 1628, when Milton was nineteen. The writing of such a piece was natural enough for a young poet who had done four Latin poems on the death of conspicuous elders, and in this case he could not feel much more personal loss (however much he sympathized with the parents); there was the further difficulty that little could be said about an infant's soul and experience. But in filling the void with mythology and rhetoric, as in the Latin poems, Milton car-ried classical reference to more functional complexity, developing the contrast between the inadequacy of the pagan vision of death and the full assurance of Christian consolation.

The stanza, which was to appear again in the prelude of the *Nativity* and in *The Passion*, was used by the Spenserian Phineas Fletcher in poems not published until 1633 (Milton might possibly have seen them in manuscript, but he was not less capable than Fletcher of invention); it may be described as a Spenserian stanza with the fifth and sixth lines omitted, or as rhyme royal with a final Alexandrine. Milton's compound adjectives perhaps point to Sylvester (cf. the early Psalms, above). But the fluidity and decorative sweetness of the texture belong to the larger Elizabethan tradition, especially the Spenserian.

I

O fairest flower, no sooner blown but blasted,
Soft silken primrose fading timelessly,
Summer's chief honor, if thou hadst outlasted
Bleak Winter's force that made thy blossom dry;
For he, being amorous on that lovely dye   5
    That did thy cheek envermeil, thought to kiss
But killed, alas, and then bewailed his fatal bliss.

II

For since grim Aquilo his charioteer
By boist'rous rape th' Athenian damsel got,
He thought it touched his deity full near   10
If likewise he some fair one wedded not,
Thereby to wipe away th' infámous blot
    Of long-uncoupled bed and childless eld,
Which 'mongst the wanton gods a foul reproach was held.

III

So mounting up in icy-pearlèd car,   15
Through middle empire of the freezing air
He wandered long, till thee he spied from far;
There ended was his quest, there ceased his care.
Down he descended from his snow-soft chair,
    But all unwares with his cold-kind embrace   20
Unhoused thy virgin soul from her fair biding-place.

IV

Yet art thou not inglorious in thy fate;
For so Apollo with unweeting hand
Whilom did slay his dearly lovèd mate,
Young Hyacinth, born on Eurotas' strand,   25
Young Hyacinth, the pride of Spartan land;
    But then transformed him to a purple flower:
Alack, that so to change thee Winter had no power!

V

Yet can I not persuade me thou art dead,
Or that thy corse corrupts in earth's dark womb,   30
Or that thy beauties lie in wormy bed,
Hid from the world in a low-delvèd tomb;
Could Heav'n for pity thee so strictly doom?
    Oh no! for something in thy face did shine
Above mortality that showed thou wast divine.   35

1–2. While the idea is traditional, critics cite *The Passionate Pilgrim* (1599), sonnet 10: "Sweet rose, fair flower, untimely plucked, soon vaded,/Plucked in the bud, and vaded in the spring." timelessly: unseasonably.

5–7. A common conceit, e.g., Sidney, *Astrophel and Stella* 22.14; Shakespeare, *Venus and Adonis* 1110.

8. Aquilo, the north wind (the Greek Boreas), carried off the Athenian princess Orithyia.

22–28. Cf. Spenser, *F.Q.* 3.6.45.

25. Eurotas: a river in Laconia.

VI

Resolve me then, O Soul most surely blest
(If so it be that thou these plaints dost hear),
Tell me, bright Spirit, where'er thou hoverest,
Whether above that high first-moving sphere,
Or in the Elysian fields (if such there were);   40
    Oh say me true if thou wert mortal wight,
And why from us so quickly thou didst take thy flight.

VII

Wert thou some star which from the ruined roof
Of shaked Olympus by mischance didst fall;
Which careful Jove in nature's true behoof   45
Took up, and in fit place did reinstall?
Or did of late Earth's sons besiege the wall
    Of sheeny heav'n, and thou some goddess fled
Amongst us here below to hide thy nectared head?

VIII

Or wert thou that just maid who once before   50
Forsook the hated earth, O tell me sooth,
And cam'st again to visit us once more?
Or wert thou [Mercy], that sweet smiling youth?
Or that crowned matron, sage white-robèd Truth?
    Or any other of that heav'nly brood   55
Let down in cloudy throne to do the world some good?

IX

Or wert thou of the golden-wingèd host,
Who having clad thyself in human weed
To earth from thy prefixèd seat didst post,
And after short abode fly back with speed,   60
As if to show what creatures heav'n doth breed,
    Thereby to set the hearts of men on fire
To scorn the sordid world, and unto heav'n aspire?

X

But oh why didst thou not stay here below
To bless us with thy Heav'n-loved innocence,   65
To slake his wrath whom sin hath made our foe,
To turn swift-rushing black perdition hence,
Or drive away the slaughtering pestilence,
    To stand 'twixt us and our deservèd smart?
But thou canst best perform that office where thou art.   70

39. Glossary, "first moved."
47. Earth's sons: the Giants who tried to overthrow the gods.
50. maid: glossary, "Astraea."
53. To fill out a defective line (presumably due to a printer's error), editors have commonly supplied "Mercy" (cf. *Nativity* 141–46);

"youth" seems to be female. "Virtue" and "Peace" have also been suggested (cf. Milton's Prolusion 4 for the linking of Astraea, Peace, and Truth), but "Peace" by itself would be unmetrical.
57. host: angels.   66. his: God's.
68. On the plague of 1625–26, see Elegy 3.

XI

Then thou the mother of so sweet a child,
Her false-imagined loss cease to lament,
And wisely learn to curb thy sorrows wild;
Think what a present thou to God hast sent,
And render him with patience what he lent;   75
　This if thou do he will an offspring give,
That till the world's last end shall make thy name to live.

(1628)

76–77. Anne Phillips was about to give birth to another child (Elizabeth, baptized April 9, 1628); but Milton seems rather to be thinking of the immortality, promised to the faithful, which is better than children (Isa. 56.5).

Naturam non pati senium

Heu quam perpetuis erroribus acta fatiscit
Avia mens hominum, tenebrisque immersa profundis
Oedipodioniam volvit sub pectore noctem!
Quae vesana suis metiri facta deorum
Audet, et incisas leges adamante perenni   5
Assimilare suis, nulloque solubile saeclo
Consilium fati perituris alligat horis.
　Ergone marcescet sulcantibus obsita rugis
Naturae facies, et rerum publica mater
Omniparum contracta uterum sterilescet ab aevo?   10
Et se fassa senem male certis passibus ibit
Sidereum tremebunda caput? Num tetra vetustas
Annorumque aeterna fames, squalorque situsque
Sidera vexabunt? An et insatiabile Tempus
Esuriet Caelum, rapietque in viscera patrem?   15
Heu, potuitne suas imprudens Iupiter arces
Hoc contra munisse nefas, et Temporis isto
Exemisse malo, gyrosque dedisse perennes?
Ergo erit ut quandoque sono dilapsa tremendo
Convexi tabulata ruant, atque obvius ictu   20
Stridat uterque polus, superaque ut Olympius aula
Decidat, horribilisque retecta Gorgone Pallas;
Qualis in Aegaeam proles Iunonia Lemnon
Deturbata sacro cecidit de limine caeli.
Tu quoque, Phoebe, tui casus imitabere nati   25
Praecipiti curru subitaque ferere ruina
Pronus, et extincta fumabit lampade Nereus,
Et dabit attonito feralia sibila ponto.
Tunc etiam aerei divulsis sedibus Haemi
Dissultabit apex, imoque allisa barathro   30
Terrebunt Stygium deiecta Ceraunia Ditem,

In superos quibus usus erat, fraternaque bella.
  At pater omnipotens fundatis fortius astris
Consuluit rerum summae, certoque peregit
Pondere fatorum lances, atque ordine summo   35
Singula perpetuum iussit servare tenorem.
Volvitur hinc lapsu mundi rota prima diurno,
Raptat et ambitos socia vertigine caelos.
Tardior haud solito Saturnus, et acer ut olim
Fulmineum rutilat cristata casside Mavors.   40
Floridus aeternum Phoebus iuvenile coruscat,
Nec fovet effetas loca per declivia terras
Devexo temone deus; sed semper amica
Luce potens eadem currit per signa rotarum.
Surgit odoratis pariter formosus ab Indis   45
Aethereum pecus albenti qui cogit Olympo,
Mane vocans, et serus agens in pascua coeli;
Temporis et gemino dispertit regna colore.
Fulget, obitque vices alterno Delia cornu,
Caeruleumque ignem paribus complectitur ulnis.   50
Nec variant elementa fidem, solitoque fragore
Lurida perculsas iaculantur fulmina rupes.
Nec per inane furit leviori murmure Corus,
Stringit et armiferos aequali horrore Gelonos
Trux Aquilo, spiratque hiemem, nimbosque volutat.   55
Utque solet, Siculi diverberat ima Pelori
Rex maris, et rauca circumstrepit aequora concha
Oceani tubicen, nec vasta mole minorem
Aegaeona ferunt dorso Balearica cete.
Sed neque, Terra, tibi saecli vigor ille vetusti   60
Priscus abest; servatque suum Narcissus odorem;
Et puer ille suum tenet et puer ille decorem,
Phoebe, tuusque, et, Cypri, tuus; nec ditior olim
Terra datum sceleri celavit montibus aurum
Conscia, vel sub aquis gemmas. Sic denique in aevum   65
Ibit cunctarum series iustissima rerum,
Donec flamma orbem populabitur ultima, late
Circumplexa polos, et vasti culmina caeli;
Ingentique rogo flagrabit machina mundi.

                              (1628?)

THAT NATURE DOES NOT SUFFER FROM OLD AGE

MILTON did not date this poem but it was probably written in the early summer of 1628. On July 2, 1628, he wrote to his friend Alexander Gill that he was sending him a printed copy of a piece he had lately written for a Fellow of the College to use in a Commencement disputation. This might have been the *Platonic Idea*, but *Nature* seems more likely. It is a tiny contribution to a large and protracted debate, in and outside of England, on the question whether nature, including man, was in a process of perpetual decay and the related but contrary theory of the progress of civilization. The deteriorationist view had a prominent spokesman in Godfrey Goodman (*The Fall of Man*, 1616). The most massive denial of that view came from another cleric, George Hakewill (*An Apology of the Power and Providence of God*, 1627). Milton's poem is too unphilosophical to have needed a knowledge of Hakewill, although he says many similar things and may have read him or other discussions. After an introductory

deprecation of man's irreligious irrationality, he gives an ironic paragraph to imagining the general effects of alleged decay, and the final paragraph to a survey of nature, also in mythological terms, and an assertion of its unchanging strength and order. A number of the mythological allusions, though put to a different use, are the same as those in the *Fair Infant*, written in the late winter of 1628 — which is a straw in favor of *Nature* as the poem done a few months later.

Alas, how weary grows the wandering mind of man, driven on by continual errors, and, plunged in deep darkness, what Oedipean night[3] it carries within! In his folly man dares to measure the acts of the gods by his own[4] and to compare his laws with those engraved on everlasting adamant, and he binds to the passing hours the decrees of fate[7] which no age can alter.

Shall then the face of nature[9] be furrowed with wrinkles and wither? Shall the common mother of things contract her all-creating womb and grow barren with age? Shall she, confessing herself old, move with feet unsteady and starry head shaking? Shall the stars suffer from foul senility and the eternal hunger of the years and squalor and decay? Shall insatiable Time swallow up Heaven and take his father into his own entrails?[15] Alas, could not unforeseeing Jupiter have fortified his citadels against this catastrophe, could he not have freed them from that evil work of time and given them ceaseless revolutions? Some day, then, it will come about that the floor of heaven will collapse and fall with a tremendous sound, that both poles will groan under the blow, and that the Olympian will tumble from his celestial court and Pallas too, with her horrible Gorgon-shield uncovered.[22] So on Aegean Lemnos fell the offspring[23] of Juno, thrown from the sacred threshold of heaven. You also, Phoebus, will repeat the fate of your son[25] in your headlong chariot and be struck down in sudden ruin; and with the quenching of your light Nereus will send up steam and fearful hissing from his astonished waters. Then too the bases of lofty Haemus[29] will be rent and the summit torn asunder, and the Ceraunian mountains,[31] once used against the gods in fratricidal wars, will be dashed down to the lowest depths of hell and terrify Stygian Dis.

But the omnipotent father, consulting on the sum of things,[34] founded the stars more strongly, fixed the scales of the fates with sure balance,[35] and decreed that all things in the great order should maintain their perpetual course. Hence the prime wheel[37] of the world makes a daily rotation and, imparting its whirling motion, turns the enclosed spheres. Saturn is not slower than his wont, and, fierce as ever,

3. night: blindness.
4. Cf. Isa. 55.8.
7. God's will.
9. The earth.
15. Cronos, son of Heaven and Earth, who devoured his and Rhea's children (though she saved Zeus), was equated with Chronos or Saturn (*Tempus*, Time). In keeping with the imagined decay of things, Milton reverses the myth and has Time devouring his father, Heaven.

22. Pallas Athene's shield bore the head of the Gorgon Medusa.
23. Glossary, "Vulcan."
25. Phaethon.
29. A Thracian mountain or range.
31. On the coast of Epirus. The allusion is to the wars of Giants and Titans against the gods.
34. Cf. *P.L.* 6.673.
35. Cf. *P.L.* 4.996–1002.
37. See glossary, "first moved."

Mars sends forth a ruddy blaze from his crested helmet.[40] Phoebus[41] shines with the freshness of eternal youth, nor does the god let his chariot sink to warm the exhausted soil of low-lying lands, but, powerful with his friendly light, drives always through the same signs of the zodiac. No less beautiful, there rises from the spicy Indies the star[45] that shepherds the heavenly flock on white Olympus,[46] calling them at dawn and at evening sending them forth to the pastures of heaven, dividing the kingdoms of time with double light. Delia shines and wanes with alternating horns[49] and clasps her heavenly fire with unchanged arms. Nor do the elements betray their faith; with their accustomed crash lurid lightning-bolts strike and shatter cliffs. Corus[53] rages through the void with no gentler sound, and no less severely does angry Aquilo freeze the warlike Geloni[54] as he breathes out winter and rolls the clouds. As always, the king[57] of the sea pounds the base of Sicilian Pelorus and Ocean's trumpeter[58] blows his hoarse shell over the waters; the Balearic[59] whales bear on their backs an Aegaeon[59] no less vast in bulk. Nor, Earth, do you lack that first vigor of the early age: Narcissus keeps his fragrance; and your favorite boy,[63] Phoebus, and yours,[63] Cypris, retain their beauty; nor in old times did a richer earth guiltily conceal more gold — the source of crime — in the mountains or more gems under the sea. So, in brief, the perfect sequence of things will go on forever, until the last conflagration shall destroy the universe, enveloping the poles and the summits of vast heaven, and in a monstrous pyre the fabric of the world shall be consumed.[69]

40. The planet Mars has been noted for its red light.
41. The sun-god, the sun. Various writers, e.g. Spenser (*F.Q.*, bk. 5, proem) and Hakewill referred — to use the latter's words — to "a supposed approach of the Sun nearer the earth than in former ages."
45. The planet Venus, as Lucifer the morning star and Hesperus the evening star.
46. The sky.
49. The "horns" fit the crescent moon and the bow of the goddess-huntress Delia (Diana).
53. The northwest wind.

54. Glossary, "Scythians."
57. Neptune.
58. Triton.
59. Mediterranean islands near Spain (Majorca and Minorca).   Aegaeon: glossary, "Briareos."
63. boy: glossary, "Hyacinth"; Milton is here speaking of the flower.   yours: Adonis, i.e. the anemone.
69. 2 Pet. 3.10. Hakewill, while rejecting the theory of nature's decay, of course accepted — and had a chapter on — the Christian belief in a final conflagration of the world.

At a Vacation Exercise in the College, Part Latin, Part English

The Latin speeches ended, the English thus began.

Anno Aetatis 19 [At the age of 19]

IN JULY, 1628, Milton acted as "Father" or "Dictator" at a College assembly which, coming just before the long vacation, was both academic and festive. His Latin speech, printed as his sixth Prolusion, carried on this double vein. The nature of the occasion and his office for the day — an evidence of his growing popularity — prompted a genially urbane discourse; the latter half of it was a less happy effort in the kind of humor expected at such a time. Then followed these English verses, in which Milton took his hearers into his confidence. His poetry hitherto had been almost wholly in Latin. Now he salutes his native language, avows his distaste for the trifling themes and eccentric style of some student poets, and goes on, in couplets of more smoothness and eloquence, to sketch the "graver" subjects that attract him —

nature and the cosmos and "kings and queens and heroes old." Lines 33–35 invite comparison with parts of Milton's third Prolusion; and in 33–39 he might be said to make over the end of the first book of the *Iliad* in the spirit of Plato's *Phaedrus* 246–47. The lines were first published in the second edition of Milton's *Poems* (1673).

Hail, native language, that by sinews weak
Didst move my first endeavoring tongue to speak,
And mad'st imperfect words with childish trips,
Half unpronounced, slide through my infant lips,
Driving dumb Silence from the portal door,   5
Where he had mutely sat two years before:
Here I salute thee and thy pardon ask
That now I use thee in my latter task:
Small loss it is that thence can come unto thee;
I know my tongue but little grace can do thee.   10
Thou need'st not be ambitious to be first;
Believe me, I have thither packed the worst:
And, if it happen as I did forecast,
The daintiest dishes shall be served up last.
I pray thee then deny me not thy aid   15
For this same small neglect that I have made;
But haste thee straight to do me once a pleasure,
And from thy wardrobe bring thy chiefest treasure;
Not those new-fangled toys and trimming slight
Which takes our late fantastics with delight,   20
But cull those richest robes and gay'st attire
Which deepest spirits and choicest wits desire.
I have some naked thoughts that rove about
And loudly knock to have their passage out,
And weary of their place do only stay   25
Till thou hast decked them in thy best array;
That so they may without suspect or fears
Fly swiftly to this fair assembly's ears;
Yet I had rather, if I were to choose,
Thy service in some graver subject use,   30
Such as may make thee search thy coffers round,
Before thou clothe my fancy in fit sound:
Such where the deep transported mind may soar
Above the wheeling poles, and at heav'n's door
Look in, and see each blissful deity   35
How he before the thunderous throne doth lie,
Listening to what unshorn Apollo sings
To the touch of golden wires, while Hebe brings
Immortal nectar to her kingly sire;
Then passing through the spheres of watchful fire,   40

8. latter: later.
18. wardrobe: see glossary.
27. suspect: suspicion.
33. deep: high (cf. *altus*).
37. unshorn: the stock classical epithet.
40. In old cosmic theory a sphere of fire (the fourth element) was between the sphere of air and the sphere of the moon; thus it could be called a "watchful" guardian of the changeless supralunary region against the flux of the sublunary world.

And misty regions of wide air next under,
And hills of snow and lofts of pilèd thunder,
May tell at length how green-eyed Neptune raves,
In Heav'n's defiance mustering all his waves;
Then sing of secret things that came to pass   45
When beldam Nature in her cradle was;
And last of kings and queens and heroes old,
Such as the wise Demodocus once told
In solemn songs at king Alcinous' feast,
While sad Ulysses' soul and all the rest   50
Are held with his melodious harmony
In willing chains and sweet captivity.
But fie, my wand'ring Muse, how thou dost stray!
Expectance calls thee now another way;
Thou know'st it must be now thy only bent   55
To keep in compass of thy Predicament:
Then quick about thy purposed business come,
That to the next I may resign my room.

Then ENS *is represented as Father of the Predicaments, his ten sons, whereof the eldest stood for* SUBSTANCE *with his Canons, which* ENS, *thus speaking, explains:*

Good luck befriend thee, son; for at thy birth
The fairy ladies danced upon the hearth;   60
Thy drowsy nurse hath sworn she did them spy
Come tripping to the room where thou didst lie,
And sweetly singing round about thy bed
Strew all their blessings on thy sleeping head.
She heard them give thee this, that thou should'st still   65
From eyes of mortals walk invisible;
Yet there is something that doth force my fear,
For once it was my dismal hap to hear
A Sibyl old, bow-bent with crooked age,
That far events full wisely could presage,   70
And in time's long and dark prospective-glass
Foresaw what future days should bring to pass:
"Your son," said she, "(nor can you it prevent)
Shall subject be to many an *Accident.*
O'er all his brethren he shall reign as king,   75
Yet every one shall make him underling;
And those that cannot live from him asunder
Ungratefully shall strive to keep him under;
In worth and excellence he shall outgo them,
Yet being above them, he shall be below them;   80
From others he shall stand in need of nothing,
Yet on his brothers shall depend for clothing.

42. lofts: glossary, "mid-air."
48–52. *Odyssey* 8.73 f., 266 f., 499 f.
53. Cf. Horace, *Od.* 3.3.70.
56. Predicament: one of the ten Aristotelian categories. The primary one is substance, which is subject to and known through the other nine, quantity, quality, relation, etc. Milton, as "Father," is Ens, absolute being.
71. A glass for foreseeing the future.

To find a foe it shall not be his hap,
And peace shall lull him in her flow'ry lap;
Yet shall he live in strife, and at his door   85
Devouring war shall never cease to roar;
Yea, it shall be his natural property
To harbor those that are at enmity."
What power, what force, what mighty spell, if not
Your learned hands, can loose this Gordian knot?   90

The next, QUANTITY *and* QUALITY, *spake in prose; then* RELATION *was
called by his name.*

Rivers arise; whether thou be the son
Of utmost Tweed, or Ouse, or gulfy Dun,
Or Trent, who like some Earth-born giant spreads
His thirty arms along the indented meads,
Or sullen Mole that runneth underneath,   95
Or Severn swift, guilty of maiden's death,
Or rocky Avon, or of sedgy Lea,
Or coaly Tyne, or ancient hallowed Dee,
Or Humber loud, that keeps the Scythian's name,
Or Medway smooth, or royal-towered Thame.   100

The rest was prose.

(1628)

91. Rivers: the name of two of the students representing the Predicaments.
92 f. With the possible exception of the Dun, Milton's rivers are all among those catalogued in Spenser, *F.Q.* 4.11.24–47 (and full notes are in the Variorum edition of Spenser); there were also descriptions in prose.
92. Ouse: see glossary and *F.Q.*, stanza 34 and 37.6.
93–94. Trent . . . thirty arms: cf. *F.Q.* 35.9, "thirty sundry streames."

95. Mole . . . underneath: cf. *F.Q.* 32.8–9.
96. Severn: cf. *F.Q.* 30.6 and *Comus* 824 f.
97. rocky Avon: cf. *F.Q.* 31.6–9.
98. Tyne: the river that has Newcastle at its mouth and flows through a coal-mining region.   hallowed Dee: see glossary and *F.Q.* 39.3–4.
99. Humber: a legendary Scythian king who, after unsuccessfully invading Britain, was drowned in the Humber; cf. *F.Q.* 30.7, 37.8–9, 38.

De Idea Platonica quemadmodum Aristoteles intellexit

Dicite, sacrorum praesides nemorum deae,
Tuque O noveni perbeata numinis
Memoria mater, quaeque in immenso procul
Antro recumbis otiosa Aeternitas,
Monumenta servans, et ratas leges Iovis,   5
Caelique fastos atque ephemeridas deum,
Quis ille primus cuius ex imagine
Natura sollers finxit humanum genus,
Aeternus, incorruptus, aequaevus polo,
Unusque et universus, exemplar Dei?   10

Haud ille Palladis gemellus innubae
Interna proles insidet menti Iovis;
Sed quamlibet natura sit communior,
Tamen seorsus extat ad morem unius,
Et, mira, certo stringitur spatio loci;   15
Seu sempiternus ille siderum comes
Caeli pererrat ordines decemplicis,
Citimumve terris incolit lunae globum;
Sive inter animas corpus adituras sedens
Obliviosas torpet ad Lethes aquas;   20
Sive in remota forte terrarum plaga
Incedit ingens hominis archetypus gigas,
Et diis tremendus erigit celsum caput,
Atlante maior portitore siderum.
Non, cui profundum caecitas lumen dedit,   25
Dircaeus augur vidit hunc alto sinu;
Non hunc silenti nocte Pleiones nepos
Vatum sagaci praepes ostendit choro;
Non hunc sacerdos novit Assyrius, licet
Longos vetusti commemoret atavos Nini,   30
Priscumque Belon, inclytumque Osiridem.
Non ille trino gloriosus nomine
Ter magnus Hermes (ut sit arcani sciens)
Talem reliquit Isidis cultoribus.
At tu perenne ruris Academi decus   35
(Haec monstra si tu primus induxti scholis)
Iam iam poetas urbis exules tuae
Revocabis, ipse fabulator maximus,
Aut institutor ipse migrabis foras.

(1628–29?)

ON THE PLATONIC IDEA
AS ARISTOTLE UNDERSTOOD IT

THIS OBVIOUSLY academic poem, probably of 1628–29, may have been written for a not wholly serious public occasion (see the headnote to *Nature*, above). Though the manner is half-burlesque, the theme is large and important: Plato versus Aristotle. Milton, a devoted Platonist, poses as a literal-minded Aristotelian who is sceptical of Platonic idealism or "realism" and fastens on the particular question of the reality of the Platonic or Neoplatonic Idea or archetype of man. The irony is directed against Aristotelianism, not Platonism.

Say, you goddesses[1] who preside over the sacred groves, and you, Memory, blessed mother of the ninefold divinity,[3] and you, Eternity,[4] who lie at ease far away in a

1. Possibly Diana and her nymphs; more probably the nine Muses.
3. The Muses.
4. This personification of Eternity goes back to Claudian's *On Stilicho's Consulship* (2.424–40) and Boccaccio's *Genealogy of the Gods,* c. 1.

huge cave, preserving the records and fixed laws of Jove, the calendars of heaven and the journals of the gods, say who was that first being — eternal, incorruptible, coeval with the heavens, single and universal, an image of God — from whose likeness cunning Nature molded the human race? He does not dwell a child unborn in the mind of Jove, a twin of virgin Athene. But although men participate in his nature, yet he exists by himself as a separate individual, and — strange to relate — is confined to definite limits of space. Does that perpetual companion of the stars wander through the ten spheres of heaven, or does he inhabit the moon's globe that is nearest to the earth? Or does he sit in a torpor by Lethe's waters of forgetfulness, among spirits about to enter a body? Or perhaps that archetype of man is a huge giant who stalks in some remote region of the earth, a being with uplifted head, fearful to the gods, taller than Atlas the supporter of the stars. Never was this archetype perceived by the deep mind of the Dircean seer,[26] to whom blindness brought piercing light. Nor was he shown in the silent night to the wise band of prophets by the wing-footed grandson[27] of Pleïone. The Assyrian priest did not know him, though he could recount the long line of old Ninus'[30] ancestors, and primeval Belus and renowned Osiris. Nor did he who is illustrious with his triple name, thrice-great Hermes, for all his secret lore, leave such a being to the worshipers of Isis.[34] But you, everlasting glory of the rural Academy, if you first brought these monstrosities into the philosophic schools, you surely must now recall the poets, those exiles from your city,[37] since you yourself are the greatest maker of fables, or else you, the founder, must go into exile yourself.

26. The Theban Tiresias.
27. Hermes (Mercury).
30. Ninus: glossary.
34. Egyptians.
37. Plato's exclusion of poets from his ideal state (*Rep.* 377–98, 599–608), on the ground that they undermined morality and religion through their immoral fictions, was continually cited and opposed by Renaissance defenders of poetry.

Elegia quinta. Anno aetatis 20

In adventum veris

In se perpetuo Tempus revolubile gyro
    Iam revocat Zephyros vere tepente novos;
Induiturque brevem Tellus reparata iuventam,
    Iamque soluta gelu dulce virescit humus.
Fallor? an et nobis redeunt in carmina vires,   5
    Ingeniumque mihi munere veris adest?
Munere veris adest, iterumque vigescit ab illo
    (Quis putet?) atque aliquod iam sibi poscit opus.
Castalis ante oculos, bifidumque cacumen oberrat,
    Et mihi Pirenen somnia nocte ferunt;
Concitaque arcano fervent mihi pectora motu,   10
    Et furor, et sonitus me sacer intus agit.
Delius ipse venit, video Peneide lauro
    Implicitos crines, Delius ipse venit.
Iam mihi mens liquidi raptatur in ardua coeli,   15
    Perque vagas nubes corpore liber eo;

Perque umbras, perque antra feror, penetralia vatum,
  Et mihi fana patent interiora deum.
Intuiturque animus toto quid agatur Olympo,
  Nec fugiunt oculos Tartara caeca meos.   20
Quid tam grande sonat distento spiritus ore?
  Quid parit haec rabies, quid sacer iste furor?
Ver mihi, quod dedit ingenium, cantabitur illo;
  Profuerint isto reddita dona modo.
Iam, Philomela, tuos, foliis adoperta novellis,   25
  Instituis modulos, dum silet omne nemus.
Urbe ego, tu silva, simul incipiamus utrique,
  Et simul adventum veris uterque canat.
Veris io rediere vices; celebremus honores
  Veris, et hoc subeat Musa perennis opus.   30
Iam sol, Aethiopas fugiens Tithoniaque arva,
  Flectit ad Arctoas aurea lora plagas.
Est breve noctis iter, brevis est mora noctis opacae,
  Horrida cum tenebris exulat illa suis.
Iamque Lycaonius plaustrum caeleste Bootes   35
  Non longa sequitur fessus ut ante via;
Nunc etiam solitas circum Iovis atria toto
  Excubias agitant sidera rara polo.
Nam dolus, et caedes, et vis cum nocte recessit,
  Neve giganteum dii timuere scelus.   40
Forte aliquis scopuli recubans in vertice pastor,
  Roscida cum primo sole rubescit humus;
"Hac," ait, "hac certe caruisti nocte puella,
  Phoebe, tua, celeres quae retineret equos."
Laeta suas repetit silvas, pharetramque resumit   45
  Cynthia, luciferas ut videt alta rotas,
Et tenues ponens radios gaudere videtur
  Officium fieri tam breve fratris ope.
"Desere," Phoebus ait, "thalamos, Aurora, seniles;
  Quid iuvat effeto procubuisse toro?   50
Te manet Aeolides viridi venator in herba;
  Surge, tuos ignes altus Hymettus habet."
Flava verecundo dea crimen in ore fatetur,
  Et matutinos ocius urget equos.
Exuit invisam Tellus rediviva senectam,   55
  Et cupit amplexus, Phoebe, subire tuos;
Et cupit, et digna est; quid enim formosius illa,
  Pandit ut omniferos luxuriosa sinus,
Atque Arabum spirat messes, et ab ore venusto
  Mitia cum Paphiis fundit amoma rosis?   60
Ecce, coronatur sacro frons ardua luco,
  Cingit ut Idaeam pinea turris Opim;
Et vario madidos intexit flore capillos,
  Floribus et visa est posse placere suis.
Floribus effusos ut erat redimita capillos,   65
  Taenario placuit diva Sicana deo.

Aspice, Phoebe; tibi faciles hortantur amores,
   Mellitasque movent flamina verna preces.
Cinnamea Zephyrus leve plaudit odorifer ala,
   Blanditiasque tibi ferre videntur aves.   70
Nec sine dote tuos temeraria quaerit amores
   Terra, nec optatos poscit egena toros;
Alma salutiferum medicos tibi gramen in usus
   Praebet, et hinc titulos adiuvat ipsa tuos.
Quod si te pretium, si te fulgentia tangunt   75
   Munera (muneribus saepe coemptus amor),
Illa tibi ostentat quascunque sub aequore vasto,
   Et superiniectis montibus, abdit opes.
Ah quoties, cum tu clivoso fessus Olympo
   In vespertinas praecipitaris aquas,   80
"Cur te," inquit, "cursu languentem, Phoebe, diurno
   Hesperiis recipit caerula mater aquis?
Quid tibi cum Tethy? quid cum Tartesside lympha?
   Dia quid immundo perluis ora salo?
Frigora, Phoebe, mea melius captabis in umbra: 85
   Huc ades, ardentes imbue rore comas.
Mollior egelida veniet tibi somnus in herba;
   Huc ades, et gremio lumina pone meo.
Quaque iaces circum mulcebit lene susurrans
   Aura per humentes corpora fusa rosas.   90
Nec me (crede mihi) terrent Semeleia fata,
   Nec Phaetonteo fumidus axis equo;
Cum tu, Phoebe, tuo sapientius uteris igni,
   Huc ades et gremio lumina pone meo."
Sic Tellus lasciva suos suspirat amores;   95
   Matris in exemplum cetera turba ruunt.
Nunc etenim toto currit vagus orbe Cupido,
   Languentesque fovet solis ab igne faces.
Insonuere novis lethalia cornua nervis,
   Triste micant ferro tela corusca novo.   100
Iamque vel invictam tentat superasse Dianam,
   Quaeque sedet sacro Vesta pudica foco.
Ipsa senescentem reparat Venus annua formam,
   Atque iterum tepido creditur orta mari.
Marmoreas iuvenes clamant *Hymenaee* per urbes;   105
   Litus *io Hymen* et cava saxa sonant.
Cultior ille venit tunicaque decentior apta;
   Puniceum redolet vestis odora crocum.
Egrediturque frequens ad amoeni gaudia veris
   Virgineos auro cincta puella sinus.   110
Votum est cuique suum, votum est tamen omnibus unum,
   Ut sibi quem cupiat det Cytherea virum.
Nunc quoque septena modulatur arundine pastor,
   Et sua quae iungat carmina Phyllis habet.
Navita nocturno placat sua sidera cantu,   115
   Delphinasque leves ad vada summa vocat.

Iupiter ipse alto cum coniuge ludit Olympo,
　　Convocat et famulos ad sua festa deos.
Nunc etiam Satyri, cum sera crepuscula surgunt,
　　Pervolitant celeri florea rura choro,　　　　　　　　120
Sylvanusque sua cyparissi fronde revinctus,
　　Semicaperque deus, semideusque caper.
Quaeque sub arboribus Dryades latuere vetustis
　　Per iuga, per solos expatiantur agros.
Per sata luxuriat fruticetaque Maenalius Pan;　　　　　125
　　Vix Cybele mater, vix sibi tuta Ceres;
Atque aliquam cupidus praedatur Oreada Faunus,
　　Consulit in trepidos dum sibi nympha pedes,
Iamque latet, latitansque cupit male tecta videri,
　　Et fugit, et fugiens pervelit ipsa capi.　　　　　　130
Dii quoque non dubitant caelo praeponere silvas,
　　Et sua quisque sibi numina lucus habet.
Et sua quisque diu sibi numina lucus habeto,
　　Nec vos arborea, dii, precor, ite domo.
Te referant miseris te, Iupiter, aurea terris　　　　　135
　　Saecla! quid ad nimbos, aspera tela, redis?
Tu saltem lente rapidos age, Phoebe, iugales
　　Qua potes, et sensim tempora veris eant.
Brumaque productas tarde ferat hispida noctes,
　　Ingruat et nostro serior umbra polo.　　　　　　　140

(1629)

ELEGY V

On the Coming of Spring
At the age of 20

ELEGY 5, written apparently in April or May, 1629, is, it seems to be agreed, much the best of Milton's early Latin poems and one of the two or three best he ever wrote. He feels the sensuous intoxications of springtime with an intensity that no translation can fatally cool or dilute. While the poem is Ovidian in its mythological rhetoric, in spirit it is nearer to the pictures in Lucretius' exordium and Virgil's third *Georgic* (209–83) of sexual vitality surging through the natural world. If the young poet's "paganism" is completely innocent, his surrender to it is also complete; there is no reassuring allusion to moly as at the end of Elegy 1, and the gods who in the *Nativity* are put to rout are here entreated not to leave the earth. But there is a kind of moral control implied in the artistic control: what may, after the prelude, appear to be a formless outpouring is a logically ordered account of the effects of spring in the heavens, on the earth, in man, and in the gods.

Now, as the spring grows warm, Time, revolving in its perpetual round, again calls back the zephyrs. Mother earth, refreshed, puts on her brief youth and now, loosened from frost, the ground turns green and sweet. Am I deceived, or is my power of song also returning, and has inspiration come to me through the bounty of spring? Through the bounty of spring it has come and again gains strength — who would believe it? — and now demands some outlet for itself. The Castalian fountain and the double peak[9] float before my eyes, and dreams at night bring Pirene[10] to me. My breast kindles and burns with mysterious fire; I am carried away by poetic fervor and the divine agitation within me. The Delian[13] himself appears — I see his hair bound with Daphne's laurel — the Delian himself appears. Now my mind is rapt to the heights of the clear sky and, free of the body, I pass through the wandering clouds. Through shadows I am borne, and through caverns, the secret sanctuaries of poets, and the inner shrines of the gods are revealed to me. My spirit beholds what is done all over Olympus, and dark Tartarus is not concealed from my eyes. What lofty strain will my soul pour from open lips? What will this madness, this sacred fury, bring to birth? Spring, which gave the inspiration, shall be its theme; so shall the gift repay the giver.

Now, Philomela, in your covert of new leaves, you begin to tune your notes, while all the woods are still. I in the city and you in the forest, together let us begin, together let us proclaim the arrival of spring. Heigh, now comes in the sweet of the year! Let us celebrate the glories of the spring, and let the Muse undertake her perennial[30] task. Now the sun, fleeing from Ethiopia and the lands of Tithonus, turns his golden reins toward northern zones.[32] Short is the night's journey, short the stay of murky night; she is banished with her horrid darkness. And now Lycaonian[35] Bootes does not, as before in his long course, wearily follow the celestial Wain. Now too in all the heavens only a few stars keep their accustomed watch about the halls of Jove, for fraud and slaughter and violence have vanished with night, and the gods fear no attack from the giants. Perhaps some shepherd, reclining on the top of a cliff while the dewy earth grows red beneath the rising sun, may say: "This night, Phoebus, this night you surely did not have your love with you, to delay your swift horses." Cynthia, when from on high she sees the wheels of the Light-bringer,[46] lays aside her pallid rays and seems to rejoice that her own task has been shortened by her brother's aid; joyfully she goes back to her forest and resumes her quíver. "Aurora," cries Phoebus, "leave the bed of your aged spouse.[50] What pleasure is there in lying beside a sapless old man? For you the hunter,[51] grandson of Aeolus, is waiting in the green fields. Get up! Your lover is already on the slopes of Hymettus." The fair goddess with rosy face admits her fault, and urges the horses of the dawn to a swifter gallop.

Earth, reviving, casts off hateful old age and longs, Phoebus, to feel your embraces. She longs for them and she is worthy of them. For what is more beautiful than earth when she voluptuously lays bare her fertile bosom and breathes forth the fragrance of Arabian harvests and from her lovely lips pours balsam and Paphian roses? See, her lofty brow is crowned with a sacred grove, as a turret of pines crowns Idaean Ops. And she braids her dewy hair with many-colored flowers and with her flowers she seems to possess potent charms, as the Sicanian goddess,[65] when her flowing locks were twined with blossoms, charmed the Taenarian god.[66] Look, Phoebus, willing loves call to you, and the winds of spring carry sweet prayers. The odorous Zephyr gently fans his cinnamon-scented wings and the birds seem to proffer you their blandishments. Earth does not boldly, without a dowry, seek your love; not

---

9. Parnassus.
10. Pirene: a fountain in Corinth associated with the Muses.
13. Delian: Phoebus Apollo.
30. The *quotannis* of 1645, which involved a false quantity pointed out by Salmasius, became *perennis* in 1673.

32. The sun has left the equator for the north, i.e. the vernal equinox.
35. Northern (glossary: "Callisto").
46. The sun.   50. Tithonus.
51. Cephalus.
65. Proserpine.
66. Pluto.

empty-handed does she claim the bridal she desires. Graciously she furnishes you with wholesome herbs for medicines and so enhances your fame. If a reward, if resplendent gifts can move you (love is often bought with gifts), she lays out before you all the riches that she hides in the great ocean and under the piled mountains. Ah, how many times when you, wearied from steep Olympus,[79] have plunged at evening into western waters, she cries:

"Why, Phoebus, when you are faint after your daily journey, does the blue mother[82] receive you into the Hesperian sea? What have you to do with Tethys? What have you to do with Tartessian tides? Why do you bathe your divine face in foul brine? You will enjoy coolness better in my shade. Come hither, wet your glowing hair in dew. Softer sleep will visit you in the cool grass. Come hither, and lay your splendors in my lap. Where you lie, the gently whispering breeze will soothe our bodies couched on dewy roses. I do not, believe me, fear the fate of Semele, nor the smoking axle of Phaethon's chariot. When you use your fire more wisely, Phoebus, come hither and lay your splendors in my lap."

Thus the wanton earth breathes her amorous desires, and all creatures follow headlong their mother's example. Now indeed Cupid runs at large over the whole world and feeds his dying torch from the sun's fire. His deadly bow resounds with new strings, and his arrows, bright with new tips, have a fatal gleam. And now he tries to conquer even the invincible Diana, and chaste Vesta, who sits by the sacred hearth. Venus herself, with the return of spring, repairs her aging beauty and seems again to have risen from the warm sea. Through marble cities the young men shout *Hymenaeus! Io Hymen*[106] echoes from the shore and hollow rocks. Hymen himself appears in festal array, with a graceful and becoming tunic; his fragrant robe exhales the perfume of the purple crocus. And throngs of girls go forth to enjoy the lovely spring, their maiden breasts girdled with gold. Every one has her own prayer, yet every one's is the same, that Cytherea may grant her the man of her desire.

Now too the shepherd plays on his seven-reed pipe, and Phyllis has her songs to match his music. The sailor propitiates his stars with nightly singing and brings up the lively dolphins to the surface of the waves.[116] On high Olympus Jove himself sports with his queen and calls even the menial gods to his feast. And now, when twilight comes on, the satyrs in quick-moving bands flit through the blossoming countryside, and Silvanus, crowned with his cypress wreath, a god half-goat, a goat half-god. The dryads who have been hiding under the ancient trees roam about the hills and deserted meadows. Maenalian Pan riots through the sown fields and copses; Mother Cybele and Ceres are hardly safe from him. The lustful Faunus seeks to possess some oread, while the nymph flies on trembling feet. Now she hides and hiding, ill concealed, wishes to be seen; she flees and, fleeing, would willingly be caught. Even the gods are not slow to leave heaven for the woods, and every grove has its own deities.

And long may every grove have its own deities! Gods, I pray, do not forsake your silvan home. May the golden age restore you, Jove, to the wretched earth! Why return to the clouds, your cruel armory?[136] Do you at least, Phoebus, hold in if you can your swift team and let the springtime pass slowly. Let rough winter be tardy in bringing back its long nights, and let the shades fall later than their wont upon our sky!

79. The sky.   82. Tethys.
106. Cf. the refrain in Catullus, 61.
116. Dolphins were traditionally fond of music.
136. The clouds from which Jove sent his thunderbolts.

Song: On May Morning

THIS LYRIC, a miniature choral song, is in substance a distillation of Elegy 5. If the conjectural 1629–30 is correct, the poem may be said to inaugurate the Jonsonian vein more amply displayed in the *Epitaph on the Marchioness of Winchester* and *L'Allegro* and *Il Penseroso*. In contrast with, say, the rich color and detail of Spenser, or the extravagant conceits and compound epithets of Sylvester, Milton's manner is one of restrained and elegant simplicity and urbanity.

> Now the bright morning star, day's harbinger,
> Comes dancing from the east, and leads with her
> The flow'ry May, who from her green lap throws
> The yellow cowslip and the pale primrose.
> Hail, bounteous May, that dost inspire   5
> Mirth and youth and warm desire!
> Woods and groves are of thy dressing,
> Hill and dale doth boast thy blessing.
> Thus we salute thee with our early song,
> And welcome thee, and wish thee long.   10
>
> (1629–30?)

On the Morning of Christ's Nativity

MILTON'S first great English poem, one of the great English odes, was written at Christmas, 1629, a few weeks after his twenty-first birthday. While its youthful exuberance may not be quite flawless, the little adverse criticism it has received — on its slighting of the Gospel story, its supposedly artificial conceits, and its supposedly monotonous rhythm — may be thought mostly wrongheaded. Milton's theme is the idea of the Incarnation, its significance as a religious and historical event. The young poet is already a master of form. The prelude states the central, traditional paradox, the contrast between the human infant and his divine power, and links the poet, writing before dawn in London, with "the star-led wizards" on their way to Bethlehem. The first eight stanzas of the Hymn give the cosmic and historical setting: nature, conscious of her imperfections, awaits the advent of her Creator (the conceits belong to the old religious view of half-animate nature and are quite distinct from "the pathetic fallacy"). In the second movement the angelic music, blending with the music of the spheres, announces the new and closer harmony between heaven and earth; it also recalls the music of Creation, the first supreme event, and then casts forward to the third event, the day of judgment. Since the Incarnation prepares the way for redemption and eternity, the third movement describes the first stage in fallen man's recovery of truth and righteousness, the overthrow of the pagan gods and idolatrous religions — a bravura passage in which the young poet is somewhat carried away by his first grand orchestration of exotic names. Here, and throughout, images of darkness and discord are in contrast with the dominant images of light and music. This poem has the first of Milton's great quiet endings: in two narrative and pictorial lines of subtle simplicity he reasserts the central paradox and the central theme of order and the new bond between heaven and man.

The style is much more Miltonic than it was in the *Death of a Fair Infant* of less than a year before, but it is still in the

Spenserian tradition. The tone ranges from the sweet to the plangent. The stanzaic form used in the prelude is that of the *Fair Infant;* the stanza of the Hymn may be Milton's own invention. While the internal music of the stanzas varies a good deal, the comparative regularity of the pattern may seem wholly appropriate to a song of jubilation. Along with the Bible many things may have made general or particular contributions, from Virgil's fourth or "Messianic" eclogue to Tasso's *Canzone Sopra la Cappella del Presepio* and Giles Fletcher's *Christ's Victory and Triumph* (1610). In his *Poems* of 1645 Milton placed the *Nativity* first.

I

This is the month, and this the happy morn,
Wherein the Son of heav'n's eternal King,
Of wedded Maid and Virgin Mother born,
Our great redemption from above did bring;
For so the holy sages once did sing,   5
     That he our deadly forfeit should release,
And with his Father work us a perpetual peace.

II

That glorious form, that light unsufferable,
And that far-beaming blaze of majesty,
Wherewith he wont at heav'n's high council-table   10
To sit the midst of Trinal Unity,
He laid aside; and here with us to be,
     Forsook the courts of everlasting day,
And chose with us a darksome house of mortal clay.

III

Say, Heav'nly Muse, shall not thy sacred vein   15
Afford a present to the infant God?
Hast thou no verse, no hymn, or solemn strain,
To welcome him to this his new abode,
Now while the heav'n, by the sun's team untrod,
     Hath took no print of the approaching light,   20
And all the spangled host keep watch in squadrons bright?

IV

See how from far upon the eastern road
The star-led wizards haste with odors sweet!
O run, prevent them with thy humble ode,
And lay it lowly at his blessèd feet;   25
Have thou the honor first thy Lord to greet,
     And join thy voice unto the angel quire,
From out his secret altar touched with hallowed fire.

5. sages: the Old Testament prophets.
8–14. Phil. 2.6–8.
11. Trinal Unity: the Trinity.
15. Heav'nly Muse: glossary, "Urania."
21. The stars above London become the angelic host above the shepherds. Throughout the Hymn the mixture of tenses telescopes past and present.
24. wizards: the Magi or three wise men (Matt. 2.1 f.).
28. Isa. 6.6–7.

THE HYMN

I

It was the winter wild
While the Heav'n-born child   30
 All meanly wrapped in the rude manger lies;
Nature in awe to him
Had doffed her gaudy trim,
 With her great Master so to sympathize;
It was no season then for her   35
To wanton with the sun, her lusty paramour.

II

Only with speeches fair
She woos the gentle air
 To hide her guilty front with innocent snow,
And on her naked shame,   40
Pollute with sinful blame,
 The saintly veil of maiden white to throw,
Confounded that her Maker's eyes
Should look so near upon her foul deformities.

III

But he her fears to cease   45
Sent down the meek-eyed Peace;
 She, crowned with olive green, came softly sliding
Down through the turning sphere,
His ready harbinger,
 With turtle wing the amorous clouds dividing,   50
And waving wide her myrtle wand,
She strikes a universal peace through sea and land.

IV

No war or battle's sound
Was heard the world around:
 The idle spear and shield were high uphung;   55
The hookèd chariot stood
Unstained with hostile blood;
 The trumpet spake not to the armèd throng;
And kings sat still with awful eye,
As if they surely knew their sovran Lord was by.   60

V

But peaceful was the night
Wherein the Prince of Light
 His reign of peace upon the earth began:

35–36. Cf. Elegy 5.55 f.
42. Rev. 3.18.
46–52. Peace is described as if a figure in a contemporary masque. Cf. 141–48.
 47. olive: a symbol of peace.
 48. sphere: the firmament, which in the old astronomy turned daily about the earth.

50. turtle: turtle dove.
52–60. Christian writers (e.g., Augustine, *City of God* 18.46) saw a fulfilment of Old Testament prophecy in the peace prevailing in the Roman empire at the time of Christ's birth.
 56. hookèd: with projecting blades.

The winds with wonder whist
Smoothly the waters kissed,   65
   Whispering new joys to the mild ocëan,
Who now hath quite forgot to rave,
While birds of calm sit brooding on the charmèd wave.

VI

The stars with deep amaze
Stand fixed in steadfast gaze,   70
   Bending one way their precious influence,
And will not take their flight
For all the morning light,
   Or Lucifer that often warned them thence;
But in their glimmering orbs did glow,   75
Until their Lord himself bespake, and bid them go.

VII

And though the shady gloom
Had given day her room,
   The sun himself withheld his wonted speed,
And hid his head for shame,   80
As his inferior flame
   The new-enlightened world no more should need;
He saw a greater Sun appear
Than his bright throne or burning axletree could bear.

VIII

The shepherds on the lawn,   85
Or ere the point of dawn,
   Sat simply chatting in a rustic row;
Full little thought they than
That the mighty Pan
   Was kindly come to live with them below;   90
Perhaps their loves, or else their sheep,
Was all that did their silly thoughts so busy keep.

IX

When such music sweet
Their hearts and ears did greet,
   As never was by mortal finger strook,   95
Divinely warbled voice
Answering the stringèd noise,
   As all their souls in blissful rapture took;

65. whist: hushed (cf. the same rhyme in *The Tempest* 1.2.377–78).

68. birds: halcyons, whose nesting time at the winter solstice (December 22) was associated with fair weather at sea.

74. Lucifer: the morning star, Venus (in Elegy 3.50 and Elegy 5.46 Lucifer is the sun).

84. Cf. the myth of Phaethon.

86. Or ere: before.

88. than: a variant form of "then."

90. kindly: beneficently and as one of the human race or "kind."

92. silly: simple, innocent.

The air such pleasure loth to lose,
With thousand echoes still prolongs each heav'nly close.   100

X

Nature that heard such sound
Beneath the hollow round
   Of Cynthia's seat, the airy region thrilling,
Now was almost won
To think her part was done,   105
   And that her reign had here its last fulfilling;
She knew such harmony alone
Could hold all heav'n and earth in happier unïon.

XI

At last surrounds their sight
A globe of circular light,   110
   That with long beams the shamefaced Night arrayed;
The helmèd Cherubim
And sworded Seraphim
   Are seen in glittering ranks with wings displayed,
Harping in loud and solemn quire   115
With unexpressive notes to Heaven's new-born heir.

XII

Such music (as 'tis said)
Before was never made,
   But when of old the sons of morning sung,
While the Creator great   120
His constellations set,
   And the well-balanced world on hinges hung,
And cast the dark foundations deep,
And bid the welt'ring waves their oozy channel keep.

XIII

Ring out, ye crystal spheres,   125
Once bless our human ears
   (If ye have power to touch our senses so),
And let your silver chime
Move in melodious time,
   And let the bass of heav'n's deep organ blow;   130
And with your ninefold harmony
Make up full consort to th' angelic symphony.

---

102. round: sphere of the moon (Cynthia, Diana).
106. its: see glossary.
112–13. Glossary, "angels."
119. Cf. Job 38.6–7 (and *P.L.* 7.252–60).
122. Cf. Job 26.7, Ovid, *Met.* 1.12–13 (and *P.L.* 7.242).
124. Cf. Ovid, *Met.* 1.30–31, 36 f.
125 f. In the Pythagorean-Platonic-Christian tradition the moving spheres of the planets made music which would be audible to the sinless or disembodied soul; cf. Plato, *Rep.* 617; Cicero, *Rep.* 6.17–18; *The Merchant of Venice* 5.1.60–65; Milton, Prolusion 2 and *Arcades* 68 f.
131–32. The music of the nine spheres blending with that of the nine orders of angels.

XIV

For if such holy song
Enwrap our fancy long,
 Time will run back and fetch the age of gold,   135
And speckled Vanity
Will sicken soon and die,
 And leprous Sin will melt from earthly mold,
And hell itself will pass away,
And leave her dolorous mansions to the peering day.   140

XV

Yea, Truth and Justice then
Will down return to men,
 Orbed in a rainbow; and, like glories wearing,
Mercy will sit between,
Throned in celestial sheen,   145
 With radiant feet the tissued clouds down steering;
And heav'n as at some festival
Will open wide the gates of her high palace hall.

XVI

But wisest Fate says no,
This must not yet be so;   150
 The Babe lies yet in smiling infancy,
That on the bitter cross
Must redeem our loss,
 So both himself and us to glorify;
Yet first, to those ychained in sleep,   155
The wakeful trump of doom must thunder through the deep,

XVII

With such a horrid clang
As on Mount Sinai rang
 While the red fire and smold'ring clouds outbrake:
The aged Earth, aghast   160
With terror of that blast,
 Shall from the surface to the center shake,
When at the world's last session
The dreadful Judge in middle air shall spread his throne.

135. Cf. Virgil, *Ecl.* 4; Ovid, *Met.* 1.89 f.
136. The stains of sin; cf. Horace, *Od.* 4.5.22.
140. peering: appearing.
141–46. A combination of the classical Astraea or Justice (Virgil, *Ecl.* 4.6, Ovid, *Met.* 1.149–50) with Ps. 85.10–11: "Mercy and Truth are met together; righteousness and peace have kissed each other."
143–44. The 1645 reading (altered in 1673) was: "Th' enameled arras of the rainbow wearing,/And Mercy set between."
146. tissued: woven, especially with gold or silver thread.

151. infancy. The word seems to include its literal sense, "not speaking."
155–64. The last judgment (cf. *P.L.* 3.323 f.).
155. ychained. The "y" is a literary relic of the Old English participial prefix "ge"; a frequent archaism in Spenser. sleep: death.
156. 1 Thess. 4.16.
157–59. When Moses received the Ten Commandments (Exod. 19.16–18).
160. Cf. Milton's early *Psalm 114*, line 15.
161. Cf. Spenser, *F.Q.* 1.8.4.6, "the terror of that blast."
164. 1 Thess. 4.17.

XVIII

And then at last our bliss   165
Full and perfect is,
     But now begins; for from this happy day
Th' old Dragon under ground,
In straiter limits bound,
     Not half so far casts his usurpèd sway,   170
And wroth to see his kingdom fail,
Swinges the scaly horror of his folded tail.

XIX

The oracles are dumb,
No voice or hideous hum
     Runs through the archèd roof in words deceiving.   175
Apollo from his shrine
Can no more divine,
     With hollow shriek the steep of Delphos leaving.
No nightly trance or breathèd spell
Inspires the pale-eyed priest from the prophetic cell.   180

XX

The lonely mountains o'er,
And the resounding shore,
     A voice of weeping heard, and loud lament;
From haunted spring and dale
Edged with poplar pale,   185
     The parting Genius is with sighing sent;
With flow'r-inwoven tresses torn
The nymphs in twilight shade of tangled thickets mourn.

XXI

In consecrated earth,
And on the holy hearth,   190
     The Lars and Lemures moan with midnight plaint;
In urns and altars round,
A drear and dying sound
     Affrights the flamens at their service quaint;
And the chill marble seems to sweat,   195
While each peculiar power forgoes his wonted seat.

XXII

Peor and Baälim
Forsake their temples dim,
     With that twice-battered god of Palestine,

---

168. Dragon: Satan (Rev. 12.9, 20.2).
172. Swinges: lashes about.
173 f. In Christian tradition the pagan gods were regarded as devils (cf. *P.L.* 1.364 f.); for oracles, cf. *P.R.* 1.430–64.
181–88. A stanza touched by the feeling that animates Elegy 5.

191. Lars: *Lares,* Roman tutelary gods of the home.   Lemures: spirits of the dead.
194. flamens: ancient Roman priests.
195. sweat: cf. Virgil, *Georg.* 1.480.
197–213. For most of the deities see the glossary.
199. Dagon.

And moonèd Ashtaroth,   200
Heav'n's queen and mother both,
  Now sits not girt with tapers' holy shine;
The Libyc Hammon shrinks his horn,
In vain the Tyrian maids their wounded Thammuz mourn.

XXIII

And sullen Moloch, fled,   205
Hath left in shadows dread
  His burning idol all of blackest hue;
In vain with cymbals' ring
They call the grisly king,
  In dismal dance about the furnace blue;   210
The brutish gods of Nile as fast,
Isis and Orus, and the dog Anubis haste.

XXIV

Nor is Osiris seen
In Memphian grove or green,
  Trampling the unshow'red grass with lowings loud;   215
Nor can he be at rest
Within his sacred chest,
  Naught but profoundest hell can be his shroud;
In vain with timbreled anthems dark
The sable-stolèd sorcerers bear his worshiped ark.   220

XXV

He feels from Judah's land
The dreaded Infant's hand,
  The rays of Bethlehem blind his dusky eyn;
Nor all the gods beside
Longer dare abide,   225
  Not Typhon huge ending in snaky twine:
Our Babe, to show his Godhead true,
Can in his swaddling bands control the damnèd crew.

XXVI

So when the sun in bed,
Curtained with cloudy red,   230
  Pillows his chin upon an orient wave,
The flocking shadows pale
Troop to th' infernal jail;
  Each fettered ghost slips to his several grave,
And the yellow-skirted fays   235
Fly after the night-steeds, leaving their moon-loved maze.

212. Anubis: an Egyptian god, son of Osiris, represented with a jackal's head.
215. unshow'red: without rain.
219. timbreled: accompanied by tambourines.
220. sable-stolèd: black-robed.
223. eyn (archaic): eyes.

227–28. In spite of the antipagan context, the lines suggest the infant Hercules strangling the serpents.
232–36. Cf. *A Midsummer Night's Dream* 3.2.378–87; *Hamlet* 1.1.149–55.
236. Night had a chariot corresponding to that of Dawn.

XXVII

But see, the Virgin blest
Hath laid her Babe to rest.
   Time is our tedious song should here have ending;
Heaven's youngest-teemèd star   240
Hath fixed her polished car,
   Her sleeping Lord with handmaid lamp attending;
And all about the courtly stable
Bright-harnessed angels sit in order serviceable.

240. youngest-teemèd: latest born.   243–44. Cf. 30–31.
241. Matt. 2.9.

Elegia sexta

Ad Carolum Diodatum ruri commorantem

Qui, cum Idibus Decemb. scripsisset, et sua carmina excusari postulasset si solito minus essent bona, quod inter lautitias quibus erat ab amicis exceptus, haud satis felicem operam Musis dare se posse affirmabat, hunc habuit responsum.

Mitto tibi sanam non pleno ventre salutem,
   Qua tu distento forte carere potes.
At tua quid nostram prolectat Musa Camenam,
   Nec sinit optatas posse sequi tenebras?
Carmine scire velis quam te redamemque colamque,   5
   Crede mihi, vix hoc carmine scire queas,
Nam neque noster amor modulis includitur arctis,
   Nec venit ad claudos integer ipse pedes.
Quam bene solennes epulas, hilaremque Decembrim,
   Festaque coelifugam quae coluere Deum,   10
Deliciasque refers, hiberni gaudia ruris,
   Haustaque per lepidos Gallica musta focos.
Quid quereris refugam vino dapibusque poesin?
   Carmen amat Bacchum, carmina Bacchus amat.
Nec puduit Phoebum virides gestasse corymbos,   15
   Atque hederam lauro praeposuisse suae.
Saepius Aoniis clamavit collibus *Euoe*
   Mista Thyoneo turba novena choro.
Naso Corallaeis mala carmina misit ab agris;
   Non illic epulae, non sata vitis erat.   20
Quid nisi vina, rosasque, racemiferumque Lyaeum
   Cantavit brevibus Teia Musa modis?
Pindaricosque inflat numeros Teumesius Euan,
   Et redolet sumptum pagina quaeque merum;
Dum gravis everso currus crepat axe supinus,   25
   Et volat Eleo pulvere fuscus eques.

Quadrimoque madens lyricen Romanus Iaccho
    Dulce canit Glyceran, flavicomamque Chloen.
Iam quoque lauta tibi generoso mensa paratu
    Mentis alit vires, ingeniumque fovet.   30
Massica fecundam despumant pocula venam,
    Fundis et ex ipso condita metra cado.
Addimus his artes, fusumque per intima Phoebum
    Corda; favent uni Bacchus, Apollo, Ceres.
Scilicet haud mirum tam dulcia carmina per te   35
    Numine composito tres peperisse deos.
Nunc quoque Thressa tibi caelato barbitos auro
    Insonat arguta molliter icta manu;
Auditurque chelys suspensa tapetia circum,
    Virgineos tremula quae regat arte pedes.   40
Illa tuas saltem teneant spectacula Musas,
    Et revocent quantum crapula pellit iners.
Crede mihi, dum psallit ebur comitataque plectrum
    Implet odoratos festa chorea tholos,
Percipies tacitum per pectora serpere Phoebum,   45
    Quale repentinus permeat ossa calor,
Perque puellares oculos digitumque sonantem
    Irruet in totos lapsa Thalia sinus.
Namque Elegia levis multorum cura deorum est,
    Et vocat ad numeros quemlibet illa suos;   50
Liber adest elegis, Eratoque, Ceresque, Venusque,
    Et cum purpurea matre tenellus Amor.
Talibus inde licent convivia larga poetis,
    Saepius et veteri commaduisse mero.
At qui bella refert, et adulto sub Iove caelum,   55
    Heroasque pios, semideosque duces,
Et nunc sancta canit superum consulta deorum,
    Nunc latrata fero regna profunda cane,
Ille quidem parce Samii pro more magistri
    Vivat, et innocuos praebeat herba cibos;   60
Stet prope fagineo pellucida lympha catillo,
    Sobriaque e puro pocula fonte bibat.
Additur huic scelerisque vacans et casta iuventus,
    Et rigidi mores, et sine labe manus;
Qualis veste nitens sacra et lustralibus undis   65
    Surgis ad infensos augur iture Deos.
Hoc ritu vixisse ferunt post rapta sagacem
    Lumina Tiresian, Ogygiumque Linon,
Et lare devoto profugum Calchanta, senemque
    Orpheon edomitis sola per antra feris;   70
Sic dapis exiguus, sic rivi potor Homerus
    Dulichium vexit per freta longa virum,
Et per monstrificam Perseiae Phoebados aulam,
    Et vada femineis insidiosa sonis,
Perque tuas, rex ime, domos, ubi sanguine nigro   75
    Dicitur umbrarum detinuisse greges.

Diis etenim sacer est vates, divumque sacerdos,
    Spirat et occultum pectus et ora Iovem.
At tu si quid agam scitabere (si modo saltem
    Esse putas tanti noscere siquid agam),   80
Paciferum canimus caelesti semine regem,
    Faustaque sacratis saecula pacta libris;
Vagitumque Dei, et stabulantem paupere tecto
    Qui suprema suo cum patre regna colit;
Stelliparumque polum, modulantesque aethere turmas,   85
    Et subito elisos ad sua fana deos.
Dona quidem dedimus Christi natalibus illa;
    Illa sub auroram lux mihi prima tulit.
Te quoque pressa manent patriis meditata cicutis;
    Tu mihi, cui recitem, iudicis instar eris.   90

(1629)

ELEGY VI

To Charles Diodati visiting in the country

A reply to a letter of December 13, in which Diodati had asked indulgence
if his verses were not up to the mark, because, lavishly entertained as he was
by his friends, he could not, he said, offer fitting service to the Muses.

MILTON's prefatory note gives a sufficient key to this epistle, written a few days after Christmas, 1629. The poem might be said to embody two small academic prolusions. In the first part Milton carries on Diodati's mood with half-playful, half-serious praise of vinous and amorous poetry. But then he turns, with entire seriousness, to picture the heroic poet as an ascetic priest of the Pythagorean kind. This exalted ideal leads naturally into the concluding outline of the English poem he has just been writing, the *Nativity*. Thus both poems — written within a few weeks of his coming of age — are an indirect statement of his own high poetic resolves for the future. Whether or not he had by this time given up the idea of taking orders, he sees the truly heroic poet in quasi-religious terms.

I, with no full stomach, send you wishes for the good health that you, with your high living, may be in want of. But why does your Muse challenge mine and not allow her to enjoy the obscurity she desires? If you would like to know, through a poem, how warmly I cherish you and return your affection, that, I assure you, you could hardly learn from verse, for my love is not to be confined within poetic meters and is too strong and sound to limp on elegiac feet.[8]

How well you describe the accustomed feasts and the joys of December, and the celebrations that commemorate the God who came down from heaven, the pleasures and the merry-making of winter in the country, and the drinking of French wine by the jolly fireside! But why do you complain that poetry flees from wine and feasting? Song loves Bacchus and Bacchus loves song. Phoebus was not ashamed to wear the green clusters and to set the ivy above his own laurel. Many a time on the Aonian hills the choir of the nine,[18] mingled with the Thyonean[18]

8. See the note on Elegy 1.92.
18. The Muses. Thyonean: Bacchic (from Bacchus' mother, Semele, known as Thyone after Jove took her to heaven).

throng, have raised the cry *Euoe!*[17] Ovid sent bad verses from the Corallian[19] land, for there conviviality was lacking and the vine was not planted. Did the Teian Muse[22] sing in his short measures of anything but wine and roses and Lyaeus[21] with his branches of grapes? Teumesian[23] Bacchus inspired Pindar's odes, and every page smacks of his deep draughts, as he tells of the broken axle, the crash of the heavy chariot, and the racing horseman black with Elean[26] dust. The Roman lyrist,[27] mellowed by four-year-old wine, sings sweetly of Glycera and golden-haired Chloe. Now likewise the well-spread and luxurious table strengthens your mind and warms your genius. Your Massic[31] cups foam into rich song and from the wine jar itself you pour out verses stored within. To these stimulants artistry is added, and the fire of Apollo kindling your secret heart. Upon you Bacchus, Apollo, and Ceres bestow their gifts; it is no wonder, surely, that through the united power of three deities you have given birth to such charming lines.

Now also for you the gold-chased Thracian[37] lute is sounding, under the soft touch of a skilled hand, and in tapestried rooms are heard the tuneful rhythms of the lyre that direct the girls' dancing feet. Let such scenes occupy your Muses at least, and call back the inspiration that sluggish indulgence drives away. Believe me, while the music of ivory keys[43] and the lute fills the lofty perfumed halls and leads the festive dance, you will feel Apollo stealing silently through your heart, as a sudden heat penetrates your marrow; and from the eyes and fingers of the fair musicians Thalia[48] will flood into your whole being.

For light elegy has the patronage of many gods and calls whom she will to her measures; Bacchus presides over elegies, and Erato[51] and Ceres and Venus, and tender Love along with his rosy mother. Such poets, then, may be allowed lavish feasts and drenching brimmers of old wine. But he[55] who tells of wars and of heaven under the ripe sway of Jove, of pious heroes and godlike leaders, who sings now of the solemn decrees of the gods above, now of the infernal kingdoms where the fierce dog[58] howls — such a poet must live sparingly, after the manner of the Samian teacher,[59] and take plain herbs for his food. He should have beside him a little beechen bowl of crystal water and drink sober draughts from the clear spring. And his youth must be free from evil, and chaste, his character upright, his hand without stain. He must be such as you, augur-priest, when, in the shining purity of sacred vestments and lustral water, you go forth to face the hostile gods. By this rule, they say, wise Tiresias lived, after his sight was gone, and Ogygian Linus,[68] and Calchas,[69] an exile from his doomed hearth, and aged Orpheus when he had tamed the wild beasts among the lonely caves. Thus Homer,[71] who took little food and drank of the stream, carried the Dulichian hero[72]

17. The festal cry of Bacchic devotees.
19. The Coralli were one of the barbarous peoples in the region of Ovid's exile.
21. Lyaeus: Bacchus.
22. Anacreon of Teos.
23. Teumesian: Boeotian.
26. See the note on *P.L.* 2.530.
27. Horace.
31. Wine produced on the Campanian Mount Massicus.
37. So called because of the Thracian Orpheus.
43. Of the virginal or harpsichord.
48. The Muse of comedy and social verse.
51. The Muse of lyrical and amatory verse.
55 f. Some Roman poets (e.g. Virgil, *Ecl.* 6; Horace, *Od.* 1.6 and 2.12; Ovid, *Amores* 1.1, etc.) repudiated heroic in favor of rustic

or convivial or erotic themes; Milton reverses the shift.
58. Cerberus.
59. Pythagoras (born at Samos *c.* 580 B.C.) established a religious and ascetic society in southern Italy.
68. A mythical bard of Thebes (Ogygia) who taught Orpheus. The ascetic habits ascribed to these prophets and poets seem to be largely Milton's invention.
69. The prophet in the Greek army at Troy, who later helped to colonize Pamphylia.
71. Boccaccio (*Genealogy of the Gods* 14.19) gave a picture of Homer as a sort of rugged hermit.
72. Odysseus, ruler of Ithaca and a small adjacent island, Dulichium.

over the wide seas and through the monster-making palace of the daughter[73] of the sun-god and Perseis, past the seductive shores of the Sirens' music,[74] and through your courts, king of the underworld,[75] where, it is said, with an offering of dark blood he summoned troops of the shades.[76] For the true poet is sacred to the gods, he is a priest of the gods; and his inmost soul and his lips breathe out Jove.

Now if you would like to know what I am doing (if indeed you care to hear of my occupations), I am singing the prince of peace, the son of Heaven, and the blessed ages promised in the sacred books — the cries of the infant God, and the lodgement in a poor stable of him who with his Father rules the realms above; I am singing of the starry sky and the hymns of the angelic host in the upper air, and the pagan gods suddenly destroyed at their own shrines. This is my gift for the birthday of Christ; the first light of dawn brought it to me. For you also are waiting these verses, simply fashioned on my native pipes, and you, when I recite them to you, shall be my judge.[90]

73. Circe.
74. *Odyssey* 12.45 f., 165 f.
75. Pluto.
76. *Odyssey* 11.34 f.
90. The translation of the last sentence assumes that Milton is carrying on his reference to the *Nativity,* written as a gift for Christ, brought by the dawn as a gift to the poet, and now, as a sort of gift, awaiting Diodati's judgment. A recent suggestion about these much-discussed lines is that Milton is referring to Diodati's native or ancestral language, Italian, and to the sheaf of Italian poems which, on this view, Milton had lately written.

The Passion

SINCE the first stanza of this poem alludes to the *Nativity,* it was presumably written just before the following Easter, 1630. The inspiration of the *Nativity* probably led to an uninspired resolution to follow it up. *The Passion* has some beautiful lines but, instead of getting into its subject, it wanders further and further away. Milton's note at the end, the only note of its kind, indicates his dissatisfaction.

I

Erewhile of music and ethereal mirth,
Wherewith the stage of air and earth did ring,
And joyous news of heav'nly Infant's birth,
My muse with angels did divide to sing;
But headlong joy is ever on the wing,
   In wintry solstice like the shortened light
Soon swallowed up in dark and long outliving night.   5

II

For now to sorrow must I tune my song,
And set my harp to notes of saddest woe,
Which on our dearest Lord did seize ere long,   10
Dangers, and snares, and wrongs, and worse than so,
Which he for us did freely undergo.
   Most perfect Hero, tried in heaviest plight
Of labors huge and hard, too hard for human wight.

13–14. Cf. Hercules.

III

He, sov'ran Priest, stooping his regal head,   15
That dropped with odorous oil down his fair eyes,
Poor fleshly tabernacle enterèd,
His starry front low-roofed beneath the skies;
O what a mask was there, what a disguise!
    Yet more: the stroke of death he must abide,   20
Then lies him meekly down fast by his brethren's side.

IV

These latest scenes confine my roving verse,
To this horizon is my Phoebus bound;
His Godlike acts, and his temptations fierce,
And former sufferings otherwhere are found;   25
Loud o'er the rest Cremona's trump doth sound;
    Me softer airs befit, and softer strings
Of lute, or viol still, more apt for mournful things.

V

Befriend me, Night, best patroness of grief,
Over the pole thy thickest mantle throw,   30
And work my flattered fancy to belief
That heav'n and earth are colored with my woe;
My sorrows are too dark for day to know.
    The leaves should all be black whereon I write,
And letters where my tears have washed, a wannish white.   35

VI

See, see the chariot and those rushing wheels
That whirled the prophet up at Chebar flood;
My spirit some transporting Cherub feels,
To bear me where the towers of Salem stood,
Once glorious towers, now sunk in guiltless blood;   40
    There doth my soul in holy vision sit
In pensive trance, and anguish, and ecstatic fit.

VII

Mine eye hath found that sad sepulchral rock
That was the casket of heav'n's richest store,
And here though grief my feeble hands uplock,   45
Yet on the softened quarry would I score
My plaining verse as lively as before;
    For sure so well instructed are my tears,
That they would fitly fall in ordered characters.

15–16. Heb. 1.9, 9.11.
22. latest: 1645, latter.
26. The *Christiad,* a Latin epic on the life of Christ by M. G. Vida (1485–1566) of Cremona.
28. still: subdued.

37. prophet: Ezekiel 1.
39. Salem: Jerusalem.
43. rock: Christ's tomb (Matt. 27.60 and the other Gospels).
46. quarry: stone.

VIII

Or should I thence hurried on viewless wing   50
    Take up a weeping on the mountains wild,
    The gentle neighborhood of grove and spring
    Would soon unbosom all their echoes mild,
    And I (for grief is easily beguiled)
        Might think the infection of my sorrows loud   55
    Had got a race of mourners on some pregnant cloud.

This subject the author finding to be above the years he had when he wrote it, and nothing satisfied with what was begun, left it unfinished.

(1630)

51. Jer. 9.10.   56. Glossary, "Ixion."

Sonnet I

MILTON's first English sonnet, written in the spring of perhaps 1630, is somewhat akin to Elegy 7 (though far from expressing any intense feeling) and much more to the Italian sonnets that follow. It may indeed have been an experimental prelude to amatory ventures in another language. The sonnet is a piece of graceful artifice, half humorous in its use of the medieval fancy that, if a lover in springtime heard the nightingale before the cuckoo, he would be successful in love.

O nightingale, that on yon bloomy spray
    Warbl'st at eve, when all the woods are still,
    Thou with fresh hope the lover's heart dost fill,
    While the jolly Hours lead on propitious May;
Thy liquid notes that close the eye of day,   5
    First heard before the shallow cuckoo's bill,
    Portend success in love; O if Jove's will
    Have linked that amorous power to thy soft lay,
Now timely sing, ere the rude bird of hate
    Foretell my hopeless doom in some grove nigh,   10
    As thou from year to year hast sung too late
For my relief, yet hadst no reason why:
    Whether the Muse or Love call thee his mate,
    Both them I serve, and of their train am I.
                                            (1629–30?)

1–2. Cf. Elegy 5.25–26.   4. jolly Hours: cf. *Iliad* 21.450.

ITALIAN POEMS

THE SIX Italian poems, which may have been written in 1630 (see, however, the last note on Elegy 6), link themselves in theme with Elegy 7 and the English Sonnet 1. We do not know if Milton was in love with someone or only in love with love and poetry and things Italian; actual experience is suggested by some circumstantiality, but that kind of evidence is unreliable. At any rate the poems enlarge our picture of the young man and young artist who, perhaps not long after writing the *Nativity*, could play the role of the courtly romantic lover. Yet his amorousness is far from that of Carew or Suckling. As he said later in his *Apology for Smectymnuus,* he turned away from the sensuality of Ovid and his fellows to the idealism of Dante and Petrarch. Thus he ends Sonnet 3 on a religious note (whether personal or conventional), and his own voice is clearly heard in Sonnet 6 in the account of himself as an almost disciplined Stoic. The poems vary in quality, from the originality of Sonnet 6 and the Canzone to the weakness of Sonnet 5, but they attest the young Milton's considerable mastery of Italian and the Italian sonneteers' language of love. Italian influences, poetic and critical, were to count a good deal in his poetry of the next forty years.

Sonnet II

Donna leggiadra, il cui bel nome onora
   L' erbosa val di Reno e il nobil varco,
   Ben è colui d' ogni valore scarco
   Qual tuo spirto gentil non innamora,
Che dolcemente mostrasi di fuora,   5
   De' suói atti soavi giammai parco,
   E i don', che son d'Amor saette ed arco,
   Là onde l' alta tua virtù s' infiora.
Quando tu vaga parli, o lieta canti,
   Che mover possa duro alpestre legno, 10
   Guardi ciascun agli occhi ed agli orecchi
L' entrata, chi di te si trova indegno;
   Grazia sola di sù gli vaglia, innanti
   Che 'l disio amoroso al cuor s' invecchi.
                    (1629–30?)

Beautiful lady, whose fair name honors the green valley of the Reno and the famous ford,[2] truly he is devoid of all worth who does not love your noble spirit, which is sweetly expressed in the unfailing bounty of its gracious looks and the gifts that are the arrows and bow of Love, in that place[8] where your high virtue blooms. When you in your beauty speak, or give forth happy song that could move tough mountain-trees,[10] let every man who finds himself unworthy of you watch well the portals of his eyes and ears. Only grace from above can avail him to prevent amorous desire from rooting itself in his heart.

2. In Italian fashion Milton identifies his lady's name as Emilia by alluding to the Aemilian province of Italy through which flow the Reno and the Rubicon. The ford is that in the Rubicon associated with Julius Caesar's fateful return to Italy.
   8. Her eyes.
   10. Like Orpheus.

Sonnet III

Qual in colle aspro, al imbrunir di sera,
   L' avvezza giovinetta pastorella
   Va bagnando l' erbetta strana e bella,
   Che mal si spande a disusata spera
Fuor di sua natia alma primavera,   5
   Così Amor meco insù la lingua snella
   Desta il fior novo di strania favella,
   Mentre io di te, vezzosamente altera,
Canto, dal mio buon popol non inteso,

As on a rough hillside, in darkening twilight, the young shepherdess, accustomed to the place, waters a strange and beautiful little plant which grows weakly in an alien air, far from its own nourishing springtime, so on my ready tongue Love awakens the unwonted flower of foreign speech, while of you in your charming pride I sing, not understood by my good countrymen, and ex-

E 'l bel Tamigi cangio col bel Arno. 10
Amor lo volse, ed io, a l' altrui peso,
Seppi ch' Amor cosa mai volse indarno.

Deh! foss' il mio cuor lento e 'l duro seno
A chi pianta dal ciel sì buon terreno.
(1629–30?)

10. The river that flows through Florence,
a city noted for the purity of its Italian speech.
14. The sensuous young poet is perhaps
uneasily aware that he — or "nature's part" in
him — is more instinctively responsive to love

change the fair Thames for the fair Arno.[10]
Love willed it, and from others' cost I have
learned that Love never willed anything in
vain. Ah, would that my sluggish heart and
stony breast might be as fertile soil for Him
who sows from heaven.[14]

than to religion, but the Petrarchan tradition
made much of both the analogy and the conflict between the love of woman and the
love of God.

Canzone

Ridonsi donne e giovani amorosi,
M' accostandosi attorno, e "Perchè scrivi,
Perchè tu scrivi in lingua ignota e strana,
Verseggiando d' amor, e com t' osi?
Dinne, se la tua speme sia mai vana,   5
E de' pensieri lo miglior t' arrivi!"
Così mi van burlando: "Altri rivi,
Altri lidi t' aspettan ed altre onde,
Nelle cui verdi sponde
Spuntati ad or ad or a la tua chioma   10
L' immortal guiderdon d' eterne frondi.
Perchè alle spalle tue soverchia soma?"
    Canzon, dirotti, e tu per me rispondi:
Dice mia Donna, e 'l suo dir è il mio cuore,
"Questa è lingua di cui si vanta Amore." 15
(1629–30?)

The Italian canzone was (to ignore its internal complications) composed of a series of
irregular paragraphs with lines of irregular
length, like *Lycidas*. Milton's Canzone is only
a single such paragraph, like a madrigal —
and like *On Time* and *At a Solemn Music*.

Amorous young men and women[1] crowd
around me, laughing: "Why, O why, do you
write in an unknown foreign tongue, making verses about love? How do you dare?
Tell us, if your hope is not to be ever vain
and the best of your wishes is to be fulfilled?" Thus they make fun of me: "Other
streams, other shores are waiting for you,
and other waters on whose green banks even
now is growing for your hair the immortal
chaplet of undying leaves. Why add a needless burden to your shoulders?" Canzone,[13]
I will tell you, and you answer for me: my
lady says — and her words are my heart —
"This is the language of which Love boasts."

1. These young people are of course English and in England.
13. The common envoy of the canzone, in
which the poet addressed his poem (cf. Spenser's *Epithalamion* and the partly similar conclusion of *Lycidas*).

Sonnet IV

Diodati — e te 'l dirò con maraviglia —
    Quel ritroso io, ch' Amor spreggiar
        soléa
    E de' suoi lacci spesso mi ridéa,
    Già caddi, ov' uom dabben talor s'
        impiglia.
Nè treccie d' oro, nè guancia vermiglia   5
    M' abbaglian sì, ma sotto nùova idea
    Pellegrina bellezza che 'l cuor bea,
    Portamenti alti onesti, e nelle ciglia
Quel sereno fulgor d' amabil nero,
    Parole adorne di lingua più d' una,   10
    E 'l cantar che di mezzo l' emisfero

Diodati — and I tell you with wonder —
I, that stubborn one who used to mock
Love and often laughed at his snares, have
now fallen where a good man is sometimes
caught. It is not golden hair or a rosy cheek
that so bewitches me, but a foreign beauty
of a new pattern rejoices my heart — proud
modesty of bearing, in her eyes that clear
sheen of lovely black, speech adorned by
more than one language, and a gift of song

Traviar ben può la faticosa Luna;
   E degli occhi suoi avventa sì gran fuoco
   Che l' incerar gli orecchi mi fia poco.
                  (1629–30?)

This sonnet, addressed to Milton's friend, is a miniature variation on the theme of Elegy 7. The praise of a dark Italian beauty is a backsliding from the celebration of English girls in Elegy 1.

that might well drive the laboring moon[12] astray in the middle of the sky, and from her eyes darts such a potent fire that wax in my ears would be of little use.[14]

12. In eclipse (cf. Virgil, *Ecl.* 8.69 and *Georg.* 2.478, and *P.L.* 2.665).
14. Odysseus stopped his men's ears with wax to prevent their being tempted by the Sirens' song.

Sonnet V

Per certo i bei vostr' occhi, Donna mia,
   Esser non può che non sian lo mio sole;
   Sì mi percuoton forte, come ei suole
   Per l' arene di Libia chi s' invia,
Mentre un caldo vapor (nè sentì pria)   5
   Da quel lato si spinge ove mi duole,
   Che forse amanti nelle lor parole
   Chiaman sospir; io non so che si sia.
Parte rinchiusa e turbida si cela
   Scosso mi il petto, e poi n' uscendo poco   10
   Quivi d' attorno o s' agghiaccia o s' ingiela;
Ma quanto agli occhi giunge a trovar loco
   Tutte le notti a me suol far piovose,
   Finchè mia Alba rivien colma di rose.
                  (1629–30?)

6. The side where the heart is.

Surely your beautiful eyes, my lady, cannot be other than my sun; they beat upon me as strongly as the sun upon the traveler through Libyan sands. At the same time a hot vapor — which I never felt before — presses upon me from that side where my pain is.[6] Perhaps lovers in their language call it a sigh; I do not know what it may be. A turbulent part, enclosed and hidden in my breast, makes it throb; and then a little escaping freezes and turns to ice. But the part of it that finds lodging in my eyes makes all my nights rainy,[13] until my Dawn returns, full of roses.

13. With tears.

Sonnet VI

Giovane piano, e semplicetto amante,
   Poichè fuggir me stesso in dubbio sono,
   Madonna, a voi del mio cuor l' umil dono
   Farò divoto; io certo a prove tante
L' ebbi fedele, intrepido, costante,   5
   Di pensieri leggiadro, accorto, e buono;
   Quando rugge il gran mondo, e scocca il tuono,
   S' arma di se, e d' intero diamante,
Tanto del forse e d' invidia sicuro,
   Di timori, e speranze al popol use,   10
   Quanto d' ingegno e d' alto valor vago,
E di cetra sonora, e delle Muse.
   Sol troverete in tal parte men duro
   Ove Amor mise l' insanabil ago.
                  (1629–30?)

Young, gentle, and simple-hearted lover that I am, since I am in doubt whether to flee from myself, lady, in devotion to you I will offer the humble gift of my heart. In many tests I have found it faithful, fearless, and steadfast, and in its thoughts gracious, discreet, and good. When the great world is in commotion and the thunder crashes, it arms itself with itself, with solid adamant — as secure against fortune, envy, and the fears and hopes of the mass of men, as it is eagerly desirous of powers of mind and high courage, and the melodious lyre, and the Muses.[7-12] Only in one place is it less invulnerable — there where Love planted his incurable wound.

7–12. Cf. Horace, *Od.* 3.3.1–8, 3.29.55 f.

On Shakespeare. 1630

THIS POEM — Milton's first English one to be published — was printed in and presumably written for the Second Folio of Shakespeare (1632); it may have been requested by the printer. Such a tribute, in addition to some specific allusions, is welcome evidence of the young poet's recognition of Shakespeare, and is a partial confirmation of many apparent echoes in Milton's poetry. The conception of Shakespeare as an untutored natural genius (lines 9–10) became current quite early, for example in Jonson's poem in the First Folio (1623), although

Jonson praised his art also (cf. *L'Allegro* 131–34). Milton doubtless remembered Jonson's line (22): "Thou art a monument, without a tomb." He may have known and consciously echoed an epitaph on Sir Edward Stanley which was ascribed to Shakespeare:

Not monumental stones preserves our fame;
Nor sky-aspiring pyramids our name;
The memory of him for whom this stands
Shall outlive marble and defacers' hands . . .

The general idea is as old as Horace, *Odes* 3.30.

What needs my Shakespeare for his honored bones
The labor of an age in pilèd stones,
Or that his hallowed relics should be hid
Under a star-ypointing pyramid?
Dear son of memory, great heir of fame,   5
What need'st thou such weak witness of thy name?
Thou in our wonder and astonishment
Hast built thyself a livelong monument.
For whilst to th' shame of slow-endeavoring art
Thy easy numbers flow, and that each heart   10
Hath from the leaves of thy unvalued book
Those Delphic lines with deep impression took,
Then thou, our fancy of itself bereaving,
Dost make us marble with too much conceiving;
And so sepúlchred in such pomp dost lie,
That kings for such a tomb would wish to die.

(1630)

1 (and 6). What: Why.
4. See the note on *Nativity* 155. The archaic "y" does not belong with a present participle.
5. son of memory: i.e. brother of the Muses (cf. *Idea Platonica* 2–3).
11. unvalued: invaluable.
14. Cf. *Il Penseroso* 42 and William

Browne, *On the Countess Dowager of Pembroke:*
Marble piles let no man raise
To her name, for after-days
Some kind woman, born as she,
Reading this, like Niobe
Shall turn marble, and become
Both her mourner and her tomb.

[Epilogue to the Elegies]

Haec ego mente olim laeva, studioque supino
    Nequitiae posui vana trophaea meae.
Scilicet abreptum sic me malus impulit error,
    Indocilisque aetas prava magistra fuit,

Donec Socraticos umbrosa Academia rivos 5
Praebuit, admissum dedocuitque iugum.
Protinus extinctis ex illo tempore flammis,
Cincta rigent multo pectora nostra gelu,
Unde suis frigus metuit puer ipse sagittis,
Et Diomedeam vim timet ipsa Venus. 10
(1630 or later?)

THIS EPILOGUE followed Elegy 7 in Milton's *Poems* but evidently applied to more than that one piece; presumably he had Elegies 1 and 5 also in mind. These three were more or less in the erotic tradition of the elegy and would be the trophies of his wantonness for which he apologized. Elegy 7 was placed last of his elegies, out of chronological order, perhaps because the apology would have been quite inappropriate after Elegy 6, the latest in time of composition. The poet has now, thanks to Plato, moved beyond his youthful Ovidian phase.

These verses, vain trophies of my wantonness, with misguided mind and idle zeal I once hung up. So far in truth did mischievous error carry me away, and heedless youth was a bad teacher — until the shady Academy offered its Socratic streams and taught me how to cast off the yoke I had accepted. From that time onward the flames were extinguished, and my breast has been armed with a thick layer of ice, so that Cupid himself fears the cold for his arrows and even Venus dreads my Diomedean strength.[10]

10. Aphrodite (Venus) appeared in battle at Troy to protect her son Aeneas and was wounded by Diomedes (*Iliad* 5.334–417).

On the University Carrier

who sickened in the time of his vacancy, being forbid to go to London by reason of the plague

THOMAS HOBSON, who kept a livery in Cambridge and whose system of hiring out horses gave birth to the phrase "Hobson's choice," for over sixty years drove a wagon weekly between Cambridge and London. He had to stop, at the age of about 86, in the spring of 1630, when Cambridge was quarantined by the plague. He died on January 1, 1631, and many students wrote verses of affectionate jocosity in memory of the well-known veteran. Milton's second poem — more closely packed with puns than the other — was first printed, with variations, in the sixth edition of an anthology, *A Banquet of Jests* (1640), and both were included in *Wit Restor'd* (1658); neither book gave Milton's name. Authentic versions of both pieces were printed in his *Poems* of 1645.

Here lies old Hobson, Death hath broke his girt,
And here, alas, hath laid him in the dirt;
Or else, the ways being foul, twenty to one
He's here stuck in a slough, and overthrown.
'Twas such a shifter, that if truth were known, 5
Death was half glad when he had got him down;

1. girt: saddle-girth.

For he had any time this ten years full
Dodged with him betwixt Cambridge and *The Bull*.
And surely Death could never have prevailed,
Had not his weekly course of carriage failed;   10
But lately finding him so long at home,
And thinking now his journey's end was come,
And that he had ta'en up his latest inn,
In the kind office of a chamberlain
Showed him his room where he must lodge that night,   15
Pulled off his boots, and took away the light.
If any ask for him, it shall be said,
"Hobson has supped, and's newly gone to bed."

(1631)

Another on the Same

Here lieth one who did most truly prove
That he could never die while he could move;
So hung his destiny never to rot
While he might still jog on and keep his trot;
Made of sphere-metal, never to decay   5
Until his revolution was at stay.
Time numbers motion, yet (without a crime
'Gainst old truth) motion numbered out his time;
And like an engine moved with wheel and weight,
His principles being ceased, he ended straight.   10
Rest, that gives all men life, gave him his death,
And too much breathing put him out of breath;
Nor were it contradiction to affirm
Too long vacation hastened on his term.
Merely to drive the time away he sickened,   15
Fainted, and died, nor would with ale be quickened;
"Nay," quoth he, on his swooning bed outstretched,
"If I may not carry, sure I'll ne'er be fetched,
But vow, though the cross doctors all stood hearers,
For one carrier put down to make six bearers."   20
Ease was his chief disease, and to judge right,
He died for heaviness that his cart went light.
His leisure told him that his time was come,
And lack of load made his life burdensome,
That even to his last breath (there be that say't)   25
As he were pressed to death, he cried "More weight!"
But had his doings lasted as they were,
He had been an immortal carrier.

5. sphere-metal: the indestructible material
of the heavens.
7. Time . . . motion: a traditional commonplace (Plato, *Timaeus* 37–38).

10. principles: powers.
26. Like convicted persons being pressed to
death and longing for a quick end.

Obedient to the moon he spent his date
In course reciprocal, and had his fate   30
Linked to the mutual flowing of the seas,
Yet (strange to think) his wain was his increase.
His letters are delivered all and gone,
Only remains this superscription.

(1631)

29–31. The ebb and flow of the tides as caused by the moon.

An Epitaph on the Marchioness of Winchester

JANE PAULET, wife of the Catholic Marquis of Winchester, died on April 15, 1631, aged twenty-three, after giving birth to a dead boy; the cause of her death was an infected abscess in her cheek. Although the poem contains some biographical details, there is no evidence for Milton's having been acquainted with her or her family; but, since she was not a public figure like a bishop, he would hardly have written such a poem without any warrant. Possibly some Cambridge poets planned a collection of elegies. Though slighter than Henry King's great *Exequy*, and of course not inspired by any such personal grief, Milton's poem on the premature death of a noble and exemplary young wife and mother has lines of comparable tenderness and poignancy. This was his first poem in couplets of seven or eight syllables and mixed iambics and trochaics — the pattern to be used with even finer felicity in *L'Allegro* and *Il Penseroso*. The poem also inaugurated a new phase in the evolution of Milton's style; its Jonsonian simplicity may be measured by comparison with the Spenserian *Fair Infant* of three years earlier. (Jonson's own elegy on the Marchioness was a somewhat external and declamatory piece.)

This rich marble doth inter
The honored wife of Winchester,
A viscount's daughter, an earl's heir,
Besides what her virtues fair
Added to her noble birth,   5
More than she could own from earth.
Summers three times eight save one
She had told; alas, too soon,
After so short time of breath,
To house with darkness and with death.   10
Yet had the number of her days
Been as complete as was her praise,
Nature and fate had had no strife
In giving limit to her life.
Her high birth and her graces sweet   15
Quickly found a lover meet;
The virgin quire for her request
The god that sits at marriage feast;
He at their invoking came
But with a scarce well-lighted flame;   20

18. god: Hymen (cf. *L'Allegro* 125–26).

And in his garland as he stood,
Ye might discern a cypress bud.
Once had the early matrons run
To greet her of a lovely son,
And now with second hope she goes,   25
And calls Lucina to her throes;
But whether by mischance or blame,
Atropos for Lucina came,
And with remorseless cruelty
Spoiled at once both fruit and tree: 30
The hapless babe before his birth
Had burial, yet not laid in earth,
And the languished mother's womb
Was not long a living tomb.
So have I seen some tender slip,   35
Saved with care from winter's nip,
The pride of her carnation train,
Plucked up by some unheedy swain,
Who only thought to crop the flow'r
New shot up from vernal show'r;   40
But the fair blossom hangs the head
Sideways as on a dying bed,
And those pearls of dew she wears
Prove to be presaging tears
Which the sad morn had let fall   45
On her hast'ning funeral.
Gentle Lady, may thy grave
Peace and quiet ever have;
After this thy travail sore
Sweet rest seize thee evermore,   50
That to give the world increase
Shortened hast thy own life's lease;
Here, besides the sorrowing
That thy noble house doth bring,
Here be tears of perfect moan   55
Wept for thee in Helicon,
And some flowers and some bays
For thy hearse to strew the ways,
Sent thee from the banks of Came,
Devoted to thy virtuous name;   60
Whilst thou, bright saint, high sitt'st in glory,
Next her much like to thee in story,

---

22. A symbol of death.
24. The Marchioness had given birth to a son in 1629, seven years after her marriage.
26. Lucina: the Roman goddess of child-birth.
28. Atropos: the third of the three Fates, who cut the thread of life.

30. An echo of the last line of Milton's *Apologus?*
43–45. Cf. *In quintum Novembris* 135–36.
47–48. Cf. the dirge in *Cymbeline* (4.2.280–81).
50. seize: possess.   55. perfect: sincere.
59. Came: the river Cam at Cambridge.

That fair Syrian shepherdess,
Who after years of barrenness
The highly favored Joseph bore   65
To him that served for her before,
And at her next birth much like thee,
Through pangs fled to felicity,
Far within the bosom bright
Of blazing Majesty and Light;   70
There with thee, new-welcome saint,
Like fortunes may her soul acquaint,
With thee there clad in radiant sheen,
No marchioness, but now a queen.

(1631)

63. Rachel, Jacob's wife, who died in giving birth to Benjamin (Gen. 29–30 and 35.16–20). Dante had linked Rachel with Beatrice (*Par.* 32.7–9).

L'ALLEGRO and IL PENSEROSO

L'Allegro and *Il Penseroso* may have been written in Milton's last long vacation in 1631, when he was 22, or perhaps in the following summer. They are the most felicitous lyrical products of the young poet's Jonsonian phase, which had begun with the *Epitaph on the Marchioness of Winchester;* along with Jonson's classical symmetry, clarity, and urbanity, the poems have a refined purity of vision, a delicacy and charm of phrase and tone and rhythm, that are beyond the master's reach. The structural line — with contrasting images of light and darkness — is provided by patterns of an ideal day and night, although these short periods overlap and take in different seasons as well as quite diverse scenes. (In his first academic Prolusion, on the comparative superiority of day or night, Milton had remarked that the theme was more suitable for verse than prose.) The two poems, obviously designed as companion pieces, are linked together by constant parallels and contrasts, all governed by "decorum" and contributing to the unified wholes. The universal abstractions, Mirth and Melancholy (the latter is really Contemplation, of an especially Platonic cast), are given substance through outdoor and indoor settings and a variety of allusion, and details are generalized and idealized in keeping with the themes; the picture of meditative and studious solitude is less concrete than the world of people whom the cheerful man observes. Milton's temperament was flexible enough to enable him to distill both states of mind — and Mirth as well as Contemplation has an affinity with heaven. While the twin poems are creations of pure poetry, they remind us of various literary genres, the academic disputation, the pastoral, the "character," the emblem, and the encomium. Critics have seen an initial suggestion in the verses prefixed to the third edition (1628) of Robert Burton's *Anatomy of Melancholy;* there seem to be echoes of a number of poets, more than the notes can take account of. The metrical pattern of both poems carries on, with appropriate modulations, that of the preceding *Epitaph.*

L'Allegro

Hence, loathèd Melancholy,
   Of Cerberus and blackest Midnight born,
In Stygian cave forlorn
   'Mongst horrid shapes, and shrieks, and sights unholy,
Find out some uncouth cell,   5
   Where brooding darkness spreads his jealous wings,
And the night-raven sings;
   There under ebon shades and low-browed rocks,
As ragged as thy locks,
   In dark Cimmerian desert ever dwell.   10
But come, thou Goddess fair and free,
In heav'n yclept Euphrosyne,
And by men heart-easing Mirth,
Whom lovely Venus at a birth

1–10. The melancholy here banished is not casual depression or the contemplative state celebrated in *Il Penseroso* but the disease recognized in medical tradition.

9. ragged: rugged.
12. yclept: called (see note on *Nativity* 155). Euphrosyne: glossary, "Graces."

With two sister Graces more   15
To ivy-crownèd Bacchus bore;
Or whether (as some sager sing)
The frolic wind that breathes the spring,
Zephyr, with Aurora playing,
As he met her once a-Maying,   20
There on beds of violets blue,
And fresh-blown roses washed in dew,
Filled her with thee, a daughter fair,
So buxom, blithe, and debonair.
Haste thee, Nymph, and bring with thee   25
Jest and youthful Jollity,
Quips and Cranks, and wanton Wiles,
Nods and Becks and wreathèd Smiles,
Such as hang on Hebe's cheek,
And love to live in dimple sleek;   30
Sport that wrinkled Care derides,
And Laughter holding both his sides.
Come, and trip it as ye go
On the light fantastic toe,
And in thy right hand lead with thee   35
The mountain nymph, sweet Liberty;
And if I give thee honor due,
Mirth, admit me of thy crew,
To live with her, and live with thee,
In unreprovèd pleasures free;   40
To hear the lark begin his flight,
And singing startle the dull night,
From his watch-tow'r in the skies,
Till the dappled dawn doth rise;
Then to come in spite of sorrow   45
And at my window bid good-morrow,
Through the sweet-briar or the vine,
Or the twisted eglantine;
While the cock with lively din
Scatters the rear of darkness thin,   50
And to the stack or the barn door
Stoutly struts his dames before;
Oft list'ning how the hounds and horn
Cheerly rouse the slumb'ring morn,
From the side of some hoar hill,   55
Through the high wood echoing shrill;
Sometime walking, not unseen,
By hedgerow elms, on hillocks green,

15. Cf. Horace, *Od.* 4.7.5.
22. Cf. *Taming of the Shrew* 2.1.174.
24. buxom, blithe: in *Pericles*, prologue 23.
debonair: graceful, gracious.
27. Cranks: odd turns of speech.
28. Becks: upward nods.
33. ye: 1673, you.

39. Cf. Marlowe's pastoral lyric, "Come live with me and be my love."
45. The subject of "to come," as of the preceding infinitives, is the poet, who greets the new day at his window.   spite: defiance.
55. hoar: gray, from lack of foliage or early morning mist or hoar frost.

Right against the eastern gate,
Where the great sun begins his state,   60
Robed in flames and amber light,
The clouds in thousand liveries dight;
While the ploughman near at hand
Whistles o'er the furrowed land,
And the milkmaid singeth blithe,   65
And the mower whets his scythe,
And every shepherd tells his tale
Under the hawthorn in the dale.
Straight mine eye hath caught new pleasures,
Whilst the landscape round it measures: 70
Russet lawns and fallows gray,
Where the nibbling flocks do stray;
Mountains on whose barren breast
The laboring clouds do often rest;
Meadows trim with daisies pied,   75
Shallow brooks and rivers wide.
Towers and battlements it sees
Bosomed high in tufted trees,
Where perhaps some beauty lies,
The cynosure of neighboring eyes.   80
Hard by, a cottage chimney smokes
From betwixt two aged oaks,
Where Corydon and Thyrsis met
Are at their savory dinner set
Of herbs and other country messes,   85
Which the neat-handed Phillis dresses;
And then in haste her bow'r she leaves,
With Thestylis to bind the sheaves;
Or if the earlier season lead,
To the tanned haycock in the mead.   90
Sometimes with secure delight
The upland hamlets will invite,
When the merry bells ring round,
And the jocund rebecks sound
To many a youth and many a maid   95
Dancing in the chequered shade;
And young and old come forth to play
On a sunshine holiday,
Till the livelong daylight fail:
Then to the spicy nut-brown ale,   100
With stories told of many a feat,
How fairy Mab the junkets eat;

---

59. eastern gate: cf. *Midsummer Night's Dream* 3.2.391.

60. state: stately progress (of Phoebus the sungod).

67. tells his tale: either "counts his sheep" (as in George Wither, *Fair Virtue* 691), or "tells his story" (as in Wither, *Shepherd's Hunting, Ecl.* 3.24). In Wither, as in Virgil, *Ecl.* 6.85, the counting is an evening opera-tion; in Virgil, *Ecl.* 3.34 (where Dryden translates "takes the tale"), it is done twice a day.

70. landscape: glossary.

75. pied: variegated (cf. *Love's Labor's Lost* 5.2.904).

94. rebecks: primitive violins.

102. Mab. See *Romeo and Juliet* 1.4.53 f. eat: past tense.

She was pinched and pulled, she said,
And he, by friar's lantern led,
Tells how the drudging goblin sweat   105
To earn his cream-bowl duly set,
When in one night, ere glimpse of morn,
His shadowy flail hath threshed the corn
That ten day-laborers could not end;
Then lies him down the lubber fiend,   110
And stretched out all the chimney's length,
Basks at the fire his hairy strength;
And crop-full out of doors he flings,
Ere the first cock his matin rings.
Thus done the tales, to bed they creep,   115
By whispering winds soon lulled asleep.
Towered cities please us then,
And the busy hum of men,
Where throngs of knights and barons bold
In weeds of peace high triumphs hold,   120
With store of ladies, whose bright eyes
Rain influence, and judge the prize
Of wit or arms, while both contend
To win her grace whom all commend.
There let Hymen oft appear   125
In saffron robe, with taper clear,
And pomp, and feast, and revelry,
With masque and antique pageantry:
Such sights as youthful poets dream
On summer eves by haunted stream.   130
Then to the well-trod stage anon,
If Jonson's learned sock be on,
Or sweetest Shakespeare, Fancy's child,
Warble his native wood-notes wild;
And ever against eating cares   135
Lap me in soft Lydian airs,
Married to immortal verse,
Such as the meeting soul may pierce
In notes with many a winding bout
Of linkèd sweetness long drawn out,   140
With wanton heed and giddy cunning,
The melting voice through mazes running,
Untwisting all the chains that tie
The hidden soul of harmony;

103–04. She, he: members of the story-telling group.
104. friar's lantern: will-o'-the-wisp. In 1673 the line read "And by the Friars Lanthorn led."
105. goblin: Robin Goodfellow, Puck.
110. lubber fiend: drudging spirit.
132. sock: the light shoe of ancient comic actors, a symbol of comedy.
133–34. Shakespeare is characterized partly in contrast with the learned Jonson (cf. *On Shakespeare* 9–10), partly in terms of the out-door comedies the mirthful man would enjoy.
135. eating cares: cf. Horace, *Od.* 2.11.18.
136. Lydian: sensuous, relaxing (the young Milton is less severe than Plato, *Rep.* 398–99).
136–37. Cf. Horace, *Od.* 4.15.30.
136–44. Since Milton links music with song he seems to be thinking, not so much of the unaccompanied madrigal or part-song, but of the solo "air" or Italian aria.
139. bout: turn, involution.

That Orpheus' self may heave his head   145
From golden slumber on a bed
Of heaped Elysian flow'rs, and hear
Such strains as would have won the ear
Of Pluto, to have quite set free
His half-regained Eurydice.   150
These delights if thou canst give,
Mirth, with thee I mean to live.

(1631–32?)

Il Penseroso

Hence, vain deluding Joys,
 The brood of Folly without father bred,
How little you bestead,
 Or fill the fixèd mind with all your toys;
Dwell in some idle brain,   5
 And fancies fond with gaudy shapes possess,
As thick and numberless
 As the gay motes that people the sunbeams,
Or likest hovering dreams,
 The fickle pensioners of Morpheus' train.   10
But hail, thou Goddess sage and holy,
Hail, divinest Melancholy,
Whose saintly visage is too bright
To hit the sense of human sight,
And therefore to our weaker view   15
O'erlaid with black, staid Wisdom's hue;
Black, but such as in esteem
Prince Memnon's sister might beseem,
Or that starred Ethiop queen that strove
To set her beauty's praise above   20
The sea-nymphs, and their powers offended.
Yet thou art higher far descended:
Thee bright-haired Vesta long of yore
To solitary Saturn bore;
His daughter she (in Saturn's reign   25
Such mixture was not held a stain).
Oft in glimmering bow'rs and glades
He met her, and in secret shades

1–10. The vain joys here dismissed are empty levity, not the refined Mirth celebrated in *L'Allegro*.

8. Cf. *Wife of Bath's Tale* 868.

10. pensioners: attendants. Morpheus: god of dreams.

16. "Melancholy" means literally "black bile," one of the four humors (glossary). The "black" or darkened skin associated with this Milton links with the benign kind of melancholy that accompanied genius and philosophical and poetical contemplation.

18. Memnon: glossary.

19–21. Like a number of other writers, Milton has Cassiopeia boast of her own beauty, not that of her daughter Andromeda; she was made a constellation.

23. Vesta, the Roman goddess of the hearth, adds the idea of the purity of celestial fire.

24 f. Saturn: glossary.

Of woody Ida's inmost grove,
While yet there was no fear of Jove.   30
Come, pensive Nun, devout and pure,
Sober, steadfast, and demure,
All in a robe of darkest grain,
Flowing with majestic train,
And sable stole of cypress lawn   35
Over thy decent shoulders drawn.
Come, but keep thy wonted state,
With even step and musing gait,
And looks commercing with the skies,
Thy rapt soul sitting in thine eyes;   40
There held in holy passion still,
Forget thyself to marble, till
With a sad leaden downward cast
Thou fix them on the earth as fast.
And join with thee calm Peace and Quiet,   45
Spare Fast, that oft with gods doth diet,
And hears the Muses in a ring
Aye round about Jove's altar sing;
And add to these retired Leisure,
That in trim gardens takes his pleasure;   50
But first, and chiefest, with thee bring
Him that yon soars on golden wing,
Guiding the fiery-wheelèd throne,
The Cherub Contemplatïon;
And the mute Silence hist along,   55
'Less Philomel will deign a song,
In her sweetest, saddest plight,
Smoothing the rugged brow of Night,
While Cynthia checks her dragon yoke
Gently o'er th' accustomed oak.   60
Sweet bird, that shunn'st the noise of folly,
Most musical, most melancholy!
Thee, chauntress, oft the woods among
I woo to hear thy even-song;
And missing thee, I walk unseen   65
On the dry smooth-shaven green,
To behold the wand'ring moon
Riding near her highest noon,
Like one that had been led astray
Through the heav'n's wide pathless way;   70

30. Jove: Zeus (Jupiter), who was brought up on Mount Ida in Crete, later overthrew his father Cronos (Saturn).
37. Cf. Jonson, *Queen and huntress* 4: "State in wonted manner keep."
39. Cf. Ovid, *Ars Amatoria* 3.549, *commercia caeli*.
42. Cf. *On Shakespeare* 14.
43. leaden: glossary, "Saturn."

45–46. Cf. Elegy 6.55 f.
47–48. Cf. Prolusion 2 (*Works*, 12, 155).
52–54. Ezek. 1 and 10.
55. hist: summon with the quiet exclamation "hist."
59. Cynthia (the moon) is given the dragon-chariot associated with Hecate, the goddess in her underworld aspect.

And oft, as if her head she bowed,
Stooping through a fleecy cloud.
Oft on a plat of rising ground
I hear the far-off curfew sound
Over some wide-watered shore,   75
Swinging slow with sullen roar;
Or if the air will not permit,
Some still removèd place will fit,
Where glowing embers through the room
Teach light to counterfeit a gloom,   80
Far from all resort of mirth,
Save the cricket on the hearth,
Or the bellman's drowsy charm,
To bless the doors from nightly harm.
Or let my lamp at midnight hour   85
Be seen in some high lonely tow'r,
Where I may oft outwatch the Bear,
With thrice great Hermes, or unsphere
The spirit of Plato to unfold
What worlds or what vast regions hold   90
The immortal mind that hath forsook
Her mansion in this fleshly nook;
And of those daemons that are found
In fire, air, flood, or under ground,
Whose power hath a true consent   95
With planet or with element.
Sometime let gorgeous Tragedy
In sceptered pall come sweeping by,
Presenting Thebes, or Pelops' line,
Or the tale of Troy divine,   100
Or what (though rare) of later age
Ennobled hath the buskined stage.
But, O sad Virgin, that thy power
Might raise Musaeus from his bower,
Or bid the soul of Orpheus sing   105
Such notes as, warbled to the string,
Drew iron tears down Pluto's cheek
And made hell grant what love did seek;
Or call up him that left half told
The story of Cambuscan bold,   110
Of Camball and of Algarsife,
And who had Canace to wife,

83. bellman: the night-watchman calling the hours.
87. That is, stay up all night, since the Great Bear does not set.
88. Hermes: glossary, "Hermes Trismegistus."   unsphere: call back.
93–96. Glossary, "element."
98. pall: robe.
99. Thebes: tragedies concerning Oedipus and his family.   Pelops' line: Pelops was the ancestor of Atreus and Thyestes, Agamemnon, Orestes, Electra, and Iphigenia.
102. The buskin, a high shoe worn by ancient tragic actors, corresponds to the "sock" of *L'Allegro* 132.
104. Musaeus: a mythical Greek poet.
108. Pluto's conditional release of Eurydice (glossary, "Orpheus"; *L'Allegro* 145 f.).
109–15. Chaucer's unfinished *Squire's Tale.*

That owned the virtuous ring and glass,
And of the wondrous horse of brass,
On which the Tartar king did ride; 115
And if aught else great bards beside
In sage and solemn tunes have sung,
Of tourneys and of trophies hung,
Of forests and enchantments drear,
Where more is meant than meets the ear. 120
Thus, Night, oft see me in thy pale career,
Till civil-suited Morn appear,
Not tricked and frounced as she was wont
With the Attic boy to hunt,
But kerchieft in a comely cloud, 125
While rocking winds are piping loud,
Or ushered with a shower still,
When the gust hath blown his fill,
Ending on the rustling leaves,
With minute drops from off the eaves. 130
And when the sun begins to fling
His flaring beams, me, Goddess, bring
To archèd walks of twilight groves,
And shadows brown that Sylvan loves,
Of pine or monumental oak, 135
Where the rude axe with heavèd stroke
Was never heard the nymphs to daunt,
Or fright them from their hallowed haunt.
There in close covert by some brook,
Where no profaner eye may look, 140
Hide me from Day's garish eye,
While the bee with honied thigh,
That at her flow'ry work doth sing,
And the waters murmuring
With such consort as they keep, 145
Entice the dewy-feathered Sleep;
And let some strange mysterious dream
Wave at his wings in airy stream
Of lively portraiture displayed,
Softly on my eyelids laid. 150
And as I wake, sweet music breathe
Above, about, or underneath,
Sent by some Spirit to mortals good,
Or th' unseen Genius of the wood.

116–20. Chiefly, no doubt, *The Faerie Queene*, by "our sage and serious poet Spenser" (*Areopagitica*, *Works*, 4, 311); also, Tasso's *Gerusalemme Liberata* and parts of Ariosto's *Orlando Furioso*.

122. civil-suited: plainly dressed (cf. *Romeo and Juliet* 3.2.10–11). frounced: with hair curled.

124. Attic boy: Cephalus.

126. rocking winds: that cause to rock (Sandys used "rocking winds" in translating Ovid, *Met*. 7.585–86).

130. minute drops: drops falling at intervals of a minute.

141. Cf. "garish sun," *Romeo and Juliet* 3.2.25.

144–46. Cf. Horace, *Epod*. 2.27–28.

148–50. Wave . . . laid: come floating with the wings of Sleep as they settle on my eyes.

But let my due feet never fail   155
To walk the studious cloister's pale,
And love the high embowèd roof,
With antique pillars massy proof,
And storied windows richly dight,
Casting a dim religious light.   160
There let the pealing organ blow
To the full-voiced quire below,
In service high and anthems clear,
As may with sweetness, through mine ear,
Dissolve me into ecstasies,   165
And bring all heav'n before mine eyes.
And may at last my weary age
Find out the peaceful hermitage,
The hairy gown and mossy cell,
Where I may sit and rightly spell   170
Of every star that heav'n doth shew,
And every herb that sips the dew,
Till old experience do attain
To something like prophetic strain.
These pleasures, Melancholy, give,   175
And I with thee will choose to live.
(1631–32?)

156. pale: enclosure.
157. embowèd: vaulted.
158. antique: glossary, "antic."
160. Cf. More's *Utopia*, tr. R. Robinson (Everyman's Library, pp. 107–08): "Because they thought that overmuch light doth disperse men's cogitations, whereas in dim and doubtful light they be gathered together, and more earnestly fixed upon religion and devotion."
170–71. spell Of: interpret.

Ad Patrem

Nunc mea Pierios cupiam per pectora fontes
Irriguas torquere vias, totumque per ora
Volvere laxatum gemino de vertice rivum;
Ut tenues oblita sonos audacibus alis
Surgat in officium venerandi Musa parentis.   5
Hoc utcunque tibi gratum, pater optime, carmen
Exiguum meditatur opus, nec novimus ipsi
Aptius a nobis quae possint munera donis
Respondere tuis, quamvis nec maxima possint
Respondere tuis, nedum ut par gratia donis   10
Esse queat vacuis quae redditur arida verbis.
Sed tamen haec nostros ostendit pagina census,
Et quod habemus opum charta numeravimus ista,
Quae mihi sunt nullae, nisi quas dedit aurea Clio,
Quas mihi semoto somni peperere sub antro,   15
Et nemoris laureta sacri, Parnassides umbrae.
    Nec tu vatis opus divinum despice carmen,

Quo nihil aethereos ortus et semina caeli,
Nil magis humanam commendat origine mentem,
Sancta Prometheae retinens vestigia flammae.   20
Carmen amant superi, tremebundaque Tartara carmen
Ima ciere valet, divosque ligare profundos,
Et triplici duros Manes adamante coercet.
Carmine sepositi retegunt arcana futuri
Phoebades, et tremulae pallentes ora Sibyllae;   25
Carmina sacrificus sollennes pangit ad aras,
Aurea seu sternit motantem cornua taurum,
Seu cum fata sagax fumantibus abdita fibris
Consulit et tepidis Parcam scrutatur in extis.
Nos etiam, patrium tunc cum repetemus Olympum,   30
Aeternaeque morae stabunt immobilis aevi,
Ibimus auratis per caeli templa coronis,
Dulcia suaviloquo sociantes carmina plectro,
Astra quibus geminique poli convexa sonabunt.
Spiritus et rapidos qui circinat igneus orbes   35
Nunc quoque sidereis intercinit ipse choreis
Immortale melos et inenarrabile carmen,
Torrida dum rutilus compescit sibila Serpens,
Demissoque ferox gladio mansuescit Orion,
Stellarum nec sentit onus Maurusius Atlas.   40
Carmina regales epulas ornare solebant,
Cum nondum luxus, vastaeque immensa vorago
Nota gulae, et modico spumabat coena Lyaeo.
Tum de more sedens festa ad convivia vates,
Aesculea intonsos redimitus ab arbore crines,   45
Heroumque actus imitandaque gesta canebat,
Et chaos, et positi late fundamina mundi,
Reptantesque deos, et alentes numina glandes,
Et nondum Aetnaeo quaesitum fulmen ab antro.
Denique quid vocis modulamen inane iuvabit,   50
Verborum sensusque vacans, numerique loquacis?
Silvestres decet iste choros, non Orphea, cantus,
Qui tenuit fluvios et quercubus addidit aures,
Carmine, non cithara, simulacraque functa canendo
Compulit in lacrimas: habet has a carmine laudes.   55
    Nec tu perge, precor, sacras contemnere Musas,
Nec vanas inopesque puta, quarum ipse peritus
Munere mille sonos numeros componis ad aptos,
Millibus et vocem modulis variare canoram
Doctus, Arionii merito sis nominis haeres.   60
Nunc tibi quid mirum si me genuisse poetam
Contigerit, caro si tam prope sanguine iuncti
Cognatas artes studiumque affine sequamur?
Ipse volens Phoebus se dispertire duobus,
Altera dona mihi, dedit altera dona parenti;   65
Dividuumque deum genitorque puerque tenemus.
    Tu tamen ut simules teneras odisse Camenas,

Non odisse reor, neque enim, pater, ire iubebas
Qua via lata patet, qua pronior area lucri,
Certaque condendi fulget spes aurea nummi;   70
Nec rapis ad leges, male custoditaque gentis
Iura, nec insulsis damnas clamoribus aures.
Sed magis excultam cupiens ditescere mentem,
Me procul urbano strepitu, secessibus altis
Abductum, Aoniae iucunda per otia ripae,   75
Phoebaeo lateri comitem sinis ire beatum.
Officium cari taceo commune parentis;
Me poscunt maiora. Tuo, pater optime, sumptu
Cum mihi Romuleae patuit facundia linguae
Et Latii veneres, et quae Iovis ora decebant   80
Grandia magniloquis elata vocabula Graiis,
Addere suasisti quos iactat Gallia flores,
Et quam degeneri novus Italus ore loquelam
Fundit, barbaricos testatus voce tumultus,
Quaeque Palaestinus loquitur mysteria vates.   85
Denique quicquid habet coelum, subiectaque coelo
Terra parens, terraeque et coelo interfluus aer,
Quicquid et unda tegit pontique agitabile marmor,
Per te nosse licet, per te, si nosse libebit;
Dimotaque venit spectanda scientia nube,   90
Nudaque conspicuos inclinat ad oscula vultus,
Ni fugisse velim, ni sit libasse molestum.
    I nunc, confer opes, quisquis malesanus avitas
Austriaci gazas Peruanaque regna praeoptas.
Quae potuit maiora pater tribuisse, vel ipse   95
Iupiter, excepto, donasset ut omnia, coelo?
Non potiora dedit, quamvis et tuta fuissent,
Publica qui iuveni commisit lumina nato
Atque Hyperionios currus, et frena diei,
Et circum undantem radiata luce tiaram.   100
Ergo ego, iam doctae pars quamlibet ima catervae,
Victrices hederas inter laurosque sedebo;
Iamque nec obscurus populo miscebor inerti,
Vitabuntque oculos vestigia nostra profanos.
Este procul vigiles Curae, procul este Querelae,   105
Invidiaeque acies transverso tortilis hirquo;
Saeva nec anguiferos extende, Calumnia, rictus;
In me triste nihil, foedissima turba, potestis,
Nec vestri sum iuris ego; securaque tutus
Pectora vipereo gradiar sublimis ab ictu.   110
    At tibi, care pater, postquam non aequa merenti
Posse referre datur, nec dona rependere factis,
Sit memorasse satis, repetitaque munera grato
Percensere animo, fidaeque reponere menti.
    Et vos, O nostri, iuvenilia carmina, lusus,   115
Si modo perpetuos sperare audebitis annos,
Et domini superesse rogo, lucemque tueri,

Nec spisso rapient oblivia nigra sub Orco,
Forsitan has laudes, decantatumque parentis
Nomen, ad exemplum, sero servabitis aevo.   120
(1631–32?)

TO HIS FATHER

MILTON left this poem undated and little help is given by the supposedly chronological order of the poems as printed, since this one comes between the *Idea Platonica* (1628–29?) and the Greek Psalm of November–December, 1634. Orthodox modern opinion favors *c.* 1637 — some scholars prefer *c.* 1634 — on the ground that the publication or the composition of *Comus* would have sealed Milton's commitment to poetry. This may be thought a very tenuous argument. The problem of a profession would have come up between father and son before the son left Cambridge, certainly by his last year, 1631–32. Moreover, the tone of the poem as a whole and lines 73–76 in particular suggest that he is writing at Cambridge; and his themes are akin to those of *Il Penseroso* (1631–32?) and the seventh Prolusion (1631–32?). Although Milton had been brought up with the expectation of becoming a clergyman, he does not here refer to that possibility, which must have become dim before he left the university. On the other hand, while he expresses full confidence in his poetic vocation, he hardly approaches the high religious vein of the sonnet "How soon hath Time" (written presumably on his twenty-fourth birthday, December 9, 1632) and the subsequent religious writings up through *Comus*. Milton addresses his father with much affection and gratitude and no little tact: if he is committed to poetry, it is because he has been given a fitting education by a father who is himself a composer, a fellow votary of the Muses.

Now I wish that the Pierian waters would wind their refreshing way through my breast, and that the whole stream flowing from the twin peaks[3] would pour over my lips, so that my Muse, forgetting trivial strains, might rise on bold wings to pay tribute to my revered father. The poem she is meditating is a small effort, and perhaps not very pleasing to you, my dear father; yet I do not know what I can more fitly offer in return for your gifts to me, though my greatest gifts could never match yours, much less can yours be equalled by the barren gratitude expressed in mere words. This page, however, shows the extent of my property, and all my wealth I have counted up on this paper, for I own nothing except what I have received from golden Clio,[14] from dreams in a secluded cave, from the laurel copses of the sacred wood, the shady places of Parnassus.

Do not scorn the poet's work, divine song, which more than anything else proclaims the celestial source of the human mind, its heavenly seed, and still keeps holy sparks of the Promethean fire. The high gods love song, and song has the power to stir the trembling depths of Tartarus and to bind the gods below, and it chains the unfeeling shades with triple adamant. In song Apollo's priestesses[25] and tremulous, pale-faced Sibyls[25] reveal the secrets of the far-off future. The sacrificial priest utters songs at the hallowed altars, whether he is slaying the bull that tosses its gilded horns or when his prophetic eye discerns things to come hidden in the smoking flesh and seeks destiny in the warm entrails. We too, at that day

3. twin peaks: of Parnassus.
14. Clio (see glossary) is golden partly because she is here a substitute for gold coin.
25. priestesses: especially at the Delphic oracle of Apollo.   Sibyls: especially the one who guided Aeneas to Hades (*Aen.* 6.10 f.).

when we return to our native Olympus and the fixed ages of changeless eternity
have begun, we too shall move with golden crowns[32] through the spaces of heaven,
blending sweet songs with the soft notes of the lyre, so that the sound shall ring
through the starry vault from pole to pole. Even now the fiery Spirit[35] who circles
the swift spheres is himself singing, in harmony with their celestial music, his immortal melody, an unutterable song; while the glowing Serpent[38] checks his hot
hissing, fierce Orion, grown gentle, lowers his sword, and Maurusian[40] Atlas feels
no longer the weight of the stars.

Songs were wont to adorn royal feasts, when as yet luxury was not known, nor
the bottomless pit of the monstrous gullet, when modest wines foamed on the table.
Then, as the custom was, the bard sat at the festal board, his unshorn hair bound
with oak leaves, and sang of the inspiring deeds and achievements of heroes, of
chaos and the broad foundations[46] of the world, of creeping gods[48] and divinities
nourished by acorns, of the thunderbolt not yet sought from the bowels of Etna.[49]
In brief, of what use is the idle modulation of the voice if it lacks words and sense
and rhythmical speech? That kind of music suits woodland singers, not Orpheus,
who by his song, not his lyre, held back rivers, gave ears to the oak trees, and by his
singing drew tears from the shades of the dead. Such fame he owes to song.

Do not, then, I pray, persist in contempt for the sacred Muses, nor think them
vain and worthless, since by their gift you yourself marry a thousand notes to fitting measures, and have the skill to take the singer's voice through countless variations, so that you deserve to be called the heir of Arion. Now, if you have happened
to beget a poet, why is it strange that we, who are so closely joined in blood, should
cultivate sister arts and related studies? Apollo himself, wishing to divide himself
between us two, bestowed some gifts on me, others on my father, and we, father and
son, together possess the divided god.

Yet though you pretend to hate the delicate Muses, I do not believe you really
hate them. For, father, you did not enjoin me to go where the broad way lies open,
where money slides more easily into the hand, and the golden hope of piling up
wealth shines bright and sure; nor do you drive me into the law and the ill-guarded
statutes of our country and thus condemn my ears to noisy stupidity. But, desiring
rather that my mind should be cultivated and enriched, you have removed me from
the city's din to the deep retreats of happy leisure by the Aonian stream, and you
allow me to walk, a blessed companion, by the side of Apollo.[76]

I say nothing of a dear father's ordinary care, for I must speak of greater things.
At your expense, generous father, when I had gained command of the tongue of
Romulus and the graces of Latin, and the lofty language of the eloquent Greeks, fit
for the lips of Jove himself, you persuaded me to add the flowers that France boasts,
and the speech the modern Italian pours from his decadent mouth, showing by his
utterance the effects of the barbarian invasions,[83] and the mysteries delivered by the
Palestinian prophet.[85] Lastly, whatever is contained in the sky, and in mother earth
below the sky, and in the air that flows between earth and sky, all that is covered by

32. crowns: Rev. 4.4, 14.2.
35. Lately interpreted, in Neoplatonic terms,
as Milton's own disembodied spirit.
38. Serpent: the constellation.
40. Maurusian: Mauretanian, Moroccan.
46. foundations: cf. *Aen.* 1.740–46, *Nativity* 123.
48. creeping gods: cf. *Nativity* 211, *P.L.*
1.481–82, 489.
49. Jove's thunderbolts were forged by Vulcan under Etna.
76. Lines 73–76 are commonly taken as a

reference to Horton, but they seem rather to
refer to Cambridge: removal from the city's
din to lettered peace fits removal from London
to Cambridge but not removal from Cambridge
to Horton (or Hammersmith).
83. Milton is not condemning the modern
Italian's enunciation but speaking of the Italian
language as a corruption of Latin — which
is historically correct though not in Milton's
normal vein of feeling about Italian.
85. prophet. That is, the Hebrew of the
Old Testament as a whole. Milton is more

water and the restless waves of the sea — all this, through you, I have been enabled to know, and through you I shall be, if I have the desire. From behind a cloud science[90] comes forth to be viewed and, naked, bends her bright face to my kisses, unless I should find her irksome and wish to escape.

Go now, heap up riches, whoever is mad enough to prefer the ancient treasures of Austria and the Peruvian realms. What greater wealth could a father have given, or Jove himself, though he had given all things except heaven? Not more potent gifts (even if they had been safe) did he bestow who granted his young son[98] the common light of the world, Hyperion's[99] chariot, and the reins of day, and the tiara radiating luminous waves. Therefore I am now one among the learned band,[101] however low my place, and shall sit with a victor's ivy and laurel. Then I shall not mingle, unknown, with the dull crowd, and my footsteps shall shun the sight of profane eyes. Be off, wakeful cares, be off, complaints, and the goatish squint of envy's crooked eye. Spiteful Calumny, do not open your snake-filled jaws, you can do me no harm, loathsome swarm; I am not under your power. With a breast safe and secure I shall walk above the reach of your viper stroke.

But for you, dear father, since I cannot make a return equal to your deserts, or repay gifts with deeds, may it be enough that I have recorded them, that I gratefully count over your repeated benefits and cherish them in a faithful heart.

And you, my youthful poems and diversions,[115] if only you dare hope to enjoy lasting life and survive your master's pyre and see the light, and dark oblivion does not carry you down to crowded Orcus, perhaps these praises, and the name of the father they celebrate, you will preserve as an example to a distant age.

---

explicit here about the private tutoring his father provided than he is in the personal passages in the *Reason of Church Government* (1642) and the *Second Defence of the English People* (1654). In these lines, and those that follow, he seems to say that, in addition to school work in Latin and Greek, he was privately instructed in French, Italian, Hebrew (this he would have in his last year at school), natural science, and perhaps geography. Cf. Elegy 4.

90. science. Perhaps *scientia* should be rendered by the broad word "knowledge," but the rest of the sentence seems to support the narrower meaning; Milton used the same image of "philosophy" in his sixth Prolusion (1628).

98. son: Phaethon, son of Apollo.

99. Hyperion: father of the sun-god, usually the sun itself.

101–10. These lines imply no special vanity in Milton; they express the Renaissance humanist-poet's creed, derived from Horace, Ovid, and others.

115. Apropos of the date, discussed in the headnote, if Milton had already written *Comus* he would surely not use such words of so serious and ambitious a work.

Arcades

THE COUNTESS DOWAGER of Derby was the widow of Queen Elizabeth's Lord Keeper, Sir Thomas Egerton, later Lord Ellesmere (who had had John Donne as his secretary), but she was known by the title that came from her first husband; to go back further, she was one of the three daughters of Sir John Spencer who had received dedications from their kinsman, Edmund Spenser. Her home, Harefield, was some ten miles from Horton (the Miltons may not have been living there yet). It is almost certain that the performance was managed by the court musician, Henry Lawes, who later produced *Comus;* he was musical tutor in the family of the Countess' stepson, the Earl of Bridgewater, and was probably, through his music, an old acquaintance of the elder Milton, a composer, and his poet-son. *Arcades* is the first work transcribed in the manuscript (preserved at Trinity College, Cambridge) in which Milton began to copy his poems; but that fact does not help much to narrow down the conjectural date, 1630–34. The

Arcades: dwellers in Arcadia (glossary).

Countess became 70 about 1630 and that or another birthday might have furnished the occasion. It seems unlikely that, after the solemn self-dedication of Sonnet 7 (probably December 9, 1632), Milton would soon have written a mainly secular piece (even though it includes a passage of exalted and quasi-religious Platonism). A closer guess might be the spring or summer of 1632. When asked to supply such a script, Milton would no doubt have reviewed Ben Jonson, and *Arcades* seems to show marks of imitation, both in the lyrics and in the figure and speech of the Genius. It is a courtly and graceful miniature, pastoral and mythological.

Part of an entertainment presented to the Countess Dowager of Derby at Harefield by some noble persons of her family, who appear on the scene in pastoral habit, moving toward the seat of state, with this song.

I. SONG

Look, nymphs, and shepherds, look,
What sudden blaze of majesty
Is that which we from hence descry,
Too divine to be mistook:
    This, this is she 5
To whom our vows and wishes bend;
Here our solemn search hath end.

Fame, that her high worth to raise
Seemed erst so lavish and profuse,
We may justly now accuse 10
Of detraction from her praise:
    Less than half we find expressed;
    Envy bid conceal the rest.

Mark what radiant state she spreads
In circle round her shining throne, 15
Shooting her beams like silver threads.
This, this is she alone,
    Sitting like a goddess bright
    In the center of her light.

Might she the wise Latona be, 20
Or the towered Cybele,
Mother of a hundred gods?
Juno dares not give her odds;
    Who had thought this clime had held
    A deity so unparalleled? 25

As they come forward, the Genius of the Wood appears,
and turning toward them, speaks.

Gen. Stay, gentle swains, for though in this disguise,
I see bright honor sparkle through your eyes;

---

12. Cf. 1 Kings 10.7.
20–23. Latona, Cybele, Juno: glossary.

26. Genius: glossary and *Il Penseroso* 154.
27. honor: noble descent (cf. "gentle," 26).

Of famous Arcady ye are, and sprung
Of that renownèd flood, so often sung,
Divine Alphéus, who by secret sluice   30
Stole under seas to meet his Arethuse;
And ye, the breathing roses of the wood,
Fair silver-buskined nymphs as great and good,
I know this quest of yours and free intent
Was all in honor and devotion meant   35
To the great mistress of yon princely shrine,
Whom with low reverence I adore as mine,
And with all helpful service will comply
To further this night's glad solemnity,
And lead ye where ye may more near behold   40
What shallow-searching Fame hath left untold,
Which I full oft, amidst these shades alone,
Have sat to wonder at and gaze upon.
For know by lot from Jove I am the pow'r
Of this fair wood, and live in oaken bow'r,   45
To nurse the saplings tall, and curl the grove
With ringlets quaint and wanton windings wove.
And all my plants I save from nightly ill
Of noisome winds and blasting vapors chill;
And from the boughs brush off the evil dew,   50
And heal the harms of thwarting thunder blue,
Or what the cross dire-looking planet smites,
Or hurtful worm with cankered venom bites.
When ev'ning gray doth rise, I fetch my round
Over the mount and all this hallowed ground,   55
And early ere the odorous breath of morn
Awakes the slumb'ring leaves, or tasseled horn
Shakes the high thicket, haste I all about,
Number my ranks, and visit every sprout
With puissant words and murmurs made to bless.   60
But else in deep of night, when drowsiness
Hath locked up mortal sense, then listen I
To the celestial Sirens' harmony,
That sit upon the nine enfolded spheres
And sing to those that hold the vital shears   65
And turn the adamantine spindle round,
On which the fate of gods and men is wound.
Such sweet compulsion doth in music lie,
To lull the daughters of Necessity,
And keep unsteady Nature to her law,   70
And the low world in measured motion draw
After the heavenly tune, which none can hear
Of human mold with gross unpurgèd ear;

46. curl: adorn (cf. Jonson, *To Sir Robert Wroth* 17, "the curled woods").

52. cross . . . planet: malign Saturn (cf. *Epitaphium Damonis* 80).

63 f. Not the Homeric Sirens but those described in Plato's myth of Er (*Rep.* 616–17), the angelic intelligences who attend the celestial spheres; these turn on a spindle which rests on the knees of Necessity, mother of the three Fates.

72–73. Cf. *Nativity* 125 f. and note.

And yet such music worthiest were to blaze
The peerless height of her immortal praise   **75**
Whose luster leads us, and for her most fit,
If my inferior hand or voice could hit
Inimitable sounds; yet as we go,
Whate'er the skill of lesser gods can show,
I will assay, her worth to celebrate,   **80**
And so attend ye toward her glittering state;
Where ye may all that are of noble stem
Approach, and kiss her sacred vesture's hem.

II. SONG

O'er the smooth enameled green
Where no print of step hath been,   **85**
 Follow me as I sing,
 And touch the warbled string.
Under the shady roof
Of branching elm star-proof,
  Follow me;   **90**
I will bring you where she sits,
Clad in splendor as befits
  Her deity.
Such a rural Queen
All Arcadia hath not seen.   **95**

III. SONG

Nymphs and shepherds, dance no more
 By sandy Ladon's lilied banks;
On old Lycaeus or Cyllene hoar,
 Trip no more in twilight ranks;
Though Erymanth your loss deplore,   **100**
 A better soil shall give ye thanks.
From the stony Maenalus
Bring your flocks and live with us;
Here ye shall have greater grace,
To serve the Lady of this place.   **105**
 Though Syrinx your Pan's mistress were,
 Yet Syrinx well might wait on her.
  Such a rural Queen
All Arcadia hath not seen.

(1632?)

82. stem: family.
89. Cf. Spenser, *F.Q.* 1.1.7.6.
97. Ladon: a river in Arcadia.

98–102. Names of Arcadian mountains associated mainly with Pan.

Sonnet VII

THIS SONNET seems to have been written on Milton's twenty-fourth birthday (December 9, 1632), not on his twenty-third. (Titles containing the words "age of twenty-three" and the like are late editorial additions and have no authority.) The date is important in regard to Milton's state of mind. He had become a literary and intellectual figure in the Cambridge world, but now he has been for six months an obscure student under his father's roof, beginning the years of hard reading by which he hoped to prepare himself for the unknown future; meanwhile his contemporaries are forging ahead. This religious self-dedication is a landmark in Milton's early development; the poems that followed it appear (though some dates are uncertain) to have been all more or less religious. In a letter written early in 1633 to a friend (perhaps his old tutor, Thomas Young), who had warned him against indulgence in study and urged an active life,

presumably in the ministry, Milton replied with an account of his earnest reflections. Having in mind the parables of the talents and the vineyard, he still thinks he should not be anxious about "being late, so it give advantage to be more fit." But he included a copy of the sonnet as proof "that I am something suspicious of myself, and do take notice of a certain belatedness in me."

Compared with most of the later sonnets, this one is strictly regular in its formal divisions; and the sestet, though deeply charged with feeling, is plain, unfigurative statement.

How soon hath Time, the subtle thief of youth,
    Stol'n on his wing my three and twentieth year!
    My hasting days fly on with full career,
    But my late spring no bud or blossom shew'th.
Perhaps my semblance might deceive the truth,   5
    That I to manhood am arrived so near,
    And inward ripeness doth much less appear,
    That some more timely-happy spirits endu'th.
Yet be it less or more, or soon or slow,
    It shall be still in strictest measure ev'n   10
    To that same lot, however mean or high,
Toward which Time leads me, and the will of Heav'n;
    All is, if I have grace to use it so,
    As ever in my great Task-Master's eye.

(December 9, 1632?)

2. Milton apparently means "my first 23 years."

8. Among contemporaries who might have been in Milton's mind was his friend and junior, Diodati (see the headnotes to Elegy 1 and the *Epitaphium Damonis*).

9–14. Milton may be giving a Christian turn to lines 41–43 of Pindar's fourth Nemean ode: "But whatever excellence Lord Destiny gave me, well I know that creeping time will bring its appointed fulfilment."

13. All is, if: i.e. all depends on whether.

On Time

THIS and the next two poems form a group which apparently followed close upon Sonnet 7. Milton's gambit in the first one is explained by the subtitle in the Cambridge Manuscript, "To be set on a clock case." In most Renaissance poets the idea of time inspired neopagan and amatory variations, gay or sober, on the Horatian text *carpe diem*, though some could sound a religious

note. Milton is wholly religious in his contrast between earthly flux and sin and the eternal purity and joy of the soul's life in heaven. The form, a paragraph with lines of irregular length and irregular rhymes, is that of an Italian madrigal; the slow movement, the manipulation of phrase and rhythm, gives full weight to every word.

Fly, envious Time, till thou run out thy race,
    Call on the lazy leaden-stepping hours,
Whose speed is but the heavy plummet's pace;
    And glut thyself with what thy womb devours,

3. plummet: the weight that moves the works of the clock.

Which is no more than what is false and vain,   5
And merely mortal dross;
So little is our loss,
So little is thy gain.
For when as each thing bad thou hast entombed,
And last of all thy greedy self consumed,   10
Then long Eternity shall greet our bliss
With an individual kiss;
And Joy shall overtake us as a flood,
When every thing that is sincerely good
And perfectly divine,   15
With Truth, and Peace, and Love shall ever shine
About the supreme throne
Of him t' whose happy-making sight alone
When once our heav'nly-guided soul shall climb,
Then all this earthy grossness quit,   20
Attired with stars, we shall for ever sit,
    Triumphing over Death, and Chance, and thee, O Time.
                                            (1632?)

12. A kiss given to every individual soul;   21. Attired with stars: like figures of
or perhaps "undividable," "eternal."   pagan myth changed into constellations; also,
  14. sincerely: purely, wholly.   in old tradition the stars were of ethereal, in-
  18. happy-making   sight: "the beatific destructible substance.
vision" (cf. *P.L.* 1.684, 3.61–62).

Upon the Circumcision

SINCE the circumcision of the infant Jesus   flags after the opening lines. The stanza
is commemorated on January 1, Milton pre-   form is close to that of Petrarch's canzone
sumably wrote this poem on or about that   to the Blessed Virgin (*Vergine bella, che di
day, 1633. His choice of a theme may have   Sol vestita*) and that of Tasso's *Alla Beatis-
been prompted more by the church calendar   sima Vergine in Loreto.*
than by authentic inspiration, since the poem

Ye flaming Powers, and wingèd Warriors bright,
That erst with music and triumphant song
First heard by happy watchful shepherds' ear,
So sweetly sung your joy the clouds along
Through the soft silence of the list'ning night;   5
Now mourn, and if sad share with us to bear
Your fiery essence can distill no tear,
Burn in your sighs, and borrow
Seas wept from our deep sorrow;
He who with all heav'n's heraldry whilere   10
Entered the world, now bleeds to give us ease;
Alas, how soon our sin
    Sore doth begin
        His infancy to seize!

1. Powers: glossary, "angels."   10. whilere: lately.

O more exceeding love, or law more just? 15
Just law indeed, but more exceeding love!
For we by rightful doom remédiless
Were lost in death, till he that dwelt above
High-throned in secret bliss, for us frail dust
Emptied his glory, ev'n to nakedness; 20
And that great cov'nant which we still transgress
Entirely satisfied,
And the full wrath beside
Of vengeful justice bore for our excess,
And seals obedience first with wounding smart 25
This day, but O ere long,
Huge pangs and strong
Will pierce more near his heart.

(1633?)

17–20. Cf. *Nativity* 1–14 and notes.   21. cov'nant: Gen. 17.7–10 and glossary.

At A Solemn Music

THIS POEM was probably written early in 1633. The Cambridge Manuscript has two drafts and a fair copy. Milton takes up again the double theme of *On Time*, but in reverse order: here he moves from the harmony of heaven down to the sinful discords of earth, though the last lines return to the celestial vision. Obviously the whole poem works out a musical metaphor. As in *On Time*, the irregular lines and slow movement elicit full and fresh value from even the most ordinary words. The first 24 lines constitute a single sentence.

Blest pair of Sirens, pledges of heav'n's joy,
Sphere-born harmonious sisters, Voice and Verse,
Wed your divine sounds, and mixed power employ
Dead things with inbreathed sense able to pierce,
And to our high-raised phantasy present 5
That undisturbèd song of pure concent,
Aye sung before the sapphire-colored throne
To him that sits thereon,
With saintly shout and solemn jubilee,
Where the bright Seraphim in burning row 10
Their loud uplifted angel-trumpets blow,
And the Cherubic host in thousand quires
Touch their immortal harps of golden wires,
With those just spirits that wear victorious palms,
Hymns devout and holy psalms 15
Singing everlastingly;

The title means "At a Concert of Sacred Music."
1–2. Voice and Verse are the earthly counterparts of the Platonic Sirens of *Arcades* 63 f.
5. phantasy: imagination.
6. concent: harmony.
7–16. Ezek. 1.26, Rev. 7.9–15.
14. just spirits: the redeemed (cf. *Comus* 9–11).

That we on earth with undiscording voice
May rightly answer that melodious noise;
As once we did, till disproportioned sin
Jarred against Nature's chime, and with harsh din   20
Broke the fair music that all creatures made
To their great Lord, whose love their motion swayed
In perfect diapason, whilst they stood
In first obedience and their state of good.
O may we soon again renew that song,   25
And keep in tune with heav'n, till God ere long
To his celestial consort us unite,
To live with him, and sing in endless morn of light.

(1633?)

18. noise: cf. Ps. 100.1, "Make a joyful   23. diapason: concord.
noise unto the Lord."

COMUS

THE QUALITY of *Arcades* led Henry Lawes to turn again to Milton with a larger commission, the writing of a masque for the inauguration of the Earl of Bridgewater as Lord President of Wales. To the young poet, who was pursuing his private studies at home and had not written anything for some time, the invitation provided no doubt an agreeable interlude. His "Mask" — the handy but illogical title *Comus* was first adopted in the eighteenth century for stage performances — was presented at Ludlow Castle in Shropshire on September 29, 1634. Lawes, the producer and composer of music for the songs, took the role of the Attendant Spirit. The parts of the Elder and Second Brother and the Lady were acted by the Earl's children, Viscount Brackley and Thomas and Lady Alice Egerton, who, though only eleven, nine, and fifteen respectively, had already appeared in masques at court.

From the accession of King James in 1603 up to 1640, two years before the outbreak of the civil war, masques were a favorite form of entertainment at court and sometimes at noble houses. The masque gained artistic status especially through the partnership of Ben Jonson and the great stage designer and architect, Inigo Jones, and the genre attracted many other poets and dramatists from Samuel Daniel and Thomas Campion to Thomas Carew and James Shirley. As a rule the masque did not attempt to be dramatic; the libretto, allegorical or mythological or both, might touch a serious theme, but it was mainly an excuse for an abundance of spectacle, music, and dancing. Court productions were lavish and expensive.

Arcades, though a miniature, was closer to the standard type than *Comus,* which developed a moral and religious theme through a semi-dramatic story and elaborate and weighty speeches. The acting version, however, was somewhat shorter than the one we read: it did not contain the Lady's most impassioned reply to Comus and some other passages (lines 195–225, 737–55, 779–806, 997, 1000–1011), which appeared in the text published by Lawes in 1637 and in that of Milton's *Poems* (1645). Also, the Attendant Spirit's epilogue was, in shorter form, a prologue. Up to a point Milton followed the conventions: he furnished a modicum of spectacle, singing, and dancing, and, in Comus and his beast-headed crew, he exploited the "antimasque," the grotesque feature often contrasted with the ordered beauty of the whole. But in its treatment of a serious subject, and in the texture of the poetry, *Comus* was far above the normal masque — and very far above the spurious "Platonics" in vogue at the Caroline court. The masque was soon in demand for reading and

Lawes had so many requests for copies that in 1637 he printed it, evidently with Milton's consent, though he withheld his name.

Many "sources" have been suggested as contributing to Milton's plot or theme or pastoral atmosphere: George Peele's *Old Wives' Tale,* John Fletcher's *Faithful Shepherdess,* the Latin fable *Comus* (1608) by the Dutch Erycius Puteanus; *The Tempest;* William Browne's *Inner Temple Masque* (1615), on the myth of Circe, and Jonson's *Pleasure Reconciled to Virtue* (1618), in which Comus appeared as a crude belly-god (neither of these masques was in print in 1634); another masque of Jonson's, *Hymenaei* (printed in 1606 and 1616); and Tasso's famous pastoral play, *Aminta,* and an Italian musical drama, *La Catena d'Adone* (1626). But, whether or not Milton knew some or all of these works, they would be far less important than Homer and Ovid and Spenser. Homer's tale of Odysseus and Circe was for the Renaissance the great *exemplum* of heroic virtue confronted by sensual temptation, and it was elaborately reworked by such major poets as Ariosto, Tasso, and Spenser. (Milton, in his first rendering of the conflict between good and evil, gave the story a fresh turn by making Comus the son of Circe and the inheritor of her magical powers.) Spenser had used the idea in book two of *The Faerie Queene,* the book of temperance, and in his third book he had the parallel episode of the virtuous Amoret held captive by the sensual Busyrane. Spenser was Milton's great predecessor in the poetic and figurative treatment of moral and religious ideas, and in *Areopagitica* Milton was to refer to the Cave of Mammon and the Bower of Bliss devised by "our sage and serious poet Spenser, whom I dare be known to think a better teacher than Scotus or Aquinas."

The allegorical interpretation of the Homeric tale was a universal commonplace — Milton alluded to it at the end of his first Latin elegy — and it was fully set forth in the commentary that George Sandys in 1632 added to his translation of Ovid's *Metamorphoses* (p. 479). Whether or not Milton had looked into the book — and such a lover of Ovid may well have done so — some of Sandys' phrases are suggestive. Ulysses, "being fortified by an immortal power, was not subject to mutation. For the divine and celestial soul, subsisting through the bounty of the Creator, can by no assault of nature be violated, nor can that be converted into a beast which so highly participates of reason. . . ." Circe's allurements cannot be resisted "but by the divine assistance, Moly, the gift of Mercury, which signifies temperance. . . ." Men whose appetites "revolt from the sovereignty of reason (by which we are only like unto God, and armed against depraved affections)" can never "return into their country (from whence the soul deriveth her celestial original) unless disenchanted and cleansed from their former impurity."

The Platonic coloring of Sandys' comments brings us to what is by far the best of all introductions to *Comus* and to much of Milton's earlier poetry, his own account, in *An Apology for Smectymnuus* (1642), of the growth of his youthful ideal of chastity and the reading that fostered it. That all-important passage is quoted in full near the beginning of this volume, and it needs to be read and reread.

Thus *Comus* is not a mere negative exposition of chastity as abstinence from vice but a positive and all-embracing celebration of the Platonic and Christian love of the good. Like all Christian humanists, Milton sees the highest pagan ethics, with the special inspiration of Platonic love, as a strong ally of Christian ethics, and he recognizes both the difference between them and their necessary fusion. The Second Brother is immature and anxious. The confident Elder Brother, somewhat in the manner of a contemporary student delivering academic speeches, appeals less to religious faith than to classical reason. The Lady represents a mature blending of the two. Sabrina, who is invoked to free the Lady, may stand for the divine grace that must reinforce rational temperance. The Attendant Spirit is a Neoplatonic daemon who has the virtually Christian function of a guardian angel. The first paragraph of his opening speech renews the theme of *On Time* and *At a Solemn Music,* the contrast between heaven (here a Platonic-Christian heaven) and sin-worn earth; and his epilogue is a religious benediction upon the victory won, a religious injunction to love the true freedom of goodness.

Comus, it may be added, is a gentleman of cultivated sensibility; his inward corruption is shown — as Satan's is to be, on a grand scale — by the ironic method of self-revelation. His central speech to the Lady on Nature's bounties (706 f.) is a unique piece of writing; its vivid, sprawling immediacy of tactual and visual images has the effect of betraying the speaker's moral disorder.

Most of *Comus* is written in blank verse — Milton's first venture in that medium — and it varies in movement from the smooth and semi-lyrical to the irregular and colloquial. In point of style, the masque may almost be called a mosaic of different styles, which range from Elizabethan pastoralism to Augustan classicism, though every line bears the stamp of its author. One must quote the famous eulogy included in the letter of advice on travel which Sir Henry Wotton sent to Milton in April, 1638, and which was prefixed to *Comus* in the *Poems* of 1645: "Wherein I should much commend the tragical part, if the lyrical did not ravish me with a certain Doric delicacy in your songs and odes, whereunto I must plainly confess to have seen yet nothing parallel in our language: *Ipsa mollities.*" Whatever the experimental variety of texture, the masque as a whole is unified by the young poet's passionate purity of vision, which casts its spell with the opening,

> Before the starry threshold of Jove's court
> My mansion is,

and culminates in the incantation,

> Or if virtue feeble were,
> Heav'n itself would stoop to her.

A MASKE

PRESENTED

At Ludlow Castle,

1 6 3 4 :

On *Michaelmaſſe night*, *before the*
RIGHT HONORABLE,

IOHN *Earle of Bridgewater* , *Vicount* BRACKLY,
Lord Præſident of WALES , And one of
His MAIESTIES moſt honorable
Privie Counſell.

Eheu quid volui miſero mihi ! ſloribus auſtrum
Perditus ————

LONDON

Printed for HYMPHREY ROBINSON,
at the ſigne of the *Three Pidgeons* in
Pauls Church-yard. 1 6 3 7.

A

M A S K

Of the same

A U T H O R

Presented
At LUDLOW-Castle,
1634.

Before
The Earl of Bridgewater
Then President of Wales.

Anno Dom. 1645

To the Right Honorable John, Lord Viscount Brackley,
son and heir-apparent to the Earl of Bridgewater, &c.

My Lord,

This Poem, which received its first occasion of birth from yourself and others of your noble family, and much honor from your own person in the performance, now returns again to make a final dedication of itself to you. Although not openly acknowledged by the author, yet it is a legitimate off-spring, so lovely, and so much desired, that the often copying of it hath tired my pen to give my several friends satisfaction, and brought me to a necessity of producing it to the public view; and now to offer it up, in all rightful devotion, to those fair hopes and rare endowments of your much-promising youth, which give a full assurance, to all that know you, of a future excellence. Live, sweet Lord, to be the honor of your name; and receive this as your own from the hands of him who hath by many favors been long obliged to your most honored parents, and, as in this representation your attendant Thyrsis, so now in all real expression

Your faithful and most humble Servant,
H. LAWES.

THE PERSONS.

The Attendant Spirit, afterwards in the habit of Thyrsis.
Comus with his crew.
The Lady.
1. Brother.
2. Brother.
Sabrina the Nymph.

The chief persons which presented were
The Lord Brackley
Mr. Thomas Egerton his Brother
The Lady Alice Egerton

The first scene discovers a wild wood.
The Attendant Spirit descends or enters.

Before the starry threshold of Jove's court
My mansion is, where those immortal shapes
Of bright aërial Spirits live insphered
In regions mild of calm and serene air,
Above the smoke and stir of this dim spot   5
Which men call Earth, and with low-thoughted care,
Confined and pestered in this pinfold here,
Strive to keep up a frail and feverish being,
Unmindful of the crown that Virtue gives,
After this mortal change, to her true servants   10
Amongst the enthroned gods on sainted seats.
Yet some there be that by due steps aspire
To lay their just hands on that golden key
That opes the palace of Eternity:
To such my errand is, and but for such   15
I would not soil these pure ambrosial weeds
With the rank vapors of this sin-worn mold.
      But to my task. Neptune, besides the sway
Of every salt flood and each ebbing stream,
Took in by lot 'twixt high and nether Jove   20
Imperial rule of all the sea-girt isles
That like to rich and various gems inlay

1–17. Cf. Plato, *Phaedo* 109–10. Here, as in *Comus* generally, classical and Christian images and ideas are blended.

2. mansion: John 14.2.

4. Cf. *Odyssey* 6.43–44. The Cambridge Manuscript contains, after line 4, a passage of 14 lines which Milton deleted. The main part of the passage was this:

Amidst th' Hesperian gardens, on whose banks
Bedewed with nectar and celestial songs
Eternal roses grow, and hyacinth
And fruits of golden rind, on whose fair tree
The scaly-harnessed dragon ever keeps
His unenchanted eye; and round the verge
And sacred limits of this blissful isle
The jealous ocean, that old river, winds
His far-extended arms, till with steep fall
Half his waste flood the wide Atlantic fills
And half the slow, unfadomed Stygian pool. . . .

5. smoke and stir. Cf. Horace, *Od.* 3.29.12, *fumum et opes strepitumque Romae.*

7. pinfold: pen for animals.

9. crown: 1 Cor. 9.25; Rev. 2.10.

10. mortal change: death.

11. Rev. 4.4.

12–14. Cf. *Aen.* 6.129–31.

13. key: cf. *Lycidas* 111.

17. mold: the earth? the flesh?

20. Jove (Jupiter, Zeus) ruled the heavens, Pluto ("nether Jove") the underworld, and Neptune (Poseidon) the sea.

The unadornèd bosom of the deep,
Which he, to grace his tributary gods,
By course commits to several government, 25
And gives them leave to wear their sapphire crowns
And wield their little tridents. But this isle,
The greatest and the best of all the main,
He quarters to his blue-haired deities;
And all this tract that fronts the falling sun 30
A noble peer of mickle trust and power
Has in his charge, with tempered awe to guide
An old and haughty nation proud in arms;
Where his fair offspring, nursed in princely lore,
Are coming to attend their father's state 35
And new-entrusted scepter; but their way
Lies through the perplexed paths of this drear wood,
The nodding horror of whose shady brows
Threats the forlorn and wand'ring passenger.
And here their tender age might suffer peril, 40
But that by quick command from soveran Jove
I was despatched for their defense and guard;
And listen why, for I will tell ye now
What never yet was heard in tale or song
From old or modern bard in hall or bow'r. 45
    Bacchus, that first from out the purple grape
Crushed the sweet poison of misusèd wine,
After the Tuscan mariners transformed,
Coasting the Tyrrhene shore, as the winds listed,
On Circe's island fell. (Who knows not Circe, 50
The daughter of the Sun? whose charmèd cup
Whoever tasted, lost his upright shape,
And downward fell into a groveling swine.)
This nymph that gazed upon his clust'ring locks,
With ivy berries wreathed, and his blithe youth, 55
Had by him, ere he parted thence, a son
Much like his father, but his mother more,
Whom therefore she brought up and Comus named;
Who, ripe and frolic of his full-grown age,
Roving the Celtic and Iberian fields, 60
At last betakes him to this ominous wood,
And, in thick shelter of black shades imbow'red,
Excels his mother at her mighty art,
Off'ring to every weary traveler
His orient liquor in a crystal glass, 65

30. tract: Wales and the Welsh-English border.

31. peer: the Earl of Bridgewater. mickle: great.

33. proud in arms: cf. *Aen.* 1.21.

37. Cf. *Aen.* 9.391–92.

37–39. A wood is a traditional symbol for life and its hazards; cf. Dante, *Inf.* 1; Spenser, *F.Q.* 1.1.7 f.

43. ye: 1673, you.

48. Bacchus, carried off by pirates, changed them into dolphins (Ovid, *Met.* 3.605–86). Milton's phrase is a Latinism for "after the transformation of."

58. The Greek name Comus means "revelry" or "band of revelers"; he had been personified by Renaissance writers (starting from the *Imagines* of the ancient Philostratus).

To quench the drouth of Phoebus, which as they taste
(For most do taste through fond intemperate thirst),
Soon as the potion works, their human count'nance,
Th' express resemblance of the gods, is changed
Into some brutish form of wolf, or bear,   70
Or ounce, or tiger, hog, or bearded goat,
All other parts remaining as they were;
And they, so perfect is their misery,
Not once perceive their foul disfigurement,
But boast themselves more comely than before   75
And all their friends, and native home forget
To roll with pleasure in a sensual sty.
Therefore when any favored of high Jove
Chances to pass through this advent'rous glade,
Swift as the sparkle of a glancing star   80
I shoot from heav'n to give him safe convoy,
As now I do. But first I must put off
These my sky-robes, spun out of Iris' woof,
And take the weeds and likeness of a swain
That to the service of this house belongs,   85
Who with his soft pipe and smooth-dittied song
Well knows to still the wild winds when they roar,
And hush the waving woods; nor of less faith,
And in this office of his mountain watch
Likeliest, and nearest to the present aid   90
Of this occasion. But I hear the tread
Of hateful steps; I must be viewless now.

*Comus enters with a charming-rod in one hand, his glass in the other;
with him a rout of monsters headed like sundry sorts of wild beasts, but
otherwise like men and women, their apparel glistering. They come in
making a riotous and unruly noise, with torches in their hands.*

Comus. The star that bids the shepherd fold
Now the top of heav'n doth hold,
And the gilded car of day   95
His glowing axle doth allay
In the steep Atlantic stream;
And the slope sun his upward beam
Shoots against the dusky pole,
Pacing toward the other goal   100
Of his chamber in the east.

66. drouth of Phoebus: thirst caused by
the sun's heat.
69. Gen. 1.27.
72–77. Circe's victims, while completely
transformed, remembered that they had been
human. Milton, in having the face only
changed, may have followed such a precedent
as Ariosto (*O.F.* 6.60–66) for convenience of
stage presentation.
75–76. The early editions have no comma
after "before" and have one (in 1637 a semi-
colon) after "friends." Modern editors sometimes reverse the punctuation to make more
obvious sense, though the original reading was
probably Milton's intention; the "friends"
are fellow victims of Comus.
80. glancing: shooting, gleaming.
93. star: Hesperus (Venus).   fold: put
sheep in the fold.
95–97. Cf. Elegy 5.81 f.
96. allay: temper, cool.
98. upward. The sun is now below the
horizon.
100–01. Ps. 19.4–5.

Meanwhile welcome joy and feast,
Midnight shout and revelry,
Tipsy dance and jollity.
Braid your locks with rosy twine   105
Dropping odors, dropping wine.
Rigor now is gone to bed,
And Advice with scrupulous head,
Strict Age, and sour Severity,
With their grave saws in slumber lie.   110
We that are of purer fire
Imitate the starry quire,
Who in their nightly watchful spheres
Lead in swift round the months and years.
The sounds and seas with all their finny drove   115
Now to the moon in wavering morris move,
And on the tawny sands and shelves
Trip the pert fairies and the dapper elves;
By dimpled brook and fountain brim
The wood-nymphs, decked with daisies trim,   120
Their merry wakes and pastimes keep:
What hath night to do with sleep?
Night hath better sweets to prove,
Venus now wakes, and wakens Love.
Come, let us our rites begin;   125
'Tis only daylight that makes sin,
Which these dun shades will ne'er report.
Hail, goddess of nocturnal sport,
Dark-veiled Cotytto, t' whom the secret flame
Of midnight torches burns; mysterious dame,   130
That ne'er art called but when the dragon womb
Of Stygian darkness spets her thickest gloom,
And makes one blot of all the air,
Stay thy cloudy ebon chair
Wherein thou rid'st with Hecat', and befriend   135
Us thy vowed priests, till utmost end
Of all thy dues be done, and none left out,
Ere the blabbing eastern scout,
The nice Morn on th' Indian steep,
From her cabined loop-hole peep,   140
And to the tell-tale Sun descry
Our concealed solemnity.
Come, knit hands, and beat the ground,
In a light fantastic round.

105. rosy twine: intertwined roses.
113. watchful spheres: see glossary, "sphere"; Plato, *Timaeus* 40; and *Vacation Exercise* 40 and note.
115. finny drove: in Spenser, *F.Q.* 3.8.29.9.
116. morris: morris dance.
118. pert: lively. dapper: small and nimble.

129. Cotytto: a Thracian divinity celebrated in licentious nocturnal rites.
132. spets: spits.
139. Morn: Aurora. Indian steep: cf. *A Midsummer Night's Dream* 2.1.69.
141. descry: reveal.

The Measure.

Break off, break off, I feel the different pace   145
Of some chaste footing near about this ground.
Run to your shrouds within these brakes and trees;
Our number may affright: some virgin sure
(For so I can distinguish by mine art)
Benighted in these woods. Now to my charms   150
And to my wily trains; I shall ere long
Be well stocked with as fair a herd as grazed
About my mother Circe. Thus I hurl
My dazzling spells into the spongy air,
Of power to cheat the eye with blear illusion,   155
And give it false presentments, lest the place
And my quaint habits breed astonishment,
And put the damsel to suspicious flight,
Which must not be, for that's against my course;
I, under fair pretense of friendly ends,   160
And well-placed words of glozing courtesy
Baited with reasons not unplausible,
Wind me into the easy-hearted man,
And hug him into snares. When once her eye
Hath met the virtue of this magic dust,   165
I shall appear some harmless villager
Whom thrift keeps up about his country gear.
But here she comes; I fairly step aside,
And hearken, if I may, her business here.

The Lady enters.

Lady. This way the noise was, if mine ear be true,   170
My best guide now. Methought it was the sound
Of riot and ill-managed merriment,
Such as the jocund flute or gamesome pipe
Stirs up among the loose unlettered hinds,
When for their teeming flocks and granges full   175
In wanton dance they praise the bounteous Pan,
And thank the gods amiss. I should be loth
To meet the rudeness and swilled insolence
Of such late wassailers; yet O where else
Shall I inform my unacquainted feet   180
In the blind mazes of this tangled wood?
My brothers, when they saw me wearied out
With this long way, resolving here to lodge
Under the spreading favor of these pines,

154. spongy: absorbing.
155. blear: deceptive.
156. presentments: pictures.
167. This line did not appear in the 1673 edition and is omitted in the *Works*, so that, from here on, the Columbia line-numbering differs from that of most other editions.
168. fairly: quietly.

169. This, the reading of the Manuscript and of 1637 and 1645, was changed in the 1673 Errata to "And hearken, if I may her business hear" — perhaps by a printer who did not understand Milton's use of "hearken" as a transitive verb.
175. granges: barns.

Stepped as they said to the next thicket side   185
To bring me berries, or such cooling fruit
As the kind hospitable woods provide.
They left me then when the gray-hooded Ev'n,
Like a sad votarist in palmer's weed,
Rose from the hindmost wheels of Phoebus' wain.   190
But where they are, and why they came not back,
Is now the labor of my thoughts; 'tis likeliest
They had engaged their wand'ring steps too far,
And envious darkness, ere they could return,
Had stole them from me. Else, O thievish Night,   195
Why shouldst thou, but for some felonious end,
In thy dark lantern thus close up the stars
That Nature hung in heav'n, and filled their lamps
With everlasting oil, to give due light
To the misled and lonely traveler?   200
This is the place, as well as I may guess,
Whence even now the tumult of loud mirth
Was rife, and perfect in my list'ning ear,
Yet naught but single darkness do I find.
What might this be? A thousand fantasies   205
Begin to throng into my memory
Of calling shapes, and beck'ning shadows dire,
And airy tongues that syllable men's names
On sands and shores and desert wildernesses.
These thoughts may startle well, but not astound   210
The virtuous mind, that ever walks attended
By a strong siding champion, Conscïence.
O welcome, pure-eyed Faith, white-handed Hope,
Thou hovering angel girt with golden wings,
And thou unblemished form of Chastity,   215
I see ye visibly, and now believe
That He, the supreme Good, t' whom all things ill
Are but as slavish officers of vengeance,
Would send a glist'ring guardian if need were
To keep my life and honor unassailed.   220
Was I deceived, or did a sable cloud
Turn forth her silver lining on the night?
I did not err, there does a sable cloud
Turn forth her silver lining on the night,
And casts a gleam over this tufted grove.   225
I cannot hallo to my brothers, but
Such noise as I can make to be heard farthest
I'll venture, for my new-enlivened spirits
Prompt me; and they perhaps are not far off.

189. a . . . weed: a sober person under a religious vow, in the garb of a pilgrim to the Holy Land.
195–225. These lines were not in the acting version; they appeared in the editions of 1637 and 1645.

204. single: only, total.
212. siding: defending.
221–24. The repeated lines suggest a symbolic confirmation of the inward assurance of lines 216–20.

SONG

Sweet Echo, sweetest nymph that liv'st unseen   230
    Within thy airy shell
    By slow Maeander's margent green,
And in the violet-embroidered vale
    Where the lovelorn nightingale
Nightly to thee her sad song mourneth well: 235
Canst thou not tell me of a gentle pair
    That likest thy Narcissus are?
      O if thou have
    Hid them in some flow'ry cave,
      Tell me but where,   240
    Sweet queen of parley, daughter of the sphere;
So may'st thou be translated to the skies,
And give resounding grace to all heav'n's harmonies.

Comus. Can any mortal mixture of earth's mold
Breath such divine enchanting ravishment?   245
Sure something holy lodges in that breast,
And with these raptures moves the vocal air
To testify his hidden residence;
How sweetly did they float upon the wings
Of silence, through the empty-vaulted night,   250
At every fall smoothing the raven down
Of darkness till it smiled. I have oft heard
My mother Circe with the Sirens three,
Amidst the flow'ry-kirtled Naiades,
Culling their potent herbs and baleful drugs,   255
Who as they sung would take the prisoned soul
And lap it in Elysium; Scylla wept,
And chid her barking waves into attention,
And fell Charybdis murmured soft applause.
Yet they in pleasing slumber lulled the sense,   260
And in sweet madness robbed it of itself;
But such a sacred and home-felt delight,
Such sober certainty of waking bliss,
I never heard till now. I'll speak to her,
And she shall be my queen. Hail, foreign wonder,   265
Whom certain these rough shades did never breed,
Unless the goddess that in rural shrine
Dwell'st here with Pan or Sylvan, by blest song
Forbidding every bleak unkindly fog
To touch the prosperous growth of this tall wood.   270
    Lady. Nay, gentle shepherd, ill is lost that praise
That is addressed to unattending ears.
Not any boast of skill, but éxtreme shift

---

231. airy shell: an actual cavern (MS., "cell"; cf. Ovid, *Met.* 3.394) or vault of air.
232. Maeander: a winding river in Asia Minor.
241. Cf. *At a Solemn Music* 2.
251. fall: cadence.
253. The Sirens whose singing put a spell upon sailors (*Odyssey* 12.47 f., 165 f.).

How to regain my severed company
Compelled me to awake the courteous Echo   275
To give me answer from her mossy couch.
    Comus. What chance, good lady, hath bereft you thus?
    Lady. Dim darkness and this leavy labyrinth.
    Comus. Could that divide you from near-ushering guides?
    Lady. They left me weary on a grassy turf.   280
    Comus. By falsehood, or discourtesy, or why?
    Lady. To seek i' th' valley some cool friendly spring.
    Comus. And left your fair side all unguarded, lady?
    Lady. They were but twain, and purposed quick return.
    Comus. Perhaps forestalling night prevented them.   285
    Lady. How easy my misfortune is to hit!
    Comus. Imports their loss, beside the present need?
    Lady. No less than if I should my brothers lose.
    Comus. Were they of manly prime, or youthful bloom?
    Lady. As smooth as Hebe's their unrazored lips.   290
    Comus. Two such I saw, what time the labored ox
In his loose traces from the furrow came,
And the swinked hedger at his supper sat;
I saw them under a green mantling vine
That crawls along the side of yon small hill,   295
Plucking ripe clusters from the tender shoots;
Their port was more than human, as they stood.
I took it for a faëry vision
Of some gay creatures of the element,
That in the colors of the rainbow live   300
And play i' th' plighted clouds. I was awe-strook,
And as I passed, I worshiped; if those you seek,
It were a journey like the path to heav'n
To help you find them.
    Lady.   Gentle villager,
What readiest way would bring me to that place?   305
    Comus. Due west it rises from this shrubby point.
    Lady. To find out that, good shepherd, I suppose,
In such a scant allowance of star-light,
Would overtask the best land-pilot's art,
Without the sure guess of well-practised feet.   310
    Comus. I know each lane and every alley green,
Dingle or bushy dell of this wild wood,
And every bosky bourn from side to side,
My daily walks and ancient neighborhood,
And if your stray attendance be yet lodged,   315
Or shroud within these limits, I shall know
Ere morrow wake or the low-roosted lark
From her thatched pallet rouse; if otherwise,

277–90. Dialogue in single lines, the sticho-mythia of Greek drama.
293. swinked hedger: weary hedge-clipper, laborer.
301. plighted: folded.
313. bosky bourn: brook bordered with bushes.
318. thatched pallet: straw nest.

I can conduct you, lady, to a low
But loyal cottage, where you may be safe   320
Till further quest.
    Lady.   Shepherd, I take thy word,
And trust thy honest-offered courtesy,
Which oft is sooner found in lowly sheds
With smoky rafters, than in tap'stry halls
And courts of princes, where it first was named,   325
And yet is most pretended. In a place
Less warranted than this, or less secure,
I cannot be, that I should fear to change it.
Eye me, blest Providence, and square my trial
To my proportioned strength. Shepherd, lead on.   330
                       [*Exeunt.*]

The two Brothers.

    Eld. Bro. Unmuffle, ye faint stars, and thou, fair moon,
That wont'st to love the traveler's benison,
Stoop thy pale visage through an amber cloud
And disinherit Chaos, that reigns here
In double night of darkness and of shades;   335
Or if your influence be quite dammed up
With black usurping mists, some gentle taper,
Though a rush-candle from the wicker hole
Of some clay habitation, visit us
With thy long leveled rule of streaming light,   340
And thou shalt be our star of Arcady,
Or Tyrian Cynosure.
    Sec. Bro.   Or if our eyes
Be barred that happiness, might we but hear
The folded flocks penned in their wattled cotes,
Or sound of pastoral reed with oaten stops,   345
Or whistle from the lodge, or village cock
Count the night-watches to his feathery dames,
'Twould be some solace yet, some little cheering,
In this close dungeon of innumerous boughs.
But O that hapless virgin, our lost sister,   350
Where may she wander now, whither betake her
From the chill dew, amongst rude burs and thistles?
Perhaps some cold bank is her bolster now,
Or 'gainst the rugged bark of some broad elm
Leans her unpillowed head fraught with sad fears.   355
What if in wild amazement and affright,
Or, while we speak, within the direful grasp

323–25. A traditional and especially pastoral sentiment; cf. Aeschylus, *Agamemnon* 772 f.; Horace, *Od.* 3.29.14–16; etc.
326. yet: still.
334. disinherit: dispossess.
341. star of Arcady: constellation of the Great Bear (glossary, "Callisto"), by which Greek mariners steered.
342. Tyrian Cynosure: the North or Pole Star in the Little Bear (glossary, "Callisto"), by which Phoenician sailors navigated.
344. wattled cotes: sheepfolds made of plaited branches.

Of savage hunger or of savage heat?
   Eld. Bro. Peace, brother, be not over-exquisite
To cast the fashion of uncertain evils; 360
For grant they be so, while they rest unknown,
What need a man forestall his date of grief,
And run to meet what he would most avoid?
Or if they be but false alarms of fear,
How bitter is such self-delusïon? 365
I do not think my sister so to seek,
Or so unprincipled in virtue's book,
And the sweet peace that goodness bosoms ever,
As that the single want of light and noise
(Not being in danger, as I trust she is not) 370
Could stir the constant mood of her calm thoughts,
And put them into misbecoming plight.
Virtue could see to do what Virtue would
By her own radiant light, though sun and moon
Were in the flat sea sunk. And Wisdom's self 375
Oft seeks to sweet retired solitude,
Where with her best nurse, Contemplatïon,
She plumes her feathers and lets grow her wings,
That in the various bustle of resort
Were all to-ruffled, and sometimes impaired. 380
He that has light within his own clear breast
May sit i' th' center and enjoy bright day,
But he that hides a dark soul and foul thoughts
Benighted walks under the mid-day sun;
Himself is his own dungeon.
   Sec. Bro.   'Tis most true 385
That musing meditation most affects
The pensive secrecy of desert cell,
Far from the cheerful haunt of men and herds,
And sits as safe as in a senate-house;
For who would rob a hermit of his weeds, 390
His few books, or his beads, or maple dish,
Or do his gray hairs any violence?
But beauty, like the fair Hesperian tree
Laden with blooming gold, had need the guard
Of dragon-watch with unenchanted eye 395
To save her blossoms and defend her fruit
From the rash hand of bold Incontinence.
You may as well spread out the unsunned heaps
Of miser's treasure by an outlaw's den,
And tell me it is safe, as bid me hope 400
Danger will wink on opportunity,

373–74. Cf. Spenser, *F.Q.* 1.1.12.9.
377–78. For the image of wings see Plato, *Phaedrus* 246 f.
380. to-ruffled: much ruffled ("to" is an archaic intensive prefix).
382. center: glossary.

395. unenchanted: that cannot be enchanted. Cf. the canceled lines quoted in the note on 4 above.
401. Danger: power. wink on: close the eyes to.

And let a single helpless maiden pass
Uninjured in this wild surrounding waste.
Of night or loneliness it recks me not;
I fear the dread events that dog them both,   405
Lest some ill-greeting touch attempt the person
Of our unowned sister.
    Eld. Bro.   I do not, brother,
Infer as if I thought my sister's state
Secure without all doubt or controversy;
Yet where an equal poise of hope and fear   410
Does arbitrate th' event, my nature is
That I incline to hope rather than fear,
And gladly banish squint suspicïon.
My sister is not so defenseless left
As you imagine; she has a hidden strength   415
Which you remember not.
    Sec. Bro.   What hidden strength,
Unless the strength of Heav'n, if you mean that?
    Eld. Bro. I mean that too, but yet a hidden strength
Which, if Heav'n gave it, may be termed her own:
'Tis chastity, my brother, chastity.   420
She that has that is clad in cómplete steel,
And like a quivered nymph with arrows keen
May trace huge forests and unharbored heaths,
Infamous hills and sandy perilous wilds,
Where, through the sacred rays of chastity,   425
No savage fierce, bandit, or mountaineer
Will dare to soil her virgin purity.
Yea, there where very desolation dwells,
By grots and caverns shagged with horrid shades,
She may pass on with unblenched majesty,   430
Be it not done in pride or in presumption.
Some say no evil thing that walks by night,
In fog or fire, by lake or moorish fen,
Blue meager hag, or stubborn unlaid ghost,
That breaks his magic chains at curfew time,   435
No goblin or swart fairy of the mine,
Hath hurtful power o'er true virginity.
Do ye believe me yet, or shall I call
Antiquity from the old schools of Greece
To testify the arms of chastity?   440
Hence had the huntress Dian her dread bow,
Fair silver-shafted queen for ever chaste,

---

404. it recks me not: I am not concerned about.

407. unowned: unprotected.

422. quivered nymph: nymph with a quiver of arrows, a follower of the huntress Diana, goddess of chastity.

423. unharbored: without shelter.

430. unblenched: fearless.

433. fire: cf. *L'Allegro* 104.

434. hag: evil spirit in female form.

434. unlaid: unexorcised, wandering from his proper abode.

435. Spirits might walk between curfew time (eight or nine o'clock) and the first crowing of the cock. Cf. *Nativity* 229–36.

435. fairy . . . mine: underground spirit.

439. schools: philosophical schools, teachings.

Wherewith she tamed the brinded lioness
And spotted mountain-pard, but set at naught
The frivolous bolt of Cupid; gods and men 445
Feared her stern frown, and she was queen o' th' woods.
What was that snaky-headed Gorgon shield
That wise Minerva wore, unconquered virgin,
Wherewith she freezed her foes to cóngealed stone,
But rigid looks of chaste austerity, 450
And noble grace that dashed brute violence
With sudden adoration and blank awe?
So dear to Heav'n is saintly chastity
That when a soul is found sincerely so,
A thousand liveried angels lackey her, 455
Driving far off each thing of sin and guilt,
And in clear dream and solemn visïon
Tell her of things that no gross ear can hear,
Till oft converse with heav'nly habitants
Begin to cast a beam on th' outward shape, 460
The unpolluted temple of the mind,
And turns it by degrees to the soul's essence,
Till all be made immortal. But when lust,
By unchaste looks, loose gestures, and foul talk,
But most by lewd and lavish act of sin, 465
Lets in defilement to the inward parts,
The soul grows clotted by contagion,
Imbodies and imbrutes, till she quite lose
The divine property of her first being.
Such are those thick and gloomy shadows damp 470
Oft seen in charnel vaults and sepulchres
Lingering, and sitting by a new-made grave,
As loth to leave the body that it loved,
And linked itself by carnal sensualty
To a degenerate and degraded state. 475
    Sec. Bro. How charming is divine philosophy!
Not harsh and crabbed, as dull fools suppose,
But musical as is Apollo's lute,
And a perpetual feast of nectared sweets,
Where no crude surfeit reigns.
    Eld. Bro.   List, list, I hear 480
Some far-off hallo break the silent air.
    Sec. Bro. Methought so too; what should it be?
    Eld. Bro.   For certain,
Either some one like us night-foundered here,
Or else some neighbor woodman, or at worst,
Some roving robber calling to his fellows. 485
    Sec. Bro. Heav'n keep my sister! Again, again, and near!

---

448. Minerva: glossary, "Pallas Athene."
458. Cf. *Arcades* 72–73.
463–75. A free paraphrase of Plato, *Phaedo*
81.

474. sensualty (1645): sensuality (1637, 1673).
478. Cf. *Love's Labor's Lost* 4.3.342–43.
483. night-foundered: benighted.

Best draw, and stand upon our guard.
    Eld. Bro.   I'll hallo;
If he be friendly, he comes well; if not,
Defense is a good cause, and Heav'n be for us.
    The Attendant Spirit, habited like a shepherd.
That hallo I should know; what are you? speak.   490
Come not too near, you fall on iron stakes else.
    Spir. What voice is that? my young lord? speak again.
    Sec. Bro. O brother, 'tis my father's shepherd, sure.
    Eld. Bro. Thyrsis, whose artful strains have oft delayed
The huddling brook to hear his madrigal,   495
And sweetened every musk-rose of the dale,
How cam'st thou here, good swain? Hath any ram
Slipped from the fold, or young kid lost his dam,
Or straggling wether the pent flock forsook?
How couldst thou find this dark sequestered nook?   500
    Spir. O my loved master's heir, and his next joy,
I came not here on such a trivial toy
As a strayed ewe, or to pursue the stealth
Of pilfering wolf; not all the fleecy wealth
That doth enrich these downs is worth a thought   505
To this my errand, and the care it brought.
But O my virgin lady, where is she?
How chance she is not in your company?
    Eld. Bro. To tell thee sadly, shepherd, without blame
Or our neglect, we lost her as we came.   510
    Spir. Ay me unhappy, then my fears are true.
    Eld. Bro. What fears, good Thyrsis? Prithee briefly shew.
    Spir. I'll tell ye. 'Tis not vain or fabulous
(Though so esteemed by shallow ignorance)
What the sage poets, taught by th' heav'nly Muse,   515
Storied of old in high immortal verse
Of dire Chimeras and enchanted isles,
And rifted rocks whose entrance leads to hell;
For such there be, but unbelief is blind.
    Within the navel of this hideous wood,   520
Immured in cypress shades, a sorcerer dwells,
Of Bacchus and of Circe born, great Comus,
Deep skilled in all his mother's witcheries,
And here to every thirsty wanderer
By sly enticement gives his baneful cup,   525
With many murmurs mixed, whose pleasing poison
The visage quite transforms of him that drinks,
And the inglorious likeness of a beast

---

491. iron stakes: their swords.
493. MS., fathers; edd., father.
495. huddling: hurrying.
495–512. A passage of rhymed couplets.
506. To: compared with.
513–19. The allegorical interpretation of pagan myth began before Plato and continued throughout the Christian era (and was early extended to the Bible); cf. *Comus* itself and the quotations from Sandys in the headnote. One motive was the common belief that pagan myth was not merely fiction but a partly distorted version of Hebraic and Christian truth; cf. *P.L.* 10.581–84 and note.
520. navel: center.

Fixes instead, unmolding reason's mintage
Charáctered in the face; this have I learnt   530
Tending my flocks hard by i' th' hilly crofts
That brow this bottom glade, whence night by night
He and his monstrous rout are heard to howl
Like stabled wolves, or tigers at their prey,
Doing abhorrèd rites to Hecate   535
In their obscurèd haunts of inmost bow'rs.
Yet have they many baits and guileful spells
T' inveigle and invite th' unwary sense
Of them that pass unweeting by the way.
This evening late, by then the chewing flocks   540
Had ta'en their supper on the savory herb
Of knot-grass dew-besprent, and were in fold,
I sat me down to watch upon a bank
With ivy canopied, and interwove
With flaunting honeysuckle, and began,   545
Wrapped in a pleasing fit of melancholy,
To meditate my rural minstrelsy,
Till fancy had her fill. But ere a close
The wonted roar was up amidst the woods,
And filled the air with barbarous dissonance,   550
At which I ceased, and listened them a while,
Till an unusual stop of sudden silence
Gave respite to the drowsy frighted steeds
That draw the litter of close-curtained Sleep.
At last a soft and solemn-breathing sound   555
Rose like a steam of rich distilled perfumes,
And stole upon the air, that even Silence
Was took ere she was ware, and wished she might
Deny her nature and be never more,
Still to be so displaced. I was all ear,   560
And took in strains that might create a soul
Under the ribs of Death, but O ere long
Too well I did perceive it was the voice
Of my most honored lady, your dear sister.
Amazed I stood, harrowed with grief and fear,   565
And "O poor hapless nightingale," thought I,
"How sweet thou sing'st, how near the deadly snare!"
Then down the lawns I ran with headlong haste
Through paths and turnings often trod by day,
Till guided by mine ear I found the place   570
Where that damned wizard, hid in sly disguise
(For so by certain signs I knew), had met

530. Charáctered: engraved.
531. crofts: small enclosed fields.
532. brow: overlook.
540. then: the time that.
547. meditate . . . minstrelsy: play on
shepherd's pipe (cf. Virgil, *Ecl.* 1.2).
553. drowsy frighted: frightened though

drowsy. This is the reading of the editions of
1637, 1645, and 1673; some editors prefer
the "drowsy flighted" of the MS.
555. steam (1637, 1645); 1673, stream.
559–60. be . . . displaced: no longer exist,
if she could always be destroyed by such
music.

Already, ere my best speed could prevent,
The aidless innocent lady, his wished prey,
Who gently asked if he had seen such two,   575
Supposing him some neighbor villager;
Longer I durst not stay, but soon I guessed
Ye were the two she meant; with that I sprung
Into swift flight, till I had found you here;
But furder know I not.

  Sec. Bro.   O night and shades,   580
How are ye joined with hell in triple knot
Against th' unarmèd weakness of one virgin
Alone and helpless! Is this the confidence
You gave me, brother?

  Eld. Bro.   Yes, and keep it still,
Lean on it safely; not a period   585
Shall be unsaid for me. Against the threats
Of malice or of sorcery, or that power
Which erring men call chance, this I hold firm:
Virtue may be assailed, but never hurt,
Surprised by unjust force, but not enthralled;   590
Yea, even that which mischief meant most harm
Shall in the happy trial prove most glory.
But evil on itself shall back recoil,
And mix no more with goodness, when at last,
Gathered like scum, and settled to itself,   595
It shall be in eternal restless change
Self-fed and self-consumed; if this fail,
The pillared firmament is rottenness,
And earth's base built on stubble. But come, let's on.
Against th' opposing will and arm of Heav'n   600
May never this just sword be lifted up;
But for that damned magician, let him be girt
With all the grisly legïons that troop
Under the sooty flag of Acheron,
Harpies and Hydras, or all the monstrous forms   605
'Twixt Africa and Ind, I'll find him out,
And force him to restore his purchase back,
Or drag him by the curls to a foul death,
Cursed as his life.

  Spir.   Alas, good vent'rous youth,
I love thy courage yet, and bold emprise,   610
But here thy sword can do thee little stead;
Far other arms and other weapons must
Be those that quell the might of hellish charms.
He with his bare wand can unthread thy joints,
And crumble all thy sinews.

  Eld. Bro.   Why, prithee, shepherd,   615

580. furder: 1673, further.
585. period: sentence.
586. for me: by me, for my part.

598. firmament: sphere of fixed stars.
605. Cf. *P.L.* 2.628 and note.
607. purchase: prey.

How durst thou then thyself approach so near
As to make this relation?
     Spir   Care and utmost shifts
How to secure the lady from surprisal
Brought to my mind a certain shepherd lad,
Of small regard to see to, yet well skilled   620
In every virtuous plant and healing herb
That spreads her verdant leaf to th' morning ray.
He loved me well, and oft would beg me sing;
Which when I did, he on the tender grass
Would sit, and hearken even to ecstasy,   625
And in requital ope his leathern scrip,
And show me simples of a thousand names,
Telling their strange and vigorous faculties;
Amongst the rest a small unsightly root,
But of divine effect, he culled me out;   630
The leaf was darkish, and had prickles on it,
But in another country, as he said,
Bore a bright golden flow'r, but not in this soil;
Unknown, and like esteemed, and the dull swain
Treads on it daily with his clouted shoon;   635
And yet more med'cinal is it than that moly
That Hermes once to wise Ulysses gave;
He called it haemony, and gave it me,
And bade me keep it as of sovran use
'Gainst all enchantments, mildew blast, or damp,   640
Or ghastly Furies' apparition;
I pursed it up, but little reck'ning made,
Till now that this extremity compelled,
But now I find it true; for by this means
I knew the foul enchanter though disguised,   645
Entered the very lime-twigs of his spells,
And yet came off. If you have this about you
(As I will give you when we go), you may
Boldly assault the necromancer's hall;
Where if he be, with dauntless hardihood   650
And brandished blade rush on him, break his glass,
And shed the luscious liquor on the ground,
But seize his wand. Though he and his cursed crew
Fierce sign of battle make, and menace high,

---

619 f. The account of the "shepherd lad" with his "simples" (medicinal herbs) may be only a dramatic invention or may include a half-playful tribute to Milton's friend Diodati, the medical student (cf. *Epitaphium Damonis* 150–52).

620. small . . . to: unimpressive appearance.

632. another country: heaven? Cf. the quotations from Sandys in the headnote.

635. clouted shoon: hobnailed and/or patched shoes.

636. moly: the magical plant, given by Hermes to Odysseus, which protected him from Circe's spells (*Odyssey* 10.287 f.).

638. haemony: glossary, "Haemonia." The plant apparently represents Platonic-Christian temperance (see the headnote above); if it were religious faith or divine grace, its efficacy would surely be less limited than it proves to be.

646. lime-twigs. Birds were once caught by lime smeared on branches.

651–52. Cf. Spenser, *F.Q.* 2.12.57.

Or like the sons of Vulcan vomit smoke,   655
Yet will they soon retire, if he but shrink.
    Eld Bro. Thyrsis, lead on apace, I'll follow thee,
And some good angel bear a shield before us.

*The scene changes to a stately palace, set out with all manner of deli-
ciousness: soft music, tables spread with all dainties. Comus appears with
his rabble, and the Lady set in an enchanted chair, to whom he offers his
glass, which she puts by, and goes about to rise.*

    Comus. Nay, lady, sit; if I but wave this wand,
Your nerves are all chained up in alablaster,   660
And you a statue, or as Daphne was
Root-bound, that fled Apollo.
    Lady.   Fool, do not boast;
Thou canst not touch the freedom of my mind
With all thy charms, although this corporal rind
Thou hast immanacled, while Heav'n sees good.   665
    Comus. Why are you vexed, lady? why do you frown?
Here dwell no frowns, nor anger; from these gates
Sorrow flies far. See, here be all the pleasures
That fancy can beget on youthful thoughts,
When the fresh blood grows lively, and returns   670
Brisk as the April buds in primrose season.
And first behold this cordial julep here
That flames and dances in his crystal bounds,
With spirits of balm and fragrant syrups mixed.
Not that nepenthes which the wife of Thone   675
In Egypt gave to Jove-born Helena
Is of such power to stir up joy as this,
To life so friendly, or so cool to thirst.
Why should you be so cruel to yourself,
And to those dainty limbs which Nature lent   680
For gentle usage and soft delicacy?
But you invert the cov'nants of her trust,
And harshly deal like an ill borrower
With that which you received on other terms,
Scorning the unexempt condition   685
By which all mortal frailty must subsist,
Refreshment after toil, ease after pain,
That have been tir'd all day without repast,
And timely rest have wanted; but, fair virgin,
This will restore all soon.
    Lady.   'Twill not, false traitor,   690
'Twill not restore the truth and honesty
That thou hast banished from thy tongue with lies.
Was this the cottage and the safe abode

---

655. Cf. *Aen.* 8.193–261.   676. Helena: Helen of Troy, daughter of
675–76. See the *Odyssey* 4.219–30.   Zeus.
675. nepenthes: magic potion, opiate.   685. unexempt: universal.

Thou told'st me of? What grim aspécts are these,
These ugly-headed monsters? Mercy guard me! 695
Hence with thy brewed enchantments, foul deceiver;
Hast thou betrayed my credulous innocence
With vizored falsehood and base forgery,
And wouldst thou seek again to trap me here
With lickerish baits fit to ensnare a brute? 700
Were it a draught for Juno when she banquets,
I would not taste thy treasonous offer; none
But such as are good men can give good things,
And that which is not good is not delicious
To a well-governed and wise appetite. 705
    Comus. O foolishness of men! that lend their ears
To those budge doctors of the Stoic fur,
And fetch their precepts from the Cynic tub,
Praising the lean and sallow Abstinence.
Wherefore did Nature pour her bounties forth 710
With such a full and unwithdrawing hand,
Covering the earth with odors, fruits, and flocks,
Thronging the seas with spawn innumerable,
But all to please and sate the curious taste?
And set to work millions of spinning worms, 715
That in their green shops weave the smooth-haired silk
To deck her sons; and that no corner might
Be vacant of her plenty, in her own loins
She hutched th' all-worshiped ore and precious gems
To store her children with. If all the world 720
Should in a pet of temperance feed on pulse,
Drink the clear stream, and nothing wear but frieze,
Th' All-giver would be unthanked, would be unpraised,
Not half his riches known, and yet despised,
And we should serve him as a grudging master, 725
As a penurious niggard of his wealth,
And live like Nature's bastards, not her sons,
Who would be quite surcharged with her own weight,
And strangled with her waste fertility;
Th' earth cumbered, and the winged air darked with plumes; 730
The herds would over-multitude their lords,
The sea o'erfraught would swell, and th' unsought diamonds
Would so emblaze the forehead of the deep,
And so bestud with stars, that they below
Would grow inured to light, and come at last 735
To gaze upon the sun with shameless brows.

---

700. lickerish: tempting.
  707. budge: stiff, formal (from a kind of fur used on doctoral hoods or robes).
  708. Cynic tub. Diogenes, the Cynic philosopher of Athens, was said to have lived in a tub to show his scorn for luxury.
  719. hutched: laid away, hoarded.

721. pet: fit.
722. frieze: coarse woollen cloth.
733. deep: the earth, the vault of hell. Some minerals were thought to reproduce themselves.
734. they below: inhabitants of the underworld.

List, lady, be not coy, and be not cozened
With that same vaunted name Virginity;
Beauty is Nature's coin, must not be hoarded,
But must be current, and the good thereof   740
Consists in mutual and partaken bliss,
Unsavory in th' enjoyment of itself.
If you let slip time, like a neglected rose
It withers on the stalk with languished head.
Beauty is Nature's brag, and must be shown   745
In courts, at feasts, and high solemnities
Where most may wonder at the workmanship;
It is for homely features to keep home,
They had their name thence; coarse complexïons
And cheeks of sorry grain will serve to ply   750
The sampler, and to tease the housewife's wool.
What need a vermeil-tinctured lip for that,
Love-darting eyes, or tresses like the morn?
There was another meaning in these gifts,
Think what, and be advised; you are but young yet.   755
    Lady. I had not thought to have unlocked my lips
In this unhallowed air, but that this juggler
Would think to charm my judgment, as mine eyes,
Obtruding false rules pranked in reason's garb.
I hate when vice can bolt her arguments,   760
And virtue has no tongue to check her pride.
Impostor, do not charge most innocent Nature,
As if she would her children should be riotous
With her abundance; she, good cateress,
Means her provision only to the good,   765
That live according to her sober laws
And holy dictate of spare Temperance.
If every just man that now pines with want
Had but a moderate and beseeming share
Of that which lewdly pampered luxury   770
Now heaps upon some few with vast excess,
Nature's full blessings would be well dispensed
In unsuperfluous even proportïon,
And she no whit encumbered with her store;
And then the Giver would be better thanked,   775
His praise due paid, for swinish gluttony
Ne'er looks to Heav'n amidst his gorgeous feast,
But with besotted base ingratitude

---

737. cozened: cheated.
737–55. Comus' specious arguments for the use of nature's bounties (706–36) shift in 737–55 (lines which were not in the acting version) to a non-sequitur, a plea for sexual license in the common vein of Renaissance libertinism: e.g., Marlowe, *Hero and Leander* 1.215 f., 315 f.; some of Donne's early poems; Thomas Randolph, *Muses' Looking Glass* 2.3 ("Nature has been bountiful . . .").

743–44. Cf. *A Midsummer Night's Dream* 1.1.76–78.
751. tease: comb, card.
752. vermeil: vermilion.
753. Love-darting eyes: cf. Sylvester, 2.3.4.849, "love-darting eyn."
759. pranked: dressed up.
760. bolt: sift, refine.

Crams, and blasphemes his Feeder. Shall I go on?
Or have I said enough? To him that dares   780
Arm his profane tongue with contemptuous words
Against the sun-clad power of Chastity,
Fain would I something say, yet to what end?
Thou hast nor ear nor soul to apprehend
The sublime notion and high mystery   785
That must be uttered to unfold the sage
And serious doctrine of Virginity,
And thou art worthy that thou shouldst not know
More happiness than this thy present lot.
Enjoy your dear wit and gay rhetoric   790
That hath so well been taught her dazzling fence;
Thou art not fit to hear thyself convinced.
Yet should I try, the uncontrollèd worth
Of this pure cause would kindle my rapt spirits
To such a flame of sacred vehemence   795
That dumb things would be moved to sympathize,
And the brute Earth would lend her nerves, and shake,
Till all thy magic structures, reared so high,
Were shattered into heaps o'er thy false head.
    Comus. She fables not. I feel that I do fear   800
Her words set off by some superior power;
And though not mortal, yet a cold shudd'ring dew
Dips me all o'er, as when the wrath of Jove
Speaks thunder and the chains of Erebus
To some of Saturn's crew. I must dissemble,   805
And try her yet more strongly. Come, no more,
This is mere moral babble, and direct
Against the canon laws of our foundation;
I must not suffer this, yet 'tis but the lees
And settlings of a melancholy blood;   810
But this will cure all straight; one sip of this
Will bathe the drooping spirits in delight
Beyond the bliss of dreams. Be wise, and taste.

*The Brothers rush in with swords drawn, wrest his glass out of his hand,
and break it against the ground; his rout make sign of resistance, but are
all driven in; the Attendant Spirit comes in.*

    Spir. What, have you let the false enchanter scape?
O ye mistook, ye should have snatched his wand   815
And bound him fast; without his rod reversed,

779–806. These lines were not in the acting version or the Cambridge Manuscript; they
appeared in the editions of 1637 and 1645.
In 762–99 the Lady replies, mainly in rational
terms, to Comus' first argument and urges
temperance and fair distribution of nature's
blessings. In 779–99, replying to his second
argument, she rises to an impassioned religious affirmation of the beauty of chastity.

785. mystery: cf. *Apology for Smectymnuus*
(quoted early in this volume).

791. fence: art of fencing.

792. convinced: confuted.

797. brute Earth: cf. Horace, *Od.* 1.34.9.

805. Saturn's crew: the rebel Titans imprisoned in the underworld.

808. canon laws . . . foundation. Cf.
Comus' pose of priesthood in 93–144.

810. melancholy: glossary, "humors."

816–17. The formula for undoing Circe's
spells (Ovid, *Met.* 14.300–01) and Busyrane's
(Spenser, *F.Q.* 3.12.36).

And backward mutters of dissevering power,
We cannot free the lady that sits here
In stony fetters fixed and motionless;
Yet stay, be not disturbed; now I bethink me,   820
Some other means I have which may be used,
Which once of Meliboeus old I learnt,
The soothest shepherd that e'er piped on plains.
    There is a gentle Nymph not far from hence,
That with moist curb sways the smooth Severn stream;   825
Sabrina is her name, a virgin pure;
Whilom she was the daughter of Locrine,
That had the scepter from his father Brute.
She, guiltless damsel, flying the mad pursuit
Of her enragèd stepdame Guendolen,   830
Commended her fair innocence to the flood
That stayed her flight with his cross-flowing course;
The water-nymphs that in the bottom played
Held up their pearlèd wrists and took her in,
Bearing her straight to aged Nereus' hall,   835
Who, piteous of her woes, reared her lank head,
And gave her to his daughters to imbathe
In nectared lavers strewed with asphodel,
And through the porch and inlet of each sense
Dropped in ambrosial oils, till she revived   840
And underwent a quick immortal change,
Made goddess of the river. Still she retains
Her maiden gentleness, and oft at eve
Visits the herds along the twilight meadows,
Helping all urchin blasts, and ill-luck signs   845
That the shrewd meddling elf delights to make,
Which she with precious vialed liquors heals;
For which the shepherds at their festivals
Carol her goodness loud in rustic lays,
And throw sweet garland wreaths into her stream   850
Of pansies, pinks, and gaudy daffodils.
And, as the old swain said, she can unlock
The clasping charm and thaw the numbing spell,
If she be right invoked in warbled song;
For maidenhood she loves, and will be swift   855
To aid a virgin such as was herself
In hard-besetting need. This will I try,
And add the power of some adjuring verse.

822. Meliboeus: Spenser.
    824 f. The story of Sabrina — a legend of
the Severn river very appropriate for a masque
given at Ludlow — had been told in *The
Faerie Queene* 2.10.14–19; Milton adapts it
to his own purposes and theme. Sabrina,
though here enveloped in classical allusions,
may represent divine grace.
    828. Brute: the great-grandson of Aeneas

and the legendary founder of Britain.
    836. lank: drooping.
    845. urchin ("hedgehog"): caused by evil
spirits (cf. *The Tempest* 2.2.5–12).
    846. elf: any mischievous sprite or Puck
in particular (*A Midsummer Night's Dream*
2.1.33, etc.).
    852. swain: Meliboeus (cf. 822).

SONG

Sabrina fair,
  Listen where thou art sitting   860
Under the glassy, cool, translucent wave,
  In twisted braids of lilies knitting
The loose train of thy amber-dropping hair;
  Listen for dear honor's sake,
  Goddess of the silver lake,   865
  Listen and save.
Listen and appear to us
In name of great Oceanus,
By the earth-shaking Neptune's mace,
And Tethys' grave majestic pace,   870
By hoary Nereus' wrinkled look,
And the Carpathian wizard's hook,
By scaly Triton's winding shell,
And old soothsaying Glaucus' spell,
By Leucothea's lovely hands,   875
And her son that rules the strands,
By Thetis' tinsel-slippered feet,
And the songs of Sirens sweet,
By dead Parthenope's dear tomb,
And fair Ligea's golden comb,   880
Wherewith she sits on diamond rocks
Sleeking her soft alluring locks;
By all the nymphs that nightly dance
Upon thy streams with wily glance,
Rise, rise, and heave thy rosy head   885
From thy coral-paven bed,
And bridle in thy headlong wave,
Till thou our summons answered have.
                Listen and save.

Sabrina rises, attended by water-nymphs, and sings.

  By the rushy-fringèd bank,   890
Where grows the willow and the osier dank,
  My sliding chariot stays,
Thick set with agate, and the azurn sheen
  Of turkis blue, and emerald green,
    That in the channel strays.   895

---

868. Oceanus: god of the river encircling the earth.

872. Carpathian . . . hook: the staff of Proteus (glossary).

873. Triton was Neptune's trumpeter. winding: having winding passages (cf. Ovid, *Met.* 1.333 f.).

874. Glaucus: a mortal who became a sea-god and prophet.

875–76. Ino became a sea-divinity under the name of Leucothea; mother of Melicertes (see note on *Lycidas* 164).

878. See note on 253.

879. Parthenope: see note on *To Leonora* (3).

880. Ligea: a name given to one of Homer's Sirens.

894. turkis: turquoise.

895. Colors that shift in the rippling water ("strays" having a plural sense)?

Whilst from off the waters fleet
Thus I set my printless feet
O'er the cowslip's velvet head,
   That bends not as I tread.
Gentle swain, at thy request   900
   I am here.
   Spir. Goddess dear,
We implore thy powerful hand
To undo the charmèd band
Of true virgin here distressed,   905
Through the force and through the wile
Of unblest enchanter vile.
   Sab. Shepherd, 'tis my office best
To help ensnarèd chastity.
Brightest lady, look on me;   910
Thus I sprinkle on thy breast
Drops that from my fountain pure
I have kept of precious cure,
Thrice upon thy finger's tip,
Thrice upon thy rubied lip;   915
Next this marble venomed seat,
Smeared with gums of glutinous heat,
I touch with chaste palms moist and cold.
Now the spell hath lost his hold;
And I must haste ere morning hour   920
To wait in Amphitrite's bow'r.

Sabrina descends, and the Lady rises out of her seat.

   Spir. Virgin, daughter of Locrine,
Sprung of old Anchises' line,
May thy brimmèd waves for this
Their full tribute never miss   925
From a thousand petty rills,
That tumble down the snowy hills;
Summer drouth or singèd air
Never scorch thy tresses fair,
Nor wet October's torrent flood   930
Thy molten crystal fill with mud;
May thy billows roll ashore
The beryl and the golden ore;
May thy lofty head be crowned
With many a tower and terrace round,   935
And here and there thy banks upon
With groves of myrrh and cinnamon.
   Come, lady, while Heaven lends us grace,
Let us fly this cursèd place,

---

897. printless feet: cf. *The Tempest* 5.1.34.
904. band: bondage.
921. Amphitrite: wife of Poseidon (Neptune).

923. Anchises was the father of Aeneas (see the note on 828 above).
934–35. Cf. *Arcades* 21.

Lest the sorcerer us entice 940
With some other new device.
Not a waste or needless sound
Till we come to holier ground;
I shall be your faithful guide
Through this gloomy covert wide, 945
And not many furlongs thence
Is your father's residence,
Where this night are met in state
Many a friend to gratulate
His wished presence, and beside 950
All the swains that there abide
With jigs and rural dance resort;
We shall catch them at their sport,
And our sudden coming there
Will double all their mirth and cheer. 955
Come, let us haste, the stars grow high,
But Night sits monarch yet in the mid sky.

*The scene changes, presenting Ludlow Town and the President's Castle;
then come in Country Dancers, after them the Attendant Spirit, with the
two Brothers and the Lady.*

SONG

Spir. *Back, shepherds, back, enough your play*
Till next sunshine holiday;
Here be without duck or nod 960
Other trippings to be trod
Of lighter toes, and such court guise
As Mercury did first devise
With the mincing Dryades
On the lawns and on the leas. 965

This second Song presents them to their father and mother.

Noble Lord, and Lady bright,
I have brought ye new delight.
Here behold so goodly grown
Three fair branches of your own;
Heav'n hath timely tried their youth, 970
Their faith, their patience, and their truth,
And sent them here through hard assays
With a crown of deathless praise,
    To triumph in victorious dance
O'er sensual folly and intemperance. 975

The dances ended, the Spirit epiloguizes.

957. Cf. *Aen.* 3.512, 5.738, 835.
960. duck: curtsy.

964. mincing Dryades: wood-nymphs dancing daintily.
970. timely: early.

Spir. To the ocean now I fly,
And those happy climes that lie
Where day never shuts his eye,
Up in the broad fields of the sky.
There I suck the liquid air   980
All amidst the gardens fair
Of Hesperus, and his daughters three
That sing about the golden tree.
Along the crispèd shades and bow'rs
Revels the spruce and jocund Spring;   985
The Graces and the rosy-bosomed Hours
Thither all their bounties bring,
That there eternal summer dwells,
And west winds with musky wing
About the cedarn alleys fling   990
Nard and cassia's balmy smells.
Iris there with humid bow
Waters the odorous banks that blow
Flowers of more mingled hue
Than her purfled scarf can shew,   995
And drenches with Elysian dew
(List, mortals, if your ears be true)
Beds of hyacinth and roses,
Where young Adonis oft reposes,
Waxing well of his deep wound   1000
In slumber soft, and on the ground
Sadly sits th' Assyrian queen;
But far above in spangled sheen
Celestial Cupid, her famed son, advanced,
Holds his dear Psyche sweet entranced   1005
After her wand'ring labors long,
Till free consent the gods among
Make her his eternal bride,
And from her fair unspotted side
Two blissful twins are to be born,   1010
Youth and Joy; so Jove hath sworn.

976–99. When the masque was acted it opened with these lines, somewhat abridged and altered. Cf. *The Tempest* 5.1.88–94 and pictures of earthly paradises in Spenser (*F.Q.* 3.6) et al.
984. crispèd shades: trees or bushes with leaves curled by the wind.
985. spruce: dainty, elegant.
989. musky: perfumed.
995. purfled: fringed with embroidered colors.
997. Cf. 458 and *Arcades* 71–73.
999–1002. Milton seems to follow Spenser's interpretation (*F.Q.* 3.6.46 f.) of the love of Venus ("th' Assyrian queen") as symbolizing the perpetual cycle of physical generation within the order of nature.

1000–11. These lines and 997 were added in the 1637 edition.
1003–11. Apuleius' tale of Cupid and Psyche had lent itself to Christian interpretation as representing the love of Christ for the human soul. Milton, writing in the Platonic-Christian tradition, emphasizes the Platonic love of the good that engenders knowledge and virtue (cf. *Apology for Smectymnuus*, quoted early in this book). In *Comus*, which displays the victory of knowledge and virtue, Milton makes Psyche's progeny "Youth and Joy" ("Pleasure" in Apuleius and Spenser, *F.Q.* 3.6.50), perhaps because Comus had claimed to embody both, whereas they are the possession of the good.

But now my task is smoothly done,
I can fly, or I can run
Quickly to the green earth's end,
Where the bowed welkin slow doth bend,   1015
And from thence can soar as soon
To the corners of the moon.
  Mortals that would follow me,
Love Virtue, she alone is free;
She can teach ye how to climb   1020
Higher than the sphery chime;
Or if Virtue feeble were,
Heav'n itself would stoop to her.

(1634)

1015. bowed welkin: vaulted sky.
1017. corners: horns (cf. the note on *Naturam* 49 and *Macbeth* 3.5.23).

1019. Comus, who claimed to be free, is a slave to sensuality.
1021. sphery chime: the music of the spheres (above the spheres is heaven).

Psalm 114

Ἰσραὴλ ὅτε παῖδες, ὅτ' ἀγλαὰ φῦλ' Ἰακώβου
Αἰγύπτιον λίπε δῆμον, ἀπεχθέα, βαρβαρόφωνον,
Δὴ τότε μοῦνον ἔην ὅσιον γένος υἷες Ἰούδα·
Ἐν δὲ θεὸς λαοῖσι μέγα κρείων βασίλευεν.
Εἶδε, καὶ ἐντροπάδην φυγάδ' ἐρρώησε θάλασσα   5
Κύματι εἰλυμένη ῥοθίῳ, ὃ δ' ἄρ' ἐστυφελίχθη
Ἱρὸς Ἰορδάνης ποτὶ ἀργυροειδέα πηγήν.
Ἐκ δ' ὄρεα σκαρθμοῖσιν ἀπειρέσια κλονέοντο,
Ὡς κριοὶ σφριγόωντες ἐϋτραφερῷ ἐν ἀλωῇ.
Βαιότεραι δ' ἅμα πᾶσαι ἀνασκίρτησαν ἐρίπναι,   10
Οἷα παραὶ σύριγγι φίλῃ ὑπὸ μητέρι ἄρνες.
Τίπτε σύ γ' αἰνὰ θάλασσα πέλωρ φυγάδ' ἐρρώησας;
Κύματι εἰλυμένη ῥοθίῳ; τί δ' ἄρ' ἐστυφελίχθης
Ἱρὸς Ἰορδάνη ποτὶ ἀργυροειδέα πηγήν;
Τίπτ' ὄρεα σκαρθμοῖσιν ἀπειρέσια κλονέεσθε   15
Ὡς κριοὶ σφριγόωντες ἐϋτραφερῷ ἐν ἀλωῇ;
Βαιότεραι τί δ' ἄρ' ὕμμες ἀνασκιρτήσατ' ἐρίπναι,
Οἷα παραὶ σύριγγι φίλῃ ὑπὸ μητέρι ἄρνες;
Σείεο γαῖα τρέουσα θεὸν μεγάλ' ἐκκτυπέοντα,
Γαῖα θεὸν τρείουσ' ὕπατον σέβας Ἰσσακίδαο   20
Ὅς τε καὶ ἐκ σπιλάδων ποταμοὺς χέε μορμύροντας
Κρήνην τ' ἀέναον πέτρης ἀπὸ δακρυοέσσης.

IN A LETTER of December 4, 1634, to his friend Alexander Gill, Milton reported that, on a sudden impulse, he had just translated Psalm 114 into Greek heroic verse, the first bit of Greek composition he had done since leaving school. Like the English version of this Psalm which he had made in boyhood (the first poem in this volume), the Greek translation is freely embroidered.

When the children of Israel, when the glorious tribes of Jacob, left the land of Egypt, a hateful land, of barbarous speech, then the sons of Judah were the one holy race. Among those peoples Almighty God was king. The sea saw this, and coiling up its roaring waves reverently gave strength to the fugitive. The sacred Jordan was pushed back to its silver source. The huge mountains leaped and bounded, like lusty rams in a flourishing meadow. At the same time all the smaller crags skipped like lambs, at the sound of the pipe, about their loving mother. Why, dread monstrous sea, did you give strength to the fugitive, coiling up your roaring waves? Why, sacred Jordan, were you pushed back to your silver source? Why, huge mountains, did you leap and bound, like lusty rams in a flourishing meadow? Why did you smaller crags skip like lambs, at the sound of the pipe, about their loving mother? Shake, earth, in fear of the Lord who makes a mighty sound; earth, fear the Lord, the Most High God of the seed of Isaac, who poured roaring rivers from the cliffs, and an everlasting fountain from the dripping rock.

Lycidas

In August, 1637, Edward King, a graduate of Christ's College and a candidate for holy orders, was drowned in a shipwreck in the Irish Sea. He was the son of an English official in Ireland, he had received some academic distinctions, and he had contributed Latin verses to academic anthologies. His youth and character and the manner of his death may have helped, along with his family's prominence, to evoke from Cambridge friends an honor usually reserved for more illustrious personages, a volume of elegies in Latin, Greek, and English, *Justa Edouardo King* (1638). Milton, who was immersed in his books at Horton (and had not written anything since *Comus* except a Greek version of a Psalm), was presumably invited to join in the memorial. He does not appear to have been a particular friend of King, although in the small world of Christ's College — some 260 students and dons — everyone would have been acquainted with everyone else; and Milton would have been remembered by the older men as a poet. *Lycidas*, signed "J.M." was the last and longest poem in a very mediocre collection. In the Cambridge Manuscript Milton dated it November, 1637, the month before his twenty-ninth birthday. The poem, coming near the end of the Horton period, links itself with the sonnet "How soon hath Time," written at the beginning.

The pastoral elegy, a main branch of the pastoral genre, had its great model in Virgil's fifth Eclogue (with which the tenth, though not an elegy, went along). During the Renaissance the original Greek elegies added their influence — Theocritus' first Idyll, Bion's *Epitaph for Adonis*, and the *Epitaph for Bion* ascribed to Moschus; this last was the first elegy on an actual poet conceived as a shepherd. Renaissance poets inherited a standard though flexible set of conventions, such as the appeal to local divinities or the Muses who had not saved the dead poet, the lament of nature for its departed singer, the procession of individual mourners, and, in the Christianized tradition, the banishment of grief by the thought of resurrection and immortality. One main reason for the very long life of the pastoral convention, both in the elegy and in its other branches, was that from the beginning it had been a dramatic mask for any kind of utterance, private or public; behind an established and impersonal pattern and *persona*, the poet enjoyed complete freedom.

In the nineteenth century *Lycidas* was recognized as the greatest of pastoral elegies, but generally in a quite inadequate way; even if Dr. Johnson's complaints were set aside, the poem was still a supreme neoclassical exercise. It has been only in the past generation that criticism has shown the reverberating depths and complexities of both its theme and its art, so that, for some people, *Lycidas* now stands out as perhaps the greatest short poem in English. But a brief note cannot provide more than some suggestions.

The main premise, for the Christian poet, is that the drowning of Edward King was not merely a grievous accident but a positive act of God. From that grows the central question Milton wrestles with, one of the oldest questions man had asked: "Why should the just man suffer? How can the premature death of the good, how can the existence of evil, be reconciled with God's providence?" Milton's mother had died in the spring of 1637, but he was affected very differently by the death of a virtuous and promising contemporary on the threshold of service in God's church, the church he himself had turned away from. Milton had now spent five years in private study to prepare himself for his unknown future, for labor under his great Task-Master's eye: what if he too should be unaccountably cut off before his life's work is begun, before his entrusted talents have borne fruit? But while his personal situation helps to explain the passionate intensity of the poem, it is barely registered. In the opening lines the poet's sense of unripeness merges with the fate of young Lycidas in the general idea of unfulfilment; in lines 20–23 there are the references to "my destined urn" and "my sable shroud"; and in the lines that follow the two "shepherds" are associated in the picture of carefree youth enjoying, with no thought of death's striking one of them, the apparent order and serenity of nature. But the personal is soon absorbed into the universal. Even pastoral nature reveals something perverse and fatal at the heart of things. Even Orpheus, the archetypal poet, was swept away. Is there any value in virtue, talent, and labor that give no promise of survival and fulfilment? What is to be the final answer is stated in lines 76–84, yet at this point it does not bring assurance, and the pressure of doubt and fear continues and mounts.

The several mourners widen, in oblique terms, the questioning of God's ways. The whole poem develops in a dialectic of emotion, image, style, and rhythm, and some of the most radical contrasts lead into the climax. The harsh denunciation of the clergy, the hireling shepherds, is followed by the lyrical invocation of flowers; but this reminder of nature's beauty is ironical, a "false surmise," since there is no hearse to strew them on. The fact calls up the thought of Lycidas' helpless body tossing in the sea, a reminder of nature's violence that is heightened by the volume of sound. But this final note of despair yields immediately to a final affirmation, which comes now not as mere statement but with the complete assurance of a beatific vision. The sun is the grand image of death as rebirth, and "the dear might of him that walked the waves" attests the divine love that envelops fragile life. The triumphant vindication of God's ways to men enables the poet to return gently to the pastoral world of order and to face the future without fear.

While the poet's conflicting emotions surge back and forth under our eyes, they are held under the most impersonal artistic control. One means toward that combined effect is the framework of the pastoral convention, which Milton re-creates and transcends. Another means is his adaptation of the pattern of the Italian canzone, the use of paragraphs and lines of irregular length and irregularly interwoven rhymes; the power of the orchestration is felt at once, though its subtleties must be studied. One formal element of the canzone, the poet's concluding address to his poem (here in *ottava rima*) becomes, as we have seen, an integral and highly significant part of the whole; it is one of Milton's great, simple, quiet endings, suggesting far more than it says.

In this monody the author bewails a learned friend, unfortunately drowned in his passage from Chester on the Irish Seas, 1637. And by occasion foretells the ruin of our corrupted clergy, then in their height.

Yet once more, O ye laurels, and once more,
Ye myrtles brown, with ivy never sere,
I come to pluck your berries harsh and crude,
And with forced fingers rude
Shatter your leaves before the mellowing year.
Bitter constraint, and sad occasion dear,
Compels me to disturb your season due;
For Lycidas is dead, dead ere his prime,
Young Lycidas, and hath not left his peer.

The prefatory note was added in 1645, when Anglican censorship was no longer operative (in 1638 the censor presumably had not read the poem — or lines 113–31). The changes Milton made in composition and revision are more fully recorded in such large editions as the Columbia *Works* and those of H. F. Fletcher (facsimile) and H. Darbishire.

1. There are ten unrhymed lines: 1, 13, 15, 22, 39, 51, 82, 91, 92, 161.

1–2. laurels, myrtles, ivy: evergreens associated respectively with Apollo, Venus, and Bacchus, and with crowns of honor, especially poetical honor (cf. *Ad Patrem* 102, *Mansus* 6, 92).

6. dear: grievous.

8. Lycidas: a traditional pastoral name.

Who would not sing for Lycidas? He. knew
Himself to sing, and build the lofty rhyme.
He must not float upon his wat'ry bier
Unwept, and welter to the parching wind,
Without the meed of some melodious tear.
   Begin then, Sisters of the sacred well 15
That from beneath the seat of Jove doth spring,
Begin, and somewhat loudly sweep the string.
Hence with denial vain, and coy excuse;
So may some gentle Muse
With lucky words favor my destined urn, 20
And as he passes turn,
And bid fair peace be to my sable shroud.
For we were nursed upon the self-same hill,
Fed the same flock, by fountain, shade, and rill.
   Together both, ere the high lawns appeared 25
Under the opening eyelids of the morn,
We drove afield, and both together heard
What time the gray-fly winds her sultry horn,
Batt'ning our flocks with the fresh dews of night,
Oft till the star that rose, at ev'ning, bright 30
Toward heav'n's descent had sloped his westering wheel.
Meanwhile the rural ditties were not mute,
Tempered to th' oaten flute;
Rough Satyrs danced, and Fauns with clov'n heel
From the glad sound would not be absent long, 35
And old Damoetas loved to hear our song.
   But O the heavy change, now thou art gone,
Now thou art gone, and never must return!
Thee, Shepherd, thee the woods and desert caves,
With wild thyme and the gadding vine o'ergrown, 40
And all their echoes mourn.
The willows and the hazel copses green
Shall now no more be seen
Fanning their joyous leaves to thy soft lays.
As killing as the canker to the rose, 45
Or taint-worm to the weanling herds that graze,
Or frost to flowers, that their gay wardrobe wear,
When first the white-thorn blows;
Such, Lycidas, thy loss to shepherd's ear.

10. Who . . . Lycidas? Cf. Virgil, *Ecl.*
10.3.   knew: knew how. In the MS. and two printed texts of 1638 Milton (apparently) wrote in "well" before "knew"; the reading of 1645 and 1673, followed here, may have been an oversight or, more probably, he may have changed his mind about what, without further change, would have been awkwardly hypermetrical.

15. Sisters: glossary, "Muses." For the invocation, cf. Theocritus, *Id.* 1.64.

19. Muse: here a poet. With 19–22, cf. *Mansus* 85 f.

26. opening: 1638, glimmering.

29. Batt'ning: feeding, fattening.

30. star: evening star (Hesperus); cf. *Comus* 93.

30. 1638: Oft till the ev'n-star bright.

31. 1638: burnished wheel.

36. Damoetas: a pastoral name, perhaps for some Cambridge don.

45. canker: canker-worm (cf. *Arcades* 53).

46. taint-worm: some kind of parasite.

47. wardrobe: glossary.

48. white-thorn: hawthorn.

Where were ye, Nymphs, when the remorseless deep   50
Closed o'er the head of your loved Lycidas?
For neither were ye playing on the steep
Where your old bards, the famous Druids, lie,
Nor on the shaggy top of Mona high,
Nor yet where Deva spreads her wizard stream.   55
Ay me, I fondly dream,
Had ye been there! — for what could that have done?
What could the Muse herself that Orpheus bore,
The Muse herself, for her enchanting son
Whom universal nature did lament,   60
When by the rout that made the hideous roar
His gory visage down the stream was sent,
Down the swift Hebrus to the Lesbian shore?
Alas! what boots it with uncessant care
To tend the homely slighted shepherd's trade,   65
And strictly meditate the thankless Muse?
Were it not better done as others use,
To sport with Amaryllis in the shade,
Or with the tangles of Neaera's hair?
Fame is the spur that the clear spirit doth raise   70
(That last infirmity of noble mind)
To scorn delights, and live laborious days;
But the fair guerdon when we hope to find,
And think to burst out into sudden blaze,
Comes the blind Fury with th' abhorrèd shears,   75
And slits the thin-spun life. "But not the praise,"
Phoebus replied, and touched my trembling ears:
"Fame is no plant that grows on mortal soil,
Nor in the glistering foil
Set off to th' world, nor in broad rumor lies,   80
But lives and spreads aloft by those pure eyes
And perfect witness of all-judging Jove;
As he pronounces lastly on each deed,
Of so much fame in heav'n expect thy meed."

50. Cf. Theocritus, *Id.* 1.66–69, Virgil, *Ecl.* 10.9–12.

52–55. Places along the west coast of England and Wales.

52. steep: perhaps the island of Bardsey, south of Anglesey.

54. Mona: the island of Anglesey.

55. Deva: glossary, "Dee."

56. fondly: foolishly.

58 f. Orpheus: glossary. Cf. Ovid, *Amores* 3.9.21.

63. Hebrus: a Thracian river flowing into the Aegean Sea.   Lesbian: of Lesbos, the large island near Asia Minor; cf. Ovid, *Met.* 11.15–60.

66. Cf. Virgil, *Ecl.* 1.2.

67. Cf. Virgil, *Ecl.* 2.14–15.   use: are wont to do.

68. Cf. Virgil, *Ecl.* 1.4–5.

69. Cf. Horace, *Od.* 3.14.21–22.   Or with: 1638, Hid in.

70. The classic English expression of a commonplace that goes back at least to Ovid, *Ex Ponto* 4.2.36. Cf. Milton's letter sent to Diodati about the time he was writing *Lycidas* (*Works*, 12, 27; *C.P.W.*, 1, 326–27).

71. Another great commonplace. Cf. Tacitus, *Hist.* 4.6 (and Owen Felltham, *Resolves*, "Of Fame"); also Boethius, *Consolatio Philosophiae* 2.7.

75. The function of Atropos, the Fate who cuts the thread of life, is here given to a "blind Fury," perhaps to emphasize her apparent irresponsibility.

77. Cf. Virgil, *Ecl.* 6.3–4.

79. glistering foil: the bright setting (gold or silver leaf) of a jewel.

O fountain Arethuse, and thou honored flood,   85
Smooth-sliding Mincius, crowned with vocal reeds,
That strain I heard was of a higher mood.
But now my oat proceeds,
And listens to the herald of the sea
That came in Neptune's plea.   90
He asked the waves, and asked the felon winds,
What hard mishap hath doomed this gentle swain?
And questioned every gust of rugged wings
That blows from off each beakèd promontory;
They knew not of his story,   95
And sage Hippotades their answer brings,
That not a blast was from his dungeon strayed;
The air was calm, and on the level brine
Sleek Panope with her all sisters played.
It was that fatal and perfidious bark,   100
Built in th' eclipse, and rigged with curses dark,
That sunk so low that sacred head of thine.

     Next Camus, reverend sire, went footing slow,
His mantle hairy, and his bonnet sedge,
Inwrought with figures dim, and on the edge   105
Like to that sanguine flower inscribed with woe.
"Ah, who hath reft," quoth he, "my dearest pledge?"
Last came, and last did go,
The Pilot of the Galilean lake;
Two massy keys he bore of metals twain   110
(The golden opes, the iron shuts amain).
He shook his mitred locks, and stern bespake:
"How well could I have spared for thee, young swain,
Enow of such as for their bellies' sake
Creep and intrude and climb into the fold!   115
Of other care they little reck'ning make
Than how to scramble at the shearers' feast,
And shove away the worthy bidden guest.

---

86. Mincius: a north-Italian river associated with the birthplace of Virgil (and cf. his *Ecl.* 7.12), here linked with Theocritus (the Sicilian Arethusa) as representing pastoral poetry.

88. oat: oaten or pastoral pipe (cf. *Comus* 345).

89. herald . . . sea: Triton. See the note on *Comus* 873.

92. What hard mishap: in Spenser, *F.Q.* 2.4.16.8.

96. Hippotades: Aeolus (glossary). For "sage," cf. *Aen.* 1.56–66.

99. Panope: a sea nymph, one of the fifty daughters of Nereus.

101. in th' eclipse: i.e. ill-omened. In 97–101 the poet is groping in the natural world for some apparent cause of the wreck.

103. Camus: god of the river Cam, representing Cambridge University.

106. flower: glossary, "Hyacinth."

107. The poet is still, in pastoral terms, expressing bewilderment over an inexplicable act of God.   pledge: child (cf. *pignora*, Elegy 4.42).

109. St. Peter, the Galilean fisherman (Luke 5.3), traditionally the first bishop ("mitred locks"), to whom Jesus gave the keys of heaven (Matt. 16.19).

113–31. Milton's first attack on the Anglican clergy. In the third of his anti-episcopal tracts (*Animadversions*, 1642) he quoted the similar lines from Spenser's *Shepherd's Calendar* (*May* 103–31). Ecclesiastical satire was a traditional element of pastorals (if not of pastoral elegies); its special relevance here is that God has ended the life of the exemplary Edward King while He allows hireling shepherds to infest His church. Cf. Ezek. 34; 2 Pet. 2; Dante, *Par.* 27.19–66, 29.103–26.

114–15. Phil. 3.19; John 10.1.

118. worthy . . . guest: Matt. 22.8.

Blind mouths! that scarce themselves know how to hold
A sheep-hook, or have learned aught else the least   120
That to the faithful herdman's art belongs!
What recks it them? What need they? They are sped;
And when they list, their lean and flashy songs
Grate on their scrannel pipes of wretched straw;
The hungry sheep look up, and are not fed,   125
But swoln with wind, and the rank mist they draw,
Rot inwardly, and foul contagion spread;
Besides what the grim wolf with privy paw
Daily devours apace, and nothing said;
But that two-handed engine at the door   130
Stands ready to smite once, and smite no more."
    Return, Alphéus, the dread voice is past
That shrunk thy streams; return, Sicilian Muse,
And call the vales, and bid them hither cast
Their bells and flow'rets of a thousand hues.   135
Ye valleys low where the mild whispers use
Of shades and wanton winds and gushing brooks,
On whose fresh lap the swart star sparely looks,
Throw hither all your quaint enameled eyes,
That on the green turf suck the honied show'rs,   140
And purple all the ground with vernal flow'rs.
Bring the rathe primrose that forsaken dies,
The tufted crowtoe, and pale jessamine,
The white pink, and the pansy freaked with jet,
The glowing violet, ·   145
The musk-rose, and the well-attired woodbine,
With cowslips wan that hang the pensive head,
And every flower that sad embroidery wears.
Bid amaranthus all his beauty shed,
And daffadillies fill their cups with tears,   150
To strew the laureate hearse where Lycid lies.
For so to interpose a little ease,
Let our frail thoughts dally with false surmise;
Ay me! whilst thee the shores and sounding seas
Wash far away, where'er thy bones are hurled,   155
Whether beyond the stormy Hebrides,
Where thou perhaps under the whelming tide

123. flashy: empty, worthless.
124. scrannel: thin and harsh (cf. Virgil, *Ecl.* 3.27).
128. wolf: a traditional term of abuse in anti-Catholic writings (Matt. 7.15; John 10.12–13; Acts 20.29). Puritans especially were disturbed by what they regarded as Romanist tendencies in Laud's Church of England and by recent conversions in the circle of Queen Henrietta, a French Catholic.
129. nothing: 1638, little.
130–31. This, the most notorious crux in Milton, apparently means an instrument of God's justice, whatever further meanings the metaphor includes. Cf. "the axe of God's refor- mation hewing at the old and hollow trunk of papacy" (*Of Reformation touching Church Discipline, Works*, 3, 1, 47) and *P.L.* 6.250–01, 317–23; cf. also Ps. 149.6–9, Matt. 3.10 and 26.31, Luke 3.9.
138. swart star: Sirius, the Dog Star, associated with the parched herbage of late summer.   sparely: seldom.
142–50. Cf. the floral catalogue in Spenser, *April* 38 f.
142. rathe: early.   forsaken: in the shade, out of the sun's reach.
144. freaked: splashed.
157. whelming: 1638, humming.

Visit'st the bottom of the monstrous world;
Or whether thou, to our moist vows denied,
Sleep'st by the fable of Bellerus old,   160
Where the great Vision of the guarded mount
Looks toward Namancos and Bayona's hold:
Look homeward, Angel, now, and melt with ruth;
And, O ye dolphins, waft the hapless youth.
    Weep no more, woeful shepherds, weep no more,   165
For Lycidas, your sorrow, is not dead,
Sunk though he be beneath the wat'ry floor;
So sinks the day-star in the ocean bed,
And yet anon repairs his drooping head,
And tricks his beams, and with new-spangled ore   170
Flames in the forehead of the morning sky:
So Lycidas sunk low, but mounted high,
Through the dear might of him that walked the waves,
Where, other groves and other streams along,
With nectar pure his oozy locks he laves,   175
And hears the unexpressive nuptial song
In the blest kingdoms meek of joy and love.
There entertain him all the saints above,
In solemn troops and sweet societies
That sing, and singing in their glory move,   180
And wipe the tears for ever from his eyes.
Now, Lycidas, the shepherds weep no more;
Henceforth thou art the Genius of the shore,
In thy large recompense, and shalt be good
To all that wander in that perilous flood.   185
    Thus sang the uncouth swain to th' oaks and rills,
While the still morn went out with sandals gray;
He touched the tender stops of various quills,
With eager thought warbling his Doric lay.
And now the sun had stretched out all the hills,   190
And now was dropped into the western bay;
At last he rose, and twitched his mantle blue:
To-morrow to fresh woods, and pastures new.

                         (1637)

---

158. monstrous: inhabited by monsters.

160. Bellerus: an imaginary giant from whom Land's End (the extremity of Cornwall) might have got its Roman name, Bellerium.

161. mount: St. Michael's Mount, off the Cornish coast.

162. Places on the coast of Spain.   hold: fortress.

163. Angel: St. Michael.   melt with ruth: in Chaucer, *Troilus* 1.582, and Spenser, *F.Q.* 3.7.9.5–7.

164. Dolphins carried to shore the dead body of Melicertes, who became the sea-god Palaemon; the Romans identified him with Portunus, the god of harbors. Cf. the story of Arion.

168. day-star: the sun.

173. Matt. 14.25–26.

176. nuptial song: for "the marriage of the Lamb" (Rev. 19.7–9); cf. the end of the passage from *An Apology for Smectymnuus* quoted earlier in this book.

177. This line was lacking in 1638.

181. Rev. 7.17, 21.4.

183. Genius: see glossary, the note on 164 above, and Virgil, *Ecl.* 5.64–65.

186–93. See the end of the headnote and cf. Virgil, *Ecl.* 10.70–77.

190. Cf. Virgil, *Ecl.* 1.83.

192. twitched: pulled up.

193. Cf. P. Fletcher, *Purple Island* 6.77.6: "To-morrow shall ye feast in pastures new."

Ad Salsillum poetam Romanum aegrotantem
Scazontes

O Musa gressum quae volens trahis claudum,
Vulcanioque tarda gaudes incessu,
Nec sentis illud in loco minus gratum
Quam cum decentes flava Deiope suras
Alternat aureum ante Iunonis lectum,   5
Adesdum et haec s'is verba pauca Salsillo
Refer, Camena nostra cui tantum est cordi,
Quamque ille magnis praetulit immerito divis.
Haec ergo alumnus ille Londini Milto,
Diebus hisce qui suum linquens nidum   10
Polique tractum (pessimus ubi ventorum,
Insanientis impotensque pulmonis
Pernix anhela sub Iove exercet flabra)
Venit feraces Itali soli ad glebas,
Visum superba cognitas urbes fama   15
Virosque doctaeque indolem iuventutis,
Tibi optat idem hic fausta multa, Salsille,
Habitumque fesso corpori penitus sanum;
Cui nunc profunda bilis infestat renes,
Praecordiisque fixa damnosum spirat.   20
Nec id pepercit impia quod tu Romano
Tam cultus ore Lesbium condis melos.
O dulce divum munus, O Salus, Hebes
Germana! Tuque, Phoebe, morborum terror
Pythone caeso, sive tu magis Paean   25
Libenter audis, hic tuus sacerdos est.
Querceta Fauni, vosque rore vinoso
Colles benigni, mitis Euandri sedes,
Siquid salubre vallibus frondet vestris,
Levamen aegro ferte certatim vati.   30
Sic ille caris redditus rursum Musis
Vicina dulci prata mulcebit cantu.
Ipse inter atros emirabitur lucos
Numa, ubi beatum degit otium aeternum,
Suam reclivis semper Aegeriam spectans;   35
Tumidusque et ipse Tibris hinc delinitus
Spei favebit annuae colonorum;
Nec in sepulcris ibit obsessum reges,
Nimium sinistro laxus irruens loro;
Sed frena melius temperabit undarum,   40
Adusque curvi salsa regna Portumni.

(1638)

TO SALZILLI, THE ROMAN POET, WHEN HE WAS ILL

Scazons

THIS POEM was apparently written during the first of Milton's two sojourns in Rome, in or about November, 1638, as an acknowledgment of the extravagant quatrain in which Salzilli had ranked him above Homer, Virgil, and Tasso (and which was printed in Milton's *Poems* of 1645 along with commendatory pieces from other Italian friends). The poem to Salzilli expresses friendly gratitude and sympathy but bears some obvious marks of manufacture.

O Muse, who willingly drag a halting foot[1] and enjoy Vulcan's slow gait, and do not think it less pleasing in its way than the graceful ankles of fair Dëiope when she dances before Juno's golden couch,[5] come, and carry if you will these few words to Salzilli, who thinks so highly of my verse and ranks it undeservedly above that of the great godlike poets.[8] These lines go to you from that Milton, a nursling of London, who lately left his nest and his tract of the heavens (where the worst[11] of winds, its lungs swelling with wild rage, swiftly drives its furious gusts under the sky), and came to the fruitful soil of Italy to see its proudly famous cities, its men, and the learning and talent of the young. That Milton offers you many good wishes, Salzilli, and sound health for your worn body, whose kidneys suffer from excessive bile[19] which spreads harm from its center in your vitals, and in its wickedness has not spared you, although you, a cultured poet, have poured Lesbian song from Roman lips.[22] O sweet gift of the gods, O Health,[23] sister of Hebe! And you, Phoebus, who in slaying the Python became the foe of diseases — or Paean, if you prefer that name — this man is your priest.[26] Oak-groves of Faunus, and you hills rich in juicy grapes, the seat of mild Evander,[28] if any medicinal plant grows in your valleys, do you vie with one another in bringing aid to the sick poet. Then he, restored to the dear Muses, will gladden the neighboring fields with sweet song. Numa[34] himself will wonder, among the dark groves where, reclining, he spends the blessed leisure of eternity in contemplation of his Egeria. And even swelling Tiber, soothed by his song, will favor the farmers' yearly hope, and will not, with his left rein loose,[39] pour in a flood over kings in their tombs, but will better bridle his waves, as far as the salty realms of curving Portumnus.[41]

1. In the scazontic or choliambic meter a "limping" effect is given by the substitution in the last foot of a spondee or trochee for an iamb.

5. Juno offered the nymph Deiopea to Aeolus if he would send a storm against the Trojan fleet (*Aen.* 1.65–75); the detail in the text may be Milton's invention.

8. See the headnote.

11. Aquilo, the north wind.

19. Glossary: "humors." Black bile caused melancholy.

22. Adapting to Latin the Greek lyric tradition of Alcaeus and Sappho, both natives of Lesbos.

23. Health: a Roman goddess (*Salus*).

26. Apollo is referred to as both the god of healing (in this role he had the epithet of Paean) and the god of poetry.

28. Evander founded a city on the Tiber, where he welcomed Aeneas (*Aen.* 8.51–584).

34. Numa, the second of Rome's legendary kings, was said to learn religious and civil wisdom from the nymph Egeria.

39. The low left bank of the Tiber was especially subject to floods (Horace, *Od.* 1.2.13–20).

41. The name of Portumnus or Portunus, the Roman god of harbors and gates, seems here to suggest both the curving shore and the sea itself, or perhaps the temple which tradition placed at the mouth of the Tiber.

Mansus

Joannes Baptista Mansus, Marchio Villensis, vir ingenii laude, tum literarum studio, nec non et bellica virtute apud Italos clarus in primis est. Ad quem Torquati Tassi Dialogus extat de Amicitia scriptus; erat enim Tassi amicissimus; ab quo etiam inter Campaniae principes celebratur, in illo poemate cui titulus GERUSALEMME CONQUISTATA, lib. 20.

> Fra cavalier magnanimi, è cortesi
> Risplende il Manso . . .

Is authorem Neapoli commorantem summa benevolentia prosecutus est, multaque ei detulit humanitatis officia. Ad hunc itaque hospes ille, antequam ab ea urbe discederet, ut ne ingratum se ostenderet, hoc carmen misit.

Haec quoque, Manse, tuae meditantur carmina laudi
Pierides; tibi, Manse, choro notissime Phoebi,
Quandoquidem ille alium haud aequo est dignatus honore,
Post Galli cineres, et Mecaenatis Hetrusci.
Tu quoque, si nostrae tantum valet aura Camenae,   5
Victrices hederas inter laurosque sedebis.
Te pridem magno felix concordia Tasso
Iunxit, et aeternis inscripsit nomina chartis.
Mox tibi dulciloquum non inscia Musa Marinum
Tradidit; ille tuum dici se gaudet alumnum,   10
Dum canit Assyrios divum prolixus amores,
Mollis et Ausonias stupefecit carmine nymphas.
Ille itidem moriens tibi soli debita vates
Ossa, tibi soli, supremaque vota reliquit.
Nec manes pietas tua cara fefellit amici;   15
Vidimus arridentem operoso ex aere poetam.
Nec satis hoc visum est in utrumque, et nec pia cessant
Officia in tumulo; cupis integros rapere Orco,
Qua potes, atque avidas Parcarum eludere leges:
Amborum genus, et varia sub sorte peractam   20
Describis vitam, moresque, et dona Minervae;
Aemulus illius Mycalen qui natus ad altam
Rettulit Aeolii vitam facundus Homeri.
Ergo ego te, Clius et magni nomine Phoebi,
Manse pater, iubeo longum salvere per aevum,   25
Missus Hyperboreo iuvenis peregrinus ab axe.
Nec tu longinquam bonus aspernabere Musam,
Quae nuper, gelida vix enutrita sub Arcto,
Imprudens Italas ausa est volitare per urbes.
Nos etiam in nostro modulantes flumine cygnos   30
Credimus obscuras noctis sensisse per umbras,
Qua Thamesis late puris argenteus urnis
Oceani glaucos perfundit gurgite crines;
Quin et in has quondam pervenit Tityrus oras.
Sed neque nos genus incultum, nec inutile Phoebo,   35

Qua plaga septeno mundi sulcata Trione
Brumalem patitur longa sub nocte Booten.
Nos etiam colimus Phoebum, nos munera Phoebo,
Flaventes spicas, et lutea mala canistris,
Halantemque crocum (perhibet nisi vana vetustas) 40
Misimus, et lectas Druidum de gente choreas.
(Gens Druides antiqua, sacris operata deorum,
Heroum laudes imitandaque gesta canebant.)
Hinc quoties festo cingunt altaria cantu
Delo in herbosa Graiae de more puellae, 45
Carminibus laetis memorant Corineida Loxo,
Fatidicamque Upin, cum flavicoma Hecaerge,
Nuda Caledonio variatas pectora fuco.
Fortunate senex, ergo quacunque per orbem
Torquati decus et nomen celebrabitur ingens, 50
Claraque perpetui succrescet fama Marini,
Tu quoque in ora frequens venies plausumque virorum,
Et parili carpes iter immortale volatu.
Dicetur tum sponte tuos habitasse penates
Cynthius, et famulas venisse ad limina Musas. 55
At non sponte domum tamen idem et regis adivit
Rura Pheretiadae caelo fugitivus Apollo,
Ille licet magnum Alciden susceperat hospes;
Tantum, ubi clamosos placuit vitare bubulcos,
Nobile mansueti cessit Chironis in antrum, 60
Irriguos inter saltus frondosaque tecta,
Peneium prope rivum: ibi saepe sub ilice nigra,
Ad citharae strepitum, blanda prece victus amici,
Exilii duros lenibat voce labores.
Tum neque ripa suo, barathro nec fixa sub imo 65
Saxa stetere loco; nutat Trachinia rupes,
Nec sentit solitas, immania pondera, silvas;
Emotaeque suis properant de collibus orni,
Mulcenturque novo maculosi carmine lynces.
Diis dilecte senex, te Iupiter aequus oportet 70
Nascentem et miti lustrarit lumine Phoebus,
Atlantisque nepos; neque enim nisi carus ab ortu
Diis superis poterit magno favisse poetae.
Hinc longaeva tibi lento sub flore senectus
Vernat, et Aesonios lucratur vivida fusos, 75
Nondum deciduos servans tibi frontis honores,
Ingeniumque vigens, et adultum mentis acumen.
O mihi si mea sors talem concedat amicum,
Phoebaeos decorasse viros qui tam bene norit,
Si quando indigenas revocabo in carmina reges, 80
Arturumque etiam sub terris bella moventem;
Aut dicam invictae sociali foedere mensae
Magnanimos heroas, et (O modo spiritus adsit)
Frangam Saxonicas Britonum sub Marte phalanges.
Tandem ubi non tacitae permensus tempora vitae, 85

Annorumque satur cineri sua iura relinquam,
Ille mihi lecto madidis astaret ocellis;
Astanti sat erit si dicam "Sim tibi curae";
Ille meos artus liventi morte solutos
Curaret parva componi molliter urna.   90
Forsitan et nostros ducat de marmore vultus,
Nectens aut Paphia myrti aut Parnasside lauri
Fronde comas; at ego secura pace quiescam.
Tum quoque, si qua fides, si praemia certa bonorum,
Ipse ego caelicolum semotus in aethera divum,   95
Quo labor et mens pura vehunt atque ignea virtus,
Secreti haec aliqua mundi de parte videbo
(Quantum fata sinunt), et tota mente serenum
Ridens purpureo suffundar lumine vultus,
Et simul aethereo plaudam mihi laetus Olympo.   100

(1638)

MANSO

In addition to his introductory note to the poem, Milton in his *Second Defence of the English People* (1654) gratefully recalled Manso's hospitality; he also cited his host's parting remark that he would have been still more attentive if Milton had been less outspoken on religious topics (the same reservation was made in Manso's complimentary distich which was printed in Milton's *Poems* of 1645). Since Milton wrote *Mansus* before he left Naples, it must have been done in or about December, 1638. Although in origin a bread-and-butter epistle, it became much more than that, and is indeed one of Milton's two or three best Latin poems. At home Milton had not been acquainted with writers, and such poems as had been published were known only to small circles, so that he had had little external support for his choice of a poetic vocation; but his reception by Italian literary men, and especially courtesies from the friend and benefactor of Tasso and Marino, kindled his aspirations and heightened his confidence. Thus, while paying warm tribute to the venerable patron of letters, he gently punctures Italian complacency with a reminder of the culture and poetry of England, and ends with an impressive personal passage. This — which includes the first statement of his intending to write an Arthurian epic — is not so egotistical as it may sound; it is in one way a continuation of the tribute to Manso as a literary patron and it is also an impersonal vindication of poetry. The form it takes, and its unexpected intensity, have led to the suggestion that Milton had already learned of his friend Diodati's death in England (August, 1638).

John Baptista Manso, Marquis of Villa, is one of the most distinguished men in Italy, for both intellectual eminence and literary interests, and for military prowess also. There is extant a dialogue on friendship which Torquato Tasso addressed to him, for he was a close friend of the poet, who celebrated him among Campanian leaders in the poem called *Jerusalem Conquered*, book 20:

Among high-souled and courteous knights
Manso shines.

When the present author was visiting Naples, the Marquis was extremely kind to him and showed him many gracious attentions. Before he left the city, therefore, the author sent him this poem, that he might not seem ungrateful.

These lines too,[1] Manso, the Pierides are meditating in your praise, for you, Manso, who are widely known to Phoebus' choir because, since the death of Gallus and Etruscan Maecenas,[4] on no one else has the god bestowed equal honor. You also, if the breath of my Muse has the power, shall sit among victorious ivy and laurels.[6]

You in the past were linked with the great Tasso in a happy friendship which has written your names in enduring records. Soon afterward the Muse, well knowing what she did, entrusted to you the sweet-voiced Marino.[9] He was proud to be called your disciple when he wrote his copious poem on the Assyrian loves of the gods[11] and with his soft verse entranced Ausonian girls. So when he died the poet, conscious of his debt, left his body to you alone, and to you alone his last wishes. And his shade has not been deceived by your loyal devotion, for we have seen the poet smiling from his sculptured bronze.[16] But this service did not seem enough for either poet, and your pious offices did not end at the tomb. For, so far as you could, you desired to preserve them from Orcus unharmed and evade the greedy laws of the Fates; so you set forth their family history, the varying fortunes of their lives, their characters, and their gifts from Minerva.[21] Thus you rival the man born near lofty Mycale who wrote the eloquent life of Aeolian Homer.[23] Therefore, father Manso, in the name of Clio and of great Phoebus, I, a young traveler come from Hyperborean skies, wish you health and long life. And you in your courtesy will not scorn a distant Muse, who, though meagerly nourished under the cold Bear,[28] has lately been rash enough to wing her way through Italian cities.[29] I believe that in the darkness of night I too have heard swans singing on my river, where the silver Thames with pure urns wets her blue-gray locks in the wide swell of the sea.[33] Indeed, long ago Tityrus arrived at these shores.[34]

For we are no uncultivated race worthless to Phoebus, we who pass our long nights under wintry Bootes in that part of the world furrowed by the sevenfold Wain. We too are worshipers of Phoebus, and — unless antiquity reports falsely — we have sent him our gifts, golden spikes of grain, baskets of yellow apples, the fragrant crocus, and choirs chosen from Druid stock. The Druids, an ancient race, skilled in service of the gods, used to sing the praises of heroes and deeds worthy of emulation.[43] Hence, as often as Greek girls in grassy Delos circle their altars with

1. Manso had received many poetic tributes.
4. Gallus: the poet and friend of Virgil (*Ecl.* 10). Maecenas: the patron of Horace, Virgil, and others, whose name has long been a symbol for patronage. His Etruscan descent was referred to by Horace and Propertius.
6. This line is almost identical with line 102 of *Ad Patrem*.
9. Giambattista Marino (1569–1625) was addicted to conceits which have made Marinism a critical term.
11. Marino's prolix *L'Adone* (1623) treated the love of Venus (Semitic Astarte; Assyrian Ishtar) and Adonis (Babylonian Thammuz).
16. Marino's monument at Naples.
21. Manso wrote a life of Tasso, published in part in 1621; his manuscript life of Marino has been lost.
23. Herodotus (whose birthplace, Halicarnassus in Asia Minor, was not very near Mycale) is not now credited with the life of Homer. Western Asia Minor was settled by Aeolian Greeks.

28. For Milton's consciousness of climatic influence, cf. *P.L.* 9.44–45.
28. Bear: see glossary, "Callisto," "Bootes."
29. Milton had shown poems to Italian friends and been invited to read in public (cf. *Epitaphium Damonis* 125 f.).
33. The reference to English poets ("swans") doubtless includes Shakespeare and Jonson, to whom Milton had already paid tribute, and Spenser and others. The association of personified rivers with urns was a classical commonplace.
34. An allusion to Chaucer's visits to Italy. In the *Shepherd's Calendar* (*February* 92, *June* 81, *December* 4) Spenser had used the Virgilian "Tityrus" for Chaucer.
43. The Druids were described by Julius Caesar (*Gallic War* 6.14) and William Camden (*Britain*, tr. P. Holland, 1610, p. 4) as both priests and bards. This line is almost identical with line 46 of *Ad Patrem*.

festal chant in the traditional way, their joyful songs commemorate Loxo, daughter of Corineus,[46] prophetic Upis, and golden-haired Hecaërge, damsels whose bare breasts were colored with Caledonian dye.[48]

Fortunate old man![49] For wherever through the world the glory and great name of Tasso shall be honored, and wherever the lustrous fame of immortal Marino shall spread, your name and praise also shall be often on men's lips, and you on equal wing shall share the way to immortality. Then it will be said that Cynthius[55] was a voluntary guest in your house, and that the Muses came as servants to your door. For it was not willingly that Apollo, when he was an exile from heaven, came to the home and fields of King Pheretiades,[57] although the king had been the host of great Alcides. Only, when he wished to escape from the noisy ploughmen, he sought refuge in the famous cave of gentle Chiron, among the well-watered glades and leafy shelters beside the river Peneus. There under the dark oak, yielding to his friend's persuasive urging, he would often, to the sound of the lyre, relieve the hard labors of his exile with song. Then neither the bank of the stream nor the rocks fixed in the lowest abyss remained in their places; the Trachinian cliff[66] swayed and no longer felt the huge weight of its accustomed woods; the ash-trees, dislodged, hastened from their hills, and the spotted lynxes were tamed by the wondrous song.[69]

Old man beloved by the gods, when you were born kindly Jupiter and Phoebus and the grandson of Atlas[72] must have shed their gracious light upon you, for no one, unless from birth he was dear to the gods, could have befriended a great poet. Hence your old age is green with lingering blossoms and gains the vigor of Aesonian spindles;[75] your brow still preserves its honors unfallen,[76] and your spirit is strong, your ripe mind acute. O if my fate would grant to me such a friend, who knows well how to honor the votaries of Phoebus — if ever I shall call back into verse our native kings, and Arthur waging wars even under the earth,[81] or shall tell of the great-hearted heroes united in the invincible fellowship of the table;[82] and — if only inspiration be with me — I shall break the Saxon battalions under British arms! And when at last I have measured the term of a not silent life and, full of years, I pay my debt to death, if that friend might stand with moist eyes beside my bed, I should be content if I might say to him as he stood there, "Let me be your care." He would see to it that my limbs, loosened by gray death, were gently laid to rest in a small urn. And perhaps he would carve my face in marble, binding my hair with leaves of Paphian myrtle or Parnassian laurel, and I should lie in perfect peace. Then too, if faith has meaning, if rewards are assured for the good, I myself, carried away to the home of the heavenly gods to which labor and a pure mind and ardent virtue

46. Corineus: one of the followers of the legendary Trojan Brute when he came to Britain (Geoffrey of Monmouth, 1.12 f.).

48. The idea of British Druidesses going to Delos with offerings for Apollo and Artemis is developed from concrete hints in Herodotus (4.35), Callimachus' *Hymn to Delos*, etc.

49. The phrase is from Virgil, *Ecl.* 1.46.

55. Cynthius: an epithet for Apollo (from Mount Cynthus on the island of Delos, where he was born).

57. When Apollo killed the Cyclopes (in reprisal for Zeus's killing of Apollo's son Aesculapius), he was punished by being sent to be herdsman to King Admetus (Pheretiades: son of Pheres). The point of 56–69 is that Manso had befriended Tasso and Marino as Admetus and Chiron had entertained Apollo.

66. Trachinian cliff: Mount Oeta in Thessaly, near the town of Trachis.

69. Apollo as musician and singer is given powers like those of Orpheus.

72. grandson of Atlas: Mercury.

75. spindles. The condensed phrase means that Manso, with his youth renewed like that of Aeson (see glossary), cheated the Fates who spin human destinies.

76. Milton took the aged Manso's abundant hair to be his own. Masson remarked that "the old nobleman's wig was a good one, and he had worn it carefully when he and Milton were together."

81. In tradition Arthur was alive in the other world and destined to return to rule over the Britons. On 80–84, see the headnote.

82. table: the Round Table.

lead, shall see these things, as far as the fates allow, from some part of that secret world, and, with my mind wholly serene and my smiling face suffused with rosy light, I shall in joy know myself blessed in ethereal Olympus.[100]

100. Olympus: heaven.

Ad Leonoram Romae canentem

Angelus unicuique suus (sic credite gentes)
   Obtigit aethereis ales ab ordinibus.
Quid mirum, Leonora, tibi si gloria maior?
   Nam tua praesentem vox sonat ipsa Deum.
Aut Deus, aut vacui certe mens tertia coeli,   5
   Per tua secreto guttura serpit agens;
Serpit agens, facilisque docet mortalia corda
   Sensim immortali assuescere posse sono.
Quod si cuncta quidem Deus est, per cunctaque fusus,
   In te una loquitur, cetera mutus habet.   10

(1638–39)

TO LEONORA SINGING AT ROME

DURING his Italian tour Milton had two sojourns in Rome in 1638–39; we do not know which one gave him the opportunity to hear the famous Leonora Baroni sing. His three epigrams do not fall short of her countrymen's praises in a volume of *Applausi* got out in 1639; and the first one, if its religious parallels seem rather bold for an earnest Christian, is typical of Milton's linking music with divine beauty and order.

To everyone — so believe, nations — a winged angel from the heavenly ranks gives protection.[2] What wonder, Leonora, if you have greater glory? For your voice declares God's own presence. Either God or at least the third mind,[5] quitting heaven, moves with secret power in your throat — moves with power, and graciously teaches mortal hearts how they can insensibly become accustomed to immortal sounds. But, if God is all things and interpenetrates all,[9] in you alone he speaks, and in silence holds all else.

2. Belief in a guardian angel was a traditional element of Christianity.

5. Since elsewhere in the epigram Milton clearly is thinking of the Christian God, he must here be surely referring to the third person of the Trinity, the Holy Ghost. Cf. 2 Cor. 12.2 and 4, 1 John 5.7; and *Comus* 244 f.

9. This is not pantheism but an allusion, in somewhat unguarded language, to the orthodox belief in God's omnipresence. E.g., cf. Du Bartas' Protestant and ultra-orthodox epic of creation, in Sylvester, 1.3.808: "I find God everywhere"; and 828–29: "Th' Almighty voice, which built this mighty ball, Still, still rebounds and echoes over all."

Ad eandem

Altera Torquatum cepit Leonora poetam,
  Cuius ab insano cessit amore furens.
Ah miser ille tuo quanto felicius aevo
  Perditus, et propter te, Leonora, foret!
Et te Pieria sensisset voce canentem   5
  Aurea maternae fila movere lyrae,
Quamvis Dircaeo torsisset lumina Pentheo
  Saevior, aut totus desipuisset iners,
Tu tamen errantes caeca vertigine sensus
  Voce eadem poteras composuisse tua;   10
Et poteras aegro spirans sub corde quietem
  Flexanimo cantu restituisse sibi.

(1638–39)

TO THE SAME

Another Leonora enchanted the poet Torquato,[1] who went mad through passionate love for her. Ah, wretched man, how much more happily he might have been destroyed, Leonora, in your time and for your sake! He would have heard you singing with Pierian voice as you touched the golden strings of your mother's lyre![6] Even if his eyes had rolled more wildly than those of Dircean Pentheus,[7] or if his mind had completely collapsed, yet you with your voice could have set right his faculties wandering in blind disorder; and, breathing peace into his sick heart, you could with your soul-animating song have restored him to himself.

1. The name of Torquato Tasso (1544–95) was connected with several Leonoras, chiefly Leonora d'Este, the sister of his patron, the Duke of Ferrara; but his recurrent insanity had other and more substantial causes.

6. Leonora's mother was a musician.
7. The king of Thebes, who opposed the Dionysian rites and was torn to pieces by the maddened Bacchantes.

Ad eandem

Credula quid liquidam Sirena, Neapoli, iactas,
  Claraque Parthenopes fana Acheloiados,
Litoreamque tua defunctam Naiada ripa
  Corpora Chalcidico sacra dedisse rogo?
Illa quidem vivitque, et amoena Tibridis unda   5
  Mutavit rauci murmura Pausilipi.
Illic Romulidum studiis ornate secundis,
  Atque homines cantu detinet atque deos.

(1638–39)

TO THE SAME

Why, credulous Naples, do you boast of your clear-voiced Siren and the famous shrine of Parthenope, Achelous' daughter, of the naiad of the shore who died on your coast and whose sacred body was burned on a Chalcidian pyre?[4] She still lives, and has exchanged the noises of hoarse Pausilipus[6] for the pleasant waves of the Tiber. There she is honored by the warm applause of the sons of Romulus and holds men and gods spellbound with her song.[8]

4. Since Leonora was born in Naples, Milton (like some poets of the *Applausi*) uses a local myth: that Parthenope, one of the Sirens, had been washed ashore near Naples and been given a tomb there. Her name was the original name of the city.
6. Leonora had left Naples for Rome. The allusion may be to the noise of traffic going through the tunnel under Mount Posilipo or — more logically, in view of the reference to the Tiber — to the sound of waves at the foot of the mountain.
8. Cf. the Sirens, Orpheus, et al.

Epitaphium Damonis

ARGUMENTUM

Thyrsis et Damon, eiusdem viciniae pastores, eadem studia sequuti a pueritia amici erant, ut qui plurimum. Thyrsis, animi causa profectus, peregre de obitu Damonis nuntium accepit. Domum postea reversus, et rem ita esse comperto, se suamque solitudinem hoc carmine deplorat. Damonis autem sub persona hic intelligitur Carolus Deodatus, ex urbe Hetruriae Luca paterno genere oriundus, cetera Anglus; ingenio, doctrina, clarissimisque ceteris virtutibus, dum viveret, iuvenis egregius.

> Himerides nymphae (nam vos et Daphnin et Hylan,
> Et plorata diu meministis fata Bionis),
> Dicite Sicelicum Thamesina per oppida carmen:
> Quas miser effudit voces, quae murmura Thyrsis,
> Et quibus assiduis exercuit antra querelis,   5
> Fluminaque, fontesque vagos, nemorumque recessus,
> Dum sibi praereptum queritur Damona, neque altam
> Luctibus exemit noctem, loca sola pererrans.
> Et iam bis viridi surgebat culmus arista,
> Et totidem flavas numerabant horrea messes,   10
> Ex quo summa dies tulerat Damona sub umbras,
> Nec dum aderat Thyrsis; pastorem scilicet illum
> Dulcis amor Musae Thusca retinebat in urbe.
> Ast ubi mens expleta domum pecorisque relicti
> Cura vocat, simul assueta seditque sub ulmo,   15
> Tum vero amissum, tum denique, sentit amicum,
> Coepit et immensum sic exonerare dolorem:
>   "Ite domum impasti, domino iam non vacat, agni.
> Hei mihi! quae terris, quae dicam numina coelo,
> Postquam te immiti rapuerunt funere, Damon;   20
> Siccine nos linquis, tua sic sine nomine virtus

Ibit, et obscuris numero sociabitur umbris?
At non ille animas virga qui dividit aurea
Ista velit, dignumque tui te ducat in agmen,
Ignavumque procul pecus arceat omne silentum.   25
    "Ite domum impasti, domino iam non vacat, agni.
Quicquid erit, certe, nisi me lupus ante videbit,
Indeplorato non comminuere sepulcro,
Constabitque tuus tibi honos, longumque vigebit
Inter pastores. Illi tibi vota secundo   30
Solvere post Daphnin, post Daphnin dicere laudes
Gaudebunt, dum rura Pales, dum Faunus amabit;
Si quid id est, priscamque fidem coluisse, piumque,
Palladiasque artes, sociumque habuisse canorum.
    "Ite domum impasti, domino iam non vacat, agni.   35
Haec tibi certa manent, tibi erunt haec praemia, Damon.
At mihi quid tandem fiet modo? quis mihi fidus
Haerebit lateri comes, ut tu saepe solebas
Frigoribus duris, et per loca feta pruinis,
Aut rapido sub sole, siti morientibus herbis?   40
Sive opus in magnos fuit eminus ire leones,
Aut avidos terrere lupos praesepibus altis?
Quis fando sopire diem cantuque solebit?
    "Ite domum impasti, domino iam non vacat, agni.
Pectora cui credam? quis me lenire docebit   45
Mordaces curas, quis longam fallere noctem
Dulcibus alloquiis, grato cum sibilat igni
Molle pirum, et nucibus strepitat focus, at malus Auster
Miscet cuncta foris, et desuper intonat ulmo?
    "Ite domum impasti, domino iam non vacat, agni.   50
Aut aestate, dies medio dum vertitur axe,
Cum Pan aesculea somnum capit abditus umbra,
Et repetunt sub aquis sibi nota sedilia nymphae,
Pastoresque latent, stertit sub sepe colonus,
Quis mihi blanditiasque tuas, quis tum mihi risus,   55
Cecropiosque sales referet, cultosque lepores?
    "Ite domum impasti, domino iam non vacat, agni.
At iam solus agros, iam pascua solus oberro,
Sicubi ramosae densantur vallibus umbrae;
Hic serum expecto; supra caput imber et Eurus   60
Triste sonant, fractaeque agitata crepuscula silvae.
    "Ite domum impasti, domino iam non vacat, agni.
Heu quam culta mihi prius arva procacibus herbis
Involvuntur, et ipsa situ seges alta fatiscit!
Innuba neglecto marcescit et uva racemo,   65
Nec myrteta iuvant; ovium quoque taedet, at illae
Moerent, inque suum convertunt ora magistrum.
    "Ite domum impasti, domino iam non vacat, agni.
Tityrus ad corylos vocat, Alphesiboeus ad ornos,
Ad salices Aegon, ad flumina pulcher Amyntas,   70
Hic gelidi fontes, hic illita gramina musco,

Hic Zephyri, hic placidas interstrepit arbutus undas;
Ista canunt surdo, frutices ego nactus abibam.
 "Ite domum impasti, domino iam non vacat, agni.
Mopsus ad haec, nam me redeuntem forte notarat   75
(Et callebat avium linguas, et sidera Mopsus)
'Thyrsi, quid hoc?' dixit, 'quae te coquit improba bilis?
Aut te perdit amor, aut te male fascinat astrum,
Saturni grave saepe fuit pastoribus astrum,
Intimaque obliquo figit praecordia plumbo.'   80
 "Ite domum impasti, domino iam non vacat, agni.
Mirantur nymphae, et 'quid te, Thyrsi, futurum est?
Quid tibi vis?' aiunt, 'non haec solet esse iuventae
Nubila frons, oculique truces, vultusque severi;
Illa choros, lususque leves, et semper amorem   85
Iure petit; bis ille miser qui serus amavit.'
 "Ite domum impasti, domino iam non vacat, agni.
Venit Hyas, Dryopeque, et filia Baucidis Aegle
Docta modos, citharaeque sciens, sed perdita fastu,
Venit Idumanii Chloris vicina fluenti;   90
Nil me blanditiae, nil me solantia verba,
Nil me, si quid adest, movet, aut spes ulla futuri.
 "Ite domum impasti, domino iam non vacat, agni.
Hei mihi quam similes ludunt per prata iuvenci,
Omnes unanimi secum sibi lege sodales,   95
Nec magis hunc alio quisquam secernit amicum
De grege, sic densi veniunt ad pabula thoes,
Inque vicem hirsuti paribus iunguntur onagri;
Lex eadem pelagi, deserto in litore Proteus
Agmina phocarum numerat, vilisque volucrum   100
Passer habet semper quicum sit, et omnia circum
Farra libens volitet, sero sua tecta revisens;
Quem si sors letho obiecit, seu milvus adunco
Fata tulit rostro, seu stravit arundine fossor,
Protinus ille alium socio petit inde volatu.   105
Nos durum genus, et diris exercita fatis
Gens, homines, aliena animis, et pectore discors;
Vix sibi quisque parem de millibus invenit unum;
Aut, si sors dederit tandem non aspera votis,
Illum inopina dies, qua non speraveris hora,   110
Surripit, aeternum linquens in saecula damnum.
 "Ite domum impasti, domino iam non vacat, agni.
Heu quis me ignotas traxit vagus error in oras
Ire per aereas rupes, Alpemque nivosam!
Ecquid erat tanti Romam vidisse sepultam   115
(Quamvis illa foret, qualem dum viseret olim
Tityrus ipse suas et oves et rura reliquit),
Ut te tam dulci possem caruisse sodale,
Possem tot maria alta, tot interponere montes,
Tot silvas, tot saxa tibi, fluviosque sonantes?   120
Ah! certe extremum licuisset tangere dextram,

Et bene compositos placide morientis ocellos,
Et dixisse 'Vale! nostri memor ibis ad astra.'
    "Ite domum impasti, domino iam non vacat, agni.
Quamquam etiam vestri nunquam meminisse pigebit,   125
Pastores Thusci, Musis operata iuventus,
Hic Charis, atque Lepos; et Thuscus tu quoque Damon,
Antiqua genus unde petis Lucumonis ab urbe.
O ego quantus eram, gelidi cum stratus ad Arni
Murmura, populeumque nemus, qua mollior herba,   130
Carpere nunc violas, nunc summas carpere myrtos,
Et potui Lycidae certantem audire Menalcam.
Ipse etiam tentare ausus sum, nec puto multum
Displicui; nam sunt et apud me munera vestra,
Fiscellae, calathique, et cerea vincla cicutae: 135
Quin et nostra suas docuerunt nomina fagos
Et Datis et Francinus; erant et vocibus ambo
Et studiis noti, Lydorum sanguinis ambo.
    "Ite domum impasti, domino iam non vacat, agni.
Haec mihi tum laeto dictabat roscida luna,   140
Dum solus teneros claudebam cratibus hoedos.
Ah quoties dixi, cum te cinis ater habebat,
'Nunc canit, aut lepori nunc tendit retia Damon,
Vimina nunc texit, varios sibi quod sit in usus';
Et quae tum facili sperabam mente futura   145
Arripui voto levis, et praesentia finxi,
'Heus, bone, numquid agis? nisi te quid forte retardat,
Imus? et arguta paulum recubamus in umbra,
Aut ad aquas Colni, aut ubi iugera Cassibelauni?
Tu mihi percurres medicos, tua gramina, succos,   150
Helleborumque, humilesque crocos, foliumque hyacinthi,
Quasque habet ista palus herbas, artesque medentum.'
Ah pereant herbae, pereant artesque medentum,
Gramina, postquam ipsi nil profecere magistro.
Ipse etiam, nam nescio quid mihi grande sonabat   155
Fistula, ab undecima iam lux est altera nocte,
Et tum forte novis admoram labra cicutis:
Dissiluere tamen rupta compage, nec ultra
Ferre graves potuere sonos: dubito quoque ne sim
Turgidulus; tamen et referam; vos cedite, silvae.   160
    "Ite domum impasti, domino iam non vacat, agni.
Ipse ego Dardanias Rutupina per aequora puppes
Dicam, et Pandrasidos regnum vetus Inogeniae,
Brennumque Arviragumque duces, priscumque Belinum,
Et tandem Armoricos Britonum sub lege colonos;   165
Tum gravidam Arturo fatali fraude Iogernen,
Mendaces vultus, assumptaque Gorlois arma,
Merlini dolus. O mihi tum si vita supersit,
Tu procul annosa pendebis, fistula, pinu
Multum oblita mihi, aut patriis mutata Camenis   170
Brittonicum strides, quid enim? omnia non licet uni,

Non sperasse uni licet omnia; mi satis ampla
Merces, et mihi grande decus (sim ignotus in aevum
Tum licet, externo penitusque inglorius orbi)
Si me flava comas legat Usa, et potor Alauni,   175
Vorticibusque frequens Abra, et nemus omne Treantae,
Et Thamesis meus ante omnes, et fusca metallis
Tamara, et extremis me discant Orcades undis.
   "Ite domum impasti, domino iam non vacat, agni.
Haec tibi servabam lenta sub cortice lauri,   180
Haec, et plura simul; tum quae mihi pocula Mansus,
Mansus, Chalcidicae non ultima gloria ripae,
Bina dedit, mirum artis opus, mirandus et ipse,
Et circum gemino caelaverat argumento:
In medio rubri maris unda, et odoriferum ver,   185
Litora longa Arabum, et sudantes balsama silvae;
Has inter Phoenix, divina avis, unica terris,
Caeruleum fulgens diversicoloribus alis,
Auroram vitreis surgentem respicit undis;
Parte alia polus omnipatens, et magnus Olympus: 190
Quis putet? hic quoque Amor, pictaeque in nube pharetrae,
Arma corusca, faces, et spicula tincta pyropo;
Nec tenues animas, pectusque ignobile vulgi
Hinc ferit; at, circum flammantia lumina torquens,
Semper in erectum spargit sua tela per orbes   195
Impiger, et pronos nunquam collimat ad ictus:
Hinc mentes ardere sacrae, formaeque deorum.
   "Tu quoque in his, nec me fallit spes lubrica, Damon,
Tu quoque in his certe es; nam quo tua dulcis abiret
Sanctaque simplicitas, nam quo tua candida virtus?   200
Nec te Lethaeo fas quaesivisse sub Orco;
Nec tibi conveniunt lacrimae, nec flebimus ultra.
Ite procul, lacrimae; purum colit aethera Damon,
Aethera purus habet, pluvium pede reppulit arcum;
Heroumque animas inter, divosque perennes,   205
Aethereos haurit latices et gaudia potat
Ore sacro. Quin tu, coeli post iura recepta,
Dexter ades, placidusque fave, quicunque vocaris;
Seu tu noster eris Damon, sive aequior audis
Diodotus, quo te divino nomine cuncti   210
Coelicolae norint, silvisque vocabere Damon.
Quod tibi purpureus pudor, et sine labe iuventus
Grata fuit, quod nulla tori libata voluptas,
En etiam tibi virginei servantur honores!
Ipse caput nitidum cinctus rutilante corona,   215
Laetaque frondentis gestans umbracula palmae
Aeternum perages immortales hymenaeos,
Cantus ubi, choreisque furit lyra mista beatis,
Festa Sionaeo bacchantur et orgia thyrso."

                             (1639–40)

ELEGY FOR DAMON

As MILTON SAYS in his prefatory note, he had learned, while in Italy, of the death in England (August, 1638) of his one close friend, Charles Diodati. After leaving Oxford in 1629, Diodati had for a time studied theology at Geneva and then turned to his father's profession, medicine, which he was practising when he died. Milton returned to England about August 1, 1639, and soon settled in London and began to take private pupils. The elegy was apparently written late in 1639 or early in 1640 and was privately printed in 1640 or later. Milton used not only the conventions of the pastoral elegy but Latin, the language of his earlier letters to Diodati in verse and prose. In some features, for example the refrain, he imitated the ancient Greek elegists whom he invoked in his opening lines. He probably knew Castiglione's Latin elegy *Alcon*. Milton's poem has some concrete and very moving passages, especially on old companionship and present loneliness, but the elegy as a whole, though commonly placed at the head of his Latin poems, may be thought an imperfect success. Unlike most pastoral elegies, it is wholly concerned with the feelings of a single mourner, the poet; and yet, in spite of or because of his very real grief, Milton is unwontedly diffuse and seems to pad the poem with pastoral artifice which is seldom re-created with anything like the power and intensity of *Lycidas*.

Thyrsis and Damon, shepherds of the same countryside, from childhood shared the same pursuits and were united in the closest friendship. Thyrsis, while seeking improvement abroad, heard news of Damon's death. When he returned home and found that it was true, he mourned for himself and his loneliness in this poem. "Damon" represents Charles Diodati, whose father's family belonged to the Tuscan city of Lucca but who himself was in all other respects an Englishman; while his short life lasted, he was distinguished in mind, in learning, and in all notable virtues.

Nymphs of Himera,[1] since you remember Daphnis[1] and Hylas and the long-lamented fate of Bion,[2] sing a Sicilian elegy through the cities of the Thames — the words and sighs that sorrowing Thyrsis[4] uttered, the unceasing complaints that he poured out to caves and rivers and winding brooks and the recesses of the woods, as he bewailed the untimely loss of Damon.[7] The deep night also witnessed his grief, as he wandered through lonely ways. Twice already had the stalk grown up with its green ear, and twice had the barns stored their yellow harvest, since that fatal day which carried Damon to the shades.[11] And Thyrsis was not by his side, because love of the sweet Muse held that shepherd in a Tuscan city.[13] But when his mind had its fill of study, and the care of the flock left behind called him home, he sat down under the accustomed elm and then indeed he realized that his friend was gone. And thus he sought by utterance to lighten the heavy weight of his sorrow:

1. Himera: a Sicilian river. The nymphs are the Muses of Sicilian or Greek pastoral elegy.   Daphnis: the dead shepherd of Theocritus' first *Idyll*, the fountain-head of pastoral elegy.

2. Bion: the author of the *Lament for Adonis* who was himself commemorated in the *Lament for Bion* that goes under the name of Moschus, the first pastoral elegy on a dead poet conceived as a shepherd.

4. Thyrsis. Milton gives himself the name of the shepherd who mourns for Daphnis in Theocritus, *Id.* 1.

7. Damon. The name Milton uses for Diodati is common in pastoral literature; he may also have thought of the famous friendship of Damon and Pythias.

11. Two autumn harvests have passed since Diodati's death (August, 1638); see the headnote.   shades. Pagan references to death, here and later, are repudiated before the poem ends.   13. city: Florence.

"*Go home unfed, my lambs, your master has no time for you now.*[18] Ah me, what powers on earth or in heaven shall I appeal to, since they have swept you away, Damon, to cruel death? And will you leave me thus? Is such a man to sink into oblivion and be added to the crowd of nameless shades? But that he[23] would not wish who marshals souls with his golden wand; he would lead you into a company worthy of you and would keep far off the whole ignoble herd of the silent dead.

"*Go home unfed, my lambs, your master has no time for you now.* Whatever may happen, assuredly — unless a wolf's eye first strike me dumb[27] — you shall not crumble in the grave unwept. Your fair fame shall stand fast and long shall flourish among the shepherds. To you, next after Daphnis,[31] they shall pay their vows; next after Daphnis', they shall rejoice to sing your praises, so long as Pales and Faunus shall love the fields — if it means anything to have been true to ancient faith and piety, to know the arts of Pallas, and to have had a poet for your friend.

"*Go home unfed, my lambs, your master has no time for you now.* For you, Damon, these rewards cannot fail; they shall be yours. But what now is to become of me? What faithful comrade will be always at my side, as you used to be when cold was biting and the fields were in the grip of frost, or when under the hot sun green things were dying of thirst, whether it was our task to face great lions or frighten hungry wolves from the high sheepfolds? Who now will lull the day to rest with conversation and song?

"*Go home unfed, my lambs, your master has no time for you now.* Whom shall I confide in? Who will help me to soothe devouring cares, or to beguile the long night with delightful talk, while the ripe pear hisses by the cheerful fire, and nuts crack open on the hearth, and the wicked south wind makes hurly-burly outdoors and the elm-tops groan?

"*Go home unfed, my lambs, your master has no time for you now.* Or in summer, when the sun is in mid-career, when Pan is asleep in the shade of the oak and the nymphs seek their haunts in the depths of the water, when shepherds take their ease and the ploughman snores under the hedge, who then will bring back to me your charm, your laughter and Cecropian salt,[56] your urbane humor?

"*Go home unfed, my lambs, your master has no time for you now.* But now alone I wander through the fields, alone through the pastures; where branches deepen the shadows in the valleys, there I wait for evening. Over my head rain and the east wind make a moaning sound, and the forest twilight is shaken by the swaying trees.

"*Go home unfed, my lambs, your master has no time for you now.* Alas, how my once well-tilled fields are overgrown with shameless weeds, and the tall grain splits open with mold. Unwedded to the tree, the neglected grapevine droops, and the myrtles afford no pleasure. I am weary even of my sheep, and they turn sad eyes upon their master.

"*Go home unfed, my lambs, your master has no time for you now.* Tityrus[69] calls me to the hazels, Alphesiboeus to the ash trees, Aegon to the willows, fair Amyntas

18. The words of the refrain are modeled on line 44 in Virgil, *Ecl.* 7. Milton uses the refrain 17 times; it occurs 19 times in Theocritus, *Id.* 1.

23. he: Hermes, Mercury.

27. Superstition said that a man became dumb if he was seen by a wolf before he saw it (Virgil, *Ecl.* 9.53–54).

31. next after Daphnis. Milton is setting

himself, as poet, below Theocritus.

56. Cecropian salt: Attic salt, i.e. wit (from Cecrops, the first king of Athens).

69–90. The pastoral convention of a procession of mourners is changed to a group of friends who come to divert or comfort Thyrsis (cf. Virgil, *Ecl.* 10.19 f.). The names are common in pastoral writing.

to the streams. 'Here are cool springs, here is turf soft with moss, here are zephyrs, here the arbutus whispers to the quiet water.' But they sing to deaf ears; I slip away from them into the bushes.

"*Go home unfed, my lambs, your master has no time for you now.* Then came Mopsus — by chance he had seen me returning — Mopsus, who was versed in the language of birds and in the stars. 'Thyrsis, what does this mean?' he said. 'What attack of bile[77] torments you? You are either dying of love or bewitched by an evil star. Saturn's star has often been baneful to shepherds; his glancing leaden shaft pierces the inmost vitals.'[80]

"*Go home unfed, my lambs, your master has no time for you now.* The nymphs are filled with wonder. 'What is to become of you, Thyrsis? What is it you desire?' they say. 'It is not for youth to have a clouded brow, grim eyes, and gloomy face. Youth rightly seeks dances and merry games and always love; twice wretched is he who loves too late.'

"*Go home unfed, my lambs, your master has no time for you now.* Hyas and Dryope came, and Aegle, daughter of Baucis — Aegle, skilled mistress of the harp but spoiled by pride — and Chloris came, from the nearby Idumanian river.[90] But their charms and consolations cannot move me; there is no comfort in the present nor any hope for the future.

"*Go home unfed, my lambs, your master has no time for you now.* Ah me, how like one another are the young steers sporting in the pastures, all companions, of one mind, linked by one law; and no one singles out a particular friend from the herd. So the wolves come in packs to feed, and the shaggy wild asses have mates in turn. The same law holds for the sea; on the deserted shore Proteus numbers his troops of seals. Even the lowest of birds, the sparrow, has always a mate with whom to flit about happily among all the heaps of grain, and returns late to his own nest. And if by chance his mate is carried off by death, whether it comes from the hawk's curved beak or the peasant's arrow, forthwith he seeks another companion for his flights. But we men are a hard race, driven by cruel fates, with minds alien to one another and hearts discordant. Scarcely can you find one friend among thousands; or if destiny, at length yielding to your prayers, has granted one, an unexpected day and hour snatch him away, leaving for ever an irreparable loss.

"*Go home unfed, my lambs, your master has no time for you now.* Alas, what restless impulse sent me traveling to unknown shores, over the towering crags of the snowy Alps?[114] Was it worth so much to have seen buried Rome[115] — or even the ancient city that Tityrus[117] left his sheep and his lands to see — that I could let myself be cut off from so dear a friend, that I could put between us all the deep seas, and mountains and woods and rocks and roaring rivers? O, I might at the end have touched his right hand and closed his eyes at the moment of his quiet death, and have said 'Farewell! remember me as you rise to the stars.'[123]

"*Go home unfed, my lambs, your master has no time for you now.* And yet I shall never weary of your memory, Tuscan shepherds,[126] young men devoted to

---

77. bile. See the note on *To Salzilli* 19.

80. The planet Saturn was associated with cold, wet weather (see glossary also).

90. river: the Chelmer in Essex — the only place-name in the passage, though Chloris, if representing an actual person, remains a ghost.

114. Milton went to Italy by ship from Nice to Genoa; in returning he traveled "by way of Verona, Milan, and the Pennine Alps, and Lake

Leman" to Geneva (*Second Defence*).

115. Rome: i.e. the antiquities.

117. Tityrus: the Tityrus of Virgil's *Ecl.* 1, who saw the Rome of Augustus.

123. Cf. *Mansus* 85–90

126. Other recollections of Milton's Florentine friends appear in the *Second Defence* and in letters.

the Muses, for with you dwell Grace and Charm — and you too, Damon, were a Tuscan and traced your descent from the old city of Lucumo.[128] Ah, how great I felt when I lay beside the cool, murmuring Arno,[129] on the soft grass of a poplar grove, where I could pluck now violets, now shoots of myrtle, and listen to Menalcas and Lycidas contending in song! I too was bold enough to try, and I do not think I greatly displeased you, my hearers, for I have with me your gifts, baskets of reed and wicker and pipes fastened with wax;[135] and Dati and Francini, both renowned poet-scholars and both of Lydian blood, taught their beech trees my name.[138]

"Go home unfed, my lambs, your master has no time for you now. These things the moist moon used to say to me, then when I was happy, while alone I shut the young kids in their folds. Ah, how many times, when you were dark ashes, I said, 'Now Damon is singing, or stretching nets for the hare, now he is weaving reeds together for his various uses.' And all the hopes that my mind freely spun for the future, I lightly changed from wishful fancy into present reality. 'Well, good friend, are you busy? Unless perhaps you have something to do, let us go and lie down for a while in the whispering shade, by the waters of Colne or on the ground Cassivellaunus once held.[149] You shall run over for me your medicinal plants and juices — hellebore, the lowly crocus, the hyacinth leaf, all the herbs that the marsh yields — and explain the physicians' arts.'

"Ah, may the herbs and plants perish, and the physicians' arts, since they did not avail for their master! As for me, my pipe was sounding I know not what grand strain — it is now eleven nights and a day since then — perhaps I had set my lips to new pipes. But the fastenings broke, the pipes fell apart and could no longer sustain the noble notes. Though I may reveal some vanity, yet I will tell the tale. Give place, woodlands.[160]

"Go home unfed, my lambs, your master has no time for you now. I am going to tell of Dardanian ships in the Rutupian seas[162] and the ancient kingdom of Inogene, Pandrasus' daughter,[163] and of the chieftains Brennus and Arviragus, and old Belinus,[164] and the Armorican settlers who came at length under British law;[165] then of Igraine's conceiving Arthur through Uther's fateful deception, when by Merlin's guile he assumed the face and arms of Gorlois.[168] And then, my pastoral

---

128. Lucca, the city from which Diodati's forebears came, as Milton says in his prefatory note; he made a point of visiting the city.

129. Arno: the river that runs through Florence (cf. *P.L.* 1.290).

135. The pastoral convention of a singing-match (cf. Theocritus, *Id.* 8, Virgil, *Ecl.* 3, etc.) represents the readings Milton had heard and shared in Florentine academies. The pastoral gifts represent books or poems.

138. Two particular friends, Carlo Dati and Antonio Francini (whose tributes to Milton were printed, with others, in his *Poems* of 1645), are said to be of Lydian descent because Tuscany was settled by Lydian emigrants from Asia Minor.

149. Colne: a river near Horton. The territory of the British chieftain, north of the Thames, included Horton and St. Albans.

160. Cf. Virgil, *Ecl.* 10.63. In 155–60 Milton is thinking of the British epic (already referred to in *Manso*) which is outlined in 162 f. His pastoral pipe was inadequate for epic strains; the incoherent phrases reflect a

conflict between poetical pride and modesty.

162. Rutupiae was identified by Camden with Richborough in Kent; the phrase means the strait of Dover, the English Channel.

163. According to Geoffrey of Monmouth (1.3–11), Pandrasus was a king of Greece whose daughter Ignoge or Inogen was married to Brutus (Brute), the Trojan founder of Britain.

164. The legendary Brennus and Belinus, British princes, achieved continental conquests; their taking of Rome was telescoped with the historical capture of Rome (390 B.C.) by the Gauls under a chief named Brennus. Arviragus was a son of King Cymbeline who married the daughter of Claudius Caesar after submitting to Rome, but later revolted.

165. Constantine's colony of British veterans on the west coast of Gaul, now Brittany.

168. King Uther Pendragon was enabled by the magician Merlin to gain access to Igraine in the form of her husband, Gorlois, and begot a son, Arthur.

pipe, if life still remains to me, you shall hang forgotten on an old pine far away; or else, changed, you shall sound forth a British theme in native strains.[171] Indeed, one man cannot do all things, nor even hope to do all. For me it would be ample reward and great honor — though I remain unknown and inglorious throughout the rest of the world — if only fair-haired Ouse[175] should read me, and he who drinks of the Alne,[175] and the Humber[176] with its many whirlpools, and every forest by the Trent,[176] and before all my Thames, and the mineral-darkened Tamar,[178] and if the Orkneys far out in the sea should learn my song.

"*Go home unfed, my lambs, your master has no time for you now.* These things I was keeping for you in the pliant bark of the laurel,[180] these and more besides. I was saving the two cups[181] that Manso gave me, Manso, not the least glory of the Chalcidian shore; they are works of marvelous art, and the giver himself is a marvel. Around the cups runs an engraving with a double theme. In the middle are the waves of the Red Sea,[185] and fragrant spring, the long shores of Arabia, and woods exuding balsam. Among the trees the phoenix,[187] that divine bird unique on earth, gleams blue with many-colored wings, and watches Aurora rise over the shimmering water. In another place are the vast expanse of sky and great Olympus. Here also — who would believe it? — is Love, with his quiver painted against a cloud, his flashing arms, his torches, his darts tinged wth fiery bronze. From this height he does not attack frivolous spirits and the vulgar hearts of the crowd, but, casting around his burning eyes, he sends his darts in a ceaseless shower up through the spheres and never aims a downward shot. Hence he kindles only sanctified minds and the souls of the gods.[197]

"You also, Damon, are among these — for no vain hope deceives me — you also are assuredly one of them; for where else should go your sweet and pure simplicity, your shining virtues? It would be sin to look for you in the Lethean underworld. Nothing is here for tears, and I will weep no more. Away, my tears! In the pure ether pure Damon dwells, and spurns the rainbow with his foot. Among the souls of heroes and the immortal gods, he drains ethereal draughts and drinks joy with holy lips. And now, since you have been granted the rights of heaven, stand by my side and gently favor me, by whatever name you are called.[208] Whether you are to be my Damon or prefer to be Diodati (by that divine name, 'God-given,' you will be known to all the heavenly host), in the woods you will still be Damon. Because maiden modesty was dear to you, and spotless youth, because you did not taste the pleasures of marriage, see, for you are reserved virginal honors.[214] Your

---

171. In 168–78 Milton looks forward to laying aside pastoral verse and writing an epic in English, even though that will restrict his audience to Britain.

175. Ouse: glossary. There was an Alne river in both Northumberland and Hampshire.

176. The Latin Abra probably means the Humber. The Trent rises in Staffordshire and joins the Ouse to form the Humber.

178. The Tamar flows between Devon and Cornwall, through a mining region.

180. Milton probably means written in laurel bark (cf. Virgil, *Ecl.* 5.13–14).

181. The cups presented by Manso may be actual cups or, more probably, are used as conventional pastoral gifts which here stand for books, perhaps two written by Manso. At any rate the presents gave Milton hints for the symbolic development of Christian and Platonic parallels and contrasts between earthly and

heavenly life and love. The pattern on the bowl in Theocritus, *Id.* 1, has to do with earth only.

185. Red Sea. Milton apparently used the name in the ancient sense for the Arabian and Persian Gulfs, the Indian Ocean.

187. phoenix: glossary.

197. Cupid here is not the blind, irresponsible bow-boy of romantic or sensual love but a symbol of Platonic and Christian love in angelic natures.

208. Damon is presented in classical terms as a deified mortal who can — like a Catholic saint — help people on earth (cf. *Lycidas* 182–85).

214. virginal honors. See Rev. 14.1–4 and the end of the extract from Milton's *Apology for Smectymnuus* (quoted at the end of the general introduction).

radiant head shall be bound with a glittering crown and, with shadowing branches of the joyous palm in your hands, you shall for ever enact the immortal marriage, where hymns[218] and the ecstatic sound of the lyre mingle with the choric dances of the blessed, and festal throngs revel under the thyrsus of Zion."[219]

(1639–40)

218. hymns: cf. Rev. 7.9–10, 19.6–8.
219. The conclusion is a notable example of the Renaissance fusion of pagan and Christian symbols and ideas. The picture of Damon welcomed into the immortality of heaven is similar to the climax of *Lycidas*, but, however genuine the emotion, the result seems strained and hectic and nowhere near the earlier vision.

TRANSLATIONS FROM

Of Reformation Touching Church Discipline in England (1641)

In the first of his five anti-episcopal tracts Milton translated bits from Dante, Petrarch, and Ariosto, "three the famousest men for wit and learning that Italy at this day glories of," as witnesses "for a received opinion even among men professing the Romish faith, that Constantine marred all in the Church" (*Works*, 3, 1, 26–27; *C.P.W.*, 1, 558–60). The point of the excerpts can be best appreciated in the setting of Milton's prose:

"Dante in his 19. Canto of *Inferno* [115–17] hath thus, as I will render it you in English blank verse:

> Ah Constantine, of how much ill was cause
> Not thy conversion, but those rich domains
> That the first wealthy pope received of thee.

"So in his 20. Canto of *Paradise* [55–60] he makes the like complaint, and Petrarch seconds him in the same mind in his 108. Sonnet which is wiped out by the Inquisitor in some editions; speaking of the Roman Antichrist as merely bred up by Constantine:

> Founded in chaste and humble poverty,
> 'Gainst them that raised thee dost thou lift thy horn,
> Impudent whore, where hast thou placed thy hope?
> In thy adulterers, or thy ill-got wealth?
> Another Constantine comes not in haste.

"Ariosto of Ferrara, after both these in time but equal in fame, following the scope of his poem in a difficult knot how to restore Orlando his chief hero to his lost senses, brings Astolfo the English knight up into the moon, where St. John, as he feigns, met him (canto 34):

> And to be short, at last his guide him brings
> Into a goodly valley, where he sees
> A mighty mass of things strangely confused,
> Things that on earth were lost, or were abused.[1]

[1] These four lines Milton quoted from Sir John Harington's translation (1591), canto 34, stanza 72. The next four lines, from stanza 79, have several verbal echoes of Harington.

"And amongst these so abused things listen what he met withal, under the conduct of the Evangelist:

> Then passed he to a flow'ry mountain green,
> Which once smelt sweet, now stinks as odiously;
> This was that gift (if you the truth will have)
> That Constantine to good Sylvestro gave."

TRANSLATION FROM

The Reason of Church Government (1642)

When I die, let the earth be rolled in flames.[1]

---

[1] A saying of the emperor Tiberius found in various forms in Dio Cassius (58.23.4) and other ancient writers. The phrase is in Milton's *Works*, 3, 1, 202; *C.P.W.*, 1, 770.

TRANSLATIONS FROM

An Apology for Smectymnuus (1642)

In his fifth and last anti-episcopal tract, by way of showing "what force of teaching there is sometimes in laughter," Milton translated Horace, *Sat.* 1.1.24–26:

> — laughing to teach the truth
> What hinders? as some teachers give to boys
> Junkets and knacks, that they may learn apace;

and ibid., 1.10.14–15:

> Jesting decides great things
> Stronglier, and better oft than earnest can.

In justifying his hard words about the bishops he appealed to "what Electra in Sophocles, a wise virgin, answered her wicked mother, who thought herself too violently reproved by her the daughter [*Electra*, 624–25]":

> 'Tis you that say it, not I, you do the deeds,
> And your ungodly deeds find me the words.

The two passages are close together in the *Works*, 3, 1, 318–19, and *C.P.W.*, 1, 904–05.

SONNETS AND OTHER VERSE, 1642–1658

SONNETS I and VII and the five Italian sonnets belong to Milton's youth. The seventeen sonnets of 1642–58, the occasional utterances of a period given almost wholly to prose and public affairs, fall into two groups, private and public. Some of the former show Milton's genius for friendship, especially with the young. They are more or less relaxed and genial and sometimes recall Horace's urbane invitations to friends; yet even these may glance at great things and have a massive dignity. The sonnets on public men and events recall the Horace of exalted patriotic odes and the heroic sonnets of such moderns as Tasso. In Milton's hand, as Wordsworth said,

The thing became a trumpet, whence he blew
Soul-animating strains — alas, too few!

Such a devotee of Italian as Milton naturally broke away from the Elizabethan pattern of three quatrains and a couplet and adopted the Italian octave and sestet. But he recreated the form in English, with his eye especially, it appears, on Giovanni della Casa (whose poems he had bought in 1629). He uses run-on lines and strong medial pauses and often disregards normal word-order and a strict division between octave and sestet, so that, in spite of the rhymes — which may be, as in the *Massacre at Piedmont*, notably sonorous and emphatic — the sonnet becomes in effect a paragraph of blank verse. In keeping with his heroic themes, Milton's style is elevated in various ways, but these ways, such as periphrasis, are functional, not inflationary.

Sonnet VIII

THE CIVIL WAR had begun on August 22, 1642. After the battle of Edgehill (October 23), the royalist forces advanced on London, causing great alarm; but they turned back on November 13 in the face of a hastily mustered army. The Cambridge Manuscript recorded two titles (which Milton did not use in print), *On his door when the city expected an assault,* which was cancelled in favor of *When the assault was intended to the city.* The idea of putting the sonnet on his door was only a poetic device. It is a quite impersonal consideration, amidst the violence of war, of the value of poetry, in terms of its "eternizing" power, as ancient and Renaissance poets often wrote of it.

> Captain or colonel, or knight in arms,
>   Whose chance on these defenseless doors may seize,
>   If deed of honor did thee ever please,
>   Guard them, and him within protect from harms;
> He can requite thee, for he knows the charms   5
>   That call fame on such gentle acts as these,
>   And he can spread thy name o'er lands and seas,
>   Whatever clime the sun's bright circle warms.

1. colonel: three syllables.   8. Cf. Horace, *Od.* 4.14.1–6.

Lift not thy spear against the Muses' bow'r:
>The great Emathian conqueror bid spare   10
>The house of Pindarus, when temple and tow'r
Went to the ground; and the repeated air
>Of sad Electra's poet had the power
>To save th' Athenian walls from ruin bare.

(1642)

10. According to tradition, the Macedonian Alexander the Great spared Pindar's house when he razed Thebes in 335 B.C.
12. repeated air: the recital of the air.
12–14. Plutarch (*Lysander*) says that, at the end of the Peloponnesian War (404 B.C.), the victorious Spartans refrained from destroying Athens when one of their officers sang the first chorus of Euripides' *Electra*.

Sonnet IX

THE YOUNG GIRL here addressed is unknown. Among her family and friends she had evidently been regarded as a prig, and the poet gives her religious reassurance. The sonnet was presumably written later than Sonnet 8 (November, 1642) and it was included in the *Poems* of 1645.

Lady that in the prime of earliest youth
>Wisely hast shunned the broad way and the green,
>And with those few art eminently seen
>That labor up the hill of heav'nly Truth,
The better part with Mary and with Ruth   5
>Chosen thou hast; and they that overween,
>And at thy growing virtues fret their spleen,
>No anger find in thee, but pity and ruth.
Thy care is fixed and zealously attends
>To fill thy odorous lamp with deeds of light,   10
>And hope that reaps not shame. Therefore be sure,
Thou, when the Bridegroom with his feastful friends
>Passes to bliss at the mid-hour of night,
>Hast gained thy entrance, virgin wise and pure.

(1642–45)

2–4. The classical image of the difficult ascent of the hill of virtue (Hesiod, *Works and Days*, 287–92; etc.) is combined with the biblical image of the broad path to destruction (Matt. 7.13).
2. green: Job 8.12–13, 16.

5. Mary chose to listen to Jesus rather than join her sister Martha in housework (Luke 10.42). Ruth (Ruth 1) left her home in Moab for the sake of her mother-in-law Naomi.
10–14. Cf. the parable of the wise and foolish virgins (Matt. 25.1–13).

Sonnet X

THE MANUSCRIPT title, not used in print, was *To the Lady Margaret Ley.* Milton's nephew, Edward Phillips, reported in his biography of his uncle that, after Mrs. Milton left him, "Our author, now as it were a single man again, made it his chief diversion now and then in an evening, to visit the Lady Margaret Lee, daughter to the . . . Earl of Marlborough. . . . This lady being a woman of great wit and ingenuity had a particular honor for him, and took much delight in his company, as likewise her husband Captain Hobson, a very accomplished gentleman." The Earl, who had held high posts under King James and King Charles, died in March, 1629, shortly after the violent break-up of the last parliament to be held until 1640. Captain Hobson, who married Lady Margaret in 1641, was in the parliamentary army; they were neighbors of Milton in Aldersgate Street. This sonnet, like earlier ones, was included in the *Poems* of 1645; it was evidently written between the end of 1642 and the end of 1645.

> Daughter to that good Earl, once President
> Of England's Council and her Treasury,
> Who lived in both unstained with gold or fee,
> And left them both, more in himself content,
> Till the sad breaking of that parliament   5
> Broke him, as that dishonest victory
> At Chaeronea, fatal to liberty,
> Killed with report that old man eloquent;
> Though later born than to have known the days
> Wherein your father flourished, yet by you,   10
> Madam, methinks I see him living yet:
> So well your words his noble virtues praise
> That all both judge you to relate them true,
> And to possess them, honored Margaret.
>   (1642–45)

6. dishonest: shameful (cf. Latin *inhonestus*).

8. old man. Isocrates, the Greek teacher of rhetoric, was said to have starved himself to death after Philip of Macedon defeated Athens and Thebes at Chaeronea (338 B.C.) and reduced these city-states to subjection.

FROM THE TITLE PAGE OF

Areopagitica (1644)

> This is true Liberty: when free-born men,
> Having to advise the public, may speak free,
> Which he who can, and will, deserves high praise;
> Who neither can nor will may hold his peace.
> What can be juster in a state than this?
>   Euripides, *Suppliants*, 438–41.

F R O M *Tetrachordon* (1645)

Whom do we count a good man, whom but he
Who keeps the laws and statutes of the Senate,
Who judges in great suits and controversies,
Whose witness and opinion wins the cause?
But his own house and the whole neighborhood
Sees his foul inside through his whited skin.*

* Horace, *Epistles*, 1.16.40–45 (Milton, *Works*, 4, 137; *C.P.W.*, 2, 639).

In Effigiei Eius Sculptorem

'Αμαθεῖ γεγράφθαι χειρὶ τήνδε μὲν εἰκόνα
Φαίης τάχ' ἂν, πρὸς εἶδος αὐτοφυὲς βλέπων·
Τὸν δ' ἐκτυπωτὸν οὐκ ἐπιγνόντες, φίλοι,
Γελᾶτε φαύλου δυσμίμημα ζωγράφου.
(1645)

ON THE ENGRAVER OF HIS PORTRAIT

WHEN FACED with the portrait of himself which was to be the frontispiece of his *Poems* of 1645, and which had been done by William Marshall, the most popular engraver of the day, the handsome Milton, with good reason, did not relish it. He wrote this quatrain which the Greekless Marshall duly inscribed below the portrait. Nemesis in time brought some censure of Milton's Greek and also the complaint that the point of the epigram seems to be rather blunted than sharpened by the last two lines.

Looking at the original, you would perhaps say that this likeness was made by an unskilled hand. Since, friends, you cannot recognize the person represented, laugh at the poor reproduction of a bad artist.

SONNETS XI AND XII

SONNETS 11 and 12 record Milton's feelings about the attacks from Presbyterians — with whom he had allied himself in 1641–42 in writing against prelacy — on the liberal view of divorce that he urged in pamphlets of 1643–45. Like most of the sonnets that follow, they were first printed in the second edition of Milton's *Poems* (1673). In the Cambridge Manuscript (where the two are in reverse order), above "I did but prompt" is the title *On the detraction which followed upon my writing certain treatises*, which may have been intended to cover both. These sonnets were probably written in 1645 or early 1646, since they were numbered and printed between Sonnet 10 (included in the *Poems* of 1645–46) and Sonnet 13 of February 9, 1646. Sonnet 11, with its colloquial style and jocose rhymes, expresses a half-humorous contempt for an age which is puzzled by a Greek title but can swallow the Scottish names that have been made familiar through Scotland's involvement in the civil war. In Sonnet 12 journalistic invective includes a touch of Miltonic sublimity (6–7) and a statement (10–12) of a central Miltonic principle.

Sonnet XI

A book was writ of late called *Tetrachordon,*
   And woven close, both matter, form, and style;
   The subject new: it walked the town a while,
   Numb'ring good intellects; now seldom pored on.
Cries the stall-reader, "Bless us! what a word on   5
   A title-page is this!"; and some in file
   Stand spelling false, while one might walk to Mile-
   End Green. Why is it harder, sirs, than *Gordon,*
Colkitto, or *Macdonnel,* or *Galasp?*
   Those rugged names to our like mouths grow sleek   10
   That would have made Quintilian stare and gasp.
Thy age, like ours, O soul of Sir John Cheke,
   Hated not learning worse than toad or asp,
   When thou taught'st Cambridge and King Edward Greek.
                         (1645–46)

1. *Tetrachordon,* Milton's third tract on divorce, and his fourth, *Colasterion,* were published simultaneously on March 4, 1645. "Tetrachordon," a Greek musical term for a four-tone scale, was used because Milton was expounding, as his title page said, the four chief biblical passages on marriage and divorce.
7. spelling false: misinterpreting.
8. Mile-End Green: at the east end of London.
11. Quintilian (born *c.* 35–40 A.D.), the great Roman authority on rhetoric, reprehended barbarous foreign words (*Instit.* 1.5.8, etc.).
12–14. Cheke's age did not hate Greek, as Milton's does (we would say "unlike"). Sir John Cheke (1514–57) was the first professor of Greek at Cambridge (1540–51) and tutor of Prince, later King, Edward. At the beginning and end of *Tetrachordon* Milton spoke of the reign of Edward VI (1547–53) as the "best and purest," "the purest and sincerest" age of the English Reformation; the latter reference included praise of Cheke's learning and piety.

Sonnet XII

On the Same

I did but prompt the age to quit their clogs
   By the known rules of ancient liberty,
   When straight a barbarous noise environs me
   Of owls and cuckoos, asses, apes, and dogs;
As when those hinds that were transformed to frogs
   Railed at Latona's twin-born progeny,
   Which after held the sun and moon in fee.
But this is got by casting pearl to hogs,
   That bawl for freedom in their senseless mood,
   And still revolt when truth would set them free.   10
   License they mean when they cry liberty;
For who loves that must first be wise and good:
   But from that mark how far they rove we see,
   For all this waste of wealth and loss of blood.
                         (1645–46)

2. known rules: see the note on Sonnet 11.1.
7. fee: full possession. When Latona, with her new-born twins, Apollo and Diana, was fleeing from the wrath of Juno, she approached a lake to get a drink but was driven off by peasants, who were punished by being transformed into frogs (Ovid, *Met.* 6.332–81). The "twin-born progeny" may glance at Milton's twin pamphlets (see Sonnet 11, note 1). Cf. Spenser, *F.Q.* 2.12.13.4–7.

Sonnet XIII

To My Friend Mr. Henry Lawes

HENRY LAWES (1595/96–1662), the distinguished court musician and composer, has been noticed already in connection with *Arcades* and *Comus*. This sonnet, which Milton dated February 9, 1646, was — according to a Manuscript title — written for publication with Lawes's *Airs and Dialogues*. But the first part of this work was not published until 1653 and the sonnet was printed, with the title given above, in Lawes's *Choice Psalms* (1648), a book Lawes courageously dedicated to Charles I, who was then in captivity. Lawes's royalism did not cause any breach of friendship with Milton, and Milton showed courage and magnanimity in allowing his poem to appear along with such a dedication. His tribute emphasized a quality for which Lawes's music was noted, the bringing out of the full expressive power of the words. His compositions included settings for songs by Milton (as the title page of the *Poems* of 1645 indicated) and many other poets, such as Jonson, Herrick, Carew, Lovelace, and Waller.

> Harry, whose tuneful and well-measured song
>   First taught our English music how to span
>   Words with just note and accent, not to scan
>   With Midas' ears, committing short and long,
> Thy worth and skill exempts thee from the throng,   5
>   With praise enough for Envy to look wan;
>   To after age thou shalt be writ the man
>   That with smooth air couldst humor best our tongue.
> Thou honor'st verse, and verse must lend her wing
>   To honor thee, the priest of Phoebus' quire,   10
>   That tun'st their happiest lines in hymn or story.
> Dante shall give Fame leave to set thee higher
>   Than his Casella, whom he wooed to sing,
>   Met in the milder shades of Purgatory.

(1646)

2. span: join, fit (in view of the Elizabethan composers, Lawes could hardly be called the first English musician to fit words and notes together with due regard to accent).

4. King Midas adjudged Pan a better musician than Apollo, who thereupon changed his ears to those of an ass.   committing: forcing together (i.e. short syllables and long notes and vice versa).

10. priest . . . quire: cf. Horace, *Od.* 3.1.3.

11. story. A note in *Choice Psalms* said that the reference was to Lawes's setting for William Cartwright's *Complaint of Ariadne*.

13. Casella. Dante met the Florentine musician on the threshold of Purgatory (*Purg.* 2.76–119). Here, as elsewhere, Milton dignifies persons he admires by linking them with illustrious figures of the past.

On the New Forcers of Conscience
Under the Long Parliament

THIS SPECIMEN of a sonnet with a "tail" or (as here) successive tails — a kind Milton knew from Italian verse — was not included in the numbered series. It was written probably in 1646. In July, 1643 the Westminster Assembly, composed mainly of divines, met under parliamentary auspices to reorganize the church on the Presbyterian model. But five Independent ministers, who wished to carry on with their own congregations, started what turned into a full-scale pamphlet debate on uniformity versus toleration or freedom of conscience. Parliamentary ordinances of 1646 established the Presbyterian system (March 14), authorized the ordination of ministers by "classical" presbyteries within their respective bounds (August 28), and abolished archbishops and bishops (October 9). But the actual results fell far short of Presbyterian hopes. Milton of course is strongly opposed to Presbyterian rigidity and intolerance.

> Because you have thrown off your prelate lord,
>> And with stiff vows renounced his liturgy
>> To seize the widowed whore, Plurality,
>> From them whose sin ye envied, not abhorred,
> Dare ye for this adjure the civil sword   5
>> To force our consciences that Christ set free,
>> And ride us with a classic hierarchy
>> Taught ye by mere A. S. and Rutherford?
> Men whose life, learning, faith, and pure intent
>> Would have been held in high esteem with Paul   10
>> Must now be named and printed heretics
> By shallow Edwards and Scotch what-d'ye-call!
>> But we do hope to find out all your tricks,
>> Your plots and packing, worse than those of Trent,
>>> That so the parliament   15
> May with their wholesome and preventive shears

1. Episcopacy was formally abolished in January, 1643.

2. The Book of Common Prayer was banned in August, 1645.

3. Plurality. Milton sees Presbyterian clergymen, like a number of their Anglican predecessors, as greedily receiving the income from more than one living.

7. The system of presbyteries or regional synods (Latin *classes*) ordered by parliament would be as tyrannical as the episcopal hierarchy had been.

8. A.S.: Adam Stuart or Stewart, a Scottish Presbyterian divine who, in London, wrote actively against the Independents. Samuel Rutherford, a professor of divinity at St. Andrews and one of the four Scottish Commissioners who attended the Westminster Assembly, was another champion of Presbyterianism (one who, in 1649, could argue for a sort of Protestant Inquisition).

8–10. Men like the Independent divines referred to in the headnote.

12. The English Presbyterian Thomas Edwards attacked the Independents' *Apologetical Narration* and the idea of toleration in *Antapologia* (1644); in *Gangraena* (1646) he catalogued and denounced many current "heresies."

12. Scotch what-d'ye-call: Robert Baillie, the bitterest foe of Independency among the Scottish Commissioners.

14. packing: trickery. Trent: the Catholic Council of Trent (1545–63), which was called to combat Protestantism (and which, in *Areopagitica*, Milton saw as the main inventor of censorship).

Clip your phylacteries, though baulk your ears,
                        And succor our just fears,
When they shall read this clearly in your charge:
New Presbyter is but old Priest writ large.   20

(1646?)

17. phylacteries: amulets with Mosaic texts worn by pious Jews and connoting hypocrisy (Matt. 23.5).   baulk: spare. A veiled reference (which in a canceled line had been explicit) to the Presbyterian pamphleteer, William Prynne, who in 1637, for attacking prelacy, had suffered severe punishment, including the loss of what remained of his ears, which had been partly cut off in 1634 because of an alleged reflection on the queen.

20. This famous line rests on an etymological pun, the word "priest" being derived indirectly from the Greek "presbyter" (which means literally "elder"). Milton had said similar things in *Areopagitica*.

Sonnet XIV

THE MANUSCRIPT title is *On the religious memory of Mrs. Catharine Thomason, my Christian friend, deceased December, 1646.* Her husband, George Thomason, a bookseller, earned the gratitude of modern scholars by collecting over 22,000 books, pamphlets, and newspapers of 1640–61 and dating most of them. The sonnet was evidently written in December, 1646.

When Faith and Love, which parted from thee never,
        Had ripened thy just soul to dwell with God,
        Meekly thou didst resign this earthy load
        Of death, called life, which us from life doth sever.
Thy works and alms and all thy good endeavor   5
        Stayed not behind, nor in the grave were trod;
        But, as Faith pointed with her golden rod,
        Followed thee up to joy and bliss for ever.
Love led them on, and Faith, who knew them best
        Thy handmaids, clad them o'er with purple beams   10
        And azure wings, that up they flew so dressed,
And spake the truth of thee in glorious themes
        Before the Judge, who thenceforth bid thee rest
        And drink thy fill of pure immortal streams.

(1646)

2. Gal. 3.11.
4. 2 Cor. 5.1–4.
5. Acts 10.4.

6. Rev. 14.13.
12. MS.: spake . . . in; 1673: speak . . . on.
14. Rev. 22.1 and 17.

Jan. 23. 1646 [i.e. 1647]

Ad Joannem Rousium
Oxoniensis Academiae Bibliothecarium

De libro Poematum amisso, quem ille sibi denuo mitti postulabat, ut cum aliis nostris in Bibliotheca publica reponeret, Ode.

Strophe 1

Gemelle cultu simplici gaudens liber,
Fronde licet gemina,
Munditieque nitens non operosa,
Quam manus attulit
Iuvenilis olim,   5
Sedula, tamen haud nimii poetae;
Dum vagus Ausonias nunc per umbras,
Nunc Britannica per vireta lusit
Insons populi, barbitoque devius
Indulsit patrio, mox itidem pectine Daunio   10
Longinquum intonuit melos
Vicinis, et humum vix tetigit pede;

Antistrophe

Quis te, parve liber, quis te fratribus
Subduxit reliquis dolo,
Cum tu missus ab urbe,   15
Docto iugiter obsecrante amico,
Illustre tendebas iter
Thamesis ad incunabula
Caerulei patris,
Fontes ubi limpidi   20
Aonidum, thyasusque sacer
Orbi notus per immensos
Temporum lapsus redeunte coelo,
Celeberque futurus in aevum?

Strophe 2

Modo quis deus, aut editus deo,   25
Pristinam gentis miseratus indolem
(Si satis noxas luimus priores
Mollique luxu degener otium)
Tollat nefandos civium tumultus,
Almaque revocet studia sanctus   30
Et relegatas sine sede Musas
Iam pene totis finibus Angligenum;
Immundasque volucres
Unguibus imminentes
Figat Apollinea pharetra,   35
Phineamque abigat pestem procul amne Pegaseo?

Antistrophe

Quin tu, libelle, nuntii licet mala
Fide, vel oscitantia,
Semel erraveris agmine fratrum,
Seu quis te teneat specus,   40
Seu qua te latebra, forsan unde vili
Callo tereris institoris insulsi,
Laetare felix, en iterum tibi
Spes nova fulget posse profundam
Fugere Lethen, vehique superam   45
In Iovis aulam remige penna;

Strophe 3

Nam te Rousius sui
Optat peculi, numeroque iusto
Sibi pollicitum queritur abesse,
Rogatque venias ille cuius inclyta   50
Sunt data virum monumenta curae:
Teque adytis etiam sacris
Voluit reponi quibus et ipse praesidet
Aeternorum operum custos fidelis,
Quaestorque gazae nobilioris   55
Quam cui praefuit Ion,
Clarus Erechtheides,
Opulenta dei per templa parentis
Fulvosque tripodas, donaque Delphica,
Ion Actaea genitus Creusa.   60

Antistrophe

Ergo tu visere lucos
Musarum ibis amoenos,
Diamque Phoebi rursus ibis in domum
Oxonia quam valle colit
Delo posthabita,   65
Bifidoque Parnassi iugo:
Ibis honestus,
Postquam egregiam tu quoque sortem
Nactus abis, dextri prece sollicitatus amici.
Illic legeris inter alta nomina   70
Authorum, Graiae simul et Latinae
Antiqua gentis lumina et verum decus.

Epodos

Vos tandem haud vacui mei labores,
Quicquid hoc sterile fudit ingenium,
Iam sero placidam sperare iubeo   75
Perfunctam invidia requiem, sedesque beatas
Quas bonus Hermes
Et tutela dabit solers Rousi,

Quo neque lingua procax vulgi penetrabit, atque longe
Turba legentum prava facesset;   80
At ultimi nepotes,
Et cordatior aetas
Iudicia rebus aequiora forsitan
Adhibebit integro sinu.
Tum livore sepulto,   85
Si quid meremur sana posteritas sciet
Rousio favente.

Ode tribus constat Strophis, totidemque Antistrophis una demum epodo clausis, quas, tametsi omnes nec versuum numero, nec certis ubique colis exacte respondeant, ita tamen secuimus, commode legendi potius, quam ad antiquos concinendi modos rationem spectantes. Alioquin hoc genus rectius fortasse dici monostrophicum debuerat. Metra partim sunt κατὰ σχέσιν, partim ἀπολελυμένα. Phaleucia quae sunt, spondaeum tertio loco bis admittunt, quod idem in secundo loco Catullus ad libitum fecit.

(1647)

TO JOHN ROUS

Librarian of the University of Oxford

An ode about a lost copy of my *Poems*, which Rous asked to have replaced, so that he might deposit it in the public library with my other books.

MILTON had sent a copy of his *Poems* to Rous, along with copies of the eleven pamphlets he had so far published, for deposit in the Bodleian. The volume of poems had been stolen or lost in transit. In sending another copy Milton enclosed this ode, dated January 23, 1646 (i.e. 1647); it was printed in the 1673 edition. The poem is, like the less ample and less personal sonnet, "Captain or colonel," an expression of Milton's feelings, in wartime, about the permanent value of poetry and learning. He writes, not as a partisan, but as a disinterested poet and scholar who sees civil strife against the large background of the cultural tradition. His manner blends dignity with urbane playfulness, and, in regard to the quality and destiny of his poems, he displays a mixture of humility and confidence. The ode was an experiment in the Pindaric form; Milton's appended note indicates his awareness of the technical problems and of his own deliberate licenses.

Book of twin parts, happy in a single cover but with double leaf,[2] shining with an unstudied elegance once given it by a youthful hand — a zealous hand but not yet that of an assured poet — while he sported with wandering freedom now in Ausonian shades, now in English fields,[8] unconcerned with the public world,[9] and, following his own devices, he indulged his native lute or then with Daunian quill sounded a foreign air to his neighbors, his feet scarcely touching the ground.[12]

2. leaf. The section of Latin poems had a separate title page and separate pagination.

7–8. Some Latin poems were written in Italy, others — all the English, Italian, and Greek, and most of the Latin — in England.

9. world. Most of Milton's early poems were, in modern terms, more "private" than "public."

9–10. Milton repeats the facts of 7–8, now with reference to the languages used, English and Latin chiefly. There may be a special reference to the Italian pieces (cf. the *Canzone*).

12. ground: in poetic ecstasy.

Little book, who thievishly abstracted you and left your brothers when you, sent from the city at the urgent request of my learned friend, were making the famous journey to the cradle of blue Father Thames,[18] where the clear fountains of the Aonides[21] are, and the sacred dance[21] which has been famous in the world while the firmament has turned through vast stretches of time and will be famous for ever?

But what god or demigod, remembering with pity the ancient character of our race — if we have made enough atonement for our past sins, our degenerate idleness and effeminate luxury[28] — will put an end to the wicked broils of civil war, and with his sacred power will bring back our nourishing studies and the banished Muses who have been left with scarcely any refuge in all England?[32] Who with the shafts of Apollo[35] will transfix the foul birds that threaten us with their claws and drive the plague of Phineus[36] far from the Pegasean stream?[36]

Yet, little book, although because of a messenger's dishonesty or sleepy carelessness you once wandered from your brothers' company — and may be now in some cave or den where perhaps you are rubbed by the coarse hard hand of a stupid huckster — you may rejoice in good fortune. Behold, there shines again a new hope that you may escape the depths of Lethe and may be carried on oaring wing to the high court of Jove.

For Rous, in whose care are the renowned memorials of men, wishes to add you to his possessions and complains that you are missing from the full number promised, and asks that you come to him. You he desires to place in the hallowed sanctuaries over which he himself presides, the faithful custodian of immortal works, the guardian of treasure more illustrious than the golden tripods and Delphic offerings which were entrusted to Ion[56] in the rich temple of his divine father — Ion the son of Erechtheus' daughter, Actaean[60] Creusa.

So you shall go to see the lovely groves of the Muses, and shall go again to the noble home of Phoebus, where he dwells in Oxford's valley in preference to Delos or twin-peaked Parnassus. You shall go with honor, since you depart in assurance of a notable destiny and at the request of a favoring friend. There you shall be read among the exalted names of authors who were the ancient luminaries and true glory of the Greek and Latin peoples.

You, then, my labors — whatever this barren brain has brought forth — have not been in vain. Now at last I bid you hope for quiet rest, beyond the reach of ill-will, and for the blessed abode provided by kind Hermes[77] and the watchful protection of Rous; there the babbling tongue of the populace will not penetrate and the crowd of vulgar readers will be far away. But our remote descendants in a wiser

---

18. The river Isis, on which Oxford lies, joins the Thames.

21. Aonides: glossary, "Aonia."   dance: of Bacchic celebrants — here Oxford scholars and writers.

25–36. Cf. Horace, *Od.* 1.2.25–52, etc.

27–28. The idea of war as the punishment of degeneracy is recurrent in Milton's writings.

30–32. Oxford was the royalist headquarters from 1642 until the town's surrender to Fairfax in June, 1646; normal academic pursuits almost ceased.

35. Cf. Apollo's slaying of the Python (glossary).

36. Phineus: a king and seer whose food was defiled or devoured by the Harpies (glossary).

36. stream: the Thames, i.e. Oxford.

56. In Euripides' *Ion*, Ion, the son of Apollo and Creusa (daughter of Erechtheus, king of Athens), is guardian of Apollo's shrine.

60. Actaean: Attic (Acte was an early name for Attica).

77. Hermes as the god of eloquence, the lyre, and prudence, and marshal of the shades of the dead.

age will perhaps see things with impartial mind and juster judgment. Then, when malice is buried, a sane posterity will know, thanks to Rous, if these poems have any merit.

> The ode has three strophes and the same number of antistrophes and ends with an epode. Although the sections do not all have the same number of lines and do not everywhere strictly correspond, I have divided them in this way with regard to convenient reading rather than conformity to ancient rules of versification. In other respects a poem of this form should perhaps be more correctly called monostrophic. The meters are partly in regular patterns, partly free. In two Phalaecian lines a spondee is allowed in the third foot, a practice Catullus followed at will in the second foot.

F R O M

The History of Britain (1670)

The first four books of this work were written during 1646–48. While avowing his scepticism, Milton rehearsed some of the hallowed legendary lore. The Trojan Brutus, the prospective founder of Britain, consulted an oracle of Diana on a Mediterranean island: the first passage is his petition to Diana, the second the oracle's response. Both are renderings of bits of Latin verse in Geoffrey of Monmouth's *History of the Kings of Britain*, I.11 (Milton's *Works*, 10, 11–12).

> Goddess of Shades, and Huntress, who at will
> Walk'st on the rolling sphere and through the deep,
> On thy third reign, the earth, look now and tell
> What land, what seat of rest, thou bidd'st me seek,
> What certain seat, where I may worship thee
> For aye, with temples vowed and virgin quires.

> Brutus, far to the west, in th' ocean wide
> Beyond the realm of Gaul, a land there lies,
> Sea-girt it lies, where giants dwelt of old;
> Now void, it fits thy people. Thither bend
> Thy course, there shalt thou find a lasting seat;
> There to thy sons another Troy shall rise,
> And kings be born of thee, whose dreaded might
> Shall awe the world and conquer nations bold.

In book four (*Works*, 10, 194) Milton referred, with a snort of contempt, to a tale in the medieval historian, Matthew of Westminster, about the murder of the child-king, Kenelm, being reported to the pope "by a dove dropping a written note on the altar at Rome." The note was, in translation:

> Low in a mead of kine under a thorn,
> Of head bereft li'th poor Kenelm king-born.

PSALMS LXXX–LXXXVIII

IN THE HEADNOTE to Milton's earliest English verses something was said of the general incentive for the widespread practice of versifying the Psalms. For Milton in 1648 that general incentive had the added impetus given by the Westminster Assembly's active concern with providing a new Psalter for the more or less Presbyterianized Church of England and the Scottish Kirk. Whether or not this group of Psalms gave Milton personal comfort during the second civil war (as other groups would have done), what the early anonymous biographer said of his later life — that "David's Psalms were in esteem with him above all poetry" — was no doubt true of his earlier years, as his own references would suggest. While Milton's prefatory note and marginalia indicate that he worked from the Hebrew, it has been shown that, like other men, he consulted and often echoed various English versions (among them perhaps the colonial Bay Psalm Book). Along with religious motives Milton may have felt an impulse toward poetical exercise, though it cannot be said that these versions make attractive reading.

April, 1648

Nine of the Psalms done into meter, wherein all but what is in a different character are the very words of the text, translated from the original.

Psalm LXXX

1 Thou, Shepherd that dost Israel *keep,*
   Give ear *in time of need,*
Who leadest like a flock of sheep
   Thy lovèd Joseph's seed,
That   sitt'st   between   the   Cherubs
   bright,   5
Between their wings outspread,
Shine forth, *and from thy cloud give*
   light,
   And on our foes thy dread.
2 In Ephraim's view and Benjamin's,
   And in Manasseh's sight,   10
Awake [1] thy strength, come, and *be seen*
   To save us *by thy might.*
3 Turn us again, *thy grace divine*
   To us, O God, *vouchsafe;*
Cause thou thy face on us to shine,   15
   And then we shall be safe.
4 Lord God of Hosts, how long wilt thou,
   How long wilt thou declare
Thy [2] smoking wrath *and angry brow,*
   Against thy people's prayer?   20
5 Thou feed'st them with the bread of
   tears,
   Their bread with tears they eat,
And mak'st them [3] largely drink the tears

Wherewith their cheeks are wet.
6 A strife thou mak'st us *and a prey*   25
   To every neighbor foe;
Among themselves they [1] laugh, they
   [1] play,
   And [1] flouts at us they throw.
7 Return us, *and thy grace divine,*
   O God of Hosts, *vouchsafe;*   30
Cause thou thy face on us to shine,
   And then we shall be safe.
8 A Vine from Egypt thou hast brought,
   Thy free love made it thine,
   And drov'st out nations *proud and*
      haut   35
   To plant this *lovely* Vine.
9 Thou didst prepare for it a place,
   And root it deep and fast,
That it *began to grow apace,*
   And filled the land *at last.*   40
10 With her *green* shade *that* covered *all*
   The hills were *overspread;*
   Her boughs as *high* as cedars tall
      Advanced their lofty head.
11 Her branches *on the western side*   45
   Down to the sea she sent,
   And *upward* to that river *wide*
      Her other branches *went.*

[1] *Gnorera.*   [3] *Shalish.*
[2] *Gnashanta.*

[1] *Jilgnagu.*
35. haut: haughty.

12 Why hast thou laid her hedges low,
   And broken down her fence,   50
That all may pluck her, as they go,
   With rudest violence?
13 The *tuskèd* boar out of the wood
   Upturns it by the roots;
Wild beasts there browse, and make
      their food   55
   Her grapes and tender shoots.
14 Return now, God of Hosts, look down
   From heav'n, thy seat divine;
Behold *us, but without a frown,*
   And visit this *thy* Vine.   60
15 Visit this Vine, which thy right hand
   Hath set, and planted *long,*
And the young branch, that for thyself
   Thou hast made firm and strong.
16 But now it is consumed with fire,   65
   And cut *with axes* down;
They perish at thy dreadful ire,
   At thy rebuke and frown.
17 Upon the man of thy right hand
   Let thy *good* hand be *laid;*   70
Upon the Son of Man, whom thou
   Strong for thyself hast made.
18 So shall we not go back from thee
   To ways of sin and shame:
Quicken us thou; then *gladly* we   75
   Shall call upon thy name.
19 Return us, *and thy grace divine,*
   Lord God of Hosts, *vouchsafe;*
Cause thou thy face on us to shine,
   And then we shall be safe.   80

Psalm LXXXI

1 To God our strength sing loud *and clear,*
   Sing loud to God *our King,*
To Jacob's God, *that all may hear*
   Loud acclamations ring.
2 Prepare a hymn, prepare a song,   5
   The timbrel hither bring;
The *cheerful* psalt'ry bring along,
   And harp *with* pleasant *string.*
3 Blow, *as is wont,* in the new moon
   With trumpets' *lofty sound,*   10
Th' appointed time, the day whereon
   Our solemn feast *comes round.*
4 This was a statute *giv'n of old*
   For Israel *to observe,*
A law of Jacob's God *to hold,*   15
   From whence they might not swerve.
5 This he a testimony ordained

In Joseph, *not to change,*
Whenas he passed through Egypt-land;
   The tongue I heard was strange.   20
6 From burden *and from slavish toil*
   I set his shoulder free;
His hands from pots *and miry soil*
   Delivered were *by me.*
7 When trouble did thee sore assail,   25
   On me then didst thou call,
And I to free thee *did not fail,*
   And led thee out of thrall.
I answered thee in[1] thunder deep,
   With clouds encompassed round;   30
I tried thee at the water *steep*
   Of Meribah *renowned.*
8 Hear, O my people, *hearken well:*
   I testify to thee,
Thou ancient stock of Israel,   35
   If thou wilt list to me:
9 Throughout the land of thy abode
   No alien God shall be,
Nor shalt thou to a foreign god
   In honor bend thy knee.   40
10 I am the Lord thy God which brought
   Thee out of Egypt-land;
Ask large enough, and I, *besought,*
   Will grant thy full demand.
11 And yet my people would not *hear,*   45
   Nor hearken to my voice;
And Israel, *whom I loved so dear,*
   Misliked me for his choice.
12 Then did I leave them to their will
   And to their wand'ring mind;   50
Their own conceits they followed still,
   Their own devices blind.
13 O that my people would *be wise,*
   To serve me *all their days,*
And O that Israel would *advise*   55
   To walk my *righteous* ways!
14 Then would I soon bring down their foes
   That now so proudly rise,
And turn my hand against *all those*
   That are their enemies.   60
15 Who hate the Lord should *then be fain*
   To bow to him and bend,
But *they, his people, should remain,*
   Their time should have no end.   65
16 And he would feed them *from the shock*
   With flour of finest wheat,   66
And satisfy them from the rock
   With honey *for their meat.*

[1] *Be Sether ragnam.*

32. Meribah: Exod. 17.7.

Psalm LXXXII

1 God in the [1] great [1] assembly stands
  Of kings and lordly states;
   [2] Among the gods [2] on both his hands
   He judges and debates.
2 How long will ye [3] pervert the right   5
   With [3] judgment false and wrong,
   Favoring the wicked *by your might,*
   Who thence grow bold and strong?
3 [4] Regard the [4] weak and fatherless;
   [4] Despatch the [4] poor man's cause;   10
   And [5] raise the man in deep distress
   By [5] just and equal laws.
4 Defend the poor and desolate,
   And rescue from the hands
   Of wicked men the low estate   15
   Of him *that help demands.*
5 They know not, nor will understand,
   In darkness they walk on;
   The earth's foundations all are [6] moved,
   And [6] out of order gone.   20
6 I said that ye were gods, yea all
   The sons of God most high;
7 But ye shall die like men, and fall
   As other princes *die.*
8 Rise, God, [7] judge thou the earth *in*
   might,   25
   This *wicked* earth [7] redress,
   For thou art he who shalt by right
   The nations all possess.

Psalm LXXXIII

1 Be not thou silent *now at length,*
   O God, hold not thy peace,
   Sit thou not still, O God *of strength;*
   We cry and do not cease.
2 For lo thy *furious* foes *now* [8] swell   5
   And [8] storm outrageously,
   And they that hate thee *proud and fell*
   Exalt their heads full high.
3 Against thy people they [9] contrive
   [10] Their plots and counsels deep;   10
   [11] Them to ensnare they chiefly strive
   [12] Whom thou dost hide and keep.
4 "Come, let us cut them off," say they,
   "Till they no nation be,

That Israel's name for ever may   15
Be lost in memory."
5 For they consult [1] with all their might,
   And all as one in mind
   Themselves against thee they unite
   And in firm union bind.   20
6 The tents of Edom, and the brood
   Of *scornful* Ishmael,
   Moab, with them of Hagar's blood,
   That in the desert dwell,
7 Gebal and Ammon *there* conspire,   25
   And *hateful* Amalek,
   The Philistines, and they of Tyre
   Whose bounds the sea doth check.
8 With them *great* Ashur also bands,
   And doth confirm the knot;   30
   All these have lent their armèd hands
   To aid the sons of Lot.
9 Do to them as to Midian *bold*
   That wasted all the coast,
   To Sisera, and as *is told*   35
   Thou didst to Jabin's *host,*
   When at the brook of Kishon *old*
   They were repulsed and slain,
10 At Endor quite cut off, and rolled
    As dung upon the plain.   40
11 As Zeb and Oreb evil sped,
    So let their princes speed;
    As Zeba and Zalmunna *bled,*
    So let their princes *bleed.*
12 *For they amidst their pride* have said,   45
    "By right now shall we seize
    [2] God's houses, and *will now invade*
    [2] Their stately palaces."
13 My God, oh make them as a wheel,
    No quiet let them find;   50
    Giddy and *restless* let *them reel,*
    Like stubble from the wind.
14 *As, when* an *aged* wood takes fire
    Which on a sudden strays,   55
    The *greedy* flame runs higher and higher,
    Till all the mountains blaze;   56
15 So with thy whirlwind them pursue,
    And with thy tempest chase;
16 [3] And till they [3] yield thee honor due,
    Lord, fill with shame their face.   60
17 Ashamed and troubled let them be,
    Troubled and shamed for ever,

1 *Bagnadath-el.*
2 *Bekerev.*
3 *Tishphetu gnavel.*
4 *Shiphtu-dal.*
5 *Hatzdiku.*
6 *Jimmotu.*

7 *Shiphta.*
8 *Jehemajun.*
9 *Jagnarimu.*
10 *Sod.*
11 *Jithjagnatsu gnal.*
12 *Tsephuneca.*

1 *Lev jachdau.*
2 *Neoth Elohim* bears both.
3 They seek thy name: *Heb.*

21 f. For the names of peoples and princes
see an index to the Bible.

Ever confounded, and so die
With shame, *and scape it never.*

18 Then shall they know that thou, whose name   65
Jehovah is, alone
Art the most high, *and thou the same*
O'er all the earth *art One.*

Psalm LXXXIV

1 How lovely are thy dwellings fair!
O Lord of Hosts, how dear
The *pleasant* tabernacles are
Where thou dost dwell so near!

2 My soul doth long and almost die   5
Thy courts, O Lord, to see;
My heart and flesh aloud do cry,
O living God, for thee.

3 There ev'n the sparrow, *freed from wrong,*
Hath found a house of *rest;*   10
The swallow there, to lay her young,
Hath built her *brooding* nest;
Ev'n *by* thy altars, Lord of Hosts,
They find their safe abode;
And home they fly from round the coasts
Toward thee, my King, my God.   16

4 Happy who in thy house reside
Where thee they ever praise;

5 Happy whose strength in thee doth bide,
And in their hearts thy ways.   20

6 They pass through Baca's *thirsty* vale,
That dry and barren ground,
As through a fruitful wat'ry dale
Where springs and show'rs abound.

7 They journey on from strength to strength   25
With joy and gladsome cheer,
Till all before *our* God *at length*
In Sion do appear.

8 Lord God of Hosts, hear *now* my prayer,
O Jacob's God, give ear: 30

9 Thou, God, our shield, look on the face
Of thy anointed *dear.*

10 For one day in thy courts *to be*
Is better *and more blest*
Than *in the joys of vanity*   35
A thousand days *at best.*
I in the temple of my God
Had rather keep a door

Than dwell in tents *and rich abode*
With sin *for evermore.*   40

11 For God the Lord, both sun and shield,
Gives grace and glory *bright;*
No good from them shall be withheld
Whose ways are just and right.

12 Lord *God* of Hosts *that reign'st on high,*
That man is *truly* blest   46
Who *only* on thee doth rely,
And in thee only rest.

Psalm LXXXV

1 Thy land to favor graciously
Thou hast not, Lord, been slack;
Thou hast from *hard* captivity
Returnèd Jacob back.

2 Th' iniquity thou didst forgive   5
That wrought thy people woe,
And all their sin *that did thee grieve*
Hast hid *where none shall know.*

3 Thine anger all thou hadst removed,
And *calmly* didst return   10
From thy [1] fierce wrath, which we had proved
Far worse than fire to burn.

4 God of our saving health and peace,
Turn us, and us restore;
Thine indignation cause to cease   15
Toward us, *and chide no more.*

5 Wilt thou be angry without end,
For ever angry thus?
Wilt thou thy frowning ire extend
From age to age on us?   20

6 Wilt thou not [2] turn and *hear our voice,*
And us again [2] revive,
That so thy people may rejoice,
By thee preserved alive?

7 Cause us to see thy goodness, Lord,   25
To us thy mercy shew;
Thy saving health to us afford,
And life in us renew.

8 *And now* what God the Lord will speak
I will *go straight and* hear,   30
For to his people he speaks peace,
And to his saints *full dear;*
To his dear saints he will speak peace;
But let them never more
Return to folly, *but surcease*   35
To trespass as before.

[1] *Heb.:* The burning heat of thy wrath.
[2] *Heb.:* Turn to quicken us.

9 Surely to such as do him fear
  Salvation is at hand,
And glory shall *ere long appear*
  To dwell within our land.   40
10 Mercy and Truth, *that long were missed,*
  Now *joyfully* are met;
Sweet Peace and Righteousness have
  kissed,
  And hand in hand are set.
11 Truth from the earth *like to a flow'r*   45
  Shall bud and blossom *then,*
And Justice from her heavenly bow'r
  Look down *on mortal men.*
12 The Lord will also then bestow
  Whatever thing is good;   50
Our land shall forth in plenty throw
  Her fruits *to be our food.*
13 Before him Righteousness shall go,
  His royal harbinger;
Then [1] will he come, and not be slow;
  His footsteps cannot err.   56

Psalm LXXXVI

1 Thy *gracious* ear, O Lord, incline;
  O hear me, *I thee pray,*
For I am poor, and almost pine
  With need *and sad decay.*
2 Preserve my soul, for [2] I have trod   5
  Thy ways, and love the just;
Save thou thy servant, O my God,
  Who *still* in thee doth trust.
3 Pity me, Lord, for daily thee
  I call; 4 O make rejoice   10
Thy servant's soul! for, Lord, to thee
  I lift my soul *and voice,*
5 For thou art good; thou, Lord, art
  prone
To pardon, thou to all
Art full of mercy, thou *alone,*   15
  To them that on thee call.
6 Unto my supplication, Lord,
  Give ear, and to the cry
Of my *incessant* prayers afford
  Thy hearing graciously.   20
7 I in the day of my distress
  Will call on thee *for aid;*
For thou wilt *grant* me *free access,*
  And answer *what I prayed.*

1 *Heb.:* He will set his steps to the way.
2 *Heb.:* I am good, loving, a doer of good
and holy things.

8 Like thee among the gods is none,   25
  O Lord; nor any works
Of all that other gods have done
  Like to thy *glorious* works.
9 The nations all whom thou hast made
  Shall come, *and all shall frame*   30
To bow them low before thee, Lord,
  And glorify thy name.
10 For great thou art, and wonders great
  By thy strong hand are done;
Thou *in thy everlasting seat*   35
  Remainest God alone.
11 Teach me, O Lord, thy way *most right;*
  I in thy truth will bide;
To fear thy name my heart unite;
  So shall it never slide.   40
12 Thee will I praise, O Lord my God,
  Thee honor and adore
With my whole heart, and blaze
  abroad
Thy name for evermore.
13 For great thy mercy is toward me,   45
  And thou hast freed my soul,
Ev'n from the lowest hell set free,
  From deepest darkness foul.
14 O God, the proud against me rise,
  And violent men are met   50
To seek my life, and in their eyes
  No fear of thee have set.
15 But thou, Lord, art the God most
  mild,
  Readiest thy grace to shew,
Slow to be angry, and *art styled*   55
  Most merciful, most true.
16 Oh turn to me *thy face at length,*
  And me have mercy on;
Unto thy servant give thy strength,
  And save thy handmaid's son.   60
17 Some sign of good to me afford,
  And let my foes *then* see
And be ashamed, because thou, Lord,
  Dost help and comfort me.

Psalm LXXXVII

1 Among the holy mountains *high*
  Is his foundation fast;
There seated in his sanctuary,
  His temple there is placed.
2 Sion's *fair* gates the Lord loves more   5
  Than all the dwellings *fair*
Of Jacob's *land, though there be store,*
  And all within his care.

3 City of God, most glorious things
    Of thee *abroad* are spoke;   10
I mention Egypt, *where proud kings*
    Did our forefathers yoke;
4 I mention Babel to my friends,
    Philistia *full of scorn,*
And Tyre with Ethiop's *utmost ends:*   15
    Lo this man there was born.
5 But *twice that praise shall in our ear*
    Be said of Sion *last:*
This and this man was born in her;
    High God shall fix her fast.   20
6 The Lord shall write it in a scroll
    That ne'er shall be outworn,
When he the nations doth enroll,
    That this man there was born.
7 Both they who sing and they who dance
    With sacred songs are there;   26
In thee *fresh brooks and soft streams*
    glance,
    And all my fountains *clear.*

Psalm LXXXVIII

1 LORD GOD, that dost me save and keep,
    All day to thee I cry,
And all night long before thee *weep,*
    Before thee *prostrate lie.*
2 Into thy presence let my prayer   5
    With sighs devout ascend,
And to my cries, that *ceaseless* are,
    Thine ear with favor bend.
3 For cloyed with woes and trouble store
    Surcharged my soul doth lie;   10
My life *at death's uncheerful door*
    Unto the grave draws nigh.
4 Reckoned I am with them that pass
    Down to the *dismal* pit;
I am a [1] man, but weak, alas,   15
    And for that name unfit,
5 From life discharged and parted quite
    Among the dead *to sleep,*
And like the slain *in bloody fight*
    That in the grave lie *deep,*   20
Whom thou rememberest no more,
    Dost never more regard:
Them from thy hand delivered o'er
    Death's hideous house hath barred.

[1] *Heb.:* A man without manly strength.

6 Thou in the lowest pit *profound*   25
    Hast set me *all forlorn,*
Where thickest darkness *hovers round,*
    In horrid deeps *to mourn.*
7 Thy wrath *from which no shelter saves*
    Full sore doth press on me;   30
[1] Thou break'st upon me all thy waves,
    [1] And all thy waves break me.
8 Thou dost my friends from me estrange,
    And mak'st me odious,
Me to them odious, *for they change,*   35
    And I here pent up thus.
9 Through sorrow and affliction great
    Mine eye grows dim and dead;
Lord, all the day I thee entreat,
    My hands to thee I spread.   40
10 Wilt thou do wonders on the dead?
    Shall the deceased arise
And praise thee *from their loathsome bed*
    With pale and hollow eyes?
11 Shall they thy loving-kindness tell   45
    On whom the grave *hath hold,*
Or they *who* in perdition *dwell*
    Thy faithfulness *unfold?*
12 In darkness can thy mighty *hand*
    Or wondrous acts be known,   50
Thy justice in the *gloomy* land
    Of *dark* oblivion?
13 But I to thee, O Lord, do cry
    Ere yet my life be spent,
And *up to thee* my prayer *doth hie*   55
    Each morn, and thee prevent.
14 Why wilt thou, Lord, my soul forsake
    And hide thy face from me,
15 That am already bruised, and [2] shake
    With terror sent from thee;   60
Bruised and afflicted and *so low*
    As ready to expire,
While I thy terrors undergo,
    Astonished with thine ire?
16 Thy fierce wrath over me doth flow,   65
    Thy threat'nings cut me through;
17 All day they round about me go,
    Like waves they me pursue.
18 Lover and friend thou hast removed
    And severed from me far;   70
They *fly me now* whom I have loved,
    And as in darkness are.

[1] The Hebrew bears both.
[2] *Heb.: Prae concussione.*

Sonnet XV

THE MANUSCRIPT title is *On the Lord General Fairfax at the siege of Colchester.* Sir Thomas Fairfax, the chief parliamentary general, had won the decisive battle of Naseby (1645). When royalists renewed the war in 1648, Fairfax besieged Colchester. The sonnet must have been written before the town surrendered (August 27) and also before the battle of Preston (August 17), in which Cromwell defeated the Scots, "the false North" of line 7. The

exhortation of the sestet was not fulfilled: Fairfax, who did not approve of the execution of King Charles or the invasion of Scotland, in 1650 retired into private life. Milton praised him again in his *Second Defence of the English People* (1654). This sonnet was first printed, along with that addressed to Cromwell (16) and "Cyriack, this three years' day" (22), by Edward Phillips in 1694.

> Fairfax, whose name in arms through Europe rings,
>   Filling each mouth with envy or with praise,
>   And all her jealous monarchs with amaze,
>   And rumors loud that daunt remotest kings,
> Thy firm unshaken virtue ever brings   5
>   Victory home, though new rebellions raise
>   Their Hydra heads, and the false North displays
>   Her broken league to imp their serpent wings.
> O yet a nobler task awaits thy hand;
>   For what can war but endless war still breed,   10
>   Till truth and right from violence be freed,
> And public faith cleared from the shameful brand
>   Of public fraud? In vain doth valor bleed
>   While avarice and rapine share the land.

(1648)

7. Hydra: glossary (cf. Horace, *Od.* 4.4.61–62). North. Although the Presbyterian Scots had made an alliance with the English parliament (the Solemn League and Covenant of 1643), negotiations with the king led to a Scottish royalist invasion in July, 1648 (see the headnote).

8. imp: the grafting of new feathers to the stumps of broken ones (a traditional metaphor from falconry); hence "strengthen."

11–14. One of Milton's many expressions of disillusionment with the Long Parliament: here, in particular, with the financial disorder and dishonesty that attended the raising of money, the confiscation and sale of royalists' estates, etc.

FROM

The Tenure of Kings and Magistrates (1649)

There can be slain
No sacrifice to God more acceptable
Than an unjust and wicked king.*

* Seneca, *Hercules Furens* 922–24 (Milton's *Works,* 5, 19; *C.P.W.,* 3, 213).

[In Salmasii Hundredam]

Quis expedivit Salmasio suam Hundredam,
Picamque *docuit nostra verba conari?*
Magister artis venter, et iacobaei
Centum, exulantis viscera marsupii regis.
Quod si dolosi spes refulserit nummi,   5
Ipse, Antichristi qui modo primatum Papae
Minatus uno est dissipare sufflatu,
Cantabit ultro Cardinalitium *melos.*

(1651)

A G A I N S T   T H E   H U N D R E D   O F   S A L M A S I U S

CLAUDIUS SALMASIUS (Claude de Saumaise, 1588–1653), a French Protestant and perhaps the chief classical scholar in Europe, in 1649 published *Defensio Regia,* an attack on the English regicides. As Secretary for Foreign Languages, Milton made the official reply, *Pro Populo Anglicano Defensio* (1651) — in Latin, since it was addressed to Europe at large. His belaboring of Salmasius' private character and circumstances included this epigram (*Works,* 7, 428).

Salmasius had been ostentatious and pedantic on matters of English law and government, including the term "hundred," a subdivision of an English county. The epigram plays on that and the hundred gold jacobuses Salmasius was said to have received as a reward from Charles II. Milton's italics (rendered by quotation marks in the translation) indicated phrases that he was borrowing from the Roman satirist Persius (*Prologus* 8–14).

"Who helped" Salmasius with his *hundred* and "taught the magpie to attempt our words? His master in the art was his belly," and a hundred jacobuses, from the belly of the exiled king's purse. "But, if there shines the alluring hope of money," this same man — who lately threatened with one breath to blow to pieces the supremacy of the pope,[7] the Antichrist — will gladly "sing the tune" of Cardinals.

7. Salmasius in an earlier book had challenged papal authority, so that his apparent change of front was resented by English revolutionists.

Sonnet XIX

MILTON'S EYES had been weak from childhood and his sight began to fail noticeably about 1644. By early 1650, when he was assigned the task of answering Salmasius' attack on the regicides, he had nearly lost the sight of one eye; although warned about the effect of continued labor, he persevered. Blindness became complete in the winter of 1651–52. The dating of the sonnet has been much debated. The main point on one side is that its place among the printed sonnets would put composition in 1655; but in fact the sonnets are not all in strictly chronological order, and this one seems very clearly, in substance and tone, to express Milton's first reaction to total blindness. His forty-third birthday was just behind him (or possibly just ahead), and he had not yet written the heroic poem which he had put aside at the call of public duty. The sonnet takes us back to "How soon hath Time" of 1632, though now the parable of the talents has become a more oppressive reality; yet Milton's faith in Providence remains humbly steadfast. The only text of the sonnet is that of the *Poems* of 1673.

When I consider how my light is spent,
        Ere half my days, in this dark world and wide,
        And that one talent which is death to hide
        Lodged with me useless, though my soul more bent
To serve therewith my Maker, and present   5
        My true account, lest he returning chide,
        "Doth God exact day-labor, light denied?"
        I fondly ask. But Patience, to prevent
That murmur, soon replies: "God doth not need
        Either man's work or his own gifts; who best   10
        Bear his mild yoke, they serve him best. His state
Is kingly: thousands at his bidding speed,
        And post o'er land and ocean without rest;
        They also serve who only stand and wait."

(1652?)

2. Ere half my days. Since Milton had become 43 on December 9, 1651, this phrase would seem to stretch his expected span well beyond the Psalmist's three score and ten. He might have been thinking of his mature working life, of his father's having reached 84 or more, or possibly of Plato's hundred-year term (*Rep.* 615).

3. talent: Matt. 25.14–30.
7. John 9.4.
11. yoke: Matt. 11.29–30.
14. They: i.e. angels. Milton is presumably thinking, not of two distinct orders of angels, but of all angels as God's envoys, some being sent on missions, others waiting to be sent. Cf. *P.L.* 3.648–53; Spenser, *F.Q.* 2.8.1–2.

Sonnet XVI

THE MANUSCRIPT title is *To the Lord General Cromwell, May 1652, on the proposals of certain ministers at the Committee for Propagation of the Gospel.* The Committee, appointed by parliament and dominated by Independents, was considering a kind of state-controlled Congregationalism — which Milton the individualist saw as a new Established Church. The pattern of the sonnet is akin to that on Fairfax, the praise of martial prowess being followed by a summons to the works of peace, in this case the preservation of religious liberty. Milton doubtless sent a copy of the sonnet to Cromwell. It was first printed by Edward Phillips in 1694.

Cromwell, our chief of men, who through a cloud
        Not of war only, but detractions rude,
        Guided by faith and matchless fortitude
        To peace and truth thy glorious way hast ploughed,
And on the neck of crownèd Fortune proud   5
        Hast reared God's trophies and his work pursued,
        While Darwen stream, with blood of Scots imbrued,

1–2. cloud . . . of war: cf. *Aen.* 10.809.
5. crownèd Fortune: King Charles and his son.

7. The battle of Preston (see the headnote to Sonnet 15).

And Dunbar field resounds thy praises loud,
    And Worcester's laureate wreath; yet much remains
    To conquer still: peace hath her victories   10
    No less renowned than war; new foes arise
Threat'ning to bind our souls with secular chains.
    Help us to save free conscience from the paw
    Of hireling wolves whose gospel is their maw.

                    (1652)

8. Dunbar. On September 3, 1650, Cromwell defeated the Scots at Dunbar in Scotland. 9. Worcester. On September 3, 1651, Cromwell defeated the Scots and Charles II; Charles escaped into exile. 14. The "wolves" (John 10.12) are not now the Roman Catholics of *Lycidas* 128 but Puritans.

Sonnet XVII

THIS SONNET, which Milton sent to Vane on July 3, 1652, has the Manuscript title *To Sir Henry Vane the younger.* It was first printed in George Sikes's *Life and Death of Sir Henry Vane* (1662) and then by Edward Phillips (1694). Sir Henry Vane (1613–62) was one of the ablest and most high-minded of Puritan leaders. In 1636–37, as the youthful governor of Massachusetts, he had defended the "enthusiast," Anne Hutchinson, against rigid orthodoxy, and in the Westminster Assembly (cf. headnote to *On the New Forcers of Conscience*) he had spoken for religious liberty.

He had lately been negotiating with Dutch ambassadors who had lingered in London, although war between Holland and England had already begun, and who were given their passports a few days before the sonnet was written. As in some other laudatory sonnets, Milton enhances his subject's dignity through an illustrious historical parallel. The recognizing of a clear division between church and state, for which Vane is praised, was a main article of Milton's creed. Vane was executed in 1662 by the Restoration government.

Vane, young in years, but in sage counsel old,
    Than whom a better senator ne'er held
    The helm of Rome, when gowns, not arms, repelled
    The fierce Epirot and the African bold;
Whether to settle peace or to unfold   5
    The drift of hollow states, hard to be spelled,
    Then to advise how war may best, upheld,
    Move by her two main nerves, iron and gold,
In all her equipage; besides, to know
    Both spiritual power and civil, what each means,   10
    What severs each, thou hast learnt, which few have done.
The bounds of either sword to thee we owe.
    Therefore on thy firm hand Religion leans
    In peace, and reckons thee her eldest son.

                    (1652)

4. Epirot. Pyrrhus, king of Epirus, invaded Italy in 281 B.C. His ambassador reported that the Roman senate was an assembly of kings. African: Hannibal the Carthaginian, who invaded Italy in 218 B.C. 6. hollow: a pun on "Holland," "the Low Countries," and the idea of subtlety or duplicity. 6. be spelled: understand. 8. Vane had brought the navy to a degree of efficiency which made possible the victories of Blake.

PSALMS I–VIII

THE HEADNOTE to the Psalms of 1648 is relevant here. By August, 1653, Milton had been blind for at least a year and a half, and it is again a question if his choice of Psalms involved personal consolation. It is obvious at any rate that he has abandoned the usual simple meter for experimentation.

Psalm I. *Done into Verse*, 1653

Blest is the man who hath not walked astray
In counsel of the wicked, and i' th' way
Of sinners hath not stood, and in the seat
Of scorners hath not sat. But in the great
Jehovah's Law is ever his delight,   5
And in his Law he studies day and night.
He shall be as a tree which planted grows
By wat'ry streams, and in his season knows
To yield his fruit, and his leaf shall not fall,
And what he takes in hand shall prosper
      all.   10
Not so the wicked; but as chaff which
      fanned
The wind drives, so the wicked shall not
      stand
In judgment, or abide their trial then,
Nor sinners in th' assembly of just men.
For the Lord knows th' upright way of the
      just,   15
And the way of bad men to ruin must.

Psalm II. *Done* Aug. 8, 1653

Terzetti

Why do the Gentiles tumult, and the na-
      tions
   Muse a vain thing, the kings of th' earth
      upstand
   With power, and princes in their congre-
      gations
Lay deep their plots together through each
      land
   Against the Lord and his Messiah dear? 5
   "Let us break off," say they, "by strength
      of hand
Their bonds, and cast from us, no more to
      wear,
   Their twisted cords." He who in heaven
      doth dwell
   Shall laugh, the Lord shall scoff them,
      then severe

Speak to them in his wrath, and in his fell 10
   And fierce ire trouble them. "But I,"
      saith he,
   "Anointed have my king (though ye
      rebel)
On Sion my holy hill." A firm decree
   I will declare; the Lord to me hath said,
   "Thou art my Son; I have begotten
      thee   15
This day; ask of me, and the grant is made;
   As thy possession I on thee bestow
   Th' heathen, and as thy conquest to be
      swayed
Earth's utmost bounds: them shalt thou
      bring full low
   With iron scepter bruised, and them dis-
      perse   20
   Like to a potter's vessel shivered so."
And now be wise at length, ye kings averse,
   Be taught, ye judges of the earth; with
      fear
   Jehovah serve, and let your joy converse
With trembling; kiss the Son, lest he ap-
      pear   25
   In anger and ye perish in the way,
   If once his wrath take fire like fuel sere.
Happy all those who have in him their
      stay.

Psalm III. Aug. 9, 1653

When he fled from Absalom

Lord, how many are my foes,
   How many those
That in arms against me rise!
   Many are they
· That of my life distrustfully thus say,   5
"No help for him in God there lies."

---

12. Milton's parenthetical insertion is of interest. See the note on *P.L.* 5.603–15.
13. holy. In Milton's spelling the last sylla-ble is elided to make a ten-syllable line.

But thou, Lord, art my shield, my glory;
    Thee through my story
Th' exalter of my head I count.
    Aloud I cried   10
Unto Jehovah; he full soon replied
And heard me from his holy mount.
I lay and slept, I waked again,
    For my sustain
Was the Lord. Of many millions   15
    The populous rout
I fear not, though encamping round about
They pitch against me their pavilions.
Rise, Lord, save me, my God, for thou
    Hast smote ere now   20
    On the cheek-bone all my foes,
    Of men abhorred
Hast broke the teeth. This help was from
    the Lord;
Thy blessing on thy people flows.

Psalm IV. Aug. 10, 1653

Answer me when I call,
God of my righteousness;
In straits and in distress
Thou didst me disenthrall
And set at large; now spare,   5
    Now pity me, and hear my earnest prayer.
Great ones, how long will ye
My glory have in scorn?
How long be thus forborne
Still to love vanity,   10
To love, to seek, to prize
    Things false and vain and nothing else
    but lies?
Yet know the Lord hath chose,
Chose to himself apart,
The good and meek of heart   15
(For whom to choose he knows);
Jehovah from on high
    Will hear my voice what time to him I
    cry.
Be awed, and do not sin,
Speak to your hearts alone,   20
Upon your beds, each one,
And be at peace within.
Offer the offerings just
    Of righteousness, and in Jehovah trust.
Many there be that say   25
"Who yet will show us good?"
Talking like this world's brood;
But, Lord, thus let me pray,
On us lift up the light,

Lift up the favor of thy count'nance
    bright.   30
Into my heart more joy
And gladness thou hast put
Than when a year of glut
Their stores doth over-cloy
And from their plenteous grounds   35
    With vast increase their corn and wine
    abounds.
In peace at once will I
Both lay me down and sleep;
For thou alone dost keep
Me safe where'er I lie;   40
As in a rocky cell
    Thou, Lord, alone in safety mak'st me
    dwell.

Psalm V. Aug. 12, 1653

Jehovah, to my words give ear,
    My meditation weigh;
The voice of my complaining hear,
My King and God, for unto thee I pray.
Jehovah, thou my early voice   5
    Shalt in the morning hear;
I' th' morning I to thee with choice
Will rank my prayers, and watch till thou
    appear.
For thou art not a God that takes
    In wickedness delight;   10
    Evil with thee no biding makes;
Fools or mad men stand not within thy
    sight.
All workers of iniquity
    Thou hat'st; and them unblest
Thou wilt destroy that speak a lie;   15
The bloody and guileful man God doth de-
    test.
But I will in thy mercies dear,
    Thy numerous mercies, go
Into thy house; I in thy fear
Will towards thy holy temple worship
    low.   20
    Lord, lead me in thy righteousness,
    Lead me, because of those
    That do observe if I transgress;
Set thy ways right before, where my step
    goes.
    For in his falt'ring mouth unstable   25
    No word is firm or sooth;
    Their inside, troubles miserable;

---

16. bloody. In Milton's spelling the last
syllable is elided to make a ten-syllable line.

An open grave their throat, their tongue they
   smooth.
   God, find them guilty, let them fall
      By their own counsels quelled;   30
   Push them in their rebellions all
Still on; for against thee they have rebelled;
   Then all who trust in thee shall bring
      Their joy, while thou from blame
   Defend'st them; they shall ever sing   35
And shall triumph in thee, who love thy
   name.
   For thou, Jehovah, wilt be found
      To bless the just man still;
   As with a shield thou wilt surround
Him with thy lasting favor and good will. 40

Psalm VI. Aug. 13, 1653

Lord, in thine anger do not reprehend me,
   Nor in thy hot displeasure me correct;
Pity me, Lord, for I am much deject,
   Am very weak and faint; heal and amend
   me,
For all my bones, that even with anguish
   ache,   5
   Are troubled, yea, my soul is troubled
   sore.
And thou, O Lord, how long? turn, Lord, re-
   store
   My soul, O save me for thy goodness'
   sake,
For in death no remembrance is of thee;
   Who in the grave can celebrate thy
   praise?   10
Wearied I am with sighing out my days,
   Nightly my couch I make a kind of sea;
My bed I water with my tears; mine eye
   Through grief consumes, is waxen old and
   dark
I' th' midst of all mine enemies that mark. 15
   Depart, all ye that work iniquity.
Depart from me, for the voice of my weep-
   ing
   The Lord hath heard; the Lord hath
   heard my prayer;
My supplication with acceptance fair
   The Lord will own, and have me in his
   keeping.   20
Mine enemies shall all be blank and dashed
   With much confusion; then grow red with
   shame;
They shall return in haste the way they
   came
And in a moment shall be quite abashed.

Psalm VII. Aug. 14, 1653

Upon the words of Chush the Benjamite
against him

Lord, my God, to thee I fly;
Save me and secure me under
Thy protection while I cry,
Lest as a lion (and no wonder)
He haste to tear my soul asunder,   5
Tearing and no rescue nigh.

Lord, my God, if I have thought
Or done this, if wickedness
Be in my hands, if I have wrought
Ill to him that meant me peace,   10
Or to him have rendered less,
And not freed my foe for naught,

Let th' enemy pursue my soul
And overtake it, let him tread
My life down to the earth and roll   15
In the dust my glory dead,
In the dust, and there outspread
Lodge it with dishonor foul.

Rise, Jehovah, in thine ire;
Rouse thyself amidst the rage   20
Of my foes that urge like fire;
And wake for me, their fury assuage;
Judgment here thou didst engage
And command, which I desire.

So th' assemblies of each nation   25
Will surround thee, seeking right;
Thence to thy glorious habitation
Return on high and in their sight.
Jehovah judgeth most upright
All people from the world's foundation.   30

Judge me, Lord, be judge in this
According to my righteousness,
And the innocence which is
Upon me: cause at length to cease
Of evil men the wickedness   35
And their power that do amiss.

But the just establish fast,
Since thou art the just God that tries
Hearts and reins. On God is cast
My defense, and in him lies,   40
In him who both just and wise
Saves th' upright of heart at last.

---

22. fury. The last syllable is elided.

God is a just judge and severe,
And God is every day offended;
If th' unjust will not forbear,   45
His sword he whets, his bow hath bended
Already, and for him intended
The tools of death, that waits him near.

(His arrows purposely made he
For them that persecute.) Behold,   50
He travails big with vanity,
Trouble he hath conceived of old
As in a womb, and from that mold
Hath at length brought forth a lie.

He digged a pit, and delved it deep,   55
And fell into the pit he made;
His mischief, that due course doth keep,
Turns on his head, and his ill trade
Of violence will undelayed
Fall on his crown with ruin steep.   60

Then will I Jehovah's praise
According to his justice raise,
And sing the name and deity
Of Jehovah the most high.

Psalm VIII. Aug. 14, 1653

O Jehovah, our Lord, how wondrous great
  And glorious is thy name through all the
  earth!
So as above the heavens thy praise to set
  Out of the tender mouths of latest birth,

Out of the mouths of babes and sucklings
  thou   5
  Hast founded strength, because of all thy
  foes,

To stint th' enemy, and slack th' avenger's
  brow
  That bends his rage thy providence to oppose.

When I behold thy heavens, thy fingers' art,
  The moon and stars which thou so bright
  hast set   10
In the pure firmament, then saith my heart,
  O what is man that thou rememb'rest yet,

And think'st upon him; or of man begot
  That him thou visit'st and of him art
  found?
Scarce to be less than gods, thou mad'st his
  lot,   15
  With honor and with state thou hast him
  crowned.

O'er the works of thy hand thou mad'st him
  lord,
  Thou hast put all under his lordly feet,
All flocks and herds, by thy commanding
  word,
  All beasts that in the field or forest
  meet;   20

Fowl of the heavens, and fish that through
  the wet
  Sea-paths in shoals do slide, and know no
  dearth.
O Jehovah, our Lord, how wondrous great
  And glorious is thy name through all the
  earth!

                                              (1653)

_____

7. stint: check.

[In Salmasium]

Gaudete, scombri, et quicquid est piscium salo,
Qui frigida hieme incolitis algentes freta.
Vestrum misertus ille Salmasius eques
Bonus amicire nuditatem cogitat;
Chartaeque largus apparat papyrinos   5
Vobis cucullos praeferentes Claudii
Insignia, nomenque et decus, Salmasii,
Gestetis ut per omne cetarium forum
Equitis clientes, scriniis mungentium
Cubito virorum et capsulis gratissimos.   10

(1654)

AGAINST SALMASIUS

THIS SECOND epigram appeared in 1654 in Milton's *Pro Populo Anglicano Defensio Secunda* (*Works*, 8, 56). It turns on the gibes of ancient Roman poets about paper containing bad verses as fit for wrapping fish: Salmasius has written, not for scholars, but for the "bookshelves" of the fishmongers.

Rejoice, you mackerel and all fish in the salt water, you freezing inhabitants of the seas in cold winter. The good knight Salmasius,[3] in pity for you, is considering how to clothe your nakedness. Generous with his stationery, he is preparing for you paper cowls, which bear the insignia, the name and rank, of Claudius Salmasius, so that through the whole fish-market you may carry the knight's clients, who are very welcome for the chests and boxes of the men who wipe their noses on their elbows.[10]

3. Salmasius eques: "the salmon knight" (*salmo*, salmon). Here and in line 9 "knight" is used in the ancient Roman sense of membership in the equestrian order. Salmasius actually was of ancient and noble descent.
10. The fishmongers.

Sonnet XXII

THIS SONNET dates itself (line 1) as of early 1655 (or possibly the end of 1654). It is very different in spirit and tone from "When I consider." Here Milton has rallied from the calamitous shock of blindness and is sustained in fortitude by the thought of his first and second *Defence of the English People* (1651, 1654) and by the "better guide," his faith in God's providence and the light of conscience. The sonnet was first printed in 1694 by Edward Phillips, who entitled it *To Mr Cyriack Skinner upon his Blindness.* For Skinner see the headnote to Sonnet 21 below.

> Cyriack, this three years' day these eyes, though clear
>   To outward view of blemish or of spot,
>   Bereft of light their seeing have forgot;
>   Nor to their idle orbs doth sight appear
> Of sun or moon or star throughout the year,   5
>   Or man or woman. Yet I argue not
>   Against Heav'n's hand or will, nor bate a jot
>   Of heart or hope, but still bear up and steer
> Right onward. What supports me, dost thou ask?
>   The conscience, friend, to have lost them overplied   10
>   In liberty's defense, my noble task,
> Of which all Europe talks from side to side.
>   This thought might lead me through the world's vain masque,
>   Content though blind, had I no better guide.
>
> (1655)

1. this . . . day. The sonnet is being composed on the third anniversary of the day when Milton found himself completely blind (see the headnote on Sonnet 19). It must therefore have preceded the *Massacre in Piedmont* (Sonnet 18), which could not have been composed before the end of April, 1655.

2. Milton evidently derived some small satisfaction from his not being disfigured, since he mentions the fact also in the personal passage of the *Second Defence* and in a letter of September 28, 1654, to his continental friend, Leonard Philaras; in this letter he described his symptoms and their onset.

4–6. Cf. the invocation to Light, *P.L.* 3.40–44.

7. bate: abate, slacken.

8. bear up: a nautical term for putting a ship before the wind.

10. conscience: consciousness.

12. A pardonable exaggeration, although Milton's discomfiture of Salmasius in 1651 and Alexander More in 1654 did occasion considerable talk abroad. The Manuscript has "talks"; Phillips' version gave "rings."

Sonnet XVIII

On the late Massacre in Piedmont

THIS UTTERANCE was inspired by an event of April 24, 1655, when Italian troops massacred the Piedmontese "Protestants" (known, from their medieval founder's name, Valdes, as Vaudois or Waldensians) among whom they had been billeted. In his role as Secretary, Milton drafted letters of protest which Cromwell sent to the Duke of Savoy, France, and the Protestant countries of Europe. Milton's combined invective and prayer has often been likened to the imprecations of the Hebrew prophets, and it is in fact largely cast in biblical language, harsh, compassionate, simple, and fervent. The only text of the sonnet is that of *Poems* (1673).

Avenge, O Lord, thy slaughtered saints, whose bones
    Lie scattered on the Alpine mountains cold,
    Ev'n them who kept thy truth so pure of old
    When all our fathers worshiped stocks and stones,
Forget not; in thy book record their groans   5
    Who were thy sheep, and in their ancient fold
    Slain by the bloody Piemontese that rolled
    Mother with infant down the rocks. Their moans
The vales redoubled to the hills, and they
        To heav'n. Their martyred blood and ashes sow   10
    O'er all th' Italian fields, where still doth sway
The triple tyrant, that from these may grow
    A hundredfold, who, having learnt thy way,
    Early may fly the Babylonian woe.

                                            (1655)

1. Rev. 6.9–10.
4. The sect was supposed to have originated in apostolic times. stocks and stones: Jer. 2.27.
5. book: see the note on *P.L.* 1.363.
9–10. Cf. Virgil, *Ecl.* 6.84.
10–14. Cf. the parable of the sower (Matt. 13.3–9) and the myth of the warriors who sprang from the dragon's teeth sowed by Cadmus. The idea of the blood of martyrs as the seed of the church goes back at least to

Tertullian, *Apologeticus* 50.
12. triple tyrant: the pope as wearer of the triple crown and claiming the keys of earth, heaven, and hell.
14. Many Reformation writers, including Spenser (*F.Q.*, Book 1), identified the papacy with the corrupt Babylon of Rev. 14.8, 17.5, 18.10. The Catholic Petrarch had done so in his Sonnet 108, which Milton partly translated in *Of Reformation* (see above); the sonnet contained the phrase *Fontana di dolore*.

Sonnet XX

EDWARD LAWRENCE (1633–57), the eldest son of Henry Lawrence (who wrote several theological tracts and was president of Cromwell's Council, 1654–59), became a member of parliament but died before he could fulfill his apparent promise of mind and character. His virtues were praised in a poem by Sir William Davenant; and he was the recipient of four letters from the German Henry Oldenburg, a friend of Milton who later was the first secretary of the Royal Society. This sonnet was apparently composed in 1655, in the late autumn or early winter.

Lawrence, of virtuous father virtuous son,
    Now that the fields are dank and ways are mire,
    Where shall we sometimes meet, and by the fire
    Help waste a sullen day, what may be won
From the hard season gaining? Time will run   5
    On smoother, till Favonius reinspire
    The frozen earth, and clothe in fresh attire
    The lily and rose, that neither sowed nor spun.
What neat repast shall feast us, light and choice,
    Of Attic taste, with wine, whence we may rise   10

1. Cf. Horace, *Od.* 1.16.1.
4. Cf. Horace, *Od.* 2.7.6.
6. Favonius: the west wind of spring (cf. Horace, *Od.* 1.4.1, 3.7.2).

8. Matt. 6.28.
10. Attic: defined by Milton's adjectives in line 9. Cf. the traditional phrase "Attic salt" for cultivated wit (*Epitaphium Damonis* 56).

To hear the lute well touched, or artful voice
Warble immortal notes and Tuscan air?
He who of those delights can judge, and spare
To interpose them oft, is not unwise.

(1655)

12. Tuscan: glossary.
13–14. Apparently a playful echo of a distich in the elementary school text, *Catonis Disticha* (London, 1628), 3.5.
13. spare: afford, spare time to (a meaning supported by the echo of *Cato* and by the conclusion of Sonnet 21).

14. unwise. The word recalls the Stoic and Epicurean ideal of the wise man who leads a disciplined life, perhaps also the parable of the wise and foolish virgins (cf. the end of Sonnet 9).

Sonnet XXI

CYRIACK SKINNER (1627–1700), grandson of Sir Edward Coke (who had been the great champion of the common law and opponent of excessive claims made for the royal prerogative by James and Charles), was himself a lawyer of liberal interests, a friend and former pupil of Milton. He has been put forward as the probable author of the early anonymous life of the poet. The sonnet was apparently composed in 1655.

Cyriack, whose grandsire on the royal bench
Of British Themis, with no mean applause
Pronounced and in his volumes taught our laws,
Which others at their bar so often wrench,
Today deep thoughts resolve with me to drench   5
In mirth that after no repenting draws;
Let Euclid rest and Archimedes pause,
And what the Swede intends, and what the French.
To measure life learn thou betimes, and know
Toward solid good what leads the nearest way;   10
For other things mild Heav'n a time ordains,
And disapproves that care, though wise in show,
That with superfluous burden loads the day,
And when God sends a cheerful hour, refrains.

(1655)

3. volumes: *Reports* (1600 f.) and *Institutes of the Laws of England* (1628–44).
7. The Greek Euclid and Archimedes represent mathematics and science.
7 f. Cf. Horace, *Od.* 2.11.1–4.
8. Swede. The young Charles X of Sweden, nephew of Gustavus Adolphus, spent his short reign, 1654–60, in attacks on Poland and Denmark. intends: in MS.; 1673, intend. French. French policy was at this time directed by Cardinal Mazarin.

Sonnet XXIII

MILTON'S FIRST WIFE (Mary Powell) had died in 1652. In November, 1656 he married Katherine Woodcock (b. 1628), who gave birth to a child in October, 1657, and died in February, 1658, when she was just short of thirty; the child died six weeks later. The sonnet, one of Milton's finest, is a very moving expression of devoted love, tenderness, and reverence from a man in whom Dr. Johnson and others have seen "something like a Turkish contempt of females." The octave is a grand and simple illustration of Milton's joining of classical, Hebraic, and Christian ideas and images.

Methought I saw my late espousèd saint
    Brought to me like Alcestis from the grave,
    Whom Jove's great son to her glad husband gave,
    Rescued from death by force, though pale and faint.
Mine, as whom washed from spot of child-bed taint   5
    Purification in the old Law did save,
    And such as yet once more I trust to have
    Full sight of her in heaven without restraint,
Came vested all in white, pure as her mind.
    Her face was veiled, yet to my fancied sight   10
    Love, sweetness, goodness in her person shined
So clear as in no face with more delight.
    But O as to embrace me she inclined,
    I waked, she fled, and day brought back my night.

(1658)

1. late . . . saint: i.e. the woman I lately married, now one of the blessed in heaven.

3. son: Heracles.   husband: Admetus.

4. death. In Euripides' play Death is personified as a figure with whom Heracles must contend.

6. Law: the ceremony for the purification of women after childbirth (Lev. 12). The reference is an external comparison which is not tied up with the precise circumstances of his wife's death.

7. once more. Milton had apparently never seen his second wife, so that in his dream her face is veiled (as Alcestis' would be). When he hopes "once more" to have "Full sight of her in heaven without restraint," the condensed phrasing evidently means that his present visionary sight of her will become a full reality in heaven.

9. Rev. 7.13–14.

PARADISE LOST

THE COMPOSITION of *Paradise Lost* was begun probably in 1657–58 and was completed by the summer of 1665, when Milton, driven by the Great Plague to Chalfont St. Giles in Buckinghamshire, gave the manuscript to his young Quaker friend, Thomas Ellwood, to read. It was published in 1667 as a poem in ten books, at the price of three shillings. Milton was given an initial payment of £5 and £5 more when the first edition of 1300 copies was exhausted; his widow received £8 when she sold all rights in 1680. In issues of 1668–69 Milton added the preface and a prose "argument" for the whole poem. In the second edition of 1674, the year of his death, the ten books became twelve, books 7 and 10 being divided into two each; the argument was broken up into sections prefixed to the individual books; and there were changes in minutiae.

We do not know how composition proceeded, whether in approximately the sequence we have or in diverse blocks later joined together. One passage, the deeply moving personal statement in the invocation of book 7 (lines 23–38), must obviously be dated after the Restoration. That passage is one reminder that for the blind poet night was a favorite time for composition, so that in the morning he "wanted to be milked." A favorite posture for dictation, we are told, was sitting with one leg thrown over the arm of his chair. There is no need of enlarging upon the ever-present handicaps of blindness and dependence upon other eyes and hands for transcribing, altering, arranging and rearranging, consulting books, and the later difficulties of proofreading. In whatever order Milton composed the poem, there must have been a great deal of revision, since the more we read it the more we see of its architectural design, not merely in the narrative as a whole but in innumerable links and contrasts in the smallest details.

Milton's first large ambition, as he said in *Mansus* and *Epitaphium Damonis,* was the writing of an Arthurian epic. But soon after his return from Italy he set down a list of nearly a hundred subjects for dramas, from biblical and British history, and he made four outlines, of increasing fullness, for a drama on Adam and Eve. The outlines indicate that this would have been semi-allegorical, in a form akin to that of modern Italian musical dramas. Edward Phillips reported that the first part of Satan's address to the sun (4.32–41) was written early as the opening speech of a tragedy. Milton shifted to the epic partly, we may suppose, because in Renaissance theory that was the grandest of poetic

Paradiſe loſt.

A
POEM

Written in
TEN BOOKS

By *JOHN MILTON*.

Licenſed and Entred according
to Order.

L O N D O N

Printed, and are to be ſold by *Peter Parker*
under *Creed* Church neer *Aldgate* ; And by
Robert Boulter at the *Turks Head* in *Biſhopſgate-ſtreet* ;
And *Matthias Walker*, under St. *Dunſtons* Church
in *Fleet-ſtreet*, 1667.

forms, but mainly because he needed more freedom and amplitude than drama allowed. Many parts of the narrative, however, are strongly dramatic.

As the *Nativity* reminds us, world-history was seen in a frame of three events: the creation and the fall of man; the life and death of Christ; and the end of the world and the day of judgment. All three have a place in *Paradise Lost:* the redemptive mission of Christ as the high point in the heavenly council and in Michael's revelation to Adam; and the new and perfect world of eternity — so far had the revolutionist's hopes receded — as the theme of recurrent allusion. The creation and the fall had over the centuries been the subject of many narratives and dramas as well as of much theological commentary; how much of these two large bodies of material Milton knew we cannot say, and we need not greatly care, since *Paradise Lost* has dwarfed all other imaginative treatments. In his youth Milton had shared the general esteem for Du Bartas' Protestant epic, called *Divine Weeks and Works* in Josuah Sylvester's popular translation. He had probably read two dramas, the *Adamus Exul* (1601) of Hugo Grotius (whom he had met in Paris) and *L'Adamo* (1613) of Giambattista Andreini. But possible "sources" and analogues are of interest mainly as evidence of what tradition prescribed or allowed in the necessary enlargement of the first chapters of Genesis. Within limits, a Christian author was free to use his imagination. He was in a position somewhat like that of a Greek dramatist reworking a familiar myth, with the important difference that in essentials the biblical story was sacred truth and, through its long sequel, of infinite meaning for both the poet and his readers. Milton could build on the strong foundation of traditional belief and emotional prepossessions. *Paradise Lost* would not be the poetic achievement it is if it had not been inspired by its author's own passionate religious vision.

In composing a heroic poem Milton, as a Renaissance humanist steeped in classical literature, inevitably followed Homer, whom he was said to have known by heart, and especially Virgil, the supreme formal model of neoclassical theory. *Lycidas* and other early poems show how Milton liked to work in a traditional pattern and how he transformed it in the process; in *Paradise Lost* the same artistic instinct works on a grand scale. We have such elements of epic convention as the invocation of the Muse; the plunge *in medias res;* the roll-call and council of leaders; the narrative recapitulation of events preceding the point at which the poem began; war and preliminary verbal combat; the prophetic unfolding of future history; and, throughout, the participation of divine beings in the action. But all these things are re-created on a new plane. Invocations of the Muse signalize changes of scene or focus and become earnest prayers for divine help. The roll-call of the chief rebels (1.376 f.) is, as in the seventh book of the *Aeneid,* a list of the enemies of Providence, but in Milton the list also pictures the spread of idolatry in the fallen world of history. The council in hell is a full and powerful debate which individualizes some leaders and reveals — like the description of hell that follows — the blindness of minds cut off from God. The contrasted council in heaven proclaims Milton's central belief in the free will and responsibility of man along with the divine means of his redemption. Raphael's long narrative (books 5–7) is not like Odysseus' story of personal adventures or Aeneas' larger account of the fall of Troy and the quest of a new home: Raphael tells of the ordered and evolutionary chain of being; of God's nomination of the Son as his vicegerent, the intermediary between God and man, the active agent of good in the world; of Satan's revolt and the war in heaven, an object-lesson for Adam and a kind of monstrous, anti-heroic burlesque of all war; of the contrasted work of peace, the Son's creation of the world. In the last two books the repentant Adam receives a spiritual education in being shown the grim course of human history, a prophetic picture very different from Aeneas' vision of Roman destiny; even Christianity becomes corrupt. While Milton the artist could imitate or draw upon Homer and Virgil and countless other classical authors, the invocations of books 1, 3, 7, and 9 declare at once his attachment to pagan poetry and his consciousness of soaring "Above th' Aonian mount," of dealing with higher Christian truth.

Even these bald data suggest the special problems that confronted Milton. In Homer the human theme was implicit in the material; the philosophic Virgil's dual theme was partly abstract — the place of Rome in history and the "pilgrim's progress" of the hero; but Milton went far beyond Virgil in using the concrete heroic medium in the attempt to

> assert Eternal Providence,
> And justify the ways of God to men.

His *dramatis personae* are God, the Son, and the good angels, Satan and other angelic rebels, the allegorical Sin and Death, and Adam and Eve, superhuman ideal figures who become ordinary human beings only when they sin. But what may seem to be heavy liabilities are in the main converted into assets, since the whole poem assumes the character of an archetypal myth of the nature and destiny of man seen against his cosmic background. Such a theme suited Milton's religious and poetic imagination; he was not, like Shakespeare, drawn directly to particular human scenes, persons, and passions. In its thematic design *Paradise Lost* is a Christian tragicomedy, a tragic reading of human experience which ends with a mixture of sadness, faith, and hope, a vision of perfection lost and partly recovered.

The once conventional label, "the Puritan epic," is almost completely meaningless. Only a few lines here and there reveal the indomitable republican, and the theology is in all essentials simply traditional Christianity, acceptable alike to Protestant and Catholic. For the theology of the poem Milton's huge Latin treatise, *De Doctrina Christiana* (finished about 1658–60), is in general an explicit and reliable guide. His chief heresies — the anti-Trinitarian subordination of the Son to the Father; the creation of the world out of God's own substance, not out of nothing; and the death of the soul along with the body until the resurrection — are spelled out in the treatise but in the poem are so inconspicuous that among generations of devout readers few observed their presence. Milton's religious creed, though it necessarily included elements of mystery, was of course much more definite than that of modern liberal Protestantism, but a modern reader of *Paradise Lost,* who may have no religious creed at all, does not need more than imaginative sympathy with a religious view of the world and man — and that he must have in order to read Dante or the undoctrinaire Shakespeare.

An epic in the heroic pattern virtually required that God and the Son should be speaking characters, and such anthropomorphism may seem to make the poem more fundamentalist than it is. Also, the dividing of the attributes of Deity, justice and mercy, between God and the Son has the effect at times of making God seem harsh, especially as God's utterance is reverently kept plain and bare, while the Son speaks throughout in the tone and rhythm of love. But God is a partly metaphysical Absolute and First Cause, the fountain of life and light and goodness, and divine reason is moral law, which the "right reason" of man can apprehend. God is not the Absolute Will of Calvinism: He vehemently rejects the Calvinistic doctrine of election and reprobation, and the "elect" are, in the liberal Arminian sense, all believers. No conviction of Milton's is more central and passionate than man's free will, and freedom must include freedom to err. At the same time he seems, in his later years, to have lost something of the buoyant confidence of *Areopagitica*, and, while he continues to stress reason and moral choice, he puts still more stress on humility, obedience, and love.

Satan's revolt against the new authority of the Son is not offered as an explanation of the origin of evil; that is part of the total "myth," and evil is seen as a universal fact of history and experience. The Devil of Christian tradition receives a few sentences in the *Christian Doctrine* because of biblical allusions to him and the war in heaven; but the Satan of the poem is one of the great figures of world-literature. Milton, though intoxicated by the idea of God and divine order, had the imagination needed to create a grand rebel. (We might recall that fine phrase from the *Doctrine and Discipline of Divorce*, 2.17: "as no man apprehends what vice is so well as he who is truly virtuous, no man knows hell like him who converses most in heaven.") Satan is a superhuman version of the heroes of classical epics, but their virtues are in him perverted as well as magnified; and he is in total contrast with the true heroism of Milton's two protagonists, the heavenly and sinless Son and the guilty but repentant and illuminated Adam. Milton was bold in giving the first two books, books of extraordinary energy and magnificence, to his cosmic villain; yet it is misleading to say, as many have said, that Satan's initial grandeur is later progressively degraded. Satan's first speech, a tremendous piece of rhetoric, is a full revelation of his egocentric pride and passion, and his later speeches and actions, from his relations with Sin and Death to his final metamorphosis, only deepen our sense of a nature wholly committed to evil. His first soliloquy (4.32–113) does give him a new dimension. Like the soliloquies of villains in Shakespeare, it is an acknowledgment of the speaker's wickedness, but, in revealing the conscience that his fellow-rebels lack, Satan takes on tragic potentialities; these, however, are not allowed to develop as he perseveres in evil. Since evil, whatever its triumphs, cannot ultimately prevail against God and good, Satan and his followers are seen throughout in the light of irony.

Irony, compassionate irony, also envelops the innocent Adam and Eve. One of Milton's finest strokes was to withhold his account of them until we accompany Satan into the garden, so that, though we do not see with his eyes, the picture of idyllic bliss is from the first overshadowed by its destroyer. Adam and Eve represent ideal perfection, ideal harmony with each other, with nature, and with God, and during their days of innocence they and their paradisal abode are kept at a mythic and aesthetic distance, through generalized description and ceremonial grace of speech. Milton very skilfully prepared for the fall, preserving the innocence of the pair while building up hints of latent weaknesses; indeed the first hints appear in Eve's first speech. Satan's temptations of Eve are more relevant now than they were in Milton's age, when science was only beginning to nourish *hybris*: Satan plays on the human desire for knowledge and power beyond the limits of human wisdom and stirs up Eve's ambition to be a goddess among the gods. Adam, in book 8, questions the cosmic economy but recognizes the folly of speculation on things remote from man's true ends; yet in the same book he delivers a eulogy of Eve which amounts to idolatry, to abdication of his responsibility to himself and God. The process of the actual fall, in book 9, is a remarkable stretch of close-up drama. Eve and Adam re-enact the sins of Satan and in so doing they sink to the merely human level, or below it. The process of recovery involves the panorama of human history and all its evils, but includes Christ's mission on earth, and the fallen Everyman and Everywoman gain a new understanding of sin and life and love. It is that dark picture of the fallen world that actualizes, so to speak, the total myth of the poem, and that gives full meaning to the marvelous last lines, lines of the utmost narrative simplicity and the most poignant emotional complexity.

Milton's central stage is the hearts of Adam and Eve, but the immensity of his cosmic stage is a religious, imaginative, and aesthetic fact of prime importance. While Raphael's account of a geocentric or heliocentric universe and other pas-sages are noncommittal, Milton naturally used the old and familiar system, which kept man's earth as a fixed and focal center. But the whole Ptolemaic world, our stellar world, is only a point in the universe of the poet's imagining; as it hangs in chaos, suspended from heaven, it looks to Satan like a small star beside the moon. Chaos, an almost boundless sea of raging elements, fills the space between heaven above and hell below (hell is not, as usual, inside the earth). Yet Milton's imagination is equal to its self-imposed task, and our sense of vast space is part of our aesthetic response. For an oblique example, Satan, flying up toward the gates of hell, looks far off like ships from the East Indies that "Ply stemming nightly toward the pole" — as if we, from a point above the globe, were seeing a wide expanse of ocean. Milton has nothing of Pascal's horror of the silence of infinite space, nor is he disturbed, as some men were, by the idea of a plurality of inhabited worlds, because God is present everywhere, even in chaos. And Milton, though not at all a mystic, sounds a half-mystical note whenever he touches that grand manifestation of divine order, the "starry dance" of the planets in their courses.

Paradise Lost is a network of dynamic parallels and contrasts both massive and minute — the Son and Satan, good and evil, love and hate, humility and pride, reason and passion, liberty and servitude, order and anarchy, natural sim-plicity and artificial luxury, upward and downward movement, time and timeless-ness, and so on. Such abstract ideas are made vividly alive through dramatic speech, action, and imagery, often through the subtle and repeated use of single words. Heaven and hell and Eden are both places and states of mind, so that nearly all physical description is more or less symbolic and carries an explicit or implicit moral judgment. Milton associates God and goodness with "holy Light," and the contrast between light and darkness is the most central and persistent strain of imagery; the symbolism is no less potent than simple, and it takes the most varied forms. Another conspicuous strain is the mythological. As in Renaissance art generally, classical myth is a storehouse of symbols of beauty, power, and horror beyond the limits of the human and actual, and in *Paradise Lost* these are naturally most abundant in the pictures of hell and of Eden. In weaving such allusions into a fabric of religious truth Milton often includes an apology, yet in themselves they may embody his most evocative art — witness the lines on Mulciber (1.740–48) and Proserpine (4.268–72) — and at the same time are related to the total theme. The latter example is a reminder of Milton's use of the epic simile. While Homer's similes are commonly drawn from the varied peacetime activities of a simple civilization, Milton's are more heterogeneous in substance and more closely illustrative. Mythological, biblical, geographical, historical, and scientific similes and allusions not only enrich our imaginative apprehension but bind the remote fable to the world, the fallen world, of history. Perhaps an exception should be made of the mythological similes in the descriptions of the garden and of Eve, where Milton's nostalgic theme is the pure beauty of prelapsarian innocence and nature's fecundity — though even these carry ominous or ironic overtones.

The language and style of *Paradise Lost* are unique in English poetry in their combined simplicity and sublimity. Any long poem, like Homer's and Virgil's, must be stylized, and Milton's theme required a style that would raise the mind above everyday affairs to the contemplation of first and last things. He echoed the Bible, both its phrases and ideas, more than any other book. Hebrew, Greek, and Latin poetry, and the precepts and practice of such modern Italians as Tasso, suggested ways of attaining elevation, magnificence, and force: compressed and elliptical syntax, the wrenching of normal word-order and the placing of words and phrases for degrees of emphasis, the long and complex periodic sentence, periphrasis, the novel and arresting and sometimes ambiguous use of words, including recurrent echoes and verbal plays. Such elements of the grand style — among them the most direct simplicity — had emerged in *Lycidas* and the heroic sonnets, and were further developed in the muscular toughness and energy of the prose tracts. They are not devices for mechanical inflation; periphrasis, for example, does not merely record a fact but carries a judgment on its significance. And Milton continually blends the general with the particular, the sensory with the moral and religious, so that his generalized style is both substantial and powerfully and complexly suggestive. Style and rhythm go along with imagination in creating the Miltonic world.

Milton is one of the boldest manipulators of language in English poetry (or in all poetry), and a number of critics, from Addison and Dr. Johnson onward, have complained that the English of *Paradise Lost* is almost a foreign idiom. To correct this conventional impressionistic opinion one has only to open the poem almost anywhere and read. The charge that it contains an un-English predominance of Latinate diction is simply not true; for instance, the first lines of the invocation to Light (3.1 f.), being theological and technical, are Latinate, but the main body of that incomparable passage is normal English. In general, diction varies with the nature of the occasion, and the flexible mixture of the elevated and the plain achieves the most varied effects. The syntax does not trouble us unless we are unable to read poetry without parsing; more important is the positive fact that Milton's fluid syntax is one of his most subtle instruments of expression, for both evoking emotion and controlling responses. But for all his learning and all the wealth of association and suggestion in his resonant language, Milton is much more accessible to the common reader than much of the poetry of our own time.

Milton was no less bold as a creator of rhythm than as a creator of style. His use of blank verse for a long poem was, as he said in his vigorous preface, an unprecedented innovation, and he exploited all the possibilities of expressive rhythm that his material invited or allowed and that his extraordinary ear could invent. The general looseness of his conception of blank verse was a charter of liberty. His basic principles can be defined only in imprecise terms: the unit is the ten-syllable line (often achieved through elision); syllables are most commonly grouped in pairs; and those pairs are most commonly iambic. Such principles left room for endless variations on an endlessly variable norm. Some of these had appeared in the sonnets, where the pattern of rhyme might be nearly lost through the combination of run-on lines and strong medial pauses or full stops. But the continuous flow of the epic gave much richer opportunities for the free orchestration of much larger units. As T. S. Eliot, a master of rhythm, has said, Milton's blank verse is never monotonous. And the inexhaustible pleasures of sound, in major or minor keys, are of course not merely aural; they have such functional expressiveness that, more than most poets, Milton must be read aloud. Rhythm goes along with substance and style to distinguish descriptions of hell and heaven, Eden and chaos; to characterize individual speakers in heaven and hell, God and the Son, the blunt Moloch and the sinuous Belial, the public harangues and the soliloquies of Satan; and the elaborate harmonies of the innocent Adam and Eve change with temptation and sin to semi-colloquial rhythms as well as syntax.

This short survey can only set up a few headings in regard to the theme, material, structure, and texture of *Paradise Lost*. During the last twenty-five years there have been more books written on the poem than on any other work in English literature except perhaps one or two plays of Shakespeare, and for the last five years the exception may not hold. Sophisticated and perceptive criticism has found in *Paradise Lost* more and more to excite and capture the modern reader, a uniquely powerful blend of splendor, simplicity, and subtlety. But, with all the excellent guidance available, that reader must tune his faculties to concert pitch and experience the poem for himself. If his imagination cannot go along with Milton's passionate faith in God and freewill and the attainment of a "paradise within," he can at least hardly fail to respond to a compassionate myth of the precarious human situation, a myth which in one way or another comprehends all that mankind has felt and thought and done throughout the course of history.

Paradiſe Loſt.

A
POEM
IN
TWELVE BOOKS.

The Author
JOHN MILTON.

𝔗𝔥𝔢 𝔖𝔢𝔠𝔬𝔫𝔡 𝔈𝔡𝔦𝔱𝔦𝔬𝔫
Reviſed and Augmented by the
ſame Author.

LONDON,
Printed by *S. Simmons* next door to the
Golden Lion in *Alderſgate-ſtreet,* 1674.

ON PARADISE LOST*

When I beheld the poet blind, yet bold,
In slender book his vast design unfold —
Messiah crowned, God's reconciled decree,
Rebelling angels, the forbidden tree,
Heaven, hell, earth, chaos, all — the argu-
    ment   5
Held me a while misdoubting his intent,
That he would ruin (for I saw him strong)
The sacred truths to fable and old song
(So Samson groped the temple's posts in
    spite),
The world o'erwhelming to revenge his
    sight.   10
  Yet as I read, soon growing less severe,
I liked his project, the success did fear —
Through that wide field how he his way
    should find
O'er which lame faith leads understanding
    blind;
Lest he perplexed the things he would ex-
    plain,   15
And what was easy he should render vain.
  Or if a work so infinite he spanned,
Jealous I was that some less skilful hand
(Such as disquiet always what is well,
And by ill imitating would excel)   20
Might hence presume the whole creation's
    day
To change in scenes, and show it in a play.
  Pardon me, mighty poet, nor despise
My causeless, yet not impious, surmise.
But I am now convinced, and none will
    dare   25
Within thy labors to pretend a share.
Thou hast not missed one thought that
    could be fit,
And all that was improper dost omit;

So that no room is here for writers left,
But to detect their ignorance or theft.   30
  The majesty which through thy work doth
    reign
Draws the devout, deterring the profane.
And things divine thou treat'st of in such
    state
As them preserves, and thee, inviolate.
At once delight and horror on us seize;   35
Thou sing'st with so much gravity and ease,
And above human flight dost soar aloft
With plume so strong, so equal, and so soft.
The bird named from that Paradise you sing
So never flags, but always keeps on wing.   40
  Where could'st thou words of such a com-
    pass find?
Whence furnish such a vast expense of
    mind?
Just Heav'n, thee like Tiresias to requite,
Rewards with prophecy thy loss of sight.
  Well might'st thou scorn thy readers to
    allure   45
With tinkling rhyme, of thy own sense se-
    cure;
While the Town-Bayes writes all the while
    and spells,
And like a pack-horse tires without his
    bells.
Their fancies like our bushy points appear;
The poets tag them, we for fashion wear.   50
I too, transported by the mode, offend,
And, while I meant to *praise* thee, must
    commend.
Thy verse created like thy theme sublime,
In number, weight, and measure, needs not
    rhyme.

                   A.M.

* A commendatory poem by Andrew Marvell
prefixed to the second edition (1674).
  18. John Aubrey recorded Dryden's calling
on Milton to ask permission to turn *Paradise
Lost* into a drama in rhyme: "Mr. Milton received him civilly and told him he would give
him leave to tag his verses." Tags were metal
points attached to the ends of ribbons.

  39–40. Birds of Paradise were traditionally
thought to have no feet and hence to be always
in flight.
  47. "Bayes" was a common nickname for
Dryden (from the Duke of Buckingham's
satirical play, *The Rehearsal*).
  49. bushy points: tasseled fasteners for hose.
  54. rhyme. See the note on Milton's preface.

Paradise Lost

THE VERSE[1]

The measure is English heroic verse without rhyme, as that of Homer in Greek and of Virgil in Latin, rhyme being no necessary adjunct or true ornament of poem or good verse, in longer works especially, but the invention of a barbarous age, to set off wretched matter and lame meter — graced indeed since by the use of some famous modern poets, carried away by custom, but much to their own vexation, hindrance, and constraint to express many things otherwise, and for the most part worse, than else they would have expressed them. Not without cause, therefore, some both Italian and Spanish poets of prime note have rejected rhyme both in longer and shorter works, as have also long since our best English tragedies, as a thing of itself, to all judicious ears, trivial and of no true musical delight; which consists only in apt numbers, fit quantity[2] of syllables, and the sense variously drawn out from one verse into another, not in the jingling sound of like endings, a fault avoided by the learned ancients both in poetry and all good oratory. This neglect then of rhyme so little is to be taken for a defect, though it may seem so perhaps to vulgar readers, that it rather is to be esteemed an example set, the first in English, of ancient liberty recovered to heroic poem from the troublesome and modern bondage of rhyming.

Book I

THE ARGUMENT

This first book proposes, first in brief, the whole subject, man's disobedience, and the loss thereupon of Paradise wherein he was placed: then touches the prime cause of his fall, the Serpent, or rather Satan in the Serpent; who, revolting from God, and drawing to his side many legions of angels, was by the command of God driven out of heaven with all his crew into the great deep. Which action passed over, the poem hastes into the midst of things, presenting Satan with his angels now fallen into hell — described here, not in the center (for heaven and earth may be supposed as yet not made, certainly not yet accursed), but in a place of utter darkness, fitliest called Chaos. Here Satan with his angels lying on the burning lake, thunderstruck and astonished, after a certain space recovers, as from confusion; calls up him who, next in order and dignity, lay by him; they confer of their miserable fall. Satan awakens all his legions, who lay till then in the same manner confounded.

[1] This preface was not in the first issue of *P.L.* but was added in one of the later issues of 1668. Milton's vigorous defense of his bold innovation, the use of blank verse for a heroic poem, and his censure of rhyme may in part reflect the recent debate between Dryden and Sir Robert Howard.

[2] quantity: number.

They rise: their numbers, array of battle, their chief leaders named, according to the idols known afterwards in Canaan and the countries adjoining. To these Satan directs his speech, comforts them with hope yet of regaining heaven, but tells them lastly of a new world and new kind of creature to be created, according to an ancient prophecy or report in heaven; for that angels were long before this visible creation was the opinion of many ancient fathers. To find out the truth of this prophecy, and what to determine thereon, he refers to a full council. What his associates thence attempt. Pandemonium, the palace of Satan, rises, suddenly built out of the deep; the infernal peers there sit in council.

O<small>F</small> MAN's first disobedience, and the fruit
Of that forbidden tree, whose mortal taste
Brought death into the world, and all our woe,
With loss of Eden, till one greater Man
Restore us, and regain the blissful seat,   5
Sing, Heav'nly Muse, that on the secret top
Of Oreb, or of Sinai, didst inspire
That shepherd who first taught the chosen seed
In the beginning how the heav'ns and earth
Rose out of Chaos; or if Sion hill   10
Delight thee more, and Siloa's brook that flowed
Fast by the oracle of God, I thence
Invoke thy aid to my advent'rous song,
That with no middle flight intends to soar
Above th' Aonian mount, while it pursues   15
Things unattempted yet in prose or rhyme.
And chiefly thou, O Spirit, that dost prefer
Before all temples th' upright heart and pure,
Instruct me, for thou know'st; thou from the first
Wast present, and with mighty wings outspread   20
Dove-like sat'st brooding on the vast abyss
And mad'st it pregnant: what in me is dark
Illumine, what is low raise and support;
That to the highth of this great argument
I may assert Eternal Providence,   25

BOOK I. 1. fruit: both "fruit" and "result."
2. mortal: both "human" and "fatal."
4. one greater Man: Christ, in theological tradition "the second Adam"; cf. Rom. 5.19, 1 Cor. 15.21, *P.L.* 3.285–89, 12.386 f., *P.R.* 1.1–7, 4.606–09.
6. Heav'nly Muse: glossary, "Urania."
8. shepherd: Moses, the supposed author of Genesis, etc. God first spoke to him when he watched sheep on Mount Horeb (Exod. 3.1 f.) and gave him the law on Sinai when he was "shepherd" of his people (Exod. 19 f., 34).
11. Siloa: the brook and pool near the temple ("oracle": 1 Kings 6.19–20) of Jerusalem (Isa. 8.6; John 9.1–11). The reference corresponds to the fountains of the pagan Muses.

14. Cf. the three traditional styles or levels of rhetoric, "lofty, mean [i.e. "middle"], or lowly" (*Of Education*).
16. From Ariosto, *O.F.* 1.2.2.
17. Spirit. Not the third person of the Trinity, who Milton says may not be invoked (*C.D.* 1.6), but a personification of God's creative power and wisdom; cf. Gen. 1.2, the apocryphal Wisdom of Solomon 7–8, *P.L.* 7.5 f., and, in the passage quoted above from the *Reason of Church Government*, the sentence "Neither do I think it shame. . . ."
18. Ps. 15.1–2, 1 Cor. 3.16.
21. Gen. 1.2. Dove-like: Matt. 3.16, Mark 1.10, Luke 3.22, John 1.32.

And justify the ways of God to men.
    Say first, for heav'n hides nothing from thy view,
Nor the deep tract of hell, say first what cause
Moved our grand parents in that happy state,
Favored of Heav'n so highly, to fall off   30
From their Creator, and transgress his will
For one restraint, lords of the world besides?
Who first seduced them to that foul revolt?
Th' infernal Serpent; he it was whose guile,
Stirred up with envy and revenge, deceived   35
The mother of mankind, what time his pride
Had cast him out from heav'n, with all his host
Of rebel angels, by whose aid aspiring
To set himself in glory above his peers,
He trusted to have equaled the Most High,   40
If he opposed; and with ambitious aim
Against the throne and monarchy of God
Raised impious war in heav'n and battle proud
With vain attempt. Him the Almighty Power
Hurled headlong flaming from th' ethereal sky   45
With hideous ruin and combustion down
To bottomless perdition, there to dwell
In adamantine chains and penal fire,
Who durst defy th' Omnipotent to arms.
Nine times the space that measures day and night   50
To mortal men, he with his horrid crew
Lay vanquished, rolling in the fiery gulf
Confounded though immortal. But his doom
Reserved him to more wrath; for now the thought
Both of lost happiness and lasting pain   55
Torments him; round he throws his baleful eyes,
That witnessed huge affliction and dismay
Mixed with obdúrate pride and steadfast hate.
At once as far as angels ken he views
The dismal situation waste and wild: 60
A dungeon horrible, on all sides round
As one great furnace flamed, yet from those flames
No light, but rather darkness visible
Served only to discover sights of woe,
Regions of sorrow, doleful shades, where peace   65

26. justify: show the justice of.
27–32. Cf. *Aen.* 1.8–11.
34 f. The serpent of Gen. 3 was in tradition identified with Satan (Rev. 12.9 f., 20.1–3, etc.). For the question and answer, cf. *Iliad* 1.8 f.
44 f. Luke 10.18, 2 Pet. 2.4, Jude 6, Rev. 20.1–3.
50. The Titans, overthrown by Zeus, fell nine days and nights from heaven to earth and nine more down to Tartarus (Hesiod, *Theog.* 720 f.).

53–54. The transition from the general exordium *in medias res*.
57. witnessed: reflected, expressed.
59. angels ken. Since in Milton's time the possessive apostrophe was quite commonly not used, "ken" may be either a noun (as in 3.622, 11.379) or a verb (as, with an object, in 5.265, 11.396, *P.R.* 2.286); here it is probably a verb.
63. No light. In theological tradition the fires of hell gave forth no light. visible: that can be seen through (cf. Job 10.22).

And rest can never dwell, hope never comes
That comes to all; but torture without end
Still urges, and a fiery deluge, fed
With ever-burning sulphur unconsumed:
Such place Eternal Justice had prepared   70
For those rebellious, here their prison ordained
In utter darkness, and their portion set
As far removed from God and light of heav'n
As from the center thrice to th' utmost pole.
O how unlike the place from whence they fell!   75
There the companions of his fall, o'erwhelmed
With floods and whirlwinds of tempestuous fire,
He soon discerns, and welt'ring by his side
One next himself in power, and next in crime,
Long after known in Palestine, and named   80
Beelzebub. To whom th' Arch-Enemy,
And thence in heav'n called Satan, with bold words
Breaking the horrid silence thus began:
    "If thou beest he — but O how fall'n! how changed
From him, who in the happy realms of light   85
Clothed with transcendent brightness didst outshine
Myriads though bright — if he whom mutual league,
United thoughts and counsels, equal hope
And hazard in the glorious enterprise,
Joined with me once, now misery hath joined   90
In equal ruin: into what pit thou seest
From what highth fall'n, so much the stronger proved
He with his thunder, and till then who knew
The force of those dire arms? Yet not for those,
Nor what the potent Victor in his rage   95
Can else inflict, do I repent or change,
Though changed in outward luster, that fixed mind
And high disdain, from sense of injured merit,
That with the mightiest raised me to contend,
And to the fierce contention brought along   100
Innumerable force of Spirits armed

66. hope: cf. Dante, *Inf.* 3.9; Euripides, *Troades* 681–82.

70–71. Matt. 25.41

72. utter: outer (Matt. 8.12, 22.13). Hell was commonly placed deep in the interior of the earth; in Milton's vast universe it is below his invented Chaos, at the top of which the Ptolemaic world of spheres (glossary) hangs from heaven.

74. center, pole: glossary. "Thrice" is indefinite, not an exact measurement; cf. *Iliad* 8.16; Hesiod, *Theog.* 720–21; *Aen.* 6.578–79.

81. Arch-Enemy. The name Satan means "adversary" (1 Pet. 5.8; cf. *P.L.* 10.386–87).

84–85. how . . . From him. Cf. Isa. 14.12: "How art thou fallen from heaven, O Lucifer, son of the morning"; *Aen.* 2.274–75: *ei mihi, qualis erat! quantum mutatus ab illo Hectore.*

87. If [thou beest] he.

89. glorious enterprise. This, the first of countless phrases which ironically reveal Satan's false scale of values, may echo the *glorioso acquisto* and *alta impresa* of Tasso, *G.L.* 1.1 and 6. The whole speech, like Satan's later speeches (apart from soliloquies), repudiates all religious and moral principles and glorifies egoistic pride and passion.

91–94. Satan's incoherent unfinished phrases reflect his agitation.

94–97. Cf. Aeschylus, *Prometheus Bound* 987–96.

97–98. fixed mind . . . high disdain: in Spenser, *F.Q.* 4.7.16.5, 1.1.19.6.

98. merit: contrasted throughout with the real merit of the Son (3.290, 309, 319, etc.).

That durst dislike his reign, and me preferring,
His utmost power with adverse power opposed
In dubious battle on the plains of heav'n,
And shook his throne. What though the field be lost?   105
All is not lost; the unconquerable will,
And study of revenge, immortal hate,
And courage never to submit or yield:
And what is else not to be overcome?
That glory never shall his wrath or might   110
Extort from me. To bow and sue for grace
With suppliant knee, and deify his power
Who from the terror of this arm so late
Doubted his empire, that were low indeed,
That were an ignominy and shame beneath   115
This downfall; since by fate the strength of gods
And this empyreal substance cannot fail,
Since through experience of this great event,
In arms not worse, in foresight much advanced,
We may with more successful hope resolve   120
To wage by force or guile eternal war
Irreconcilable to our grand Foe,
Who now triumphs, and in th' excess of joy
Sole reigning holds the tyranny of heav'n."
So spake th' apostate Angel, though in pain,   125
Vaunting aloud, but racked with deep despair;
And him thus answered soon his bold compeer:
"O Prince, O Chief of many thronèd Powers,
That led th' embattled Seraphim to war
Under thy conduct, and in dreadful deeds   130
Fearless, endangered heav'n's perpetual King,
And put to proof his high supremacy,
Whether upheld by strength, or chance, or fate;
Too well I see and rue the dire event,
That with sad overthrow and foul defeat   135
Hath lost us heav'n, and all this mighty host
In horrible destruction laid thus low,
As far as gods and heav'nly essences
Can perish: for the mind and spirit remains
Invincible, and vigor soon returns,   140
Though all our glory extinct, and happy state
Here swallowed up in endless misery.
But what if he our Conqueror (whom I now
Of force believe almighty, since no less
Than such could have o'erpow'red such force as ours)   145
Have left us this our spirit and strength entire
Strongly to suffer and support our pains,

109. And what else is this state of mind than not to be defeated?
114. Doubted: feared for.
115. ignominy: pronounced *ignomy* (and in 2.207).
128–29. Powers, Seraphim: glossary, "angels."
144. Of force: perforce.

That we may so suffice his vengeful ire,
Or do him mightier service as his thralls
By right of war, whate'er his business be,   150
Here in the heart of hell to work in fire,
Or do his errands in the gloomy deep?
What can it then avail though yet we feel
Strength undiminished, or eternal being
To undergo eternal punishment?"   155
   Whereto with speedy words th' Arch-Fiend replied:
"Fall'n Cherub, to be weak is miserable,
Doing or suffering: but of this be sure,
To do aught good never will be our task,
But ever to do ill our sole delight,   160
As being the contrary to his high will
Whom we resist. If then his providence
Out of our evil seek to bring forth good,
Our labor must be to pervert that end,
And out of good still to find means of evil;   165
Which ofttimes may succeed, so as perhaps
Shall grieve him, if I fail not, and disturb
His inmost counsels from their destined aim.
But see the angry Victor hath recalled
His ministers of vengeance and pursuit   170
Back to the gates of heav'n; the sulphurous hail
Shot after us in storm, o'erblown hath laid
The fiery surge, that from the precipice
Of heav'n received us falling, and the thunder,
Winged with red lightning and impetuous rage,   175
Perhaps hath spent his shafts, and ceases now
To bellow through the vast and boundless deep.
Let us not slip th' occasion, whether scorn
Or satiate fury yield it from our Foe.
Seest thou yon dreary plain, forlorn and wild,   180
The seat of desolation, void of light,
Save what the glimmering of these livid flames
Casts pale and dreadful? Thither let us tend
From off the tossing of these fiery waves,
There rest, if any rest can harbor there,   185
And reassembling our afflicted powers,
Consult how we may henceforth most offend
Our Enemy, our own loss how repair,
How overcome this dire calamity,
What reinforcement we may gain from hope;   190
If not, what resolution from despair."
   Thus Satan talking to his nearest mate
With head uplift above the wave, and eyes
That sparkling blazed; his other parts besides

---

155. To: so as to.
157. Cherub: glossary, "angels."
162–65. A statement, from Satan's point of view, of Milton's theme; cf. 211–20 below and 12.469 f.
167. fail: mistake.

Prone on the flood, extended long and large   195
Lay floating many a rood, in bulk as huge
As whom the fables name of monstrous size,
Titanian or Earth-born, that warred on Jove,
Briareos or Typhon, whom the den
By ancient Tarsus held, or that sea-beast   200
Leviathan, which God of all his works
Created hugest that swim th' ocean stream:
Him haply slumb'ring on the Norway foam,
The pilot of some small night-foundered skiff,
Deeming some island, oft, as seamen tell,   205
With fixèd anchor in his scaly rind
Moors by his side under the lee, while night
Invests the sea, and wishèd morn delays:
So stretched out huge in length the Arch-Fiend lay
Chained on the burning lake; nor ever thence   210
Had ris'n or heaved his head, but that the will
And high permission of all-ruling Heaven
Left him at large to his own dark designs,
That with reiterated crimes he might
Heap on himself damnation, while he sought   215
Evil to others, and enraged might see
How all his malice served but to bring forth
Infinite goodness, grace and mercy shown
On man by him seduced, but on himself
Treble confusion, wrath and vengeance poured.   220
    Forthwith upright he rears from off the pool
His mighty stature; on each hand the flames
Driv'n backward slope their pointing spires, and rolled
In billows, leave i' th' midst a horrid vale.
Then with expanded wings he steers his flight   225
Aloft, incumbent on the dusky air
That felt unusual weight, till on dry land
He lights, if it were land that ever burned
With solid, as the lake with liquid fire,
And such appeared in hue; as when the force   230
Of subterranean wind transports a hill
Torn from Pelorus, or the shattered side

197–200. Both Titans, represented by Briareos, and Giants, represented by Typhon, warred against the supreme power (see glossary). The two attempts (often confused in ancient and later story) could be taken in Christian tradition as a parallel to, or pagan version of, Satan's pride and revolt.
200–08. Leviathan: the biblical sea-monster (Job 41, Ps. 104.26, Isa. 27.1), often regarded as a whale; linked also with the Dragon (Satan) of Rev. (*P.L.* 4.1f. and notes). In various medieval stories the monster was mistaken by sailors for an island and in bestiaries its submerging with an anchored ship was likened to Satan's drawing men to hell.

202. The Greek idea of the ocean as a stream encircling the earth.
204. night-foundered: benighted (as in *Comus* 483), or perhaps "in danger of sinking."
206–08. Cf. Acts 27.26–29.
222–24. Cf. the Israelites' miraculous passage through the Red Sea (Exod. 14.21 f.).
229–30. This, the MS. reading, seems more logical than that of the first two editions (fire; . . . hue,), which would restrict the simile to color or appearance only.
230–37. Cf. *Aen.* 3.570–77; Lucretius, 6.680–93; Ovid, *Met.* 15.298–306.

Of thund'ring Etna, whose combustible
And fueled entrails thence conceiving fire,
Sublimed with mineral fury, aid the winds, 235
And leave a singèd bottom all involved
With stench and smoke: such resting found the sole
Of unblest feet. Him followed his next mate,
Both glorying to have scaped the Stygian flood
As gods, and by their own recovered strength, 240
Not by the sufferance of supernal power.
  "Is this the region, this the soil, the clime,"
Said then the lost Archangel, "this the seat
That we must change for heav'n, this mournful gloom
For that celestial light? Be it so, since he 245
Who now is sovran can dispose and bid
What shall be right: fardest from him is best,
Whom reason hath equaled, force hath made supreme
Above his equals. Farewell, happy fields,
Where joy for ever dwells! Hail, horrors, hail, 250
Infernal world, and thou, profoundest hell,
Receive thy new possessor: one who brings
A mind not to be changed by place or time.
The mind is its own place, and in itself
Can make a heav'n of hell, a hell of heav'n. 255
What matter where, if I be still the same,
And what I should be, all but less than he
Whom thunder hath made greater? Here at least
We shall be free; th' Almighty hath not built
Here for his envy, will not drive us hence: 260
Here we may reign secure, and in my choice
To reign is worth ambition, though in hell:
Better to reign in hell than serve in heav'n.
But wherefore let we then our faithful friends,
Th' associates and copartners of our loss, 265
Lie thus astonished on th' oblivious pool,
And call them not to share with us their part
In this unhappy mansion, or once more
With rallied arms to try what may be yet
Regained in heav'n, or what more lost in hell?" 270
  So Satan spake, and him Beelzebub
Thus answered: "Leader of those armies bright,

---

235. Sublimed: vaporized (from alchemy).
237–38. Gen. 8.9.
239. Stygian flood: here the lake of fire.
254–55. For good Christians like Benjamin Whichcote (*Aphorisms* 100, 202, 464, 583), Sir Thomas Browne (*Religio Medici* 1.49, 51), and Milton, heaven and hell were states of mind as well as places, but the idea that both were merely mental was a traditional heresy; the mind's independence of circumstance was a central Stoic doctrine.

254. its: see glossary.
257. all but: scarcely.
263. The shade of Achilles felt otherwise (*Odyssey* 11.489–91). Cf. Plutarch, *Julius Caesar* 11; P. Fletcher, *Purple Island* 7.10: "In heav'n they scorned to serve, so now in hell they reign."
266. oblivious: causing forgetfulness (like Lethe).
267–68. Rev. 21.8; John 14.2 (cf. *P.L.* 2.462, 6.738).

Which but th' Omnipotent none could have foiled,
If once they hear that voice, their liveliest pledge
Of hope in fears and dangers, heard so oft   275
In worst extremes, and on the perilous edge
Of battle when it raged, in all assaults
Their surest signal, they will soon resume
New courage and revive, though now they lie
Groveling and prostrate on yon lake of fire,   280
As we erewhile, astounded and amazed;
No wonder, fall'n such a pernicious highth!"
    He scarce had ceased when the superior Fiend
Was moving toward the shore; his ponderous shield,
Ethereal temper, massy, large, and round,   285
Behind him cast; the broad circumference
Hung on his shoulders like the moon, whose orb
Through optic glass the Tuscan artist views
At ev'ning from the top of Fesole,
Or in Valdarno, to descry new lands,   290
Rivers or mountains in her spotty globe.
His spear, to equal which the tallest pine
Hewn on Norwegian hills, to be the mast
Of some great ammiral, were but a wand,
He walked with to support uneasy steps   295
Over the burning marl, not like those steps
On heaven's azure; and the torrid clime
Smote on him sore besides, vaulted with fire.
Nathless he so endured, till on the beach
Of that inflamèd sea, he stood and called   300
His legions, angel forms, who lay entranced,
Thick as autumnal leaves that strow the brooks
In Vallombrosa, where th' Etrurian shades
High over-arched embow'r; or scattered sedge
Afloat, when with fierce winds Orion armed   305
Hath vexed the Red Sea coast, whose waves o'erthrew
Busiris and his Memphian chivalry,
While with perfidious hatred they pursued
The sojourners of Goshen, who beheld
From the safe shore their floating carcasses   310

288. Tuscan artist: the "Italian expert," Galileo (1564–1642), who lived for a time near Florence on the hill of Fiesole, above the valley of the Arno river, in his *Sidereus Nuncius* (1610) reported his telescopic observations of the moon. In 1638–39 Milton had visited him.
292–94. Cf. *Aen.* 3.659; Cowley, *Davideis* 3 (ed. Waller, p. 334).
294. ammiral: admiral's ship.
296. marl: soil.
299. Nathless: nevertheless.
302. The germ of the simile was traditional (*Iliad* 2.468, 800, 6.146–49; *Aen.* 6.309–10; Dante, *Inf.* 3.112–14), but as usual Milton

adds concrete particulars for his own purposes.
303. Vallombrosa: a "shady valley" about 18 miles from Florence in Tuscany (ancient Etruria).
307. The Pharaoh who first oppressed the Israelites and whose daughter found Moses (Exod. 1–2) was sometimes identified with the cruel king Busiris (Ralegh, *History of the World* 1.2.2.7; G. Sandys, *Ovid*, 1632, p. 321); a later Busiris was linked with the exodus in a book Milton knew, the *Chronicle* of Carion revised by Melanchthon.
309. Goshen: the Egyptian home of the Israelites, east of the Nile Delta (Gen. 47.27).

And broken chariot wheels; so thick bestrown,
Abject and lost lay these, covering the flood,
Under amazement of their hideous change.
He called so loud that all the hollow deep
Of hell resounded: "Princes, Potentates,   315
Warriors, the flow'r of heav'n, once yours, now lost,
If such astonishment as this can seize
Eternal Spirits; or have ye chos'n this place
After the toil of battle to repose
Your wearied virtue, for the ease you find   320
To slumber here, as in the vales of heav'n?
Or in this abject posture have ye sworn
To adore the Conqueror, who now beholds
Cherub and Seraph rolling in the flood
With scattered arms and ensigns, till anon   325
His swift pursuers from heav'n gates discern
Th' advantage, and descending tread us down
Thus drooping, or with linkèd thunderbolts
Transfix us to the bottom of this gulf?
Awake, arise, or be for ever fall'n!"   330
    They heard, and were abashed, and up they sprung
Upon the wing, as when men wont to watch
On duty, sleeping found by whom they dread,
Rouse and bestir themselves ere well awake.
Nor did they not perceive the evil plight   335
In which they were, or the fierce pains not feel;
Yet to their general's voice they soon obeyed
Innumerable. As when the potent rod
Of Amram's son in Egypt's evil day
Waved round the coast, up called a pitchy cloud   340
Of locusts, warping on the eastern wind,
That o'er the realm of impious Pharaoh hung
Like night, and darkened all the land of Nile:
So numberless were those bad angels seen
Hovering on wing under the cope of hell   345
'Twixt upper, nether, and surrounding fires;
Till, as a signal giv'n, th' uplifted spear
Of their great Sultan waving to direct
Their course, in even balance down they light
On the firm brimstone, and fill all the plain;   350
A multitude, like which the populous North
Poured never from her frozen loins, to pass
Rhene or the Danaw, when her barbarous sons

---

312. Abject: cast down.
335. Nor . . . not: a classical idiom.
339. Amram's son: Moses (Exod. 6.20).
340. pitchy cloud: used, in the plural, by
Sandys in rendering Ovid's *picea caligine* (*Met.*
1.265) and *piceis nubibus* (ibid., 11.549).
341. locusts: Exod. 10.12 f.   warping:
tacking, veering.

348. Sultan: a word which, in view of the
Turks' westward advance in the 15th and 16th
centuries, had the sinister connotation of the
modern *Führer*.
351 f. The barbarian invasions of Europe in
the early Middle Ages.
353. The Rhine; the Danube.

Came like a deluge on the South, and spread
Beneath Gibraltar to the Libyan sands.   355
Forthwith from every squadron and each band
The heads and leaders thither haste where stood
Their great commander; godlike shapes and forms
Excelling human, princely dignities,
And powers that erst in heaven sat on thrones;   360
Though of their names in heav'nly records now
Be no memorial, blotted out and razed
By their rebellion from the Books of Life.
Nor had they yet among the sons of Eve
Got them new names, till wand'ring o'er the earth,   365
Through God's high sufferance for the trial of man,
By falsities and lies the greatest part
Of mankind they corrupted to forsake
God their Creator, and th' invisible
Glory of him that made them to transform   370
Oft to the image of a brute, adorned
With gay religions full of pomp and gold,
And devils to adore for deities:
Then were they known to men by various names,
And various idols through the heathen world.   375
    Say, Muse, their names then known, who first, who last,
Roused from the slumber on that fiery couch,
At their great emperor's call, as next in worth
Came singly where he stood on the bare strand,
While the promiscuous crowd stood yet aloof.   380
    The chief were those who from the pit of hell,
Roaming to seek their prey on earth, durst fix
Their seats long after next the seat of God,
Their altars by his altar, gods adored
Among the nations round, and durst abide   385
Jehovah thund'ring out of Sion, throned
Between the Cherubim; yea, often placed
Within his sanctuary itself their shrines,
Abominations; and with cursèd things
His holy rites and solemn feasts profaned,   390
And with their darkness durst affront his light.
First Moloch, horrid king besmeared with blood
Of human sacrifice, and parents' tears,
Though for the noise of drums and timbrels loud

---

363. Books of Life: God's record of the
righteous (Exod. 32.32–33; Ps. 69.28; Rev.
3.5, 20.15, 21.27).
    370–73. Deut. 32.17; Rom. 1.23; 1 Cor.
10.20–21; etc.
    374 f. Milton naturally used the patristic
and later tradition that the fallen angels became the gods of the heathen religions (cf.
Nativity 173 f.). The roll-call of leaders is akin
to that of *Aen.* 7.641 f., where the Italian followers of Turnus who band together against

Aeneas are opposing the will of Providence.
Milton's catalogue recalls places where the
enemies of God and Israel were overthrown,
relates his fable to the corrupted world of
history, and signalizes some of the debaters of
book 2. The Homeric and Virgilian catalogues
begin with an invocation (*Iliad* 2.484; *Aen.*,
loc. cit.).
    382. 1 Pet. 5.8.
    383–91. 2 Kings 16, 17, 21, etc.; Ps. 80.1.

Their children's cries unheard, that passed through fire   395
To his grim idol. Him the Ammonite
Worshiped in Rabba and her wat'ry plain,
In Argob and in Basan, to the stream
Of utmost Arnon. Nor content with such
Audacious neighborhood, the wisest heart   400
Of Solomon he led by fraud to build
His temple right against the temple of God
On that opprobrious hill, and made his grove
The pleasant valley of Hinnom, Tophet thence
And black Gehenna called, the type of hell.   405
Next Chemos, th' óbscene dread of Moab's sons,
From Aroer to Nebo, and the wild
Of southmost Abarim; in Hesebon
And Horonaim, Seon's realm, beyond
The flow'ry dale of Sibma clad with vines,   410
And Elealè to th' Asphaltic pool:
Peor his other name, when he enticed
Israel in Sittim on their march from Nile
To do him wanton rites, which cost them woe.
Yet thence his lustful orgies he enlarged   415
Even to that hill of scandal, by the grove
Of Moloch homicide, lust hard by hate;
Till good Josiah drove them thence to hell.
With these came they who, from the bord'ring flood
Of old Euphrates to the brook that parts   420
Egypt from Syrian ground, had general names
Of Baalim and Ashtaroth, those male,
These feminine. For Spirits when they please
Can either sex assume, or both; so soft
And uncompounded is their essence pure,   425
Not tied or manacled with joint or limb,
Nor founded on the brittle strength of bones,
Like cumbrous flesh; but in what shape they choose,
Dilated or condensed, bright or obscure,
Can execute their airy purposes,   430
And works of love or enmity fulfill.
For those the race of Israel oft forsook
Their living Strength, and unfrequented left
His righteous altar, bowing lowly down

397–420. The towns, districts, etc., are east of the Jordan and the Dead Sea; a number of them are named in Isa. 15 and 16.

400. wisest heart: 1 Kings 4.29–31.

403. that . . . hill: Mount of Olives (1 Kings 11.7; 2 Kings 23.13).

404–05. Hinnom: near Jerusalem, where human sacrifices were offered to false gods (2 Kings 23.10; Jer. 7.31, 19.5–6).

406. Chemos: a Moabite god related to Moloch and Baal-Peor (Num. 21.29; Judges 11.24; 1 Kings 11.7).

411. pool: the Dead Sea.

413–14. Sittim: Num. 25.1–9.

416. hill of scandal: Mount of Olives (cf. 403 and note).

418. Josiah abolished idolatry and human sacrifices (2 Kings 22–23; 2 Chron. 34.1–7).

420. brook: Besor, the boundary between Palestine and Egypt (1 Sam. 30.10, 21).

423–31. Such angelic powers — which are turned to account later in *P.L.* — had the authority of traditional demonology.

To bestial gods; for which their heads as low 435
Bowed down in battle, sunk before the spear
Of despicable foes. With these in troop
Came Astoreth, whom the Phoenicians called
Astarte, queen of heav'n, with crescent horns;
To whose bright image nightly by the moon 440
Sidonian virgins paid their vows and songs;
In Sion also not unsung, where stood
Her temple on th' offensive mountain, built
By that uxorious king, whose heart though large,
Beguiled by fair idolatresses, fell 445
To idols foul. Thammuz came next behind,
Whose annual wound in Lebanon allured
The Syrian damsels to lament his fate
In amorous ditties all a summer's day,
While smooth Adonis from his native rock 450
Ran purple to the sea, supposed with blood
Of Thammuz yearly wounded: the love-tale
Infected Sion's daughters with like heat,
Whose wanton passions in the sacred porch
Ezekiel saw, when by the vision led 455
His eye surveyed the dark idolatries
Of alienated Judah. Next came one
Who mourned in earnest, when the captive ark
Maimed his brute image, head and hands lopped off
In his own temple, on the grunsel edge, 460
Where he fell flat, and shamed his worshipers:
Dagon his name, sea monster, upward man
And downward fish; yet had his temple high
Reared in Azotus, dreaded through the coast
Of Palestine, in Gath and Ascalon, 465
And Accaron and Gaza's frontier bounds.
Him followed Rimmon, whose delightful seat
Was fair Damascus, on the fertile banks
Of Abbana and Pharphar, lucid streams.
He also against the house of God was bold: 470
A leper once he lost and gained a king,
Ahaz his sottish conqueror, whom he drew
God's altar to disparage and displace
For one of Syrian mode, whereon to burn
His odious off'rings, and adore the gods 475
Whom he had vanquished. After these appeared

438. Astoreth: glossary, "Ashtoreth."
441. Sidonian: of Sidon, the Phoenician city on the northern coast of Palestine.
443. offensive mountain: see 403, 416, above.
444. king: Solomon (1 Kings 4.29, 11.1 f.).
446. Thammuz: glossary, "Adonis," and G. Sandys' commentary on Ovid's tenth book.
455. Ezek. 8.12–14.
457–66. See 1 Sam. 5.1–5.

460. grunsel: threshold.
467. Rimmon: a Syrian god (2 Kings 5.18).
464. Azotus: Ashdod, a Philistine city (like those named just below, in the southern coastal region of Palestine).
471. The Syrian general, Naaman, cured of leprosy by the water of Jordan, acknowledged the God of Israel (2 Kings 5).
472. Ahaz, king of Judah, adopted the Syrian religion (2 Kings 16).

A crew who under names of old renown,
Osiris, Isis, Orus, and their train,
With monstrous shapes and sorceries abused
Fanatic Egypt and her priests, to seek   480
Their wand'ring gods disguised in brutish forms
Rather than human. Nor did Israel scape
Th' infection when their borrowed gold composed
The calf in Oreb; and the rebel king
Doubled that sin in Bethel and in Dan,   485
Lik'ning his Maker to the grazèd ox —
Jehovah, who in one night when he passed
From Egypt marching, equaled with one stroke
Both her first-born and all her bleating gods.
Belial came last, than whom a Spirit more lewd   490
Fell not from heaven, or more gross to love
Vice for itself. To him no temple stood
Or altar smoked; yet who more oft than he
In temples and at altars, when the priest
Turns atheist, as did Eli's sons, who filled   495
With lust and violence the house of God?
In courts and palaces he also reigns
And in luxurious cities, where the noise
Of riot ascends above their loftiest tow'rs,
And injury and outrage; and when night   500
Darkens the streets, then wander forth the sons
Of Belial, flown with insolence and wine.
Witness the streets of Sodom, and that night
In Gibeah, when the hospitable door
Exposed a matron to avoid worse rape.   505
These were the prime in order and in might;
The rest were long to tell, though far renowned,
Th' Ionian gods, of Javan's issue held
Gods, yet confessed later than Heav'n and Earth,
Their boasted parents; Titan, Heav'n's first-born,   510
With his enormous brood, and birthright seized
By younger Saturn; he from mightier Jove,
His own and Rhea's son, like measure found;
So Jove usurping reigned. These, first in Crete

478. Cf. *Nativity* 211 f.
481–82. Cf. Ovid, *Met.* 5.321 f.
482–84. Aaron made a golden calf as an idol for the Israelites (Exod. 32 and 12.35).
484. rebel king: Jereboam, who set up two golden calves (1 Kings 12.28–29').
486. Cf. Ps. 106.19–20.
487. he: Jehovah, as identified with the people of Israel.
487–89. God's punishment of the Egyptians (Exod. 12.12–30).
495. The past tense shifts to the present "Turns." For "Eli's sons" see 1 Sam. 2.12–17 (and Milton's *Ready and Easy Way, Works,* 6, 138).

501–02. The biblical phrase "sons of Belial" was a Puritan label for men and parties they accounted wicked.   flown: flushed and — metaphorically — swollen.
503–05. Gen. 19.4–14 and Judges 19.12–30.
508. Javan: son of Japheth (Gen. 10.2) and supposed ancestor of the Ionians (Greeks).
509. Heav'n and Earth: in Greek mythology, Uranus and Ge, progenitors of Titans, Giants, and gods (Hesiod, *Theog.* 126 f.).
510. Titan: in late tradition (e.g. Lactantius, *Div. Inst.* 1.14) the eldest son of Uranus and older brother of Saturn and father of the "enormous brood" of Titans.

And Ida known, thence on the snowy top   515
Of cold Olympus ruled the middle air,
Their highest heav'n; or on the Delphian cliff,
Or in Dodona, and through all the bounds
Of Doric land; or who with Saturn old
Fled over Adria to th' Hesperian fields,   520
And o'er the Celtic roamed the utmost isles.
    All these and more came flocking; but with looks
Downcast and damp, yet such wherein appeared
Obscure some glimpse of joy, to have found their Chief
Not in despair, to have found themselves not lost   525
In loss itself; which on his count'nance cast
Like doubtful hue. But he, his wonted pride
Soon recollecting, with high words, that bore
Semblance of worth, not substance, gently raised
Their fainted courage, and dispelled their fears.   530
Then straight commands that at the warlike sound
Of trumpets loud and clarions be upreared
His mighty standard; that proud honor claimed
Azazel as his right, a Cherub tall;
Who forthwith from the glittering staff unfurled   535
Th' imperial ensign, which full high advanced
Shone like a meteor streaming to the wind,
With gems and golden luster rich emblazed,
Seraphic arms and trophies; all the while
Sonorous metal blowing martial sounds;   540
At which the universal host upsent
A shout that tore hell's concave, and beyond
Frighted the reign of Chaos and old Night.
All in a moment through the gloom were seen
Ten thousand banners rise into the air   545
With orient colors waving; with them rose
A forest huge of spears; and thronging helms
Appeared, and serried shields in thick array
Of depth immeasurable. Anon they move
In perfect phalanx to the Dorian mood   550
Of flutes and soft recorders; such as raised
To highth of noblest temper heroes old
Arming to battle, and instead of rage
Deliberate valor breathed, firm and unmoved
With dread of death to flight or foul retreat,   555
Nor wanting power to mitigate and swage
With solemn touches troubled thoughts, and chase

517–18. The oracle of Apollo at Delphi and that of Zeus at Dodona in northern Greece.
519. Doric land: the southern half of Greece.
519–20. In some myths Saturn crossed the Adriatic Sea and reigned in Italy.
521. isles: Britain and adjacent islands.

530. fainted: so the MS. and ed. 1; ed. 2, fainting.
534. Azazel: in Jewish occult tradition a commander of devils and Satan's standard-bearer.
549 f. The description is adapted from the account of the Spartans marching in Plutarch's *Lycurgus* 22.

Anguish and doubt and fear and sorrow and pain
From mortal or immortal minds. Thus they,
Breathing united force with fixèd thought,   560
Moved on in silence to soft pipes that charmed
Their painful steps o'er the burnt soil; and now
Advanced in view they stand, a horrid front
Of dreadful length and dazzling arms, in guise
Of warriors old with ordered spear and shield,   565
Awaiting what command their mighty Chief
Had to impose. He through the armèd files
Darts his experienced eye, and soon traverse
The whole battalion views, their order due,
Their visages and stature as of gods;   570
Their number last he sums. And now his heart
Distends with pride, and hard'ning in his strength
Glories; for never, since created man,
Met such embodied force as named with these
Could merit more than that small infantry   575
Warred on by cranes: though all the giant brood
Of Phlegra with th' heroic race were joined
That fought at Thebes and Ilium, on each side
Mixed with auxiliar gods; and what resounds
In fable or romance of Uther's son   580
Begirt with British and Armoric knights;
And all who since, baptized or infidel,
Jousted in Aspramont or Montalban,
Damasco, or Marocco, or Trebisond,
Or whom Biserta sent from Afric shore   585
When Charlemain with all his peerage fell
By Fontarabbia. Thus far these beyond
Compare of mortal prowess, yet observed
Their dread commander. He above the rest
In shape and gesture proudly eminent   590
Stood like a tow'r; his form had yet not lost
All her original brightness, nor appeared
Less than Archangel ruined, and th' excess
Of glory obscured: as when the sun new ris'n

571–72. 1 Chron. 21.1–7; Dan. 5.20.
573. since . . . man: a Latinism, "since the creation of man."
575. small infantry: see 780 below (and *Iliad* 3.3–6).
577. Phlegra: the western tip of Chalcidice, in the north Aegean, where the Giants fought with the gods (placed by some writers in the volcanic region near Naples).
578. The wars of "the seven against Thebes" and of Troy.
580. Uther's son: King Arthur.
581. Armoric: of Brittany.
583. Aspramont: in Calabria, the "toe" of Italy, where, in romance, Charlemagne fought the Saracens.   Montalban: Rinaldo's castle

in southern France, in Italian romances of Charlemagne.
584. Damasco: Damascus (Ariosto, *O.F.* 17; etc.).
584. Trebisond: on the south coast of the Black Sea.
585. Biserta: the Tunisian seaport.
586–87. In orthodox story not Charlemagne but one of his peers, Roland (Orlando in Italian), was killed in a rearguard action at Roncevaux, about 40 miles from Fontarabbia. Milton perhaps forgot or followed a variant version or altered the data to magnify the conflict between Christians and Saracens.
592. her: glossary, "its."

Looks through the horizontal misty air   595
Shorn of his beams, or from behind the moon
In dim eclipse disastrous twilight sheds
On half the nations, and with fear of change
Perplexes monarchs. Darkened so, yet shone
Above them all th' Archangel; but his face   600
Deep scars of thunder had intrenched, and care
Sat on his faded cheek, but under brows
Of dauntless courage, and considerate pride
Waiting revenge. Cruel his eye, but cast
Signs of remorse and passion to behold   605
The fellows of his crime, the followers rather
(Far other once beheld in bliss), condemned
For ever now to have their lot in pain,
Millions of Spirits for his fault amerced
Of heav'n, and from eternal splendors flung   610
For his revolt, yet faithful how they stood,
Their glory withered: as when heaven's fire
Hath scathed the forest oaks or mountain pines,
With singèd top their stately growth though bare
Stands on the blasted heath. He now prepared   615
To speak; whereat their doubled ranks they bend
From wing to wing, and half enclose him round
With all his peers: attention held them mute.
Thrice he assayed, and thrice in spite of scorn,
Tears such as angels weep burst forth; at last   620
Words interwove with sighs found out their way:
  "O myriads of immortal Spirits, O Powers
Matchless, but with th' Almighty, and that strife
Was not inglorious, though th' event was dire,
As this place testifies, and this dire change   625
Hateful to utter. But what power of mind
Foreseeing or presaging, from the depth
Of knowledge past or present, could have feared
How such united force of gods, how such
As stood like these, could ever know repulse?   630
For who can yet believe, though after loss,
That all these puissant legions, whose exile
Hath emptied heav'n, shall fail to re-ascend
Self-raised, and repossess their native seat?
For me, be witness all the host of heav'n,   635
If counsels different, or danger shunned
By me, have lost our hopes. But he who reigns
Monarch in heav'n, till then as one secure
Sat on his throne, upheld by old repute,
Consent or custom, and his regal state   640

597. disastrous: ill-starred, ominous.
603. considerate: conscious, thoughtful.
609. amerced: fined, deprived.
619. Thrice . . . thrice: cf. *Iliad* 21.176–77,

Odyssey 11.206–07, *Aen.* 6.700–01, Spenser,
F.Q. 1.11.41.
  633. emptied: cf. 2.692 and 5.710 and
notes.

Put forth at full, but still his strength concealed,
Which tempted our attempt, and wrought our fall.
Henceforth his might we know, and know our own,
So as not either to provoke, or dread
New war, provoked; our better part remains   645
To work in close design, by fraud or guile,
What force effected not; that he no less
At length from us may find, who overcomes
By force hath overcome but half his foe.
Space may produce new worlds; whereof so rife   650
There went a fame in heav'n that he ere long
Intended to create, and therein plant
A generation, whom his choice regard
Should favor equal to the sons of heaven.
Thither, if but to pry, shall be perhaps   655
Our first eruption, thither or elsewhere;
For this infernal pit shall never hold
Celestial Spirits in bondage, nor th' abyss
Long under darkness cover. But these thoughts
Full counsel must mature. Peace is despaired,   660
For who can think submission? War then, war
Open or understood must be resolved."
    He spake; and to confirm his words, out flew
Millions of flaming swords, drawn from the thighs
Of mighty Cherubim; the sudden blaze   665
Far round illumined hell. Highly they raged
Against the Highest, and fierce with graspèd arms
Clashed on their sounding shields the din of war,
Hurling defiance toward the vault of heav'n.
    There stood a hill not far whose grisly top   670
Belched fire and rolling smoke; the rest entire
Shone with a glossy scurf, undoubted sign
That in his womb was hid metallic ore,
The work of sulphur. Thither winged with speed
A numerous brígade hastened: as when bands   675
Of pioneers with spade and pickaxe armed
Forerun the royal camp, to trench a field
Or cast a rampart. Mammon led them on,
Mammon, the least erected Spirit that fell
From heav'n, for ev'n in heav'n his looks and thoughts   680
Were always downward bent, admiring more
The riches of heav'n's pavement, trodden gold,
Than aught divine or holy else enjoyed
In vision beatific. By him first

---

650 f. Theologians had disagreed as to
whether the world and man were created before or after Satan's revolt; Milton follows the
latter view (7.150 f., 184 f., and *C.D.* 1.7.)
but for dramatic reasons — as here and in
2.345 f. — has God's purpose known in heaven
before the revolt.

674. sulphur. In scientific tradition metals
were formed through combinations of mercury
and sulphur.
682. Rev. 21.21; cf. *Iliad* 4.2.
684. vision beatific: the theological term for
the supreme experience of "seeing" God (Matt.
5.8); cf. *On Time* 18, *P.L.* 3.60–62.

Men also, and by his suggestion taught,   685
Ransacked the center, and with impious hands
Rifled the bowels of their mother earth
For treasures better hid. Soon had his crew
Opened into the hill a spacious wound
And digged out ribs of gold. Let none admire   690
That riches grow in hell; that soil may best
Deserve the precious bane. And here let those
Who boast in mortal things, and wond'ring tell
Of Babel, and the works of Memphian kings,
Learn how their greatest monuments of fame,   695
And strength and art are easily outdone
By Spirits reprobate, and in an hour
What in an age they with incessant toil
And hands innumerable scarce perform.
Nigh on the plain in many cells prepared,   700
That underneath had veins of liquid fire
Sluiced from the lake, a second multitude
With wondrous art founded the massy ore,
Severing each kind, and scummed the bullion dross.
A third as soon had formed within the ground   705
A various mold, and from the boiling cells
By strange conveyance filled each hollow nook,
As in an organ from one blast of wind
To many a row of pipes the sound-board breathes.
Anon out of the earth a fabric huge   710
Rose like an exhalation, with the sound
Of dulcet symphonies and voices sweet,
Built like a temple, where pilasters round
Were set, and Doric pillars overlaid
With golden architrave; nor did there want   715
Cornice or frieze, with bossy sculptures grav'n;
The roof was fretted gold. Not Babylon,
Nor great Alcairo such magnificence
Equaled in all their glories, to enshrine
Belus or Serapis their gods, or seat   720
Their kings, when Egypt with Assyria strove
In wealth and luxury. Th' ascending pile
Stood fixed her stately highth, and straight the doors

685–88. Cf. Ovid, *Met.* 1.138 f., Horace, *Od.* 3.3.49.

688–707. Cf. Virgil, *Georg.* 4.170–78.

692. precious bane: cf. Boethius, *Consolatio Philosophiae* 2, met. 5.30, *pretiosa pericula*; Ovid, loc. cit.

694. Babel: presumably the tower (see glossary), since Babylon is mentioned in 717.
   works: the Pyramids.

703. founded (MS. and ed. 1): smelted? The "found out" (i.e. "discovered") of ed. 2, sometimes taken as the correction of a technical error, seems superfluous at this stage (cf. 690).

704. scummed: skimmed.

710–12. We are reminded of the music of Apollo and Amphion that raised the walls of Troy and Thebes.

714–17. Details range from classical temples and the temple of Jerusalem (1 Kings 6.7, 21, 35) to St. Peter's in Rome and architectural devices in Stuart masques; the total effect is of excessive artifice and opulence which, in Milton as in Spenser, is associated with evil.

716. bossy: in relief.

718. Alcairo: ancient Memphis, near modern Cairo.

720. Serapis: a Graeco-Egyptian form of Osiris as god of the underworld.

Op'ning their brazen folds discover wide
Within, her ample spaces, o'er the smooth   725
And level pavement; from the archèd roof
Pendent by subtle magic many a row
Of starry lamps and blazing cressets fed
With naphtha and asphaltus yielded light
As from a sky. The hasty multitude   730
Admiring entered, and the work some praise,
And some the architect: his hand was known
In heav'n by many a tow'red structure high,
Where sceptered angels held their residence,
And sat as princes, whom the súpreme King   735
Exalted to such power, and gave to rule,
Each in his hierarchy, the orders bright.
Nor was his name unheard or unadored
In ancient Greece, and in Ausonian land
Men called him Mulciber; and how he fell   740
From heav'n, they fabled, thrown by angry Jove
Sheer o'er the crystal battlements: from morn
To noon he fell, from noon to dewy eve,
A summer's day; and with the setting sun
Dropped from the zenith like a falling star,   745
On Lemnos th' Aégean isle. Thus they relate,
Erring; for he with this rebellious rout
Fell long before; nor aught availed him now
To have built in heav'n high tow'rs; nor did he scape
By all his engines, but was headlong sent   750
With his industrious crew to build in hell.
    Meanwhile the wingèd heralds by command
Of sovran power, with awful ceremony
And trumpet's sound, throughout the host proclaim
A solemn council forthwith to be held   755
At Pandemonium, the high capitol
Of Satan and his peers; their summons called
From every band and squarèd regiment
By place or choice the worthiest; they anon
With hundreds and with thousands trooping came   760
Attended. All access was thronged, the gates
And porches wide, but chief the spacious hall
(Though like a covered field, where champions bold
Wont ride in armed, and at the Soldan's chair
Defied the best of paynim chivalry   765
To mortal combat or career with lance)
Thick swarmed, both on the ground and in the air,
Brushed with the hiss of rustling wings. As bees

726–30. Cf. *Aen.* 1.726–27.
740. Mulciber: glossary, "Vulcan." Cf. *Iliad* 1.590–94.
746–48. See the notes on 1.197–200 and 4.250–51.
756. Pandemonium: palace for "all the demons."

768–75. Cf. *Iliad* 2.87–90; Virgil, *Aen.* 1.430–36 and especially *Georg.* 4, *passim.* The traditional likening of a human community to exemplary bees here points up the very different character of the fallen angels and somewhat deflates the grandeur of Pandemonium.

In springtime, when the sun with Taurus rides,
Pour forth their populous youth about the hive   770
In clusters; they among fresh dews and flowers
Fly to and fro, or on the smoothèd plank,
The suburb of their straw-built citadel,
New rubbed with balm, expatiate and confer
Their state affairs: so thick the airy crowd   775
Swarmed and were straitened; till the signal giv'n,
Behold a wonder! they but now who seemed
In bigness to surpass Earth's giant sons,
Now less than smallest dwarfs, in narrow room
Throng numberless, like that Pygmean race   780
Beyond the Indian mount, or fairy elves,
Whose midnight revels by a forest side
Or fountain some belated peasant sees,
Or dreams he sees, while overhead the moon
Sits arbitress, and nearer to the earth   785
Wheels her pale course; they on their mirth and dance
Intent, with jocund music charm his ear;
At once with joy and fear his heart rebounds.
Thus incorporeal Spirits to smallest forms
Reduced their shapes immense, and were at large,   790
Though without number still, amidst the hall
Of that infernal court. But far within,
And in their own dimensions like themselves,
The great Seraphic Lords and Cherubim
In close recess and secret conclave sat,   795
A thousand demi-gods on golden seats,
Frequent and full. After short silence then
And summons read, the great consult began.

Book II

THE ARGUMENT

The consultation begun, Satan debates whether another battle be to be hazarded for the recovery of heaven: some advise it, others dissuade. A third proposal is preferred, mentioned before by Satan, to search the truth of that prophecy or tradition in heaven concerning another world, and another kind of creature, equal or not much inferior to themselves, about this time to be created. Their doubt who shall be sent on this difficult search; Satan, their chief, undertakes alone the voyage; is honored and applauded. The council

769. The sun is in the zodiacal sign of the Bull during April 19–May 20.
774. expatiate: walk abroad.
780. Pygmean: of a race of pygmies usually placed in Asia.
781. mount: Himalayas.

783–84. Cf. *Aen.* 6.451–54 and *A Midsummer Night's Dream* 2.1.28–29, 141, etc.
795. conclave: a word commonly used of cardinals assembled to elect a pope (cf. "Synod" in 2.391).

thus ended, the rest betake them several ways and to several employments, as their inclinations lead them, to entertain the time till Satan return. He passes on his journey to hell gates, finds them shut, and who sat there to guard them; by whom at length they are opened, and discover to him the great gulf between hell and heaven; with what difficulty he passes through, directed by Chaos, the power of that place, to the sight of this new world which he sought.

HIGH on a throne of royal state, which far
Outshone the wealth of Ormus and of Ind,
Or where the gorgeous East with richest hand
Show'rs on her kings barbaric pearl and gold,
Satan exalted sat, by merit raised   5
To that bad eminence; and from despair
Thus high uplifted beyond hope, aspires
Beyond thus high, insatiate to pursue
Vain war with Heav'n, and by success untaught,
His proud imaginations thus displayed: 10
    "Powers and Dominions, Deities of heav'n,
For since no deep within her gulf can hold
Immortal vigor, though oppressed and fall'n,
I give not heav'n for lost. From this descent
Celestial Virtues rising will appear   15
More glorious and more dread than from no fall,
And trust themselves to fear no second fate.
Me though just right and the fixed laws of heav'n
Did first create your leader, next, free choice,
With what besides, in council or in fight,   20
Hath been achieved of merit, yet this loss,
Thus far at least recovered, hath much more
Established in a safe unenvied throne
Yielded with full consent. The happier state
In heav'n, which follows dignity, might draw   25
Envy from each inferior; but who here
Will envy whom the highest place exposes
Foremost to stand against the Thunderer's aim
Your bulwark, and condemns to greatest share
Of endless pain? Where there is then no good   30
For which to strive, no strife can grow up there
From faction; for none sure will claim in hell

BOOK II. 1–485. Councils of leaders are naturally held in many epics from the *Iliad* (1.54 f.) onward; one infernal council is in Tasso, *G.L.*, canto 4. Milton's debate outdoes them all in amplitude and power, realistic verisimilitude, and the individualizing of speakers through style and tone as well as ideas.

1–6. Cf. Spenser's enthroned Lucifera, *F.Q.* 1.4.8.

2. Ormus: a famously rich city in the Persian Gulf.

3–4. An eastern custom at coronations; cf. *Antony and Cleopatra* 2.5.45–46; Virgil, *Aen.* 2.504, *barbarico . . . auro.*

3. the gorgeous East: in *Love's Labor's Lost* 4.3.223.

5. merit: see the note on 1.98.

15. Virtues: glossary, "angels."

20. council. The original "counsel" could mean either "counsel" or "council."

28. Thunderer: a classical epithet for Zeus and Jupiter (cf. *In quintum Novembris* 204).

Precedence, none whose portion is so small
Of present pain that with ambitious mind
Will covet more. With this advantage then   35
To union, and firm faith, and firm accord,
More than can be in heav'n, we now return
To claim our just inheritance of old,
Surer to prosper than prosperity
Could have assured us; and by what best way,   40
Whether of open war or covert guile,
We now debate; who can advise, may speak."
     He ceased, and next him Moloch, sceptered king,
Stood up, the strongest and the fiercest Spirit
That fought in heav'n, now fiercer by despair.   45
His trust was with th' Eternal to be deemed
Equal in strength, and rather than be less
Cared not to be at all; with that care lost
Went all his fear: of God, or hell, or worse
He recked not, and these words thereafter spake: 50
     "My sentence is for open war. Of wiles,
More unexpert, I boast not: them let those
Contrive who need, or when they need, not now.
For while they sit contriving, shall the rest,
Millions that stand in arms and longing wait   55
The signal to ascend, sit ling'ring here,
Heav'n's fugitives, and for their dwelling-place
Accept this dark opprobrious den of shame,
The prison of his tyranny who reigns
By our delay? No, let us rather choose,   60
Armed with hell flames and fury, all at once
O'er heav'n's high tow'rs to force resistless way,
Turning our tortures into horrid arms
Against the Torturer; when to meet the noise
Of his almighty engine he shall hear   65
Infernal thunder, and for lightning see
Black fire and horror shot with equal rage
Among his angels, and his throne itself
Mixed with Tartarean sulphur and strange fire,
His own invented torments. But perhaps   70
The way seems difficult and steep to scale
With upright wing against a higher foe?
Let such bethink them, if the sleepy drench
Of that forgetful lake benumb not still,
That in our proper motion we ascend   75
Up to our native seat; descent and fall
To us is adverse. Who but felt of late,

56. sit ling'ring here. The phrase is in the very different context of Henry Vaughan's "They are all gone into the world of light," line 2.
74. forgetful lake: cf. 1.266.

75–81. Since angels are of heavenly substance (1.117), it is their nature to rise; Milton may also be ironically recalling the traditional Graeco-Christian principle that all things tend toward God. Cf. *Aen.* 6.126–29.

When the fierce foe hung on our broken rear
Insulting, and pursued us through the deep,
With what compulsion and laborious flight   80
We sunk thus low? Th' ascent is easy then;
Th' event is feared? Should we again provoke
Our stronger, some worse way his wrath may find
To our destruction, if there be in hell
Fear to be worse destroyed: what can be worse   85
Than to dwell here, driv'n out from bliss, condemned
In this abhorrèd deep to utter woe;
Where pain of unextinguishable fire
Must exercise us without hope of end
The vassals of his anger, when the scourge   90
Inexorably, and the torturing hour
Calls us to penance? More destroyed than thus
We should be quite abolished and expire.
What fear we then? What doubt we to incense
His utmost ire? Which to the highth enraged   95
Will either quite consume us, and reduce
To nothing this essential, happier far
Than miserable to have eternal being;
Or if our substance be indeed divine,
And cannot cease to be, we are at worst   100
On this side nothing; and by proof we feel
Our power sufficient to disturb his heav'n,
And with perpetual inroads to alarm,
Though inaccessible, his fatal throne;
Which if not victory is yet revenge."   105
    He ended frowning, and his look denounced
Desperate revenge, and battle dangerous
To less than gods. On th' other side up rose
Belial, in act more graceful and humane;
A fairer person lost not heav'n; he seemed   110
For dignity composed and high exploit:
But all was false and hollow, though his tongue
Dropped manna, and could make the worse appear
The better reason, to perplex and dash
Maturest counsels: for his thoughts were low;   115
To vice industrious, but to nobler deeds
Timorous and slothful: yet he pleased the ear,
And with persuasive accent thus began:
    "I should be much for open war, O Peers,
As not behind in hate, if what was urged   120
Main reason to persuade immediate war
Did not dissuade me most, and seem to cast
Ominous conjecture on the whole success:

---

79. Insulting. The word includes the primary Latin sense of "springing upon."
89. exercise: torment.
97. essential: essence.
106. denounced: threatened.

108–18. Cf. *Aen.* 11.336–42.
113–14. make . . . reason: the charge brought against the Greek Sophists and Socrates (Plato, *Apology* 18 B).

When he who most excels in fact of arms,
In what he counsels and in what excels 125
Mistrustful, grounds his courage on despair
And utter dissolution, as the scope
Of all his aim, after some dire revenge.
First, what revenge? The tow'rs of heav'n are filled
With armèd watch, that render all access 130
Impregnable; oft on the bordering deep
Encamp their legions, or with óbscure wing
Scout far and wide into the realm of Night,
Scorning surprise. Or could we break our way
By force, and at our heels all hell should rise 135
With blackest insurrection, to confound
Heav'n's purest light, yet our great Enemy
All incorruptible would on his throne
Sit unpolluted, and th' ethereal mold
Incapable of stain would soon expel 140
Her mischief, and purge off the baser fire,
Victorious. Thus repulsed, our final hope
Is flat despair; we must exasperate
Th' almighty Victor to spend all his rage,
And that must end us, that must be our cure, 145
To be no more. Sad cure! for who would lose,
Though full of pain, this intellectual being,
Those thoughts that wander through eternity,
To perish rather, swallowed up and lost
In the wide womb of uncreated Night, 150
Devoid of sense and motion? And who knows,
Let this be good, whether our angry Foe
Can give it, or will ever? How he can
Is doubtful; that he never will is sure.
Will he, so wise, let loose at once his ire, 155
Belike through impotence, or unaware,
To give his enemies their wish, and end
Them in his anger, whom his anger saves
To punish endless? 'Wherefore cease we then?'
Say they who counsel war; 'we are decreed, 160
Reserved, and destined to eternal woe;
Whatever doing, what can we suffer more,
What can we suffer worse?' Is this then worst,
Thus sitting, thus consulting, thus in arms?
What when we fled amain, pursued and strook 165
With Heav'n's afflicting thunder, and besought
The deep to shelter us? This hell then seemed
A refuge from those wounds. Or when we lay
Chained on the burning lake? That sure was worse.

---

148. Cf. *Areopagitica* (*Works*, 4, 320): "minds that can wander beyond all limit and satiety."

151. Cf. *Measure for Measure* 3.1.120: "This sensible warm motion."
156. Belike: no doubt (ironical).
165. What: how was it.

What if the breath that kindled those grim fires   170
Awaked should blow them into sevenfold rage
And plunge us in the flames? Or from above
Should intermitted vengeance arm again
His red right hand to plague us? What if all
Her stores were opened and this firmament   175
Of hell should spout her cataracts of fire,
Impendent horrors, threat'ning hideous fall
One day upon our heads; while we perhaps
Designing or exhorting glorious war,
Caught in a fiery tempest shall be hurled   180
Each on his rock transfixed, the sport and prey
Of racking whirlwinds, or for ever sunk
Under yon boiling ocean, wrapped in chains;
There to converse with everlasting groans,
Unrespited, unpitied, unreprieved,   185
Ages of hopeless end? This would be worse.
War therefore, open or concealed, alike
My voice dissuades; for what can force or guile
With him, or who deceive his mind, whose eye
Views all things at one view? He from heav'n's highth   190
All these our motions vain, sees and derides;
Not more almighty to resist our might
Than wise to frustrate all our plots and wiles.
Shall we then live thus vile, the race of heav'n
Thus trampled, thus expelled to suffer here   195
Chains and these torments? Better these than worse,
By my advice; since fate inevitable
Subdues us, and omnipotent decree,
The Victor's will. To suffer, as to do,
Our strength is equal, nor the law unjust   200
That so ordains: this was at first resolved,
If we were wise, against so great a foe
Contending, and so doubtful what might fall.
I laugh when those who at the spear are bold
And vent'rous, if that fail them, shrink and fear   205
What yet they know must follow, to endure
Exile, or ignominy, or bonds, or pain,
The sentence of their Conqueror. This is now
Our doom; which if we can sustain and bear,
Our súpreme Foe in time may much remit   210
His anger, and perhaps, thus far removed,
Not mind us not offending, satisfied
With what is punished; whence these raging fires
Will slacken, if his breath stir not their flames.
Our purer essence then will overcome   215
Their noxious vapor, or inured not feel,

170. Isa. 30.33.   182. racking: driving, torturing (cf. 1.126).
174. red right hand: Horace, *Od.* 1.2.2–3.   190–91. Cf. Ps. 2.4.
180–82. The punishment of the impious   207. ignominy. See note on 1.115.
Ajax son of Oileus (*Aen.* 1.44–45, 6.75).

Or changed at length, and to the place conformed
In temper and in nature, will receive
Familiar the fierce heat, and void of pain;
This horror will grow mild, this darkness light,   220
Besides what hope the never-ending flight
Of future days may bring, what chance, what change
Worth waiting, since our present lot appears
For happy though but ill, for ill not worst,
If we procure not to ourselves more woe."   225
    Thus Belial with words clothed in reason's garb,
Counseled ignoble ease, and peaceful sloth,
Not peace; and after him thus Mammon spake:
    "Either to disenthrone the King of heav'n
We war, if war be best, or to regain   230
Our own right lost. Him to unthrone we then
May hope when everlasting fate shall yield
To fickle chance, and Chaos judge the strife:
The former, vain to hope, argues as vain
The latter; for what place can be for us   235
Within heav'n's bound, unless heav'n's Lord supreme
We overpower? Suppose he should relent
And publish grace to all, on promise made
Of new subjection; with what eyes could we
Stand in his presence humble, and receive   240
Strict laws imposed, to celebrate his throne
With warbled hymns, and to his Godhead sing
Forced halleluiahs; while he lordly sits
Our envied Sovran, and his altar breathes
Ambrosial odors and ambrosial flowers,   245
Our servile offerings? This must be our task
In heav'n, this our delight; how wearisome
Eternity so spent in worship paid
To whom we hate. Let us not then pursue,
By force impossible, by leave obtained   250
Unácceptáble, though in heav'n, our state
Of splendid vassalage, but rather seek
Our own good from ourselves, and from our own
Live to ourselves, though in this vast recess,
Free, and to none accountable, preferring   255
Hard liberty before the easy yoke
Of servile pomp. Our greatness will appear
Then most conspicuous, when great things of small,
Useful of hurtful, prosperous of adverse
We can create, and in what place soe'er   260
Thrive under evil, and work ease out of pain
Through labor and endurance. This deep world
Of darkness do we dread? How oft amidst
Thick clouds and dark doth heav'n's all-ruling Sire

224. For . . . for: compared with.
249. pursue: seek to regain.
256. easy yoke: Matt. 11.30.

263–68. Exod. 19.16–20; Deut. 4.11–12;
2 Chron. 5.13, 6.1; Ps. 18.11–13, 97.2.

Choose to reside, his glory unobscured,   265
And with the majesty of darkness round
Covers his throne; from whence deep thunders roar,
Must'ring their rage, and heav'n resembles hell!
As he our darkness, cannot we his light
Imitate when we please? This desert soil   270
Wants not her hidden luster, gems and gold;
Nor want we skill or art, from whence to raise
Magnificence; and what can heav'n show more?
Our torments also may in length of time
Become our elements, these piercing fires   275
As soft as now severe, our temper changed
Into their temper; which must needs remove
The sensible of pain. All things invite
To peaceful counsels, and the settled state
Of order, how in safety best we may   280
Compose our present evils, with regard
Of what we are and where, dismissing quite
All thoughts of war. Ye have what I advise."
   He scarce had finished, when such murmur filled
Th' assembly as when hollow rocks retain   285
The sound of blust'ring winds, which all night long
Had roused the sea, now with hoarse cadence lull
Seafaring men o'erwatched, whose bark by chance
Or pinnace anchors in a craggy bay
After the tempest. Such applause was heard   290
As Mammon ended, and his sentence pleased,
Advising peace; for such another field
They dreaded worse than hell: so much the fear
Of thunder and the sword of Michaël
Wrought still within them; and no less desire   295
To found this nether empire, which might rise
By policy, and long process of time,
In emulation opposite to heav'n.
Which when Beelzebub perceived, than whom,
Satan except, none higher sat, with grave   300
Aspect he rose, and in his rising seemed
A pillar of state; deep on his front engraven
Deliberation sat and public care;
And princely counsel in his face yet shone,
Majestic though in ruin: sage he stood,   305
With Atlantean shoulders fit to bear
The weight of mightiest monarchies; his look
Drew audience and attention still as night
Or summer's noontide air, while thus he spake:
   "Thrones and imperial Powers, offspring of heav'n,   310
Ethereal Virtues; or these titles now

---

278. sensible: what is felt by the senses.   284–88. Cf. *Iliad* 2.144–46; *Aen.* 10.96 f.
282. where: ed. 1; ed. 2, were.   306. Atlantean: glossary, "Atlas."

Must we renounce, and changing style be called
Princes of hell? For so the popular vote
Inclines, here to continue, and build up here
A growing empire; doubtless! while we dream   315
And know not that the King of heav'n hath doomed
This place our dungeon, not our safe retreat
Beyond his potent arm, to live exempt
From Heav'n's high jurisdiction, in new league
Banded against his throne, but to remain   320
In strictest bondage, though thus far removed,
Under th' inevitable curb, reserved
His captive multitude. For he, be sure,
In highth or depth, still first and last will reign
Sole king, and of his kingdom lose no part   325
By our revolt, but over hell extend
His empire, and with iron scepter rule
Us here, as with his golden those in heav'n.
What sit we then projecting peace and war?
War hath determined us, and foiled with loss   330
Irreparable; terms of peace yet none
Vouchsafed or sought; for what peace will be giv'n
To us enslaved, but custody severe,
And stripes, and arbitrary punishment
Inflicted? And what peace can we return,   335
But to our power hostility and hate,
Untamed reluctance, and revenge though slow,
Yet ever plotting how the Conqueror least
May reap his conquest, and may least rejoice
In doing what we most in suffering feel?   340
Nor will occasion want, nor shall we need
With dangerous expedition to invade
Heav'n, whose high walls fear no assault or siege
Or ambush from the deep. What if we find
Some easier enterprise? There is a place   345
(If ancient and prophetic fame in heav'n
Err not), another world, the happy seat
Of some new race called man, about this time
To be created like to us, though less
In power and excellence, but favored more   350
Of him who rules above; so was his will
Pronounced among the gods, and by an oath,
That shook heav'n's whole circumference, confirmed.
Thither let us bend all our thoughts, to learn
What creatures there inhabit, of what mold   355
Or substance, how endued, and what their power,
And where their weakness, how attempted best,

324–25. Rev. 1.11, 21.6, 22.13; 1 Tim.   336. to: to the utmost of.
6.15.   345 f. Cf. 1.650 f. and note.
    327. iron scepter: Ps. 2.9, Rev. 2.27, 12.5,   352–53. Gen. 22.16, Heb. 6.17, 12.26,
19.15.   Isa. 13.12–13; cf. *Iliad* 1.530, *Aen.* 9.106.

By force or subtlety. Though heav'n be shut,
And heav'n's high Arbitrator sit secure
In his own strength, this place may lie exposed,   360
The utmost border of his kingdom, left
To their defense who hold it; here perhaps
Some advantageous act may be achieved
By sudden onset, either with hell fire
To waste his whole creation, or possess   365
All as our own, and drive as we were driven,
The puny habitants; or if not drive,
Seduce them to our party, that their God
May prove their foe, and with repenting hand
Abolish his own works. This would surpass   370
Common revenge, and interrupt his joy
In our confusion, and our joy upraise
In his disturbance; when his darling sons,
Hurled headlong to partake with us, shall curse
Their frail original, and faded bliss,   375
Faded so soon. Advise if this be worth
Attempting, or to sit in darkness here
Hatching vain empires." Thus Beelzebub
Pleaded his devilish counsel, first devised
By Satan, and in part proposed; for whence,   380
But from the author of all ill, could spring
So deep a malice, to confound the race
Of mankind in one root, and earth with hell
To mingle and involve, done all to spite
The great Creator? But their spite still serves   385
His glory to augment. The bold design
Pleased highly those infernal States, and joy
Sparkled in all their eyes; with full assent
They vote: whereat his speech he thus renews:
    "Well have ye judged, well ended long debate,   390
Synod of gods, and like to what ye are,
Great things resolved; which from the lowest deep
Will once more lift us up, in spite of fate,
Nearer our ancient seat; perhaps in view
Of those bright confines, whence with neighboring arms   395
And opportune excursion we may chance
Re-enter heav'n; or else in some mild zone
Dwell not unvisited of heav'n's fair light
Secure, and at the bright'ning orient beam
Purge off this gloom; the soft delicious air   400
To heal the scar of these corrosive fires
Shall breathe her balm. But first whom shall we send
In search of this new world, whom shall we find

---

367. puny: both "younger, later born"
(*puis né*) and "weak."
375. original (ed. 1, originals): Adam.
377. sit in darkness: Ps. 107.10–11.

380. in part proposed: in 1.650 f.
387. States: statesmen, "estates" of parliament.
402–04. Cf. Isa. 6.8.

Sufficient? Who shall tempt with wand'ring feet
The dark unbottomed infinite abyss   405
And through the palpable obscure find out
His uncouth way, or spread his airy flight
Upborne with indefatigable wings
Over the vast abrupt, ere he arrive
The happy isle; what strength, what art can then   410
Suffice, or what evasion bear him safe
Through the strict senteries and stations thick
Of angels watching round? Here he had need
All circumspection, and we now no less
Choice in our suffrage; for on whom we send,   415
The weight of all and our last hope relies."
     This said, he sat; and expectation held
His look suspense, awaiting who appeared
To second, or oppose, or undertake
The perilous attempt: but all sat mute,   420
Pondering the danger with deep thoughts; and each
In other's count'nance read his own dismay
Astonished. None among the choice and prime
Of those heav'n-warring champions could be found
So hardy as to proffer or accept   425
Alone the dreadful voyage; till at last
Satan, whom now transcendent glory raised
Above his fellows, with monarchal pride
Conscious of highest worth, unmoved thus spake:
     "O Progeny of heav'n, empyreal Thrones,   430
With reason hath deep silence and demur
Seized us, though undismayed. Long is the way
And hard, that out of hell leads up to light;
Our prison strong, this huge convex of fire,
Outrageous to devour, immures us round   435
Ninefold, and gates of burning adamant
Barred over us prohibit all egress.
These passed, if any pass, the void profound
Of unessential Night receives him next
Wide gaping, and with utter loss of being   440
Threatens him, plunged in that abortive gulf.
If thence he scape into whatever world,
Or unknown region, what remains him less
Than unknown dangers and as hard escape?
But I should ill become this throne, O Peers,   445
And this imperial sov'ranty, adorned
With splendor, armed with power, if aught proposed
And judged of public moment, in the shape

404. tempt: attempt.
406. palpable obscure. Cf. Exod. 10.21.
The adjective in place of a noun (cf. "abrupt"
in 409) intensifies the horror of the unknown.
412. senteries: sentries.
431. demur: hesitation.

432–33. Cf. *Aen.* 6.128–29.
434. convex: the vault of hell.
438. profound. Cf. Lucretius, 1.439: *vacuum . . . inane;* 1008: *inane profundum.*
439. unessential: uncreated, without substance (cf. 2.150).

Of difficulty or danger could deter
Me from attempting. Wherefore do I assume   450
These royalties, and not refuse to reign,
Refusing to accept as great a share
Of hazard as of honor, due alike
To him who reigns, and so much to him due
Of hazard more, as he above the rest   455
High honored sits? Go therefore, mighty Powers,
Terror of heav'n, though fall'n; intend at home,
While here shall be our home, what best may ease
The present misery, and render hell
More tolerable, if there be cure or charm   460
To respite or deceive, or slack the pain
Of this ill mansion; intermit no watch
Against a wakeful foe, while I abroad
Through all the coasts of dark destruction seek
Deliverance for us all: this enterprise   465
None shall partake with me." Thus saying rose
The monarch, and prevented all reply;
Prudent, lest from his resolution raised
Others among the chief might offer now
(Certain to be refused) what erst they feared;   470
And so refused might in opinion stand
His rivals, winning cheap the high repute
Which he through hazard huge must earn. But they
Dreaded not more th' adventure than his voice
Forbidding, and at once with him they rose;   475
Their rising all at once was as the sound
Of thunder heard remote. Towards him they bend
With awful reverence prone; and as a god
Extol him equal to the Highest in heav'n.
Nor failed they to express how much they praised,   480
That for the general safety he despised
His own: for neither do the Spirits damned
Lose all their virtue; lest bad men should boast
Their specious deeds on earth, which glory excites,
Or close ambition varnished o'er with zeal.   485
    Thus they their doubtful consultations dark
Ended rejoicing in their matchless Chief:
As when from mountain tops the dusky clouds
Ascending, while the north wind sleeps, o'erspread
Heav'n's cheerful face, the louring element   490
Scowls o'er the darkened landscape snow or show'r;
If chance the radiant sun with farewell sweet
Extend his ev'ning beam, the fields revive,

452. Refusing: i.e. if I refuse.
457. intend: consider (with 456–57 cf. 7.162).
461. deceive: beguile, relieve.
482–85. Bad men cannot boast of speciously public-spirited acts prompted by vainglorious personal ambition, since even the fallen angels have that poor remnant of virtue.
488–95. Cf. Spenser, *Amoretti* 40.
489. while . . . sleeps: cf. *Iliad* 5.524.
490. Heav'n's cheerful face: in Spenser, *F.Q.* 2.12.34.7.

The birds their notes renew, and bleating herds
Attest their joy, that hill and valley rings.   495
O shame to men! Devil with devil damned
Firm concord holds, men only disagree
Of creatures rational, though under hope
Of heavenly grace; and God proclaiming peace,
Yet live in hatred, enmity, and strife   500
Among themselves, and levy cruel wars,
Wasting the earth, each other to destroy:
As if (which might induce us to accord)
Man had not hellish foes enow besides,
That day and night for his destruction wait.   505
 The Stygian council thus dissolved; and forth
In order came the grand infernal peers;
Midst came their mighty Paramount, and seemed
Alone th' antagonist of Heav'n, nor less
Than hell's dread emperor, with pomp supreme   510
And god-like imitated state; him round
A globe of fiery Seraphim enclosed
With bright emblazonry and horrent arms.
Then of their session ended they bid cry
With trumpet's regal sound the great result.   515
Toward the four winds four speedy Cherubim
Put to their mouths the sounding alchemy
By herald's voice explained; the hollow abyss
Heard far and wide, and all the host of hell
With deaf'ning shout returned them loud acclaim.   520
Thence more at ease their minds and somewhat raised
By false presumptuous hope, the rangèd powers
Disband, and wand'ring each his several way
Pursues, as inclination or sad choice
Leads him perplexed, where he may likeliest find   525
Truce to his restless thoughts, and entertain
The irksome hours, till his great Chief return.
Part on the plain, or in the air sublime
Upon the wing, or in swift race contend,
As at th' Olympian games or Pythian fields;   530
Part curb their fiery steeds, or shun the goal
With rapid wheels, or fronted brígades form:
As when to warn proud cities war appears
Waged in the troubled sky, and armies rush

513. horrent: bristling.
515–16. Matt. 24.30–31.
517. sounding alchemy: trumpets made of material resembling gold.
521–628. The epic convention of games in honor of a dead hero (*Iliad* 23.257 f.; *Aen.* 5.104 f., 577 f.) is re-created: the fallen angels' restless, futile activities, physical and mental (along with the horrors of the hell they explore), reflect their blind anarchy of spirit — and anticipate the occupations and state of mind of fallen man on earth.

527. his: ed. 2, this.
530. The Olympic games were held in the plain of Olympia in Elis, the Pythian games at Delphi.
531–32. shun . . . wheels. Cf. Horace, *Od.* 1.1.4–5.
533–38. Such visions of armies in the sky have been heard of in many centuries, including the twentieth. G. Sandys (*Ovid,* 1632, p. 527) told of such a sight reported in 1629; cf. *Julius Caesar* 2.2.19–20.

To battle in the clouds; before each van   535
Prick forth the airy knights, and couch their spears,
Till thickest legions close; with feats of arms
From either end of heav'n the welkin burns.
Others with vast Typhoean rage more fell
Rend up both rocks and hills, and ride the air   540
In whirlwind; hell scarce holds the wild uproar;
As when Alcides from Oechalia crowned
With conquest, felt th' envenomed robe, and tore
Through pain up by the roots Thessalian pines,
And Lichas from the top of Oeta threw   545
Into th' Euboic sea. Others more mild,
Retreated in a silent valley, sing
With notes angelical to many a harp
Their own heroic deeds and hapless fall
By doom of battle; and complain that fate   550
Free virtue should enthrall to force or chance.
Their song was partial, but the harmony
(What could it less when Spirits immortal sing?)
Suspended hell, and took with ravishment
The thronging audience. In discourse more sweet   555
(For eloquence the soul, song charms the sense)
Others apart sat on a hill retired,
In thoughts more elevate, and reasoned high
Of providence, foreknowledge, will, and fate,
Fixed fate, free will, foreknowledge absolute,   560
And found no end, in wand'ring mazes lost.
Of good and evil much they argued then,
Of happiness and final misery,
Passion and apathy, and glory and shame,
Vain wisdom all, and false philosophy;   565
Yet with a pleasing sorcery could charm
Pain for a while or anguish, and excite
Fallacious hope, or arm th' obdurèd breast
With stubborn patience as with triple steel.
Another part, in squadrons and gross bands,   570
On bold adventure to discover wide
That dismal world, if any clime perhaps
Might yield them easier habitation, bend

542–46. Hercules, tortured by the poisoned robe his wife had sent him (thinking it would restore his love), hurled the bringer, Lichas, into the sea; Oechalia was in the large Greek island of Euboea, Mount Oeta in southern Thessaly. Milton follows Ovid, *Met.* 9.134 f.

546–69. These intellectual pursuits, not properly a part of epic games, were perhaps suggested by Virgil's account of the blessed (*Aen.* 6.637 f.) and by musical contests held at some of the ancient Greek festivals.

552. partial: prejudiced.

556. Cf. *Of Education* (*Works*, 4, 286): "To which [logic and rhetoric] poetry would be made subsequent, or indeed rather prece-

dent, as being less subtle and fine, but more simple, sensuous, and passionate."

558–65. The metaphysical and ethical philosophies of the Greeks and Romans, the elevated but inadequate products of the natural reason. Cf. *P.R.* 4.285 f.

559–60. A Miltonic "turn," a repetition which here suggests "wand'ring mazes" and gives emotional emphasis.

564. apathy: the Stoic ideal of freedom from passion.

569. triple steel: a variation on Horace's "triple bronze" (*Od.* 1.3.9).

570. gross: compact.

Four ways their flying march, along the banks
Of four infernal rivers that disgorge   575
Into the burning lake their baleful streams:
Abhorrèd Styx, the flood of deadly hate;
Sad Acheron of sorrow, black and deep;
Cocytus, named of lamentation loud
Heard on the rueful stream; fierce Phlegethon,   580
Whose waves of torrent fire inflame with rage.
Far off from these a slow and silent stream,
Lethe, the river of oblivion, rolls
Her wat'ry labyrinth, whereof who drinks
Forthwith his former state and being forgets,   585
Forgets both joy and grief, pleasure and pain.
Beyond this flood a frozen continent
Lies dark and wild, beat with perpetual storms
Of whirlwind and dire hail, which on firm land
Thaws not, but gathers heap, and ruin seems   590
Of ancient pile; all else deep snow and ice,
A gulf profound as that Serbonian bog
Betwixt Damiata and Mount Casius old,
Where armies whole have sunk; the parching air
Burns frore, and cold performs th' effect of fire.   595
Thither by harpy-footed Furies haled,
At certain revolutions all the damned
Are brought; and feel by turns the bitter change
Of fierce extremes, extremes by change more fierce,
From beds of raging fire to starve in ice   600
Their soft ethereal warmth, and there to pine
Immovable, infixed, and frozen round,
Periods of time; thence hurried back to fire.
They ferry over this Lethean sound
Both to and fro, their sorrow to augment,   605
And wish and struggle, as they pass, to reach
The tempting stream, with one small drop to lose
In sweet forgetfulness all pain and woe,
All in one moment, and so near the brink;
But fate withstands, and to oppose th' attempt   610
Medusa with Gorgonian terror guards
The ford, and of itself the water flies
All taste of living wight, as once it fled
The lip of Tantalus. Thus roving on
In cónfused march forlorn, th' advent'rous bands,   615

575–81. The four rivers of Hades, each name being given its meaning (cf. *Aen.* 6.265, 295–97, 323, 439).

582–86. Lethe: cf. *Aen.* 6.705–15.

587 f. Medieval tradition provided cold as well as heat in hell (cf. Dante, *Inf.* 32–34; *Measure for Measure* 3.1.122–23).

589. dire hail: Horace, *Od.* 1.2.1–2.

592–94. Lake Serbonis, east of the Nile delta; Damiata, on the most eastern mouth of the Nile (alluded to by Dante, *Inf.* 14.104,

Ariosto, *O.F.* 15.64, and Tasso, *G.L.* 15.16). Following Diodorus Siculus (1.30), G. Sandys spoke of "whole armies . . . devoured" there (*Relation*, 1615, p. 137).

595. frore: frosty.

600. starve: have die, freeze.

611. Medusa: one of the three Gorgons whose face turned beholders to stone.

614. Tantalus: condemned by Zeus to remain in a pool whose water eluded his attempts to drink.

With shudd'ring horror pale, and eyes aghast,
Viewed first their lamentable lot, and found
No rest. Through many a dark and dreary vale
They passed, and many a region dolorous,
O'er many a frozen, many a fiery Alp,   620
Rocks, caves, lakes, fens, bogs, dens, and shades of death,
A universe of death, which God by curse
Created evil, for evil only good,
Where all life dies, death lives, and Nature breeds,
Perverse, all monstrous, all prodigious things,   625
Abominable, inutterable, and worse
Than fables yet have feigned, or fear conceived,
Gorgons and Hydras, and Chimeras dire.
    Meanwhile the Adversary of God and man,
Satan, with thoughts inflamed of highest design,   630
Puts on swift wings, and toward the gates of hell
Explores his solitary flight; sometimes
He scours the right-hand coast, sometimes the left;
Now shaves with level wing the deep, then soars
Up to the fiery concave tow'ring high: 635
As when far off at sea a fleet descried
Hangs in the clouds, by equinoctial winds
Close sailing from Bengala, or the isles
Of Ternate and Tidore, whence merchants bring
Their spicy drugs: they on the trading flood   640
Through the wide Ethiopian to the Cape
Ply stemming nightly toward the pole. So seemed
Far off the flying Fiend. At last appear
Hell bounds high reaching to the horrid roof,
And thrice threefold the gates; three folds were brass,   645
Three iron, three of adamantine rock,
Impenetrable, impaled with circling fire,
Yet unconsumed. Before the gates there sat
On either side a formidable shape;
The one seemed woman to the waist, and fair,   650
But ended foul in many a scaly fold

618–28. The physical horrors of hell, "A universe of death," suggest the spiritual darkness and "death" of the wicked angels and the contrasted order and fullness of life in heaven.
628. Cf. *Aen.* 6.288–89; Tasso, *G.L.* 4.5.
637. winds: trade winds, monsoons.
638. Bengala: Bengal.
639. Ternate, Tidore: islands of the Moluccas, south of the Philippines.
640. trading flood: the sea current followed by merchant ships.
641. Ethiopian: the Indian Ocean off Africa. Cape: Cape of Good Hope.
642. Ply stemming: beat against the wind, making headway.   pole: South Pole.
648 f. The unexpected, unique, and powerful allegory of Sin and Death (resumed in 10.229 f.) is based on James 1.15: "Then when lust hath conceived, it bringeth forth sin; and sin, when it is finished, bringeth forth death." The episode is a vision of the nihilistic horror and power of evil; it drives home the true character of Satan, which his "heroic" leadership in hell had partly disguised; and it constitutes a monstrous parody of the Trinity, marked by phrases in lines 728, 827, and 868–70. The chief ancient prototypes of Sin are Scylla (line 660 and glossary), who from patristic times had the allegorical meaning of sin, and the woman-serpent Echidna (Hesiod, *Theog.* 298); among poetical descendants was Spenser's Error (*F.Q.* 1.1.14–15). Virgil (*Aen.* 6.286) had placed "double-shaped Scyllas" at the gates of hell; cf. Statius, *Theb.* 4.533.

Voluminous and vast, a serpent armed
With mortal sting. About her middle round
A cry of hell-hounds never ceasing barked
With wide Cerberean mouths full loud, and rung   655
A hideous peal; yet, when they list, would creep,
If aught disturbed their noise, into her womb,
And kennel there, yet there still barked and howled,
Within unseen. Far less abhorred than these
Vexed Scylla bathing in the sea that parts   660
Calabria from the hoarse Trinacrian shore;
Nor uglier follow the night-hag, when called
In secret, riding through the air she comes,
Lured with the smell of infant blood, to dance
With Lapland witches, while the laboring moon   665
Eclipses at their charms. The other shape —
If shape it might be called that shape had none
Distinguishable in member, joint, or limb,
Or substance might be called that shadow seemed,
For each seemed either — black it stood as Night,   670
Fierce as ten Furies, terrible as hell,
And shook a dreadful dart; what seemed his head
The likeness of a kingly crown had on.
Satan was now at hand, and from his seat
The monster moving onward came as fast   675
With horrid strides; hell trembled as he strode.
Th' undaunted Fiend what this might be admired,
Admired, not feared; God and his Son except,
Created thing naught valued he nor shunned;
And with disdainful look thus first began: 680
    "Whence and what art thou, execrable Shape,
That dar'st, though grim and terrible, advance
Thy miscreated front athwart my way
To yonder gates? Through them I mean to pass,
That be assured, without leave asked of thee.   685
Retire, or taste thy folly, and learn by proof,
Hell-born, not to contend with Spirits of heav'n."
    To whom the goblin full of wrath replied:
"Art thou that traitor angel, art thou he,
Who first broke peace in heav'n and faith, till then   690
Unbroken, and in proud rebellious arms
Drew after him the third part of heav'n's sons
Conjured against the Highest, for which both thou
And they, outcast from God, are here condemned

652. voluminous: in coils.
    653. mortal sting: cf. Spenser, *F.Q.* 1.1.15.4;
1 Cor. 15.55–56.
    654. cry: pack.
    661. Calabria: the "toe" of Italy.
    662. night-hag: Hecate, whose association
with witchcraft is used in *Macbeth*, 3.5, 4.1.
    665. Lapland: the north part of Europe, a

traditional home of witches.   laboring: suffering eclipse (Virgil, *Georg.* 2.478; Ovid, *Met.*
7.207).
    673. Rev. 6.2.
    692. third part: Rev. 12.4; cf. *P.L.* 1.633.
    693. Conjured: sworn together (cf. *In quin-
tum Novembris* 202).

To waste eternal days in woe and pain?   695
And reckon'st thou thyself with Spirits of heav'n,
Hell-doomed, and breath'st defiance here and scorn
Where I reign king, and to enrage thee more,
Thy king and lord? Back to thy punishment,
False fugitive, and to thy speed add wings,   700
Lest with a whip of scorpions I pursue
Thy ling'ring, or with one stroke of this dart
Strange horror seize thee, and pangs unfelt before."
      So spake the grisly terror, and in shape,
So speaking and so threat'ning, grew tenfold   705
More dreadful and deform. On th' other side,
Incensed with indignation Satan stood
Unterrified, and like a comet burned,
That fires the length of Ophiuchus huge
In th' arctic sky, and from his horrid hair   710
Shakes pestilence and war. Each at the head
Leveled his deadly aim; their fatal hands
No second stroke intend; and such a frown
Each cast at th' other, as when two black clouds
With heav'n's artillery fraught, come rattling on   715
Over the Caspian, then stand front to front
Hov'ring a space, till winds the signal blow
To join their dark encounter in mid-air:
So frowned the mighty combatants that hell
Grew darker at their frown, so matched they stood;   720
For never but once more was either like
To meet so great a foe. And now great deeds
Had been achieved, whereof all hell had rung,
Had not the snaky sorceress that sat
Fast by hell gate, and kept the fatal key,   725
Ris'n, and with hideous outcry rushed between.
      "O father, what intends thy hand," she cried,
"Against thy only son? What fury, O son,
Possesses thee to bend that mortal dart
Against thy father's head? And know'st for whom?   730
For him who sits above and laughs the while
At thee ordained his drudge, to execute
Whate'er his wrath, which he calls justice, bids,
His wrath which one day will destroy ye both."
      She spake, and at her words the hellish pest   735
Forbore; then these to her Satan returned:
      "So strange thy outcry, and thy words so strange
Thou interposest, that my sudden hand
Prevented spares to tell thee yet by deeds

---

701. whip of scorpions: 1 Kings 12.11.
709. Ophiuchus ("Serpent-bearer"): a northern constellation.
710–11. "Comet" in Greek means "long-haired," i.e. with a tail; comets were tradition-ally ominous. Cf. *Aen.* 10.272–275.
718. mid-air: glossary.
722. so great a foe: Christ (cf. *P.R.* 4.618 f.; 1 Cor. 15.26).

What it intends; till first I know of thee,   740
What thing thou art, thus double-formed, and why
In this infernal vale first met thou call'st
Me father, and that phantasm call'st my son.
I know thee not, nor ever saw till now
Sight more detestable than him and thee."   745
   T' whom thus the portress of hell gate replied:
"Hast thou forgot me then, and do I seem
Now in thine eye so foul? Once deemed so fair
In heav'n, when at th' assembly, and in sight
Of all the Seraphim with thee combined   750
In bold conspiracy against heav'n's King,
All on a sudden miserable pain
Surprised thee; dim thine eyes, and dizzy swum
In darkness, while thy head flames thick and fast
Threw forth, till on the left side op'ning wide,   755
Likest to thee in shape and count'nance bright,
Then shining heav'nly fair, a goddess armed
Out of thy head I sprung. Amazement seized
All th' host of heav'n; back they recoiled afraid
At first, and called me *Sin*, and for a sign   760
Portentous held me; but familiar grown,
I pleased, and with attractive graces won
The most averse, thee chiefly, who full oft
Thyself in me thy perfect image viewing
Becam'st enamored; and such joy thou took'st   765
With me in secret, that my womb conceived
A growing burden. Meanwhile war arose,
And fields were fought in heav'n; wherein remained
(For what could else?) to our almighty Foe
Clear victory, to our part loss and rout   770
Through all the empyrean: down they fell
Driv'n headlong from the pitch of heaven, down
Into this deep, and in the general fall
I also; at which time this powerful key
Into my hand was giv'n, with charge to keep   775
These gates for ever shut, which none can pass
Without my op'ning. Pensive here I sat
Alone, but long I sat not, till my womb,
Pregnant by thee, and now excessive grown,
Prodigious motion felt and rueful throes.   780
At last this odious offspring whom thou seest,
Thine own begotten, breaking violent way
Tore through my entrails, that with fear and pain
Distorted, all my nether shape thus grew
Transformed; but he my inbred enemy   785
Forth issued, brandishing his fatal dart

749 f. The birth of Sin at the time of Satan's conceiving rebellion heightens the contrast with the birth of Athene, goddess of wisdom, from the head of Zeus. There may be also the greater contrast with the generation of the Son from the Father.

Made to destroy. I fled, and cried out *Death!*
Hell trembled at the hideous name, and sighed
From all her caves, and back resounded *Death!*
I fled, but he pursued (though more, it seems,   790
Inflamed with lust than rage) and swifter far,
Me overtook, his mother, all dismayed,
And in embraces forcible and foul
Engend'ring with me, of that rape begot
These yelling monsters that with ceaseless cry   795
Surround me, as thou saw'st, hourly conceived
And hourly born, with sorrow infinite
To me; for when they list, into the womb
That bred them they return, and howl and gnaw
My bowels, their repast; then bursting forth   800
Afresh, with conscious terrors vex me round,
That rest or intermission none I find.
Before mine eyes in opposition sits
Grim Death my son and foe, who sets them on,
And me his parent would full soon devour   805
For want of other prey, but that he knows
His end with mine involved; and knows that I
Should prove a bitter morsel, and his bane,
Whenever that shall be; so fate pronounced.
But thou, O father, I forewarn thee, shun   810
His deadly arrow; neither vainly hope
To be invulnerable in those bright arms,
Though tempered heav'nly, for that mortal dint,
Save he who reigns above, none can resist."
    She finished, and the subtle Fiend his lore   815
Soon learned, now milder, and thus answered smooth:
"Dear daughter, since thou claim'st me for thy sire,
And my fair son here show'st me, the dear pledge
Of dalliance had with thee in heav'n, and joys
Then sweet, now sad to mention, through dire change   820
Befall'n us unforeseen, unthought of, know
I come no enemy, but to set free
From out this dark and dismal house of pain
Both him and thee, and all the heav'nly host
Of Spirits that in our just pretenses armed   825
Fell with us from on high. From them I go
This uncouth errand sole, and one for all
Myself expose, with lonely steps to tread
Th' unfounded deep, and through the void immense
To search with wand'ring quest a place foretold   830
Should be, and, by concurring signs, ere now
Created vast and round, a place of bliss
In the purlieus of heav'n, and therein placed
A race of upstart creatures, to supply
Perhaps our vacant room, though more removed,   835

829. unfounded: bottomless.

Lest heav'n surcharged with potent multitude
Might hap to move new broils. Be this or aught
Than this more secret now designed, I haste
To know, and this once known, shall soon return,
And bring ye to the place where thou and Death   840
Shall dwell at ease, and up and down unseen
Wing silently the buxom air, embalmed
With odors; there ye shall be fed and filled
Immeasurably; all things shall be your prey."
He ceased, for both seemed highly pleased, and Death   845
Grinned horrible a ghastly smile, to hear
His famine should be filled, and blessed his maw
Destined to that good hour. No less rejoiced
His mother bad, and thus bespake her sire:
    "The key of this infernal pit by due   850
And by command of heav'n's all-powerful King
I keep, by him forbidden to unlock
These adamantine gates; against all force
Death ready stands to interpose his dart,
Fearless to be o'ermatched by living might.   855
But what owe I to his commands above
Who hates me, and hath hither thrust me down
Into this gloom of Tartarus profound,
To sit in hateful office here confined,
Inhabitant of heav'n and heav'nly-born,   860
Here in perpetual agony and pain,
With terrors and with clamors compassed round
Of mine own brood, that on my bowels feed?
Thou art my father, thou my author, thou
My being gav'st me; whom should I obey   865
But thee, whom follow? Thou wilt bring me soon
To that new world of light and bliss, among
The gods who live at ease, where I shall reign
At thy right hand voluptuous, as beseems
Thy daughter and thy darling, without end."   870
    Thus saying, from her side the fatal key,
Sad instrument of all our woe, she took;
And towards the gate rolling her bestial train,
Forthwith the huge portcullis high up drew,
Which but herself not all the Stygian powers   875
Could once have moved; then in the key-hole turns
Th' intricate wards, and every bolt and bar
Of massy iron or solid rock with ease
Unfastens. On a sudden open fly
With impetuous recoil and jarring sound   880
Th' infernal doors, and on their hinges grate

842. buxom air: in Spenser, *F.Q.* 1.11.37.6;
see glossary.
  850. due: right.
  868. gods . . . ease: cf. *Iliad* 6.138, *Odys-*
sey 4.805, etc.

868–70. See the note above on 648 f., and
cf. 5.597, 6.892.
  879–82. Cf. *Aen.* 6.573–74.

Harsh thunder, that the lowest bottom shook
Of Erebus. She opened, but to shut
Excelled her power; the gates wide open stood,
That with extended wings a bannered host   885
Under spread ensigns marching might pass through
With horse and chariots ranked in loose array;
So wide they stood, and like a furnace mouth
Cast forth redounding smoke and ruddy flame.
Before their eyes in sudden view appear   890
The secrets of the hoary deep, a dark
Illimitable ocean without bound,
Without dimension; where length, breadth, and highth,
And time and place are lost; where eldest Night
And Chaos, ancestors of Nature, hold   895
Eternal anarchy, amidst the noise
Of endless wars, and by confusion stand.
For Hot, Cold, Moist, and Dry, four champions fierce,
Strive here for mast'ry, and to battle bring
Their embryon atoms; they around the flag   900
Of each his faction, in their several clans,
Light-armed or heavy, sharp, smooth, swift or slow,
Swarm populous, unnumbered as the sands
Of Barca or Cyrene's torrid soil,
Levied to side with warring winds, and poise   905
Their lighter wings. To whom these most adhere,
He rules a moment; Chaos umpire sits,
And by decision more embroils the fray
By which he reigns; next him high arbiter
Chance governs all. Into this wild abyss,   910
The womb of Nature and perhaps her grave,
Of neither sea, nor shore, nor air, nor fire,
But all these in their pregnant causes mixed
Confus'dly, and which thus must ever fight,
Unless th' Almighty Maker them ordain   915
His dark materials to create more worlds,
Into this wild abyss the wary Fiend
Stood on the brink of hell and looked a while,
Pondering his voyage; for no narrow frith
He had to cross. Nor was his ear less pealed   920
With noises loud and ruinous (to compare
Great things with small) than when Bellona storms,

885–87. Cf. *Iliad* 9.383–84.
889. redounding: overflowing, rolling.
890 f. The picture of the Chaos between hell and heaven may be called modern in its emphasis on immensity (though the ancients had some notion of vast space), but the terms are traditional; cf. Ovid, *Met.* 1.5–20.
891. hoary deep: Job 41.32.
85. Nature: the created universe (cf. 2.1037–38).
898. The traditional four elements, fire, earth, water, air.
900. embryon atoms: the smallest units of matter; cf. the *semina rerum* of Lucretius, 1.59, etc.
904. Barca, Cyrene: cities of Cyrenaica, west of Egypt.
905. poise: add weight to.
911. Cf. Lucretius, 5.259: *omniparens, eadem rerum commune sepulcrum; Romeo and Juliet* 2.3.9–10.
919. frith: arm of the sea, firth.
920. pealed: assailed, deafened.
921–22. to compare . . . small: cf. Virgil, *Ecl.* 1.23, *Georg.* 4.176.
922. Bellona: Roman goddess of war.

With all her battering engines bent to raze
Some capital city; or less than if this frame
Of heav'n were falling, and these elements 925
In mutiny had from her axle torn
The steadfast earth. At last his sail-broad vans
He spreads for flight, and in the surging smoke
Uplifted spurns the ground; thence many a league
As in a cloudy chair ascending rides 930
Audacious, but that seat soon failing, meets
A vast vacuity: all unawares
Flutt'ring his pennons vain plumb down he drops
Ten thousand fadom deep, and to this hour
Down had been falling, had not by ill chance 935
The strong rebuff of some tumultuous cloud
Instinct with fire and niter hurried him
As many miles aloft. That fury stayed,
Quenched in a boggy Syrtis, neither sea,
Nor good dry land, nigh foundered on he fares, 940
Treading the crude consistence, half on foot,
Half flying; behoves him now both oar and sail.
As when a gryphon through the wilderness
With wingèd course o'er hill or moory dale,
Pursues the Arimaspian, who by stealth 945
Had from his wakeful custody purloined
The guarded gold: so eagerly the Fiend
O'er bog or steep, through strait, rough, dense, or rare,
With head, hands, wings, or feet pursues his way,
And swims or sinks, or wades, or creeps, or flies. 950
At length a universal hubbub wild
Of stunning sounds and voices all confused,
Borne through the hollow dark, assaults his ear
With loudest vehemence; thither he plies,
Undaunted to meet there whatever Power 955
Or Spirit of the nethermost abyss
Might in that noise reside, of whom to ask
Which way the nearest coast of darkness lies
Bordering on light; when straight behold the throne
Of Chaos, and his dark pavilion spread 960
Wide on the wasteful deep; with him enthroned
Sat sable-vested Night, eldest of things,
The consort of his reign; and by them stood
Orcus and Ades, and the dreaded name
Of Demogorgon; Rumor next and Chance, 965
And Tumult and Confusion all embroiled,

934. fadom: Milton's form for "fathom."
939. Syrtis: either of two gulfs near Tripoli
notorious for quicksands.
943–47. Griffins were mythical monsters
which guarded gold against the one-eyed Ari-
maspians, a mythical Scythian race.
944. moory: marshy.
959 f. Cf. *Aen.* 6.273 f.; Spenser, *F.Q.*
4.2.47.

960. Ps. 18.11.
964. Orcus: Roman name for Pluto or
Hades. Ades: Hades, Pluto.
965. Demogorgon: a mysterious deity introduced into Renaissance literature by Boccaccio's *Genealogia Deorum*; described in Milton's first Prolusion as ancestor of all the gods
and called Chaos by the ancients; cf. Spenser
(note on 959).

And Discord with a thousand various mouths.
   T' whom Satan turning boldly, thus: "Ye Powers
And Spirits of this nethermost abyss,
Chaos and ancient Night, I come no spy,   970
With purpose to explore or to disturb
The secrets of your realm, but by constraint
Wand'ring this darksome desert, as my way
Lies through your spacious empire up to light,
Alone, and without guide, half lost, I seek   975
What readiest path leads where your gloomy bounds
Confine with heav'n; or if some other place
From your dominion won, th' Ethereal King
Possesses lately, thither to arrive
I travel this profound. Direct my course;   980
Directed, no mean recompense it brings
To your behoof, if I that region lost,
All usurpation thence expelled, reduce
To her original darkness and your sway
(Which is my present journey), and once more   985
Erect the standard there of ancient Night;
Yours be th' advantage all, mine the revenge."
   Thus Satan; and him thus the Anarch old
With falt'ring speech and visage incomposed
Answered: "I know thee, stranger, who thou art,   990
That mighty leading angel, who of late
Made head against heav'n's King, though overthrown.
I saw and heard, for such a numerous host
Fled not in silence through the frighted deep
With ruin upon ruin, rout on rout,   995
Confusion worse confounded; and heav'n gates
Poured out by millions her victorious bands
Pursuing. I upon my frontiers here
Keep residence; if all I can will serve
That little which is left so to defend,   1000
Encroached on still through our intestine broils
Weak'ning the scepter of old Night: first hell
Your dungeon stretching far and wide beneath;
Now lately heaven and earth, another world
Hung o'er my realm, linked in a golden chain   1005
To that side heav'n from whence your legions fell.
If that way be your walk, you have not far;
So much the nearer danger; go and speed;
Havoc and spoil and ruin are my gain."
   He ceased; and Satan stayed not to reply,   1010

---

980. this profound: Sandys used the adjective as a noun in rendering Ovid's *fluctibus* (*Met.* 11.700) and *alta aequora* (ibid., 14.478–79).

989. incomposed: disturbed.

990. Mark 1.24.

1101. our. The early emendation "your" would seem to fit better the logic of Chaos's speech.

1004. heaven: the earth's sky (in 1006 the heaven of God).

1005. golden chain. Homer's golden chain (*Iliad* 8.18–27) had since antiquity been an especially Neoplatonic symbol of divine order in the universe, of the bond between heaven and earth.

1008. speed: both "hasten" and "prosper."

But glad that now his sea should find a shore,
With fresh alacrity and force renewed
Springs upward like a pyramid of fire
Into the wild expanse, and through the shock
Of fighting elements, on all sides round   1015
Environed, wins his way; harder beset
And more endangered than when Argo passed
Through Bosporus betwixt the justling rocks,
Or when Ulysses on the larboard shunned
Charybdis, and by th' other whirlpool steered.   1020
So he with difficulty and labor hard
Moved on, with difficulty and labor he;
But he once passed, soon after when man fell,
Strange alteration! Sin and Death amain
Following his track, such was the will of Heav'n,   1025
Paved after him a broad and beaten way
Over the dark abyss, whose boiling gulf
Tamely endured a bridge of wondrous length
From hell continued reaching th' utmost orb
Of this frail world; by which the Spirits perverse   1030
With easy intercourse pass to and fro
To tempt or punish mortals, except whom
God and good angels guard by special grace.
　　　But now at last the sacred influence
Of light appears, and from the walls of heav'n   1035
Shoots far into the bosom of dim Night
A glimmering dawn; here Nature first begins
Her fardest verge, and Chaos to retire
As from her outmost works a broken foe,
With tumult less and with less hostile din,   1040
That Satan with less toil and now with ease
Wafts on the calmer wave by dubious light,
And like a weather-beaten vessel holds
Gladly the port, though shrouds and tackle torn;
Or in the emptier waste, resembling air,   1045
Weighs his spread wings, at leisure to behold
Far off th' empyreal heav'n, extended wide
In circuit, undetermined square or round,
With opal tow'rs and battlements adorned
Of living sapphire, once his native seat;   1050
And fast by hanging in a golden chain

1017. Argo: the ship of Jason and his Argonauts.
1018. Bosporus: the strait between the Sea of Marmora and the Black Sea. justling rocks: the Symplegades. Sandys had used Milton's phrase in translating Ovid's *rupibus* (*Met.* 14.190); cf. Sandys' *Relation* (1615), p. 40.
1019–20. Cf. *Odyssey* 12.234 f.; *Aen.* 3.420 f.
1026. Matt. 7.13; cf. Spenser, *F.Q.* 1.1.11.3, 1.1.28.3.
1028. bridge: see 10.252 f.

1029. utmost orb: see the note on 3.418.
1037. Nature: the created universe with the earth at its center.
1042. Wafts: sails.
1043. holds: makes for.
1048. The shape of heaven is uncertain only from Satan's distant view at the moment; tradition made it square (Rev. 21.16; *P.L.* 10.381).
1049–50. Rev. 21.19–21.
1051–52. See the notes on 1005 and 1037 above; cf. *Measure for Measure* 3.1.126.

This pendent world, in bigness as a star
Of smallest magnitude close by the moon.
Thither full fraught with mischievous revenge,
Accurst, and in a cursèd hour, he hies.   **1055**

Book III

THE ARGUMENT

God, sitting on his throne, sees Satan flying towards this world, then newly created; shows him to the Son, who sat at his right hand; foretells the success of Satan in perverting mankind; clears his own justice and wisdom from all imputation, having created man free and able enough to have withstood his tempter; yet declares his purpose of grace towards him, in regard he fell not of his own malice, as did Satan, but by him seduced. The Son of God renders praises to his Father for the manifestation of his gracious purpose towards man; but God again declares that grace cannot be extended towards man without the satisfaction of divine justice: man hath offended the majesty of God by aspiring to Godhead, and therefore with all his progeny devoted to death must die, unless someone can be found sufficient to answer for his offense, and undergo his punishment. The Son of God freely offers himself a ransom for man; the Father accepts him, ordains his incarnation, pronounces his exaltation above all names in heaven and earth; commands all the angels to adore him: they obey, and hymning to their harps in full choir, celebrate the Father and the Son. Meanwhile Satan alights upon the bare convex of this world's outermost orb; where wandering he first finds a place since called the Limbo of Vanity; what persons and things fly up thither; thence comes to the gate of heaven, described ascending by stairs, and the waters above the firmament that flow about it. His passage thence to the orb of the sun: he finds there Uriel, the regent of that orb, but first changes himself into the shape of a meaner angel, and pretending a zealous desire to behold the new creation and man whom God had placed here, inquires of him the place of his habitation, and is directed; alights first on Mount Niphates.

Hail, holy Light, offspring of Heav'n first-born,
Or of th' Eternal coeternal beam
May I express thee unblamed? since God is light,
And never but in unapproachèd light
Dwelt from eternity, dwelt then in thee,   5
Bright effluence of bright essence increate.

BOOK III. 1–55. This, the greatest of Milton's invocations of his heavenly Muse, is, like the others, an earnest prayer. Its place and substance are prompted by the change of scene from hell and chaos to heaven.

1–8. Approaching light as a religious, not a scientific phenomenon, Milton suggests three possibilities: (1) it was God's first creation (line 1; Gen. 1.3.); (2) it was not created ("increate," line 6) but was co-eternal with God; (3) its origin is an unexplained mystery (7–8).

3–4. Cf. 1 John 1.5; 1 Tim. 6.16.

Or hear'st thou rather pure ethereal stream,
Whose fountain who shall tell? Before the sun,
Before the heavens thou wert, and at the voice
Of God, as with a mantle didst invest   10
The rising world of waters dark and deep,
Won from the void and formless infinite.
Thee I revisit now with bolder wing,
Escaped the Stygian pool, though long detained
In that obscure sojourn, while in my flight   15
Through utter and through middle darkness borne
With other notes than to th' Orphéan lyre
I sung of Chaos and eternal Night,
Taught by the Heav'nly Muse to venture down
The dark descent, and up to reascend,   20
Though hard and rare. Thee I revisit safe,
And feel thy sovran vital lamp; but thou
Revisit'st not these eyes, that roll in vain
To find thy piercing ray, and find no dawn;
So thick a drop serene hath quenched their orbs,   25
Or dim suffusion veiled. Yet not the more
Cease I to wander where the Muses haunt
Clear spring, or shady grove, or sunny hill,
Smit with the love of sacred song; but chief
Thee, Sion, and the flow'ry brooks beneath   30
That wash thy hallowed feet, and warbling flow,
Nightly I visit; nor sometimes forget
Those other two equaled with me in fate,
So were I equaled with them in renown,
Blind Thamyris and blind Maeonides,   35
And Tiresias and Phineus prophets old:
Then feed on thoughts that voluntary move
Harmonious numbers, as the wakeful bird
Sings darkling, and in shadiest covert hid
Tunes her nocturnal note. Thus with the year   40

7. hear'st: art called (a classicism); cf. *Ad Salsillum* 26; *Epitaphium Damonis* 209; *Areopagitica* (*Works*, 4, 317): "for which England hears ill abroad."
8–12. Before . . . infinite: Gen. 1.1–8.
10. Ps. 104.2.
12. void . . . infinite: Chaos.
16. utter: outer (hell).   middle: Chaos.
17–18. Milton's Christian theme is above the pagan level of the so-called Orphic Hymn to Night and of the mythical poet Orpheus who visited hell.
19–21. See glossary, "Urania," and *Aen.* 6.126–29. Cf. *P.L.* 2.432–33.
25–26. drop serene . . . dim suffusion: translations of medical terms for ocular diseases, *gutta serena* and *suffusio nigra*.
26–29. Blindness has not extinguished his love of classical poetry. The lines are an inspired adaptation of Virgil, *Georg.* 2.475–89;

cf. *quarum sacra fero ingenti percussus amore* and "Smit with the love of sacred song."
30–32. As Virgil contrasts his unpretentious rural verse with the poetry of cosmic themes, Milton turns from the pagan classics to the higher visions of the Bible and Christian truth. Cf. *P.L.* 1.10–12.
32. Milton was much given to composing at night.
33–34. "If I were equal in renown as I am in blindness." Cf. the passage on his blindness in the *Second Defence* of 1654 (*Works*, 8, 63–69).
35. Thamyris: a mythical Thracian poet (*Iliad* 2.595–600). Maeonides: Homer, as a native of Maeonia in Asia Minor (cf. Ovid, *Fasti* 2.120, *Tristia* 1.1.47, 2.377).
36. Phineus: see the note on *Ad J. Rousium* 36.
38. bird: nightingale.
39. darkling: in the dark.

Seasons return; but not to me returns
Day, or the sweet approach of ev'n or morn,
Or sight of vernal bloom, or summer's rose,
Or flocks, or herds, or human face divine;
But cloud instead, and ever-during dark   45
Surrounds me, from the cheerful ways of men
Cut off, and for the book of knowledge fair
Presented with a universal blank
Of Nature's works to me expunged and razed,
And wisdom at one entrance quite shut out.   50
So much the rather thou, celestial Light,
Shine inward, and the mind through all her powers
Irradiate, there plant eyes, all mist from thence
Purge and disperse, that I may see and tell
Of things invisible to mortal sight.   55
    Now had the Almighty Father from above,
From the pure empyrean where he sits
High throned above all highth, bent down his eye,
His own works and their works at once to view.
About him all the sanctities of heaven   60
Stood thick as stars, and from his sight received
Beatitude past utterance; on his right
The radiant image of his glory sat,
His only Son. On earth he first beheld
Our two first parents, yet the only two   65
Of mankind, in the happy garden placed,
Reaping immortal fruits of joy and love,
Uninterrupted joy, unrivaled love,
In blissful solitude. He then surveyed
Hell and the gulf between, and Satan there   70
Coasting the wall of heav'n on this side Night
In the dun air sublime, and ready now
To stoop with wearied wings and willing feet
On the bare outside of this world, that seemed
Firm land imbosomed without firmament,   75
Uncertain which, in ocean or in air.
Him God beholding from his prospect high,
Wherein past, present, future he beholds,
Thus to his only Son foreseeing spake:
    "Only begotten Son, seest thou what rage   80

44. human face divine. In this climax of the brief catalogue men are fellow beings and friends (cf. 46) and are also made in the image of God.

47–50. The secondary revelation of God in his works, in nature, "the book of creatures."

51–55. The inner light that compensates for loss of physical vision (cf. *Works*, 8, 71–77). Throughout this passage, as in other invocations, Milton does not speak as an individual person but rather dramatizes himself as "the blind poet-prophet."

56–415. Milton sets forth his theme, his conception of God, the Son, the fall and redemption of man, and emphatically repudiates Calvinistic predestination and reprobation. While the heavenly council inevitably lacks the dramatic color of the infernal one, it embodies the poet's passionate concern with justice, order, love, mercy, obedience, salvation.

60. sanctities: angels.

61. his sight: the sight of him (cf. 1.683–84).

62–64. Cf. Heb. 1.3 and above, 2.868–70.

74. bare outside: see below, 418 and note.

Transports our Adversary? Whom no bounds
Prescribed, no bars of hell, nor all the chains
Heaped on him there, nor yet the main abyss
Wide interrupt can hold; so bent he seems
On desperate revenge, that shall redound   85
Upon his own rebellious head. And now
Through all restraint broke loose he wings his way
Not far off heav'n, in the precincts of light,
Directly towards the new-created world,
And man there placed, with purpose to assay   90
If him by force he can destroy, or worse,
By some false guile pervert; and shall pervert;
For man will hearken to his glozing lies,
And easily transgress the sole command,
Sole pledge of his obedience; so will fall   95
He and his faithless progeny. Whose fault?
Whose but his own? Ingrate, he had of me
All he could have; I made him just and right,
Sufficient to have stood, though free to fall.
Such I created all th' ethereal Powers   100
And Spirits, both them who stood and them who failed;
Freely they stood who stood, and fell who fell.
Not free, what proof could they have giv'n sincere
Of true allegiance, constant faith or love,
Where only what they needs must do, appeared,   105
Not what they would? What praise could they receive?
What pleasure I from such obedience paid,
When will and reason (reason also is choice)
Useless and vain, of freedom both despoiled,
Made passive both, had served necessity,   110
Not me. They therefore as to right belonged,
So were created, nor can justly accuse
Their Maker, or their making, or their fate,
As if predestination overruled
Their will, disposed by absolute decree   115
Or high foreknowledge; they themselves decreed
Their own revolt, not I. If I foreknew,
Foreknowledge had no influence on their fault,
Which had no less proved certain unforeknown.
So without least impulse or shadow of fate,   120
Or aught by me immutably foreseen,
They trespass, authors to themselves in all,
Both what they judge and what they choose; for so

---

84. interrupt: forming a breach.
96 f. Although in some lines God speaks in
the tone of Milton the pamphleteer, emphasis
on man's free will and responsible power of
choice is central in his theme; cf. *C.D.* 1.3.
108. reason . . . choice. Cf. *Areopagitica*
(*Works*, 4, 319): "Many there be that complain of divine Providence for suffering Adam

to transgress. Foolish tongues! When God
gave him reason, he gave him freedom to
choose, for reason is but choosing." True
freedom must include the freedom to err.
114 f. As in orthodox theological tradition,
God foresees man's fall but does not determine
it; cf. Milton, *C.D.* 1.3–4.

I formed them free, and free they must remain,
Till they enthrall themselves: I else must change   125
Their nature, and revoke the high decree
Unchangeable, eternal, which ordained
Their freedom; they themselves ordained their fall.
The first sort by their own suggestion fell,
Self-tempted, self-depraved; man falls deceived   130
By the other first; man therefore shall find grace,
The other none. In mercy and justice both,
Through heav'n and earth, so shall my glory excel,
But mercy first and last shall brightest shine."
   Thus while God spake, ambrosial fragrance filled   135
All heav'n, and in the blessèd Spirits elect
Sense of new joy ineffable diffused.
Beyond compare the Son of God was seen
Most glorious; in him all his Father shone
Substantially expressed, and in his face   140
Divine compassion visibly appeared,
Love without end, and without measure grace,
Which uttering thus he to his Father spake:
   "O Father, gracious was that word which closed
Thy sovran sentence, that man should find grace;   145
For which both heav'n and earth shall high extol
Thy praises, with th' innumerable sound
Of hymns and sacred songs, wherewith thy throne
Encompassed shall resound thee ever blest.
For should man finally be lost, should man   150
Thy creature late so loved, thy youngest son,
Fall circumvented thus by fraud, though joined
With his own folly? That be from thee far,
That far be from thee, Father, who art judge
Of all things made, and judgest only right.   155
Or shall the Adversary thus obtain
His end, and frustrate thine, shall he fulfill
His malice, and thy goodness bring to naught,
Or proud return though to his heavier doom,
Yet with revenge accomplished, and to hell   160
Draw after him the whole race of mankind,
By him corrupted? Or wilt thou thyself
Abolish thy creation, and unmake,
For him, what for thy glory thou hast made?
So should thy goodness and thy greatness both   165
Be questioned and blasphemed without defense."
   To whom the great Creator thus replied:
"O Son, in whom my soul hath chief delight,
Son of my bosom, Son who art alone

---

129. first sort: Satan and his followers.
136. Spirits elect: the good angels (1 Tim. 5.21).
138–42. Heb. 1.3; Matt. 9.36; John 1.14, 13.1.
153–54. Gen. 18.25.

164. The motive of "glory" is denied, or at least put in different terms, in *P.R.* 3.122 f.; cf. *P.L.* 7.188–91.
168–70. An echo of Venus' words to her son Cupid (*Aen.* 1.664) as well as of Matt. 3.17 and John 1.18.

My Word, my wisdom, and effectual might,   170
All hast thou spoken as my thoughts are, all
As my eternal purpose hath decreed:
Man shall not quite be lost, but saved who will,
Yet not of will in him, but grace in me
Freely vouchsafed; once more I will renew   175
His lapsèd powers, though forfeit and enthralled
By sin to foul exorbitant desires;
Upheld by me, yet once more he shall stand
On even ground against his mortal foe,
By me upheld, that he may know how frail   180
His fall'n condition is, and to me owe
All his deliv'rance, and to none but me.
Some I have chosen of peculiar grace
Elect above the rest; so is my will.
The rest shall hear me call, and oft be warned   185
Their sinful state, and to appease betimes
Th' incensèd Deity, while offered grace
Invites; for I will clear their senses dark,
What may suffice, and soften stony hearts
To pray, repent, and bring obedience due.   190
To prayer, repentance, and obedience due,
Though but endeavored with sincere intent,
Mine ear shall not be slow, mine eye not shut.
And I will place within them as a guide
My umpire Conscíence, whom if they will hear,   195
Light after light well used they shall attain,
And to the end persisting, safe arrive.
This my long sufferance and my day of grace
They who neglect and scorn shall never taste;
But hard be hardened, blind be blinded more,   200
That they may stumble on, and deeper fall;
And none but such from mercy I exclude.
But yet all is not done. Man disobeying,
Disloyal breaks his fealty, and sins
Against the high supremacy of Heav'n,   205
Affecting Godhead, and so losing all,
To expiate his treason hath naught left,
But to destruction sacred and devote,
He with his whole posterity must die;
Die he or justice must; unless for him   210

170. My Word: glossary. effectual might: executive agent.
183 f. In *C.D.* 1.4 Milton rejects the Calvinistic doctrine of the few predestined for salvation, the many for damnation, and, in the spirit of liberal Arminianism, takes the elect as all believers. Here in *P.L.* the means of salvation are open to all men, wicked though they may be, but some are endowed with special grace and righteousness (183–84).
188–90. Ezek. 11.19, 36.26.
206. Affecting: seeking to attain (Gen. 3.5.).

208. sacred: the same as "devote" (glossary).
210–12. This is not Puritan legalism (as it has been called), it is Catholic and Protestant orthodoxy. One of many witnesses is Bishop Lancelot Andrewes: "Fond men! if He would quit His justice or waive His truth, He could; but His justice and truth are to Him as essential, as intrinsically essential, as His mercy; of equal regard, every way as dear to Him. Justice otherwise remains unsatisfied; and satisfied it must be either on Him or on us" (*Ninety-Six Sermons*, Oxford, 1841, I, 184–85).

Some other able, and as willing, pay
The rigid satisfaction, death for death.
Say, heav'nly Powers, where shall we find such love?
Which of ye will be mortal to redeem
Man's mortal crime, and just th' unjust to save?   215
Dwells in all heaven charity so dear?"
　　He asked, but all the heav'nly quire stood mute,
And silence was in heav'n; on man's behalf
Patron or intercessor none appeared,
Much less that durst upon his own head draw   220
The deadly forfeiture, and ransom set.
And now without redemption all mankind
Must have been lost, adjudged to death and hell
By doom severe, had not the Son of God,
In whom the fulness dwells of love divine,   225
His dearest mediation thus renewed:
　　"Father, thy word is passed, man shall find grace;
And shall grace not find means, that finds her way,
The speediest of thy wingèd messengers,
To visit all thy creatures, and to all   230
Comes unprevented, unimplored, unsought?
Happy for man, so coming; he her aid
Can never seek, once dead in sins and lost;
Atonement for himself or offering meet,
Indebted and undone, hath none to bring.   235
Behold me then, me for him, life for life
I offer; on me let thine anger fall;
Account me man; I for his sake will leave
Thy bosom, and this glory next to thee
Freely put off, and for him lastly die   240
Well pleased; on me let Death wreck all his rage;
Under his gloomy power I shall not long
Lie vanquished; thou hast giv'n me to possess
Life in myself for ever; by thee I live;
Though now to Death I yield, and am his due,   245
All that of me can die, yet that debt paid,
Thou wilt not leave me in the loathsome grave
His prey, nor suffer my unspotted soul
For ever with corruption there to dwell;
But I shall rise victorious, and subdue   250
My vanquisher, spoiled of his vaunted spoil;
Death his death's wound shall then receive, and stoop
Inglorious, of his mortal sting disarmed.
I through the ample air in triumph high

213–21. Cf. the call for a volunteer to accomplish man's destruction (2.402–26).
215. just . . . save: 1 Pet. 3.18.
224–65. Cf. Satan in 2.426–66.
231. unprevented: not anticipated, not won
by prayer.
241. wreck: wreak.

242–65. The Son's assurance of resurrection
does not make easy his self-sacrifice but carries
an assurance for mankind.
243–44. Cf. John 5.26.
247–49. Cf. Ps. 16.10, Acts 2.27.
250–59. Cf. 1 Cor. 15.26, 51–56.
253. mortal sting: cf. 2.653 above.

Shall lead hell captive maugre hell, and show   255
The powers of darkness bound. Thou at the sight
Pleased, out of heaven shalt look down and smile,
While by thee raised I ruin all my foes,
Death last, and with his carcass glut the grave:
Then with the multitude of my redeemed   260
Shall enter heaven long absent, and return,
Father, to see thy face, wherein no cloud
Of anger shall remain, but peace assured
And reconcilement; wrath shall be no more
Thenceforth, but in thy presence joy entire."   265
     His words here ended, but his meek aspect
Silent yet spake, and breathed immortal love
To mortal men, above which only shone
Filial obedience: as a sacrifice
Glad to be offered, he attends the will   270
Of his great Father. Admiration seized
All heav'n, what this might mean, and whither tend,
Wond'ring; but soon th' Almighty thus replied:
     "O thou in heav'n and earth the only peace
Found out for mankind under wrath, O thou   275
My sole complacence! well thou know'st how dear
To me are all my works, nor man the least
Though last created, that for him I spare
Thee from my bosom and right hand, to save,
By losing thee a while, the whole race lost.   280
Thou therefore, whom thou only canst redeem,
Their nature also to thy nature join;
And be thyself man among men on earth,
Made flesh, when time shall be, of virgin seed,
By wondrous birth; be thou in Adam's room   285
The head of all mankind, though Adam's son.
As in him perish all men, so in thee
As from a second root shall be restored
As many as are restored; without thee, none.
His crime makes guilty all his sons; thy merit   290
Imputed shall absolve them who renounce
Their own both righteous and unrighteous deeds,
And live in thee transplanted, and from thee
Receive new life. So man, as is most just,
Shall satisfy for man, be judged and die,   295
And dying rise, and rising with him raise
His brethren, ransomed with his own dear life.
So heav'nly love shall outdo hellish hate,
Giving to death, and dying to redeem,

255. Ps. 68.18.
281–82. whom . . . Their nature: the nature
of them whom thou only.
285–89. See note on 1.4.
287. 1 Cor. 15.22.
290–91. thy merit Imputed: a technical

theological phrase. "As therefore our sins are
imputed to Christ, so the merits or righteousness of Christ are imputed to us through faith"
(Milton, *C.D.* 1.22).
     299. Giving: submitting (cf. Matt. 20.28).

So dearly to redeem what hellish hate 300
So easily destroyed, and still destroys
In those who, when they may, accept not grace.
Nor shalt thou, by descending to assume
Man's nature, lessen or degrade thine own.
Because thou hast, though throned in highest bliss 305
Equal to God, and equally enjoying
God-like fruition, quitted all to save
A world from utter loss, and hast been found
By merit more than birthright Son of God,
Found worthiest to be so by being good, 310
Far more than great or high; because in thee
Love hath abounded more than glory abounds;
Therefore thy humiliation shall exalt
With thee thy manhood also to this throne;
Here shalt thou sit incarnate, here shalt reign 315
Both God and man, Son both of God and man,
Anointed universal King. All power
I give thee; reign for ever, and assume
Thy merits; under thee as Head supreme
Thrones, Princedoms, Powers, Dominions, I reduce. 320
All knees to thee shall bow, of them that bide
In heaven, or earth, or under earth in hell;
When thou attended gloriously from heav'n
Shalt in the sky appear, and from thee send
The summoning archangels to proclaim 325
Thy dread tribunal, forthwith from all winds
The living, and forthwith the cited dead
Of all past ages to the general doom
Shall hasten, such a peal shall rouse their sleep.
Then all thy saints assembled, thou shalt judge 330
Bad men and angels; they arraigned shall sink
Beneath thy sentence; hell, her numbers full,
Thenceforth shall be for ever shut. Meanwhile
The world shall burn, and from her ashes spring
New heav'n and earth, wherein the just shall dwell, 335
And after all their tribulations long
See golden days, fruitful of golden deeds,
With joy and love triumphing, and fair truth.
Then thou thy regal scepter shalt lay by,
For regal scepter then no more shall need; 340
God shall be all in all. But all ye gods,
Adore him, who to compass all this dies,
Adore the Son, and honor him as me."

312. Phil. 1.9.
317–19. Matt. 28.18, Eph. 4.15, Heb. 1.9.
317–22. See note on 5.603–15.
321. Phil. 2.10.
323–24. Matt. 24.30–31.
327–29. 1 Cor. 15.51–52, 1 Thess. 4.16–17.

333–35. 2 Pet. 3.12–13, Rev. 21.1.
333–41. This vision of eternity, which recurs in similar terms throughout the poem, has replaced Milton's earlier revolutionary dreams of a grand reformation on earth.
340. need: be needed.
341. God . . . all: 1 Cor. 15.28.

No sooner had th' Almighty ceased, but all
The multitude of angels with a shout   345
Loud as from numbers without number, sweet
As from blest voices, uttering joy, heav'n rung
With jubilee, and loud hosannas filled
Th' eternal regions. Lowly reverent
Towards either throne they bow, and to the ground   350
With solemn adoration down they cast
Their crowns inwove with amarant and gold,
Immortal amarant, a flow'r which once
In Paradise, fast by the Tree of Life
Began to bloom, but soon for man's offense   355
To heav'n removed where first it grew, there grows
And flow'rs aloft shading the fount of life,
And where the river of bliss through midst of heav'n
Rolls o'er Elysian flow'rs her amber stream;
With these that never fade the Spirits elect   360
Bind their resplendent locks inwreathed with beams;
Now in loose garlands thick thrown off, the bright
Pavement, that like a sea of jasper shone,
Impurpled with celestial roses smiled.
Then crowned again their golden harps they took,   365
Harps ever tuned, that glittering by their side
Like quivers hung, and with preamble sweet
Of charming symphony they introduce
Their sacred song, and waken raptures high;
No voice exempt, no voice but well could join   370
Melodious part, such concord is in heav'n.
     Thee, Father, first they sung omnipotent,
Immutable, immortal, infinite,
Eternal King; thee Author of all being,
Fountain of light, thyself invisible   375
Amidst the glorious brightness where thou sitt'st
Throned inaccessible, but when thou shad'st
The full blaze of thy beams, and through a cloud
Drawn round about thee like a radiant shrine,
Dark with excessive bright thy skirts appear,   380
Yet dazzle heav'n, that brightest Seraphim
Approach not, but with both wings veil their eyes.
Thee next they sang, of all creation first,
Begotten Son, Divine Similitude,
In whose conspicuous count'nance, without cloud   385

344–417. The symbolic picture of heavenly order and harmony is contrasted with the heterogeneous distractions of the fallen angels in 2.521 f.
349–52. Rev. 4.4–10.
353. amarant: glossary.
357–58. Rev. 7.17, 22.1–2; *Aen.* 6.656–59.
363. sea of jasper: Rev. 4.6.
373. This line is in Sylvester, 1.1.56.
375–79. 1 Tim. 6.16.

380–81. Cf. Henry Vaughan, *The Night:* "There is in God, some say, A deep but dazzling darkness."
381–82. Isa. 6.2.
383. The phrase applied to the Son, "of all creation first," is one reminder of the anti-Trinitarian heresy that Milton set forth in *C.D.* 1.5: the Son is not co-equal with the Father. Cf. Col. 1.15.

Made visible, th' Almighty Father shines,
Whom else no creature can behold; on thee
Impressed the effulgence of his glory abides,
Transfused on thee his ample Spirit rests.
He heav'n of heavens and all the Powers therein   390
By thee created, and by thee threw down
Th' aspiring Dominations. Thou that day
Thy Father's dreadful thunder didst not spare,
Nor stop thy flaming chariot wheels, that shook
Heav'n's everlasting frame, while o'er the necks   395
Thou drov'st of warring angels disarrayed.
Back from pursuit, thy Powers with loud acclaim
Thee only extolled, Son of thy Father's might,
To execute fierce vengeance on his foes,
Not so on man; him through their malice fall'n,   400
Father of mercy and grace, thou didst not doom
So strictly, but much more to pity incline.
No sooner did thy dear and only Son
Perceive thee purposed not to doom frail man
So strictly, but much more to pity inclined,   405
He to appease thy wrath, and end the strife
Of mercy and justice in thy face discerned,
Regardless of the bliss wherein he sat
Second to thee, offered himself to die
For man's offense. O unexampled love,   410
Love nowhere to be found less than divine!
Hail, Son of God, Saviour of men, thy name
Shall be the copious matter of my song
Henceforth, and never shall my harp thy praise
Forget, nor from thy Father's praise disjoin.   415
　　Thus they in heav'n, above the starry sphere,
Their happy hours in joy and hymning spent.
Meanwhile upon the firm opacous globe
Of this round world, whose first convex divides
The luminous inferior orbs, enclosed   420
From Chaos and th' inroad of Darkness old,
Satan alighted walks. A globe far off
It seemed, now seems a boundless continent
Dark, waste, and wild, under the frown of Night
Starless exposed, and ever-threat'ning storms   425
Of Chaos blust'ring round, inclement sky;
Save on that side which from the wall of heav'n,
Though distant far, some small reflection gains
Of glimmering air less vexed with tempest loud:
Here walked the Fiend at large in spacious field.   430

389. Spirit: God's power, not the third person of the Trinity (cf. 7.165).
390–99. See books 6 and 7.
418. globe: the created universe (also in 422 and 498). Most modern commentators have thought that Milton conceived of his universe as encased in a hard outer shell, the "first convex," though this has been disputed. See glossary, "sphere" and "first moved."

As when a vulture on Imaus bred,
Whose snowy ridge the roving Tartar bounds,
Dislodging from a region scarce of prey
To gorge the flesh of lambs or yeanling kids
On hills where flocks are fed, flies toward the springs   435
Of Ganges or Hydaspes, Indian streams,
But in his way lights on the barren plains
Of Sericana, where Chineses drive
With sails and wind their cany wagons light:
So on this windy sea of land, the Fiend   440
Walked up and down alone bent on his prey,
Alone, for other creature in this place,
Living or lifeless, to be found was none,
None yet; but store hereafter from the earth
Up hither like aërial vapors flew   445
Of all things transitory and vain, when sin
With vanity had filled the works of men:
Both all things vain, and all who in vain things
Built their fond hopes of glory or lasting fame,
Or happiness in this or th' other life;   450
All who have their reward on earth, the fruits
Of painful superstition and blind zeal,
Naught seeking but the praise of men, here find
Fit retribution, empty as their deeds;
All th' unaccomplished works of Nature's hand,   455
Abortive, monstrous, or unkindly mixed,
Dissolved on earth, fleet hither, and in vain,
Till final dissolution, wander here,
Not in the neighboring moon, as some have dreamed;
Those argent fields more likely habitants,   460
Translated saints, or middle Spirits hold
Betwixt th' angelical and human kind.
Hither of ill-joined sons and daughters born,
First from the ancient world those giants came
With many a vain exploit, though then renowned;   465
The builders next of Babel on the plain
Of Sennaär, and still with vain design
New Babels, had they wherewithal, would build;

---

431 f. Imaus: mountains extending from the Himalayas to the Arctic Ocean. The simile is one of the many items in Milton's stripping Satan of the specious grandeur he had maintained in hell.

434. yeanling: newly born.

436. Hydaspes: the river Jhelum in the Punjab.

438. Sericana: the part of China north of India.

439. cany: made of cane or bamboo.

444–97. The "Paradise of Fools," inspired by Ariosto, *O.F.* 34, from which Milton translated a few lines in *Of Reformation* (see above), and by Plato's myth of Er (*Rep.* 615–

16), is an unexpected and grotesque addition to Chaos; it is a sort of limbo, a wild hurricane which contains exemplars of misguided and infantile pride and folly less wicked than those sent to hell.

452. painful: earnest, grievous.

456. unkindly: unnaturally.

459. some: Ariosto (see note on 444–97 above).

461. Translated saints: Enoch (Gen. 5.24); Elijah (2 Kings 2.11).

463–65. Gen. 6.2–4; see note on 11.574–627 below.

467. Sennaär: Shinar, Babylonia (Gen. 11 and below, 12.38 f.).

Others came single: he who to be deemed
A god, leaped fondly into Etna flames,   470
Empedocles; and he who to enjoy
Plato's Elysium, leaped into the sea,
Cleombrotus; and many more too long,
Embryos and idiots, eremites and friars
White, black, and gray, with all their trumpery.   475
Here pilgrims roam, that strayed so far to seek
In Golgotha him dead who lives in heav'n;
And they who to be sure of Paradise,
Dying put on the weeds of Dominic,
Or in Franciscan think to pass disguised;   480
They pass the planets seven, and pass the fixed,
And that crystálline sphere whose balance weighs
The trepidation talked, and that first moved;
And now Saint Peter at heav'n's wicket seems
To wait them with his keys, and now at foot   485
Of heav'n's ascent they lift their feet, when lo!
A violent cross wind from either coast
Blows them transverse ten thousand leagues awry
Into the devious air; then might ye see
Cowls, hoods and habits with their wearers tossed   490
And fluttered into rags; then relics, beads,
Indulgences, dispenses, pardons, bulls,
The sport of winds. All these upwhirled aloft
Fly o'er the backside of the world far off
Into a limbo large and broad, since called   495
The Paradise of Fools; to few unknown
Long after, now unpeopled and untrod.
    All this dark globe the Fiend found as he passed,
And long he wandered, till at last a gleam
Of dawning light turned thitherward in haste   500
His traveled steps; far distant he descries
Ascending by degrees magnificent
Up to the wall of heaven a structure high,

469–73. Both suicides are cited in Lactantius, *Div. Inst.* 3.18. For Empedocles, the Greek philosopher, cf. Horace, *Ars Poetica* 464–66. Cleombrotus was said to have committed suicide after reading Plato's *Phaedo* in order to enjoy at once a better life (cf. Augustine, *City of God* 1.21).

474–75. friars White, black, and gray: the Carmelite, Dominican, and Franciscan orders respectively. Milton's anti-Catholicism in 474–93 is in keeping with his habitual (and anti-Anglican) stress on the inward spirit and his dislike of ritual.

477. Golgotha: the scene of Christ's crucifixion.

478–79. Particular examples are the Italian humanist and poet, Angelo Poliziano (1454–94), who on his death-bed was dressed in Dominican garb, and Guido da Montefeltro, who in old age became a Franciscan (Dante, *Inf.* 27).

481–82. Glossary: "sphere."

483. trepidation: the supposedly oscillating precession of the equinoxes attributed by medieval astronomers to the combined movements of the eighth sphere and a ninth sphere invented for the purpose (Copernicus' explanation was a slow rotation of the earth's axis).   first moved: glossary.

485. keys: cf. *Lycidas* 110 and note.

492. dispenses: ecclesiastical dispensations (in the Roman Catholic Church).

495. limbo: a lesser hell, for infants and the righteous who lived before Christ.

501. traveled: includes the sense of "travailed," "tired."

501–25. As lines 516–17 indicate, Milton does not think of the ladder as identical with the golden chain of 2.1051.

At top whereof, but far more rich appeared
The work as of a kingly palace gate 505
With frontispiece of diamond and gold
Embellished; thick with sparkling orient gems
The portal shone, inimitable on earth
By model, or by shading pencil drawn.
The stairs were such as whereon Jacob saw 510
Angels ascending and descending, bands
Of guardians bright, when he from Esau fled
To Padan-Aram in the field of Luz,
Dreaming by night under the open sky,
And waking cried, "This is the gate of heav'n.' 515
Each stair mysteriously was meant, nor stood
There always, but drawn up to heav'n sometimes
Viewless, and underneath a bright sea flowed
Of jasper, or of liquid pearl, whereon
Who after came from earth, sailing arrived, 520
Wafted by angels, or flew o'er the lake
Rapt in a chariot drawn by fiery steeds.
The stairs were then let down, whether to dare
The Fiend by easy ascent, or aggravate
His sad exclusion from the doors of bliss. 525
Direct against which opened from beneath,
Just o'er the blissful seat of Paradise,
A passage down to th' earth, a passage wide,
Wider by far than that of after-times
Over Mount Sion, and, though that were large, 530
Over the Promised Land to God so dear,
By which, to visit oft those happy tribes,
On high behests his angels to and fro
Passed frequent, and his eye with choice regard
From Paneas the fount of Jordan's flood 535
To Beërsaba, where the Holy Land
Borders on Egypt and the Arabian shore;
So wide the op'ning seemed, where bounds were set
To darkness, such as bound the ocean wave.
Satan from hence, now on the lower stair 540
That scaled by steps of gold to heaven gate,
Looks down with wonder at the sudden view
Of all this world at once. As when a scout
Through dark and desert ways with peril gone
All night, at last by break of cheerful dawn 545
Obtains the brow of some high-climbing hill,
Which to his eye discovers unaware
The goodly prospect of some foreign land

510–15. Gen. 28; John 1.51.
516. mysteriously: mystically, allegorically.
518–19. The waters above the firmament (cf. the "argument" to book 3).
520–22. Like Lazarus (Luke 16.22) or Elijah (cf. Milton's first epigram on the Gun-

powder Plot and *On the Death of the Bishop of Ely* 49).
535. Paneas: in the extreme north of Palestine.
536. Beërsaba: at the southern end of Palestine.

First seen, or some renowned metropolis
With glistering spires and pinnacles adorned,   550
Which now the rising sun gilds with his beams:
Such wonder seized, though after heaven seen,
The Spirit malign, but much more envy seized
At sight of all this world beheld so fair.
Round he surveys, and well might, where he stood   555
So high above the circling canopy
Of Night's extended shade; from eastern point
Of Libra to the fleecy star that bears
Andromeda far off Atlantic seas
Beyond th' horizon; then from pole to pole   560
He views in breadth, and without longer pause
Down right into the world's first region throws
His flight precipitant, and winds with ease
Through the pure marble air his oblique way
Amongst innumerable stars, that shone   565
Stars distant, but nigh hand seemed other worlds:
Or other worlds they seemed, or happy isles,
Like those Hesperian Gardens famed of old,
Fortunate fields, and groves and flow'ry vales,
Thrice happy isles, but who dwelt happy there   570
He stayed not to inquire. Above them all
The golden sun in splendor likest heaven
Allured his eye. Thither his course he bends
Through the calm firmament (but up or down,
By center, or eccentric, hard to tell,   575
Or longitude) where the great luminary
Aloof the vulgar constellations thick,
That from his lordly eye keep distance due,
Dispenses light from far; they as they move
Their starry dance in numbers that compute   580
Days, months, and years, towards his all-cheering lamp
Turn swift their various motions, or are turned
By his magnetic beam, that gently warms
The universe, and to each inward part
With gentle penetration, though unseen,   585
Shoots invisible virtue even to the deep:
So wondrously was set his station bright.
     There lands the Fiend, a spot like which perhaps

558. Libra: the Scales or Balance in the zodiac.   fleecy star: Aries, the Ram.
559. Andromeda: a northern constellation, above Aries.
564. marble: bright, liquid.
568. Hesperian Gardens: cf. *Comus* 980 f. and glossary.
570. The possibility of other inhabited worlds, an idea revived with the new astronomy, disturbed some people (e.g. Robert Burton) on religious grounds; Milton, with his intense faith in God's order and omnipresence, remained untroubled.
571. Above: more than.

571–612. The picture of the sun, on which Satan now lands, mingles everyday notions with traditional scientific and alchemical conceptions of its light and life-giving power.
574–76. Milton allows for either a Ptolemaic (geocentric) or a Copernican (heliocentric) view of the universe. (He nowhere takes account of the Tychonic compromise.)
577. Aloof: apart from.
580. starry dance. Milton's unmystical imagination approached the mystical in his idea of the planetary system as an example and symbol of divine order. Cf. 5.620–27 and Plato, *Timaeus* 40.

Astronomer in the sun's lucent orb
Through his glazed optic tube yet never saw.   590
The place he found beyond expression bright,
Compared with aught on earth, metal or stone;
Not all parts like, but all alike informed
With radiant light, as glowing iron with fire.
If metal, part seemed gold, part silver clear;   595
If stone, carbuncle most or chrysolite,
Ruby or topaz, to the twelve that shone
In Aaron's breast-plate, and a stone besides,
Imagined rather oft than elsewhere seen,
That stone, or like to that, which here below   600
Philosophers in vain so long have sought,
In vain, though by their powerful art they bind
Volátile Hermes, and call up unbound
In various shapes old Proteus from the sea,
Drained through a limbec to his native form.   605
What wonder then if fields and regions here
Breathe forth elixir pure, and rivers run
Potable gold, when with one virtuous touch
Th' arch-chemic sun, so far from us remote,
Produces, with terrestrial humor mixed,   610
Here in the dark so many precious things
Of color glorious and effect so rare?
Here matter new to gaze the Devil met
Undazzled; far and wide his eye commands,
For sight no obstacle found here, nor shade,   615
But all sunshine, as when his beams at noon
Culminate from th' equator, as they now
Shot upward still direct, whence no way round
Shadow from body opaque can fall, and the air,
Nowhere so clear, sharpened his visual ray   620
To objects distant far, whereby he soon
Saw within ken a glorious angel stand,
The same whom John saw also in the sun.
His back was turned, but not his brightness hid;
Of beaming sunny rays, a golden tiar   625
Circled his head, nor less his locks behind
Illustrious on his shoulders fledge with wings
Lay waving round; on some great charge employed

589–90. Galileo's telescope had revealed sun spots.
596–98. Exod. 28.17–20.
600–01. The "philosopher's stone," the substance, long sought by alchemists, which would transmute the baser metals into gold and, as an elixir (607–08), cure disease and prolong life.
602–03. bind . . . Hermes: fix or solidify mercury, the prime material of alchemical experiments and readily vaporized.
603–05. Proteus, since he could take many forms (see glossary), lent himself to alchemical metaphor.
605. limbec: alembic.

606. here: in the sun.
607–08. elixir: the liquid form of the philosopher's stone, supposedly found in "potable" (drinkable) gold; see note on 600–01.
609. arch-chemic: chief of alchemists.
611. Here . . . dark: on earth, under ground. The sun's rays were traditionally thought to create precious stones in the ground (cf. *Comus* 732–36, *P.L.* 6.477–81).
622 f. Uriel (cf. 648–58, 690) is not a biblical angel but belonged to Jewish tradition.
623. Rev. 19.17.
625. tiar: tiara.
627. Illustrious: shining.

He seemed, or fixed in cogitation deep.
Glad was the Spirit impure, as now in hope   630
To find who might direct his wand'ring flight
To Paradise, the happy seat of man,
His journey's end and our beginning woe.
But first he casts to change his proper shape,
Which else might work him danger or delay: 635
And now a stripling Cherub he appears,
Not of the prime, yet such as in his face
Youth smiled celestial, and to every limb
Suitable grace diffused, so well he feigned.
Under a coronet his flowing hair   640
In curls on either cheek played, wings he wore
Of many a colored plume sprinkled with gold,
His habit fit for speed succinct, and held
Before his decent steps a silver wand.
He drew not nigh unheard; the angel bright,   645
Ere he drew nigh, his radiant visage turned,
Admonished by his ear, and straight was known
Th' Archangel Uriel, one of the sev'n
Who in God's presence, nearest to his throne,
Stand ready at command, and are his eyes   650
That run through all the heav'ns, or down to th' earth
Bear his swift errands over moist and dry,
O'er sea and land. Him Satan thus accosts:
    "Uriel, for thou of those sev'n Spirits that stand
In sight of God's high throne, gloriously bright,   655
The first art wont his great authentic will
Interpreter through highest heav'n to bring,
Where all his sons thy embassy attend;
And here art likeliest by supreme decree
Like honor to obtain, and as his eye   660
To visit oft this new creation round;
Unspeakable desire to see, and know
All these his wondrous works, but chiefly man,
His chief delight and favor, him for whom
All these his works so wondrous he ordained,   665
Hath brought me from the quires of Cherubim
Alone thus wand'ring. Brightest Seraph, tell
In which of all these shining orbs hath man
His fixèd seat, or fixèd seat hath none,
But all these shining orbs his choice to dwell;   670
That I may find him, and with secret gaze
Or open admiration him behold
On whom the great Creator hath bestowed
Worlds, and on whom hath all these graces poured;
That both in him and all things, as is meet,   675
The Universal Maker we may praise;
Who justly hath driv'n out his rebel foes

---

637. prime: early youth.   648–53. Rev. 1.4, 4.5, 8.2, Zech. 4.10;
643. succinct: girt up.   Milton, *C.D.* 1.9.

To deepest hell, and to repair that loss
Created this new happy race of men
To serve him better: wise are all his ways." 680
    So spake the false dissembler unperceived;
For neither man nor angel can discern
Hypocrisy, the only evil that walks
Invisible, except to God alone,
By his permissive will, through heav'n and earth; 685
And oft though wisdom wake, suspicion sleeps
At wisdom's gate, and to simplicity
Resigns her charge, while goodness thinks no ill
Where no ill seems: which now for once beguiled
Uriel, though regent of the sun, and held 690
The sharpest-sighted Spirit of all in heav'n;
Who to the fraudulent impostor foul
In his uprightness answer thus returned:
"Fair Angel, thy desire which tends to know
The works of God, thereby to glorify 695
The great Work-master, leads to no excess
That reaches blame, but rather merits praise
The more it seems excess, that led thee hither
From thy empyreal mansion thus alone,
To witness with thine eyes what some perhaps 700
Contented with report hear only in heav'n:
For wonderful indeed are all his works,
Pleasant to know, and worthiest to be all
Had in remembrance always with delight;
But what created mind can comprehend 705
Their number, or the wisdom infinite
That brought them forth, but hid their causes deep?
I saw when at his word the formless mass,
This world's material mold, came to a heap:
Confusion heard his voice, and wild uproar 710
Stood ruled, stood vast infinitude confined;
Till at his second bidding darkness fled,
Light shone, and order from disorder sprung.
Swift to their several quarters hasted then
The cumbrous elements, earth, flood, air, fire, 715
And this ethereal quintessence of heav'n
Flew upward, spirited with various forms,
That rolled orbicular, and turned to stars
Numberless, as thou seest, and how they move;
Each had his place appointed, each his course; 720
The rest in circuit walls this universe.
Look downward on that globe whose hither side
With light from hence, though but reflected, shines;
That place is earth the seat of man, that light
His day, which else as th' other hemisphere 725

706–07. Prov. 3.19.
708–21. This brief account of creation combines biblical and classical myth: Gen. 1; Plato,

Timaeus; Ovid, *Met.* 1.5 f.; etc. Cf. *P.L.*
7.239–42.
  716. quintessence: glossary.

Night would invade, but there the neighboring moon
(So call that opposite fair star) her aid
Timely interposes, and her monthly round
Still ending, still renewing, through mid-heav'n,
With borrowed light her countenance triform   730
Hence fills and empties to enlighten th' earth,
And in her pale dominion checks the night.
That spot to which I point is Paradise,
Adam's abode, those lofty shades his bow'r.
Thy way thou canst not miss, me mine requires."   735
　　Thus said, he turned, and Satan bowing low,
As to superior Spirits is wont in heaven,
Where honor due and reverence none neglects,
Took leave, and toward the coast of earth beneath,
Down from th' ecliptic, sped with hoped success,   740
Throws his steep flight in many an airy wheel,
Nor stayed, till on Niphates' top he lights.

Book IV

THE ARGUMENT

　　Satan, now in prospect of Eden, and nigh the place where he must now attempt the bold enterprise which he undertook alone against God and man, falls into many doubts with himself, and many passions, fear, envy, and despair; but at length confirms himself in evil, journeys on to Paradise, whose outward prospect and situation is described, overleaps the bounds, sits in the shape of a cormorant on the Tree of Life, as highest in the Garden, to look about him. The Garden described; Satan's first sight of Adam and Eve; his wonder at their excellent form and happy state, but with resolution to work their fall; overhears their discourse; thence gathers that the Tree of Knowledge was forbidden them to eat of, under penalty of death; and thereon intends to found his temptation by seducing them to transgress; then leaves them a while, to know further of their state by some other means. Meanwhile Uriel, descending on a sunbeam, warns Gabriel, who had in charge the gate of Paradise, that some evil Spirit had escaped the deep, and passed at noon by his sphere, in the shape of a good angel, down to Paradise; discovered after by his furious gestures in the mount. Gabriel promises to find him ere morning. Night coming on, Adam and Eve discourse of going to their rest: their bower described; their evening worship. Gabriel, drawing forth his bands of night-watch to walk the round of Paradise, appoints two strong angels to Adam's bower, lest the evil Spirit should be there doing some harm to Adam or Eve sleeping; there they find him at the ear of Eve, tempting her in a dream, and

---

730. triform: Ovid, *Met.* 7.177 and glossary, "Diana."
740. ecliptic: the apparent orbit of the sun around the earth.

742. Niphates: a mountain in Armenia on the Assyrian border.

bring him, though unwilling, to Gabriel; by whom questioned, he scornfully
answers, prepares resistance, but hindered by a sign from heaven, flies out of
Paradise.

O FOR that warning voice, which he who saw
Th' Apocalypse heard cry in heaven aloud,
Then when the Dragon, put to second rout,
Came furious down to be revenged on men,
"Woe to the inhabitants on earth!" that now,   5
While time was, our first parents had been warned
The coming of their secret foe, and scaped,
Haply so scaped, his mortal snare; for now
Satan, now first inflamed with rage, came down,
The tempter ere th' accuser of mankind,   10
To wreck on innocent frail man his loss
Of that first battle, and his flight to hell:
Yet not rejoicing in his speed, though bold,
Far off and fearless, nor with cause to boast,
Begins his dire attempt, which nigh the birth   15
Now rolling, boils in his tumultuous breast,
And like a devilish engine back recoils
Upon himself; horror and doubt distract
His troubled thoughts, and from the bottom stir
The hell within him, for within him hell   20
He brings, and round about him, nor from hell
One step no more than from himself can fly
By change of place. Now conscience wakes despair
That slumbered, wakes the bitter memory
Of what he was, what is, and what must be   25
Worse; of worse deeds worse sufferings must ensue.
Sometimes towards Eden which now in his view
Lay pleasant, his grieved look he fixes sad,
Sometimes towards heav'n and the full-blazing sun,
Which now sat high in his meridian tow'r.   30
Then much revolving, thus in sighs began:
   "O thou that with surpassing glory crowned
Look'st from thy sole dominion like the god
Of this new world; at whose sight all the stars
Hide their diminished heads; to thee I call,   35
But with no friendly voice, and add thy name,

BOOK IV. 1. he: St. John.
1–5. Rev. 12.3–12.
10. Rev. 12.10.
11. wreck: wreak.
17. engine: cannon.
20–23. Cf. Marlowe, *Dr. Faustus* (*Works,*
ed. C. F. T. Brooke), 553–55.
27–28. The name "Eden" means "pleasure."
32–113. Satan's speech, like soliloquies of
villains in Elizabethan drama, is a confession
of evil, quite unlike his harangues to his followers in hell. In 1.604–21 he showed compassion for the host he had misled, but here his
pangs of conscience in relation to God give
him tragic potentialities that set him apart from
his fellows; these, however, are not allowed to
develop. The soliloquy is in contrast with the
poet's invocation to Light which opened book
3. According to Edward Phillips, Milton's
nephew and biographer, lines 32–41 at least
were written very early as the first speech in
a tragedy. Cf. Euripides, *Phoenissae* 1 f.

O sun, to tell thee how I hate thy beams
That bring to my remembrance from what state
I fell, how glorious once above thy sphere;
Till pride and worse ambition threw me down   40
Warring in heav'n against heav'n's matchless King.
Ah wherefore? He deserved no such return
From me, whom he created what I was
In that bright eminence, and with his good
Upbraided none; nor was his service hard.   45
What could be less than to afford him praise,
The easiest recompense, and pay him thanks,
How due! Yet all his good proved ill in me,
And wrought but malice; lifted up so high
I sdained subjection, and thought one step higher   50
Would set me highest, and in a moment quit
The debt immense of endless gratitude,
So burthensome still paying, still to owe;
Forgetful what from him I still received,
And understood not that a grateful mind   55
By owing owes not, but still pays, at once
Indebted and discharged; what burden then?
O had his powerful destiny ordained
Me some inferior angel, I had stood
Then happy; no unbounded hope had raised   60
Ambition. Yet why not? Some other Power
As great might have aspired, and me though mean
Drawn to his part; but other Powers as great
Fell not, but stand unshaken, from within
Or from without, to all temptations armed.   65
Hadst thou the same free will and power to stand?
Thou hadst. Whom hast thou then or what to accuse,
But Heav'n's free love dealt equally to all?
Be then his love accurst, since love or hate,
To me alike, it deals eternal woe.   70
Nay cursed be thou, since against his thy will
Chose freely what it now so justly rues.
Me miserable! which way shall I fly
Infinite wrath, and infinite despair?
Which way I fly is hell; myself am hell;   75
And in the lowest deep a lower deep
Still threat'ning to devour me opens wide,
To which the hell I suffer seems a heav'n.
O then at last relent: is there no place
Left for repentance, none for pardon left?   80
None left but by submission; and that word
Disdain forbids me, and my dread of shame

37. John 3.20.
43–45. Ezek. 28.15, 17; James 1.5.
50. sdained: disdained.
51. quit: requite, pay.

63–67. Cf. 3.100 f. and 5.535–40 and note.
66 (and 67, 71). thou: Satan himself.
75. Cf. 4.20–23 and 1.254–55.
79–80. Heb. 12.17.

Among the Spirits beneath, whom I seduced
With other promises and other vaunts
Than to submit, boasting I could subdue   85
Th' Omnipotent. Ay me, they little know
How dearly I abide that boast so vain,
Under what torments inwardly I groan;
While they adore me on the throne of hell,
With diadem and scepter high advanced,   90
The lower still I fall, only supreme
In misery; such joy ambition finds.
But say I could repent and could obtain
By act of grace my former state; how soon
Would highth recall high thoughts, how soon unsay   95
What feigned submission swore: ease would recant
Vows made in pain, as violent and void.
For never can true reconcilement grow
Where wounds of deadly hate have pierced so deep;
Which would but lead me to a worse relapse   100
And heavier fall: so should I purchase dear
Short intermission bought with double smart.
This knows my Punisher; therefore as far
From granting he, as I from begging peace.
All hope excluded thus, behold instead   105
Of us outcast, exiled, his new delight,
Mankind created, and for him this world.
So farewell hope, and with hope farewell fear,
Farewell remorse! All good to me is lost;
Evil, be thou my good; by thee at least   110
Divided empire with heav'n's King I hold
By thee, and more than half perhaps will reign;
As man ere long, and this new world shall know."
    Thus while he spake, each passion dimmed his face
Thrice changed with pale, ire, envy, and despair,   115
Which marred his borrowed visage, and betrayed
Him counterfeit, if any eye beheld.
For heav'nly minds from such distempers foul
Are ever clear. Whereof he soon aware,
Each perturbation smoothed with outward calm,   120
Artificer of fraud; and was the first
That practised falsehood under saintly show,
Deep malice to conceal, couched with revenge:
Yet not enough had practised to deceive
Uriel once warned, whose eye pursued him down   125
The way he went, and on th' Assyrian mount
Saw him disfigured, more than could befall
Spirit of happy sort: his gestures fierce

---

94. act of grace: pardon.
110. Isa. 5.20.
115. changed with pale: dimmed to paleness.

116. borrowed visage: cf. 3.634 f.
123. couched: joined in concealment.
126. Assyrian mount: Niphates (3.742).

He marked and mad demeanor, then alone,
As he supposed, all unobserved, unseen.   130
So on he fares, and to the border comes
Of Eden, where delicious Paradise,
Now nearer, crowns with her enclosure green
As with a rural mound the champaign head
Of a steep wilderness, whose hairy sides   135
With thicket overgrown, grotesque and wild,
Access denied; and overhead up grew
Insuperable highth of loftiest shade,
Cedar, and pine, and fir, and branching palm,
A sylvan scene, and as the ranks ascend   140
Shade above shade, a woody theater
Of stateliest view. Yet higher than their tops
The verdurous wall of Paradise up sprung;
Which to our general sire gave prospect large
Into his nether empire neighboring round.   145
And higher than that wall a circling row
Of goodliest trees loaden with fairest fruit,
Blossoms and fruits at once of golden hue,
Appeared, with gay enameled colors mixed;
On which the sun more glad impressed his beams   150
Than in fair evening cloud, or humid bow,
When God hath show'red the earth; so lovely seemed
That landscape. And of pure now purer air
Meets his approach, and to the heart inspires
Vernal delight and joy, able to drive   155
All sadness but despair; now gentle gales
Fanning their odoriferous wings dispense
Native perfumes, and whisper whence they stole
Those balmy spoils. As when to them who sail
Beyond the Cape of Hope, and now are past   160
Mozambic, off at sea north-east winds blow
Sabaean odors from the spicy shore
Of Araby the Blest, with such delay
Well pleased they slack their course, and many a league
Cheered with the grateful smell old ocean smiles;   165
So entertained those odorous sweets the Fiend
Who came their bane, though with them better pleased
Than Asmodëus with the fishy fume,
That drove him, though enamored, from the spouse
Of Tobit's son, and with a vengeance sent   170
From Media post to Egypt, there fast bound.

---

134. champaign head: plateau.
140–42. sylvan scene . . . theater: Cf. *Aen.*
1.164–65, *silvis   scaena   coruscis/desuper;*
Spenser, *F.Q.* 3.5.39.4–6.
145. nether empire: the land surrounding
Paradise.
151. humid bow: rainbow (*Comus* 992).
153. of pure: after pure.

160. Hope: Good Hope.
161. Mozambique, on the east coast of
Africa.
162. Sabaean: of Saba (Sheba; modern
Yemen) in southwest Arabia. Cf. 2 Chron. 9.9;
Song of Solomon; Diodorus Siculus, 3.46; many
English allusions.
168–71. Asmodëus: glossary, "Asmadai."

Now to th' ascent of that steep savage hill
Satan had journeyed on, pensive and slow;
But further way found none, so thick entwined,
As one continued brake, the undergrowth   175
Of shrubs and tangling bushes had perplexed
All path of man or beast that passed that way.
One gate there only was, and that looked east
On th' other side; which when th' Arch-Felon saw,
Due entrance he disdained, and in contempt   180
At one slight bound high overleaped all bound
Of hill or highest wall, and sheer within
Lights on his feet. As when a prowling wolf,
Whom hunger drives to seek new haunt for prey,
Watching where shepherds pen their flocks at eve   185
In hurdled cotes amid the field secure,
Leaps o'er the fence with ease into the fold;
Or as a thief bent to unhoard the cash
Of some rich burgher, whose substantial doors,
Cross-barred and bolted fast, fear no assault,   190
In at the window climbs, or o'er the tiles:
So clomb this first grand thief into God's fold;
So since into his church lewd hirelings climb.
Thence up he flew, and on the Tree of Life,
The middle tree and highest there that grew,   195
Sat like a cormorant; yet not true life
Thereby regained, but sat devising death
To them who lived; nor on the virtue thought
Of that life-giving plant, but only used
For prospect, what well used had been the pledge   200
Of immortality. So little knows
Any, but God alone, to value right
The good before him, but perverts best things
To worst abuse, or to their meanest use.
　　Beneath him with new wonder now he views   205
To all delight of human sense exposed
In narrow room Nature's whole wealth, yea more,
A heav'n on earth, for blissful Paradise
Of God the garden was, by him in the east
Of Eden planted; Eden stretched her line   210
From Auran eastward to the royal tow'rs

172. savage: cf. above, 135–36; below, 224.
176. perplexed: cf. *Comus* 37.
183–93. John 10.1, 10–13; Acts 20.29; cf. *Aen.* 9.59–64.
186. hurdled cotes: cf. *Comus* 344 and note.
193. Cf. *Lycidas* 115 and note.   lewd: base.
194. Tree of Life: Gen. 2.9.
196. A cormorant was a traditional symbol of greed; cf. 3.431 f.

205 f. The picture, which contains all the elements of traditional earthly paradises, is a non-realistic symbol of idyllic pastoral perfection and innocence, reflecting the spiritual state of Adam and Eve as the picture of hell reflected that of the fallen angels. The tradition combined the myth of prelapsarian Eden with that of the classical golden age. It was a grand stroke of irony to describe Paradise when Satan enters it.
211. Auran: probably the Haran of Gen. 11.31, in Mesopotamia.

Of great Seleucia, built by Grecian kings,
Or where the sons of Eden long before
Dwelt in Telassar. In this pleasant soil
His far more pleasant garden God ordained;   215
Out of the fertile ground he caused to grow
All trees of noblest kind for sight, smell, taste;
And all amid them stood the Tree of Life,
High eminent, blooming ambrosial fruit
Of vegetable gold; and next to life   220
Our death, the Tree of Knowledge, grew fast by,
Knowledge of good bought dear by knowing ill.
Southward through Eden went a river large,
Nor changed his course, but through the shaggy hill
Passed underneath ingulfed, for God had thrown   225
That mountain as his garden mold, high raised
Upon the rapid current, which through veins
Of porous earth with kindly thirst up drawn,
Rose a fresh fountain, and with many a rill
Watered the garden; thence united fell   230
Down the steep glade, and met the nether flood,
Which from his darksome passage now appears,
And now divided into four main streams
Runs diverse, wand'ring many a famous realm
And country whereof here needs no account;   235
But rather to tell how, if art could tell,
How from that sapphire fount the crispèd brooks,
Rolling on orient pearl and sands of gold,
With mazy error under pendent shades
Ran nectar, visiting each plant, and fed   240
Flow'rs worthy of Paradise, which not nice art
In beds and curious knots, but Nature boon
Poured forth profuse on hill and dale and plain,
Both where the morning sun first warmly smote
The open field, and where the unpierced shade   245
Imbrowned the noontide bow'rs. Thus was this place,
A happy rural seat of various view;
Groves whose rich trees wept odorous gums and balm,
Others whose fruit burnished with golden rind
Hung amiable, Hesperian fables true,   250
If true, here only, and of delicious taste.

214. Telassar: a city of Eden (2 Kings 19.12; Isa. 37.12).
214–15. pleasant: see note on 4.27–28.
219. blooming: bearing.   221. Gen. 2.9.
222. Cf. *Areopagitica* (*Works*, 4, 311): "that doom which Adam fell into of knowing good and evil, that is to say, of knowing good by evil." Despite Milton's emphasis on the actuality of evil and on reason as choice, he has a nostalgia for the lost innocence of Eden; cf. 4.317–18, 774–75, etc.
223–35. Gen. 2.10–14. In 9.71–73 the river is said to be the Tigris.

226. garden mold: rich topsoil.
239. error: wandering (Latin sense).
240. Ran nectar: cf. Ovid, *Met.* 1.111.
241–42. nice . . . knots: as in a formal garden.   boon: bountiful.
246. Imbrowned: darkened.
250–51. Hesperian fables: see glossary and note on 1.740. The phrase "If true, here only" is a reminder that up through Milton's age mythographers often saw in pagan myth a distorted version of biblical truth — a view which helped to sanction Christian writers' use of it.

Betwixt them lawns, or level downs, and flocks
Grazing the tender herb, were interposed,
Or palmy hillock, or the flow'ry lap
Of some irriguous valley spread her store,   255
Flow'rs of all hue, and without thorn the rose.
Another side, umbrageous grots and caves
Of cool recess, o'er which the mantling vine
Lays forth her purple grape, and gently creeps
Luxuriant; meanwhile murmuring waters fall   260
Down the slope hills, dispersed, or in a lake,
That to the fringèd bank with myrtle crowned
Her crystal mirror holds, unite their streams.
The birds their quire apply; airs, vernal airs,
Breathing the smell of field and grove, attune   265
The trembling leaves, while universal Pan,
Knit with the Graces and the Hours in dance,
Led on th' eternal spring. Not that fair field
Of Enna, where Prosérpine gathering flow'rs,
Herself a fairer flow'r, by gloomy Dis   270
Was gathered, which cost Ceres all that pain
To seek her through the world; nor that sweet grove
Of Daphne by Orontes, and th' inspired
Castalian spring, might with this Paradise
Of Eden strive; nor that Nyseian isle   275
Girt with the river Triton, where old Cham,
Whom Gentiles Ammon call and Libyan Jove,
Hid Amalthea and her florid son
Young Bacchus from his stepdame Rhea's eye;
Nor where Abassin kings their issue guard,   280
Mount Amara, though this by some supposed
True Paradise, under the Ethiop line
By Nilus' head, enclosed with shining rock,
A whole day's journey high, but wide remote
From this Assyrian garden, where the Fiend   285
Saw undelighted all delight, all kind
Of living creatures new to sight and strange.
    Two of far nobler shape erect and tall,
God-like erect, with native honor clad

255. irriguous: well-watered.
256. The absence of thorns, implied in Gen.
3.18, is explicit in patristic and later tradition.
258. mantling vine: cf. *Comus* 294.
266. universal Pan: "whose body and habit
expresseth Universal Nature, as his name im-
porteth" (Sandys, *Ovid*, 1632, p. 483).
266–74. For names see the glossary.
268–72. The most beautiful of similes is a
veiled anticipation of the fate of Eve.
275. Nyseian isle: Nysa, in the Tunisian
river Triton in north Africa.
276–77. Cham: Ham, Noah's son, was often
identified with Jupiter Ammon.
278–79. Amalthea: in some myths the

mother of Bacchus by the Libyan King Ammon
or Jupiter Ammon (Diodorus Siculus, 3.67–
68).
281. Amara: a hill with palaces where Abyssinian ("Abassin") princes were brought up in
seclusion.
282. Ethiop line: equator.
288 f. As ideal man and woman, husband
and wife, Adam and Eve, like their paradisal
surroundings, are kept at an aesthetic distance.
288–89. In both classical and Christian
traditions man's erect stature distinguished him
from the brutes and linked him with God. Cf.
Ovid, *Met.* 1.84–86.

In naked majesty seemed lords of all,   290
And worthy seemed, for in their looks divine
The image of their glorious Maker shone,
Truth, wisdom, sanctitude severe and pure,
Severe but in true filial freedom placed;
Whence true authority in men; though both   295
Not equal, as their sex not equal seemed;
For contemplation he and valor formed,
For softness she and sweet attractive grace;
He for God only, she for God in him.
His fair large front and eye sublime declared   300
Absolute rule; and hyacinthine locks
Round from his parted forelock manly hung
Clust'ring, but not beneath his shoulders broad:
She as a veil down to the slender waist
Her unadornèd golden tresses wore   305
Disheveled, but in wanton ringlets waved
As the vine curls her tendrils, which implied
Subjection, but required with gentle sway,
And by her yielded, by him best received,
Yielded with coy submission, modest pride,   310
And sweet reluctant amorous delay.
Nor those mysterious parts were then concealed;
Then was not guilty shame; dishonest shame
Of Nature's works, honor dishonorable,
Sin-bred, how have ye troubled all mankind   315
With shows instead, mere shows of seeming pure,
And banished from man's life his happiest life,
Simplicity and spotless innocence.
So passed they naked on, nor shunned the sight
Of God or angel, for they thought no ill;   320
So hand in hand they passed, the loveliest pair
That ever since in love's embraces met,
Adam the goodliest man of men since born
His sons, the fairest of her daughters Eve.
Under a tuft of shade that on a green   325
Stood whispering soft, by a fresh fountain side
They sat them down; and after no more toil
Of their sweet gard'ning labor than sufficed
To recommend cool Zephyr, and made ease

291–92. Gen. 1.26–27.

295 f. Religious, secular, and philosophic tradition placed man above woman in the chain of being; see note on *S.A.* 1053 f.

299. The principle is illustrated by many later bits of action and speech; indeed Adam's fall turns on his violation of it.

301. hyacinthine: dark (cf. *Odyssey* 6.230–31).

301–05. 1 Cor. 11.7–15.

307–08. which implied Subjection: 1 Cor. 11.10.

310. coy: modest, shy (the word carries no hint of coquettishness).

311. Cf. Ovid, *Ars Amatoria* 2.718.

313. dishonest: unchaste.

321. hand in hand. For parallels and contrasts to this symbolic action cf. 4.488–89, 689, 739, 8.510–11, 9.385, 1037, 12.648.

323–24. An English as well as classical idiom. Cf. *A Midsummer Night's Dream* 5.1.250; Dekker: "Thou [London] art the goodliest of thy neighbors"; Browne, *Vulgar Errors* 1.1: "he [Adam] was the wisest of all men since."

More easy, wholesome thirst and appetite 330
More grateful, to their supper fruits they fell,
Nectarine fruits which the compliant boughs
Yielded them, sidelong as they sat recline
On the soft downy bank damasked with flow'rs.
The savory pulp they chew, and in the rind 335
Still as they thirsted scoop the brimming stream;
Nor gentle purpose, nor endearing smiles
Wanted, nor youthful dalliance, as beseems
Fair couple linked in happy nuptial league,
Alone as they. About them frisking played 340
All beasts of th' earth, since wild, and of all chase
In wood or wilderness, forest or den;
Sporting the lion ramped, and in his paw
Dandled the kid; bears, tigers, ounces, pards,
Gamboled before them; th' unwieldy elephant 345
To make them mirth used all his might, and wreathed
His lithe proboscis; close the serpent sly
Insinuating, wove with Gordian twine
His braided train, and of his fatal guile
Gave proof unheeded; others on the grass 350
Couched, and now filled with pasture gazing sat,
Or bedward ruminating; for the sun
Declined was hasting now with prone career
To th' ocean isles, and in th' ascending scale
Of heav'n the stars that usher evening rose: 355
When Satan still in gaze, as first he stood,
Scarce thus at length failed speech recovered sad:
    "O hell! what do mine eyes with grief behold!
Into our room of bliss thus high advanced
Creatures of other mold, earth-born perhaps, 360
Not Spirits, yet to heav'nly Spirits bright
Little inferior; whom my thoughts pursue
With wonder, and could love, so lively shines
In them divine resemblance, and such grace
The hand that formed them on their shape hath poured. 365
Ah gentle pair, ye little think how nigh
Your change approaches, when all these delights
Will vanish and deliver ye to woe,
More woe, the more your taste is now of joy;
Happy, but for so happy ill secured 370
Long to continue, and this high seat your heav'n
Ill fenced for Heav'n to keep out such a foe

---

334. damasked: variegated.
337. purpose: speech.
340 f. The golden age includes harmony in the animal world; cf. Isa. 11.6–9; Virgil, *Ecl.* 4.22–24.
341. all chase: every habitat.
348. Insinuating: winding.

354. ocean isles: the west, the Azores (cf. 592).
358–92. Satan's impulses toward love and pity for his victims, if not mere self-deception, are smothered by self-pity, envy, sardonic wit akin to that of Richard **III** or Iago, and "Machiavellian policy."
362. Little inferior: Ps. **8.5.**

As now is entered; yet no purposed foe
To you whom I could pity thus forlorn,
Though I unpitied. League with you I seek,   375
And mutual amity so strait, so close,
That I with you must dwell, or you with me
Henceforth; my dwelling haply may not please,
Like this fair Paradise, your sense, yet such
Accept your Maker's work; he gave it me,   380
Which I as freely give; hell shall unfold,
To entertain you two, her widest gates,
And send forth all her kings; there will be room,
Not like these narrow limits, to receive
Your numerous offspring; if no better place,   385
Thank him who puts me loth to this revenge
On you who wrong me not, for him who wronged.
And should I at your harmless innocence
Melt, as I do, yet public reason just,
Honor and empire with revenge enlarged   390
By conquering this new world, compels me now
To do what else though damned I should abhor."
     So spake the Fiend, and with necessity,
The tyrant's plea, excused his devilish deeds.
Then from his lofty stand on that high tree   395
Down he alights among the sportful herd
Of those four-footed kinds, himself now one,
Now other, as their shape served best his end
Nearer to view his prey, and unespied
To mark what of their state he more might learn   400
By word or action marked. About them round
A lion now he stalks with fiery glare;
Then as a tiger, who by chance hath spied
In some purlieu two gentle fawns at play,
Straight couches close, then rising, changes oft   405
His couchant watch, as one who chose his ground
Whence rushing he might surest seize them both
Gripped in each paw; when Adam first of men
To first of women Eve, thus moving speech
Turned him, all ear to hear new utterance flow: 410
     "Sole partner and sole part of all these joys,
Dearer thyself than all, needs must the Power
That made us, and for us this ample world,

381–83. Matt. 10.8; Isa. 14.9.

389–94. Throughout history, morality has been in unequal conflict with "reason of state." Milton rightly names Satan as the "tyrant" of the poem.

396–408. When Satan takes the forms of various animals (cf. 1 Pet. 5.8; Sylvester, 2.1.2.116 f.), they become beasts of prey, unlike the actual animals of Eden (4.340 f.).

406. couchant: crouching.

410. him: Adam (Eve is "all ear").

411–39. Before the fall Adam and Eve, who have world enough and time, address each other with a regal elevation fitting for the parents of the race. Here, Adam's reminding Eve of the one prohibition — which enables Satan to plan his campaign — does not necessarily imply that the pair have existed only a short time; cf. Andromache's telling Hector many things he would have known long before (*Iliad* 6.407 f.). See the note on 449 below.

411. Sole . . . sole: only; chief.

Be infinitely good, and of his good
As liberal and free as infinite,   415
That raised us from the dust and placed us here
In all this happiness, who at his hand
Have nothing merited, nor can perform
Aught whereof he hath need; he who requires
From us no other service than to keep   420
This one, this easy charge, of all the trees
In Paradise that bear delicious fruit
So various, not to taste that only Tree
Of Knowledge, planted by the Tree of Life,
So near grows death to life, whate'er death is,   425
Some dreadful thing no doubt; for well thou know'st
God hath pronounced it death to taste that Tree,
The only sign of our obedience left
Among so many signs of power and rule
Conferred upon us, and dominion giv'n   430
Over all other creatures that possess
Earth, air, and sea. Then let us not think hard
One easy prohibition, who enjoy
Free leave so large to all things else, and choice
Unlimited of manifold delights;   435
But let us ever praise him, and extol
His bounty, following our delightful task
To prune these growing plants, and tend these flow'rs,
Which were it toilsome, yet with thee were sweet."
    To whom thus Eve replied: "O thou for whom   440
And from whom I was formed flesh of thy flesh,
And without whom am to no end, my guide
And head, what thou hast said is just and right.
For we to him indeed all praises owe,
And daily thanks, I chiefly who enjoy   445
So far the happier lot, enjoying thee
Pre-eminent by so much odds, while thou
Like consort to thyself canst nowhere find.
That day I oft remember, when from sleep
I first awaked, and found myself reposed   450
Under a shade on flowers, much wond'ring where
And what I was, whence thither brought, and how.
Not distant far from thence a murmuring sound
Of waters issued from a cave and spread
Into a liquid plain, then stood unmoved   455
Pure as th' expanse of heav'n; I thither went

418–19. Cf. Acts 17.25 and Milton's Sonnet 19.9–10.

421. charge: Gen. 2.16–17.

428. In *C.D.* 1.10 Milton takes God's one prohibition as a test of obedience.

430–32. Gen. 1.26–28.

441. Gen. 2.23.

443. head: 1 Cor. 11.3.

449. That day I oft remember. Milton does not pronounce upon the traditional question of how long Adam and Eve existed before the fall, but, along with implications of a honeymoon, a number of references, like this one, imply some space of time (e.g. 4.680, 5.56, 9.2–3, 1082, 10.103, 119, 11.317 f.).

451. Ed. 1, on flowers; ed. 2, of.

With unexperienced thought, and laid me down
On the green bank, to look into the clear
Smooth lake, that to me seemed another sky.
As I bent down to look, just opposite   460
A shape within the wat'ry gleam appeared
Bending to look on me: I started back,
It started back, but pleased I soon returned,
Pleased it returned as soon with answering looks
Of sympathy and love; there I had fixed   465
Mine eyes till now, and pined with vain desire,
Had not a voice thus warned me: 'What thou seest,
What there thou seest, fair creature, is thyself,
With thee it came and goes; but follow me,
And I will bring thee where no shadow stays   470
Thy coming, and thy soft embraces, he
Whose image thou art, him thou shalt enjoy
Inseparably thine; to him shalt bear
Multitudes like thyself, and thence be called
Mother of human race.' What could I do   475
But follow straight, invisibly thus led?
Till I espied thee, fair indeed and tall,
Under a platane; yet methought less fair,
Less winning soft, less amiably mild,
Than that smooth wat'ry image; back I turned,   480
Thou following cried'st aloud, 'Return, fair Eve,
Whom fli'st thou? Whom thou fli'st, of him thou art,
His flesh, his bone; to give thee being I lent
Out of my side to thee, nearest my heart,
Substantial life, to have thee by my side   485
Henceforth an individual solace dear.
Part of my soul I seek thee, and thee claim
My other half.' With that thy gentle hand
Seized mine, I yielded, and from that time see
How beauty is excelled by manly grace   490
And wisdom, which alone is truly fair."
    So spake our general mother, and with eyes
Of conjugal attraction unreproved,
And meek surrender, half embracing leaned
On our first father; half her swelling breast   495
Naked met his under the flowing gold
Of her loose tresses hid. He in delight

460 f. Eve's behaving like Narcissus (Ovid, *Met.* 3.407 f.), while natural and blameless, gives a first faint hint of potential vanity and self-centeredness. Also, in Christian tradition, some of the newly created angels looked up to God, others fell in love with themselves; cf. Donne, *Sermons*, ed. Potter and Simpson, 3, 254.

470. stays: waits for.

478. platane: plane-tree. One of the examples, noted by Keats, of Milton's "stationing" his unlocalized characters in relation to solid objects.

481–82. Adam's words apparently echo those of the amorous Apollo to the fleeing Daphne (Ovid, *Met.* 1.504 f.) and, though no less natural and blameless than Eve's Narcissism, suggest the germ of his excessive devotion to her. The two items (cf. the note on 460 f.) are steps in Milton's preparation for the fall: Adam and Eve remain innocent but increasingly reveal their vulnerability.

483. Cf. 441 and note.

486. individual: inseparable.

487. Part . . . soul: cf. Horace, *Od.* 1.3.8, 2.17.5; Milton, Elegy 4.19–20.

Both of her beauty and submissive charms
Smiled with superior love, as Jupiter
On Juno smiles, when he impregns the clouds   500
That shed May flowers; and pressed her matron lip
With kisses pure. Aside the Devil turned
For envy, yet with jealous leer malign
Eyed them askance, and to himself thus plained:
  "Sight hateful, sight tormenting! thus these two   505
Imparadised in one another's arms,
The happier Eden, shall enjoy their fill
Of bliss on bliss, while I to hell am thrust,
Where neither joy nor love, but fierce desire,
Among our other torments not the least,   510
Still unfulfilled with pain of longing pines;
Yet let me not forget what I have gained
From their own mouths. All is not theirs, it seems;
One fatal tree there stands, of Knowledge called,
Forbidden them to taste. Knowledge forbidden?   515
Suspicious, reasonless. Why should their Lord
Envy them that? Can it be sin to know,
Can it be death? And do they only stand
By ignorance, is that their happy state,
The proof of their obedience and their faith?   520
O fair foundation laid whereon to build
Their ruin! Hence I will excite their minds
With more desire to know, and to reject
Envious commands, invented with design
To keep them low whom knowledge might exalt   525
Equal with gods. Aspiring to be such,
They taste and die; what likelier can ensue?
But first with narrow search I must walk round
This garden, and no corner leave unspied;
A chance but chance may lead where I may meet   530
Some wand'ring Spirit of heav'n, by fountain side,
Or in thick shade retired, from him to draw
What further would be learnt. Live while ye may,
Yet happy pair; enjoy, till I return,
Short pleasures, for long woes are to succeed."   535
  So saying, his proud step he scornful turned,
But with sly circumspection, and began
Through wood, through waste, o'er hill, o'er dale, his roam.
Meanwhile in utmost longitude, where heav'n
With earth and ocean meets, the setting sun   540
Slowly descended, and with right aspéct
Against the eastern gate of Paradise
Leveled his ev'ning rays. It was a rock

499–501. A traditional meteorological interpretation of myth but a kind rare in Milton. Cf. *Iliad* 14.346–51, Virgil, *Georg.* 2.325 f.

506. Imparadised: in this context a doubly potent word, perhaps remembered from Sidney's *Arcadia* (ed. Feuillerat, 1912, p. 167).

526. Cf. 1.38–40, 3.206.

539. utmost longitude: extreme west.

541–42. with right aspect: directly opposite.   Against: i.e. against the inner side of the gate.

Of alablaster, piled up to the clouds,
Conspicuous far, winding with one ascent   545
Accessible from earth, one entrance high;
The rest was craggy cliff, that overhung
Still as it rose, impossible to climb.
Betwixt these rocky pillars Gabriel sat,
Chief of th' angelic guards, awaiting night;   550
About him exercised heroic games
Th' unarmèd youth of heav'n, but nigh at hand
Celestial armory, shields, helms, and spears,
Hung high, with diamond flaming and with gold.
Thither came Uriel, gliding through the even   555
On a sunbeam, swift as a shooting star
In autumn thwarts the night, when vapors fired
Impress the air, and shows the mariner
From what point of his compass to beware
Impetuous winds. He thus began in haste: 560
    "Gabriel, to thee thy course by lot hath giv'n
Charge and strict watch that to this happy place
No evil thing approach or enter in;
This day at highth of noon came to my sphere
A Spirit, zealous, as he seemed, to know   565
More of th' Almighty's works, and chiefly man,
God's latest image. I described his way
Bent all on speed, and marked his airy gait;
But in the mount that lies from Eden north,
Where he first lighted, soon discerned his looks   570
Alien from heav'n, with passions foul obscured.
Mine eye pursued him still, but under shade
Lost sight of him; one of the banished crew,
I fear, hath ventured from the deep, to raise
New troubles; him thy care must be to find."   575
    To whom the wingèd warrior thus returned:
"Uriel, no wonder if thy perfect sight,
Amid the sun's bright circle where thou sitt'st,
See far and wide. In at this gate none pass
The vigilance here placed, but such as come   580
Well known from heav'n; and since meridian hour
No creature thence. If Spirit of other sort,
So minded, have o'erleaped these earthy bounds
On purpose, hard thou know'st it to exclude
Spiritual substance with corporeal bar.   585
But if within the circuit of these walks,
In whatsoever shape he lurk, of whom
Thou tell'st, by morrow dawning I shall know."
    So promised he, and Uriel to his charge
Returned on that bright beam, whose point now raised   590

567. God's first image was the Son (3.63,   580. vigilance: guards.
384).   described: descried.   590–92. The sun, near the horizon in 540–
568. gait: course, voyage.   43 and 556, is now below it.

Bore him slope downward to the sun now fall'n
Beneath th' Azores; whether the prime orb,
Incredible how swift, had thither rolled
Diurnal, or this less volúble earth
By shorter flight to th' east, had left him there   595
Arraying with reflected purple and gold
The clouds that on his western throne attend.
    Now came still ev'ning on, and twilight gray
Had in her sober livery all things clad;
Silence accompanied, for beast and bird,   600
They to their grassy couch, these to their nests
Were slunk, all but the wakeful nightingale;
She all night long her amorous descant sung;
Silence was pleased. Now glowed the firmament
With living sapphires; Hesperus that led   605
The starry host, rode brightest, till the moon
Rising in clouded majesty, at length
Apparent queen unveiled her peerless light,
And o'er the dark her silver mantle threw;
    When Adam thus to Eve: "Fair consort, th' hour   610
Of night, and all things now retired to rest
Mind us of like repose, since God hath set
Labor and rest, as day and night to men
Successive, and the timely dew of sleep
Now falling with soft slumbrous weight inclines   615
Our eyelids; other creatures all day long
Rove idle, unemployed, and less need rest;
Man hath his daily work of body or mind
Appointed, which declares his dignity,
And the regard of Heav'n on all his ways;   620
While other animals unactive range,
And of their doings God takes no account.
To-morrow ere fresh morning streak the east
With first approach of light, we must be ris'n,
And at our pleasant labor, to reform   625
Yon flow'ry arbors, yonder alleys green,
Our walk at noon, with branches overgrown,
That mock our scant manuring, and require
More hands than ours to lop their wanton growth.
Those blossoms also, and those dropping gums,   630
That lie bestrown unsightly and unsmooth,
Ask riddance, if we mean to tread with ease;
Meanwhile, as nature wills, night bids us rest."
    To whom thus Eve with perfect beauty adorned:

592–95. Another noncommittal allowance for either the Ptolemaic or the Copernican system (cf. 3.574 f.).

592. whether: edd. 1–6, whither.   prime orb: the sun.

594. volúble: rolling swiftly.

603. descant: song with variations.
608. Apparent: manifest.
614. dew of sleep: cf. *Richard III* 4.1.84, *Julius Caesar* 2.1.230.
627. walk: ed. 2; ed. 1, walks.

"My author and disposer, what thou bidd'st   635
Unargued I obey; so God ordains.
God is thy law, thou mine; to know no more
Is woman's happiest knowledge and her praise.
With thee conversing I forget all time,
All seasons and their change, all please alike.   640
Sweet is the breath of morn, her rising sweet,
With charm of earliest birds; pleasant the sun
When first on this delightful land he spreads
His orient beams, on herb, tree, fruit, and flow'r,
Glist'ring with dew; fragrant the fertile earth   645
After soft showers; and sweet the coming on
Of grateful ev'ning mild, then silent night
With this her solemn bird and this fair moon,
And these the gems of heav'n, her starry train:
But neither breath of morn when she ascends   650
With charm of earliest birds, nor rising sun
On this delightful land, nor herb, fruit, flow'r,
Glist'ring with dew, nor fragrance after showers,
Nor grateful ev'ning mild, nor silent night
With this her solemn bird, nor walk by moon   655
Or glittering starlight without thee is sweet.
But wherefore all night long shine these, for whom
This glorious sight, when sleep hath shut all eyes?"
     To whom our general ancestor replied:
"Daughter of God and man, accomplished Eve,   660
Those have their course to finish, round the earth,
By morrow ev'ning, and from land to land
In order, though to nations yet unborn,
Minist'ring light prepared, they set and rise;
Lest total darkness should by night regain   665
Her old possession, and extinguish life
In nature and all things; which these soft fires
Not only enlighten, but with kindly heat
Of various influence foment and warm,
Temper or nourish, or in part shed down   670
Their stellar virtue on all kinds that grow
On earth, made hereby apter to receive
Perfection from the sun's more potent ray.
These then, though unbeheld in deep of night,
Shine not in vain, nor think, though men were none,   675
That heav'n would want spectators, God want praise;
Millions of spiritual creatures walk the earth
Unseen, both when we wake, and when we sleep:

639–56. The elaborate pattern of this pastoral hymn of love is the most notable example of the non-colloquial utterance of Adam and Eve in their state of innocence; Eve's motif (656) is picked up from the last phrase of Adam's first speech (439).

640. seasons: times of day (Eden enjoys eternal spring: 4:264–68).

642. charm: song.

665–67. Cf. 2.983–86, 1034–39.

670–73. A common — and limited — principle of astrology.

677–88. A beautifully potent reminder of the angelic presences who still inhabited the seventeenth-century world.

All these with ceaseless praise his works behold
Both day and night. How often from the steep   680
Of echoing hill or thicket have we heard
Celestial voices to the midnight air,
Sole, or responsive each to other's note,
Singing their great Creator; oft in bands
While they keep watch, or nightly rounding walk,   685
With heav'nly touch of instrumental sounds
In full harmonic number joined, their songs
Divide the night, and lift our thoughts to heaven."
   Thus talking, hand in hand alone they passed
On to their blissful bower; it was a place   690
Chos'n by the sovran Planter, when he framed
All things to man's delightful use; the roof
Of thickest covert was inwoven shade,
Laurel and myrtle, and what higher grew
Of firm and fragrant leaf; on either side   695
Acanthus, and each odorous bushy shrub
Fenced up the verdant wall; each beauteous flow'r,
Iris all hues, roses, and jessamine
Reared high their flourished heads between, and wrought
Mosaic; under foot the violet,   700
Crocus, and hyacinth with rich inlay
Broidered the ground, more colored than with stone
Of costliest emblem. Other creature here,
Beast, bird, insect, or worm durst enter none;
Such was their awe of man. In shadier bower   705
More sacred and sequestered, though but feigned,
Pan or Silvanus never slept, nor nymph
Nor Faunus haunted. Here in close recess
With flowers, garlands, and sweet-smelling herbs
Espousèd Eve decked first her nuptial bed,   710
And heav'nly quires the hymenean sung,
What day the genial angel to our sire
Brought her in naked beauty more adorned,
More lovely than Pandora, whom the gods
Endowed with all their gifts, and O too like   715
In sad event, when to the unwiser son
Of Japhet brought by Hermes, she ensnared
Mankind with her fair looks, to be avenged
On him who had stole Jove's authentic fire.
   Thus at their shady lodge arrived, both stood,   720
Both turned, and under open sky adored

680. See the note on 449 above.
688. Divide: into watches.
699. flourished: luxuriant.
700 f. Cf. *Iliad* 14.347 f.
  703. emblem: inlaid work. The use of terms from art ("Mosaic," "inlay") stresses the work of God and nature.
  705. Ed. 1, shadier; ed. 2, shady.

706. feigned. Cf. 1.740 f., 4.250–51.
714 f. Pandora ("all gifts"), the maiden brought as a snare to Epimetheus ("afterthought"), brother of Prometheus ("forethought"); her box of gifts, when opened, let loose all ills upon the world (Hesiod, *Works and Days* 70 f.).
  719. authentic: original.

The God that made both sky, air, earth, and heav'n
Which they beheld, the moon's resplendent globe
And starry pole: "Thou also mad'st the night,
Maker Omnipotent, and thou the day,   725
Which we in our appointed work employed
Have finished happy in our mutual help
And mutual love, the crown of all our bliss
Ordained by thee, and this delicious place
For us too large, where thy abundance wants   730
Partakers, and uncropped falls to the ground.
But thou hast promised from us two a race
To fill the earth, who shall with us extol
Thy goodness infinite, both when we wake,
And when we seek, as now, thy gift of sleep."   735
    This said unanimous, and other rites
Observing none, but adoration pure
Which God likes best, into their inmost bow'r
Handed they went; and eased the putting off
These troublesome disguises which we wear,   740
Straight side by side were laid, nor turned, I ween,
Adam from his fair spouse, nor Eve the rites
Mysterious of connubial love refused;
Whatever hypocrites austerely talk
Of purity and place and innocence,   745
Defaming as impure what God declares
Pure, and commands to some, leaves free to all.
Our Maker bids increase; who bids abstain
But our destroyer, foe to God and man?
Hail, wedded Love, mysterious law, true source   750
Of human offspring, sole propriety
In Paradise of all things common else.
By thee adulterous lust was driv'n from men
Among the bestial herds to range; by thee
Founded in reason, loyal, just, and pure,   755
Relations dear, and all the charities
Of father, son, and brother first were known.
Far be it that I should write thee sin or blame,
Or think thee unbefitting holiest place,
Perpetual fountain of domestic sweets,   760
Whose bed is undefiled and chaste pronounced,
Present or past, as saints and patriarchs used.
Here Love his golden shafts employs, here lights
His constant lamp, and waves his purple wings,
Reigns here and revels; not in the bought smile   765
Of harlots, loveless, joyless, unendeared,

724–25. Ps. 74.16.
735. thy gift of sleep: Ps. 127.2; *Iliad*
9.713; *Aen.* 2.269.
739. Handed: hand in hand.
744–48. 1 Tim. 4.1–4; Gen. 1.28.
750. Eph. 5.31–32.

751. propriety: property, exclusive possession.
761. Heb. 13.4.
763 f. Using classical terms, Milton repudiates the tradition of Ovidian and courtly love
(glossary: "Cupid").

Casual fruition; nor in court amours,
Mixed dance, or wanton masque, or midnight ball,
Or serenate, which the starved lover sings
To his proud fair, best quitted with disdain.   770
These lulled by nightingales, embracing slept,
And on their naked limbs the flow'ry roof
Show'red roses, which the morn repaired. Sleep on,
Blest pair; and O yet happiest if ye seek
No happier state, and know to know no more.   775
    Now had night measured with her shadowy cone
Half way up hill this vast sublunar vault,
And from their ivory port the Cherubim
Forth issuing at th' accustomed hour stood armed
To their night-watches in warlike parade,   780
When Gabriel to his next in power thus spake:
    "Uzziel, half these draw off, and coast the south
With strictest watch; these other wheel the north;
Our circuit meets full west." As flame they part,
Half wheeling to the shield, half to the spear.   785
From these, two strong and subtle Spirits he called
That near him stood, and gave them thus in charge:
    "Ithuriel and Zephon, with winged speed
Search through this garden; leave unsearched no nook;
But chiefly where those two fair creatures lodge,   790
Now laid perhaps asleep secure of harm.
This ev'ning from the sun's decline arrived
Who tells of some infernal Spirit seen
Hitherward bent (who could have thought?) escaped
The bars of hell, on errand bad no doubt: 795
Such where ye find, seize fast, and hither bring."
    So saying, on he led his radiant files,
Dazzling the moon; these to the bower direct
In search of whom they sought. Him there they found
Squat like a toad, close at the ear of Eve,   800
Assaying by his devilish art to reach
The organs of her fancy, and with them forge
Illusions as he list, phantasms and dreams;
Or if, inspiring venom, he might taint
Th' animal spirits that from pure blood arise   805
Like gentle breaths from rivers pure, thence raise
At least distempered, discontented thoughts,
Vain hopes, vain aims, inordinate desires

---

769. serenate (Italian form): serenade.
769–70. The lover in the cold (see note on 2.600) outside his mistress' door — as in Ovid, *Amores* 1.6, 9; 3.11a; Propertius 1.16; Horace, *Od.* 1.25, 3.10.
773. which . . . repaired: cf. Virgil, *Georg.* 2.201–02.
774–75. know . . . more: are wise enough not to seek knowledge beyond human limits.

Cf. Virgil, *Georg.* 2.458.
776–77. The earth being smaller than the sun, its shadow forms a cone; as the sun sinks the point of the cone moves half way up from the horizon to the zenith.
785. shield . . . spear: left, right (classical terms).
793. Who: one who.
805. spirits: see glossary.

Blown up with high conceits engend'ring pride.
Him thus intent Ithuriel with his spear   810
Touched lightly; for no falsehood can endure
Touch of celestial temper, but returns
Of force to its own likeness. Up he starts
Discovered and surprised. As when a spark
Lights on a heap of nitrous powder, laid   815
Fit for the tun some magazine to store
Against a rumored war, the smutty grain
With sudden blaze diffused, inflames the air:
So started up in his own shape the Fiend.
Back stepped those two fair angels half amazed   820
So sudden to behold the grisly king;
Yet thus, unmoved with fear, accost him soon:
    "Which of those rebel Spirits adjudged to hell
Com'st thou, escaped thy prison; and transformed,
Why sat'st thou like an enemy in wait   825
Here watching at the head of these that sleep?"
    "Know ye not then," said Satan, filled with scorn,
"Know ye not me? Ye knew me once no mate
For you, there sitting where ye durst not soar;
Not to know me argues yourselves unknown,   830
The lowest of your throng; or if ye know,
Why ask ye, and superfluous begin
Your message, like to end as much in vain?"
To whom thus Zephon, answering scorn with scorn:
"Think not, revolted Spirit, thy shape the same,   835
Or undiminished brightness, to be known
As when thou stood'st in heav'n upright and pure;
That glory then, when thou no more wast good,
Departed from thee, and thou resembl'st now
Thy sin and place of doom obscure and foul.   840
But come, for thou, be sure, shalt give account
To him who sent us, whose charge is to keep
This place inviolable, and these from harm."
    So spake the Cherub, and his grave rebuke,
Severe in youthful beauty, added grace   845
Invincible. Abashed the Devil stood,
And felt how awful goodness is, and saw
Virtue in her shape how lovely; saw, and pined
His loss; but chiefly to find here observed
His luster visibly impaired; yet seemed   850
Undaunted. "If I must contend," said he,
"Best with the best, the sender not the sent;
Or all at once; more glory will be won,
Or less be lost." "Thy fear," said Zephon bold,
"Will save us trial what the least can do   855
Single against thee wicked, and thence weak."

815. nitrous powder: gunpowder.   843. these: Adam and Eve.
816. tun: barrel.

The Fiend replied not, overcome with rage;
But like a proud steed reined, went haughty on,
Champing his iron curb. To strive or fly
He held it vain; awe from above had quelled   860
His heart, not else dismayed. Now drew they nigh
The western point, where those half-rounding guards
Just met, and closing stood in squadron joined
Awaiting next command. To whom their chief
Gabriel from the front thus called aloud: 865
    "O friends, I hear the tread of nimble feet
Hasting this way, and now by glimpse discern
Ithuriel and Zephon through the shade,
And with them comes a third, of regal port,
But faded splendor wan, who by his gait   870
And fierce demeanor seems the Prince of Hell,
Not likely to part hence without contést;
Stand firm, for in his look defiance lours."
    He scarce had ended, when those two approached
And brief related whom they brought, where found,   875
How busied, in what form and posture couched.
    To whom with stern regard thus Gabriel spake:
"Why hast thou, Satan, broke the bounds prescribed
To thy transgressions, and disturbed the charge
Of others, who approve not to transgress   880
By thy example, but have power and right
To question thy bold entrance on this place;
Employed it seems to violate sleep, and those
Whose dwelling God hath planted here in bliss?"
    To whom thus Satan, with contemptuous brow: 885
"Gabriel, thou hadst in heav'n th' esteem of wise,
And such I held thee; but this question asked
Puts me in doubt. Lives there who loves his pain?
Who would not, finding way, break loose from hell,
Though thither doomed? Thou wouldst thyself, no doubt,   890
And boldly venture to whatever place
Farthest from pain, where thou mightst hope to change
Torment with ease, and soonest recompense
Dole with delight, which in this place I sought;
To thee no reason, who know'st only good,   895
But evil hast not tried. And wilt object
His will who bound us? Let him surer bar
His iron gates, if he intends our stay
In that dark durance. Thus much what was asked.
The rest is true, they found me where they say;   900
But that implies not violence or harm."
    Thus he in scorn. The warlike angel moved,
Disdainfully half smiling thus replied:
"O loss of one in heav'n to judge of wise,

---

894. Dole with delight: cf. *Hamlet* 1.2.13.   904. How great a loss to heaven of one so
896. object: urge as an objection.   well able to judge of wisdom.

Since Satan fell, whom folly overthrew,   905
And now returns him from his prison scaped,
Gravely in doubt whether to hold them wise
Or not, who ask what boldness brought him hither
Unlicensed from his bounds in hell prescribed;
So wise he judges it to fly from pain   910
However, and to scape his punishment.
So judge thou still, presumptuous, till the wrath,
Which thou incurr'st by flying, meet thy flight
Sevenfold, and scourge that wisdom back to hell.
Which taught thee yet no better, that no pain   915
Can equal anger infinite provoked.
But wherefore thou alone? Wherefore with thee
Came not all hell broke loose? Is pain to them
Less pain, less to be fled, or thou than they
Less hardy to endure? Courageous chief,   920
The first in flight from pain, hadst thou alleged
To thy deserted host this cause of flight,
Thou surely hadst not come sole fugitive."
    To which the Fiend thus answered frowning stern:
"Not that I less endure, or shrink from pain,   925
Insulting angel, well thou know'st I stood
Thy fiercest, when in battle to thy aid
The blasting volleyed thunder made all speed
And seconded thy else not dreaded spear.
But still thy words at random, as before,   930
Argue thy inexperience what behoves,
From hard assays and ill successes past,
A faithful leader, not to hazard all
Through ways of danger by himself untried.
I therefore, I alone first undertook   935
To wing the desolate abyss, and spy
This new-created world, whereof in hell
Fame is not silent, here in hope to find
Better abode, and my afflicted powers
To settle here on earth, or in mid-air;   940
Though for possession put to try once more
What thou and thy gay legions dare against;
Whose easier business were to serve their Lord
High up in heav'n, with songs to hymn his throne,
And practised distances to cringe, not fight."   945
    To whom the warrior angel soon replied:
"To say and straight unsay, pretending first
Wise to fly pain, professing next the spy,
Argues no leader but a liar traced,
Satan, and couldst thou 'faithful' add? O name,   950

911. However: in whatever way.
926–27. stood Thy fiercest: withstood thy
fiercest attack.
928. The: ed. 2, Thy.

940. mid-air: glossary.
945. Make the bows prescribed by court
etiquette.

O sacred name of faithfulness profaned!
Faithful to whom? To thy rebellious crew?
Army of fiends, fit body to fit head;
Was this your discipline and faith engaged,
Your military obedience, to dissolve   955
Allegiance to th' acknowledged Power Supreme?
And thou sly hypocrite, who now wouldst seem
Patron of liberty, who more than thou
Once fawned, and cringed, and servilely adored
Heav'n's awful Monarch? Wherefore but in hope   960
To dispossess him, and thyself to reign?
But mark what I areed thee now: Avaunt!
Fly thither whence thou fledd'st. If from this hour
Within these hallowed limits thou appear,
Back to th' infernal pit I drag thee chained,   965
And seal thee so, as henceforth not to scorn
The facile gates of hell too slightly barred."
    So threatened he, but Satan to no threats
Gave heed, but waxing more in rage replied:
    "Then when I am thy captive talk of chains,   970
Proud limitary Cherub, but ere then
Far heavier load thyself expect to feel
From my prevailing arm, though heaven's King
Ride on thy wings, and thou with thy compeers,
Used to the yoke, draw'st his triumphant wheels   975
In progress through the road of heav'n star-paved."
    While thus he spake, th' angelic squadron bright
Turned, fiery red, sharp'ning in moonèd horns
Their phalanx, and began to hem him round
With ported spears, as thick as when a field   980
Of Ceres ripe for harvest waving bends
Her bearded grove of ears, which way the wind
Sways them; the careful ploughman doubting stands
Lest on the threshing-floor his hopeful sheaves
Prove chaff. On th' other side Satan alarmed   985
Collecting all his might dilated stood,
Like Teneriffe or Atlas unremoved:
His stature reached the sky, and on his crest
Sat Horror plumed; nor wanted in his grasp
What seemed both spear and shield. Now dreadful deeds   990

---

962. areed (archaic): advise.
966. seal: Rev. 20.3.
971. limitary: guard at a frontier (cf. "limits," 964), and "limiting."
974. Cf. 6.771 and Ps. 18.10.
977–1015. Cf. the final encounter of Aeneas and Turnus (*Aen*. 12.661–952) and items in notes following.
978. moonèd horns: crescent formation.
980. ported: held aslant (cf. "port arms").
980 f. Cf. *Iliad* 2.147–48; Virgil, *Georg*. 1.226, 316 f., *Aen*. 9.661–64.

983. careful: anxious.
985. alarmed: aroused.
985–90. Cf. *Aen*. 12.697–703.
986. dilated: cf. 1.428–30.
987. Teneriffe: the high peak in the Canary Islands.   unremoved: unremovable.
990–1004. So Zeus weighs the fates of Hector and Achilles (*Iliad* 22.209 f.) and Jupiter those of Turnus and Aeneas (*Aen*. 12.725–27).

Might have ensued, nor only Paradise
In this commotion, but the starry cope
Of heav'n perhaps, or all the elements
At least had gone to wrack, disturbed and torn
With violence of this conflict, had not soon   995
Th' Eternal to prevent such horrid fray
Hung forth in heav'n his golden scales, yet seen
Betwixt Astraea and the Scorpion sign,
Wherein all things created first he weighed,
The pendulous round earth with balanced air   1000
In counterpoise, now ponders all events,
Battles and realms. In these he put two weights,
The sequel each of parting and of fight;
The latter quick up flew, and kicked the beam;
Which Gabriel spying, thus bespake the Fiend: 1005
    "Satan, I know thy strength, and thou know'st mine,
Neither our own but giv'n; what folly then
To boast what arms can do, since thine no more
Than Heav'n permits, nor mine, though doubled now
To trample thee as mire. For proof look up,   1010
And read thy lot in yon celestial sign
Where thou art weighed, and shown how light, how weak,
If thou resist." The Fiend looked up and knew
His mounted scale aloft: nor more; but fled
Murmuring, and with him fled the shades of night.   1015

Book V

THE ARGUMENT

Morning approached, Eve relates to Adam her troublesome dream; he likes
it not, yet comforts her; they come forth to their day labors; their morning
hymn at the door of their bower. God, to render man inexcusable, sends
Raphael to admonish him of his obedience, of his free estate, of his enemy near
at hand — who he is, and why his enemy, and whatever else may avail Adam
to know. Raphael comes down to Paradise; his appearance described; his coming discerned by Adam afar off, sitting at the door of his bower; he goes out
to meet him, brings him to his lodge, entertains him with the choicest fruits of
Paradise got together by Eve; their discourse at table. Raphael performs his
message, minds Adam of his state and of his enemy; relates, at Adam's request, who that enemy is, and how he came to be so, beginning from his first
revolt in heaven, and the occasion thereof; how he drew his legions after him

997–98. The constellation Libra (Scales) between Virgo (glossary: "Astraea") and the Scorpion in the zodiac.   999. Isa. 40.12.
1001. ponders: weighs (Latin sense); 1 Sam. 2.3.

1003. sequel: consequence (for Satan).
1010. To . . . mire: Isa. 10.6.
1012. Dan. 5.27.
1014–15. Cf. *Aen.* 12.951–52.

to the parts of the north, and there incited them to rebel with him, persuading all but only Abdiel, a Seraph, who in argument dissuades and opposes him, then forsakes him.

N ow Morn her rosy steps in th' eastern clime
Advancing, sowed the earth with orient pearl,
When Adam waked, so customed, for his sleep
Was airy light, from pure digestion bred,
And temperate vapors bland, which th' only sound   5
Of leaves and fuming rills, Aurora's fan,
Lightly dispersed, and the shrill matin song
Of birds on every bough; so much the more
His wonder was to find unwakened Eve
With tresses discomposed, and glowing cheek,   10
As through unquiet rest. He on his side
Leaning half-raised, with looks of cordial love
Hung over her enamored, and beheld
Beauty, which whether waking or asleep
Shot forth peculiar graces; then with voice   15
Mild, as when Zephyrus on Flora breathes,
Her hand soft touching, whispered thus: "Awake,
My fairest, my espoused, my latest found,
Heav'n's last best gift, my ever new delight,
Awake, the morning shines, and the fresh field   20
Calls us; we lose the prime, to mark how spring
Our tended plants, how blows the citron grove,
What drops the myrrh, and what the balmy reed,
How Nature paints her colors, how the bee
Sits on the bloom extracting liquid sweet."   25
    Such whispering waked her, but with startled eye
On Adam, whom embracing, thus she spake:
    "O sole in whom my thoughts find all repose,
My glory, my perfection, glad I see
Thy face, and morn returned, for I this night —   30
Such night till this I never passed — have dreamed,
If dreamed, not as I oft am wont, of thee,
Works of day past, or morrow's next design,
But of offense and trouble, which my mind
Knew never till this irksome night. Methought   35
Close at mine ear one called me forth to walk
With gentle voice; I thought it thine. It said:
'Why sleep'st thou, Eve? Now is the pleasant time,
The cool, the silent, save where silence yields
To the night-warbling bird, that now awake

BOOK V. 1–2. A variation on the Homeric formula; Ps. 97.11.
    5. which: i.e. sleep.
    5. only: mere, alone.
    17–25. For the *aubade*, cf. Song of Songs 2.10; etc.
    21. prime: early morning.

23. balmy: yielding balm.
28–135. The non-biblical incident of Eve's dream, inspired by Satan (cf. 4.799–809), is obviously a major step in Milton's preparation for the fall, even though her waking reaction is right.
40. bird: cf. 3.38–40.

Tunes sweetest his love-labored song; now reigns
Full-orbed the moon, and with more pleasing light
Shadowy sets off the face of things; in vain,
If none regard; heav'n wakes with all his eyes,
Whom to behold but thee, Nature's desire,   45
In whose sight all things joy, with ravishment
Attracted by thy beauty still to gaze?'
I rose as at thy call, but found thee not;
To find thee I directed then my walk;
And on, methought, alone I passed through ways   50
That brought me on a sudden to the tree
Of interdicted knowledge. Fair it seemed,
Much fairer to my fancy than by day;
And as I wond'ring looked, beside it stood
One shaped and winged like one of those from heav'n   55
By us oft seen; his dewy locks distilled
Ambrosia; on that tree he also gazed;
And 'O fair plant,' said he, 'with fruit surcharged,
Deigns none to ease thy load and taste thy sweet,
Nor god, nor man; is knowledge so despised?   60
Or envy, or what reserve forbids to taste?
Forbid who will, none shall from me withhold
Longer thy offered good, why else set here?'
This said he paused not, but with vent'rous arm
He plucked, he tasted; me damp horror chilled   65
At such bold words vouched with a deed so bold.
But he thus, overjoyed: 'O fruit divine,
Sweet of thyself, but much more sweet thus cropped,
Forbidden here, it seems, as only fit
For gods, yet able to make gods of men;   70
And why not gods of men, since good, the more
Communicated, more abundant grows,
The author not impaired, but honored more?
Here, happy creature, fair angelic Eve,
Partake thou also; happy though thou art,   75
Happier thou may'st be, worthier canst not be;
Taste this, and be henceforth among the gods
Thyself a goddess, not to earth confined,
But sometimes in the air, as we; sometimes
Ascend to heav'n, by merit thine, and see   80
What life the gods live there, and such live thou.'
So saying, he drew nigh, and to me held,
Even to my mouth of that same fruit held part
Which he had plucked; the pleasant savory smell
So quickened appetite that I, methought,   85
Could not but taste. Forthwith up to the clouds
With him I flew, and underneath beheld

44. eyes: stars.   60–63. Cf. 4.515 f., 9.691 f.
56–57. his . . . Ambrosia: cf. *Aen.* 1.403–   77–81. Gen. 3.5.
04.

The earth outstretched immense, a prospect wide
And various. Wond'ring at my flight and change
To this high exaltation, suddenly   90
My guide was gone, and I, methought, sunk down,
And fell asleep; but O how glad I waked
To find this but a dream!" Thus Eve her night
Related, and thus Adam answered sad:
    "Best image of myself and dearer half,   95
The trouble of thy thoughts this night in sleep
Affects me equally; nor can I like
This uncouth dream, of evil sprung, I fear;
Yet evil whence? In thee can harbor none,
Created pure. But know that in the soul   100
Are many lesser faculties that serve
Reason as chief; among these fancy next
Her office holds; of all external things,
Which the five watchful senses represent,
She forms imaginations, airy shapes,   105
Which reason joining or disjoining frames
All what we affirm or what deny, and call
Our knowledge or opinion; then retires
Into her private cell when nature rests.
Oft in her absence mimic fancy wakes   110
To imitate her; but misjoining shapes,
Wild work produces oft, and most in dreams,
Ill matching words and deeds long past or late.
Some such resemblances methinks I find
Of our last ev'ning's talk in this thy dream,   115
But with addition strange; yet be not sad.
Evil into the mind of god or man
May come and go, so unapproved, and leave
No spot or blame behind; which gives me hope
That what in sleep thou didst abhor to dream,   120
Waking thou never wilt consent to do.
Be not disheartened then, nor cloud those looks
That wont to be more cheerful and serene
Than when fair morning first smiles on the world,
And let us to our fresh employments rise   125
Among the groves, the fountains, and the flow'rs
That open now their choicest bosomed smells
Reserved from night, and kept for thee in store."
    So cheered he his fair spouse, and she was cheered,
But silently a gentle tear let fall   130
From either eye, and wiped them with her hair;

---

94. sad: seriously.
100–16. A summary of orthodox "faculty psychology."
114. resemblances: cf. 4.423 f., and 4.646 f. and 5.38 f.
117–19. While in Christian theology an omniscient God must know evil along with good (as Aquinas says), it seems likely here that "god" means "angel," as it often does in *P.L.* (e.g. 1.116, 138, 240, 629, 2.352, etc.). The capitalized "God" of the early editions tells us nothing, since capitals were used so freely.
130–31. Luke 7.37–38.

Two other precious drops that ready stood,
Each in their crystal sluice, he ere they fell
Kissed as the gracious signs of sweet remorse
And pious awe, that feared to have offended.   135
　　So all was cleared, and to the field they haste.
But first from under shady arborous roof,
Soon as they forth were come to open sight
Of day-spring, and the sun, who scarce up risen
With wheels yet hov'ring o'er the ocean brim,   140
Shot parallel to the earth his dewy ray,
Discovering in wide landscape all the east
Of Paradise and Eden's happy plains,
Lowly they bowed adoring, and began
Their orisons, each morning duly paid   145
In various style, for neither various style
Nor holy rapture wanted they to praise
Their Maker, in fit strains pronounced or sung
Unmeditated; such prompt eloquence
Flowed from their lips, in prose or numerous verse,   150
More tuneable than needed lute or harp
To add more sweetness, and they thus began:
　　"These are thy glorious works, Parent of good,
Almighty, thine this universal frame,
Thus wondrous fair; thyself how wondrous then!   155
Unspeakable, who sitt'st above these heavens,
To us invisible or dimly seen
In these thy lowest works, yet these declare
Thy goodness beyond thought, and power divine.
Speak ye who best can tell, ye sons of light,   160
Angels, for ye behold him, and with songs
And choral symphonies, day without night,
Circle his throne rejoicing, ye in heav'n;
On earth join all ye creatures to extol
Him first, him last, him midst, and without end.   165
Fairest of stars, last in the train of night,
If better thou belong not to the dawn,
Sure pledge of day, that crown'st the smiling morn
With thy bright circlet, praise him in thy sphere
While day arises, that sweet hour of prime.   170
Thou sun, of this great world both eye and soul,
Acknowledge him thy greater; sound his praise
In thy eternal course, both when thou climb'st,
And when high noon hast gained, and when thou fall'st.

---

144 f. Milton's dislike of a prescribed ritual and his emphasis on inward spirituality were manifested in his anti-episcopal tracts. Cf. *P.L.* 1.17–18, 4.736–38.

150. numerous: metrical, melodious.

153–208. This canticle grows out of Ps. 19.1, Ps. 104, and especially Ps. 148.

165. Rev. 22.13.

166–69. Fairest of stars: Hesperus (*Iliad* 22.318) or Venus and Lucifer (glossary); with 166–79 cf. Plato, *Timaeus* 38 C–E.

171. sun . . . eye and soul: cf. Ovid, *Met.* 4.227–28; Pliny, *Nat. Hist.* 2.4.13.

173 f. All things celestial and terrestrial form a pattern of motion, rising and falling in order.

Moon, that now meet'st the orient sun, now fli'st   175
With the fixed stars, fixed in their orb that flies,
And ye five other wand'ring fires that move
In mystic dance not without song, resound
His praise, who out of darkness called up light.
Air, and ye elements, the eldest birth   180
Of Nature's womb, that in quaternion run
Perpetual circle, multiform, and mix
And nourish all things, let your ceaseless change
Vary to our great Maker still new praise.
Ye mists and exhalations that now rise   185
From hill or steaming lake, dusky or gray,
Till the sun paint your fleecy skirts with gold,
In honor to the world's great Author rise;
Whether to deck with clouds the uncolored sky,
Or wet the thirsty earth with falling showers,   190
Rising or falling still advance his praise.
His praise, ye winds, that from four quarters blow,
Breathe soft or loud; and wave your tops, ye pines,
With every plant, in sign of worship wave.
Fountains, and ye that warble, as ye flow,   195
Melodious murmurs, warbling tune his praise.
Join voices, all ye living souls; ye birds,
That singing up to heaven gate ascend,
Bear on your wings and in your notes his praise;
Ye that in waters glide, and ye that walk   200
The earth, and stately tread, or lowly creep,
Witness if I be silent, morn or even,
To hill, or valley, fountain, or fresh shade
Made vocal by my song, and taught his praise.
Hail, universal Lord, be bounteous still   205
To give us only good; and if the night
Have gathered aught of evil or concealed,
Disperse it, as now light dispels the dark."
    So prayed they innocent, and to their thoughts
Firm peace recovered soon and wonted calm.   210
On to their morning's rural work they haste
Among sweet dews and flow'rs; where any row
Of fruit-trees over-woody reached too far
Their pampered boughs, and needed hands to check
Fruitless embraces. Or they led the vine   215
To wed her elm; she spoused about him twines
Her marriageable arms, and with her brings

176. fixed: glossary.
177. five other: Mercury, Venus, Mars,
Jupiter, Saturn ("planet" means "wanderer").
178. mystic dance: see 3.580 and note.
song: music of the spheres (see note on *Nativity* 125 f.).
179. Cf. 3.8–12.
181. quaternion: in fourfold combination
(cf. 414–26 and note).

189. uncolored: of one color, not variegated.
198. Cf. Shakespeare, *Cymbeline* 2.3.22
and Sonnet 29.11–12.
215–19. The "wedding" of trees and vines
— which here parallels the relations of Adam
and Eve — was traditional in antiquity, e.g.
Virgil, *Georg.* 1.2, 2.221, 360–61, 367,
Horace, *Od.* 4.5.30, *Epod.* 2.9–10.

Her dow'r, th' adopted clusters, to adorn
His barren leaves. Them thus employed beheld
With pity heav'n's high King, and to him called   220
Raphael, the sociable Spirit, that deigned
To travel with Tobias, and secured
His marriage with the seven-times-wedded maid.
    "Raphael," said he, "thou hear'st what stir on earth
Satan, from hell scaped through the darksome gulf,   225
Hath raised in Paradise, and how disturbed
This night the human pair, how he designs
In them at once to ruin all mankind.
Go therefore, half this day as friend with friend
Converse with Adam, in what bow'r or shade   230
Thou find'st him from the heat of noon retired,
To respite his day-labor with repast
Or with repose; and such discourse bring on
As may advise him of his happy state,
Happiness in his power left free to will,   235
Left to his own free will, his will though free
Yet mutable; whence warn him to beware
He swerve not, too secure. Tell him withal
His danger, and from whom; what enemy,
Late fall'n himself from heav'n, is plotting now   240
The fall of others from like state of bliss;
By violence, no, for that shall be withstood,
But by deceit and lies; this let him know,
Lest wilfully transgressing he pretend
Surprisal, unadmonished, unforewarned."   245
    So spake th' Eternal Father, and fulfilled
All justice; nor delayed the wingèd saint
After his charge received; but from among
Thousand celestial Ardors, where he stood
Veiled with his gorgeous wings, up springing light   250
Flew through the midst of heav'n; th' angelic quires
On each hand parting, to his speed gave way
Through all th' empyreal road; till at the gate
Of heav'n arrived, the gate self-opened wide
On golden hinges turning, as by work   255
Divine the sov'ran Architect had framed.
From hence, no cloud, or, to obstruct his sight,
Star interposed, however small, he sees,
Not unconform to other shining globes,
Earth and the gard'n of God, with cedars crowned   260
Above all hills: as when by night the glass
Of Galileo, less assured, observes

219 f. Raphael's beneficent mission to earth, in obvious contrast with Satan's, is partly parallelled by that of Mercury (line 285; *Aen.* 4.219–58) and other celestial messengers in the classical epics.

222–23. Tobias. See glossary, "Asmadai,"

and above, 4.168–71.
229. as . . . friend: Exod. 33.11.
244. pretend: offer as an excuse.
249. Ardors: flames, angels.
254–56. Cf. 2.879 f., 7.205 f.
261–63. Cf. 1.287–91, 3.588–90.

Imagined lands and regions in the moon;
Or pilot from amidst the Cyclades
Delos or Samos first appearing kens   265
A cloudy spot. Down thither prone in flight
He speeds, and through the vast ethereal sky
Sails between worlds and worlds, with steady wing
Now on the polar winds, then with quick fan
Winnows the buxom air; till within soar   270
Of tow'ring eagles, to all the fowls he seems
A phoenix, gazed by all, as that sole bird,
When to enshrine his relics in the sun's
Bright temple, to Egyptian Thebes he flies.
At once on th' eastern cliff of Paradise   275
He lights, and to his proper shape returns,
A Seraph winged: six wings he wore, to shade
His lineaments divine; the pair that clad
Each shoulder broad, came mantling o'er his breast
With regal ornament; the middle pair   280
Girt like a starry zone his waist, and round
Skirted his loins and thighs with downy gold
And colors dipped in heav'n; the third his feet
Shadowed from either heel with feathered mail,
Sky-tinctured grain. Like Maia's son he stood,   285
And shook his plumes, that heav'nly fragrance filled
The circuit wide. Straight knew him all the bands
Of angels under watch; and to his state
And to his message high in honor rise,
For on some message high they guessed him bound.   290
Their glittering tents he passed, and now is come
Into the blissful field, through groves of myrrh,
And flow'ring odors, cassia, nard, and balm,
A wilderness of sweets; for Nature here
Wantoned as in her prime, and played at will   295
Her virgin fancies, pouring forth more sweet,
Wild above rule or art, enormous bliss.
Him through the spicy forest onward come
Adam discerned, as in the door he sat
Of his cool bow'r, while now the mounted sun   300
Shot down direct his fervid rays to warm
Earth's inmost womb, more warmth than Adam needs;
And Eve within, due at her hour prepared
For dinner savory fruits, of taste to please

---

264. Cyclades: islands in the south Aegean.
272. phoenix: glossary.
277–85. Isa. 6.2. The colors were probably suggested by traditional descriptions of the phoenix.
282. Skirted: covered.
285. Maia's son: Hermes (Mercury). Cf. *Hamlet* 3.4.58–59.
286–87. Cf. Tasso's *G.L.*, tr. E. Fairfax, 1.14, and the aromatic phoenix.

292–93. The perfumes of the phoenix may be still in Milton's mind (Ovid, *Met.* 15.398–400); and cf. biblical references to these herbs.
294–97. Like Spenser (e.g. *F.Q.* 2.12), Milton puts nature's simplicity and fecundity above art and artifice.
297. enormous: in its literal sense, "beyond rule."
299 f. Cf. Abraham when the Lord visited him (Gen. 18.1 f.).

True appetite, and not disrelish thirst   305
Of nectarous draughts between, from milky stream,
Berry or grape: to whom thus Adam called:
    "Haste hither, Eve, and worth thy sight behold
Eastward among those trees what glorious shape
Comes this way moving; seems another morn   310
Ris'n on mid-noon; some great behest from Heav'n
To us perhaps he brings, and will vouchsafe
This day to be our guest. But go with speed,
And what thy stores contain, bring forth and pour
Abundance, fit to honor and receive   315
Our heav'nly stranger; well we may afford
Our givers their own gifts, and large bestow
From large bestowed, where Nature multiplies
Her fertile growth, and by disburd'ning grows
More fruitful; which instructs us not to spare."   320
    To whom thus Eve: "Adam, earth's hallowed mold,
Of God inspired, small store will serve, where store,
All seasons, ripe for use hangs on the stalk;
Save what by frugal storing firmness gains
To nourish, and superfluous moist consumes.   325
But I will haste and from each bough and brake,
Each plant and juiciest gourd, will pluck such choice
To entertain our angel guest, as he
Beholding shall confess that here on earth
God hath dispensed his bounties as in heav'n."   330
    So saying, with dispatchful looks in haste
She turns, on hospitable thoughts intent
What choice to choose for delicacy best,
What order, so contrived as not to mix
Tastes not well joined, inelegant, but bring   335
Taste after taste upheld with kindliest change;
Bestirs her then, and from each tender stalk
Whatever earth, all-bearing mother, yields
In India east or west, or middle shore
In Pontus or the Punic coast, or where   340
Alcinous reigned, fruit of all kinds, in coat
Rough, or smooth-rined, or bearded husk, or shell
She gathers, tribute large, and on the board
Heaps with unsparing hand; for drink the grape
She crushes, inoffensive must, and meaths   345
From many a berry, and from sweet kernels pressed
She tempers dulcet creams; nor these to hold
Wants her fit vessels pure; then strews the ground
With rose and odors from the shrub unfumed.

339. middle shore: between East and West   345. must: unfermented wine, not intoxicat-
Indies, Mediterranean.   ing ("inoffensive").   meath: mead, a sweet
341. Alcinous: king of the Phaeacians. Cf.   drink.
Odyssey 7.114–32 and below, 9.439–41.   349. unfumed: not burned for incense.
342. smooth-rined: with smooth rind.

Meanwhile our primitive great sire, to meet   350
His godlike guest, walks forth, without more train
Accompanied than with his own complete
Perfections; in himself was all his state,
More solemn than the tedious pomp that waits
On princes, when their rich retínue long   355
Of horses led and grooms besmeared with gold
Dazzles the crowd, and sets them all agape.
Nearer his presence Adam, though not awed,
Yet with submiss approach and reverence meek,
As to a superior nature, bowing low,   360
    Thus said: "Native of heav'n, for other place
None can than heav'n such glorious shape contain;
Since by descending from the thrones above,
Those happy places thou hast deigned a while
To want, and honor these, vouchsafe with us   365
Two only, who yet by sov'ran gift possess
This spacious ground, in yonder shady bow'r
To rest, and what the garden choicest bears
To sit and taste, till this meridian heat
Be over, and the sun more cool decline."   370
    Whom thus the angelic Virtue answered mild:
"Adam, I therefore came, nor art thou such
Created, or such place hast here to dwell,
As may not oft invite, though Spirits of heav'n,
To visit thee; lead on then where thy bow'r   375
O'ershades; for these mid-hours, till ev'ning rise,
I have at will." So to the sylvan lodge
They came, that like Pomona's arbor smiled
With flow'rets decked and fragrant smells, but Eve
Undecked save with herself, more lovely fair   380
Than wood-nymph, or the fairest goddess feigned
Of three that in Mount Ida naked strove,
Stood to entertain her guest from heav'n; no veil
She needed, virtue-proof; no thought infirm
Altered her cheek. On whom the Angel "Hail"   385
Bestowed, the holy salutation used
Long after to blest Mary, second Eve:
    "Hail, mother of mankind, whose fruitful womb
Shall fill the world more numerous with thy sons
Than with these various fruits the trees of God   390
Have heaped this table." Raised of grassy turf
Their table was, and mossy seats had round,
And on her ample square from side to side
All autumn piled, though spring and autumn here
Danced hand in hand. A while discourse they hold;   395
No fear lest dinner cool; when thus began

381–82. Paris's awarding of the prize of   385–87. Luke 1.28.
beauty to Aphrodite over Hera and Athene.   396. No . . . cool. Some readers, who think
   384. thought infirm: cf. Spenser, *Epithala-*   Milton should be always solemn (but would
mion 237, "thought unsound."   allow the artist's sensibility to absorb the smell

Our author: "Heav'nly stranger, please to taste
These bounties which our Nourisher, from whom
All perfect good unmeasured out descends,
To us for food and for delight hath caused   400
The earth to yield; unsavory food perhaps
To spiritual natures; only this I know,
That one celestial Father gives to all."
    To whom the Angel: "Therefore what he gives
(Whose praise be ever sung) to man in part   405
Spiritual, may of purest Spirits be found
No ingrateful food: and food alike those pure
Intelligential substances require
As doth your rational; and both contain
Within them every lower faculty   410
Of sense, whereby they hear, see, smell, touch, taste,
Tasting concoct, digest, assimilate,
And corporeal to incorporeal turn.
For know, whatever was created needs
To be sustained and fed; of elements   415
The grosser feeds the purer: earth the sea,
Earth and the sea feed air, the air those fires
Ethereal, and as lowest first the moon;
Whence in her visage round those spots, unpurged
Vapors not yet into her substance turned.   420
Nor doth the moon no nourishment exhale
From her moist continent to higher orbs.
The sun, that light imparts to all, receives
From all his alimental recompense
In humid exhalations, and at even   425
Sups with the ocean. Though in heav'n the trees
Of life ambrosial fruitage bear, and vines
Yield nectar, though from off the boughs each morn
We brush mellifluous dews, and find the ground
Covered with pearly grain; yet God hath here   430
Varied his bounty so with new delights
As may compare with heaven; and to taste
Think not I shall be nice." So down they sat,
And to their viands fell, nor seemingly
The Angel, nor in mist, the common gloss   435
Of theologians, but with keen dispatch
Of real hunger, and concoctive heat
To transubstantiate; what redounds transpires
Through Spirits with ease; nor wonder, if by fire

of cooking), resent this little vegetarian joke
— likewise the playful elephant of 4.345–47.
398–99. James 1.17.
    404 f. Aquinas said angels were pure forms
which might manifest themselves with assumed
"bodies" (cf. Donne's *Air and Angels*). Milton's angels are corporeal spirits, composed of
the same "ethereal" substance as the "empyreal" heaven (see glossary for these words).

His emphasis here on the angelic capacity for
digesting food is an embellishment of metaphysical implications and leads on to his emphasis on the goodness of matter (469 f.).
    414–26. The chain of being includes up-
ward change and interaction among the four
elements; cf. Plato, *Timaeus* 49 C; Cicero,
De Natura Deorum 2.33; and 180–83 above.
    438. redounds: is in excess.

Of sooty coal the empiric alchemist   440
Can turn, or holds it possible to turn,
Metals of drossiest ore to perfect gold,
As from the mine. Meanwhile at table Eve
Ministered naked, and their flowing cups
With pleasant liquors crowned. O innocence   445
Deserving Paradise! If ever, then,
Then had the Sons of God excuse to have been
Enamored at that sight; but in those hearts
Love unlibidinous reigned, nor jealousy
Was understood, the injured lover's hell.   450
  Thus when with meats and drinks they had sufficed,
Not burdened nature, sudden mind arose
In Adam, not to let th' occasion pass
Given him by this great conference to know
Of things above his world, and of their being   455
Who dwell in heav'n, whose excellence he saw
Transcend his own so far, whose radiant forms,
Divine effulgence, whose high power so far
Exceeded human, and his wary speech
Thus to th' empyreal minister he framed: 460
  "Inhabitant with God, now know I well
Thy favor, in this honor done to man,
Under whose lowly roof thou hast vouchsafed
To enter, and these earthly fruits to taste,
Food not of angels, yet accepted so,   465
As that more willingly thou couldst not seem
At heav'n's high feasts to have fed; yet what compare?"
  To whom the wingèd Hierarch replied:
"O Adam, one Almighty is, from whom
All things proceed, and up to him return,   470
If not depraved from good, created all
Such to perfection, one first matter all,
Endued with various forms, various degrees
Of substance, and in things that live, of life;
But more refined, more spiritous, and pure,   475
As nearer to him placed or nearer tending,
Each in their several active spheres assigned,
Till body up to spirit work, in bounds
Proportioned to each kind. So from the root
Springs lighter the green stalk, from thence the leaves   480
More airy, last the bright consummate flow'r
Spirits odórous breathes: flow'rs and their fruit,

440. empiric: experimental (with unfavorable connotation).
444. flowing cups: in *Henry V* 4.3.55.
445. crowned: a classical usage.
446–48. Sons of God: cf. Gen. 6.2–4 and
below, 11.574–627 and note.
469–500. This account of the hierarchical
chain of being (introduced by the significant
periphrasis, "the wingèd Hierarch") is largely
traditional; but it carries a traditional though
less orthodox stress on the essential goodness
of matter and its being inseparable from spirit
(cf. *C.D.* 1.7, and 1 Cor. 15). This monism
is the metaphysical basis of Milton's "optimism"
(the central basis is of course the Christian
scheme of salvation and faith in Providence).
It embodies a religious, organic, and wholly
anti-mechanistic view of nature.

Man's nourishment, by gradual scale sublimed,
To vital spirits aspire, to animal,
To intellectual; give both life and sense,   485
Fancy and understanding, whence the soul
Reason receives, and reason is her being,
Discursive, or intuitive; discourse
Is oftest yours, the latter most is ours,
Differing but in degree, of kind the same.   490
Wonder not then, what God for you saw good
If I refuse not, but convert, as you,
To proper substance. Time may come when men
With angels may participate, and find
No inconvenient diet, nor too light fare;   495
And from these corporal nutriments perhaps
Your bodies may at last turn all to spirit,
Improved by tract of time, and winged ascend
Ethereal, as we, or may at choice
Here or in heav'nly paradises dwell;   500
If ye be found obedient, and retain
Unalterably firm his love entire
Whose progeny you are. Meanwhile enjoy
Your fill what happiness this happy state
Can comprehend, incapable of more."   505
    To whom the patriarch of mankind replied:
"O favorable Spirit, propitious guest,
Well hast thou taught the way that might direct
Our knowledge, and the scale of Nature set
From center to circumference, whereon   510
In contemplation of created things
By steps we may ascend to God. But say,
What meant that caution joined, *If ye be found
Obedient?* Can we want obedience then
To him, or possibly his love desert   515
Who formed us from the dust, and placed us here
Full to the utmost measure of what bliss
Human desires can seek or apprehend?"
    To whom the Angel: "Son of heav'n and earth,
Attend: that thou art happy, owe to God;   520
That thou continu'st such, owe to thyself,
That is, to thy obedience; therein stand.
This was that caution giv'n thee; be advised.
God made thee perfect, not immutable;

483. sublimed: refined, purified.
484–87. The traditional hierarchy of "souls" comprised the vegetative, sensitive, and rational, with which plants, animals, and men are respectively endowed (each higher faculty subsuming the lower). These faculties work through a corresponding hierarchy of "spirits," natural, vital, and animal (glossary). Milton's pattern is normal in the main.
485–90. Like Protestants in general, Milton

accepts the scholastic distinction between the discursive or deliberative reason of man and angelic intuition (cf. Hooker, *Eccles. Pol.* 1.6).
496–500. Cf. 5.77 f.
503. Whose . . . are: Acts 17.28, where St. Paul quotes the phrase from Aratus' astronomical poem, *Phaenomena* 1.5.
503–05. Cf. 4.774–75 and note.
509. scale of Nature: chain of being.
524–43. Cf. 3.96 f. and note.

And good he made thee, but to persevere   525
He left it in thy power, ordained thy will
By nature free, not overruled by fate
Inextricable, or strict necessity.
Our voluntary service he requires,
Not our necessitated; such with him   530
Finds no acceptance, nor can find, for how
Can hearts not free be tried whether they serve
Willing or no, who will but what they must
By destiny, and can no other choose?
Myself and all th' angelic host that stand   535
In sight of God enthroned, our happy state
Hold, as you yours, while our obedience holds;
On other surety none; freely we serve,
Because we freely love, as in our will
To love or not; in this we stand or fall.   540
And some are fall'n, to disobedience fall'n,
And so from heav'n to deepest hell; O fall
From what high state of bliss into what woe!"
    To whom our great progenitor: "Thy words
Attentive, and with more delighted ear,   545
Divine instructor, I have heard, than when
Cherubic songs by night from neighboring hills
Aerial music send. Nor knew I not
To be both will and deed created free;
Yet that we never shall forget to love   550
Our Maker, and obey him whose command
Single is yet so just, my constant thoughts
Assured me, and still assure; though what thou tell'st
Hath passed in heav'n some doubt within me move,
But more desire to hear, if thou consent,   555
The full relation, which must needs be strange,
Worthy of sacred silence to be heard;
And we have yet large day, for scarce the sun
Hath finished half his journey, and scarce begins
His other half in the great zone of heav'n."   560
    Thus Adam made request, and Raphael,
After short pause assenting, thus began:
    "High matter thou enjoin'st me, O prime of men,
Sad task and hard, for how shall I relate
To human sense th' invisible exploits   565
Of warring Spirits; how without remorse
The ruin of so many glorious once

535–40. By way of reinforcing his central faith in the free will of man, Milton extends it to angels, who, as *P.L.* amply shows, could choose to stand or fall. Cf. 4.63–67 and *C.D.* 1.3.

546–48. Cf. 4.680 f.

557. Worthy . . . silence: cf. Horace, *Od.* 2.13.29.

563–76. The first of several apologies for a concrete and finite rendering of things celestial and infinite. It is a question if Milton is thinking in terms of Christian Platonism (nonhistorical adumbration or analogy) or of the typological interpretation of sacred history, or, whatever the difficulties of fusion, of both together. Cf. Col. 2.16–17, Heb. 8.1–5.

566. remorse: sorrow.

And perfect while they stood; how last unfold
The secrets of another world, perhaps
Not lawful to reveal? Yet for thy good   570
This is dispensed, and what surmounts the reach
Of human sense I shall delineate so,
By lik'ning spiritual to corporal forms,
As may express them best, though what if earth
Be but the shadow of heav'n, and things therein   575
Each to other like, more than on earth is thought?
      "As yet this world was not, and Chaos wild
Reigned where these heav'ns now roll, where earth now rests
Upon her center poised, when on a day
(For time, though in eternity, applied   580
To motion, measures all things durable
By present, past, and future), on such day
As heav'n's great year brings forth, th' empyreal host
Of angels by imperial summons called,
Innumerable before th' Almighty's throne   585
Forthwith from all the ends of heav'n appeared
Under their hierarchs in orders bright.
Ten thousand thousand ensigns high advanced,
Standards and gonfalons 'twixt van and rear
Stream in the air, and for distinction serve   590
Of hierarchies, of orders, and degrees;
Or in their glittering tissues bear emblazed
Holy memorials, acts of zeal and love
Recorded eminent. Thus when in orbs
Of circuit inexpressible they stood,   595
Orb within orb, the Father Infinite,
By whom in bliss embosomed sat the Son,
Amidst as from a flaming mount, whose top
Brightness had made invisible, thus spake:
      " 'Hear, all ye Angels, Progeny of Light,   600
Thrones, Dominations, Princedoms, Virtues, Powers,
Hear my decree, which unrevoked shall stand.
This day I have begot whom I declare
My only Son, and on this holy hill

571. dispensed: allowed.
577 f. The chronological beginning of the story. The epic plunge *in medias res* necessitates the later recounting (5.577 through book 7) of earlier events; cf. Odysseus' narrative of his adventures (*Odyssey* 9–12) and Aeneas' account of the fall of Troy and subsequent voyaging (*Aen.* 2–3).
578. heav'ns: sky.
578–79. earth . . . poised: cf. Ovid, *Met.* 1.12–13.
580–82. Cf. Plato, *Timaeus* 37–38. With "heav'n's great year" cf. *Timaeus* 39 D, where the great year is the point of time at which the heavenly bodies have returned to their original starting-points (every 36000 years: Plato, *Rep.* 546 f.).
589. gonfalons: banners.

587–91. Heavenly order is stressed just on the eve of Satan's revolt.
592–94. Cf. 1.536–39.
598. flaming mount: Exod. 19.16–18.
600–02. Glossary, "angels."
603–15. The Son existed before the angels, whom, as God's agent, he created (5.837–38), but he was not co-eternal or co-equal with the Father (see note on 3.383). Here, in Milton's symbolic interpretation of Ps. 2.6–7 (see his translation of this Psalm, above), the Son is not literally begotten but is proclaimed God's deputy and King and Messiah (664; cf. *C.D.* 1.5 and 7), The Son's elevation in 3.317–20 comes later in the story, fulfills that of 5.603–15, and anticipates his re-enthronement in heaven after his incarnation, death, and resurrection.

Him have anointed, whom ye now behold   605
At my right hand. Your head I him appoint;
And by myself have sworn to him shall bow
All knees in heav'n, and shall confess him Lord.
Under his great vicegerent reign abide
United as one individual soul   610
For ever happy. Him who disobeys
Me disobeys, breaks union, and that day
Cast out from God and blessèd vision, falls
Into utter darkness, deep engulfed, his place
Ordained without redemption, without end.'   615
    "So spake th' Omnipotent, and with his words
All seemed well pleased; all seemed, but were not all.
That day, as other solemn days, they spent
In song and dance about the sacred hill;
Mystical dance, which yonder starry sphere   620
Of planets and of fixed in all her wheels
Resembles nearest, mazes intricate,
Eccentric, intervolved, yet regular
Then most, when most irregular they seem;
And in their motions harmony divine   625
So smooths her charming tones that God's own ear
Listens delighted. Ev'ning now approached
(For we have also our ev'ning and our morn,
We ours for change delectable, not need);
Forthwith from dance to sweet repast they turn   630
Desirous; all in circles as they stood,
Tables are set, and on a sudden piled
With angels' food, and rubied nectar flows
In pearl, in diamond, and massy gold,
Fruit of delicious vines, the growth of heav'n.   635
On flow'rs reposed, and with fresh flow'rets crowned,
They eat, they drink, and in communion sweet
Quaff immortality and joy, secure
Of surfeit where full measure only bounds
Excess, before th' all-bounteous King, who show'red   640
With copious hand, rejoicing in their joy.
Now when ambrosial night, with clouds exhaled
From that high mount of God, whence light and shade
Spring both, the face of brightest heav'n had changed
To grateful twilight (for night comes not there   645
In darker veil) and roseate dews disposed
All but the unsleeping eyes of God to rest,
Wide over all the plain, and wider far
Than all this globous earth in plain outspread
(Such are the courts of God), th' angelic throng   650

607–08. Isa. 45.23; Phil. 2.10.
613. blessèd vision: cf. 1.684 and note.
614–15. his place: Acts 1.25.
620–27. Cf. 3.580 and note; 5.178, 7.374,
8.125, 9.103; and glossary, "sphere," "fixed,"
"eccentric."

637–40. Amplified in 1674 from the first
version to make clear the symbolic meaning.
Cf. Ps. 36.8–9.
645–46. Rev. 21.25.
647. Ps. 121.4.
649. globous: globose.

Dispersed in bands and files their camp extend
By living streams among the trees of life,
Pavilions numberless and sudden reared,
Celestial tabernacles, where they slept
Fanned with cool winds, save those who in their course   655
Melodious hymns about the sovran throne
Alternate all night long. But not so waked
Satan — so call him now, his former name
Is heard no more in heav'n; he of the first,
If not the first Archangel, great in power,   660
In favor, and pre-eminence, yet fraught
With envy against the Son of God, that day
Honored by his great Father, and proclaimed
Messiah, King anointed, could not bear
Through pride that sight, and thought himself impaired.   665
Deep malice thence conceiving and disdain,
Soon as midnight brought on the dusky hour
Friendliest to sleep and silence, he resolved
With all his legions to dislodge, and leave
Unworshiped, unobeyed, the throne supreme,   670
Contemptuous, and his next subordinate
Awak'ning, thus to him in secret spake:
    " 'Sleep'st thou, companion dear, what sleep can close
Thy eyelids? And remember'st what decree
Of yesterday, so late hath passed the lips   675
Of heav'n's Almighty? Thou to me thy thoughts
Wast wont, I mine to thee was wont to impart;
Both waking we were one; how then can now
Thy sleep dissent? New laws thou seest imposed;
New laws from him who reigns, new minds may raise   680
In us who serve, new counsels, to debate
What doubtful may ensue. More in this place
To utter is not safe. Assemble thou
Of all those myriads which we lead the chief;
Tell them that by command, ere yet dim night   685
Her shadowy cloud withdraws, I am to haste,
And all who under me their banners wave,
Homeward with flying march where we possess
The quarters of the north, there to prepare
Fit entertainment to receive our King,   690
The great Messiah, and his new commands,
Who speedily through all the hierarchies
Intends to pass triumphant, and give laws.'
    "So spake the false Archangel, and infused
Bad influence into th' unwary breast   695

661 f. Satan's envy and ambition have a limited parallel in Macbeth's reaction to Duncan's nomination of his eldest son as heir-apparent (*Macbeth* 1.4.35 f.); but the divine order is more than a dynastic affair.

664. "Messiah" means "anointed." Cf. 605 above.

671. subordinate: Beelzebub.

673. Cf. *Iliad* 2.23; *Aen.* 4.560; Tasso, *G.L.* 10.8; Milton, *In quintum Novembris* 92.

689. the north: the traditional domain of Satan (Isa. 14.13).

Of his associate; he together calls,
Or several one by one, the regent powers,
Under him regent, tells, as he was taught,
That the Most High commanding, now ere night,
Now ere dim night had disencumbered heav'n,   700
The great hierarchal standard was to move;
Tells the suggested cause, and casts between
Ambiguous words and jealousies, to sound
Or taint integrity; but all obeyed
The wonted signal, and superior voice   705
Of their great Potentate; for great indeed
His name, and high was his degree in heav'n;
His count'nance, as the morning star that guides
The starry flock, allured them, and with lies
Drew after him the third part of heav'n's host.   710
Meanwhile th' Eternal eye, whose sight discerns
Abstrusest thoughts, from forth his holy mount
And from within the golden lamps that burn
Nightly before him, saw without their light
Rebellion rising, saw in whom, how spread   715
Among the sons of morn, what multitudes
Were banded to oppose his high decree;
And smiling to his only Son thus said:
    " 'Son, thou in whom my glory I behold
In full resplendence, heir of all my might,   720
Nearly it now concerns us to be sure
Of our omnipotence, and with what arms
We mean to hold what anciently we claim
Of deity or empire: such a foe
Is rising, who intends to erect his throne   725
Equal to ours, throughout the spacious north;
Nor so content, hath in his thought to try
In battle, what our power is, or our right.
Let us advise, and to this hazard draw
With speed what force is left, and all employ   730
In our defense, lest unawares we lose
This our high place, our sanctuary, our hill.'
    "To whom the Son, with calm aspect and clear,
Lightning divine, ineffable, serene,
Made answer: 'Mighty Father, thou thy foes   735
Justly hast in derision, and secure
Laugh'st at their vain designs and tumults vain,
Matter to me of glory, whom their hate
Illustrates, when they see all regal power
Giv'n me to quell their pride, and in event   740

---

697. several: separately.

708. morning star: Lucifer (the name supposedly applied to Satan in Isa. 14.12; cf. the
note on 1.84–85).

710. third part: cf. 2.692 and note.

711–17. Cf. 647 above.

713. lamps: Rev. 4.5.

716. sons of morn: Isa. 14.12.

719–32. God, in speaking like an anxious
ruler, is being ironical, as the Son's reply indicates.

736. derision: Ps. 2.4, 59.8.

739. Illustrates: makes illustrious.

Know whether I be dextrous to subdue
Thy rebels, or be found the worst in heav'n.'
    "So spake the Son, but Satan with his powers
Far was advanced on wingèd speed, an host
Innumerable as the stars of night,   745
Or stars of morning, dew-drops, which the sun
Impearls on every leaf and every flower.
Regions they passed, the mighty regencies
Of Seraphim and Potentates and Thrones
In their triple degrees, regions to which   750
All thy dominion, Adam, is no more
Than what this garden is to all the earth
And all the sea, from one entire globose
Stretched into longitude; which having passed,
At length into the limits of the north   755
They came, and Satan to his royal seat
High on a hill, far blazing, as a mount
Raised on a mount, with pyramids and tow'rs
From diamond quarries hewn, and rocks of gold,
The palace of great Lucifer (so call   760
That structure in the dialect of men
Interpreted), which not long after, he,
Affecting all equality with God,
In imitation of that mount whereon
Messiah was declared in sight of heav'n,   765
The Mountain of the Congregation called;
For thither he assembled all his train,
Pretending so commanded to consult
About the great reception of their King,
Thither to come, and with calumnious art   770
Of counterfeited truth thus held their ears:
    " 'Thrones, Dominations, Princedoms, Virtues, Powers,
If these magnific titles yet remain
Not merely titular, since by decree
Another now hath to himself engrossed   775
All power, and us eclipsed under the name
Of King anointed, for whom all this haste
Of midnight march and hurried meeting here,
This only to consult how we may best
With what may be devised of honors new   780
Receive him coming to receive from us
Knee-tribute yet unpaid, prostration vile,
Too much to one, but double how endured,
To one and to his image now proclaimed?
But what if better counsels might erect   785
Our minds and teach us to cast off this yoke?
Will ye submit your necks, and choose to bend

750. triple degrees: glossary, "angels."   760. Lucifer: see note on 708 above.
753. globose: globe.   763. Cf. 3.206.
754. into longitude: flat.   766. Isa. 14.13.

The supple knee? Ye will not, if I trust
To know ye right, or if ye know yourselves
Natives and sons of heav'n possessed before   790
By none, and if not equal all, yet free,
Equally free; for orders and degrees
Jar not with liberty, but well consist.
Who can in reason then or right assume
Monarchy over such as live by right   795
His equals, if in power and splendor less,
In freedom equal? Or can introduce
Law and edict on us, who without law
Err not; much less for this to be our Lord,
And look for adoration, to th' abuse   800
Of those imperial titles which assert
Our being ordained to govern, not to serve?'
        "Thus far his bold discourse without control
Had audience, when among the Seraphim
Abdiel, than whom none with more zeal adored   805
The Deity, and divine commands obeyed,
Stood up, and in a flame of zeal severe
The current of his fury thus opposed:
        " 'O argument blasphémous, false, and proud!
Words which no ear ever to hear in heav'n   810
Expected, least of all from thee, ingrate,
In place thyself so high above thy peers.
Canst thou with impious obloquy condemn
The just decree of God, pronounced and sworn,
That to his only Son by right endued   815
With regal scepter, every soul in heav'n
Shall bend the knee, and in that honor due
Confess him rightful King? Unjust, thou say'st,
Flatly unjust, to bind with laws the free,
And equal over equals to let reign,   820
One over all with unsucceeded power.
Shalt thou give law to God, shalt thou dispute
With him the points of liberty, who made
Thee what thou art, and formed the pow'rs of heav'n
Such as he pleased, and circumscribed their being?   825
Yet by experience taught we know how good,
And of our good and of our dignity
How provident he is, how far from thought
To make us less; bent rather to exalt
Our happy state under one head more near   830
United. But to grant it thee unjust,
That equal over equals monarch reign:
Thyself though great and glorious dost thou count,
Or all angelic nature joined in one,

---

788. supple knee: cf. *Richard II* 1.4.33.   822–25. Rom. 9.20.
821. unsucceeded: having no successor,
everlasting.

Equal to him, begotten Son, by whom   835
As by his Word the mighty Father made
All things, ev'n thee, and all the Spirits of heav'n
By him created in their bright degrees,
Crowned them with glory, and to their glory named
Thrones, Dominations, Princedoms, Virtues, Powers? —   840
Essential Powers, nor by his reign obscured,
But more illustrious made, since he the head
One of our number thus reduced becomes,
His laws our laws, all honor to him done
Returns our own. Cease then this impious rage,   845
And tempt not these; but hasten to appease
Th' incensèd Father and th' incensèd Son
While pardon may be found, in time besought.'
    "So spake the fervent Angel; but his zeal
None seconded, as out of season judged,   850
Or singular and rash, whereat rejoiced
Th' Apostate, and more haughty thus replied:
    " 'That we were formed then, say'st thou? And the work
Of secondary hands, by task transferred
From Father to his Son? Strange point and new!   855
Doctrine which we would know whence learnt. Who saw
When this creation was? Remember'st thou
Thy making, while the Maker gave thee being?
We know no time when we were not as now;
Know none before us, self-begot, self-raised   860
By our own quick'ning power, when fatal course
Had circled his full orb, the birth mature
Of this our native heav'n, ethereal sons.
Our puissance is our own; our own right hand
Shall teach us highest deeds, by proof to try   865
Who is our equal. Then thou shalt behold
Whether by supplication we intend
Address, and to begirt th' Almighty throne
Beseeching or besieging. This report,
These tidings carry to th' anointed King;   870
And fly, ere evil intercept thy flight.'
    "He said, and as the sound of waters deep
Hoarse murmur echoed to his words applause
Through the infinite host; nor less for that
The flaming Seraph fearless, though alone   875
Encompassed round with foes, thus answered bold:
    " 'O alienate from God, O Spirit accurst,
Forsaken of all good! I see thy fall
Determined, and thy hapless crew involved
In this perfidious fraud, contagion spread   880

835–40. Col. 1.16–17.   864–65. Ps. 45.4.
836. Word: glossary.   872. Ezek. 1.24; Rev. 19.6.
853–63. Satan had spoken otherwise in his
soliloquy, 4.42–43; cf. *C.D.* 1.7.

Both of thy crime and punishment. Henceforth
No more be troubled how to quit the yoke
Of God's Messiah; those indulgent laws
Will not be now vouchsafed; other decrees
Against thee are gone forth without recall;   885
That golden scepter which thou didst reject
Is now an iron rod to bruise and break
Thy disobedience. Well thou didst advise.
Yet not for thy advice or threats I fly
These wicked tents devoted, lest the wrath   890
Impendent, raging into sudden flame
Distinguish not: for soon expect to feel
His thunder on thy head, devouring fire.
Then who created thee lamenting learn,
When who can uncreate thee thou shalt know.'   895
    "So spake the Seraph Abdiel faithful found,
Among the faithless, faithful only he;
Among innumerable false, unmoved,
Unshaken, unseduced, unterrified,
His loyalty he kept, his love, his zeal;   900
Nor number nor example with him wrought
To swerve from truth, or change his constant mind,
Though single. From amidst them forth he passed,
Long way through hostile scorn, which he sustained
Superior, nor of violence feared aught;   905
And with retorted scorn his back he turned
On those proud tow'rs to swift destruction doomed."

Book VI

THE ARGUMENT

    Raphael continues to relate how Michael and Gabriel were sent forth to battle against Satan and his angels. The first fight described; Satan and his powers retire under night. He calls a council; invents devilish engines, which, in the second day's fight, put Michael and his angels to some disorder; but they at length, pulling up mountains, overwhelmed both the force and machines of Satan. Yet, the tumult not so ending, God on the third day sends Messiah his Son, for whom he had reserved the glory of that victory. He, in the power of his Father, coming to the place, and causing all his legions to stand still on either side, with his chariot and thunder driving into the midst of his enemies, pursues them, unable to resist, towards the wall of heaven; which opening,

886–87. Cf. 2.327–28 and note.
890. wicked tents: Num. 16.26; Ps. 84.10.

906. retorted: flung back (Latin sense).
907. swift destruction: 2 Pet. 2.1.

they leap down with horror and confusion into the place of punishment prepared for them in the deep. Messiah returns with triumph to his Father.

"ALL night the dreadless angel unpursued
Through heav'n's wide champaign held his way, till Morn,
Waked by the circling Hours, with rosy hand
Unbarred the gates of light. There is a cave
Within the mount of God, fast by his throne,   5
Where light and darkness in perpetual round
Lodge and dislodge by turns, which makes through heav'n
Grateful vicissitude, like day and night;
Light issues forth, and at the other door
Obsequious darkness enters, till her hour   10
To veil the heav'n, though darkness there might well
Seem twilight here; and now went forth the Morn
Such as in highest heav'n, arrayed in gold
Empyreal; from before her vanished Night,
Shot through with orient beams; when all the plain   15
Covered with thick embattled squadrons bright,
Chariots, and flaming arms, and fiery steeds,
Reflecting blaze on blaze, first met his view.
War he perceived, war in procinct, and found
Already known what he for news had thought   20
To have reported; gladly then he mixed
Among those friendly Powers who him received
With joy and acclamations loud, that one,
That of so many myriads fall'n, yet one
Returned not lost: on to the sacred hill   25
They led him high applauded, and present
Before the seat supreme; from whence a voice
From midst a golden cloud thus mild was heard:
  " 'Servant of God, well done, well hast thou fought
The better fight, who single hast maintained   30
Against revolted multitudes the cause
Of truth, in word mightier than they in arms;
And for the testimony of truth hast borne
Universal reproach, far worse to bear
Than violence; for this was all thy care,   35
To stand approved in sight of God, though worlds
Judged thee perverse. The easier conquest now
Remains thee, aided by this host of friends,
Back on thy foes more glorious to return
Than scorned thou didst depart, and to subdue   40
By force, who reason for their law refuse,

BOOK VI. 2–4. Cf. Ovid, *Met.* 2.112–14.
3. Hours: glossary.   with rosy hand: the
Homeric "rosy-fingered."
4–7. Cf. Hesiod, *Theog.* 744–57.
19. procinct: readiness.

29. Servant of God: glossary, "Abdiel." Cf.
Matt. 25.21, 2 Tim. 4.7.
33–34. borne . . . reproach: Ps. 69.7.
36. approved . . . God: 2 Tim. 2.15.

Right reason for their law, and for their King
Messiah, who by right of merit reigns.
Go, Michael, of celestial armies prince,
And thou in military prowess next,   45
Gabriel, lead forth to battle these my sons
Invincible, lead forth my armèd saints
By thousands and by millions ranged for fight,
Equal in number to that godless crew
Rebellious; them with fire and hostile arms   50
Fearless assault, and to the brow of heav'n
Pursuing, drive them out from God and bliss
Into their place of punishment, the gulf
Of Tartarus, which ready opens wide
His fiery chaos to receive their fall.'   55
    "So spake the Sovran Voice, and clouds began
To darken all the hill, and smoke to roll
In dusky wreaths reluctant flames, the sign
Of wrath awaked; nor with less dread the loud
Ethereal trumpet from on high gan blow;   60
At which command the powers militant
That stood for heav'n, in mighty quadrate joined
Of union irresistible, moved on
In silence their bright legions, to the sound
Of instrumental harmony that breathed   65
Heroic ardor to advent'rous deeds
Under their godlike leaders, in the cause
Of God and his Messiah. On they move
Indissolubly firm; nor obvious hill,
Nor strait'ning vale, nor wood, nor stream divides   70
Their perfect ranks; for high above the ground
Their march was, and the passive air upbore
Their nimble tread; as when the total kind
Of birds in orderly array on wing
Came summoned over Eden to receive   75
Their names of thee; so over many a tract
Of heav'n they marched, and many a province wide,
Tenfold the length of this terrene. At last
Far in th' horizon to the north appeared

42. Right reason: glossary.
44–892. For the war in heaven the Bible supplied only meagre hints (Isa. 14.12 f.; Luke 10.18; 2 Pet. 2.4; Jude 6; Rev. 12.4, 7–9, etc.), and in *C.D.* 1.7 and 9 Milton barely touched it. Although he repudiated war in itself and as epic material (*P.L.* 9.27 f.), there were strong reasons for the unique war in *P.L.* It has been complained that God could have overthrown the rebels instantly (cf. 6.135 f.), that the combatants cannot be killed, that the use of artillery was an artistic mistake, that, in short, the battles are too unreal for an epic and too material for a religious symbol. But the poem needed an explosive dramatiza-tion of Satan's pride and passion, of the conflict between anarchic evil and invincible order and good, and the story is an object-lesson for Adam, an anticipation of wars on earth — as such it approaches hideous burlesque — and perhaps a typological anticipation of the last great battle that preludes the end of the world and Christ's second coming.
    56–59. Exod. 19.16, 18.
    62. quadrate: square.
    69. obvious: in the way.
    70. strait'ning: constricting.
    73–76. Cf. *Iliad* 2.459–63, *Aen.* 1.393 f., 7.699–701; Gen. 2.20.
    78. terrene: earth.

From skirt to skirt a fiery region, stretched   80
In battailous aspéct, and nearer view
Bristled with upright beams innumerable
Of rigid spears, and helmets thronged, and shields
Various, with boastful argument portrayed,
The banded powers of Satan hasting on   85
With furious expedition; for they weened
That selfsame day by fight or by surprise
To win the mount of God, and on his throne
To set the envier of his state, the proud
Aspirer, but their thoughts proved fond and vain   90
In the mid-way: though strange to us it seemed
At first, that angel should with angel war,
And in fierce hosting meet, who wont to meet
So oft in festivals of joy and love
Unanimous, as sons of one great Sire,   95
Hymning th' Eternal Father. But the shout
Of battle now began, and rushing sound
Of onset ended soon each milder thought.
High in the midst exalted as a god
Th' Apostate in his sun-bright chariot sat,   100
Idol of majesty divine, enclosed
With flaming Cherubim and golden shields;
Then lighted from his gorgeous throne, for now
'Twixt host and host but narrow space was left,
A dreadful interval, and front to front   105
Presented stood in terrible array
Of hideous length. Before the cloudy van,
On the rough edge of battle ere it joined,
Satan, with vast and haughty strides advanced,
Came tow'ring, armed in adamant and gold;   110
Abdiel that sight endured not, where he stood
Among the mightiest, bent on highest deeds,
And thus his own undaunted heart explores:
    " 'O heav'n! that such resemblance of the Highest
Should yet remain, where faith and realty   115
Remain not; wherefore should not strength and might
There fail where virtue fails, or weakest prove
Where boldest, though to sight unconquerable?
His puissance, trusting in th' Almighty's aid,
I mean to try, whose reason I have tried   120
Unsound and false; nor is it aught but just
That he who in debate of truth hath won
Should win in arms, in both disputes alike
Victor; though brutish that contést and foul,
When reason hath to deal with force, yet so   125

93. hosting: encounter.
111. Cf. *Aen.* 2.407.
114 f. (and 131 f.) Epic defiances preceding combat; here reinforcing the spiritual issues.

115. realty: sincerity, loyalty.
118. to sight: to all appearances.
120. tried: proved by trial.

Most reason is that reason overcome.'
    "So pondering, and from his armèd peers
Forth stepping opposite, half-way he met
His daring foe, at this prevention more
Incensed, and thus securely him defied: 130
    " 'Proud, art thou met? Thy hope was to have reached
The highth of thy aspiring unopposed,
The throne of God unguarded, and his side
Abandoned at the terror of thy power
Or potent tongue. Fool, not to think how vain   135
Against th' Omnipotent to rise in arms;
Who out of smallest things could without end
Have raised incessant armies to defeat
Thy folly; or with solitary hand
Reaching beyond all limit at one blow   140
Unaided could have finished thee, and whelmed
Thy legions under darkness. But thou seest
All are not of thy train; there be who faith
Prefer, and piety to God, though then
To thee not visible, when I alone   145
Seemed in thy world erroneous to dissent
From all. My sect thou seest; now learn too late
How few sometimes may know, when thousands err.'
    "Whom the grand Foe with scornful eye askance
Thus answered: 'Ill for thee, but in wished hour   150
Of my revenge, first sought for thou return'st
From flight, seditious angel, to receive
Thy merited reward, the first assay
Of this right hand provoked, since first that tongue
Inspired with contradiction durst oppose   155
A third part of the gods, in synod met
Their deities to assert, who while they feel
Vigor divine within them, can allow
Omnipotence to none. But well thou com'st
Before thy fellows, ambitious to win   160
From me some plume, that thy success may show
Destruction to the rest. This pause between
(Unanswered lest thou boast) to let thee know:
At first I thought that liberty and heav'n
To heav'nly souls had been all one; but now   165
I see that most through sloth had rather serve,
Minist'ring Spirits, trained up in feast and song;
Such hast thou armed, the minstrelsy of heav'n,
Servility with freedom to contend,
As both their deeds compared this day shall prove.'   170
    "To whom in brief thus Abdiel stern replied:
'Apostate, still thou err'st, nor end wilt find
Of erring, from the path of truth remote.

---

129. prevention: confrontation.
147. sect: a loaded word in Milton's age, when Anglicans generally scorned the noncon- formist sects.
161. success: fortune (i.e. ill).

Unjustly thou deprav'st it with the name
Of servitude to serve whom God ordains,   175
Or Nature; God and Nature bid the same,
When he who rules is worthiest, and excels
Them whom he governs. This is servitude,
To serve th' unwise, or him who hath rebelled
Against his worthier, as thine now serve thee,   180
Thyself not free, but to thyself enthralled;
Yet lewdly dar'st our minist'ring upbraid.
Reign thou in hell thy kingdom, let me serve
In heav'n God ever blest, and his divine
Behests obey, worthiest to be obeyed;   185
Yet chains in hell, not realms expect. Meanwhile,
From me returned, as erst thou saidst, from flight,
This greeting on thy impious crest receive.'
      "So saying, a noble stroke he lifted high,
Which hung not, but so swift with tempest fell   190
On the proud crest of Satan, that no sight
Nor motion of swift thought, less could his shield
Such ruin intercept. Ten paces huge
He back recoiled; the tenth on bended knee
His massy spear upstayed; as if on earth   195
Winds under ground or waters forcing way
Sidelong had pushed a mountain from his seat,
Half sunk with all his pines. Amazement seized
The rebel Thrones, but greater rage to see
Thus foiled their mightiest; ours joy filled, and shout,   200
Presage of victory and fierce desire
Of battle; whereat Michaël bid sound
Th' archangel trumpet; through the vast of heaven
It sounded, and the faithful armies rung
Hosanna to the Highest; nor stood at gaze   205
The adverse legions, nor less hideous joined
The horrid shock. Now storming fury rose,
And clamor such as heard in heav'n till now
Was never; arms on armor clashing brayed
Horrible discord, and the madding wheels   210
Of brazen chariots raged; dire was the noise
Of conflict; overhead the dismal hiss
Of fiery darts in flaming volleys flew,
And flying vaulted either host with fire.
So under fiery cope together rushed   215
Both battles main, with ruinous assault
And inextinguishable rage; all heav'n

176. In classical-Christian tradition the collective "right reason" (glossary) of mankind established the laws of nature. Cf. Hooker, *Eccles. Pol.* 1.8.3: "The general and perpetual voice of men is as the sentence of God himself. For that which all men have at all times learned, Nature herself must needs have taught; and God being the author of Nature, her voice is but his instrument."
182. lewdly: basely.
210. madding: turning furiously.
214. Cf. the picture of hell, 1.298.
216. battles main: armies.

Resounded, and had earth been then, all earth
Had to her center shook. What wonder? When
Millions of fierce encount'ring angels fought   220
On either side, the least of whom could wield
These elements, and arm him with the force
Of all their regions: how much more of power
Army against army numberless to raise
Dreadful combustion warring, and disturb,   225
Though not destroy, their happy native seat;
Had not th' Eternal King Omnipotent
From his stronghold of heav'n high overruled
And limited their might; though numbered such
As each divided legion might have seemed   230
A numerous host, in strength each armèd hand
A legion; led in fight, yet leader seemed
Each warrior single as in chief, expert
When to advance, or stand, or turn the sway
Of battle, open when, and when to close   235
The ridges of grim war; no thought of flight,
None of retreat, no unbecoming deed
That argued fear; each on himself relied,
As only in his arm the moment lay
Of victory; deeds of eternal fame   240
Were done, but infinite; for wide was spread
That war and various; sometimes on firm ground
A standing fight; then soaring on main wing
Tormented all the air; all air seemed then
Conflicting fire. Long time in even scale   245
The battle hung, till Satan, who that day
Prodigious power had shown, and met in arms
No equal, ranging through the dire attack
Of fighting Seraphim confused, at length
Saw where the sword of Michael smote, and felled   250
Squadrons at once; with huge two-handed sway
Brandished aloft the horrid edge came down
Wide-wasting; such destruction to withstand
He hasted, and opposed the rocky orb
Of tenfold adamant, his ample shield,   255
A vast circumference. At his approach
The great Archangel from his warlike toil
Surceased, and glad as hoping here to end
Intestine war in heav'n, the Arch-foe subdued
Or captive dragged in chains, with hostile frown   260
And visage all inflamed first thus began:
    " 'Author of evil, unknown till thy revolt,
Unnamed in heav'n, now plenteous as thou seest
These acts of hateful strife, hateful to all,
Though heaviest by just measure on thyself   265

229. numbered such: so numerous.   239. moment: decisive weight.
236. ridges: ranks.

And thy adherents: how hast thou disturbed
Heav'n's blessèd peace, and into Nature brought
Misery, uncreated till the crime
Of thy rebellion! how hast thou instilled
Thy malice into thousands, once upright   270
And faithful, now proved false! But think not here
To trouble holy rest; heav'n casts thee out
From all her confines. Heav'n, the seat of bliss,
Brooks not the works of violence and war.
Hence then, and evil go with thee along,   275
Thy offspring, to the place of evil, hell,
Thou and thy wicked crew! there mingle broils,
Ere this avenging sword begin thy doom,
Or some more sudden vengeance winged from God
Precipitate thee with augmented pain.'   280
  "So spake the Prince of Angels; to whom thus
The Adversary: 'Nor think thou with wind
Of airy threats to awe whom yet with deeds
Thou canst not. Hast thou turned the least of these
To flight, or if to fall, but that they rise   285
Unvanquished, easier to transact with me
That thou shouldst hope, imperious, and with threats
To chase me hence? Err not that so shall end
The strife which thou call'st evil, but we style
The strife of glory; which we mean to win,   290
Or turn this heav'n itself into the hell
Thou fablest; here however to dwell free,
If not to reign. Meanwhile, thy utmost force
(And join him named Almighty to thy aid)
I fly not, but have sought thee far and nigh.'   295
  "They ended parle, and both addressed for fight
Unspeakable; for who, though with the tongue
Of angels, can relate, or to what things
Liken on earth conspicuous, that may lift
Human imagination to such highth   300
Of godlike power? For likest gods they seemed,
Stood they or moved, in stature, motion, arms,
Fit to decide the empire of great heav'n.
Now waved their fiery swords, and in the air
Made horrid circles; two broad suns their shields   305
Blazed opposite, while expectation stood
In horror; from each hand with speed retired,
Where erst was thickest fight, th' angelic throng,
And left large field, unsafe within the wind
Of such commotion; such as (to set forth   310
Great things by small) if, Nature's concord broke,
Among the constellations war were sprung,
Two planets rushing from aspéct malign

286. easier . . . me: and think it easier to   313. aspéct: glossary (cf. 10.656–64).
deal with me than with them.

Of fiercest opposition in mid sky,
Should combat, and their jarring spheres confound.   315
Together both with next to almighty arm
Uplifted imminent, one stroke they aimed
That might determine, and not need repeat,
As not of power, at once; nor odds appeared
In might or swift prevention. But the sword   320
Of Michael from the armory of God
Was giv'n him tempered so, that neither keen
Nor solid might resist that edge: it met
The sword of Satan with steep force to smite
Descending, and in half cut sheer, nor stayed,   325
But with swift wheel reverse, deep ent'ring shared
All his right side. Then Satan first knew pain,
And writhed him to and fro convolved; so sore
The griding sword with discontinuous wound
Passed through him; but th' ethereal substance closed   330
Not long divisible, and from the gash
A stream of nectarous humor issuing flowed
Sanguine, such as celestial Spirits may bleed,
And all his armor stained, erewhile so bright.
Forthwith on all sides to his aid was run   335
By angels many and strong, who interposed
Defense, while others bore him on their shields
Back to his chariot, where it stood retired
From off the files of war; there they him laid
Gnashing for anguish and despite and shame   340
To find himself not matchless, and his pride
Humbled by such rebuke, so far beneath
His confidence to equal God in power.
Yet soon he healed; for Spirits, that live throughout
Vital in every part, not as frail man   345
In entrails, heart or head, liver or reins,
Cannot but by annihilating die;
Nor in their liquid texture mortal wound
Receive, no more than can the fluid air:
All heart they live, all head, all eye, all ear,   350
All intellect, all sense; and as they please
They limb themselves, and color, shape, or size
Assume, as likes them best, condense or rare.
    "Meanwhile in other parts like deeds deserved
Memorial, where the might of Gabriel fought,   355
And with fierce ensigns pierced the deep array

320. prevention: anticipation.
321. armory of God: Jer. 50.25.
326. shared: sheared, cut.
329. griding: cut painfully and with a grating sound.   discontinuous: breaking continuity of the bodily substance.
332. humor: angelic equivalent of blood (cf. the ichor of the Homeric gods).

334. Cf. Shakespeare, *King John* 2.1.315–16.
335. was run: i.e. it was run (a Latinism).
344–53. Cf. 1.423–31 and note.
355. the might of Gabriel: the mighty Gabriel (a classicism).

Of Moloch, furious king, who him defied,
And at his chariot wheels to drag him bound
Threatened, nor from the Holy One of heav'n
Refrained his tongue blasphémous; but anon   360
Down clov'n to the waist, with shattered arms
And uncouth pain fled bellowing. On each wing
Uriel and Raphael his vaunting foe,
Though huge and in a rock of diamond armed,
Vanquished Adramelech and Asmadai,   365
Two potent Thrones, that to be less than gods
Disdained, but meaner thoughts learned in their flight,
Mangled with ghastly wounds through plate and mail.
Nor stood unmindful Abdiel to annoy
The atheist crew, but with redoubled blow   370
Ariel and Arioch, and the violence
Of Ramiel, scorched and blasted, overthrew.
I might relate of thousands, and their names
Eternize here on earth; but those elect
Angels, contented with their fame in heav'n,   375
Seek not the praise of men: the other sort
In might though wondrous and in acts of war,
Nor of renown less eager, yet by doom
Cancelled from heav'n and sacred memory,
Nameless in dark oblivion let them dwell.   380
For strength from truth divided and from just,
Illaudable, naught merits but dispraise
And ignominy, yet to glory aspires
Vainglorious, and through infamy seeks fame:
Therefore eternal silence be their doom.   385
    "And now their mightiest quelled, the battle swerved,
With many an inroad gored; deformèd rout
Entered, and foul disorder; all the ground
With shivered armor strown, and on a heap
Chariot and charioteer lay overturned   390
And fiery foaming steeds; what stood, recoiled
O'er-wearied, through the faint Satanic host,
Defensive scarce, or with pale fear surprised,
Then first with fear surprised and sense of pain,
Fled ignominious, to such evil brought   395
By sin of disobedience, till that hour
Not liable to fear or flight or pain.
Far otherwise th' inviolable saints
In cubic phalanx firm advanced entire,
Invulnerable, impenetrably armed: 400
Such high advantages their innocence
Gave them above their foes; not to have sinned,
Not to have disobeyed; in fight they stood
Unwearied, unobnoxious to be pained

359–60. 2 Kings 19.22.   404. unobnoxious: not liable.

By wound, though from their place by violence moved.   405
   "Now Night her course began, and over heav'n
Inducing darkness, grateful truce imposed,
And silence on the odious din of war;
Under her cloudy covert both retired,
Victor and vanquished. On the foughten field   410
Michaël and his angels prevalent
Encamping, placed in guard their watches round,
Cherubic waving fires; on th' other part
Satan with his rebellious disappeared,
Far in the dark dislodged, and void of rest,   415
His potentates to council called by night,
And in the midst thus undismayed began:
   " 'O now in danger tried, now known in arms
Not to be overpowered, companions dear,
Found worthy not of liberty alone,   420
Too mean pretense, but what we more affect,
Honor, dominion, glory, and renown;
Who have sustained one day in doubtful fight
(And if one day, why not eternal days?)
What heav'n's Lord had powerfullest to send   425
Against us from about his throne, and judged
Sufficient to subdue us to his will,
But proves not so. Then fallible, it seems,
Of future we may deem him, though till now
Omniscient thought. True is, less firmly armed,   430
Some disadvantage we endured and pain,
Till now not known, but known, as soon contemned,
Since now we find this our empyreal form
Incapable of mortal injury,
Imperishable, and though pierced with wound,   435
Soon closing, and by native vigor healed.
Of evil then so small, as easy think
The remedy: perhaps more valid arms,
Weapons more violent, when next we meet,
May serve to better us, and worse our foes,   440
Or equal what between us made the odds,
In nature none. If other hidden cause
Left them superior, while we can preserve
Unhurt our minds, and understanding sound,
Due search and consultation will disclose.'   445
   "He sat; and in th' assembly next upstood
Nisroch, of Principalities the prime;
As one he stood escaped from cruel fight,
Sore toiled, his riven arms to havoc hewn,
And cloudy in aspéct thus answering spake: 450
'Deliverer from new Lords, leader to free

---

406 f. Cf. *Iliad* 8.484 f.
410–13. Cf. *Iliad* 8.553 f.
411. prevalent: prevailing, victorious.

429. Of: in.
447. Nisroch: an Assyrian god (2 Kings 19.37).

Enjoyment of our right as gods; yet hard
For gods, and too unequal work we find
Against unequal arms to fight in pain,
Against unpained, impassive; from which evil   455
Ruin must needs ensue; for what avails
Valor or strength, though matchless, quelled with pain
Which all subdues, and makes remiss the hands
Of mightiest? Sense of pleasure we may well
Spare out of life perhaps, and not repine,   460
But live content, which is the calmest life;
But pain is perfect misery, the worst
Of evils, and, excessive, overturns
All patience. He who therefore can invent
With what more forcible we may offend   465
Our yet unwounded enemies, or arm
Ourselves with like defense, to me deserves
No less than for deliverance what we owe.'
    "Whereto with look composed Satan replied:
'Not uninvented that, which thou aright   470
Believ'st so main to our success, I bring.
Which of us who beholds the bright surfáce
Of this ethereous mold whereon we stand,
This continent of spacious heav'n, adorned
With plant, fruit, flow'r ambrosial, gems and gold,   475
Whose eye so superficially surveys
These things, as not to mind from whence they grow
Deep under ground, materials dark and crude,
Of spiritous and fiery spume, till touched
With heav'n's ray, and tempered, they shoot forth   480
So beauteous, op'ning to the ambient light?
These in their dark nativity the deep
Shall yield us, pregnant with infernal flame;
Which into hollow engines long and round
Thick-rammed, at th' other bore with touch of fire   485
Dilated and infuriate shall send forth
From far with thund'ring noise among our foes
Such implements of mischief as shall dash
To pieces and o'erwhelm whatever stands
Adverse, that they shall fear we have disarmed   490
The Thunderer of his only dreaded bolt.
Nor long shall be our labor; yet ere dawn
Effect shall end our wish. Meanwhile revive;
Abandon fear; to strength and counsel joined
Think nothing hard, much less to be despaired.'   495
    "He ended, and his words their drooping cheer

---

467. to me: in my view.

470 f. The use of cannon underlines the parallel between historical man and the devils (501 f.); and lines 472 f. illustrate the perversion of good, even heavenly, things. The diabolic invention had appeared, e.g., in Ariosto, *O.F.* 9.91, 11.21–28; Spenser, *F.Q.* 1.7.13; Daniel, *Civil Wars* 6.26–27.

473. ethereous: glossary, "ethereal."

Enlightened, and their languished hope revived.
Th' invention all admired, and each how he
To be th' inventor missed; so easy it seemed
Once found, which yet unfound most would have thought   500
Impossible. Yet haply of thy race
In future days, if malice should abound,
Some one intent on mischief, or inspired
With dev'lish machination, might devise
Like instrument to plague the sons of men   505
For sin, on war and mutual slaughter bent.
Forthwith from council to the work they flew,
None arguing stood; innumerable hands
Were ready; in a moment up they turned
Wide the celestial soil, and saw beneath   510
Th' originals of Nature in their crude
Conception; sulphurous and nitrous foam
They found, they mingled, and with subtle art
Concocted and adusted they reduced
To blackest grain, and into store conveyed.   515
Part hidden veins digged up (nor hath this earth
Entrails unlike) of mineral and stone,
Whereof to found their engines and their balls
Of missive ruin; part incentive reed
Provide, pernicious with one touch to fire.   520
So all ere day-spring, under conscious night
Secret they finished, and in order set
With silent circumspection unespied.
    "Now when fair morn orient in heav'n appeared,
Up rose the victor angels, and to arms   525
The matin trumpet sung; in arms they stood
Of golden panoply, refulgent host,
Soon banded; others from the dawning hills
Looked round, and scouts each coast light-armèd scour,
Each quarter, to descry the distant foe,   530
Where lodged, or whither fled, or if for fight,
In motion or in halt. Him soon they met
Under spread ensigns moving nigh, in slow
But firm battalion; back with speediest sail
Zophiel, of Cherubim the swiftest wing,   535
Came flying, and in mid-air aloud thus cried:
    " 'Arm, warriors, arm for fight; the foe at hand,
Whom fled we thought, will save us long pursuit
This day; fear not his flight; so thick a cloud
He comes, and settled in his face I see   540
Sad resolution and secure. Let each
His adamantine coat gird well, and each
Fit well his helm, gripe fast his orbèd shield,

---

519. missive ruin: missiles of destruction.   (cf. Ovid, *Met.* 13.15; Milton, *In quintum*
incentive: kindling.   *Novembris* 150, *Naturam* 65).
    521. conscious: that witnessed their work

Borne ev'n or high; for this day will pour down,
If I conjecture aught, no drizzling shower,   545
But rattling storm of arrows barbed with fire.'
    "So warned he them, aware themselves, and soon
In order, quit of all impediment;
Instant without disturb they took alarm,
And onward move embattled; when behold   550
Not distant far with heavy pace the foe
Approaching gross and huge; in hollow cube
Training his devilish enginry, impaled
On every side with shadowing squadrons deep,
To hide the fraud. At interview both stood   555
A while; but suddenly at head appeared
Satan, and thus was heard commanding loud:
    " 'Vanguard, to right and left the front unfold,
That all may see who hate us, how we seek
Peace and composure, and with open breast   560
Stand ready to receive them, if they like
Our overture, and turn not back perverse;
But that I doubt; however, witness heaven,
Heav'n witness thou anon, while we discharge
Freely our part. Ye who appointed stand,   565
Do as you have in charge, and briefly touch
What we propound, and loud that all may hear.'
    "So scoffing in ambiguous words, he scarce
Had ended, when to right and left the front
Divided, and to either flank retired;   570
Which to our eyes discovered, new and strange,
A triple-mounted row of pillars laid
On wheels (for like to pillars most they seemed,
Or hollowed bodies made of oak or fir
With branches lopped, in wood or mountain felled),   575
Brass, iron, stony mold, had not their mouths
With hideous orifice gaped on us wide,
Portending hollow truce. At each behind
A Seraph stood, and in his hand a reed
Stood waving tipped with fire; while we suspense,   580
Collected stood within our thoughts amused;
Not long, for sudden all at once their reeds
Put forth, and to a narrow vent applied
With nicest touch. Immediate in a flame,
But soon obscured with smoke, all heav'n appeared,   585
From those deep-throated engines belched, whose roar
Emboweled with outrageous noise the air,
And all her entrails tore, disgorging foul

548. impediment: baggage (Latin).
549. took alarm: sprang to arms.
553. Training: dragging.
555. At interview: face to face.
560. composure: composition, agreement.

In 560 f. and 609 f. the puns are the cynical
jests of professional soldiers.
    581. amused: puzzled.
    587. Emboweled: disemboweled.

Their devilish glut, chained thunderbolts and hail
Of iron globes, which on the victor host   590
Leveled, with such impetuous fury smote,
That whom they hit none on their feet might stand,
Though standing else as rocks, but down they fell
By thousands, angel on archangel rolled,
The sooner for their arms; unarmed they might   595
Have easily as Spirits evaded swift
By quick contraction or remove; but now
Foul dissipation followed and forced rout;
Nor served it to relax their serried files.
What should they do? If on they rushed, repulse   600
Repeated, and indecent overthrow
Doubled, would render them yet more despised,
And to their foes a laughter; for in view
Stood ranked of Seraphim another row
In posture to displode their second tire   605
Of thunder; back defeated to return
They worse abhorred. Satan beheld their plight,
And to his mates thus in derision called:
   " 'O friends, why come not on these victors proud?
Erewhile they fierce were coming, and when we,   610
To entertain them fair with open front
And breast (what could we more?), propounded terms
Of composition, straight they changed their minds,
Flew off, and into strange vagaries fell,
As they would dance; yet for a dance they seemed   615
Somewhat extravagant and wild, perhaps
For joy of offered peace. But I suppose
If our proposals once again were heard,
We should compel them to a quick result.'
   "To whom thus Belial, in like gamesome mood: 620
'Leader, the terms we sent were terms of weight,
Of hard contents, and full of force urged home,
Such as we might perceive amused them all,
And stumbled many; who receives them right,
Had need from head to foot well understand;   625
Not understood, this gift they have besides,
They show us when our foes walk not upright.'
   "So they among themselves in pleasant vein
Stood scoffing, highthened in their thoughts beyond
All doubt of victory; Eternal Might   630
To match with their inventions they presumed
So easy, and of his thunder made a scorn,
And all his host derided, while they stood
A while in trouble. But they stood not long;
Rage prompted them at length, and found them arms   635

---

598. dissipation: scattering.
605. displode: fire.   tire: battery, volley.
623. amused: cf. 581 (a pun in 623).

625. understand: "comprehend" and "stand
firm," "be supported."
635. Cf. *Aen.* 1.150.

Against such hellish mischief fit to oppose.
Forthwith (behold the excellence, the power,
Which God hath in his mighty angels placed)
Their arms away they threw, and to the hills
(For earth hath this variety from heav'n   640
Of pleasure situate in hill and dale)
Light as the lightning glimpse they ran, they flew;
From their foundations loos'ning to and fro
They plucked the seated hills with all their load,
Rocks, waters, woods, and by the shaggy tops   645
Uplifting bore them in their hands. Amaze,
Be sure, and terror seized the rebel host,
When coming towards them so dread they saw
The bottom of the mountains upward turned,
Till on those cursèd engines' triple row   650
They saw them whelmed, and all their confidence
Under the weight of mountains buried deep,
Themselves invaded next, and on their heads
Main promontories flung, which in the air
Came shadowing, and oppressed whole legions armed.   655
Their armor helped their harm, crushed in and bruised,
Into their substance pent, which wrought them pain
Implacable, and many a dolorous groan,
Long struggling underneath, ere they could wind
Out of such prison, though Spirits of purest light,   660
Purest at first, now gross by sinning grown.
The rest in imitation to like arms
Betook them, and the neighboring hills uptore;
So hills amid the air encountered hills,
Hurled to and fro with jaculation dire,   665
That underground they fought in dismal shade;
Infernal noise; war seemed a civil game
To this uproar; horrid confusion heaped
Upon confusion rose. And now all heav'n
Had gone to wrack, with ruin overspread,   670
Had not th' Almighty Father, where he sits
Shrined in his sanctuary of heav'n secure,
Consulting on the sum of things, foreseen
This tumult, and permitted all, advised;
That his great purpose he might so fulfill,   675
To honor his anointed Son avenged
Upon his enemies, and to declare
All power on him transferred; whence to his Son,
Th' assessor of his throne, he thus began:
    " 'Effulgence of my glory, Son beloved,   680

642. Light: with swift ease (cf. Ezek. 1.14).
643 f. For the hurling of hills cf. Claudian, *Gigantomachia*, etc.
665. jaculation: throwing.

673. Consulting . . . things. Cf. Ovid, *Met.* 2.300; Milton, *Naturam* 34, *Consuluit rerum summae.*
674. advised: advisedly.
679. assessor: associate ("sitting beside").

Son in whose face invisible is beheld
Visibly, what by Deity I am,
And in whose hand what by decree I do,
Second Omnipotence, two days are passed,
Two days, as we compute the days of heav'n,   685
Since Michael and his powers went forth to tame
These disobedient; sore hath been their fight,
As likeliest was when two such foes met armed;
For to themselves I left them; and thou know'st,
Equal in their creation they were formed,   690
Save what sin hath impaired, which yet hath wrought
Insensibly, for I suspend their doom;
Whence in perpetual fight they needs must last
Endless, and no solution will be found.
War wearied hath performed what war can do,   695
And to disordered rage let loose the reins,
With mountains as with weapons armed, which makes
Wild work in heav'n, and dangerous to the main.
Two days are therefore passed, the third is thine;
For thee I have ordained it, and thus far   700
Have suffered, that the glory may be thine
Of ending this great war, since none but thou
Can end it. Into thee such virtue and grace
Immense I have transfused, that all may know
In heav'n and hell thy power above compare,   705
And this perverse commotion governed thus,
To manifest thee worthiest to be Heir
Of all things, to be Heir and to be King
By sacred unction, thy deservèd right.
Go then, thou mightiest in thy Father's might,   710
Ascend my chariot, guide the rapid wheels
That shake heav'n's basis, bring forth all my war,
My bow and thunder, my almighty arms
Gird on, and sword upon thy puissant thigh;
Pursue these sons of darkness, drive them out   715
From all heav'n's bounds into the utter deep;
There let them learn, as likes them, to despise
God and Messiah his anointed King.'
    "He said, and on his Son with rays direct
Shone full; he all his Father full expressed   720
Ineffably into his face received,
And thus the Filial Godhead answering spake:
    " 'O Father, O Supreme of heav'nly Thrones,
First, highest, holiest, best, thou always seek'st
To glorify thy Son, I always thee,   725

681–82. Col. 1.15.
691–692. yet . . . Insensibly: so far has
not shown itself.
695–96. Cf. Sonnet 15.10 and later passages
in *P.L.* and *P.R.*
701. suffered: permitted.

709. unction: anointing (cf. 3.317, 5.604–
05).
714. Ps. 45.3.
725. John 17.1, 4–5.

As is most just. This I my glory account,
My exaltation, and my whole delight,
That thou in me well pleased, declar'st thy will
Fulfilled, which to fulfill is all my bliss.
Scepter and power, thy giving, I assume,   730
And gladlier shall resign, when in the end
Thou shalt be all in all, and I in thee
For ever, and in me all whom thou lov'st.
But whom thou hat'st, I hate, and can put on
Thy terrors, as I put thy mildness on,   735
Image of thee in all things; and shall soon,
Armed with thy might, rid heav'n of these rebelled,
To their prepared ill mansion driven down
To chains of darkness, and th' undying worm,
That from thy just obedience could revolt,   740
Whom to obey is happiness entire.
Then shall thy saints unmixed, and from th' impure
Far separate, circling thy holy mount
Unfeignèd halleluiahs to thee sing,
Hymns of high praise, and I among them chief.'   745
    "So said, he o'er his scepter bowing, rose
From the right hand of Glory where he sat;
And the third sacred morn began to shine
Dawning through heav'n. Forth rushed with whirlwind sound
The chariot of Paternal Deity,   750
Flashing thick flames, wheel within wheel, undrawn,
Itself instinct with spirit, but convoyed
By four Cherubic shapes. Four faces each
Had wondrous; as with stars, their bodies all
And wings were set with eyes; with eyes the wheels   755
Of beryl, and careering fires between:
Over their heads a crystal firmament,
Whereon a sapphire throne, inlaid with pure
Amber, and colors of the show'ry arch.
He in celestial panoply all armed   760
Of radiant Urim, work divinely wrought,
Ascended; at his right hand Victory
Sat eagle-winged, beside him hung his bow
And quiver with three-bolted thunder stored,
And from about him fierce effusion rolled   765
Of smoke and bickering flame, and sparkles dire.
Attended with ten thousand thousand saints,

---

728. well pleased: Matt. 3.17, 17.5, Mark 1.11.
732. all in all: cf. 3.341 and note.
734. Ps. 139.21.
739. 2 Pet. 2.4; Jude 6; Isa. 66.24; Mark 9.44, 46, 48.
748. sacred morn: cf. *Iliad* 11.84.
749 f. The picture is based on Ezek. 1 and 10. The Son, representing the invincible power of good, is the appropriate conqueror of Satan.

757–58. Ezek. 1.26; cf. Milton, *Solemn Music* 7.
759. show'ry arch: rainbow.
761. Urim: glossary.
763–64. The eagle was the bird of Jupiter, the thunderbolt his weapon. Cf. Milton's epigram on the inventor of gunpowder.
766. bickering: quivering.
767. Jude 14; Rev. 5.11.

He onward came, far off his coming shone,
And twenty thousand (I their number heard)
Chariots of God, half on each hand, were seen.   770
He on the wings of Cherub rode sublime
On the crystálline sky, in sapphire throned,
Illustrious far and wide, but by his own
First seen; them unexpected joy surprised,
When the great ensign of Messiah blazed   775
Aloft by angels borne, his sign in heav'n;
Under whose conduct Michael soon reduced
His army, circumfused on either wing,
Under their Head embodied all in one.
Before him Power Divine his way prepared;   780
At his command the uprooted hills retired
Each to his place, they heard his voice and went
Obsequious; heav'n his wonted face renewed,
And with fresh flow'rets hill and valley smiled.
     "This saw his hapless foes, but stood obdured,   785
And to rebellious fight rallied their powers
Insensate, hope conceiving from despair.
In heav'nly Spirits could such perverseness dwell?
But to convince the proud what signs avail,
Or wonders move th' obdúrate to relent?   790
They hardened more by what might most reclaim,
Grieving to see his glory, at the sight
Took envy, and aspiring to his highth,
Stood re-embattled fierce, by force or fraud
Weening to prosper, and at length prevail   795
Against God and Messiah, or to fall
In universal ruin last, and now
To final battle drew, disdaining flight,
Or faint retreat; when the great Son of God
To all his host on either hand thus spake: 800
     " 'Stand still in bright array, ye saints, here stand,
Ye angels armed, this day from battle rest;
Faithful hath been your warfare, and of God
Accepted, fearless in his righteous cause,
And as ye have received, so have ye done   805
Invincibly. But of this cursèd crew
The punishment to other hand belongs:
Vengeance is his, or whose he sole appoints;
Number to this day's work is not ordained
Nor multitude; stand only and behold   810
God's indignation on these godless poured
By me; not you but me they have despised,

769–70. Ps. 68.17.
771. 2 Sam. 22.11.
773. Illustrious: shining.
776. sign: Matt. 24.30.
777. reduced: led back.
788. Cf. *Aen.* 1.11.

789–91. Cf. Pharaoh and the Israelites
(Exod. 7.3, etc.).
791. what . . . reclaim: the presence of
the Son.
801. Exod. 14.13.
808. Rom. 12.19, Deut. 32–35, Ps. 94.1.

Yet envied; against me is all their rage,
Because the Father, t' whom in heav'n supreme
Kingdom and power and glory appertains,   815
Hath honored me according to his will.
Therefore to me their doom he hath assigned,
That they may have their wish, to try with me
In battle which the stronger proves, they all,
Or I alone against them, since by strength   820
They measure all, of other excellence
Not emulous, nor care who them excels;
Nor other strife with them do I vouchsafe.'
    "So spake the Son, and into terror changed
His count'nance, too severe to be beheld   825
And full of wrath bent on his enemies.
At once the Four spread out their starry wings
With dreadful shade contiguous, and the orbs
Of his fierce chariot rolled, as with the sound
Of torrent floods, or of a numerous host.   830
He on his impious foes right onward drove,
Gloomy as night; under his burning wheels
The steadfast empyrean shook throughout,
All but the throne itself of God. Full soon
Among them he arrived, in his right hand   835
Grasping ten thousand thunders, which he sent
Before him, such as in their souls infixed
Plagues; they astonished all resistance lost,
All courage; down their idle weapons dropped;
O'er shields and helms and helmèd heads he rode   840
Of Thrones and mighty Seraphim prostrate,
That wished the mountains now might be again
Thrown on them as a shelter from his ire.
Nor less on either side tempestuous fell
His arrows, from the fourfold-visaged Four,   845
Distinct with eyes, and from the living wheels,
Distinct alike with multitude of eyes;
One spirit in them ruled, and every eye
Glared lightning, and shot forth pernicious fire
Among th' accurst, that withered all their strength,   850
And of their wonted vigor left them drained,
Exhausted, spiritless, afflicted, fall'n.
Yet half his strength he put not forth, but checked
His thunder in mid-volley, for he meant
Not to destroy, but root them out of heav'n.   855
The overthrown he raised, and as a herd
Of goats or timorous flock together thronged,

832. burning wheels: cf. 755–56 above and
Il Penseroso 53.
  833. 2 Sam. 22.8; Hesiod, *Theog.* 679–80,
842.
  836–38. Like Zeus (e.g., Hesiod, *Theog.*
689 f.); cf. Ps. 18.13–14.

838. Plagues: blows (Greek sense).
842–43. Hos. 10.8, Luke 23.30, Rev. 6.16.
846–47. Distinct: marked, adorned.
  853. As when Jove visited Semele (Ovid,
Met. 3.302); cf. Hesiod, *Theog.* 687–89.

Drove them before him thunderstruck, pursued
With terrors and with furies to the bounds
And crystal wall of heav'n, which op'ning wide   860
Rolled inward, and a spacious gap disclosed
Into the wasteful deep. The monstrous sight
Strook them with horror backward, but far worse
Urged them behind; headlong themselves they threw
Down from the verge of heav'n, eternal wrath   865
Burnt after them to the bottomless pit.
    "Hell heard th' unsufferable noise, hell saw
Heav'n ruining from heav'n, and would have fled
Affrighted; but strict fate had cast too deep
Her dark foundations, and too fast had bound.   870
Nine days they fell; confounded Chaos roared,
And felt tenfold confusion in their fall
Through his wild anarchy, so huge a rout
Encumbered him with ruin. Hell at last
Yawning received them whole, and on them closed,   875
Hell, their fit habitation, fraught with fire
Unquenchable, the house of woe and pain.
Disburdened heav'n rejoiced, and soon repaired
Her mural breach, returning whence it rolled.
Sole victor from th' expulsion of his foes   880
Messiah his triumphal chariot turned.
To meet him all his saints, who silent stood
Eye-witnesses of his almighty acts,
With jubilee advanced; and as they went,
Shaded with branching palm, each order bright   885
Sung triumph, and him sung victorious King,
Son, Heir, and Lord, to him dominion giv'n,
Worthiest to reign. He celebrated rode
Triumphant through mid-heav'n, into the courts
And temple of his mighty Father throned   890
On high; who into glory him received,
Where now he sits at the right hand of bliss.
    "Thus measuring things in heav'n by things on earth,
At thy request, and that thou may'st beware
By what is past, to thee I have revealed   895
What might have else to human race been hid:
The discord which befell, and war in heav'n
Among th' angelic powers, and the deep fall
Of those too high aspiring, who rebelled
With Satan, he who envies now thy state,   900
Who now is plotting how he may seduce
Thee also from obedience, that with him
Bereaved of happiness thou may'st partake
His punishment, eternal misery;

869–70. Cf. *Nativity* 123.   Her: hell's.
871. Cf. 1.50 and note.
874–75. Isa. 5.14. Raphael's narrative has

now reached the point where the poem began.
892. Heb. 1.3.
893. Cf. 5.563–76 and note; 6.297 f.

Which would be all his solace and revenge,   905
As a despite done against the Most High,
Thee once to gain companion of his woe.
But listen not to his temptations; warn
Thy weaker; let it profit thee to have heard
By terrible example the reward   910
Of disobedience. Firm they might have stood,
Yet fell; remember, and fear to transgress."

Book VII

THE ARGUMENT

Raphael, at the request of Adam, relates how and wherefore this world was first created: that God, after the expelling of Satan and his angels out of heaven, declared his pleasure to create another world, and other creatures to dwell therein; sends his Son with glory, and attendance of angels, to perform the work of creation in six days: the angels celebrate with hymns the performance thereof, and his reascension into heaven.

DESCEND from heav'n, Urania, by that name
If rightly thou art called, whose voice divine
Following, above th' Olympian hill I soar,
Above the flight of Pegasean wing.
The meaning, not the name I call; for thou   5
Nor of the Muses nine, nor on the top
Of old Olympus dwell'st, but heav'nly born,
Before the hills appeared or fountain flowed,
Thou with eternal Wisdom didst converse,
Wisdom thy sister, and with her didst play   10
In presence of th' Almighty Father, pleased
With thy celestial song. Up led by thee
Into the heav'n of heav'ns I have presumed,
An earthly guest, and drawn empyreal air,
Thy temp'ring; with like safety guided down,   15
Return me to my native element,
Lest from this flying steed unreined (as once
Bellerophon, though from a lower clime)
Dismounted, on th' Aleian field I fall,

909. weaker: Eve (1 Pet. 3.7).
BOOK VII. 1–39. The change of scene and theme from heaven to earth and from war to the great work of peace, the creation of the world, prompts a new invocation or prayer.
1. Descend from heav'n. Cf. Horace, *Od.* 3.4.1–2.   Urania: glossary and 1.6 f.
3–4. Cf. 1.15, 3.17.   Pegasus: glossary.

9–12. See Prov. 8.22–30 and apocryphal Wisdom of Solomon 7–8.
17–19. Bellerophon, the slayer of the Chimera, tried to reach heaven with his winged horse and was dropped by Zeus onto the Aleian plain in Lycia (*Iliad* 6.200–02; Pindar, *Isth.* 7.43–47.

Erroneous there to wander and forlorn.   20
Half yet remains unsung, but narrower bound
Within the visible diurnal sphere;
Standing on earth, not rapt above the pole,
More safe I sing with mortal voice, unchanged
To hoarse or mute, though fall'n on evil days,   25
On evil days though fall'n, and evil tongues;
In darkness, and with dangers compassed round,
And solitude; yet not alone, while thou
Visit'st my slumbers nightly, or when morn
Purples the east. Still govern thou my song,   30
Urania, and fit audience find, though few.
But drive far off the barbarous dissonance
Of Bacchus and his revelers, the race
Of that wild rout that tore the Thracian bard
In Rhodope, where woods and rocks had ears   35
To rapture, till the savage clamor drowned
Both harp and voice; nor could the Muse defend
Her son. So fail not thou who thee implores;
For thou art heav'nly, she an empty dream.

    Say, goddess, what ensued when Raphael,   40
The affable Archangel, had forewarned
Adam by dire example to beware
Apostasy, by what befell in heaven
To those apostates, lest the like befall
In Paradise to Adam or his race,   45
Charged not to touch the interdicted tree,
If they transgress, and slight that sole command,
So easily obeyed amid the choice
Of all tastes else to please their appetite,
Though wand'ring. He with his consorted Eve   50
The story heard attentive, and was filled
With admiration and deep muse to hear
Of things so high and strange, things to their thought
So unimaginable as hate in heav'n,
And war so near the peace of God in bliss,   55
With such confusion; but the evil soon
Driv'n back redounded as a flood on those
From whom it sprung, impossible to mix
With blessedness. Whence Adam soon repealed
The doubts that in his heart arose; and now   60
Led on, yet sinless, with desire to know
What nearer might concern him, how this world

20. Erroneous: wandering (with the suggestion of error committed).
22. diurnal sphere: the firmament revolving daily around the earth.
23. above the pole: into heaven.
24–28. On Milton's situation in and after 1660, see the Introduction.
29. Cf. 3.32, 9.22.
32–38. As in *Lycidas* 58–63, Orpheus is the archetypal poet done to death by a hostile world — here Restoration England. Cf. Ovid, *Met.* 11.15–43.
32. barbarous dissonance: in *Comus* 550.
35. Rhodope: a mountain range in Thrace.
46–50. Cf. 4.419 f.
56–59. Cf. 2.139–42.
59. repealed: dismissed, canceled.

Of heav'n and earth conspicuous first began;
When, and whereof created, for what cause,
What within Eden or without was done   65
Before his memory, as one whose drouth
Yet scarce allayed still eyes the current stream,
Whose liquid murmur heard new thirst excites,
Proceeded thus to ask his heav'nly guest:
    "Great things, and full of wonder in our ears,   70
Far differing from this world, thou hast revealed,
Divine interpreter, by favor sent
Down from the empyrean to forewarn
Us timely of what might else have been our loss,
Unknown, which human knowledge could not reach;   75
For which to the infinitely Good we owe
Immortal thanks, and his admonishment
Receive with solemn purpose to observe
Immutably his sovran will, the end
Of what we are. But since thou hast vouchsafed   80
Gently for our instruction to impart
Things above earthly thought, which yet concerned
Our knowing, as to highest Wisdom seemed,
Deign to descend now lower, and relate
What may no less perhaps avail us known: 85
How first began this heav'n which we behold
Distant so high, with moving fires adorned
Innumerable, and this which yields or fills
All space, the ambient air wide interfused
Embracing round this florid earth; what cause   90
Moved the Creator in his holy rest
Through all eternity so late to build
In Chaos, and the work begun, how soon
Absolved, if unforbid thou may'st unfold
What we, not to explore the secrets ask   95
Of his eternal empire, but the more
To magnify his works, the more we know.
And the great light of day yet wants to run
Much of his race though steep; suspense in heav'n
Held by thy voice, thy potent voice he hears,   100
And longer will delay to hear thee tell
His generation, and the rising birth
Of Nature from the unapparent deep.
Or if the star of ev'ning and the moon
Haste to thy audience, night with her will bring   105
Silence, and sleep list'ning to thee will watch,
Or we can bid his absence, till thy song
End, and dismiss thee ere the morning shine."
    Thus Adam his illustrious guest besought,

63. conspicuous: visible.   94. Absolved: completed.
72. Divine interpreter: cf. *Aen.* 4.378.   97. magnify his works: Job 36.24
79. end: purpose.   103. unapparent deep: invisible Chaos.

And thus the godlike Angel answered mild: 110
   "This also thy request with caution asked
Obtain; though to recount almighty works
What words or tongue of Seraph can suffice,
Or heart of man suffice to comprehend?
Yet what thou canst attain, which best may serve   115
To glorify the Maker, and infer
Thee also happier, shall not be withheld
Thy hearing, such commission from above
I have received, to answer thy desire
Of knowledge within bounds; beyond abstain   120
To ask, nor let thine own inventions hope
Things not revealed, which th' invisible King,
Only omniscient, hath suppressed in night,
To none communicable in earth or heaven:
Enough is left besides to search and know.   125
But knowledge is as food, and needs no less
Her temperance over appetite, to know
In measure what the mind may well contain,
Oppresses else with surfeit, and soon turns
Wisdom to folly, as nourishment to wind.   130
   "Know then, that after Lucifer from heav'n
(So call him, brighter once amidst the host
Of angels than that star the stars among)
Fell with his flaming legions through the deep
Into his place, and the great Son returned   135
Victorious with his saints, th' omnipotent
Eternal Father from his throne beheld
Their multitude, and to his Son thus spake:
   " 'At least our envious foe hath failed, who thought
All like himself rebellious, by whose aid   140
This inaccessible high strength, the seat
Of Deity supreme, us dispossessed,
He trusted to have seized, and into fraud
Drew many, whom their place knows here no more.
Yet far the greater part have kept, I see,   145
Their station; heav'n, yet populous, retains
Number sufficient to possess her realms
Though wide, and this high temple to frequent
With ministeries due and solemn rites.
But lest his heart exalt him in the harm,   150
Already done, to have dispeopled heav'n,
My damage fondly deemed, I can repair
That detriment, if such it be to lose
Self-lost, and in a moment will create
Another world, out of one man a race   155

116. infer: show, prove.
123. suppressed in night: Horace, *Od.*
3.29.29–30.
131–33. Lucifer. Cf. 5.708 and note.

139. least: so edd. 1–6. Some would read "last."
144. Job 7.10; Ps. 103.16.
150–61. See note on 1.650 f.

Of men innumerable, there to dwell,
Not here, till by degrees of merit raised
They open to themselves at length the way
Up hither, under long obedience tried,
And earth be changed to heav'n, and heav'n to earth,   160
One kingdom, joy and union without end.
Meanwhile inhabit lax, ye Powers of heav'n;
And thou my Word, begotten Son, by thee
This I perform; speak thou, and be it done.
My overshadowing Spirit and might with thee   165
I send along; ride forth, and bid the deep
Within appointed bounds be heav'n and earth;
Boundless the deep, because I am who fill
Infinitude, nor vacuous the space.
Though I uncircumscribed myself retire,   170
And put not forth my goodness, which is free
To act or not, necessity and chance
Approach not me, and what I will is fate.'
   "So spake th' Almighty, and to what he spake
His Word, the Filial Godhead, gave effect.   175
Immediate are the acts of God, more swift
Than time or motion, but to human ears
Cannot without process of speech be told,
So told as earthly notion can receive.
Great triumph and rejoicing was in heav'n   180
When such was heard declared the Almighty's will;
Glory they sung to the Most High, good will
To future men, and in their dwellings peace;
Glory to him whose just avenging ire
Had driven out th' ungodly from his sight   185
And th' habitations of the just; to him
Glory and praise, whose wisdom had ordained
Good out of evil to create; instead
Of Spirits malign a better race to bring
Into their vacant room, and thence diffuse   190
His good to worlds and ages infinite.
   "So sang the hierarchies. Meanwhile the Son
On his great expedition now appeared,
Girt with omnipotence, with radiance crowned

157–61. Cf. 3.333–41.
162. inhabit lax: dwell at ease and at large.
163. Word: glossary.
165 (and 209, 235). Spirit: God's power, not the third person of the Trinity (cf. 3.389); cf. Luke 1.35.
168–73. The metaphysical theology compressed into these lines is expounded in *C.D.* 1.7. In brief, Milton rejects the orthodox view that God created the universe out of nothing and argues that he created it out of himself: God fills all space, although he has not yet exerted his creative power ("goodness") upon the disordered elements of Chaos (cf. *Timaeus*

53), and this he now, through the Son, proceeds to do. The creation is a voluntary act, not necessitated. The "fate" here referred to is not pagan fate but what Hooker (*Eccles. Pol.* 1.2.6) described as "that order which God before all ages hath set down with himself, for himself to do all things by" (cf. *C.D.* 1.2).
170. uncircumscribed: cf. Dante, *Purg.* 11.2, *Non circonscritto.*
176 f. Another apology (cf. 5.563–76 and note) for the translation into concrete terms of mysteries beyond finite comprehension.
182–83. Luke 2.13–14.
188. Cf. 1.162–65 and note.

Of majesty divine, sapience and love   195
Immense, and all his Father in him shone.
About his chariot numberless were poured
Cherub and Seraph, Potentates and Thrones,
And Virtues, wingèd Spirits, and chariots winged,
From the armory of God, where stand of old   200
Myriads between two brazen mountains lodged
Against a solemn day, harnessed at hand,
Celestial equipage; and now came forth
Spontaneous, for within them spirit lived,
Attendant on their Lord. Heav'n opened wide   205
Her ever-during gates, harmonious sound
On golden hinges moving, to let forth
The King of Glory in his powerful Word
And Spirit coming to create new worlds.
On heav'nly ground they stood, and from the shore   210
They viewed the vast immeasurable abyss
Outrageous as a sea, dark, wasteful, wild,
Up from the bottom turned by furious winds
And surging waves, as mountains to assault
Heav'n's highth, and with the center mix the pole.   215
    " 'Silence, ye troubled waves, and thou deep, peace,'
Said then th' omnific Word, 'your discord end.'
    "Nor stayed, but on the wings of Cherubim
Uplifted, in paternal glory rode
Far into Chaos and the world unborn;   220
For Chaos heard his voice. Him all his train
Followed in bright procession to behold
Creation, and the wonders of his might.
Then stayed the fervid wheels, and in his hand
He took the golden compasses, prepared   225
In God's eternal store, to circumscribe
This universe, and all created things.
One foot he centered, and the other turned
Round through the vast profundity obscure,
And said, 'Thus far extend, thus far thy bounds,   230
This be thy just circumference, O world!'
Thus God the heav'n created, thus the earth,

200. armory of God. Cf. 6.321 and note.
201. Zech. 6.1.
204. Cf. 6.751–52; Ezek. 1.20.
205 f. Cf. the opening of the gates of hell for Satan, 2.879 f., and 5.253–56.
208. King of Glory: cf. below, 565–66, and note.
210 f. Cf. Satan's view of and voyage through Chaos (2.890 f.) and the Son's imposing of order upon it.
216. Mark 4.39.
217. omnific: all-creating.
218–19. Cf. 6.771–72.
224. fervid wheels. Cf. 6.832 and Horace, *Od.* 1.1.4–5.

224–550. The account of creation, elaborated from Gen. 1–2 with the aid of hexaemeral and secular sources and Milton's imagination, reflects, like the picture of Eden, his delight in fecundity, and it is full of bursting energy and movement — though even here, as in the ethical realm, there is the Miltonic ideal of freedom under discipline. Also, unlike many thinkers and poets, he feels no conflict between the Many and the One; the Many manifest the One.
225. compasses. Cf. Prov. 8.27; Dante, *Par.* 19.40–42.

Matter unformed and void. Darkness profound
Covered th' abyss; but on the wat'ry calm
His brooding wings the Spirit of God outspread,   235
And vital virtue infused, and vital warmth
Throughout the fluid mass, but downward purged
The black tartareous cold infernal dregs
Adverse to life; then founded, then conglobed
Like things to like, the rest to several place   240
Disparted, and between spun out the air,
And earth self-balanced on her center hung.
    " 'Let there be light,' said God; and forthwith light
Ethereal, first of things, quintessence pure,
Sprung from the deep, and from her native east   245
To journey through the airy gloom began,
Sphered in a radiant cloud, for yet the sun
Was not; she in a cloudy tabernacle
Sojourned the while. God saw the light was good;
And light from darkness by the hemisphere   250
Divided: light the day, and darkness night
He named. Thus was the first day ev'n and morn;
Nor passed uncelebrated, nor unsung
By the celestial quires, when orient light
Exhaling first from darkness they beheld,   255
Birthday of heav'n and earth; with joy and shout
The hollow universal orb they filled,
And touched their golden harps, and hymning praised
God and his works; Creator him they sung,
Both when first ev'ning was, and when first morn.   260
    "Again God said, 'Let there be firmament
Amid the waters, and let it divide
The waters from the waters.' And God made
The firmament, expanse of liquid, pure,
Transparent, elemental air, diffused   265
In circuit to the uttermost convex
Of this great round: partition firm and sure,
The waters underneath from those above
Dividing; for as earth, so he the world
Built on circumfluous waters calm, in wide   270
Crystálline ocean, and the loud misrule
Of Chaos far removed, lest fierce extremes

234–35. Cf. Gen. 1.2 and *P.L.* 1.19–22.
236–42. Cf. Ovid, *Met.* 1.24–31; Cicero, *Tusculan Disput.* 1.17.
238. tartareous: hellish (glossary, "Tartarus").
239. founded: solidified.
239–42. Cf. 3.714–21.
242. Job 26.7; *Nativity* 122.
243 f. Gen. 1.2–5; cf. *P.L.* 3.1 f.
244. Ethereal . . . quintessence: glossary.
247–48. Cf. 3.8–12 and Gen. 1.3–5, Ovid, *Met.* 1.10.
248. tabernacle: Ps. 19.4.

253–60. Cf. *Nativity* 117–24 and notes.
263 f. Gen. 1.6–7. The firmament (here the expanse of air or ether between the earth and the outermost sphere) divides the waters on the surface of the earth from the "waters . . . above the firmament" (the "Crystálline ocean" of 271). The created world is surrounded by water.
267. round: universe (the "world" of 269), partly uncreated yet but circumscribed by the Son's compass.
270. circumfluous waters: cf. Ovid, *Met.* 1.30.

Contiguous might distemper the whole frame:
And heav'n he named the firmament. So ev'n
And morning chorus sung the second day.   275
   "The earth was formed, but in the womb as yet
Of waters, embryon immature involved,
Appeared not; over all the face of earth
Main ocean flowed, not idle, but with warm
Prolific humor soft'ning all her globe,   280
Fermented the great mother to conceive,
Satiate with genial moisture; when God said,
'Be gathered now, ye waters under heav'n,
Into one place, and let dry land appear.'
Immediately the mountains huge appear   285
Emergent, and their broad bare backs upheave
Into the clouds; their tops ascend the sky.
So high as heaved the tumid hills, so low
Down sunk a hollow bottom broad and deep,
Capacious bed of waters. Thither they   290
Hasted with glad precipitance, uprolled
As drops on dust conglobing from the dry;
Part rise in crystal wall, or ridge direct,
For haste; such flight the great command impressed
On the swift floods. As armies at the call   295
Of trumpet (for of armies thou hast heard)
Troop to their standard, so the wat'ry throng,
Wave rolling after wave, where way they found,
If steep, with torrent rapture, if through plain,
Soft-ebbing; nor withstood them rock or hill;   300
But they, or under ground, or circuit wide
With serpent error wand'ring, found their way,
And on the washy ooze deep channels wore;
Easy, ere God had bid the ground be dry,
All but within those banks where rivers now   305
Stream, and perpetual draw their humid train.
The dry land earth, and the great receptacle
Of congregated waters he called seas;
And saw that it was good, and said, 'Let th' earth
Put forth the verdant grass, herb yielding seed,   310
And fruit-tree yielding fruit after her kind,
Whose seed is in herself upon the earth.'
He scarce had said, when the bare earth, till then
Desert and bare, unsightly, unadorned,
Brought forth the tender grass, whose verdure clad   315
Her universal face with pleasant green;
Then herbs of every leaf, that sudden flow'red,
Op'ning their various colors, and made gay

---

277. embryon: cf. Sylvester, 1.1.298.
278 f. Cf. Ovid, *Met.* 1.416 f.
283 f. Gen. 1.9–12; cf. Ovid, *Met.* 1.343–
45.

290–306. Elaborated from Ps. 104.8–10.
302. error: winding.
306. humid: liquid, flowing.
309 f. Gen. 1.11–12.

Her bosom, smelling sweet; and these scarce blown,
Forth flourished thick the clust'ring vine, forth crept   320
The swelling gourd, up stood the corny reed
Embattled in her field: add the humble shrub,
And bush with frizzled hair implicit. Last
Rose as in dance the stately trees, and spread
Their branches hung with copious fruit, or gemmed   325
Their blossoms. With high woods the hills were crowned,
With tufts the valleys and each fountain side,
With borders long the rivers; that earth now
Seemed like to heav'n, a seat where gods might dwell,
Or wander with delight, and love to haunt   330
Her sacred shades; though God had yet not rained
Upon the earth, and man to till the ground
None was, but from the earth a dewy mist
Went up and watered all the ground, and each
Plant of the field, which ere it was in the earth   335
God made, and every herb, before it grew
On the green stem. God saw that it was good.
So ev'n and morn recorded the third day.
      "Again th' Almighty spake: 'Let there be lights
High in th' expanse of heaven to divide   340
The day from night; and let them be for signs,
For seasons, and for days, and circling years,
And let them be for lights as I ordain
Their office in the firmament of heav'n,
To give light on the earth'; and it was so.   345
And God made two great lights, great for their use
To man, the greater to have rule by day,
The less by night altern; and made the stars,
And set them in the firmament of heav'n
To illuminate the earth, and rule the day   350
In their vicissitude, and rule the night,
And light from darkness to divide. God saw,
Surveying his great work, that it was good.
For of celestial bodies first the sun
A mighty sphere he framed, unlightsome first,   355
Though of ethereal mold; then formed the moon
Globose, and every magnitude of stars,
And sowed with stars the heav'n thick as a field.
Of light by far the greater part he took,
Transplanted from her cloudy shrine, and placed   360
In the sun's orb, made porous to receive
And drink the liquid light, firm to retain
Her gathered beams, great palace now of light.

---

321. swelling: the traditional emendation
for the "smelling" of edd. 1 and 2 (probably
caught from 319).   corny reed: grain.
322. Ed. 1, add; ed. 2, and.
323. With twigs and leaves entangled.
325. gemmed: budded (Latin).

331–37. Gen. 2.5–6.
339–53. Gen. 1.14–19.
350–52. Cf. 6.6–8.
358. Cf. Spenser, *Hymn of Heavenly Beauty*
53.

Hither, as to their fountain, other stars
Repairing, in their golden urns draw light,   365
And hence the morning planet gilds her horns;
By tincture or reflection they augment
Their small peculiar, though from human sight
So far remote, with diminution seen.
First in his east the glorious lamp was seen,   370
Regent of day, and all th' horizon round
Invested with bright rays, jocund to run
His longitude through heav'n's high road; the gray
Dawn and the Pleiades before him danced,
Shedding sweet influence. Less bright the moon,   375
But opposite in leveled west was set
His mirror, with full face borrowing her light
From him, for other light she needed none
In that aspéct, and still that distance keeps
Till night; then in the east her turn she shines,   380
Revolved on heav'n's great axle, and her reign
With thousand lesser lights dividual holds,
With thousand thousand stars, that then appeared
Spangling the hemisphere. Then first adorned
With their bright luminaries that set and rose,   385
Glad ev'ning and glad morn crowned the fourth day.
    "And God said, 'Let the waters generate
Reptile with spawn abundant, living soul;
And let fowl fly above the earth, with wings
Displayed on the op'n firmament of heav'n.'   390
And God created the great whales, and each
Soul living, each that crept, which plenteously
The waters generated by their kinds,
And every bird of wing after his kind;
And saw that it was good, and blessed them, saying,   395
'Be fruitful, multiply, and in the seas
And lakes and running streams the waters fill;
And let the fowl be multiplied on the earth.'
Forthwith the sounds and seas, each creek and bay,
With fry innumerable swarm, and shoals   400
Of fish that with their fins and shining scales
Glide under the green wave, in sculls that oft
Bank the mid-sea. Part single or with mate
Graze the seaweed their pasture, and through groves
Of coral stray, or sporting with quick glance   405
Show to the sun their waved coats dropped with gold,

364–69. Cf. Dante, *Par.* 23.28–30.
366. Galileo showed that Venus had phases like the moon (which was commonly described as having horns).
367. tincture: absorption.
368. small peculiar: own small store (of light).
373. longitude: course from east to west.

374. Job 38.31.
376. leveled: due.
382. dividual: divided, shared (modifies "reign").
387 f. Gen. 1.20–22.
402. sculls: schools.
403. Bank: make a mound or mass in.
406. dropped: flecked.

Or in their pearly shells at ease, attend
Moist nutriment, or under rocks their food
In jointed armor watch; on smooth the seal
And bended dolphins play; part huge of bulk,   410
Wallowing unwieldy, enormous in their gait,
Tempest the ocean.   There leviathan,
Hugest of living creatures, on the deep
Stretched like a promontory sleeps or swims,
And seems a moving land, and at his gills   415
Draws in, and at his trunk spouts out a sea.
Meanwhile the tepid caves and fens and shores
Their brood as numerous hatch, from the egg that soon
Bursting with kindly rupture forth disclosed
Their callow young, but feathered soon and fledge   420
They summed their pens, and soaring th' air sublime
With clang despised the ground, under a cloud
In prospect; there the eagle and the stork
On cliffs and cedar tops their eyries build.
Part loosely wing the region, part more wise,   425
In common, ranged in figure wedge their way,
Intelligent of seasons, and set forth
Their airy caravan high over seas
Flying, and over lands with mutual wing
Easing their flight; so steers the prudent crane   430
Her annual voyage, borne on winds; the air
Floats as they pass, fanned with unnumbered plumes.
From branch to branch the smaller birds with song
Solaced the woods, and spread their painted wings
Till ev'n, nor then the solemn nightingale   435
Ceased warbling, but all night tuned her soft lays.
Others on silver lakes and rivers bathed
Their downy breast; the swan, with archèd neck
Between her white wings mantling proudly, rows
Her state with oary feet; yet oft they quit   440
The dank, and rising on stiff pennons, tow'r
The mid-aerial sky.   Others on ground
Walked firm: the crested cock whose clarion sounds
The silent hours, and th' other whose gay train
Adorns him, colored with the florid hue   445
Of rainbows and starry eyes.   The waters thus
With fish replenished, and the air with fowl,
Ev'ning and morn solemnized the fifth day.

---

409. smooth: the smooth sea.
412. leviathan: see biblical references in note on 1.200–08.
421. summed their pens: reached full growth of wings.
422–23. despised: looked down upon. under . . . prospect: the ground appeared to be under a cloud.
423–24. eagle . . . cliffs: Job 39.27–28.

424. cedar . . . build: cf. *Richard III* 1.3.264.
425. region: sky.
426. wedge: move in triangular formation.
429–30. Those behind resting their heads on those in front (a bit of traditional lore).
432. Floats: undulates.
439. mantling: raised and spread.
441. tow'r: tower, soar into.
444. other: peacock.

"The sixth, and of creation last, arose
With ev'ning harps and matin, when God said,   450
'Let th' earth bring forth soul living in her kind,
Cattle and creeping things, and beast of the earth,
Each in their kind.' The earth obeyed, and straight
Op'ning her fertile womb teemed at a birth
Innumerous living creatures, perfect forms,   455
Limbed and full grown. Out of the ground up rose
As from his lair the wild beast where he wons
In forest wild, in thicket, brake, or den;
Among the trees in pairs they rose, they walked;
The cattle in the fields and meadows green: 460
Those rare and solitary, these in flocks
Pasturing at once, and in broad herds upsprung.
The grassy clods now calved, now half appeared
The tawny lion, pawing to get free
His hinder parts, then springs as broke from bonds,   465
And rampant shakes his brinded mane; the ounce,
The libbard, and the tiger, as the mole
Rising, the crumbled earth above them threw
In hillocks; the swift stag from under ground
Bore up his branching head; scarce from his mold   470
Behemoth, biggest born of earth, upheaved
His vastness; fleeced the flocks and bleating rose,
As plants; ambiguous between sea and land,
The river-horse and scaly crocodile.
At once came forth whatever creeps the ground,   475
Insect or worm: those waved their limber fans
For wings, and smallest lineaments exact
In all the liveries decked of summer's pride
With spots of gold and purple, azure and green;
These as a line their long dimension drew,   480
Streaking the ground with sinuous trace; not all
Minims of nature; some of serpent kind,
Wondrous in length and corpulence, involved
Their snaky folds, and added wings. First crept
The parsimonious emmet, provident   485
Of future, in small room large heart enclosed,
Pattern of just equality perhaps
Hereafter, joined in her popular tribes
Of commonalty; swarming next appeared
The female bee that feeds her husband drone   490

451 f. Gen. 1.24–25.
451. "Soul" is the accepted emendation for "Fowle" and "Foul" of edd. 1, 2; cf. 388 above.
457. wons: dwells.
463 f. Cf. Lucretius, 2.991–98, 5.795 f., and the warriors who sprang from the sowing of dragons' teeth in Apollonius Rhodius, *Argonautica* 3.1354 f., Ovid, *Met.* 3.104 f., 7.121 f.
467. libbard: leopard.

471. Behemoth: elephant? Cf. Job 40.15–24.
474. river-horse: hippopotamus.
482. minims: minute creatures.
483. corpulence: bulk.   involved: coiled.
484. added wings. Cf. Isa. 30.6; Herodotus 2.75; etc.
485. emmet: ant.
486. Cf. Virgil, *Georg.* 4.83.
490–92. A traditional error in regard to male and female bees.

Deliciously, and builds her waxen cells
With honey stored. The rest are numberless,
And thou their natures know'st, and gav'st them names,
Needless to thee repeated; nor unknown
The serpent, subtlest beast of all the field,   495
Of huge extent sometimes, with brazen eyes
And hairy mane terrific, though to thee
Not noxious, but obedient at thy call.
   "Now heav'n in all her glory shone, and rolled
Her motions, as the great First Mover's hand   500
First wheeled their course; earth in her rich attire
Consummate lovely smiled; air, water, earth,
By fowl, fish, beast, was flown, was swum, was walked
Frequent; and of the sixth day yet remained.
There wanted yet the master work, the end   505
Of all yet done: a creature who not prone
And brute as other creatures, but endued
With sanctity of reason, might erect
His stature, and upright with front serene
Govern the rest, self-knowing, and from thence   510
Magnanimous to correspond with heav'n,
But grateful to acknowledge whence his good
Descends; thither with heart and voice and eyes
Directed in devotion, to adore
And worship God supreme, who made him chief   515
Of all his works. Therefore the omnipotent
Eternal Father (for where is not he
Present?) thus to his Son audibly spake:
   " 'Let us make now man in our image, man
In our similitude, and let them rule   520
Over the fish and fowl of sea and air,
Beast of the field, and over all the earth,
And every creeping thing that creeps the ground.'
This said, he formed thee, Adam, thee, O man,
Dust of the ground, and in thy nostrils breathed   525
The breath of life; in his own image he
Created thee, in the image of God
Express, and thou becam'st a living soul.
Male he created thee, but thy consort
Female for race; then blessed mankind, and said,   530
'Be fruitful, multiply, and fill the earth,
Subdue it, and throughout dominion hold
Over fish of the sea, and fowl of the air,
And every living thing that moves on the earth.'
Wherever thus created, for no place   535
Is yet distinct by name, thence, as thou know'st,
He brought thee into this delicious grove,

492–93. Gen. 2.19–20.
495. Gen. 3.1.
497. mane: cf. *Aen.* 2.206–07.
505. end: crown, object.
508–10. erect: see note on 4.288–89.

511. correspond: communicate? be in harmony?
519 f. Gen. 1.26–28, 2.7.
537–44. Gen. 2.9, 15–17.

This garden, planted with the trees of God,
Delectable both to behold and taste;
And freely all their pleasant fruit for food   540
Gave thee — all sorts are here that all th' earth yields,
Variety without end; but of the Tree
Which tasted works knowledge of good and evil,
Thou may'st not; in the day thou eat'st, thou di'st;
Death is the penalty imposed, beware,   545
And govern well thy appetite, lest Sin
Surprise thee, and her black attendant Death.
    "Here finished he, and all that he had made
Viewed, and behold all was entirely good.
So ev'n and morn accomplished the sixth day;   550
Yet not till the Creator from his work
Desisting, though unwearied, up returned,
Up to the heav'n of heav'ns his high abode,
Thence to behold this new-created world,
Th' addition of his empire, how it showed   555
In prospect from his throne, how good, how fair,
Answering his great idea. Up he rode
Followed with acclamation and the sound
Symphonious of ten thousand harps that tuned
Angelic harmonies. The earth, the air   560
Resounded (thou remember'st, for thou heard'st),
The heav'ns and all the constellations rung,
The planets in their stations list'ning stood,
While the bright pomp ascended jubilant.
'Open, ye everlasting gates,' they sung,   565
'Open, ye heav'ns, your living doors; let in
The great Creator from his work returned
Magnificent, his six days' work, a world;
Open, and henceforth oft; for God will deign
To visit oft the dwellings of just men   570
Delighted, and with frequent intercourse
Thither will send his wingèd messengers
On errands of supernal grace.' So sung
The glorious train ascending. He through heav'n,
That opened wide her blazing portals, led   575
To God's eternal house direct the way,
A broad and ample road, whose dust is gold
And pavement stars, as stars to thee appear,
Seen in the Galaxy, that Milky Way
Which nightly as a circling zone thou seest   580
Powdered with stars. And now on earth the seventh
Ev'ning arose in Eden, for the sun
Was set, and twilight from the east came on,

557. idea. The only occurrence in Milton's
poetry of this word, which carries its Platonic
meaning of "ideal form, pattern." Cf. *Timaeus*
37 C; Sylvester, 1.1.97; Spenser, *Hymn in
Honor of Beauty.*
    563. Ed. 1, stations; ed. 2, station.

564. pomp: procession (Greek sense).
565–66. Ps. 24.7–9.
    579. Milky Way. Cf. Ovid, *Met.* 1.168–69;
Milton, *In obitum Praesulis Eliensis* 60.
    581. Powdered with stars. In Sylvester,
1.4.209.

Forerunning night; when at the holy mount
Of heav'n's high-seated top, th' imperial throne   585
Of Godhead, fixed for ever firm and sure,
The Filial Power arrived, and sat him down
With his great Father; for he also went
Invisible, yet stayed (such privilege
Hath Omnipresence), and the work ordained,   590
Author and end of all things, and from work
Now resting, blessed and hallowed the sev'nth day,
As resting on that day from all his work;
But not in silence holy kept: the harp
Had work and rested not, the solemn pipe,   595
And dulcimer, all organs of sweet stop,
All sounds on fret by string or golden wire
Tempered soft tunings, intermixed with voice
Choral or unison; of incense clouds
Fuming from golden censers hid the mount.   600
Creation and the six days' acts they sung:
'Great are thy works, Jehovah, infinite
Thy power; what thought can measure thee or tongue
Relate thee, greater now in thy return
Than from the giant angels? Thee that day   605
Thy thunders magnified; but to create
Is greater than created to destroy.
Who can impair thee, mighty King, or bound
Thy empire? Easily the proud attempt
Of Spirits apostate and their counsels vain   610
Thou hast repelled, while impiously they thought
Thee to diminish, and from thee withdraw
The number of thy worshipers. Who seeks
To lessen thee, against his purpose serves
To manifest the more thy might: his evil   615
Thou usest, and from thence creat'st more good.
Witness this new-made world, another heav'n
From heaven gate not far, founded in view
On the clear hyaline, the glassy sea;
Of amplitude almost immense, with stars   620
Numerous, and every star perhaps a world
Of destined habitation; but thou know'st
Their seasons; among these the seat of men,
Earth with her nether ocean circumfused,
Their pleasant dwelling-place. Thrice happy men,   625
And sons of men, whom God hath thus advanced,
Created in his image, there to dwell

591–93. Gen. 2.1–3.
597. fret: a bar on the finger-board of a musical instrument.
599. unison: solo (Latin sense).
599–600. Rev. 8.3–5.
605. giant angels: Satan and his fellows, with a glance at the wars of gods and Giants and Titans (see notes on 1.50, etc.).

619. hyaline: the waters above the firmament (cf. 263 f. and note, and Rev. 4.6, 15.2, "sea of glass").
620. immense: in literal sense, "immeasurable."
621–22. See the note on 3.570.
624. See the notes above on 263 f. and 619.

And worship him, and in reward to rule
Over his works, on earth, in sea, or air,
And multiply a race of worshipers   630
Holy and just; thrice happy if they know
Their happiness, and persevere upright.'
  "So sung they, and the empyrean rung
With halleluiahs. Thus was Sabbath kept.
And thy request think now fulfilled, that asked   635
How first this world and face of things began,
And what before thy memory was done
From the beginning, that posterity
Informed by thee might know; if else thou seek'st
Aught, not surpassing human measure, say."   640

Book VIII

THE ARGUMENT

Adam inquires concerning celestial motions, is doubtfully answered, and
exhorted to search rather things more worthy of knowledge. Adam assents,
and still desirous to detain Raphael, relates to him what he remembered since
his own creation: his placing in Paradise, his talk with God concerning solitude
and fit society, his first meeting and nuptials with Eve. His discourse with the
angel thereupon; who, after admonitions repeated, departs.

THE Angel ended, and in Adam's ear
So charming left his voice, that he a while
Thought him still speaking, still stood fixed to hear;
Then as new-waked thus gratefully replied:
"What thanks sufficient, or what recompense   5
Equal have I to render thee, divine
Historian, who thus largely hast allayed
The thirst I had of knowledge, and vouchsafed
This friendly condescension to relate
Things else by me unsearchable, now heard   10
With wonder, but delight, and, as is due,
With glory attribúted to the high
Creator? Something yet of doubt remains,
Which only thy solution can resolve.

629. Gen. 1.26, 28; Ps. 8.6.
631–32. Cf. 4.774–75 and note.
BOOK VIII. 1–4. When, for the second edition, Milton divided book 7 into books 7 and
8, lines 1–3 were added as an introduction and
line 641 of book 7 was altered to make line 4
of book 8.
  2. charming: casting a spell.

13–38. Adam's inquiry, which implies a
large flaw in the divine order, is made with a
little less diffident humility than his request in
7.80 f. The apparent disproportion in the cosmic economy was a traditional question; Milton had touched it in his seventh Prolusion at
Cambridge.

When I behold this goodly frame, this world   15
Of heav'n and earth consisting, and compute
Their magnitudes, this earth a spot, a grain,
An atom, with the firmament compared
And all her numbered stars, that seem to roll
Spaces incomprehensible (for such   20
Their distance argues and their swift return
Diurnal) merely to officiate light
Round this opacous earth, this punctual spot,
One day and night, in all their vast survey
Useless besides; reasoning I oft admire   25
How Nature wise and frugal could commit
Such disproportions, with superfluous hand
So many nobler bodies to create,
Greater so manifold, to this one use,
For aught appears, and on their orbs impose   30
Such restless revolution day by day
Repeated, while the sedentary earth,
That better might with far less compass move,
Served by more noble than herself, attains
Her end without least motion, and receives   35
As tribute, such a sumless journey brought
Of incorporeal speed, her warmth and light;
Speed, to describe whose swiftness number fails."
    So spake our sire, and by his count'nance seemed
Ent'ring on studious thoughts abstruse, which Eve   40
Perceiving where she sat retired in sight,
With lowliness majestic from her seat,
And grace that won who saw to wish her stay,
Rose, and went forth among her fruits and flow'rs,
To visit how they prospered, bud and bloom,   45
Her nursery; they at her coming sprung,
And touched by her fair tendance gladlier grew.
Yet went she not as not with such discourse
Delighted, or not capable her ear
Of what was high: such pleasure she reserved,   50
Adam relating, she sole auditress;
Her husband the relater she preferred
Before the Angel, and of him to ask
Chose rather; he, she knew, would intermix
Grateful digressions, and solve high dispute   55
With conjugal caresses; from his lip
Not words alone pleased her. O when meet now
Such pairs, in love and mutual honor joined?
With goddess-like demeanor forth she went;

15. this goodly frame: in *Hamlet* 2.2.310.
17–18. In and since antiquity it had been a commonplace that the earth was a mere speck in the cosmos.
22. officiate: provide.

23. punctual: like a point.
28 (and 34). It was also a traditional commonplace that the earth was a relatively ignoble member of the solar system.
36. sumless: incalculable.

Not unattended, for on her as queen   60
A pomp of winning Graces waited still,
And from about her shot darts of desire
Into all eyes to wish her still in sight.
And Raphael now to Adam's doubt proposed
Benevolent and facile thus replied: 65
     "To ask or search I blame thee not, for heav'n
Is as the Book of God before thee set,
Wherein to read his wondrous works, and learn
His seasons, hours, or days, or months, or years.
This to attain, whether heav'n move or earth,   70
Imports not, if thou reckon right; the rest
From man or angel the great Architect
Did wisely to conceal, and not divulge
His secrets to be scanned by them who ought
Rather admire; or if they list to try   75
Conjecture, he his fabric of the heav'ns
Hath left to their disputes, perhaps to move
His laughter at their quaint opinions wide
Hereafter, when they come to model heav'n
And calculate the stars, how they will wield   80
The mighty frame, how build, unbuild, contrive
To save appearances, how gird the sphere
With centric and eccentric scribbled o'er,
Cycle and epicycle, orb in orb.
Already by thy reasoning this I guess,   85
Who art to lead thy offspring, and supposest
That bodies bright and greater should not serve
The less not bright, nor heav'n such journeys run,
Earth sitting still, when she alone receives
The benefit. Consider first, that great   90
Or bright infers not excellence: the earth,
Though in comparison of heav'n so small,
Nor glistering, may of solid good contain
More plenty than the sun that barren shines,
Whose virtue on itself works no effect,   95
But in the fruitful earth; there first received,
His beams, unactive else, their vigor find.
Yet not to earth are those bright luminaries
Officious, but to thee, earth's habitant.
And for the heav'n's wide circuit, let it speak   100
The Maker's high magnificence, who built
So spacious, and his line stretched out so far,

---

60. Not unattended: a Homeric formula.
61. pomp: retinue.
65. facile: affable (cf. 7.41, 8.648).
66–69. The traditional recognition of God's
secondary revealing of himself in created nature. Cf. 3.47–50.
78. wide: i.e. of the mark.
82. save appearances: account for the phe-
nomena. Lines 79–84 summarize centuries of

patching up of the Ptolemaic system.
83. centric: a sphere whose center was the
earth.   eccentric: glossary.
84. epicycle: a planetary orbit whose center
was on the circumference of another circle
concentric with the earth.
91. infers: implies.
102. his line . . . far: Job 38.5.

That man may know he dwells not in his own;
An edifice too large for him to fill,
Lodged in a small partition, and the rest   105
Ordained for uses to his Lord best known.
The swiftness of those circles áttribute,
Though numberless, to his omnipotence,
That to corporeal substances could add
Speed almost spiritual; me thou think'st not slow,   110
Who since the morning hour set out from heav'n
Where God resides, and ere mid-day arrived
In Eden, distance inexpressible
By numbers that have name. But this I urge,
Admitting motion in the heav'ns, to show   115
Invalid that which thee to doubt it moved;
Not that I so affirm, though so it seem
To thee who hast thy dwelling here on earth.
God, to remove his ways from human sense,
Placed heav'n from earth so far, that earthly sight,   120
If it presume, might err in things too high,
And no advantage gain. What if the sun
Be center to the world, and other stars,
By his attractive virtue and their own
Incited, dance about him various rounds?   125
Their wand'ring course, now high, now low, then hid,
Progressive, retrograde, or standing still,
In six thou seest, and what if sev'nth to these
The planet earth, so steadfast though she seem,
Insensibly three different motions move?   130
Which else to several spheres thou must ascribe,
Moved contrary with thwart obliquities,
Or save the sun his labor, and that swift
Nocturnal and diurnal rhomb supposed,
Invisible else above all stars, the wheel   135
Of day and night; which needs not thy belief,
If earth industrious of herself fetch day
Traveling east, and with her part averse
From the sun's beam meet night, her other part
Still luminous by his ray. What if that light   140
Sent from her through the wide transpicuous air,
To the terrestrial moon be as a star
Enlight'ning her by day, as she by night
This earth, reciprocal, if land be there,

122–58. Having shown the logical validity of a geocentric system, which Adam had queried, Raphael expounds a heliocentric one, without pronouncing in favor of either.

127. Because of the earth's orbital movement, to an observer on earth the planets appeared at times to stand still and move backward.

128. six. See glossary, "sphere."

130. In Copernicus' system the earth, now considered as a planet, had three motions: daily rotation; annual rotation around the sun; and a slow motion of the earth's axis (see note on 3.483).

131. Copernicus eliminated the ninth sphere and the tenth (the *primum mobile*) and made the eighth (of fixed stars) motionless.

132. Crossing each other obliquely.

134. rhomb: glossary, "first moved."

Fields and inhabitants? Her spots thou seest   145
As clouds, and clouds may rain, and rain produce
Fruits in her softened soil, for some to eat
Allotted there; and other suns perhaps
With their attendant moons thou wilt descry,
Communicating male and female light,   150
Which two great sexes animate the world,
Stored in each orb perhaps with some that live.
For such vast room in Nature unpossessed
By living soul, desert and desolate,
Only to shine, yet scarce to cóntribute   155
Each orb a glimpse of light, conveyed so far
Down to this habitable, which returns
Light back to them, is obvious to dispute.
But whether thus these things, or whether not,
Whether the sun predominant in heav'n   160
Rise on the earth, or earth rise on the sun,
He from the east his flaming road begin,
Or she from west her silent course advance
With inoffensive pace that spinning sleeps
On her soft axle, while she paces ev'n,   165
And bears thee soft with the smooth air along —
Solicit not thy thoughts with matters hid:
Leave them to God above, him serve and fear;
Of other creatures, as him pleases best,
Wherever placed, let him dispose; joy thou   170
In what he gives to thee, this Paradise
And thy fair Eve; heav'n is for thee too high
To know what passes there; be lowly wise:
Think only what concerns thee and thy being;
Dream not of other worlds, what creatures there   175
Live, in what state, condition, or degree,
Contented that thus far hath been revealed
Not of earth only but of highest heav'n."
  To whom thus Adam, cleared of doubt, replied:
"How fully hast thou satisfied me, pure   180
Intelligence of heav'n, Angel serene,
And freed from intricacies, taught to live

145–58. On the plurality of inhabited worlds
cf. 7.621–22 and the note on 3.570.
  148–49. Such as Jupiter's satellites, discovered by Galileo.
  150. male and female: original and reflected.
  158. obvious: open.
  159–78. Cf. 7.111–30 and other angelic
cautions. Milton is not attacking science or
astronomy *per se* (witness his tributes to
Galileo), but takes astronomy as the conspicuous example of inquiry remote from central
human needs and likely to engender irreligious
pride — as the temptation of Eve was to show.
He adds Christian urgency to Socrates' concern with the moral life; and, like many men

of his century, he fears excessive "curiosity,"
intemperance in the pursuit of mere knowledge.
Cf. Donne's *Anniversaries;* Robert Burton's
"Digression of the Air" (*Anatomy of Melancholy* 2.2.3); and Ralph Cudworth's sermon to
the House of Commons, March 31, 1647: "We
think it a gallant thing to be fluttering up to
heaven with our wings of knowledge and
speculation: whereas the highest mystery of a
divine life here, and of perfect happiness hereafter, consisteth in nothing but mere obedience
to the divine will."
  164. inoffensive: unimpeded.
  182–87. Matt. 6.31–34.

The easiest way, nor with perplexing thoughts
To interrupt the sweet of life, from which
God hath bid dwell far off all anxious cares,   185
And not molest us, unless we ourselves
Seek them with wand'ring thoughts and notions vain.
But apt the mind or fancy is to rove
Unchecked, and of her roving is no end;
Till warned, or by experience taught, she learn   190
That not to know at large of things remote
From use, obscure and subtle, but to know
That which before us lies in daily life,
Is the prime wisdom; what is more, is fume,
Or emptiness, or fond impertinence,   195
And renders us in things that most concern
Unpractised, unprepared, and still to seek.
Therefore from this high pitch let us descend
A lower flight, and speak of things at hand
Useful, whence haply mention may arise   200
Of something not unseasonable to ask,
By sufferance and thy wonted favor deigned.
Thee I have heard relating what was done
Ere my remembrance: now hear me relate
My story, which perhaps thou hast not heard;   205
And day is yet not spent; till then thou seest
How subtly to detain thee I devise,
Inviting thee to hear while I relate,
Fond, were it not in hope of thy reply.
For while I sit with thee, I seem in heav'n,   210
And sweeter thy discourse is to my ear
Than fruits of palm-tree, pleasantest to thirst
And hunger both, from labor, at the hour
Of sweet repast; they satiate, and soon fill,
Though pleasant, but thy words, with grace divine   215
Imbued, bring to their sweetness no satiety."
     To whom thus Raphael answered heav'nly meek:
"Nor are thy lips ungraceful, sire of men,
Nor tongue ineloquent; for God on thee
Abundantly his gifts hath also poured   220
Inward and outward both, his image fair:
Speaking or mute all comeliness and grace
Attends thee, and each word, each motion forms.
Nor less think we in heav'n of thee on earth
Than of our fellow-servant, and inquire   225
Gladly into the ways of God with man;
For God we see hath honored thee, and set
On man his equal love. Say therefore on;

188–97. In the *Reason of Church Govern-ment* (1642) Milton contrasted "that knowl-edge that rests in the contemplation of natural causes and dimensions, which must needs be a lower wisdom, as the object is low," and "the only high valuable wisdom," the knowledge of God and goodness and true happiness in life (*Works*, 3, 1, 229).
     195. fond impertinence: foolish irrelevance.

For I that day was absent, as befell,
Bound on a voyage uncouth and obscure,   230
Far on excursion toward the gates of hell,
Squared in full legion (such command we had),
To see that none thence issued forth a spy
Or enemy, while God was in his work,
Lest he incensed at such eruption bold,   235
Destruction with Creation might have mixed.
Not that they durst without his leave attempt,
But us he sends upon his high behests
For state, as sovran King, and to inure
Our prompt obedience. Fast we found, fast shut   240
The dismal gates, and barricadoed strong;
But long ere our approaching heard within
Noise, other than the sound of dance or song,
Torment, and loud lament, and furious rage.
Glad we returned up to the coasts of light   245
Ere Sabbath ev'ning; so we had in charge.
But thy relation now; for I attend,
Pleased with thy words no less than thou with mine."
   So spake the godlike Power, and thus our sire:
"For man to tell how human life began   250
Is hard; for who himself beginning knew?
Desire with thee still longer to converse
Induced me. As new-waked from soundest sleep
Soft on the flow'ry herb I found me laid
In balmy sweat, which with his beams the sun   255
Soon dried, and on the reeking moisture fed.
Straight toward heav'n my wond'ring eyes I turned,
And gazed a while the ample sky, till raised
By quick instinctive motion up I sprung,
As thitherward endeavoring, and upright   260
Stood on my feet. About me round I saw
Hill, dale, and shady woods, and sunny plains,
And liquid lapse of murmuring streams; by these,
Creatures that lived and moved, and walked or flew,
Birds on the branches warbling; all things smiled;   265
With fragrance and with joy my heart o'erflowed.
Myself I then perused, and limb by limb
Surveyed, and sometimes went, and sometimes ran
With supple joints, as lively vigor led;
But who I was, or where, or from what cause,   270
Knew not. To speak I tried, and forthwith spake;
My tongue obeyed, and readily could name
Whate'er I saw. 'Thou sun,' said I, 'fair light,
And thou enlightened earth, so fresh and gay,
Ye hills and dales, ye rivers, woods, and plains,   275
And ye that live and move, fair creatures, tell,

257–58. Adam's first impulse is in contrast with Eve's (4.449 f.;
see the notes on 4.460 f. and 4.288–89).   268. went: walked.

Tell, if ye saw, how came I thus, how here?
Not of myself; by some great Maker then,
In goodness and in power pre-eminent.
Tell me, how may I know him, how adore,   280
From whom I have that thus I move and live,
And feel that I am happier than I know?'
While thus I called, and strayed I knew not whither,
From where I first drew air, and first beheld
This happy light, when answer none returned,   285
On a green shady bank profuse of flow'rs
Pensive I sat me down; there gentle sleep
First found me, and with soft oppression seized
My drowsèd sense, untroubled, though I thought
I then was passing to my former state   290
Insensible, and forthwith to dissolve;
When suddenly stood at my head a dream,
Whose inward apparition gently moved
My fancy to believe I yet had being,
And lived. One came, methought, of shape divine,   295
And said, 'Thy mansion wants thee, Adam, rise,
First man, of men innumerable ordained
First father; called by thee I come thy guide
To the garden of bliss, thy seat prepared.'
So saying, by the hand he took me raised,   300
And over fields and waters, as in air
Smooth sliding without step, last led me up
A woody mountain; whose high top was plain,
A circuit wide, enclosed, with goodliest trees
Planted, with walks and bowers, that what I saw   305
Of earth before scarce pleasant seemed. Each tree
Loaden with fairest fruit, that hung to the eye
Tempting, stirred in me sudden appetite
To pluck and eat; whereat I waked, and found
Before mine eyes all real, as the dream   310
Had lively shadowed. Here had new begun
My wand'ring, had not he who was my guide
Up hither from among the trees appeared,
Presence Divine. Rejoicing, but with awe,
In adoration at his feet I fell   315
Submiss. He reared me, and 'Whom thou sought'st I am,'
Said mildly, 'Author of all this thou seest
Above, or round about thee, or beneath.
This Paradise I give thee, count it thine
To till and keep, and of the fruit to eat;   320
Of every tree that in the garden grows
Eat freely with glad heart; fear here no dearth.
But of the tree whose operation brings
Knowledge of good and ill, which I have set

281. Acts 17.28; cf. note on 5.503 above.   319–33. Gen. 2.15–17.
303 f. Cf. 4.133 f.

The pledge of thy obedience and thy faith,   325
Amid the garden by the Tree of Life,
Remember what I warn thee, shun to taste,
And shun the bitter consequence. For know,
The day thou eat'st thereof, my sole command
Transgressed, inevitably thou shalt die,   330
From that day mortal, and this happy state
Shalt lose, expelled from hence into a world
Of woe and sorrow.' Sternly he pronounced
The rigid interdiction, which resounds
Yet dreadful in mine ear, though in my choice   335
Not to incur; but soon his clear aspéct
Returned, and gracious purpose thus renewed:
'Not only these fair bounds, but all the earth
To thee and to thy race I give; as lords
Possess it, and all things that therein live,   340
Or live in sea or air, beast, fish, and fowl.
In sign whereof each bird and beast behold
After their kinds; I bring them to receive
From thee their names, and pay thee fealty
With low subjection; understand the same   345
Of fish within their wat'ry residence,
Not hither summoned, since they cannot change
Their element to draw the thinner air.'
As thus he spake, each bird and beast behold
Approaching two and two, these cow'ring low   350
With blandishment, each bird stooped on his wing.
I named them as they passed, and understood
Their nature; with such knowledge God endued
My sudden apprehension. But in these
I found not what methought I wanted still,   355
And to the heav'nly Vision thus presumed:
   " 'O by what name, for thou above all these,
Above mankind, or aught than mankind higher,
Surpassest far my naming, how may I
Adore thee, Author of this universe,   360
And all this good to man, for whose well-being
So amply, and with hands so liberal
Thou hast provided all things? But with me
I see not who partakes. In solitude
What happiness? Who can enjoy alone,   365
Or all enjoying, what contentment find?'
Thus I presumptuous; and the Vision bright,
As with a smile more brightened, thus replied:
   " 'What call'st thou solitude? Is not the earth
With various living creatures, and the air   370
Replenished, and all these at thy command
To come and play before thee? Know'st thou not

330. die: be subject to death.   338–41. Gen. 1.28.
337. purpose: speech.   342–55. Gen. 2.19–20.

Their language and their ways? They also know,
And reason not contemptibly; with these
Find pastime, and bear rule; thy realm is large.'   **375**
So spake the universal Lord, and seemed
So ordering. I with leave of speech implored,
And humble deprecation, thus replied:
    " 'Let not my words offend thee, heav'nly Power;
My Maker, be propitious while I speak.   **380**
Hast thou not made me here thy substitute,
And these inferior far beneath me set?
Among unequals what society
Can sort, what harmony or true delight?
Which must be mutual, in proportion due   **385**
Giv'n and received; but in disparity,
The one intense, the other still remiss
Cannot well suit with either, but soon prove
Tedious alike. Of fellowship I speak
Such as I seek, fit to participate   **390**
All rational delight, wherein the brute
Cannot be human consort; they rejoice
Each with their kind, lion with lioness;
So fitly them in pairs thou hast combined;
Much less can bird with beast, or fish with fowl   **395**
So well converse, nor with the ox the ape;
Worse then can man with beast, and least of all.'
    "Whereto th' Almighty answered, not displeased:
'A nice and subtle happiness, I see,
Thou to thyself proposest, in the choice   **400**
Of thy associates, Adam, and wilt taste
No pleasure, though in pleasure, solitary.
What think'st thou then of me, and this my state?
Seem I to thee sufficiently possessed
Of happiness, or not? Who am alone   **405**
From all eternity; for none I know
Second to me or like, equal much less.
How have I then with whom to hold converse
Save with the creatures which I made, and those
To me inferior, infinite descents   **410**
Beneath what other creatures are to thee?'
    "He ceased; I lowly answered: 'To attain
The highth and depth of thy eternal ways
All human thoughts come short, Supreme of things;
Thou in thyself art perfect, and in thee   **415**
Is no deficience found; not so is man,
But in degree, the cause of his desire

379–80. Gen. 18.30.
387. intense . . . remiss: taut, slack (carrying on the musical metaphor).
402. in pleasure: see note on 4.27–28.
405–07. It is actually the Son — though called "th' Almighty" in 398 — who, as God's agent, had created the world and is now conversing with Adam, but he speaks for, and as if he were, the Father; these lines imply Milton's anti-Trinitarianism.
407. Cf. Horace, *Od.* 1.12.17–18.

By conversation with his like to help
Or solace his defects. No need that thou
Shouldst propagate, already infinite,   420
And through all numbers absolute, though One;
But man by number is to manifest
His single imperfection, and beget
Like of his like, his image multiplied,
In unity defective, which requires   425
Collateral love, and dearest amity.
Thou in thy secrecy although alone,
Best with thyself accompanied, seek'st not
Social communication, yet so pleased,
Canst raise thy creature to what highth thou wilt   430
Of union or communion, deified;
I by conversing cannot these erect
From prone, nor in their ways complacence find.'
Thus I emboldened spake, and freedom used
Permissive, and acceptance found, which gained   435
This answer from the gracious Voice Divine:
    " 'Thus far to try thee, Adam, I was pleased,
And find thee knowing not of beasts alone,
Which thou hast rightly named, but of thyself,
Expressing well the spirit within thee free,   440
My image, not imparted to the brute,
Whose fellowship therefore unmeet for thee
Good reason was thou freely shouldst dislike,
And be so minded still. I, ere thou spak'st,
Knew it not good for man to be alone,   445
And no such company as then thou saw'st
Intended thee, for trial only brought,
To see how thou couldst judge of fit and meet.
What next I bring shall please thee, be assured,
Thy likeness, thy fit help, thy other self,   450
Thy wish exactly to thy heart's desire.'
    "He ended, or I heard no more; for now
My earthly by his heav'nly overpowered,
Which it had long stood under, strained to the highth
In that celestial colloquy sublime,   455
As with an object that excels the sense,
Dazzled and spent, sunk down and sought repair
Of sleep, which instantly fell on me, called
By Nature as in aid, and closed mine eyes.
Mine eyes he closed, but open left the cell   460
Of fancy, my internal sight, by which
Abstract as in a trance methought I saw,

419–21. Cf. Milton, *C.D.* 1.5; Aristotle, *Eudemian Ethics* 1244b, 1245b.
421. numbers: parts (Latinism).
423. single imperfection: imperfection in being single.
427–28. alone . . . accompanied: an echo of Cicero's famous phrase, "never less alone than when alone" (*De Offic.* 3.1.1; *Rep.* 1.17.27)?
445. Gen. 2.18.
452 f. Gen. 2.21–22.
462. Abstract: withdrawn.

Though sleeping, where I lay, and saw the Shape
Still glorious before whom awake I stood;
Who stooping opened my left side, and took   465
From thence a rib, with cordial spirits warm,
And life-blood streaming fresh; wide was the wound,
But suddenly with flesh filled up and healed.
The rib he formed and fashioned with his hands;
Under his forming hands a creature grew,   470
Man-like, but different sex, so lovely fair
That what seemed fair in all the world seemed now
Mean, or in her summed up, in her contained
And in her looks, which from that time infused
Sweetness into my heart, unfelt before,   475
And into all things from her air inspired
The spirit of love and amorous delight.
She disappeared, and left me dark; I waked
To find her, or for ever to deplore
Her loss, and other pleasures all abjure: 480
When out of hope, behold her, not far off,
Such as I saw her in my dream, adorned
With what all earth or heaven could bestow
To make her amiable. On she came,
Led by her heav'nly Maker, though unseen,   485
And guided by his voice, nor uninformed
Of nuptial sanctity and marriage rites.
Grace was in all her steps, heav'n in her eye.
In every gesture dignity and love.
I overjoyed could not forbear aloud: 490
    " 'This turn hath made amends; thou hast fulfilled
Thy words, Creator bounteous and benign,
Giver of all things fair, but fairest this
Of all thy gifts, nor enviest. I now see
Bone of my bone, flesh of my flesh, my self   495
Before me. Woman is her name, of man
Extracted; for this cause he shall forgo
Father and mother, and to his wife adhere;
And they shall be one flesh, one heart, one soul.'
    "She heard me thus; and though divinely brought,   500
Yet innocence and virgin modesty,
Her virtue and the conscience of her worth,
That would be wooed, and not unsought be won,
Not obvious, not obtrusive, but retired,
The more desirable; or to say all,   505
Nature herself, though pure of sinful thought,
Wrought in her so, that seeing me, she turned;
I followed her; she what was honor knew,
And with obsequious majesty approved

---

466. cordial spirits: i.e. the vital spirits of   504. obvious: bold, forward.
the heart (see note on 5.482–87).   504–05. Cf. 4.309–11.
494–99. Gen. 2.23–24.   508. honor: Heb. 13.4.

My pleaded reason. To the nuptial bow'r   510
I led her blushing like the morn; all heav'n
And happy constellations on that hour
Shed their selectest influence; the earth
Gave sign of gratulation, and each hill;
Joyous the birds; fresh gales and gentle airs   515
Whispered it to the woods, and from their wings
Flung rose, flung odors from the spicy shrub,
Disporting, till the amorous bird of night
Sung spousal, and bid haste the ev'ning star
On his hill top, to light the bridal lamp.   520
　　"Thus I have told thee all my state, and brought
My story to the sum of earthly bliss
Which I enjoy, and must confess to find
In all things else delight indeed, but such
As used or not, works in the mind no change,   525
Nor vehement desire, these delicacies
I mean of taste, sight, smell, herbs, fruits, and flow'rs,
Walks, and the melody of birds; but here
Far otherwise, transported I behold,
Transported touch; here passion first I felt,   530
Commotion strange, in all enjoyments else
Superior and unmoved, here only weak
Against the charm of beauty's powerful glance.
Or Nature failed in me, and left some part
Not proof enough such object to sustain,   535
Or from my side subducting, took perhaps
More than enough; at least on her bestowed
Too much of ornament, in outward show
Elaborate, of inward less exact.
For well I understand in the prime end   540
Of Nature her th' inferior, in the mind
And inward faculties, which most excel;
In outward also her resembling less
His image who made both, and less expressing
The character of that dominion giv'n   545
O'er other creatures; yet when I approach
Her loveliness, so absolute she seems
And in herself complete, so well to know
Her own, that what she wills to do or say
Seems wisest, virtuousest, discreetest, best;   550
All higher knowledge in her presence falls

518. bird: nightingale (cf. 5.40–41).
519. star: Venus.
521–59. Adam's speech, which contains the seeds of catastrophe to come, is made a subtle revelation of mixed feelings, both right and wrong, which rises steadily to an impassioned climax. The uniquely disturbing force of love it is natural and right to feel, but an excess (even though passion is blended with reverence) leads Adam to ask if God left a flaw in him, to abdicate his proper place in the chain of being, and above all to let his love become idolatry, so that Eve's power over him is stronger than his own conscience and his relation to God. This second part of book 8 is closely bound up with the astronomical part: neither intellectual pride nor human love should come between man and God — or man and his integrity.
547. absolute: perfect.

Degraded, wisdom in discourse with her
Loses discount'nanced, and like folly shows;
Authority and reason on her wait,
As one intended first, not after made   555
Occasionally; and to consummate all,
Greatness of mind and nobleness their seat
Build in her loveliest, and create an awe
About her, as a guard angelic placed."
    To whom the Angel with contracted brow: 560
"Accuse not Nature, she hath done her part;
Do thou but thine, and be not diffident
Of wisdom; she deserts thee not, if thou
Dismiss not her, when most thou need'st her nigh,
By áttributing overmuch to things   565
Less excellent, as thou thyself perceiv'st.
For what admir'st thou, what transports thee so,
An outside? Fair no doubt, and worthy well
Thy cherishing, thy honoring, and thy love,
Not thy subjection. Weigh with her thyself;   570
Then value. Ofttimes nothing profits more
Than self-esteem, grounded on just and right
Well managed; of that skill the more thou know'st,
The more she will acknowledge thee her head,
And to realities yield all her shows: 575
Made so adorn for thy delight the more,
So awful, that with honor thou may'st love
Thy mate, who sees when thou art seen least wise.
But if the sense of touch whereby mankind
Is propagated seem such dear delight   580
Beyond all other, think the same vouchsafed
To cattle and each beast; which would not be
To them made common and divulged, if aught
Therein enjoyed were worthy to subdue
The soul of man, or passion in him move.   585
What higher in her society thou find'st
Attractive, human, rational, love still;
In loving thou dost well, in passion not,
Wherein true love consists not; love refines
The thoughts, and heart enlarges, hath his seat   590
In reason, and is judicious, is the scale
By which to heav'nly love thou may'st ascend,
Not sunk in carnal pleasure, for which cause
Among the beasts no mate for thee was found."
    To whom thus half abashed Adam replied: 595
"Neither her outside formed so fair, nor aught
In procreation common to all kinds

556. Occasionally: for a special purpose.
574. head: cf. 4.443 and note.
579 f. In 4.741 f. Milton went out of his
way to celebrate physical union and he is not
repudiating that here; the two passages are
complementary.

589–92. The lines have an evident Platonic
coloring.
596 f. Though Adam now expresses a cor-
rected view, he has revealed his instinctive
weakness.

(Though higher of the genial bed by far,
And with mysterious reverence I deem),
So much delights me as those graceful acts,
Those thousand decencies that daily flow
From all her words and actions, mixed with love
And sweet compliance, which declare unfeigned
Union of mind, or in us both one soul;
Harmony to behold in wedded pair   605
More grateful than harmonious sound to the ear.
Yet these subject not; I to thee disclose
What inward thence I feel, not therefore foiled,
Who meet with various objects, from the sense
Variously representing; yet still free,   610
Approve the best, and follow what I approve.
To love thou blam'st me not, for love thou say'st
Leads up to heav'n, is both the way and guide;
Bear with me then, if lawful what I ask:
Love not the heav'nly Spirits, and how their love   615
Express they, by looks only, or do they mix
Irradiance, virtual or immediate touch?"
    To whom the Angel, with a smile that glowed
Celestial rosy red, love's proper hue,
Answered: "Let it suffice thee that thou know'st   620
Us happy, and without love no happiness.
Whatever pure thou in the body enjoy'st
(And pure thou wert created) we enjoy
In eminence, and obstacle find none
Of membrane, joint, or limb, exclusive bars;   625
Easier than air with air, if Spirits embrace,
Total they mix, union of pure with pure
Desiring; nor restrained conveyance need
As flesh to mix with flesh, or soul with soul.
But I can now no more; the parting sun   630
Beyond the earth's green Cape and verdant Isles
Hesperian sets, my signal to depart.
Be strong, live happy, and love, but first of all
Him whom to love is to obey, and keep
His great command; take heed lest passion sway   635
Thy judgment to do aught which else free will
Would not admit; thine and of all thy sons
The weal or woe in thee is placed; beware.
I in thy persevering shall rejoice,
And all the blest. Stand fast; to stand or fall   640
Free in thine own arbitrement it lies.
Perfect within, no outward aid require;
And all temptation to transgress repel."

610–11. Adam's later behavior makes him unconsciously ironical in echoing, with a difference, Medea's words, "I see and approve the better and follow the worse" (Ovid, *Met.* 7.20–21).
615–29. Milton here goes beyond traditional angelology and approaches the amatory "ecstasies" of Renaissance Platonism.
631. green Cape and verdant Isles: Cape Verde and Cape Verde Islands.
634–35. 1 John 5.3.

So saying, he arose; whom Adam thus
Followed with benediction: "Since to part,   645
Go, heavenly guest, ethereal messenger,
Sent from whose sovran goodness I adore.
Gentle to me and affable hath been
Thy condescension, and shall be honored ever
With grateful memory; thou to mankind   650
Be good and friendly still, and oft return."
    So parted they, the Angel up to heav'n
From the thick shade, and Adam to his bow'r.

Book IX

THE ARGUMENT

Satan, having compassed the earth, with meditated guile returns as a mist by
night into Paradise; enters into the serpent sleeping. Adam and Eve in the
morning go forth to their labors, which Eve proposes to divide in several
places, each laboring apart: Adam consents not, alleging the danger lest that
enemy, of whom they were forewarned, should attempt her found alone. Eve,
loth to be thought not circumspect or firm enough, urges her going apart, the
rather desirous to make trial of her strength; Adam at last yields. The Serpent
finds her alone: his subtle approach, first gazing, then speaking, with much flattery extolling Eve above all other creatures. Eve, wondering to hear the Serpent
speak, asks how he attained to human speech and such understanding, not till
now; the Serpent answers that by tasting of a certain tree in the garden he
attained both to speech and reason, till then void of both. Eve requires him to
bring her to that tree, and finds it to be the Tree of Knowledge forbidden. The
Serpent, now grown bolder, with many wiles and arguments induces her at
length to eat; she, pleased with the taste, deliberates a while whether to impart thereof to Adam or not; at last brings him of the fruit; relates what persuaded her to eat thereof. Adam, at first amazed, but perceiving her lost,
resolves through vehemence of love to perish with her, and, extenuating the
trespass, eats also of the fruit. The effects thereof in them both; they seek to
cover their nakedness; then fall to variance and accusation of one another.

NO MORE of talk where God or angel guest
With man, as with his friend, familiar used
To sit indulgent, and with him partake
Rural repast, permitting him the while
Venial discourse unblamed. I now must change   5

647. whose: him whose.
651. Be good: cf. Virgil, *Ecl.* 5.65; *Lycidas*
184.
BOOK IX. 1–5. Milton may have widened
the single fact of Raphael's visit as closing a
phase in man's relations with heaven, or he

may be loosely including the colloquy in
8.295 f., or he may be imagining similar occa-
sions not narrated (as in 9.1080–82 and
11.320–23).
2. as . . . friend: cf. 5.229 and note.
5. Venial: permitted by God.

Those notes to tragic; foul distrust, and breach
Disloyal on the part of man, revolt,
And disobedience; on the part of Heav'n
Now alienated, distance and distaste,
Anger and just rebuke, and judgment giv'n,   10
That brought into this world a world of woe,
Sin and her shadow Death, and misery,
Death's harbinger. Sad task, yet argument
Not less but more heroic than the wrath
Of stern Achilles on his foe pursued   15
Thrice fugitive about Troy wall; or rage
Of Turnus for Lavinia disespoused;
Or Neptune's ire or Juno's, that so long
Perplexed the Greek and Cytherea's son;
If answerable style I can obtain   20
Of my celestial patroness, who deigns
Her nightly visitation unimplored,
And dictates to me slumb'ring, or inspires
Easy my unpremeditated verse,
Since first this subject for heroic song   25
Pleased me long choosing, and beginning late;
Not sedulous by nature to indite
Wars, hitherto the only argument
Heroic deemed, chief mast'ry to dissect
With long and tedious havoc fabled knights   30
In battles feigned (the better fortitude
Of patience and heroic martyrdom
Unsung), or to describe races and games,
Or tilting furniture, emblazoned shields,
Impresses quaint, caparisons and steeds,   35
Bases and tinsel trappings, gorgeous knights
At joust and tournament; then marshaled feast
Served up in hall with sewers and seneschals;
The skill of artifice or office mean,
Not that which justly gives heroic name   40
To person or to poem. Me of these

9–11. distaste . . . woe: cf. 1.2–3, "taste . . . woe."

14–16. The *Iliad*.

15. foe: Hector.

17. Turnus: the defender of Italy and lover of Lavinia, daughter of the king of Latium; he lost both Lavinia and his life to Aeneas.

19. the Greek: Odysseus, who suffered from the wrath of Poseidon. Cytherea's son: Aeneas, Venus' son, pursued by the anger of Juno.

21. patroness: Urania (glossary; cf. 1.1 f., 7.1 f.).

22–24. For Milton's nocturnal composition cf. 3.32 f., 7.28–30.

25–26. See the headnote.

33. races and games. See the note on 2.521–628.

34 f. The large chivalric elements in Ariosto, Tasso, Spenser, et al. The younger Milton had seen more in romance than he allows in the present context (see the note below on 40–43); cf. *Il Penseroso* 109–20, *Apology for Smectymnuus* (quoted early in this volume) and "our sage and serious poet Spenser" (*Areopagitica, Works*, 4, 311).

34. tilting furniture: equipment for tournaments.

35. Impresses: *imprese,* devices on shields.

36. Bases: housings for horses. tinsel trappings: in Spenser, *F.Q.* 3.1.15.7.

38. sewers and seneschals: waiters and stewards.

40–43. Milton's conception of true heroism is given in 12.557 f., his conception of truly heroic poetry in the invocations and in the personal passage in the *Reason of Church Government* (quoted in this volume).

Nor skilled nor studious, higher argument
Remains, sufficient of itself to raise
That name, unless an age too late, or cold
Climate, or years damp my intended wing   45
Depressed, and much they may, if all be mine,
Not hers who brings it nightly to my ear.
    The sun was sunk, and after him the star
Of Hesperus, whose office is to bring
Twilight upon the earth, short arbiter   50
'Twixt day and night, and now from end to end
Night's hemisphere had veiled the horizon round,
When Satan, who late fled before the threats
Of Gabriel out of Eden, now improved
In meditated fraud and malice, bent   55
On man's destruction, maugre what might hap
Of heavier on himself, fearless returned.
By night he fled, and at midnight returned
From compassing the earth, cautious of day,
Since Uriel, regent of the sun, descried   60
His entrance, and forewarned the Cherubim
That kept their watch; thence full of anguish driv'n,
The space of seven continued nights he rode
With darkness, thrice the equinoctial line
He circled, four times crossed the car of Night   65
From pole to pole, traversing each colure;
On the eighth returned, and on the coast averse
From entrance or Cherubic watch, by stealth
Found unsuspected way. There was a place —
Now not, though sin, not time, first wrought the change —   70
Where Tigris at the foot of Paradise
Into a gulf shot under ground, till part
Rose up a fountain by the Tree of Life;
In with the river sunk, and with it rose
Satan, involved in rising mist, then sought   75
Where to lie hid; sea he had searched and land
From Eden over Pontus, and the pool
Maeotis, up beyond the river Ob;
Downward as far antarctic; and in length
West from Orontes to the ocean barred   80
At Darien, thence to the land where flows

---

44. age too late: perhaps an allusion to general deterioration (see the headnote to *Naturam non pati senium*), or only a misgiving about the epic, even Milton's kind of epic, as belonging to an earlier age.

44–45. The traditional idea that northern climates were unfavorable to creative genius Milton alluded to in *Mansus* 28, the *Reason of Church Government* (above; *Works*, 3, 237), *Areopagitica* (ibid., 4, 296), and *History of Britain* (ibid., 10, 325).

45. wing: cf. 1.14–15, 3.13, 7.3–4.

53–54. See the end of book 4.

59. compassing the earth: Job 1.7.

60–62. Cf. 4.555 f.

64. equinoctial line: the sun's path, supposed to have been, before the fall, in the same plane as the earth's equator.

65. Night: glossary.

66. colure: one of two circles drawn from the poles through the equinoctial and solstitial points of the ecliptic.

71–73. Cf. 4.223 f.

78. Maeotis: sea of Azof.   Ob: Siberian river.

81. Darien: Isthmus of Panama.

Ganges and Indus. Thus the orb he roamed
With narrow search, and with inspection deep
Considered every creature, which of all
Most opportune might serve his wiles, and found   85
The serpent subtlest beast of all the field.
Him after long debate, irresolute
Of thoughts revolved, his final sentence chose
Fit vessel, fittest imp of fraud, in whom
To enter, and his dark suggestions hide   90
From sharpest sight; for in the wily snake,
Whatever sleights none would suspicious mark,
As from his wit and native subtlety
Proceeding, which, in other beasts observed,
Doubt might beget of diabolic pow'r   95
Active within beyond the sense of brute.
Thus he resolved, but first from inward grief
His bursting passion into plaints thus poured:
   "O earth, how like to heav'n, if not preferred
More justly, seat worthier of gods, as built   100
With second thoughts, reforming what was old!
For what God after better worse would build?
Terrestrial heav'n, danced round by other heav'ns
That shine, yet bear their bright officious lamps,
Light above light, for thee alone, as seems,   105
In thee concentring all their precious beams
Of sacred influence! As God in heav'n
Is center, yet extends to all, so thou
Centring receiv'st from all those orbs; in thee,
Not in themselves, all their known virtue appears   110
Productive in herb, plant, and nobler birth
Of creatures animate with gradual life
Of growth, sense, reason, all summed up in man.
With what delight could I have walked thee round,
If I could joy in aught, sweet interchange   115
Of hill and valley, rivers, woods, and plains,
Now land, now sea, and shores with forest crowned,
Rocks, dens, and caves; but I in none of these
Find place or refuge; and the more I see
Pleasures about me, so much more I feel   120
Torment within me, as from the hateful siege
Of contraries; all good to me becomes
Bane, and in heav'n much worse would be my state.
But neither here seek I, no nor in heav'n
To dwell, unless by mast'ring heav'n's Supreme;   125

86. Gen 3.1 (where the tempter is the serpent, not Satan in the serpent).
89. imp: offspring.
91–94. Cf. 4.347–50.
95. Doubt: suspicion.
99–178. Cf. this midnight soliloquy and that addressed to the sun in 4.32 f.

103–09. Cf. 8.15–38.
103. danced. See notes on 3.580 and 5.620–27.
109–13. Cf. 8.90–99.
113. growth, sense, reason. See note on 5.482–87.
121. siege: conflict? seat?

Nor hope to be myself less miserable
By what I seek, but others to make such
As I, though thereby worse to me redound.
For only in destroying I find ease
To my relentless thoughts; and him destroyed,   130
Or won to what may work his utter loss,
For whom all this was made, all this will soon
Follow, as to him linked in weal or woe;
In woe then, that destruction wide may range.
To me shall be the glory sole among   135
The infernal Powers, in one day to have marred
What he, Almighty styled, six nights and days
Continued making, and who knows how long
Before had been contriving? Though perhaps
Not longer than since I in one night freed   140
From servitude inglorious well-nigh half
Th' angelic name, and thinner left the throng
Of his adorers. He to be avenged,
And to repair his numbers thus impaired,
Whether such virtue spent of old now failed   145
More angels to create, if they at least
Are his created, or to spite us more,
Determined to advance into our room
A creature formed of earth, and him endow,
Exalted from so base original,   150
With heav'nly spoils, our spoils. What he decreed
He effected; man he made, and for him built
Magnificent this world, and earth his seat,
Him lord pronounced, and, O indignity!
Subjected to his service angel wings,   155
And flaming ministers to watch and tend
Their earthy charge. Of these the vigilance
I dread, and to elude, thus wrapped in mist
Of midnight vapor glide obscure, and pry
In every bush and brake, where hap may find   160
The serpent sleeping, in whose mazy folds
To hide me, and the dark intent I bring.
O foul descent! that I who erst contended
With Gods to sit the highest, am now constrained
Into a beast, and mixed with bestial slime,   165
This essence to incarnate and imbrute,
That to the height of deity aspired;
But what will not ambition and revenge
Descend to? Who aspires must down as low
As high he soared, obnoxious first or last   170
To basest things. Revenge, at first though sweet,
Bitter ere long back on itself recoils;

141. well-nigh half: cf. 2.692, 5.710, 6.156.   155–57. Ps. 104.4, 91.11.
146–47. if . . . created: cf. 4.43–44,   166. incarnate. Cf. 3.315, "Here shalt thou
5.853 f.   sit incarnate."

Let it; I reck not, so it light well aimed,
Since higher I fall short, on him who next
Provokes my envy, this new favorite   175
Of Heav'n, this man of clay, son of despite,
Whom us the more to spite his Maker raised
From dust: spite then with spite is best repaid."
    So saying, through each thicket dank or dry,
Like a black mist low creeping, he held on   180
His midnight search, where soonest he might find
The serpent. Him fast sleeping soon he found
In labyrinth of many a round self-rolled,
His head the midst, well stored with subtle wiles;
Not yet in horrid shade or dismal den,   185
Nor nocent yet, but on the grassy herb
Fearless, unfeared, he slept. In at his mouth
The Devil entered, and his brutal sense,
In heart or head, possessing soon inspired
With act intelligential, but his sleep   190
Disturbed not, waiting close th' approach of morn.
    Now whenas sacred light began to dawn
In Eden on the humid flow'rs, that breathed
Their morning incense, when all things that breathe
From th' earth's great altar send up silent praise   195
To the Creator, and his nostrils fill
With grateful smell, forth came the human pair
And joined their vocal worship to the quire
Of creatures wanting voice; that done, partake
The season, prime for sweetest scents and airs;   200
Then cómmune how that day they best may ply
Their growing work; for much their work outgrew
The hands' dispatch of two gard'ning so wide.
And Eve first to her husband thus began:
    "Adam, well may we labor still to dress   205
This garden, still to tend plant, herb, and flow'r,
Our pleasant task enjoined, but till more hands
Aid us, the work under our labor grows,
Luxurious by restraint; what we by day
Lop overgrown, or prune, or prop, or bind,   210
One night or two with wanton growth derides,
Tending to wild. Thou therefore now advise
Or hear what to my mind first thoughts present:

---

178. Cf. Aeschylus, *Prometheus Bound* 970.
186. nocent: harmful.
187–91. Keats commented: "Whose spirit does not ache at the smothering and confinement — the unwilling stillness — the 'waiting close'? Whose head is not dizzy at the possible speculations of Satan in the serpent prison? No passage of poetry ever can give a greater pain of suffocation." (*Complete Works*, ed. H. B. Forman, 3, 265).
192. sacred light. Cf. 3.1–6, 9.107.

194–99. Cf. 5.153–208.
196–97. Gen. 8.21.
199–200. partake The season: enjoy the morning.
205–25. In this speech, which opens the close-up drama of the fall, Eve, though aiming at efficiency, is unduly asserting herself, putting her work above right relations with her husband, and — as he points out (235 f.) — above God's ordinance.

Let us divide our labors, thou where choice
Leads thee, or where most needs, whether to wind   215
The woodbine round this arbor, or direct
The clasping ivy where to climb, while I
In yonder spring of roses intermixed
With myrtle, find what to redress till noon.
For while so near each other thus all day   220
Our task we choose, what wonder if so near
Looks intervene and smiles, or object new
Casual discourse draw on, which intermits
Our day's work, brought to little, though begun
Early, and th' hour of supper comes unearned."   225
    To whom mild answer Adam thus returned:
"Sole Eve, associate sole, to me beyond
Compare above all living creatures dear,
Well hast thou motioned, well thy thoughts employed
How we might best fulfill the work which here   230
God hath assigned us, nor of me shalt pass
Unpraised; for nothing lovelier can be found
In woman, than to study household good,
And good works in her husband to promote.
Yet not so strictly hath our Lord imposed   235
Labor, as to debar us when we need
Refreshment, whether food, or talk between,
Food of the mind, or this sweet intercourse
Of looks and smiles, for smiles from reason flow,
To brute denied, and are of love the food,   240
Love not the lowest end of human life.
For not to irksome toil, but to delight
He made us, and delight to reason joined.
These paths and bowers doubt not but our joint hands
Will keep from wilderness with ease, as wide   245
As we need walk, till younger hands ere long
Assist us. But if much convérse perhaps
Thee satiate, to short absence I could yield.
For solitude sometimes is best society,
And short retirement urges sweet return.   250
But other doubt possesses me, lest harm
Befall thee severed from me; for thou know'st
What hath been warned us, what malicious foe,
Envying our happiness, and of his own
Despairing, seeks to work us woe and shame   255
By sly assault; and somewhere nigh at hand
Watches, no doubt, with greedy hope to find
His wish and best advantage, us asunder,
Hopeless to circumvent us joined, where each
To other speedy aid might lend at need;   260
Whether his first design be to withdraw

218. spring: clump.   239–43. Cf. 8.586 f.
227. Sole . . . sole: cf. 4.411.   249. See the note on 8.427–28.
232–34. Prov. 31.10–31.

Our fealty from God, or to disturb
Conjugal love, than which perhaps no bliss
Enjoyed by us excites his envy more;
Or this, or worse, leave not the faithful side   265
That gave thee being, still shades thee and protects.
The wife, where danger or dishonor lurks,
Safest and seemliest by her husband stays,
Who guards her, or with her the worst endures.'
    To whom the virgin majesty of Eve,   270
As one who loves, and some unkindness meets,
With sweet austere composure thus replied:
    "Offspring of heav'n and earth, and all earth's lord,
That such an enemy we have, who seeks
Our ruin, both by thee informed I learn,   275
And from the parting angel overheard
As in a shady nook I stood behind,
Just then returned at shut of evening flow'rs.
But that thou shouldst my firmness therefore doubt
To God or thee, because we have a foe   280
May tempt it, I expected not to hear.
His violence thou fear'st not, being such
As we, not capable of death or pain,
Can either not receive, or can repel.
His fraud is then thy fear, which plain infers   285
Thy equal fear that my firm faith and love
Can by his fraud be shaken or seduced;
Thoughts, which how found they harbor in thy breast,
Adam, misthought of her to thee so dear?"
    To whom with healing words Adam replied: 290
"Daughter of God and man, immortal Eve,
For such thou art, from sin and blame entire;
Not diffident of thee do I dissuade
Thy absence from my sight, but to avoid
Th' attempt itself, intended by our foe.   295
For he who tempts, though in vain, at least asperses
The tempted with dishonor foul, supposed
Not incorruptible of faith, not proof
Against temptation. Thou thyself with scorn
And anger wouldst resent the offered wrong,   300
Though ineffectual found. Misdeem not then,
If such affront I labor to avert
From thee alone, which on us both at once
The enemy, though bold, will hardly dare,
Or daring, first on me th' assault shall light.   305
Nor thou his malice and false guile contemn;
Subtle he needs must be, who could seduce
Angels, nor think superfluous others' aid.

265. Or this: whether this be his design.
270. virgin: innocent.
276. See 8.633–43.
279–81. This note of shrillness may be said
to mark the beginning of the dramatic process
which brings Eve and Adam down from the
majestic speech and behavior of their innocence
to the merely human level.
    292. entire: free, untouched.

I from the influence of thy looks receive
Access in every virtue, in thy sight   310
More wise, more watchful, stronger, if need were
Of outward strength; while shame, thou looking on,
Shame to be overcome or overreached,
Would utmost vigor raise, and raised unite.
Why shouldst not thou like sense within thee feel   315
When I am present, and thy trial choose
With me, best witness of thy virtue tried?"
  So spake domestic Adam in his care
And matrimonial love; but Eve, who thought
Less attribúted to her faith sincere,   320
Thus her reply with accent sweet renewed:
  "If this be our condition, thus to dwell
In narrow circuit straitened by a foe,
Subtle or violent, we not endued
Single with like defense, wherever met,   325
How are we happy, still in fear of harm?
But harm precedes not sin: only our foe
Tempting affronts us with his foul esteem
Of our integrity; his foul esteem
Sticks no dishonor on our front, but turns   330
Foul on himself; then wherefore shunned or feared
By us? Who rather double honor gain
From his surmise proved false, find peace within,
Favor from Heav'n, our witness, from th' event.
And what is faith, love, virtue, unassayed   335
Alone, without exterior help sustained?
Let us not then suspect our happy state
Left so imperfect by the Maker wise
As not secure to single or combined.
Frail is our happiness, if this be so,   340
And Eden were no Eden thus exposed."
  To whom thus Adam fervently replied:
"O woman, best are all things as the will
Of God ordained them; his creating hand
Nothing imperfect or deficient left   345
Of all that he created, much less man,
Or aught that might his happy state secure,
Secure from outward force: within himself

309–14. These sentiments, though right enough in themselves, recall Adam's avowal in 8.521–59, and the epithet "domestic" (318) suggests a trace of weakness.
310. Access: accession, increase.
320. Less: too little (as with the Latin comparative).
335–36. "Of what value are faith, etc., if their unaided strength is not tested?" Some critics have found in Eve's speech the spirit of *Areopagitica*, but Milton would distinguish between her courting temptation while still in the state of innocence and meeting it in the fallen world. She is increasingly self-assertive and presumptuous, as Adam's next lines show.
339. Safe singly or together.
341. See note on 4.27–28.
343. Adam abandons ceremonial address.
348 f. Milton's central ethical principle, passionately held (cf. 3.98 f., 5.233 f., 520 f., 8.640–43; *C.D.* 1.3–4), and, in *P.L.* and the other late works, more strongly linked with obedience to God's will.

The danger lies, yet lies within his power;
Against his will he can receive no harm. 350
But God left free the will, for what obeys
Reason is free, and reason he made right,
But bid her well beware, and still erect,
Lest by some fair appearing good surprised
She dictate false, and misinform the will 355
To do what God expressly hath forbid.
Not then mistrust, but tender love enjoins,
That I should mind thee oft, and mind thou me.
Firm we subsist, yet possible to swerve,
Since reason not impossibly may meet 360
Some specious object by the foe suborned,
And fall into deception unaware,
Not keeping strictest watch, as she was warned.
Seek not temptation then, which to avoid
Were better, and most likely if from me 365
Thou sever not; trial will come unsought.
Wouldst thou approve thy constancy, approve
First thy obedience; th' other who can know,
Not seeing thee attempted, who attest?
But if thou think trial unsought may find 370
Us both securer than thus warned thou seem'st,
Go; for thy stay, not free, absents thee more;
Go in thy native innocence, rely
On what thou hast of virtue, summon all,
For God towards thee hath done his part, do thine." 375
    So spake the patriarch of mankind, but Eve
Persisted; yet submiss, though last, replied:
    "With thy permission then, and thus forewarned,
Chiefly by what thy own last reasoning words
Touched only, that our trial, when least sought, 380
May find us both perhaps far less prepared,
The willinger I go, nor much expect
A foe so proud will first the weaker seek;
So bent, the more shall shame him his repulse."
Thus saying, from her husband's hand her hand 385
Soft she withdrew, and like a wood-nymph light,
Oread or Dryad, or of Delia's train,
Betook her to the groves, but Delia's self
In gait surpassed and goddess-like deport,
Though not as she with bow and quiver armed, 390

350. A Socratic doctrine (cf. *Comus* 663).
352. Glossary, "right reason."
353. still erect: (be) always alert.
354–56. Adam's fear is to be exactly fulfilled. Cf. Hooker (1.7.7), who goes on to cite Eve: "For there was never sin committed, wherein a less good was not preferred before a greater, and that wilfully; which cannot be done without the singular disgrace of Nature, and the utter disturbance of that divine order, whereby the pre-eminence of chiefest acceptation is by the best things worthily challenged."
358. mind: remind, have in mind.
367. approve: prove.
371. securer: less on guard.
385. hand: cf. note on 4.321.
386. light. The word suggests spiritual unawareness as well as physical grace.
389. deport: deportment.

But with such gard'ning tools as art yet rude,
Guiltless of fire had formed, or angels brought.
To Pales, or Pomona, thus adorned,
Likest she seemed, Pomona when she fled
Vertumnus, or to Ceres in her prime,   395
Yet virgin of Proserpina from Jove.
Her long with ardent look his eye pursued
Delighted, but desiring more her stay.
Oft he to her his charge of quick return
Repeated, she to him as oft engaged   400
To be returned by noon amid the bow'r,
And all things in best order to invite
Noontide repast, or afternoon's repose.
O much deceived, much failing, hapless Eve,
Of thy presumed return! event perverse!   405
Thou never from that hour in Paradise
Found'st either sweet repast or sound repose;
Such ambush hid among sweet flow'rs and shades
Waited with hellish rancor imminent
To intercept thy way, or send thee back   410
Despoiled of innocence, of faith, of bliss.
For now, and since first break of dawn the Fiend,
Mere serpent in appearance, forth was come,
And on his quest, where likeliest he might find
The only two of mankind, but in them   415
The whole included race, his purposed prey.
In bow'r and field he sought, where any tuft
Of grove or garden-plot more pleasant lay,
Their tendance or plantation for delight;
By fountain or by shady rivulet   420
He sought them both, but wished his hap might find
Eve separate; he wished, but not with hope
Of what so seldom chanced, when to his wish,
Beyond his hope, Eve separate he spies,
Veiled in a cloud of fragrance, where she stood,   425
Half spied, so thick the roses bushing round
About her glowed, oft stooping to support
Each flow'r of slender stalk, whose head though gay
Carnation, purple, azure, or specked with gold,
Hung drooping unsustained; them she upstays   430
Gently with myrtle band, mindless the while,
Herself, though fairest unsupported flow'r,
From her best prop so far, and storm so nigh.
Nearer he drew, and many a walk traversed
Of stateliest covert, cedar, pine, or palm,   435

394. Ed. 1, Likest; ed. 2, Likeliest. The latter word could have the same meaning.

395. Vertumnus: Roman god of seasons and gardens, lover of Pomona (Ovid, *Met.* 14.623 f.).

413. Mere. Milton may be only saying that the serpent showed no outward sign of being possessed by Satan, or he may be rejecting an old idea that the serpent had a human or angelic face.

425–33. An overt and deeply compassionate variation on the pattern of the simile in 4.268 f.

Then voluble and bold, now hid, now seen
Among thick-woven arborets and flow'rs
Imbordered on each bank, the hand of Eve:
Spot more delicious than those gardens feigned
Or of revived Adonis, or renowned   440
Alcinous, host of old Laertes' son,
Or that, not mystic, where the sapient king
Held dalliance with his fair Egyptian spouse.
Much he the place admired, the person more.
As one who long in populous city pent,   445
Where houses thick and sewers annoy the air,
Forth issuing on a summer's morn to breathe
Among the pleasant villages and farms
Adjoined, from each thing met conceives delight,
The smell of grain, or tedded grass, or kine,   450
Or dairy, each rural sight, each rural sound;
If chance with nymph-like step fair virgin pass,
What pleasing seemed, for her now pleases more,
She most, and in her look sums all delight:
Such pleasure took the Serpent to behold   455
This flow'ry plat, the sweet recess of Eve
Thus early, thus alone; her heav'nly form
Angelic, but more soft and feminine,
Her graceful innocence, her every air
Of gesture or least action overawed   460
His malice, and with rapine sweet bereaved
His fierceness of the fierce intent it brought.
That space the Evil One abstracted stood
From his own evil, and for the time remained
Stupidly good, of enmity disarmed,   465
Of guile, of hate, of envy, of revenge;
But the hot hell that always in him burns,
Though in mid-heav'n, soon ended his delight,
And tortures him now more, the more he sees
Of pleasure not for him ordained; then soon   470
Fierce hate he recollects, and all his thoughts
Of mischief, gratulating, thus excites:
    "Thoughts, whither have ye led me, with what sweet
Compulsion thus transported to forget
What hither brought us? Hate, not love, nor hope   475
Of Paradise for hell, hope here to taste

---

436. voluble: rolling.
437. arborets: small trees, shrubs.
438. hand: handiwork.
441. Laertes' son: Odysseus.
442. not mystic. The normal meaning of
the word was "secret," "allegorical," but the
context — and Milton's habit of distinguishing
pagan fiction from scriptural truth — seem to
require the slightly later sense of "mythical";
i.e. the garden of Solomon was biblical, authentic. It would be odd if Milton denied allegorical meaning to the most famous of all religious
allegories, the Song of Songs, which he had
taken to be such in *Tetrachordon* (*Works*, 4,
86). king: Solomon, who married an
Egyptian princess (1 Kings 3.1; Song of Solomon).
450. tedded: spread out to dry.
453. for: because of.
465. Stupidly good. Incapable of any positive good, Satan is for the moment stupefied,
impotent.
467. Cf. 1.254–55, 4.20–23, 75.

Of pleasure, but all pleasure to destroy,
Save what is in destroying; other joy
To me is lost. Then let me not let pass
Occasion which now smiles: behold alone   480
The woman, opportune to all attempts,
Her husband, for I view far round, not nigh,
Whose higher intellectual more I shun,
And strength, of courage haughty, and of limb
Heroic built, though of terrestrial mold,   485
Foe not informidable, exempt from wound,
I not; so much hath hell debased, and pain
Enfeebled me, to what I was in heav'n.
She fair, divinely fair, fit love for gods,
Not terrible, though terror be in love   490
And beauty, not approached by stronger hate,
Hate stronger, under show of love well feigned,
The way which to her ruin now I tend."
    So spake the Enemy of mankind, enclosed
In serpent, inmate bad, and toward Eve   495
Addressed his way, not with indented wave,
Prone on the ground, as since, but on his rear,
Circular base of rising folds, that tow'red
Fold above fold a surging maze; his head
Crested aloft, and carbuncle his eyes;   500
With burnished neck of verdant gold, erect
Amidst his circling spires, that on the grass
Floated redundant. Pleasing was his shape,
And lovely, never since of serpent kind
Lovelier; not those that in Illyria changed   505
Hermione and Cadmus, or the god
In Epidaurus; nor to which transformed
Ammonian Jove, or Capitoline was seen,
He with Olympias, this with her who bore
Scipio, the highth of Rome. With tract oblique   510
At first, as one who sought accéss, but feared
To interrupt, sidelong he works his way.
As when a ship by skilful steersman wrought
Nigh river's mouth or foreland, where the wind
Veers oft, as oft so steers, and shifts her sail,   515

486–87. Cf. 9.283–84, 6.327.
491. not: if not.
496. indented: zigzag (cf. *As You Like It* 4.3.113).
497–503. Cf. *Aen.* 2.206–19, 5.84–89.
503. redundant: with wavy motion.
505. Illyria: region east of the Adriatic.
506. The metamorphosis of Cadmus, king of Thebes, and his queen Hermione (this form, used in Sandys' *Ovid*, was a well-known variant of the commoner Harmonia); see Ovid, *Met.* 4.563–603.
507. Epidaurus: on the east coast of Greece, the seat of Aesculapius, god of medicine, who in serpent form went to Rome to stop a plague (Ovid, *Met.* 15.622 f.).
508–10. Ammonian Jove: African Jove (cf. 4.277), in legend said to have been, in serpent form, the father of Alexander the Great. Capitoline: Jupiter Capitolinus, who, in similar legends, was the reputed father of Scipio Africanus, the conqueror of Hannibal. Both tales are in Plutarch's *Lives* (and in Sandys' commentary on book 9 of his *Ovid*).   Olympias: wife of Philip of Macedon and mother of Alexander; she is the gracious woman of Chaonia (Epirus) in Milton's Elegy 4.26.
510. tract: track.

So varied he, and of his tortuous train
Curled many a wanton wreath in sight of Eve,
To lure her eye; she busied heard the sound
Of rustling leaves, but minded not, as used
To such disport before her through the field   520
From every beast, more duteous at her call
Than at Circean call the herd disguised.
He bolder now, uncalled before her stood,
But as in gaze admiring. Oft he bowed
His turret crest, and sleek enameled neck,   525
Fawning, and licked the ground whereon she trod.
His gentle dumb expression turned at length
The eye of Eve to mark his play; he glad
Of her attention gained, with serpent tongue
Organic, or impulse of vocal air,   530
His fraudulent temptation thus began:
    "Wonder not, sovran mistress, if perhaps
Thou canst, who art sole wonder, much less arm
Thy looks, the heav'n of mildness, with disdain,
Displeased that I approach thee thus, and gaze   535
Insatiate, I thus single, nor have feared
Thy awful brow, more awful thus retired.
Fairest resemblance of thy Maker fair,
Thee all things living gaze on, all things thine
By gift, and thy celestial beauty adore,   540
With ravishment beheld, there best beheld
Where universally admired; but here
In this enclosure wild, these beasts among,
Beholders rude, and shallow to discern
Half what in thee is fair, one man except,   545
Who sees thee? (and what is one?) who shouldst be seen
A goddess among gods, adored and served
By angels numberless, thy daily train."
    So glozed the Tempter, and his proem tuned;
Into the heart of Eve his words made way,   550
Though at the voice much marveling; at length
Not unamazed she thus in answer spake:
    "What may this mean? Language of man pronounced
By tongue of brute, and human sense expressed?
The first at least of these I thought denied   555
To beasts, whom God on their creation-day
Created mute to all articulate sound;
The latter I demur, for in their looks
Much reason, and in their actions oft appears.
Thee, Serpent, subtlest beast of all the field   560
I knew, but not with human voice endued;

530. organic: as an organ or instrument.
532–48. Satan goes beyond the flattery of a
Petrarchan sonneteer or courtly amorist in
raising Eve above her station; cf. her dream,
5.35–93.

558. demur: am in doubt about (cf. 8.373–74).
560–61. Cf. 7.494–95.

Redouble then this miracle, and say,
How cam'st thou speakable of mute, and how
To me so friendly grown above the rest
Of brutal kind, that daily are in sight?   565
Say, for such wonder claims attention due."
    To whom the guileful Tempter thus replied:
"Empress of this fair world, resplendent Eve,
Easy to me it is to tell thee all
What thou command'st, and right thou shouldst be obeyed.   570
I was at first as other beasts that graze
The trodden herb, of abject thoughts and low,
As was my food, nor aught but food discerned
Or sex, and apprehended nothing high:
Till on a day roving the field, I chanced   575
A goodly tree far distant to behold,
Loaden with fruit of fairest colors mixed,
Ruddy and gold. I nearer drew to gaze;
When from the boughs a savory odor blown,
Grateful to appetite, more pleased my sense   580
Than smell of sweetest fennel or the teats
Of ewe or goat dropping with milk at ev'n,
Unsucked of lamb or kid, that tend their play.
To satisfy the sharp desire I had
Of tasting those fair apples, I resolved   585
Not to defer; hunger and thirst at once,
Powerful persuaders, quickened at the scent
Of that alluring fruit, urged me so keen.
About the mossy trunk I wound me soon,
For high from ground the branches would require   590
Thy utmost reach or Adam's: round the tree
All other beasts that saw, with like desire
Longing and envying stood, but could not reach.
Amid the tree now got, where plenty hung
Tempting so nigh, to pluck and eat my fill   595
I spared not, for such pleasure till that hour
At feed or fountain never had I found.
Sated at length, ere long I might perceive
Strange alteration in me, to degree
Of reason in my inward powers, and speech   600
Wanted not long, though to this shape retained.
Thenceforth to speculations high or deep
I turned my thoughts, and with capacious mind
Considered all things visible in heav'n,
Or earth, or middle, all things fair and good;   605
But all that fair and good in thy divine
Semblance, and in thy beauty's heav'nly ray
United I beheld; no fair to thine
Equivalent or second, which compelled

581–83. In popular lore snakes sharpened   they were also said to suck milk from sheep
their sight by rubbing their eyes on fennel;   and goats.   605. middle: the air.

Me thus, though importune perhaps, to come   610
And gaze, and worship thee of right declared
Sovran of creatures, universal dame."
    So talked the spirited sly Snake; and Eve
Yet more amazed unwary thus replied:
    "Serpent, thy overpraising leaves in doubt   615
The virtue of that fruit, in thee first proved.
But say, where grows the tree, from hence how far?
For many are the trees of God that grow
In Paradise, and various, yet unknown
To us; in such abundance lies our choice   620
As leaves a greater store of fruit untouched,
Still hanging incorruptible, till men
Grow up to their provision, and more hands
Help to disburden Nature of her bearth."
    To whom the wily Adder, blithe and glad: 625
"Empress, the way is ready, and not long,
Beyond a row of myrtles, on a flat,
Fast by a fountain, one small thicket past
Of blowing myrrh and balm; if thou accept
My conduct, I can bring thee thither soon."   630
    "Lead then," said Eve. He leading swiftly rolled
In tangles, and made intricate seem straight,
To mischief swift. Hope elevates, and joy
Brightens his crest, as when a wand'ring fire,
Compact of unctuous vapor, which the night   635
Condenses, and the cold environs round,
Kindled through agitation to a flame,
Which oft, they say, some evil Spirit attends,
Hovering and blazing with delusive light,
Misleads th' amazed night-wanderer from his way   640
To bogs and mires, and oft through pond or pool,
There swallowed up and lost, from succor far.
So glistered the dire Snake, and into fraud
Led Eve our credulous mother, to the tree
Of prohibition, root of all our woe;   645
Which when she saw, thus to her guide she spake:
    "Serpent, we might have spared our coming hither,
Fruitless to me, though fruit be here to excess,
The credit of whose virtue rest with thee,
Wondrous indeed, if cause of such effects.   650
But of this tree we may not taste nor touch;
God so commanded, and left that command
Sole daughter of his voice; the rest, we live
Law to ourselves, our reason is our law."
    To whom the Tempter guilefully replied: 655

612. universal dame: mistress (*domina*) of
the universe.
  613. spirited: inspired by a spirit (with the
common meaning added).
  624. Here "bearth" apparently suggests what
is born.

634 f. For the will-o'-the-wisp see *L'Allegro*
104, *Comus* 432–33; with 640 f., cf. *A Midsummer Night's Dream* 2.1.39.
  654. Rom. 2.14.

"Indeed? Hath God then said that of the fruit
Of all these garden trees ye shall not eat,
Yet lords declared of all in earth or air?"
　　To whom thus Eve yet sinless: "Of the fruit
Of each tree in the garden we may eat,   660
But of the fruit of this fair tree amidst
The garden, God hath said, 'Ye shall not eat
Thereof, nor shall ye touch it, lest ye die.'"
　　She scarce had said, though brief, when now more bold
The Tempter, but with show of zeal and love   665
To man, and indignation at his wrong,
New part puts on, and as to passion moved,
Fluctuates disturbed, yet comely, and in act
Raised, as of some great matter to begin.
As when of old some orator renowned   670
In Athens or free Rome, where eloquence
Flourished, since mute, to some great cause addressed,
Stood in himself collected, while each part,
Motion, each act won audience ere the tongue,
Sometimes in highth began, as no delay   675
Of preface brooking through his zeal of right:
So standing, moving, or to highth upgrown,
The Tempter all impassioned thus began:
　　"O sacred, wise, and wisdom-giving Plant,
Mother of science, now I feel thy power   680
Within me clear, not only to discern
Things in their causes, but to trace the ways
Of highest agents, deemed however wise.
Queen of this universe, do not believe
Those rigid threats of death; ye shall not die: 685
How should ye? By the fruit? It gives you life
To knowledge; by the Threat'ner? Look on me,
Me who have touched and tasted, yet both live,
And life more perfect have attained than fate
Meant me, by vent'ring higher than my lot.   690
Shall that be shut to man, which to the beast
Is open? Or will God incense his ire
For such a petty trespass, and not praise
Rather your dauntless virtue, whom the pain
Of death denounced, whatever thing death be,   695
Deterred not from achieving what might lead
To happier life, knowledge of good and evil?
Of good, how just? Of evil, if what is evil
Be real, why not known, since easier shunned?
God therefore cannot hurt ye, and be just;   700
Not just, not God; not feared then, nor obeyed:

661–63. Gen. 3.1–3.
679–732. Satan's speech — very persuasive
if his premises are accepted — develops the
plan of attack he had conceived in 4.512 f. and
launched in Eve's dream, 5.58 f.
680. science: knowledge.

681–82. Cf. Virgil, *Georg.* 2.490.
685. Gen. 3.4.
687. To: in addition to? for the gaining of?
694–95. pain . . . denounced: penalty proclaimed.

Your fear itself of death removes the fear.
Why then was this forbid? Why but to awe,
Why but to keep ye low and ignorant,
His worshipers? He knows that in the day   705
Ye eat thereof, your eyes that seem so clear,
Yet are but dim, shall perfectly be then
Opened and cleared, and ye shall be as gods,
Knowing both good and evil as they know.
That ye should be as gods, since I as man,   710
Internal man, is but proportion meet,
I of brute human, ye of human gods.
So ye shall die perhaps, by putting off
Human, to put on gods, death to be wished,
Though threatened, which no worse than this can bring.   715
And what are gods that man may not become
As they, participating godlike food?
The gods are first, and that advantage use
On our belief, that all from them proceeds;
I question it, for this fair earth I see,   720
Warmed by the sun, producing every kind,
Them nothing. If they all things, who enclosed
Knowledge of good and evil in this tree,
That whoso eats thereof, forthwith attains
Wisdom without their leave? And wherein lies   725
Th' offense, that man should thus attain to know?
What can your knowledge hurt him, or this tree
Impart against his will, if all be his?
Or is it envy, and can envy dwell
In heav'nly breasts? These, these and many more   730
Causes import your need of this fair fruit.
Goddess humane, reach then, and freely taste!"
    He ended, and his words replete with guile
Into her heart too easy entrance won.
Fixed on the fruit she gazed, which to behold   735
Might tempt alone, and in her ears the sound
Yet rung of his persuasive words, impregned
With reason, to her seeming, and with truth;
Meanwhile the hour of noon drew on, and waked
An eager appetite, raised by the smell   740
So savory of that fruit, which with desire,
Inclinable now grown to touch or taste,
Solicited her longing eye; yet first
Pausing a while, thus to herself she mused:
    "Great are thy virtues, doubtless, best of fruits,   745

705–09. Gen. 3.5.
711. Internal man: cf. 600 above.
713–14. putting off . . . gods. Satan perverts biblical ideas and phrases, Eph. 4.22–24, Col. 3.9–10, 1 Cor. 15.53.
729–30. Cf. 6.788 and note.
732. humane: probably "humane," "gracious" (cf. 2.109, *P.R.* 1.221); the meaning

"human" is possible, since the spelling does not count, but an intended oxymoron would be more logical as "Human goddess."
739–43. Gen. 3.6.
745–79. The "unwary" Eve's reason is active, but works only from complete acceptance of Satan's irreligious premises, arguments, and lies.

Though kept from man, and worthy to be admired,
Whose taste, too long forborne, at first assay
Gave elocution to the mute, and taught
The tongue not made for speech to speak thy praise.
Thy praise he also who forbids thy use   750
Conceals not from us, naming thee the Tree
Of Knowledge, knowledge both of good and evil;
Forbids us then to taste, but his forbidding
Commends thee more, while it infers the good
By thee communicated, and our want;   755
For good unknown sure is not had, or had
And yet unknown, is as not had at all.
In plain then, what forbids he but to know,
Forbids us good, forbids us to be wise?
Such prohibitions bind not. But if Death   760
Bind us with after-bands, what profits then
Our inward freedom? In the day we eat
Of this fair fruit, our doom is, we shall die.
How dies the Serpent? He hath eat'n and lives,
And knows, and speaks, and reasons, and discerns,   765
Irrational till then. For us alone
Was death invented? Or to us denied
This intellectual food, for beasts reserved?
For beasts it seems; yet that one beast which first
Hath tasted, envies not, but brings with joy   770
The good befall'n him, author unsuspect,
Friendly to man, far from deceit or guile.
What fear I then, rather what know to fear
Under this ignorance of good and evil,
Of God or death, of law or penalty?   775
Here grows the cure of all, this fruit divine,
Fair to the eye, inviting to the taste,
Of virtue to make wise; what hinders then
To reach, and feed at once both body and mind?"
   So saying, her rash hand in evil hour   780
Forth reaching to the fruit, she plucked, she eat.
Earth felt the wound, and Nature from her seat
Sighing through all her works gave signs of woe,
That all was lost. Back to the thicket slunk
The guilty Serpent, and well might, for Eve   785
Intent now wholly on her taste, naught else
Regarded; such delight till then, as seemed,
In fruit she never tasted, whether true
Or fancied so, through expectation high

758. plain: plain terms.
771. author unsuspect: unquestionable authority.
781. eat: the past tense (cf. *L'Allegro* 102).
782–84. Cf. *Aen.* 4.166–70; Hooker, quoted in the note on 354–56 above; and *P.L.* 8.511–20.

789–93. The description is clearly intended to suggest the Greek tragic sin of *hybris*, infatuated, self-sufficient pride that ignores human limitations and the divine order. Cf. 3.206, 4.513 f., 5.69 f.

Of knowledge, nor was Godhead from her thought.   790
Greedily she engorged without restraint,
And knew not eating death. Satiate at length,
And heightened as with wine, jocund and boon,
Thus to herself she pleasingly began:
   "O sovran, virtuous, precious of all trees   795
In Paradise, of operation blest
To sapience, hitherto obscured, infamed,
And thy fair fruit let hang, as to no end
Created; but henceforth my early care,
Not without song, each morning, and due praise,   800
Shall tend thee, and the fertile burden ease
Of thy full branches offered free to all;
Till dieted by thee I grow mature
In knowledge, as the gods who all things know;
Though others envy what they cannot give;   805
For had the gift been theirs, it had not here
Thus grown. Experience, next to thee I owe,
Best guide; not following thee, I had remained
In ignorance; thou open'st wisdom's way,
And giv'st accéss, though secret she retire.   810
And I perhaps am secret; Heav'n is high,
High and remote to see from thence distinct
Each thing on earth; and other care perhaps
May have diverted from continual watch
Our great Forbidder, safe with all his spies   815
About him. But to Adam in what sort
Shall I appear? Shall I to him make known
As yet my change, and give him to partake
Full happiness with me, or rather not,
But keep the odds of knowledge in my power   820
Without copartner? So to add what wants
In female sex, the more to draw his love,
And render me more equal, and perhaps,
A thing not undesirable, sometime
Superior; for inferior who is free?   825
This may be well. But what if God have seen,
And death ensue? Then I shall be no more,
And Adam wedded to another Eve
Shall live with her enjoying, I extinct;
A death to think. Confirmed then I resolve,   830
Adam shall share with me in bliss or woe.

---

792. And knew not that she was. Cf. 5.638.
795. I.e. "most virtuous, most precious" (classical idiom).
797. infamed: made infamous.
799–802. Cf. Eve's reverence for her new god, the tree, and the canticle in 5.153 f.
811–13. Job 22.13–14, Ps. 94.7.
815. "Our great Forbidder" is a shocking index to Eve's corruption, but here, as at all times before and after her fall, she thinks less about God than about Adam. Also, she now speaks, not with the majesty of innocence, but with the practical colloquialism of an ordinary jealous wife, selfishly weighing the pros and cons of domestic strategy. Cf. her lyrical asseveration of love, 4.635–58.
815. safe: harmless.
825. Eve now holds Satan's conception of freedom.

So dear I love him, that with him all deaths
I could endure, without him live no life."
   So saying, from the tree her step she turned,
But first low reverence done, as to the power   835
That dwelt within, whose presence had infused
Into the plant sciential sap, derived
From nectar, drink of gods. Adam the while
Waiting desirous her return, had wove
Of choicest flow'rs a garland to adorn   840
Her tresses, and her rural labors crown,
As reapers oft are wont their harvest queen.
Great joy he promised to his thoughts, and new
Solace in her return, so long delayed;
Yet oft his heart, divine of something ill,   845
Misgave him; he the falt'ring measure felt;
And forth to meet her went, the way she took
That morn when first they parted. By the Tree
Of Knowledge he must pass; there he her met,
Scarce from the tree returning; in her hand   850
A bough of fairest fruit that downy smiled,
New gathered, and ambrosial smell diffused.
To him she hasted; in her face excuse
Came prologue, and apology to prompt,
Which with bland words at will she thus addressed: 855
   "Hast thou not wondered, Adam, at my stay?
Thee I have missed, and thought it long, deprived
Thy presence, agony of love till now
Not felt, nor shall be twice, for never more
Mean I to try what rash untried I sought,   860
The pain of absence from thy sight. But strange
Hath been the cause, and wonderful to hear:
This tree is not as we are told, a tree
Of danger tasted, nor to evil unknown
Op'ning the way, but of divine effect   865
To open eyes, and make them gods who taste;
And hath been tasted such. The Serpent wise,
Or not restrained as we, or not obeying,
Hath eaten of the fruit, and is become
Not dead, as we are threatened, but thenceforth   870
Endued with human voice and human sense,
Reasoning to admiration, and with me
Persuasively hath so prevailed, that I
Have also tasted, and have also found
Th' effects to correspond, opener mine eyes,   875

832–33. Eve is sincere in her self-deception. For the phrasing, cf. Horace, *Od.* 3.9.24.
835–36. Cf. 799–802 and note.
837. sciential: imparting knowledge.
838 f. In the *Iliad* 22.437 f., Andromache,
not knowing that Hector has been killed, embroiders flowers and prepares his bath.

845. divine of: divining, foreseeing.
846. falt'ring measure: uneven beat (of his
heart).
852. Cf. *Aen.* 1.403–04, *Georg.* 4.415.
853–54. Eve's expression was a preface to
her verbal apology (which includes such lies
as 857–61, 877–80).

Dim erst, dilated spirits, ampler heart,
And growing up to Godhead; which for thee
Chiefly I sought, without thee can despise.
For bliss, as thou hast part, to me is bliss;
Tedious, unshared with thee, and odious soon.   880
Thou therefore also taste, that equal lot
May join us, equal joy, as equal love;
Lest thou not tasting, different degree
Disjoin us, and I then too late renounce
Deity for thee, when fate will not permit."   885
    Thus Eve with count'nance blithe her story told;
But in her cheek distemper flushing glowed.
On th' other side, Adam, soon as he heard
The fatal trespass done by Eve, amazed,
Astonied stood and blank, while horror chill   890
Ran through his veins, and all his joints relaxed;
From his slack hand the garland wreathed for Eve
Down dropped, and all the faded roses shed.
Speechless he stood and pale, till thus at length
First to himself he inward silence broke: 895
    "O fairest of creation, last and best
Of all God's works, creature in whom excelled
Whatever can to sight or thought be formed,
Holy, divine, good, amiable, or sweet!
How art thou lost, how on a sudden lost,   900
Defaced, deflow'red, and now to death devote!
Rather how hast thou yielded to transgress
The strict forbiddance, how to violate
The sacred fruit forbidd'n! Some cursèd fraud
Of enemy hath beguiled thee, yet unknown,   905
And me with thee hath ruined, for with thee
Certain my resolution is to die;
How can I live without thee, how forgo
Thy sweet converse and love so dearly joined,
To live again in these wild woods forlorn?   910
Should God create another Eve, and I
Another rib afford, yet loss of thee
Would never from my heart; no, no! I feel
The link of nature draw me: flesh of flesh,
Bone of my bone thou art, and from thy state   915

886. blithe. One of the most telling of the many significant epithets in the stage directions of this drama; Eve has no awareness of what she has done.
887. Cf. 5.10.
890. Astonied: dazed (Job 17.8; Spenser, *F.Q.* 7.6.28.6).
890–91. Cf. *Aen.* 1.92, 2.120–22, 3.29.
892–93. In Statius, *Thebaid* 7.148–50, Bacchus, with hair and garlands disordered, drops his thyrsus and grapes (unmarred) fall from his horns. Cf. *P.L.* 4.772–73.
896–97. Adam's phrases, like his own in 8.546–59 and Satan's in 9.532 f., elevate Eve above her proper station and reveal his idolatry; his whole speech is a blend of right and wrong feelings.
901. to death devote: cf. Horace, *Od.* 4.14.18.
908–10. A deeply human cry of love and loyalty, which by anticipation turns Eden without Eve into a wilderness. But what G. M. Hopkins called Adam's false chivalry saps his religious and moral integrity; cf. the corrupt patriotism of "My country, right or wrong."

Mine never shall be parted, bliss or woe."
So having said, as one from sad dismay
Recomforted, and after thoughts disturbed
Submitting to what seemed remédiless,
Thus in calm mood his words to Eve he turned: 920
"Bold deed thou hast presumed, advent'rous Eve,
And peril great provoked, who thus hast dared
Had it been only coveting to eye
That sacred fruit, sacred to abstinence,
Much more to taste it under ban to touch.   925
But past who can recall, or done undo?
Not God omnipotent, nor fate. Yet so
Perhaps thou shalt not die; perhaps the fact
Is not so heinous now, foretasted fruit,
Profaned first by the Serpent, by him first   930
Made common and unhallowed ere our taste,
Nor yet on him found deadly; he yet lives,
Lives, as thou saidst, and gains to live as man
Higher degree of life, inducement strong
To us, as likely tasting to attain   935
Proportional ascent, which cannot be
But to be gods, or angels, demi-gods.
Nor can I think that God, Creator wise,
Though threat'ning, will in earnest so destroy
Us his prime creatures, dignified so high,   940
Set over all his works, which in our fall,
For us created, needs with us must fail,
Dependent made; so God shall uncreate,
Be frustrate, do, undo, and labor lose,
Not well conceived of God, who though his power   945
Creation could repeat, yet would be loth
Us to abolish, lest the Adversary
Triumph and say: 'Fickle their state whom God
Most favors, who can please him long? Me first
He ruined, now mankind; whom will he next?'   950
Matter of scorn not to be given the Foe;
However, I with thee have fixed my lot,
Certain to undergo like doom: if death
Consort with thee, death is to me as life;
So forcible within my heart I feel   955
The bond of nature draw me to my own,
My own in thee, for what thou art is mine;
Our state cannot be severed; we are one,
One flesh; to lose thee were to lose myself."
So Adam, and thus Eve to him replied: 960
"O glorious trial of exceeding love,

921 f. On reflection, Adam accepts and re-
inforces Eve's and Satan's specious arguments.
922. Ed. 1, hast; ed. 2, hath.
947–48. Deut. 32.27.

953. Certain: resolved.
961. The line is, from Eve, unconscious
irony, since it calls up the selfless love of
Christ for man. Cf. 3.410.

Illustrious evidence, example high!
Engaging me to emulate, but short
Of thy perfection, how shall I attain,
Adam? From whose dear side I boast me sprung,   965
And gladly of our union hear thee speak,
One heart, one soul in both; whereof good proof
This day affords, declaring thee resolved,
Rather than death or aught than death more dread
Shall separate us, linked in love so dear,   970
To undergo with me one guilt, one crime,
If any be, of tasting this fair fruit,
Whose virtue (for of good still good proceeds,
Direct, or by occasion) hath presented
This happy trial of thy love, which else   975
So eminently never had been known.
Were it I thought death menaced would ensue
This my attempt, I would sustain alone
The worst, and not persuade thee, rather die
Deserted, than oblige thee with a fact   980
Pernicious to thy peace, chiefly assured
Remarkably so late of thy so true,
So faithful love unequaled; but I feel
Far otherwise th' event, not death, but life
Augmented, opened eyes, new hopes, new joys,   985
Taste so divine, that what of sweet before
Hath touched my sense, flat seems to this and harsh.
On my experience, Adam, freely taste,
And fear of death deliver to the winds."
    So saying, she embraced him, and for joy   990
Tenderly wept, much won that he his love
Had so ennobled, as of choice to incur
Divine displeasure for her sake, or death.
In recompense (for such compliance bad
Such recompense best merits) from the bough   995
She gave him of that fair enticing fruit
With liberal hand. He scrupled not to eat
Against his better knowledge, not deceived,
But fondly overcome with female charm.
Earth trembled from her entrails, as again   1000
In pangs, and Nature gave a second groan;
Sky loured and, muttering thunder, some sad drops
Wept at completing of the mortal sin

967. One . . . both: cf. Adam, 8.499, 604.
977–83. Cf. 816–33.
980. oblige: involve.
998–99. Cf. 1 Tim. 2.14; Augustine, *City of God* 14.11 and 13; Hooker, 1.7.6: "Reason therefore may rightly discern the thing which is good, and yet the will of man not incline itself thereunto, as oft as the prejudice of sensible experience doth oversway"; the note on 354–56 above; and *P.L.* 8.540–59.

1000–04. Cf. 782–84 and note on 354–56.
1003–04. sin Original. Milton's exposition in *C.D.* 1.11 makes the act embrace many sins, distrust and disobedience of God, ingratitude, presumption in aspiring to divine attributes, pride and arrogance, etc. All Adam's posterity "sinned in Adam," and all have "an innate propensity to sin," but "no one perishes, except he himself sin."

Original; while Adam took no thought,
Eating his fill, nor Eve to iterate   1005
Her former trespass feared, the more to soothe
Him with her loved society, that now
As with new wine intoxicated both
They swim in mirth, and fancy that they feel
Divinity within them breeding wings   1010
Wherewith to scorn the earth. But that false fruit
Far other operation first displayed,
Carnal desire inflaming: he on Eve
Began to cast lascivious eyes, she him
As wantonly repaid; in lust they burn,   1015
Till Adam thus 'gan Eve to dalliance move:
    "Eve, now I see thou art exact of taste,
And elegant, of sapience no small part;
Since to each meaning savor we apply,
And palate call judicious; I the praise   1020
Yield thee, so well this day thou hast purveyed.
Much pleasure we have lost, while we abstained
From this delightful fruit, nor known till now
True relish, tasting; if such pleasure be
In things to us forbidden, it might be wished   1025
For this one tree had been forbidden ten.
But come, so well refreshed, now let us play,
As meet is, after such delicious fare;
For never did thy beauty since the day
I saw thee first and wedded thee, adorned   1030
With all perfections, so inflame my sense
With ardor to enjoy thee, fairer now
Than ever, bounty of this virtuous tree."
    So said he, and forbore not glance or toy
Of amorous intent, well understood   1035
Of Eve, whose eye darted contagious fire.
Her hand he seized, and to a shady bank,
Thick overhead with verdant roof embow'red,
He led her nothing loth; flow'rs were the couch,
Pansies, and violets, and asphodel,   1040
And hyacinth, earth's freshest softest lap.
There they their fill of love and love's disport
Took largely, of their mutual guilt the seal,

1007–11. Cf. 789–93 and note.
1010–11. Cf. the Platonic image of the winged soul seeking heaven, *Comus* 377–78 and note.
1011. scorn the earth. Cf. Horace, *Od.* 3.2.24.
1011 f. The dreams of superhuman knowledge and power sink into subhuman lust. This is not in Genesis, unless by implication.
1017–20. A play on the double meaning of the Latin *sapere*, to taste and to know, be wise (cf. Cicero, *De Finibus* 2.7.24).
1027–33. Adam's sensual levity culminates

in his seeing Eve now only as an instrument of pleasure; his language echoes that of Paris to Helen and of Zeus to Hera, *Iliad* 3.442 f., 14.292 f. With 1027–28 cf. also Exod. 32.6, 1 Cor. 10.7.
1027–45. Cf. 4.689 f., 8.500–20.
1034. toy: fondling.
1037. Her hand: see note on 4.321.
1039–41. Cf. 4.700 f. and note. "Earth's freshest softest lap" suggests both the unspoiled purity of nature and human sensuality.
1042–44. fill of love . . . solace: Prov. 7.18.

The solace of their sin, till dewy sleep
Oppressed them, wearied with their amorous play.   1045
Soon as the force of that fallacious fruit,
That with exhilarating vapor bland
About their spirits had played, and inmost powers
Made err, was now exhaled, and grosser sleep
Bred of unkindly fumes, with conscious dreams   1050
Encumbered, now had left them, up they rose
As from unrest, and each the other viewing,
Soon found their eyes how opened, and their minds
How darkened; innocence, that as a veil
Had shadowed them from knowing ill, was gone;   1055
Just confidence, and native righteousness,
And honor from about them, naked left
To guilty Shame; he covered, but his robe
Uncovered more. So rose the Danite strong,
Herculean Samson, from the harlot-lap   1060
Of Philistéan Dálilah, and waked
Shorn of his strength, they destitute and bare
Of all their virtue. Silent, and in face
Confounded, long they sat, as strucken mute,
Till Adam, though not less than Eve abashed,   1065
At length gave utterance to these words constrained:
    'O Eve, in evil hour thou didst give ear
To that false worm, of whomsoever taught
To counterfeit man's voice, true in our fall,
False in our promised rising; since our eyes   1070
Opened we find indeed, and find we know
Both good and evil, good lost and evil got,
Bad fruit of knowledge, if this be to know,
Which leaves us naked thus, of honor void,
Of innocence, of faith, of purity,   1075
Our wonted ornaments now soiled and stained,
And in our faces evident the signs
Of foul concupiscence; whence evil store,
Even shame, the last of evils; of the first
Be sure then. How shall I behold the face   1080
Henceforth of God or angel, erst with joy
And rapture so oft beheld? Those heav'nly shapes
Will dazzle now this earthly, with their blaze
Insufferably bright. O might I here
In solitude live savage, in some glade   1085
Obscured, where highest woods impenetrable
To star or sunlight, spread their umbrage broad
And brown as evening! Cover me, ye pines,
Ye cedars, with innumerable boughs

1049–50. Cf. 5.3–5.
1053 f. Gen. 3.7.
1058. he: Shame. Cf. Ps. 109.29.
1059–62. Judg. 16 and Milton's drama.
1071–73. Cf. 4.774–75, etc.

1079. If "last" means "worst," "first" presumably means "lesser" (the usual glosses). If the words are used literally, "first" may mean simply "guilt."
1088–90. Hos. 10.8, Luke 23.30, Rev. 6.16.

Hide me, where I may never see them more.   1090
But let us now, as in bad plight, devise
What best may for the present serve to hide
The parts of each from other that seem most
To shame obnoxious, and unseemliest seen,
Some tree whose broad smooth leaves together sewed,   1095
And girded on our loins, may cover round
Those middle parts, that this newcomer, Shame,
There sit not, and reproach us as unclean."
     So counseled he, and both together went
Into the thickest wood; there soon they chose   1100
The fig-tree, not that kind for fruit renowned,
But such as at this day to Indians known
In Malabar or Deccan spreads her arms
Branching so broad and long, that in the ground
The bended twigs take root, and daughters grow   1105
About the mother tree, a pillared shade
High overarched, and echoing walks between;
There oft the Indian herdsman shunning heat
Shelters in cool, and tends his pasturing herds
At loop-holes cut through thickest shade. Those leaves   1110
They gathered, broad as Amazonian targe,
And with what skill they had, together sewed,
To gird their waist, vain covering if to hide
Their guilt and dreaded shame, O how unlike
To that first naked glory! Such of late   1115
Columbus found th' American so girt
With feathered cincture, naked else and wild
Among the trees on isles and woody shores.
Thus fenced, and as they thought, their shame in part
Covered, but not at rest or ease of mind,   1120
They sat them down to weep; nor only tears
Rained at their eyes, but high winds worse within
Began to rise, high passions, anger, hate,
Mistrust, suspicion, discord, and shook sore
Their inward state of mind, calm region once   1125
And full of peace, now tossed and turbulent;
For understanding ruled not, and the will
Heard not her lore, both in subjection now
To sensual appetite, who from beneath
Usurping over sovran reason claimed   1130

1090. them: "heav'nly shapes" (1082).
1100–10. The details of the description were given in many learned and popular books, e.g. John Gerard's *Herbal;* the comparison with the shields of the Amazons had appeared perhaps first in Pliny, *Nat. Hist.* 12.11.23.
1103. Malabar: southwestern coast of India. Deccan: the peninsula of southern India.
1121. They . . . weep. Cf. the Jewish exiles from Zion, Ps. 137.1.

1127–31. The traditional Platonic ethical psychology (*Rep.* 439–42) with the traditional and peculiarly Christian emphasis on the will; now the hierarchy of faculties is upset. In *C.D.* 1.12 Milton describes the first degree of spiritual death as "the loss, or at least . . . the obscuration to a great extent of that right reason which enabled man to discern the chief good, and in which consisted as it were the life of the understanding."

Superior sway. From thus distempered breast,
Adam, estranged in look and altered style,
Speech intermitted thus to Eve renewed:
    "Would thou hadst hearkened to my words, and stayed
With me, as I besought thee, when that strange   1135
Desire of wand'ring this unhappy morn,
I know not whence possessed thee; we had then
Remained still happy, not as now, despoiled
Of all our good, shamed, naked, miserable.
Let none henceforth seek needless cause to approve   1140
The faith they owe; when earnestly they seek
Such proof, conclude they then begin to fail."
    To whom, soon moved with touch of blame, thus Eve:
"What words have passed thy lips, Adam severe!
Imput'st thou that to my default, or will   1145
Of wand'ring, as thou call'st it, which who knows
But might as ill have happened thou being by,
Or to thyself perhaps? Hadst thou been there,
Or here th' attempt, thou couldst not have discerned
Fraud in the Serpent, speaking as he spake;   1150
No ground of enmity between us known
Why he should mean me ill, or seek to harm.
Was I to have never parted from thy side?
As good have grown there still a lifeless rib.
Being as I am, why didst not thou, the head,   1155
Command me absolutely not to go,
Going into such danger as thou saidst?
Too facile then, thou didst not much gainsay,
Nay didst permit, approve, and fair dismiss.
Hadst thou been firm and fixed in thy dissent,   1160
Neither had I transgressed, nor thou with me."
    To whom then first incensed Adam replied:
"Is this the love, is this the recompense
Of mine to thee, ingrateful Eve, expressed
Immutable when thou wert lost, not I,   1165
Who might have lived and joyed immortal bliss,
Yet willingly chose rather death with thee?
And am I now upbraided, as the cause
Of thy transgressing? Not enough severe,
It seems, in thy restraint. What could I more?   1170
I warned thee, I admonished thee, foretold
The danger, and the lurking enemy
That lay in wait; beyond this had been force,
And force upon free will hath here no place.

1140. approve: prove. Cf. 9.335–36.
1141. owe: own, have. Cf. Donne, *Litany*
62–63: "Let not my mind be blinder by more
light/Nor faith, by reason added, lose her
sight."

1144. With slight variations, a Homeric
formula.
1155. head: cf. 4.443 and note; 8.574.

But confidence then bore thee on, secure   1175
Either to meet no danger, or to find
Matter of glorious trial; and perhaps
I also erred in overmuch admiring
What seemed in thee so perfect, that I thought
No evil durst attempt thee, but I rue   1180
That error now, which is become my crime,
And thou th' accuser. Thus it shall befall
Him who to worth in women overtrusting
Lets her will rule; restraint she will not brook,
And left to herself, if evil thence ensue,   1185
She first his weak indulgence will accuse."
　　Thus they in mutual accusation spent
The fruitless hours, but neither self-condemning,
And of their vain contést appeared no end.

Book X

THE ARGUMENT

　　Man's transgression known, the guardian angels forsake Paradise, and return up to heaven to approve their vigilance, and are approved, God declaring that the entrance of Satan could not be by them prevented. He sends his Son to judge the transgressors; who descends and gives sentence accordingly; then in pity clothes them both, and reascends. Sin and Death, sitting till then at the gates of hell, by wondrous sympathy feeling the success of Satan in this new world, and the sin by man there committed, resolve to sit no longer confined in hell but to follow Satan their sire up to the place of man. To make the way easier from hell to this world to and fro, they pave a broad highway or bridge over Chaos, according to the track that Satan first made; then, preparing for earth, they meet him, proud of his success, returning to hell; their mutual gratulation. Satan arrives at Pandemonium; in full assembly relates, with boasting, his success against man; instead of applause is entertained with a general hiss by all his audience, transformed, with himself also, suddenly into serpents, according to his doom given in Paradise; then, deluded with a show of the Forbidden Tree springing up before them, they, greedily reaching to take of the fruit, chew dust and bitter ashes. The proceedings of Sin and Death; God foretells the final victory of his Son over them, and the renewing of all things; but for the present commands his angels to make several alterations in the heavens and elements. Adam, more and more perceiving his fallen condition, heavily bewails, rejects the condolement of Eve; she persists, and at length appeases him: then, to evade the curse likely to fall on their offspring, proposes to Adam violent ways, which he approves not, but, conceiving better hope, puts

---

1183. The "women" of the first six editions is often emended to "woman," but the discord between the plural and the singular pronouns that follow is colloquial and in keeping with Adam's agitation. Cf. "man" and "them" in 7.519–20.

her in mind of the late promise made them, that her seed should be revenged
on the Serpent, and exhorts her with him to seek peace of the offended Deity
by repentance and supplication.

MEANWHILE the heinous and despiteful act
Of Satan done in Paradise, and how
He in the Serpent had perverted Eve,
Her husband she, to taste the fatal fruit,
Was known in heav'n; for what can scape the eye   5
Of God all-seeing, or deceive his heart
Omniscient, who in all things wise and just,
Hindered not Satan to attempt the mind
Of man, with strength entire, and free will armed,
Complete to have discovered and repulsed   10
Whatever wiles of foe or seeming friend?
For still they knew, and ought to have still remembered,
The high injunction not to taste that fruit,
Whoever tempted; which they not obeying,
Incurred (what could they less?) the penalty,   15
And manifold in sin, deserved to fall.
Up into heav'n from Paradise in haste
Th' angelic guards ascended, mute and sad
For man; for of his state by this they knew,
Much wond'ring how the subtle Fiend had stol'n   20
Entrance unseen. Soon as th' unwelcome news
From earth arrived at heaven gate, displeased
All were who heard; dim sadness did not spare
That time celestial visages, yet mixed
With pity, violated not their bliss.   25
About the new-arrived, in multitudes
Th' ethereal people ran, to hear and know
How all befell. They towards the throne supreme
Accountable made haste to make appear,
With righteous plea, their utmost vigilance,   30
And easily approved; when the Most High
Eternal Father, from his secret cloud
Amidst, in thunder uttered thus his voice:
    "Assembled Angels, and ye Powers returned
From unsuccessful charge, be not dismayed,   35
Nor troubled at these tidings from the earth,
Which your sincerest care could not prevent,
Foretold so lately what would come to pass,
When first this Tempter crossed the gulf from hell.
I told ye then he should prevail and speed   40
On his bad errand; man should be seduced
And flattered out of all, believing lies

BOOK X. 19. by this (time).   40. Cf. 3.92 f.
33. Rev. 4.5.

Against his Maker; no decree of mine
Concurring to necessitate his fall,
Or touch with lightest moment of impulse   45
His free will, to her own inclining left
In even scale. But fall'n he is; and now
What rests but that the mortal sentence pass
On his transgression, death denounced that day?
Which he presumes already vain and void,   50
Because not yet inflicted, as he feared,
By some immediate stroke; but soon shall find
Forbearance no acquittance ere day end.
Justice shall not return as bounty scorned.
But whom send I to judge them? Whom but thee,   55
Vicegerent Son? To thee I have transferred
All judgment, whether in heav'n, or earth, or hell.
Easy it may be seen that I intend
Mercy colleague with justice, sending thee
Man's friend, his Mediator, his designed   60
Both ransom and Redeemer voluntary,
And destined man himself to judge man fall'n."
    So spake the Father, and unfolding bright
Toward the right hand his glory, on the Son
Blazed forth unclouded deity; he full   65
Resplendent all his Father manifest
Expressed, and thus divinely answered mild:
    "Father Eternal, thine is to decree,
Mine both in heav'n and earth to do thy will
Supreme, that thou in me thy Son beloved   70
May'st ever rest well pleased. I go to judge
On earth these thy transgressors; but thou know'st,
Whoever judged, the worst on me must light,
When time shall be; for so I undertook
Before thee, and not repenting, this obtain   75
Of right, that I may mitigate their doom
On me derived; yet I shall temper so
Justice with mercy as may illustrate most
Them fully satisfied, and thee appease.
Attendance none shall need, nor train, where none   80
Are to behold the judgment but the judged,
Those two; the third best absent is condemned,
Convict by flight, and rebel to all law;
Conviction to the Serpent none belongs."
    Thus saying, from his radiant seat he rose   85
Of high collateral glory; him Thrones and Powers,
Princedoms, and Dominations ministrant
Accompanied to heaven gate, from whence

48. rests: remains.   pass: be passed.
54. Justice shall not be scorned as bounty
has been.
55–57. John 5.22.
58. Ed. 1, may; ed. 2, might.

58–79. Cf. 3.134, 227 f., 274 f., 383 f.;
C.D. 1.15.
77. derived: diverted.
78–79. as . . . satisfied: so as may best
show justice and mercy fulfilled.

Eden and all the coast in prospect lay.
Down he descended straight; the speed of Gods   90
Time counts not, though with swiftest minutes winged.
Now was the sun in western cadence low
From noon, and gentle airs due at their hour
To fan the earth now waked, and usher in
The ev'ning cool, when he from wrath more cool   95
Came, the mild Judge and Intercessor both,
To sentence man. The voice of God they heard
Now walking in the garden, by soft winds
Brought to their ears, while day declined; they heard,
And from his presence hid themselves among   100
The thickest trees, both man and wife, till God
Approaching thus to Adam called aloud:
    "Where art thou, Adam, wont with joy to meet
My coming seen far off? I miss thee here,
Not pleased, thus entertained with solitude,   105
Where obvious duty erewhile appeared unsought.
Or come I less conspicuous, or what change
Absents thee, or what chance detains? Come forth."
He came, and with him Eve, more loth, though first
To offend, discount'nanced both, and discomposed;   110
Love was not in their looks, either to God
Or to each other, but apparent guilt,
And shame, and perturbation, and despair,
Anger, and obstinacy, and hate, and guile.
Whence Adam, falt'ring long, thus answered brief: 115
    "I heard thee in the garden, and of thy voice
Afraid, being naked, hid myself." To whom
The gracious Judge without revile replied:
    "My voice thou oft hast heard, and hast not feared,
But still rejoiced; how is it now become   120
So dreadful to thee? That thou art naked, who
Hath told thee? Hast thou eaten of the tree
Whereof I gave thee charge thou shouldst not eat?"
To whom thus Adam sore beset replied:
    "O heav'n! in evil strait this day I stand   125
Before my Judge, either to undergo
Myself the total crime, or to accuse
My other self, the partner of my life;
Whose failing, while her faith to me remains,
I should conceal, and not expose to blame   130
By my complaint; but strict necessity
Subdues me, and calamitous constraint,
Lest on my head both sin and punishment,
However insupportable, be all

---

92. cadence: sinking.
97–103. Gen. 3.8–9. Here and later "God"
means the Son, as God's vicegerent.

106. obvious: in the way, i.e. coming to
meet.   112. apparent: evident.
116–43. Gen. 3.10–12.

Devolved; though should I hold my peace, yet thou   135
Wouldst easily detect what I conceal.
This woman whom thou mad'st to be my help,
And gav'st me as thy perfect gift, so good,
So fit, so acceptáble, so divine,
That from her hand I could suspect no ill,   140
And what she did, whatever in itself,
Her doing seemed to justify the deed;
She gave me of the tree, and I did eat."
    To whom the Sovran Presence thus replied:
"Was she thy God, that her thou didst obey   145
Before his voice, or was she made thy guide,
Superior, or but equal, that to her
Thou didst resign thy manhood, and the place
Wherein God set thee above her, made of thee
And for thee, whose perfection far excelled   150
Hers in all real dignity? Adorned
She was indeed, and lovely to attract
Thy love, not thy subjection, and her gifts
Were such as under government well seemed,
Unseemly to bear rule, which was thy part   155
And person, hadst thou known thyself aright."
    So having said, he thus to Eve in few:
"Say, woman, what is this which thou hast done?"
    To whom sad Eve with shame nigh overwhelmed,
Confessing soon, yet not before her Judge   160
Bold or loquacious, thus abashed replied:
"The Serpent me beguiled and I did eat."
    Which when the Lord God heard, without delay
To judgment he proceeded on th' accused
Serpent, though brute, unable to transfer   165
The guilt on him who made him instrument
Of mischief, and polluted from the end
Of his creation; justly then accurst,
As vitiated in nature. More to know
Concerned not man (since he no further knew)   170
Nor altered his offense; yet God at last
To Satan first in sin his doom applied,
Though in mysterious terms, judged as then best;
And on the Serpent thus his curse let fall:
    "Because thou hast done this, thou art accurst   175
Above all cattle, each beast of the field;
Upon thy belly groveling thou shalt go,
And dust shalt eat all the days of thy life.
Between thee and the woman I will put
Enmity, and between thine and her seed;   180
Her seed shall bruise thy head, thou bruise his heel."

145–56. Cf. 8.561 f.   157–208. Gen. 3.13–19.
156. person: role.   165. unable: modifying "Serpent."
157. in few (words).   167. end: purpose.

So spake this oracle, then verified
When Jesus, son of Mary, second Eve,
Saw Satan fall like lightning down from heav'n,
Prince of the air; then rising from his grave   185
Spoiled Principalities and Powers, triumphed
In open show, and with ascension bright
Captivity led captive through the air,
The realm itself of Satan long usurped,
Whom he shall tread at last under our feet,   190
Ev'n he who now foretold his fatal bruise,
And to the woman thus his sentence turned:
　　"Thy sorrow I will greatly multiply
By thy conception; children thou shalt bring
In sorrow forth, and to thy husband's will   195
Thine shall submit, he over thee shall rule."
　　On Adam last thus judgment he pronounced:
"Because thou hast hearkened to the voice of thy wife,
And eaten of the tree concerning which
I charged thee, saying, 'Thou shalt not eat thereof,'   200
Cursed is the ground for thy sake; thou in sorrow
Shalt eat thereof all the days of thy life;
Thorns also and thistles it shall bring thee forth
Unbid, and thou shalt eat th' herb of the field;
In the sweat of thy face shalt thou eat bread,   205
Till thou return unto the ground, for thou
Out of the ground wast taken; know thy birth,
For dust thou art, and shalt to dust return."
　　So judged he man, both Judge and Saviour sent,
And th' instant stroke of death, denounced that day,   210
Removed far off; then pitying how they stood
Before him naked to the air, that now
Must suffer change, disdained not to begin
Thenceforth the form of servant to assume;
As when he washed his servants' feet, so now   215
As father of his family he clad
Their nakedness with skins of beasts, or slain,
Or as the snake with youthful coat repaid;
And thought not much to clothe his enemies.
Nor he their outward only with the skins   220
Of beasts, but inward nakedness, much more
Opprobrious, with his robe of righteousness
Arraying, covered from his Father's sight.
To him with swift ascent he up returned,
Into his blissful bosom reassumed   225
In glory as of old; to him appeased,
All, though all-knowing, what had passed with man

184. Luke 10.17–18.
185–90. Cf. 3.250–65; Eph. 2.2.; Col. 2.15;
Ps. 68.18; Rom. 16.20.
　213–17. Gen. 3.21; Phil. 2.7; John 13.5.

218. repaid: renewed (after being shed).
219. thought . . . much: was not reluctant.
222. Isa. 61.10. Cf. 9.1058.

Recounted, mixing intercession sweet.
Meanwhile ere thus was sinned and judged on earth,
Within the gates of hell sat Sin and Death,   230
In counterview within the gates, that now
Stood open wide, belching outrageous flame
Far into Chaos, since the Fiend passed through,
Sin opening, who thus now to Death began:
    "O son, why sit we here each other viewing   235
Idly, while Satan our great author thrives
In other worlds, and happier seat provides
For us his offspring dear? It cannot be
But that success attends him; if mishap,
Ere this he had returned, with fury driv'n   240
By his avengers, since no place like this
Can fit his punishment, or their revenge.
Methinks I feel new strength within me rise,
Wings growing, and dominion giv'n me large
Beyond this deep; whatever draws me on,   245
Or sympathy or some connatural force
Powerful at greatest distance to unite
With secret amity things of like kind
By secretest conveyance. Thou my shade
Inseparable must with me along;   250
For Death from Sin no power can separate.
But lest the difficulty of passing back
Stay his return perhaps over this gulf
Impassable, impervious, let us try
Advent'rous work, yet to thy power and mine   255
Not unagreeable, to found a path
Over this main from hell to that new world
Where Satan now prevails, a monument
Of merit high to all th' infernal host,
Easing their passage hence, for intercourse   260
Or transmigration, as their lot shall lead.
Nor can I miss the way, so strongly drawn
By this new-felt attraction and instinct."
    Whom thus the meager Shadow answered soon:
"Go whither fate and inclination strong   265
Leads thee, I shall not lag behind, nor err
The way, thou leading, such a scent I draw
Of carnage, prey innumerable, and taste
The savor of death from all things there that live;
Nor shall I to the work thou enterprisest   270
Be wanting, but afford thee equal aid."
    So saying, with delight he snuffed the smell
Of mortal change on earth. As when a flock
Of ravenous fowl, though many a league remote,

231–32. Cf. 2.883–84.
    235. why . . . here: 2 Kings 7.3; Matt.
20.6.
    261. transmigration: leaving hell to stay on
earth.

266. err: mistake.
273–78. Vultures were traditionally credited
with foreknowledge of battles (cf. Job 39.30;
Lucan, *Pharsalia* 7.831–37).

Against the day of battle, to a field   275
Where armies lie encamped, come flying, lured
With scent of living carcasses designed
For death, the following day, in bloody fight:
So scented the grim Feature, and upturned
His nostril wide into the murky air,   280
Sagacious of his quarry from so far.
Then both from out hell gates into the waste
Wide anarchy of Chaos damp and dark
Flew diverse, and with power (their power was great)
Hovering upon the waters, what they met   285
Solid or slimy, as in raging sea
Tossed up and down, together crowded drove
From each side shoaling towards the mouth of hell:
As when two polar winds blowing adverse
Upon the Cronian Sea, together drive   290
Mountains of ice, that stop th' imagined way
Beyond Petsora eastward, to the rich
Cathaian coast. The aggregated soil
Death with his mace petrific, cold and dry,
As with a trident smote, and fixed as firm   295
As Delos floating once; the rest his look
Bound with Gorgonian rigor not to move,
And with asphaltic slime; broad as the gate,
Deep to the roots of hell the gathered beach
They fastened, and the mole immense wrought on   300
Over the foaming deep high-arched, a bridge
Of length prodigious joining to the wall
Immovable of this now fenceless world,
Forfeit to Death; from hence a passage broad,
Smooth, easy, inoffensive, down to hell.   305
So, if great things to small may be compared,
Xerxes, the liberty of Greece to yoke,
From Susa his Memnonian palace high
Came to the sea, and over Hellespont
Bridging his way, Europe with Asia joined,   310
And scourged with many a stroke th' indignant waves.
Now had they brought the work by wondrous art
Pontifical, a ridge of pendent rock
Over the vexed abyss, following the track
Of Satan, to the selfsame place where he   315
First lighted from his wing, and landed safe

279–80. Cf. Virgil, *Georg.* 1.376.
285. Cf. 1.19–22.
288. shoaling: forming a shoal.
290. Cronian: Arctic.
291. imagined way: the northeast passage
to the East sought by explorers.
292. Petsora: Siberian river.
294. petrific: petrifying.
295–96. Delos: glossary.
297. Gorgonian: glossary, "Medusa."

302. wall: the outer shell of the universe;
cf. 3.418 and note.
305. inoffensive: without obstacles.
306. Cf. note on 2.921–22.
307–11. Xerxes, the Persian invader of
Greece (480 B.C.), had the waves of the
Hellespont (Dardanelles) scourged for destroying his bridge (Herodotus 7.33–35).
313. Pontifical: bridge-making (perhaps with
a satirical pun on Pontiff, *pontifex*).
315–18. See 3.418 f.

From out of Chaos to the outside bare
Of this round world. With pins of adamant
And chains they made all fast, too fast they made
And durable; and now in little space   320
The confines met of empyrean heav'n
And of this world, and on the left hand hell
With long reach interposed; three sev'ral ways
In sight to each of these three places led.
And now their way to earth they had descried,   325
To Paradise first tending, when behold
Satan in likeness of an angel bright
Betwixt the Centaur and the Scorpion steering
His zenith, while the sun in Aríes rose.
Disguised he came, but those his children dear   330
Their parent soon discerned, though in disguise.
He, after Eve seduced, unminded slunk
Into the wood fast by, and changing shape
To observe the sequel, saw his guileful act
By Eve, though all unweeting, seconded   335
Upon her husband, saw their shame that sought
Vain covertures; but when he saw descend
The Son of God to judge them, terrified
He fled, not hoping to escape, but shun
The present, fearing guilty what his wrath   340
Might suddenly inflict; that past, returned
By night, and list'ning where the hapless pair
Sat in their sad discourse and various plaint,
Thence gathered his own doom; which understood
Not instant, but of future time. With joy   345
And tidings fraught, to hell he now returned,
And at the brink of Chaos, near the foot
Of this new wondrous pontifice, unhoped
Met who to meet him came, his offspring dear.
Great joy was at their meeting, and at sight   350
Of that stupendious bridge his joy increased.
Long he admiring stood, till Sin, his fair
Enchanting daughter, thus the silence broke:
    "O Parent, these are thy magnific deeds,
Thy trophies, which thou view'st as not thine own;   355
Thou art their author and prime architect.
For I no sooner in my heart divined
(My heart, which by a secret harmony

320–24. See 3.501–43.
322. Hell was traditionally on God's left side, far below heaven (Matt. 25.33).
328–29. Centaur, Scorpion, Aries ("the Ram"): constellations in the zodiac.
345. The punctuation is that of edd. 1–6, "understood" being a past tense with the subject "he" omitted. Many editors follow the early emendation, "time, with," taking "understood" as a participle.

347. foot: upper end.
348. pontifice: bridge (see note on 313).
354–409. In this continuation of the allegory of Satan, Sin, and Death, the parody of the Trinity is carried on: Sin and Satan speak as if the building of the symbolic bridge from hell to the world were the Son's original creation approved by God.

Still moves with thine, joined in connexion sweet)
That thou on earth hadst prospered, which thy looks   360
Now also evidence, but straight I felt,
Though distant from thee worlds between, yet felt
That I must after thee with this thy son;
Such fatal consequence unites us three.
Hell could no longer hold us in her bounds,   365
Nor this unvoyageable gulf obscure
Detain from following thy illustrious track.
Thou hast achieved our liberty, confined
Within hell gates till now, thou us empow'red
To fortify thus far, and overlay   370
With this portentous bridge the dark abyss.
Thine now is all this world, thy virtue hath won
What thy hands builded not, thy wisdom gained
With odds what war hath lost, and fully avenged
Our foil in heav'n; here thou shalt monarch reign,   375
There didst not; there let him still Victor sway,
As battle hath adjudged, from this new world
Retiring, by his own doom alienated,
And henceforth monarchy with thee divide
Of all things, parted by th' empyreal bounds,   380
His quadrature, from thy orbicular world,
Or try thee now more dang'rous to his throne."
    Whom thus the Prince of Darkness answered glad:
"Fair daughter, and thou son and grandchild both,
High proof ye now have giv'n to be the race   385
Of Satan (for I glory in the name,
Antagonist of heav'n's Almighty King),
Amply have merited of me, of all
Th' infernal empire, that so near heav'n's door
Triumphal with triumphal act have met,   390
Mine with this glorious work, and made one realm
Hell and this world, one realm, one continent
Of easy thoroughfare. Therefore while I
Descend through darkness, on your road with ease
To my associate Powers, them to acquaint   395
With these successes, and with them rejoice,
You two this way, among those numerous orbs,
All yours, right down to Paradise descend;
There dwell and reign in bliss; thence on the earth
Dominion exercise and in the air,   400
Chiefly on man, sole lord of all declared;
Him first make sure your thrall, and lastly kill.
My substitutes I send ye, and create
Plenipotent on earth, of matchless might
Issuing from me: on your joint vigor now   405

364. consequence: connection.
381. quadrature: square-shaped (heaven);
cf. 2.1048 and note.

386. name: see note on 1.81.
403–05. Cf. 3.317–20, 5.606–11.

My hold of this new kingdom all depends,
Through Sin to Death exposed by my exploit.
If your joint power prevail, th' affairs of hell
No detriment need fear; go and be strong."
So saying he dismissed them; they with speed   410
Their course through thickest constellations held,
Spreading their bane; the blasted stars looked wan,
And planets, planet-strook, real eclipse
Then suffered. Th' other way Satan went down
The causey to hell gate; on either side   415
Disparted Chaos over-built exclaimed,
And with rebounding surge the bars assailed,
That scorned his indignation. Through the gate,
Wide open and unguarded, Satan passed,
And all about found desolate; for those   420
Appointed to sit there had left their charge,
Flown to the upper world; the rest were all
Far to the inland retired, about the walls
Of Pandemonium, city and proud seat
Of Lucifer, so by allusion called   425
Of that bright star to Satan paragoned.
There kept their watch the legions, while the grand
In council sat, solicitous what chance
Might intercept their Emperor sent; so he
Departing gave command, and they observed.   430
As when the Tartar from his Russian foe
By Astracan over the snowy plains
Retires, or Bactrian Sophi, from the horns
Of Turkish crescent, leaves all waste beyond
The realm of Aladule, in his retreat   435
To Tauris or Casbeen: so these, the late
Heav'n-banished host, left desert utmost hell
Many a dark league, reduced in careful watch
Round their metropolis, and now expecting
Each hour their great adventurer from the search   440
Of foreign worlds. He through the midst unmarked,
In show plebeian angel militant
Of lowest order, passed; and from the door
Of that Plutonian hall, invisible
Ascended his high throne, which under state   445
Of richest texture spread, at th' upper end
Was placed in regal luster. Down a while
He sat, and round about him saw unseen.

408. Ed. 1, prevail; ed. 2, prevails.
409. No detriment. From the formula used in ancient Rome when, in a crisis, special powers were given to the consuls.
412–14. The planets, which normally affect the earth, are themselves struck or blasted by the malign influence of Sin and Death.
415. causey: causeway.
425–26. Glossary, "Lucifer."

426. paragoned: paralleled, associated with.
432. Astracan: a city near the mouth of the Volga.
433. Bactrian Sophi: Persian ruler.   horns . . . crescent: flag, i.e. army.
435. Aladule: greater Armenia (from the name of the last king).
436. Tauris: Tabriz, in northwestern Persia. Casbeen: Kazvin, in north Persia.

At last as from a cloud his fulgent head
And shape star-bright appeared, or brighter, clad   450
With what permissive glory since his fall
Was left him, or false glitter. All amazed
At that so sudden blaze the Stygian throng
Bent their aspéct, and whom they wished beheld,
Their mighty Chief returned: loud was th' acclaim.   455
Forth rushed in haste the great consulting peers,
Raised from their dark divan, and with like joy
Congratulant approached him, who with hand
Silence, and with these words attention won:
     "Thrones, Dominations, Princedoms, Virtues, Powers,   460
For in possession such, not only of right,
I call ye and declare ye now, returned
Successful beyond hope, to lead ye forth
Triumphant out of this infernal pit
Abominable, accurst, the house of woe,   465
And dungeon of our tyrant. Now possess,
As lords, a spacious world, to our native heaven
Little inferior, by my adventure hard
With peril great achieved. Long were to tell
What I have done, what suffered, with what pain   470
Voyaged th' unreal, vast, unbounded deep
Of horrible confusion, over which
By Sin and Death a broad way now is paved
To expedite your glorious march; but I
Toiled out my uncouth passage, forced to ride   475
Th' untractable abyss, plunged in the womb
Of unoriginal Night and Chaos wild,
That jealous of their secrets fiercely opposed
My journey strange, with clamorous uproar
Protesting fate supreme; thence how I found   480
The new-created world, which fame in heav'n
Long had foretold, a fabric wonderful
Of absolute perfection, therein man
Placed in a Paradise, by our exile
Made happy. Him by fraud I have seduced   485
From his Creator, and the more to increase
Your wonder, with an apple; he thereat
Offended, worth your laughter, hath giv'n up
Both his beloved man and all his world
To Sin and Death a prey, and so to us,   490
Without our hazard, labor, or alarm,
To range in, and to dwell, and over man
To rule, as over all he should have ruled.

457. divan: Turkish council (cf. "Sultan," 1.348).
458–59. Cf. Lucan, *Pharsalia* 1.297–98.
460–61. Cf. 5.772 f.
471. unreal: unformed.
477. unoriginal: having no originator (cf.

2.962).
478–80. But see 2.1008–09.
480. Protesting fate: appealing to fate against Satan's intrusion.
481–82. fame: cf. 1.651 f., 2.345 f.

True is, me also he hath judged, or rather
Me not, but the brute serpent in whose shape   495
Man I deceived; that which to me belongs
Is enmity, which he will put between
Me and mankind; I am to bruise his heel;
His seed, when is not set, shall bruise my head.
A world who would not purchase with a bruise,   500
Or much more grievous pain? Ye have th' account
Of my performance; what remains, ye gods,
But up and enter now into full bliss?"
     So having said, a while he stood, expecting
Their universal shout and high applause   505
To fill his ear, when contrary he hears
On all sides from innumerable tongues
A dismal universal hiss, the sound
Of public scorn; he wondered, but not long
Had leisure, wond'ring at himself now more;   510
His visage drawn he felt to sharp and spare,
His arms clung to his ribs, his legs entwining
Each other, till supplanted down he fell
A monstrous serpent on his belly prone,
Reluctant, but in vain: a greater power   515
Now ruled him, punished in the shape he sinned,
According to his doom. He would have spoke,
But hiss for hiss returned with forkèd tongue
To forkèd tongue, for now were all transformed
Alike, to serpents all, as accessóries   520
To his bold riot. Dreadful was the din
Of hissing through the hall, thick swarming now
With complicated monsters, head and tail,
Scorpion and asp, and amphisbaena dire,
Cerastes horned, hydrus, and ellops drear,   525
And dipsas (not so thick swarmed once the soil
Bedropped with blood of Gorgon, or the isle
Ophiusa); but still greatest he the midst,
Now dragon grown, larger than whom the sun
Engendered in the Pythian vale on slime,   530
Huge Python, and his power no less he seemed
Above the rest still to retain. They all
Him followed issuing forth to th' open field,

504 f. The metamorphosis of Satan's follow-ers and then of himself, the final outward mani-festation of their inward state, has partial ante-cedents in Ovid, *Met.* 4.576–89, Lucan, *Phar-salia* 9.700–33, Dante, *Inf.* 24.82 f. and 25, and P. Fletcher, *Purple Island* 7.11.

513. supplanted: tripped, overthrown.
517. doom: see 175–78.
521. riot: rebellion.
523. complicated: twined together.
524–26. These various kinds of snakes be-long to traditional animal and allegorical lore (one source, Lucan, is cited above under

504 f.), and, like the scenes in hell (2.521 f.), suggest mental anarchy and turmoil.
524. amphisbaena: a fabulous snake with a head at each end.
525. Cerastes: a horned snake.   hydrus: water-snake.   ellops: perhaps the sword-fish.
526. dipsas: a serpent whose bite caused acute thirst.   soil: of Libya, which was filled with serpents when drops of blood fell from the head of Medusa (glossary).
528. Ophiusa ("serpent-island"): an ancient name for one of the Balearic islands.

Where all yet left of that revolted rout,
Heav'n-fall'n, in station stood or just array,   535
Sublime with expectation when to see
In triumph issuing forth their glorious Chief;
They saw, but other sight instead, a crowd
Of ugly serpents; horror on them fell,
And horrid sympathy; for what they saw,   540
They felt themselves now changing; down their arms,
Down fell both spear and shield, down they as fast,
And the dire hiss renewed, and the dire form
Catched by contagion, like in punishment
As in their crime. Thus was th' applause they meant   545
Turned to exploding hiss, triumph to shame
Cast on themselves from their own mouths. There stood
A grove hard by, sprung up with this their change,
His will who reigns above, to aggravate
Their penance, laden with fair fruit like that   550
Which grew in Paradise, the bait of Eve
Used by the Tempter. On that prospect strange
Their earnest eyes they fixed, imagining
For one forbidden tree a multitude
Now ris'n, to work them furder woe or shame;   555
Yet parched with scalding thirst and hunger fierce,
Though to delude them sent, could not abstain,
But on they rolled in heaps, and up the trees
Climbing, sat thicker than the snaky locks
That curled Megaera. Greedily they plucked   560
The fruitage fair to sight, like that which grew
Near that bituminous lake where Sodom flamed;
This more delusive, not the touch, but taste
Deceived; they fondly thinking to allay
Their appetite with gust, instead of fruit   565
Chewed bitter ashes, which th' offended taste
With spattering noise rejected. Oft they assayed,
Hunger and thirst constraining; drugged as oft,
With hatefulest disrelish writhed their jaws
With soot and cinders filled; so oft they fell   570
Into the same illusion, not as man
Whom they triumphed once lapsed. Thus were they plagued
And worn with famine, long and ceaseless hiss,
Till their lost shape, permitted, they resumed,
Yearly enjoined, some say, to undergo   575
This annual humbling certain numbered days,
To dash their pride, and joy for man seduced.
However, some tradition they dispersed

546. exploding: from the Latin word for an audience hissing and hooting actors from the stage.
560. Megaera: one of the three Furies, who had snakes in their hair.
562. lake: the Dead Sea; cf. the proverbial "Dead Sea fruit." Sodom: Gen. 19.24.
565. gust: gusto.
568. drugged: nauseated.
571–72. man . . . lapsed. Man, over whom they triumphed, lapsed only once.

Among the heathen of their purchase got,
And fabled how the Serpent, whom they called   580
Ophion, with Eurynome, the wide-
Encroaching Eve perhaps, had first the rule
Of high Olympus, thence by Saturn driv'n
And Ops, ere yet Dictaean Jove was born.
    Meanwhile in Paradise the hellish pair   585
Too soon arrived, Sin there in power before,
Once actual, now in body, and to dwell
Habitual habitant; behind her Death
Close following pace for pace, not mounted yet
On his pale horse; to whom Sin thus began: 590
    "Second of Satan sprung, all-conquering Death,
What think'st thou of our empire now, though earned
With travail difficult, not better far
Than still at hell's dark threshold to have sat watch,
Unnamed, undreaded, and thyself half-starved?"   595
    Whom thus the Sin-born Monster answered soon:
"To me, who with eternal famine pine,
Alike is hell, or Paradise, or heaven,
There best, where most with ravin I may meet;
Which here, though plenteous, all too little seems   600
To stuff this maw, this vast unhidebound corpse."
    To whom th' incestuous mother thus replied:
"Thou therefore on these herbs, and fruits, and flow'rs
Feed first; on each beast next, and fish, and fowl,
No homely morsels; and whatever thing   605
The scythe of Time mows down, devour unspared;
Till I in man residing through the race,
His thoughts, his looks, words, actions all infect,
And season him thy last and sweetest prey."
    This said, they both betook them several ways,   610
Both to destroy, or unimmortal make
All kinds, and for destruction to mature
Sooner or later; which th' Almighty seeing,
From his transcendent seat the saints among,
To those bright orders uttered thus his voice: 615
    "See with what heat these dogs of hell advance
To waste and havoc yonder world, which I
So fair and good created, and had still
Kept in that state, had not the folly of man
Let in these wasteful furies, who impute   620
Folly to me (so doth the Prince of Hell
And his adherents), that with so much ease

579. purchase: acquisition, prey.
581–84. Ophion ("serpent"): a Titan, first ruler of Olympus, husband of Eurynome ("wide-ruling"). The traditional identification with Satan is made, e.g., by G. Sandys in the commentary on book 1 in his *Ovid*.
584. Ops: glossary, "Rhea."   Dictaean: from Dicte, a mountain of Crete, where Jupiter was brought up.

587. actual: actualized by Adam and Eve (Milton, *C.D.* 1.11).
590. pale horse: Rev. 6.8.
601. unhidebound: with loose skin. corpse: body.
602. incestuous: cf. 2.790 f.
616–17. Cf. *Julius Caesar* 3.1.273.

I suffer them to enter and possess
A place so heav'nly, and conniving seem
To gratify my scornful enemies,   625
That laugh, as if transported with some fit
Of passion I to them had quitted all,
At random yielded up to their misrule;
And know not that I called and drew them thither,
My hell-hounds, to lick up the draff and filth   630
Which man's polluting sin with taint hath shed
On what was pure, till crammed and gorged, nigh burst
With sucked and glutted offal, at one sling
Of thy victorious arm, well-pleasing Son,
Both Sin, and Death, and yawning grave at last   635
Through Chaos hurled, obstruct the mouth of hell
For ever, and seal up his ravenous jaws.
Then heav'n and earth renewed shall be made pure
To sanctity that shall receive no stain;
Till then the curse pronounced on both precedes."   640
     He ended, and the heav'nly audience loud
Sung halleluiah, as the sound of seas,
Through multitude that sung: "Just are thy ways,
Righteous are thy decrees on all thy works;
Who can extenuate thee? Next, to the Son,   645
Destined restorer of mankind, by whom
New heav'n and earth shall to the ages rise,
Or down from heav'n descend." Such was their song,
While the Creator calling forth by name
His mighty angels gave them several charge,   650
As sorted best with present things. The sun
Had first his precept so to move, so shine,
As might affect the earth with cold and heat
Scarce tolerable, and from the north to call
Decrepit winter, from the south to bring   655
Solstitial summer's heat. To the blank moon
Her office they prescribed, to th' other five
Their planetary motions and aspécts
In sextile, square, and trine, and opposite,
Of noxious efficacy, and when to join   660
In synod unbenign, and taught the fixed
Their influence malignant when to show'r,

---

624. conniving: shutting eyes to wrong, acquiescence in.
633. sling: 1 Sam. 25.29.
638–39. 2 Pet. 3.7, 10–13.
640. precedes: prevails, operates.
641–43. Rev. 19.6.
643–44. Rev. 15.3, 16.7.
645. extenuate: lessen, disparage.
647–48. Rev. 21.1–2.
651 f. As Adam and Eve have now become ordinary sinful mortals, idyllic prelapsarian nature becomes subject to the harsh vicissitudes of the ordinary world (Gen. 3.17; Milton, *C.D.* 1.13); cf. 9.782–84, 1000–04.
657–64. The most explicitly astrological passage in *P.L.*: sextile, square, trine, and opposite describe "aspects" of the planets when they are respectively 60, 90, 120, and 180 degrees apart.
657. other   five   (planets):   glossary, "sphere."
661. synod: conjunction or linear proximity of the planets.   fixed: glossary.

Which of them rising with the sun, or falling,
Should prove tempestuous. To the winds they set
Their corners, when with bluster to confound   665
Sea, air, and shore, the thunder when to roll
With terror through the dark aerial hall.
Some say he bid his angels turn askance
The poles of earth twice ten degrees and more
From the sun's axle; they with labor pushed   670
Oblique the centric globe: some say the sun
Was bid turn reins from th' equinoctial road
Like distant breadth to Taurus with the sev'n
Atlantic Sisters, and the Spartan Twins,
Up to the Tropic Crab; thence down amain   675
By Leo and the Virgin and the Scales,
As deep as Capricorn, to bring in change
Of seasons to each clime; else had the spring
Perpetual smiled on earth with vernant flow'rs,
Equal in days and nights, except to those   680
Beyond the polar circles; to them day
Had unbenighted shone, while the low sun,
To recompense his distance, in their sight
Had rounded still th' horizon, and not known
Or east or west, which had forbid the snow   685
From cold Estotiland, and south as far
Beneath Magellan. At that tasted fruit
The sun, as from Thyestean banquet, turned
His course intended; else how had the world
Inhabited, though sinless, more than now   690
Avoided pinching cold and scorching heat?
These changes in the heav'ns, though slow, produced
Like change on sea and land, sideral blast,
Vapor, and mist, and exhalation hot,
Corrupt and pestilent. Now from the north   695
Of Norumbega, and the Samoed shore,
Bursting their brazen dungeon, armed with ice
And snow and hail and stormy gust and flaw,
Boreas and Caecias and Argestes loud
And Thrascias rend the woods and seas upturn;   700
With adverse blast upturns them from the south

668–78. Before the fall the sun's path (ecliptic) was in the same plane as the equator, so that there was only one season; now seasons are introduced through the setting of the earth's axis at an angle to the plane of the ecliptic or by the shifting of the center of the sun's orbit.
671. centric globe: the earth.
673–77. Constellations in the zodiac: Taurus, the Bull; Atlantic Sisters, the Pleiades; Spartan Twins, Gemini; Crab, Cancer; Leo, the Lion; Virgin, Virgo; Scales, Libra.
679. vernant: vernal.
686. Estotiland: an old vague name for Labrador or a supposed island near it.
687. Magellan: the strait at the tip of South America.

688. Thyestean banquet: the sons of Thyestes, killed and served to their father by his brother Atreus. For the sun, cf. Seneca, *Thyestes* 776–78.
693. sideral: from the stars.
696. Norumbega: northern New England. Samoed shore: northeastern Siberia.
697. Bursting . . . dungeon: cf. *Aen.* 1.52 f.
699–706. Most of the names of the winds were familiar from classical authors, and they with the others were listed in encyclopedias: Caecias, northeast wind; Argestes, northwest; Thrascias, north-northwest; Notus, south; Afer, southwest; Levant ("rising"), east; Ponent ("setting"), west; Sirocco and Libecchio, Italian names for southeast and southwest winds.

Notus and Afer black with thund'rous clouds
From Serraliona; thwart of these as fierce
Forth rush the Levant and the Ponent winds,
Eurus and Zephyr with their lateral noise, 705
Sirocco and Libecchio. Thus began
Outrage from lifeless things; but Discord first,
Daughter of Sin, among th' irrational
Death introduced through fierce antipathy.
Beast now with beast gan war, and fowl with fowl, 710
And fish with fish; to graze the herb all leaving,
Devour'd each other; nor stood much in awe
Of man, but fled him, or with count'nance grim
Glared on him passing. These were from without
The growing miseries, which Adam saw 715
Already in part, though hid in gloomiest shade,
To sorrow abandoned, but worse felt within,
And in a troubled sea of passion tossed,
Thus to disburden sought with sad complaint:
    "O miserable of happy! Is this the end 720
Of this new glorious world, and me so late
The glory of that glory, who now, become
Accurst of blessèd, hide me from the face
Of God, whom to behold was then my highth
Of happiness? Yet well, if here would end 725
The misery; I deserved it, and would bear
My own deservings; but this will not serve:
All that I eat or drink, or shall beget,
Is propagated curse. O voice once heard
Delightfully, 'Increase and multiply,' 730
Now death to hear! for what can I increase
Or multiply, but curses on my head?
Who of all ages to succeed, but feeling
The evil on him brought by me, will curse
My head? 'Ill fare our ancestor impure! 735
For this we may thank Adam'; but his thanks
Shall be the execration; so besides
Mine own that bide upon me, all from me
Shall with a fierce reflux on me redound,
On me as on their natural center light 740
Heavy, though in their place. O fleeting joys
Of Paradise, dear bought with lasting woes!
Did I request thee, Maker, from my clay
To mold me man, did I solicit thee
From darkness to promote me, or here place 745
In this delicious garden? As my will

---

703. Serraliona: Sierra Leone, on the west
coast of Africa.
    718. Isa. 57.20.
    720–844. Adam's soliloquy, the longest
single speech in the poem, works out of pride,
despair, and evasion into humble justification
of God's ways to men.

730. Gen. 1.28.
    738. Mine own (curses, i.e. evils).
    740–41. Things landing on their natural
center should be weightless, not heavy.
    743–44. Isa. 45.9.

Concurred not to my being, it were but right
And equal to reduce me to my dust,
Desirous to resign and render back
All I received, unable to perform   750
Thy terms too hard, by which I was to hold
The good I sought not. To the loss of that,
Sufficient penalty, why hast thou added
The sense of endless woes? Inexplicable
Thy justice seems; yet to say truth, too late   755
I thus contést; then should have been refused
Those terms whatever, when they were proposed.
Thou didst accept them; wilt thou enjoy the good,
Then cavil the conditions? And though God
Made thee without thy leave, what if thy son   760
Prove disobedient, and reproved, retort,
'Wherefore didst thou beget me? I sought it not.'
Wouldst thou admit for his contempt of thee
That proud excuse? Yet him not thy election,
But natural necessity begot.   765
God made thee of choice his own, and of his own
To serve him; thy reward was of his grace;
Thy punishment then justly is at his will.
Be it so, for I submit, his doom is fair,
That dust I am, and shall to dust return.   770
O welcome hour whenever! Why delays
His hand to execute what his decree
Fixed on this day? Why do I overlive,
Why am I mocked with death, and lengthened out
To deathless pain? How gladly would I meet   775
Mortality, my sentence, and be earth
Insensible, how glad would lay me down
As in my mother's lap! There I should rest
And sleep secure; his dreadful voice no more
Would thunder in my ears, no fear of worse   780
To me and to my offspring would torment me
With cruel expectation. Yet one doubt
Pursues me still, lest all I cannot die,
Lest that pure breath of life, the spirit of man
Which God inspired, cannot together perish   785
With this corporeal clod; then in the grave
Or in some other dismal place, who knows
But I shall die a living death? O thought
Horrid, if true! Yet why? It was but breath
Of life that sinned; what dies but what had life   790

758–68. Thou, thee, thy: i.e. Adam, Adam's.
762. Isa. 45.10.
770. Gen. 3.19; Job 34.15.
773. overlive: live on.
775 f. Job 3.10 f.
778. mother's lap. Cf. Ovid, *Met.* 1.383, 393; Spenser, *F.Q.* 5.7.9.2.

782–92. Milton puts into the mouth of the despairing Adam the so-called "mortalist heresy" which he upheld in *C.D.* 1.13: that the soul dies with the body until the resurrection.

783. all . . . die. Milton echoes the words but alters the sense of Horace, *Od.* 3.30.6.

And sin? The body properly hath neither.
All of me then shall die: let this appease
The doubt, since human reach no further knows.
For though the Lord of all be infinite,
Is his wrath also? Be it, man is not so,   795
But mortal doomed. How can he exercise
Wrath without end on man whom death must end?
Can he make deathless death? That were to make
Strange contradiction, which to God himself
Impossible is held, as argument   800
Of weakness, not of power. Will he draw out,
For anger's sake, finite to infinite
In punished man, to satisfy his rigor
Satisfied never? That were to extend
His sentence beyond dust and Nature's law,   805
By which all causes else according still
To the reception of their matter act,
Not to th' extent of their own sphere. But say
That death be not one stroke, as I supposed,
Bereaving sense, but endless misery   810
From this day onward, which I feel begun
Both in me and without me, and so last
To perpetuity: ay me, that fear
Comes thund'ring back with dreadful revolution
On my defenseless head; both Death and I   815
Am found eternal, and incorporate both,
Nor I on my part single; in me all
Posterity stands cursed. Fair patrimony
That I must leave ye, sons; O were I able
To waste it all myself, and leave ye none!   820
So disinherited how would ye bless
Me, now your curse! Ah, why should all mankind
For one man's fault thus guiltless be condemned,
If guiltless? But from me what can proceed
But all corrupt, both mind and will depraved,   825
Not to do only, but to will the same
With me? How can they then acquitted stand
In sight of God? Him after all disputes
Forced I absolve; all my evasions vain
And reasonings, though through mazes, lead me still   830
But to my own conviction: first and last
On me, me only, as the source and spring
Of all corruption, all the blame lights due;
So might the wrath. Fond wish! couldst thou support
That burden heavier than the earth to bear,   835

798–801. Cf. Milton, *C.D.* 1.2; 2 Tim.
2.13; Heb. 6.18.
805. Nature's law: "that general law which
is the origin of every thing, and under which
every thing acts" (*C.D.* 1.2). Cf. Hooker,
quoted in the note on 7.168–73.

806–08. Causes operate, not in proportion
to their own power, but in proportion to the
capacity of the object they work upon.
816. The ungrammatical "Am" expresses
Adam's shocked realization that death has become part of, identical with, himself.

Than all the world much heavier, though divided
With that bad woman? Thus what thou desir'st
And what thou fear'st, alike destroys all hope
Of refuge, and concludes thee miserable
Beyond all past example and future,   840
To Satan only like, both crime and doom.
O Conscience, into what abyss of fears
And horrors hast thou driv'n me; out of which
I find no way, from deep to deeper plunged!"
   Thus Adam to himself lamented loud   845
Through the still night, not now, as ere man fell,
Wholesome and cool and mild, but with black air
Accompanied, with damps and dreadful gloom,
Which to his evil conscience represented
All things with double terror. On the ground   850
Outstretched he lay, on the cold ground, and oft
Cursed his creation, Death as oft accused
Of tardy execution, since denounced
The day of his offense. "Why comes not Death,"
Said he, "with one thrice-ácceptáble stroke   855
To end me? Shall Truth fail to keep her word,
Justice divine not hasten to be just?
But Death comes not at call, Justice divine
Mends not her slowest pace for prayers or cries.
O woods, O fountains, hillocks, dales, and bow'rs,   860
With other echo late I taught your shades
To answer, and resound far other song."
Whom thus afflicted when sad Eve beheld,
Desolate where she sat, approaching nigh,
Soft words to his fierce passion she assayed;   865
But her with stern regard he thus repelled:
   "Out of my sight, thou serpent! that name best
Befits thee with him leagued, thyself as false
And hateful; nothing wants, but that thy shape,
Like his, and color serpentine, may show   870
Thy inward fraud, to warn all creatures from thee
Henceforth; lest that too heav'nly form, pretended
To hellish falsehood, snare them. But for thee
I had persisted happy, had not thy pride
And wand'ring vanity, when least was safe,   875
Rejected my forewarning, and disdained
Not to be trusted, longing to be seen
Though by the Devil himself, him overweening
To overreach, but with the Serpent meeting
Fooled and beguiled, by him thou, I by thee.   880
To trust thee from my side, imagined wise,

842–44. Cf. 4.75–78.
852. Job 3.1.
854–56. Cf. Sophocles, *Philoctetes* 797–98.
858–59. Cf. Horace, *Od.* 3.2.31–32.

861–62. Cf. 5.202–04; Virgil, *Ecl.* 1.4–5.
867–68. serpent. In patristic etymologizing,
"Heva," Eve's name aspirated, meant "serpent."
872. pretended: spread before as a screen.

Constant, mature, proof against all assaults,
And understood not all was but a show
Rather than solid virtue, all but a rib
Crooked by nature, bent, as now appears,   885
More to the part siníster from me drawn;
Well if thrown out, as supernumerary
To my just number found. O why did God,
Creator wise, that peopled highest heav'n
With Spirits masculine, create at last   890
This novelty on earth, this fair defect
Of Nature, and not fill the world at once
With men as angels without feminine,
Or find some other way to generate
Mankind? This mischief had not then befall'n,   895
And more that shall befall, innumerable
Disturbances on earth through female snares,
And strait conjunction with this sex. For either
He never shall find out fit mate, but such
As some misfortune brings him, or mistake,   900
Or whom he wishes most shall seldom gain,
Through her perverseness, but shall see her gained
By a far worse, or if she love, withheld
By parents, or his happiest choice too late
Shall meet, already linked and wedlock-bound   905
To a fell adversary, his hate or shame;
Which infinite calamity shall cause
To human life, and household peace confound."
        He added not, and from her turned, but Eve,
Not so repulsed, with tears that ceased not flowing,   910
And tresses all disordered, at his feet
Fell humble, and embracing them, besought
His peace, and thus proceeded in her plaint:
        "Forsake me not thus, Adam, witness Heav'n
What love sincere and reverence in my heart   915
I bear thee, and unweeting have offended,
Unhappily deceived; thy suppliant
I beg, and clasp thy knees; bereave me not
Whereon I live, thy gentle looks, thy aid,
Thy counsel in this uttermost distress,   920
My only strength and stay. Forlorn of thee,
Whither shall I betake me, where subsist?
While yet we live, scarce one short hour perhaps,
Between us two let there be peace, both joining,
As joined in injuries, one enmity   925
Against a foe by doom express assigned us,

884–88. In tradition Adam had 13 ribs on one side and Eve, made from a crooked rib, was morally defective.

886. siníster: left, with the usual meaning also.

888 f. Cf. Euripides, *Hippolytus* 616 f.

910–12. Luke 7.38.

913 f. Eve, who had initiated sin, initiates reconciliation. Her speech is in that minor key, the rhythm of love, which is heard throughout the poem chiefly on the lips of the Son.

That cruel Serpent. On me exercise not
Thy hatred for this misery befall'n,
On me already lost, me than thyself
More miserable. Both have sinned, but thou   930
Against God only, I against God and thee,
And to the place of judgment will return,
There with my cries importune Heaven, that all
The sentence from thy head removed may light
On me, sole cause to thee of all this woe,   935
Me, me only, just object of his ire."
    She ended weeping, and her lowly plight,
Immovable till peace obtained from fault
Acknowledged and deplored, in Adam wrought
Commiseration; soon his heart relented   940
Towards her, his life so late and sole delight,
Now at his feet submissive in distress,
Creature so fair his reconcilement seeking,
His counsel whom she had displeased, his aid;
As one disarmed, his anger all he lost,   945
And thus with peaceful words upraised her soon:
    "Unwary, and too desirous, as before
So now, of what thou know'st not, who desir'st
The punishment all on thyself; alas,
Bear thine own first, ill able to sustain   950
His full wrath whose thou feel'st as yet least part,
And my displeasure bear'st so ill. If prayers
Could alter high decrees, I to that place
Would speed before thee, and be louder heard,
That on my head all might be visited,   955
Thy frailty and infirmer sex forgiv'n,
To me committed and by me exposed.
But rise, let us no more contend, nor blame
Each other, blamed enough elsewhere, but strive
In offices of love, how we may light'n   960
Each other's burden in our share of woe;
Since this day's death denounced, if aught I see,
Will prove no sudden, but a slow-paced evil,
A long day's dying to augment our pain,
And to our seed (O hapless seed!) derived."   965
    To whom thus Eve, recovering heart, replied:
"Adam, by sad experiment I know
How little weight my words with thee can find,
Found so erroneous, thence by just event
Found so unfortunate; nevertheless,   970
Restored by thee, vile as I am, to place
Of new acceptance, hopeful to regain

931. Ps. 51.4.
938. Immovable: unchangeable, referring to
both Eve's being on her knees and her un-
happiness.

959. elsewhere: in heaven.
961. Gal. 6.2.

Thy love, the sole contentment of my heart
Living or dying, from thee I will not hide
What thoughts in my unquiet breast are ris'n,   975
Tending to some relief of our extremes,
Or end, though sharp and sad, yet tolerable,
As in our evils, and of easier choice.
If care of our descent perplex us most,
Which must be born to certain woe, devoured   980
By Death at last (and miserable it is
To be to others cause of misery,
Our own begotten, and of our loins to bring
Into this cursèd world a woeful race,
That after wretched life must be at last   985
Food for so foul a monster), in thy power
It lies, yet ere conception, to prevent
The race unblest, to being yet unbegot.
Childless thou art, childless remain; so Death
Shall be deceived his glut, and with us two   990
Be forced to satisfy his rav'nous maw.
But if thou judge it hard and difficult,
Conversing, looking, loving, to abstain
From love's due rites, nuptial embraces sweet,
And with desire to languish without hope,   995
Before the present object languishing
With like desire, which would be misery
And torment less than none of what we dread,
Then both ourselves and seed at once to free
From what we fear for both, let us make short,   1000
Let us seek Death, or he not found, supply
With our own hands his office on ourselves;
Why stand we longer shivering under fears
That show no end but death, and have the power,
Of many ways to die the shortest choosing,   1005
Destruction with destruction to destroy?"
    She ended here, or vehement despair
Broke off the rest; so much of death her thoughts
Had entertained as dyed her cheeks with pale.
But Adam with such counsel nothing swayed,   1010
To better hopes his more attentive mind
Laboring had raised, and thus to Eve replied:
    "Eve, thy contempt of life and pleasure seems
To argue in thee something more sublime
And excellent than what thy mind contemns;   1015
But self-destruction therefore sought refutes
That excellence thought in thee, and implies,
Not thy contempt, but anguish and regret
For loss of life and pleasure overloved.
Or if thou covet death, as utmost end   1020

979. descent: descendants.   996. object: Eve.
995. Cf. Dante, *Inf.* 4.42.   1000. short: i.e. short work.

Of misery, so thinking to evade
The penalty pronounced, doubt not but God
Hath wiselier armed his vengeful ire than so
To be forestalled; much more I fear lest death
So snatched will not exempt us from the pain   1025
We are by doom to pay; rather such acts
Of contumácy will provoke the Highest
To make death in us live. Then let us seek
Some safer resolution, which methinks
I have in view, calling to mind with heed   1030
Part of our sentence, that thy seed shall bruise
The Serpent's head; piteous amends, unless
Be meant, whom I conjecture, our grand foe
Satan, who in the serpent hath contrived
Against us this deceit. To crush his head   1035
Would be revenge indeed; which will be lost
By death brought on ourselves, or childless days
Resolved, as thou proposest; so our foe
Shall scape his punishment ordained, and we
Instead shall double ours upon our heads.   1040
No more be mentioned then of violence
Against ourselves, and wilful barrenness,
That cuts us off from hope, and savors only
Rancor and pride, impatience and despite,
Reluctance against God and his just yoke   1045
Laid on our necks. Remember with what mild
And gracious temper he both heard and judged,
Without wrath or reviling; we expected
Immediate dissolution, which we thought
Was meant by death that day, when lo, to thee   1050
Pains only in child-bearing were foretold,
And bringing forth, soon recompensed with joy,
Fruit of thy womb; on me the curse aslope
Glanced on the ground: with labor I must earn
My bread; what harm? Idleness had been worse;   1055
My labor will sustain me; and lest cold
Or heat should injure us, his timely care
Hath unbesought provided, and his hands
Clothed us unworthy, pitying while he judged;
How much more, if we pray him, will his ear   1060
Be open, and his heart to pity incline,
And teach us further by what means to shun
Th' inclement seasons, rain, ice, hail, and snow,
Which now the sky with various face begins
To show us in this mountain, while the winds   1065
Blow moist and keen, shattering the graceful locks
Of these fair spreading trees; which bids us seek
Some better shroud, some better warmth to cherish
Our limbs benumbed, ere this diurnal star
Leave cold the night, how we his gathered beams   1070

1052. John 16.21.   1069. star: the sun.

Reflected, may with matter sere foment,
Or by collision of two bodies grind
The air attrite to fire, as late the clouds,
Justling or pushed with winds rude in their shock,
Tine the slant lightning, whose thwart flame driv'n down   1075
Kindles the gummy bark of fir or pine,
And sends a comfortable heat from far,
Which might supply the sun. Such fire to use,
And what may else be remedy or cure
To evils which our own misdeeds have wrought,   1080
He will instruct us praying, and of grace
Beseeching him, so as we need not fear
To pass commodiously this life, sustained
By him with many comforts, till we end
In dust, our final rest and native home.   1085
What better can we do, than to the place
Repairing where he judged us, prostrate fall
Before him reverent, and there confess
Humbly our faults, and pardon beg, with tears
Watering the ground, and with our sighs the air   1090
Frequenting, sent from hearts contrite, in sign
Of sorrow unfeigned, and humiliation meek?
Undoubtedly he will relent and turn
From his displeasure; in whose look serene,
When angry most he seemed and most severe,   1095
What else but favor, grace, and mercy shone?"
　　So spake our father penitent, nor Eve
Felt less remorse. They forthwith to the place
Repairing where he judged them, prostrate fell
Before him reverent, and both confessed   1100
Humbly their faults, and pardon begged, with tears
Watering the ground, and with their sighs the air
Frequenting, sent from hearts contrite, in sign
Of sorrow unfeigned, and humiliation meek.

Book XI

THE ARGUMENT

　　The Son of God presents to his Father the prayers of our first parents now repenting, and intercedes for them. God accepts them, but declares that they must no longer abide in Paradise; sends Michael with a band of Cherubim

1073. attrite: rubbed.
1075. Tine: kindle.
1081. praying: if we pray.
1089–90. Cf. *Aen.* 11.191.
1090–91 and 1102–03, 11.5–6). Cf. Dante,
Inf. 4.25–27.
1098–1104. The repetition of 1086–1092

(Homeric in form rather than in tone) stresses the solemnity of their repentance. In contrast with the end of book 9, this act — following upon their purely human reconciliation — marks the beginning of their recovery, the first workings of grace (11.1 f.) in the soul of fallen man.

to dispossess them, but first to reveal to Adam future things; Michael's coming down. Adam shows to Eve certain ominous signs; he discerns Michael's approach; goes out to meet him; the Angel denounces their departure. Eve's lamentation. Adam pleads, but submits; the Angel leads him up a high hill; sets before him in vision what shall happen till the Flood.

T HUS they in lowliest plight repentant stood
Praying, for from the mercy-seat above
Prevenient grace descending had removed
The stony from their hearts, and made new flesh
Regenerate grow instead, that sighs now breathed   5
Unutterable, which the spirit of prayer
Inspired, and winged for heav'n with speedier flight
Than loudest oratory: yet their port
Not of mean suitors, nor important less
Seemed their petition than when th' ancient pair   10
In fables old, less ancient yet than these,
Deucalion and chaste Pyrrha, to restore
The race of mankind drowned, before the shrine
Of Themis stood devout. To heav'n their prayers
Flew up, nor missed the way, by envious winds   15
Blown vagabond or frustrate: in they passed
Dimensionless through heav'nly doors; then clad
With incense, where the golden altar fumed,
By their great Intercessor, came in sight
Before the Father's throne. Them the glad Son   20
Presenting, thus to intercede began:
    "See, Father, what first-fruits on earth are sprung
From thy implanted grace in man, these sighs
And prayers, which in this golden censer, mixed
With incense, I thy priest before thee bring,   25
Fruits of more pleasing savor, from thy seed
Sown with contrition in his heart, than those
Which, his own hand manuring, all the trees
Of Paradise could have produced, ere fall'n
From innocence. Now therefore bend thine ear   30
To supplication, hear his sighs though mute;
Unskilful with what words to pray, let me
Interpret for him, me his advocate
And propitiation; all his works on me,
Good or not good ingraft; my merit those   35
Shall perfect, and for these my death shall pay.

BOOK XI. 2. mercy-seat: Exod. 25.17–22; Heb. 9.5.

3. Prevenient: anticipating and promoting repentance.

3–4. Cf. 3.188–90 and note.

5–7. Rom. 8.26.

10.14. Deucalion: the Noah of classical myth, husband of Pyrrha (Ovid, *Met.* 1.318 f.).

15–16. nor . . . frustrate: not lost in the Paradise of Fools (3.444–97).

17. Dimensionless: incorporeal.

18. incense: Rev. 8.3–4.

24. golden censer: Heb. 9.4; Rev. 8.3.

33–34. 1 John 2.1–2.

34–44. Cf. 3.281–97.

Accept me, and in me from these receive
The smell of peace toward mankind; let him live
Before thee reconciled, at least his days
Numbered, though sad, till death, his doom (which I   40
To mitigate thus plead, not to reverse),
To better life shall yield him, where with me
All my redeemed may dwell in joy and bliss,
Made one with me as I with thee am one."
    To whom the Father, without cloud, serene: 45
"All thy request for man, accepted Son,
Obtain, all thy request was my decree.
But longer in that Paradise to dwell
The law I gave to Nature him forbids;
Those pure immortal elements that know   50
No gross, no unharmonious mixture foul,
Eject him tainted now, and purge him off
As a distemper, gross to air as gross,
And mortal food, as may dispose him best
For dissolution wrought by sin, that first   55
Distempered all things, and of incorrupt
Corrupted. I at first with two fair gifts
Created him endowed, with happiness
And immortality: that fondly lost,
This other served but to eternize woe,   60
Till I provided death; so death becomes
His final remedy, and after life
Tried in sharp tribulation, and refined
By faith and faithful works, to second life,
Waked in the renovation of the just,   65
Resigns him up with heav'n and earth renewed.
But let us call to synod all the blest
Through heav'n's wide bounds; from them I will not hide
My judgments, how with mankind I proceed,
As how with peccant angels late they saw,   70
And in their state, though firm, stood more confirmed."
    He ended, and the Son gave signal high
To the bright minister that watched; he blew
His trumpet, heard in Oreb since perhaps
When God descended, and perhaps once more   75
To sound at general doom. Th' angelic blast
Filled all the regions; from their blissful bow'rs
Of amarantine shade, fountain or spring,
By the waters of life, where'er they sat
In fellowships of joy, the sons of light   80
Hasted, resorting to the summons high,
And took their seats; till from his throne supreme

---

44. John 17.11, 21–23.
49. Cf. 10.805 and note.
50–53. Cf. 2.137–42, 7.56–59.
74–75. Exod. 19.13–25; cf. *Nativity* 157–
59 and *P.L.* 1.6–10.

75–76. Matt. 24.31; 1 Cor. 15.52; cf.
Nativity 155–56, 160–64.
78. amarantine: glossary, "amaranth."
79. Cf. 3.358.

Th' Almighty thus pronounced his sovran will:
"O Sons, like one of us man is become
To know both good and evil, since his taste   85
Of that defended fruit; but let him boast
His knowledge of good lost, and evil got,
Happier, had it sufficed him to have known
Good by itself, and evil not at all.
He sorrows now, repents, and prays contrite,   90
My motions in him; longer than they move,
His heart I know, how variable and vain
Self-left. Lest therefore his now bolder hand
Reach also of the Tree of Life, and eat,
And live for ever, dream at least to live   95
For ever, to remove him I decree,
And send him from the garden forth to till
The ground whence he was taken, fitter soil.
     "Michael, this my behest have thou in charge,
Take to thee from among the Cherubim   100
Thy choice of flaming warriors, lest the Fiend,
Or in behalf of man, or to invade
Vacant possession, some new trouble raise;
Haste thee, and from the Paradise of God
Without remorse drive out the sinful pair,   105
From hallowed ground th' unholy, and denounce
To them and to their progeny from thence
Perpetual banishment. Yet lest they faint
At the sad sentence rigorously urged,
For I behold them softened and with tears   110
Bewailing their excess, all terror hide.
If patiently thy bidding they obey,
Dismiss them not disconsolate; reveal
To Adam what shall come in future days,
As I shall thee enlighten; intermix   115
My cov'nant in the woman's seed renewed;
So send them forth, though sorrowing, yet in peace;
And on the east side of the garden place,
Where entrance up from Eden easiest climbs,
Cherubic watch, and of a sword the flame   120
Wide-waving, all approach far off to fright,
And guard all passage to the Tree of Life;
Lest Paradise a receptácle prove
To Spirits foul, and all my trees their prey,
With whose stol'n fruit man once more to delude."   125
     He ceased; and th' Archangelic Power prepared
For swift descent, with him the cohort bright
Of watchful Cherubim; four faces each

84–85. Gen. 3.22.
86. defended: forbidden.
86–89. Cf. 9.1071–73.
93. Self-left: left to itself.
93–98. Gen. 3.22–23. Milton adds the re-
interpretative "dream."

102. behalf of: regard to.
116. Cf. 10.179–81.
118–22. Gen. 3.24.
128–30. Cf. 6.749 f. and note.

Had, like a double Janus, all their shape
Spangled with eyes more numerous than those   130
Of Argus, and more wakeful than to drowse,
Charmed with Arcadian pipe, the pastoral reed
Of Hermes, or his opiate rod. Meanwhile
To resalute the world with sacred light,
Leucothea waked, and with fresh dews embalmed   135
The earth, when Adam and first matron Eve
Had ended now their orisons, and found
Strength added from above, new hope to spring
Out of despair, joy, but with fear yet linked;
Which thus to Eve his welcome words renewed: 140
    "Eve, easily may faith admit that all
The good which we enjoy from heav'n descends;
But that from us aught should ascend to heav'n
So prevalent as to concern the mind
Of God high-blest, or to incline his will,   145
Hard to belief may seem; yet this will prayer,
Or one short sigh of human breath, upborne
Ev'n to the seat of God. For since I sought
By prayer th' offended Deity to appease,
Kneeled and before him humbled all my heart,   150
Methought I saw him placable and mild,
Bending his ear; persuasion in me grew
That I was heard with favor; peace returned
Home to my breast, and to my memory
His promise, that thy seed shall bruise our foe;   155
Which, then not minded in dismay, yet now
Assures me that the bitterness of death
Is past, and we shall live. Whence hail to thee,
Eve rightly called mother of all mankind,
Mother of all things living, since by thee   160
Man is to live, and all things live for man."
    To whom thus Eve with sad demeanor meek:
"Ill-worthy I such title should belong
To me transgressor, who for thee ordained
A help, became thy snare; to me reproach   165
Rather belongs, distrust and all dispraise.
But infinite in pardon was my Judge,
That I, who first brought death on all, am graced
The source of life; next favorable thou,
Who highly thus to entitle me vouchsaf'st,   170
Far other name deserving. But the field
To labor calls us, now with sweat imposed,
Though after sleepless night; for see the morn,

129. Janus: Roman god of gates and begin-
nings and the four seasons; usually with two
faces, sometimes with four.
    131. Argus: glossary.
    133. opiate rod: the wand with which
Hermes could cause sleep (cf. Ovid, *Met.*
1.716).

135. Leucothea: glossary.
144. prevalent: powerful.
157. 1 Sam. 15.32.
159–60. Gen. 3.20; cf. *P.L.* 4.475, 5.388.

All unconcerned with our unrest, begins
Her rosy progress smiling; let us forth,   **175**
I never from thy side henceforth to stray,
Where'er our day's work lies, though now enjoined
Laborious, till day droop; while here we dwell,
What can be toilsome in these pleasant walks?
Here let us live, though in fall'n state, content."   **180**
      So spake, so wished much-humbled Eve, but fate
Subscribed not; Nature first gave signs, impressed
On bird, beast, air, air suddenly eclipsed
After short blush of morn. Nigh in her sight
The bird of Jove, stooped from his airy tow'r,   **185**
Two birds of gayest plume before him drove;
Down from a hill the beast that reigns in woods,
First hunter then, pursued a gentle brace,
Goodliest of all the forest, hart and hind;
Direct to th' eastern gate was bent their flight.   **190**
Adam observed, and with his eye the chase
Pursuing, not unmoved to Eve thus spake:
      "O Eve, some furder change awaits us nigh,
Which Heav'n by these mute signs in Nature shows
Forerunners of his purpose, or to warn   **195**
Us, haply too secure of our discharge
From penalty, because from death released
Some days; how long, and what till then our life,
Who knows, or more than this, that we are dust,
And thither must return and be no more?   **200**
Why else this double object in our sight
Of flight pursued in th' air and o'er the ground
One way the selfsame hour? Why in the east
Darkness ere day's mid-course, and morning-light
More orient in yon western cloud that draws   **205**
O'er the blue firmament a radiant white,
And slow descends, with something heav'nly fraught?"
      He erred not, for by this the heav'nly bands
Down from a sky of jasper lighted now
In Paradise, and on a hill made halt,   **210**
A glorious apparition, had not doubt
And carnal fear that day dimmed Adam's eye.
Not that more glorious, when the angels met
Jacob in Mahanaim, where he saw
The field pavilioned with his guardians bright;   **215**
Nor that which on the flaming mount appeared
In Dothan, covered with a camp of fire,
Against the Syrian king, who to surprise

180. Phil. 4.11.
183. eclipsed: darkened.
183–90. These first signs of nature red in tooth and claw also anticipate Michael's expulsion of Adam and Eve; cf. 9.782–84, 1000–04, 10.651 f.

185. bird of Jove: eagle (cf. *Aen.* 12.247 f.).
185. stooped (a term from falconry): swooped.
187. beast: lion.
213–15. Gen. 32.1–2.

One man, assassin-like had levied war,
War unproclaimed. The princely Hierarch   220
In their bright stand, there left his powers to seize
Possession of the garden; he alone,
To find where Adam sheltered, took his way,
Not unperceived of Adam, who to Eve,
While the great visitant approached, thus spake: 225
    "Eve, now expect great tidings, which perhaps
Of us will soon determine, or impose
New laws to be observed; for I descry
From yonder blazing cloud that veils the hill
One of the heav'nly host, and by his gait   230
None of the meanest, some great Potentate
Or of the Thrones above, such majesty
Invests him coming; yet not terrible,
That I should fear, nor sociably mild,
As Raphael, that I should much confide,   235
But solemn and sublime, whom not to offend,
With reverence I must meet, and thou retire."
    He ended; and th' Archangel soon drew nigh,
Not in his shape celestial, but as man
Clad to meet man; over his lucid arms   240
A military vest of purple flowed,
Livelier than Meliboean, or the grain
Of Sarra, worn by kings and heroes old
In time of truce; Iris had dipt the woof;
His starry helm unbuckled showed him prime   245
In manhood where youth ended; by his side
As in a glistering zodiac hung the sword,
Satan's dire dread, and in his hand the spear.
Adam bowed low; he kingly from his state
Inclined not, but his coming thus declared: 250
    "Adam, Heav'n's high behest no preface needs:
Sufficient that thy prayers are heard, and Death,
Then due by sentence when thou didst transgress,
Defeated of his seizure many days
Giv'n thee of grace, wherein thou may'st repent,   255
And one bad act with many deeds well done
May'st cover; well may then thy Lord appeased
Redeem thee quite from Death's rapacious claim;
But longer in this Paradise to dwell
Permits not; to remove thee I am come,   260
And send thee from the garden forth to till
The ground whence thou wast taken, fitter soil."
    He added not, for Adam at the news

219. One man: Elisha, miraculously saved
from the Syrians (2 Kings 6.17).
    219. assassin-like: treacherously.
    240. lucid: bright.
    242. Meliboea: a Thessalian town noted for
its purple dye.

243. Sarra: Tyre, on the Phoenician coast.
244. Iris: glossary (cf. *Comus* 83).
247–48. sword . . . dread: cf. 6.250, 320 f.

Heart-strook with chilling gripe of sorrow stood,
That all his senses bound; Eve, who unseen   265
Yet all had heard, with audible lament
Discovered soon the place of her retire:
   "O unexpected stroke, worse than of Death!
Must I thus leave thee, Paradise? Thus leave
Thee, native soil, these happy walks and shades,   270
Fit haunt of gods? Where I had hope to spend,
Quiet though sad, the respite of that day
That must be mortal to us both. O flow'rs,
That never will in other climate grow,
My early visitation, and my last   275
At ev'n, which I bred up with tender hand
From the first op'ning bud, and gave ye names,
Who now shall rear ye to the sun, or rank
Your tribes, and water from th' ambrosial fount?
Thee lastly, nuptial bower, by me adorned   280
With what to sight or smell was sweet; from thee
How shall I part, and whither wander down
Into a lower world, to this obscure
And wild, how shall we breathe in other air
Less pure, accustomed to immortal fruits?"   285
   Whom thus the Angel interrupted mild:
"Lament not, Eve, but patiently resign
What justly thou hast lost; nor set thy heart,
Thus over-fond, on that which is not thine;
Thy going is not lonely, with thee goes   290
Thy husband, him to follow thou art bound;
Where he abides, think there thy native soil."
   Adam by this from the cold sudden damp
Recovering, and his scattered spirits returned,
To Michael thus his humble words addressed: 295
   "Celestial, whether among the Thrones, or named
Of them the highest, for such of shape may seem
Prince above princes, gently hast thou told
Thy message, which might else in telling wound,
And in performing end us; what besides   300
Of sorrow and dejection and despair
Our frailty can sustain, thy tidings bring,
Departure from this happy place, our sweet
Recess, and only consolation left
Familiar to our eyes; all places else   305
Inhospitable appear and desolate,
Nor knowing us nor known. And if by prayer
Incessant I could hope to change the will
Of him who all things can, I would not cease

---

268 f. Eve's reaction is as typical of her
housewifely femininity as Adam's (315 f.) is
of his stronger religious consciousness.
   271. Fit . . . gods: unconscious irony, in
view of Eve's former ambition.
   283. to: compared with.
   297. highest: Seraphim.

To weary him with my assiduous cries; 310
But prayer against his absolute decree
No more avails than breath against the wind,
Blown stifling back on him that breathes it forth:
Therefore to his great bidding I submit.
This most afflicts me, that departing hence, 315
As from his face I shall be hid, deprived
His blessed count'nance; here I could frequent,
With worship, place by place where he vouchsafed
Presence Divine, and to my sons relate:
'On this mount he appeared, under this tree 320
Stood visible, among these pines his voice
I heard, here with him at this fountain talked.'
So many grateful altars I would rear
Of grassy turf, and pile up every stone
Of luster from the brook, in memory, 325
Or monument to ages, and thereon
Offer sweet-smelling gums and fruits and flow'rs.
In yonder nether world where shall I seek
His bright appearances, or footstep trace?
For though I fled him angry, yet recalled 330
To life prolonged and promised race, I now
Gladly behold though but his utmost skirts
Of glory, and far off his steps adore."
   To whom thus Michael with regard benign:
"Adam, thou know'st heav'n his, and all the earth, 335
Not this rock only; his omnipresence fills
Land, sea, and air, and every kind that lives,
Fomented by his virtual power and warmed.
All th' earth he gave thee to possess and rule,
No despicable gift; surmise not then 340
His presence to these narrow bounds confined
Of Paradise or Eden: this had been
Perhaps thy capital seat, from whence had spread
All generations, and had hither come
From all the ends of th' earth, to celebrate 345
And reverence thee their great progenitor.
But this pre-eminence thou hast lost, brought down
To dwell on even ground now with thy sons.
Yet doubt not but in valley and in plain
God is as here, and will be found alike 350
Present, and of his presence many a sign
Still following thee, still compassing thee round
With goodness and paternal love, his face
Express, and of his steps the track divine.
Which that thou may'st believe, and be confirmed, 355

316. Adam echoes Cain (Gen. 4.14); cf. Ps. 27.9.
330. angry: modifying "him."
335–38. Ps. 139.7–12; Jer. 23.24.
338. virtual: creative, nourishing.

355 f. As an epic convention, Michael's prophetic revelation of human history corresponds especially to Anchises' unfolding to Aeneas of the grand destiny of Rome (*Aen.* 6.754 f.), though in Michael's long record of

Ere thou from hence depart, know I am sent
To show thee what shall come in future days
To thee and to thy offspring; good with bad
Expect to hear, supernal grace contending
With sinfulness of men; thereby to learn   360
True patience, and to temper joy with fear
And pious sorrow, equally inured
By moderation either state to bear,
Prosperous or adverse: so shalt thou lead
Safest thy life, and best prepared endure   365
Thy mortal passage when it comes. Ascend
This hill; let Eve (for I have drenched her eyes)
Here sleep below while thou to foresight wak'st,
As once thou slept'st while she to life was formed."
    To whom thus Adam gratefully replied;   370
"Ascend, I follow thee, safe guide, the path
Thou lead'st me, and to the hand of Heav'n submit,
However chast'ning, to the evil turn
My obvious breast, arming to overcome
By suffering, and earn rest from labor won,   375
If so I may attain." So both ascend
In the visions of God. It was a hill
Of Paradise the highest, from whose top
The hemisphere of earth in clearest ken
Stretched out to amplest reach of prospect lay.   380
Not higher that hill nor wider looking round,
Whereon for different cause the Tempter set
Our second Adam in the wilderness,
To show him all earth's kingdoms and their glory.
His eye might there command wherever stood   385
City of old or modern fame, the seat
Of mightiest empire, from the destined walls
Of Cambalu, seat of Cathaian Can,
And Samarkand by Oxus, Temir's throne,
To Paquin of Sinaean kings, and thence   390
To Agra and Lahore of Great Mogul,
Down to the golden Chersonese, or where
The Persian in Ecbatan sat, or since

---

evil good appears rarely. Such a survey had many precedents in Christian prose and verse, old and modern, and it is an integral part of Milton's theme. It binds the sin of Adam and Eve firmly to history and shows the continual re-enactment of the fall, the eventual means of salvation through Christ, and the necessity of patient trust in Providence (lines 359–61). All of this is brought out through Adam's reactions as well as Michael's instruction.

374. obvious: exposed.
377. Ezek. 40.2 and 1.1, 8.3.
382–84. See *P.R.* 3.251 f.
385 f. The geographical panorama evokes,

economically, great tracts of time and territory, the power and magnificence of earthly conquerors and rulers.
388. Cambalu: capital of Cathay (glossary); properly Peiping.
388. Can: Khan, emperor of China.
389. Samarkand: capital of the Tartar conqueror Timur (Tamerlane) in central Asia. Oxus: Asian river flowing into the Aral Sea.
390. Paquin: Peking, Peiping.   Sinaean: Chinese.
391. Agra, Lahore: Indian capitals of the Moguls.
392. Chersonese: see note on *P.R.* 4.74.

In Hispahan, or where the Russian Ksar
In Moscow, or the Sultan in Bizance,   395
Turkéstan-born; nor could his eye not ken
Th' empire of Negus to his utmost port
Ercoco and the less marítime kings,
Mombaza, and Quiloa, and Melind,
And Sofala thought Ophir, to the realm   400
Of Congo, and Angola fardest south;
Or thence from Niger flood to Atlas mount,
The kingdoms of Almansor, Fez and Sus,
Marocco and Algiers, and Tremisen;
On Europe thence, and where Rome was to sway   405
The world. In spirit perhaps he also saw
Rich Mexico, the seat of Motezume,
And Cusco in Peru, the richer seat
Of Atabalipa, and yet unspoiled
Guiana, whose great city Geryon's sons   410
Call El Dorado. But to nobler sights
Michael from Adam's eyes the film removed
Which that false fruit that promised clearer sight
Had bred; then purged with euphrasy and rue
The visual nerve, for he had much to see;   415
And from the well of life three drops instilled.
So deep the power of these ingredients pierced,
Ev'n to the inmost seat of mental sight,
That Adam, now enforced to close his eyes,
Sunk down and all his spirits became entranced;   420
But him the gentle Angel by the hand
Soon raised, and his attention thus recalled:
    "Adam, now ope thine eyes, and first behold
Th' effects which thy original crime hath wrought
In some to spring from thee, who never touched   425
Th' excepted tree, nor with the Snake conspired,
Nor sinned thy sin, yet from that sin derive
Corruption to bring forth more violent deeds."
    His eyes he opened, and beheld a field,

394. Hispahan: Ispahan, once a Persian capital.   Ksar: Czar.
395. Bizance: Byzantium.
396. Turkestan: in central Asia.
397. Negus: Abyssinian name for king.
398. Ercoco: on the west coast of the Red Sea.
399. All three on the East African coast.
400. Sofala: in Portuguese East Africa. Ophir: some eastern region famous for wealth (1 Kings 9.28, 10.11).
401. Angola: in southwest Africa.
402. Niger: a river in west Africa.
403. Almansor (d. 1002): Muslim ruler of parts of Africa and Spain.
403–04. Fez, Sus, Tremisen: in northwest Africa.
407. Motezume: Montezuma, the Aztec emperor of Mexico conquered by Cortez.

408. Cusco: Cuzco, capital of the Inca empire.
409. Atabalipa: Atahualpa, the Inca ruler conquered by Pizarro. unspoiled: not plundered.
410. Geryon's sons: the Spanish, from a giant king overcome by Hercules.
411. El Dorado: a fabulously rich city supposed to be in Guiana or elsewhere in northern South America.
412. film removed: cf. *Aen.* 2.604–06; Tasso, *G.L.* 18.93.
413. promised: cf. 9.705–09.
414. euphrasy, rue: herbs traditionally of medicinal value for the eyes.
416. Ps. 36.9.
429–60. Gen. 4.

Part arable and tilth, whereon were sheaves   430
New-reaped, the other part sheep-walks and folds;
I' th' midst an altar as the landmark stood
Rustic, of grassy sord; thither anon
A sweaty reaper from his tillage brought
First-fruits, the green ear and the yellow sheaf,   435
Unculled, as came to hand; a shepherd next
More meek came with the firstlings of his flock,
Choicest and best; then sacrificing, laid
The inwards and their fat, with incense strewed,
On the cleft wood, and all due rites performed.   440
His off'ring soon propitious fire from heav'n
Consumed with nimble glance and grateful steam;
The other's not, for his was not sincere;
Whereat he inly raged, and as they talked,
Smote him into the midriff with a stone   445
That beat out life; he fell, and deadly pale
Groaned out his soul with gushing blood effused.
Much at that sight was Adam in his heart
Dismayed, and thus in haste to th' Angel cried:
    "O Teacher, some great mischief hath befall'n   450
To that meek man, who well had sacrificed;
Is piety thus and pure devotion paid?"
    T' whom Michael thus, he also moved, replied:
"These two are brethren, Adam, and to come
Out of thy loins; th' unjust the just hath slain,   455
For envy that his brother's offering found
From Heav'n acceptance; but the bloody fact
Will be avenged, and th' other's faith approved
Lose no reward, though here thou see him die,
Rolling in dust and gore." To which our sire: 460
    "Alas, both for the deed and for the cause!
But have I now seen Death? Is this the way
I must return to native dust? O sight
Of terror, foul and ugly to behold,
Horrid to think, how horrible to feel!"   465
    To whom thus Michaël: "Death thou hast seen
In his first shape on man; but many shapes
Of Death, and many are the ways that lead
To his grim cave, all dismal; yet to sense
More terrible at th' entrance than within.   470
Some, as thou saw'st, by violent stroke shall die,
By fire, flood, famine; by intemperance more
In meats and drinks, which on the earth shall bring
Diseases dire, of which a monstrous crew
Before thee shall appear, that thou may'st know   475
What misery th' inabstinence of Eve

433. sord: sward, turf.
447. Cf. *Aen.* 9.349, 10.908.
458–59. Heb. 11.4.
468–69. Cf. Ovid, *Met.* 4.439–40.

469–70. Cf. Seneca, *Epistles* 24.14 (echoed
in Bacon's "Of Death"); W. Drummond,
Works (ed. Kastner), 2,70.

Shall bring on men." Immediately a place
Before his eyes appeared, sad, noisome, dark,
A lazar-house it seemed, wherein were laid
Numbers of all diseased, all maladies   480
Of ghastly spasm, or racking torture, qualms
Of heart-sick agony, all feverous kinds,
Convulsions, epilepsies, fierce catarrhs,
Intestine stone and ulcer, colic pangs,
Demoniac frenzy, moping melancholy   485
And moon-struck madness, pining atrophy,
Marasmus, and wide-wasting pestilence,
Dropsies and asthmas, and joint-racking rheums.
Dire was the tossing, deep the groans; Despair
Tended the sick, busiest from couch to couch;   490
And over them triumphant Death his dart
Shook, but delayed to strike, though oft invoked
With vows, as their chief good, and final hope.
Sight so deform what heart of rock could long
Dry-eyed behold? Adam could not, but wept,   495
Though not of woman born; compassion quelled
His best of man, and gave him up to tears
A space, till firmer thoughts restrained excess,
And scarce recovering words his plaint renewed:
    "O miserable mankind, to what fall   500
Degraded, to what wretched state reserved!
Better end here unborn. Why is life giv'n
To be thus wrested from us? Rather why
Obtruded on us thus? Who if we knew
What we receive, would either not accept   505
Life offered, or soon beg to lay it down,
Glad to be so dismissed in peace. Can thus
Th' image of God in man, created once
So goodly and erect, though faulty since,
To such unsightly sufferings be debased   510
Under inhuman pains? Why should not man,
Retaining still divine similitude
In part, from such deformities be free,
And for his Maker's image sake exempt?"
    "Their Maker's image," answered Michael, "then   515
Forsook them, when themselves they vilified
To serve ungoverned appetite, and took
His image whom they served, a brutish vice,
Inductive mainly to the sin of Eve.
Therefore so abject is their punishment,   520

485–87. Added in the second edition.
486. moon-struck: lunatic.
487. Marasmus: consumption.
492–93. invoked. Cf. Sophocles, *Philoctetes* 797–98; Horace, *Od.* 2.18.38–40.
494–95. Cf. Horace, *Od.* 1.3.17–18.
496. not of woman born: cf. *Macbeth* 4.1.80, 5.3.4, etc.

497. His best of man: cf. *Macbeth* 5.8.18.
497. gave . . . tears: cf. *Henry V* 4.6.32.
504–06. Cf. Seneca, *Ad Marciam: De Consol.* 22.3; W. Drummond, *Works* (ed. Kastner), 2, 80; Donne, *Devotions* (Meditation 11); Browne, *Christian Morals* 3.25.
519. Inductive: inducing, leading to (gluttony was only part of Eve's intemperance).

Disfiguring not God's likeness, but their own,
Or if his likeness, by themselves defaced
While they pervert pure Nature's healthful rules
To loathsome sickness; worthily, since they
God's image did not reverence in themselves."   525
    "I yield it just," said Adam, "and submit.
But is there yet no other way, besides
These painful passages, how we may come
To death, and mix with our connatural dust?"
    "There is," said Michael, "if thou well observe   530
The rule of *Not too much*, by temperance taught
In what thou eat'st and drink'st, seeking from thence
Due nourishment, not gluttonous delight,
Till many years over thy head return.
So may'st thou live, till like ripe fruit thou drop   535
Into thy mother's lap, or be with ease
Gathered, not harshly plucked, for death mature:
This is old age; but then thou must outlive
Thy youth, thy strength, thy beauty, which will change
To withered weak and gray; thy senses then   540
Obtuse, all taste of pleasure must forgo
To what thou hast, and for the air of youth
Hopeful and cheerful, in thy blood will reign
A melancholy damp of cold and dry
To weigh thy spirits down, and last consume   545
The balm of life." To whom our ancestor:
    "Henceforth I fly not death, nor would prolong
Life much, bent rather how I may be quit
Fairest and easiest of this cumbrous charge,
Which I must keep till my appointed day   550
Of rend'ring up, and patiently attend
My dissolution." Michaël replied:
    "Nor love thy life, nor hate; but what thou liv'st
Live well, how long or short permit to Heav'n:
And now prepare thee for another sight."   555
    He looked and saw a spacious plain, whereon
Were tents of various hue; by some were herds
Of cattle grazing; others, whence the sound
Of instruments that made melodious chime
Was heard, of harp and organ; and who moved   560
Their stops and chords was seen: his volant touch
Instinct through all proportions low and high
Fled and pursued transverse the resonant fugue.
In other part stood one who at the forge

531. *Not too much*. An echo of the Delphic
warning and a classical maxim (cf. Aristotle,
Nicomachean Ethics 2.2.6; Seneca, *Epistles*
94.43).
535. ripe fruit: cf. Cicero, *De Senectute*
19.71.
536. mother's lap: cf. 10.778 and note.
543–46. See note on 5.482–87.

551–52. and . . . dissolution: inserted in the
second edition.
553. Nor . . . hate. Cf. Horace, *Od.* 1.9.9;
Seneca, *Epistles* 24.24, 65.18; Martial 10.47.
560. who: Jubal (Gen. 4.21).
561. volant: flying.
564. one: Tubal-cain (Gen. 4.22).

Laboring, two massy clods of iron and brass   565
Had melted (whether found where casual fire
Had wasted woods on mountain or in vale,
Down to the veins of earth, thence gliding hot
To some cave's mouth, or whether washed by stream
From underground); the liquid ore he drained   570
Into fit molds prepared; from which he formed
First his own tools; then, what might else be wrought
Fusile or grav'n in metal. After these,
But on the hither side, a different sort
From the high neighboring hills, which was their seat,   575
Down to the plain descended: by their guise
Just men they seemed, and all their study bent
To worship God aright, and know his works
Not hid, nor those things last which might preserve
Freedom and peace to men. They on the plain   580
Long had not walked, when from the tents behold
A bevy of fair women, richly gay
In gems and wanton dress; to the harp they sung
Soft amorous ditties, and in dance came on:
The men, through grave, eyed them, and let their eyes   585
Rove without rein, till in the amorous net
Fast caught, they liked, and each his liking chose;
And now of love they treat till th' ev'ning star,
Love's harbinger, appeared; then all in heat
They light the nuptial torch, and bid invoke   590
Hymen, then first to marriage rites invoked;
With feast and music all the tents resound.
Such happy interview and fair event
Of love and youth not lost, songs, garlands, flow'rs,
And charming symphonies attached the heart   595
Of Adam, soon inclined to admit delight,
The bent of Nature; which he thus expressed:
    "True opener of mine eyes, prime Angel blest,
Much better seems this vision, and more hope
Of peaceful days portends, than those two past;   600
Those were of hate and death, or pain much worse;
Here Nature seems fulfilled in all her ends."
    To whom thus Michael: "Judge not what is best
By pleasure, though to Nature seeming meet,
Created, as thou art, to nobler end   605
Holy and pure, conformity divine.
Those tents thou saw'st so pleasant, were the tents
Of wickedness, wherein shall dwell his race
Who slew his brother; studious they appear

566–73. Cf Lucretius, 5.1241–68.
  573. Fusile: formed by casting or melting.
  574–627. In Gen. 6.2–4 and some exegetical
traditions angels begot giants of the daughters
of men. Milton follows Augustine (*City of
God* 15.22–23) et al. in taking the "sons of

God" as not angels but sons of Seth who lived
west of Eden ("on the hither side").
  586. amorous net: cf. Milton, Elegy 1.60.
  588. ev'ning star: Venus.
  607–08. tents of wickedness: Ps. 84.10.

Of arts that polish life, inventors rare,   610
Unmindful of their Maker, though his Spirit
Taught them, but they his gifts acknowledged none.
Yet they a beauteous offspring shall beget;
For that fair female troop thou saw'st, that seemed
Of goddesses, so blithe, so smooth, so gay,   615
Yet empty of all good wherein consists
Woman's domestic honor and chief praise;
Bred only and completed to the taste
Of lustful appetence, to sing, to dance,
To dress, and troll the tongue, and roll the eye —   620
To these that sober race of men, whose lives
Religious titled them the Sons of God,
Shall yield up all their virtue, all their fame
Ignobly, to the trains and to the smiles
Of these fair atheists, and now swim in joy   625
(Erelong to swim at large) and laugh; for which
The world erelong a world of tears must weep."
    To whom thus Adam of short joy bereft:
"O pity and shame, that they who to live well
Entered so fair should turn aside to tread   630
Paths indirect, or in the mid-way faint!
But still I see the tenor of man's woe
Holds on the same, from woman to begin."
    "From man's effeminate slackness it begins,"
Said th' Angel, "who should better hold his place   635
By wisdom, and superior gifts received.
But now prepare thee for another scene."
    He looked and saw wide territory spread
Before him, towns, and rural works between,
Cities of men with lofty gates and tow'rs,   640
Concourse in arms, fierce faces threat'ning war,
Giants of mighty bone and bold emprise;
Part wield their arms, part curb the foaming steed,
Single or in array of battle ranged,
Both horse and foot, nor idly must'ring stood;   645
One way a band select from forage drives
A herd of beeves, fair oxen and fair kine,
From a fat meadow ground; or fleecy flock,
Ewes and their bleating lambs, over the plain,
Their booty; scarce with life the shepherds fly,   650
But call in aid, which makes a bloody fray;
With cruel tournament the squadrons join;

---

620. troll: wag.
622. Sons of God: see note above on 574–627.
626. swim: a grim glance forward to the flood.
632–33. A traditional etymology, "woman," "woe-man."
638–73. Here and elsewhere the scenes recall those depicted on Achilles' shield (*Iliad* 18.478–608) and on Aeneas' (*Aen.* 8.626–728).
642. bold emprise: cf. Ariosto, *O.F.* 1.1.2; Tasso, *G.L.* 1.6.2.
643. part . . . steed: cf. 2.531.
646–55. Cf. *Iliad* 18.527 f.
651. Ed. 2, makes; ed. 1, tacks.

Where cattle pastured late, now scattered lies
With carcasses and arms th' ensanguined field
Deserted. Others to a city strong   655
Lay siege, encamped; by battery, scale, and mine,
Assaulting; others from the wall defend
With dart and jav'lin, stones and sulphurous fire;
On each hand slaughter and gigantic deeds.
In other part the sceptered heralds call   660
To council in the city gates: anon
Gray-headed men and grave, with warriors mixed,
Assemble, and harangues are heard, but soon
In factious opposition, till at last
Of middle age one rising, eminent   665
In wise deport, spake much of right and wrong,
Of justice, of religion, truth and peace,
And judgment from above; him old and young
Exploded and had seized with violent hands,
Had not a cloud descending snatched him thence   670
Unseen amid the throng: so violence
Proceeded, and oppression, and sword-law
Through all the plain, and refuge none was found.
Adam was all in tears, and to his guide
Lamenting turned full sad: "O what are these,   675
Death's ministers, not men, who thus deal death
Inhumanly to men, and multiply
Ten-thousandfold the sin of him who slew
His brother; for of whom such massacre
Make they but of their brethren, men of men?   680
But who was that just man, whom had not Heav'n
Rescued, had in his righteousness been lost?"
     To whom thus Michael: "These are the product
Of those ill-mated marriages thou saw'st;
Where good with bad were matched, who of themselves   685
Abhor to join, and by imprudence mixed,
Produce prodigious births of body or mind.
Such were these giants, men of high renown;
For in those days might only shall be admired,
And valor and heroic virtue called;   690
To overcome in battle, and subdue
Nations, and bring home spoils with infinite
Manslaughter, shall be held the highest pitch
Of human glory, and for glory done
Of triumph, to be styled great conquerors,   695
Patrons of mankind, gods, and sons of gods,
Destroyers rightlier called and plagues of men.
Thus fame shall be achieved, renown on earth,
And what most merits fame in silence hid.

656. scale: ladder.
660–64. Cf. *Iliad* 18.503–08.
665. one: Enoch (Gen. 5.21–24).

669. Exploded: cf. 10.546 and note.
689 f. Gen. 6.4.

But he the seventh from thee, whom thou beheld'st   700
The only righteous in a world perverse,
And therefore hated, therefore so beset
With foes for daring single to be just,
And utter odious truth, that God would come
To judge them with his saints — him the Most High,   705
Rapt in a balmy cloud with wingèd steeds,
Did, as thou saw'st, receive, to walk with God
High in salvation and the climes of bliss,
Exempt from death; to show thee what reward
Awaits the good, the rest what punishment;   710
Which now direct thine eyes and soon behold."
　　He looked and saw the face of things quite changed.
The brazen throat of war had ceased to roar;
All now was turned to jollity and game,
To luxury and riot, feast and dance,   715
Marrying or prostituting, as befell,
Rape or adultery, where passing fair
Allured them; thence from cups to civil broils.
At length a reverend sire among them came,
And of their doings great dislike declared,   720
And testified against their ways; he oft
Frequented their assemblies, whereso met,
Triumphs or festivals, and to them preached
Conversion and repentance, as to souls
In prison under judgments imminent;   725
But all in vain: which when he saw, he ceased
Contending, and removed his tents far off;
Then from the mountain hewing timber tall,
Began to build a vessel of huge bulk,
Measured by cubit, length, and breadth, and highth,   730
Smeared round with pitch, and in the side a door
Contrived, and of provisions laid in large
For man and beast: when lo a wonder strange!
Of every beast, and bird, and insect small
Came sevens and pairs, and entered in, as taught   735
Their order; last the sire and his three sons
With their four wives; and God made fast the door.
Meanwhile the south wind rose, and with black wings
Wide hovering, all the clouds together drove
From under heav'n; the hills, to their supply,   740
Vapor, and exhalation dusk and moist,
Sent up amain; and now the thickened sky
Like a dark ceiling stood; down rushed the rain
Impetuous, and continued till the earth

700. he: Enoch (665 f.).
700–09. Gen. 5.18–24; Heb. 11.5; Jude
14–15.
　707. as thou saw'st: cf. 670–71.
　715. luxury: lust.
　717. fair: beautiful women.

719. sire: Noah (Gen. 6 f.; Heb. 11.7).
723–25. 1 Pet. 3.19–20.
737. God . . . door: Gen. 7.16.
738. south wind: as in Ovid, *Met.* 1.264.
743. ceiling: cf. *caelum.*

No more was seen; the floating vessel swum   745
Uplifted; and secure with beakèd prow
Rode tilting o'er the waves; all dwellings else
Flood overwhelmed, and them with all their pomp
Deep under water rolled; sea covered sea,
Sea without shore; and in their palaces   750
Where luxury late reigned, sea-monsters whelped
And stabled; of mankind, so numerous late,
All left, in one small bottom swum embarked.
How didst thou grieve then, Adam, to behold
The end of all thy offspring, end so sad,   755
Depopulation; thee another flood,
Of tears and sorrow a flood thee also drowned,
And sunk thee as thy sons; till gently reared
By th' Angel, on thy feet thou stood'st at last,
Though comfortless, as when a father mourns   760
His children, all in view destroyed at once;
And scarce to th' Angel utter'dst thus thy plaint:
    "O visions ill foreseen! better had I
Lived ignorant of future, so had borne
My part of evil only, each day's lot   765
Enough to bear; those now, that were dispensed
The burd'n of many ages, on me light
At once, by my foreknowledge gaining birth
Abortive, to torment me ere their being,
With thought that they must be. Let no man seek   770
Henceforth to be foretold what shall befall
Him or his children, evil he may be sure,
Which neither his foreknowing can prevent,
And he the future evil shall no less
In apprehension than in substance feel   775
Grievous to bear. But that care now is past;
Man is not whom to warn; those few escaped
Famine and anguish will at last consume,
Wand'ring that wat'ry desert. I had hope
When violence was ceased, and war on earth,   780
All would have then gone well, peace would have crowned
With length of happy days the race of man;
But I was far deceived; for now I see
Peace to corrupt no less than war to waste.
How comes it thus? Unfold, celestial guide,   785
And whether here the race of man will end."
    To whom thus Michael: "Those whom last thou saw'st
In triumph and luxurious wealth are they
First seen in acts of prowess eminent

750. Sea without shore: cf. Ovid, *Met.*   778. Cf. Ovid, *Met.* 1.311–12.
1.292; Sylvester, 1.2.1233.   787–807. These ideas recur often in Milton
   750–52. Cf. Ovid, *Met.* 1.299–303.   and seem to include his own age as well as
   765–66. Matt. 6.34.   earlier history.
   773–74. neither . . . and: a Latinism.

And great exploits, but of true virtue void;   790
Who having spilt much blood, and done much waste
Subduing nations, and achieved thereby
Fame in the world, high titles, and rich prey,
Shall change their course to pleasure, ease, and sloth,
Surfeit, and lust, till wantonness and pride   795
Raise out of friendship hostile deeds in peace.
The conquered also, and enslaved by war,
Shall with their freedom lost all virtue lose
And fear of God, from whom their piety feigned
In sharp contést of battle found no aid   800
Against invaders; therefore cooled in zeal,
Thenceforth shall practise how to live secure,
Worldly or dissolute, on what their lords
Shall leave them to enjoy; for th' earth shall bear
More than enough, that temperance may be tried: 805
So all shall turn degenerate, all depraved,
Justice and temperance, truth and faith forgot;
One man except, the only son of light
In a dark age, against example good,
Against allurement, custom, and a world   810
Offended; fearless of reproach and scorn,
Or violence, he of their wicked ways
Shall them admonish, and before them set
The paths of righteousness, how much more safe
And full of peace, denouncing wrath to come   815
On their impenitence; and shall return
Of them derided, but of God observed
The one just man alive; by his command
Shall build a wondrous ark, as thou beheld'st,
To save himself and household from amidst   820
A world devote to universal wrack.
No sooner he with them of man and beast
Select for life shall in the ark be lodged,
And sheltered round, but all the cataracts
Of heav'n set open on the earth shall pour   825
Rain day and night; all fountains of the deep,
Broke up, shall heave the ocean to usurp
Beyond all bounds, till inundation rise
Above the highest hills: then shall this mount
Of Paradise by might of waves be moved   830
Out of his place, pushed by the hornèd flood,
With all his verdure spoiled and trees adrift
Down the great river to the op'ning gulf,
And there take root an island salt and bare,
The haunt of seals and orcs, and sea-mews' clang: 835

808 f. Noah and Enoch are earthly counterparts of Abdiel (5.805 f., 6.1 f.).
826. fountains . . . deep: Gen. 7.11.
831. hornèd: divided, branching.
833. river: presumably the Euphrates.
gulf: the Persian Gulf.

834–35. One of Milton's most "romantic"
evocations, with a quite unromantic reason
added. Cf. Spenser, *F.Q.* 2.12.8; *Homeric
Hymn to Delian Apollo* 74–78.   sea-mews:
sea-gulls.

To teach thee that God áttributes to place
No sanctity, if none be thither brought
By men who there frequent, or therein dwell.
And now what further shall ensue, behold."
He looked, and saw the ark hull on the flood,   840
Which now abated, for the clouds were fled,
Driv'n by a keen north wind, that blowing dry
Wrinkled the face of deluge, as decayed;
And the clear sun on his wide wat'ry glass
Gazed hot, and of the fresh wave largely drew,   845
As after thirst, which made their flowing shrink
From standing lake to tripping ebb, that stole
With soft foot towards the deep, who now had stopped
His sluices, as the heav'n his windows shut.
The ark no more now floats, but seems on ground   850
Fast on the top of some high mountain fixed.
And now the tops of hills as rocks appear;
With clamor thence the rapid currents drive
Towards the retreating sea their furious tide.
Forthwith from out the ark a raven flies,   855
And after him, the surer messenger,
A dove sent forth once and again to spy
Green tree or ground whereon his foot may light;
The second time returning, in his bill
An olive leaf he brings, pacific sign: 860
Anon dry ground appears, and from his ark
The ancient sire descends with all his train;
Then with uplifted hands and eyes devout,
Grateful to Heav'n, over his head beholds
A dewy cloud, and in the cloud a bow   865
Conspicuous with three listed colors gay,
Betok'ning peace from God, and cov'nant new.
Whereat the heart of Adam, erst so sad,
Greatly rejoiced, and thus his joy broke forth:
"O thou who future things canst represent   870
As present, heav'nly instructor, I revive
At this last sight, assured that man shall live
With all the creatures, and their seed preserve.
Far less I now lament for one whole world
Of wicked sons destroyed than I rejoice   875
For one man found so perfect and so just,
That God vouchsafes to raise another world
From him, and all his anger to forget.
But say, what mean those colored streaks in heav'n,
Distended as the brow of God appeased,   880

840. hull: drift.
842. north wind. Cf. Ovid, *Met.* 1.328 (and note on 738 above); Gen. 8.1.
843. The opening of Sidney's *Arcadia*, a work Milton knew, has the phrase "wrinkles of the sea's visage" and also "hulling" (ed. Feuillerat, pp. 9–10).

848–49. Gen. 8.2.
850–54. Gen. 8.4–5; cf. Ovid, *Met.* 1.343–45.
865–901. Gen. 9.8–17. The early history of man, mainly of evil, ends on a note of partial reassurance.
866. listed: striped.

Or serve they as a flow'ry verge to bind
The fluid skirts of that same wat'ry cloud,
Lest it again dissolve and show'r the earth?"
    To whom th' Archangel: "Dextrously thou aim'st;
So willingly doth God remit his ire,   885
Though late repenting him of man depraved,
Grieved at his heart, when looking down he saw
The whole earth filled with violence, and all flesh
Corrupting each their way; yet those removed,
Such grace shall one just man find in his sight,   890
That he relents, not to blot out mankind,
And makes a covenant never to destroy
The earth again by flood, nor let the sea
Surpass his bounds, nor rain to drown the world
With man therein or beast; but when he brings   895
Over the earth a cloud, will therein set
His triple-colored bow, whereon to look
And call to mind his cov'nant. Day and night,
Seed-time and harvest, heat and hoary frost
Shall hold their course, till fire purge all things new,   900
Both heav'n and earth, wherein the just shall dwell."

Book XII

THE ARGUMENT

The Angel Michael continues from the Flood to relate what shall succeed; then, in the mention of Abraham, comes by degrees to explain who that Seed of the Woman shall be which was promised Adam and Eve in the Fall; his incarnation, death, resurrection, and ascension; the state of the church till his second coming. Adam, greatly satisfied and recomforted by these relations and promises, descends the hill with Michael; wakens Eve, who all this while had slept, but with gentle dreams composed to quietness of mind and submission. Michael in either hand leads them out of Paradise, the fiery sword waving behind them, and the Cherubim taking their stations to guard the place.

A s ONE who in his journey bates at noon,
Though bent on speed, so here the Archangel paused
Betwixt the world destroyed and world restored,
If Adam aught perhaps might interpose;
Then with transition sweet new speech resumes: 5

885–88. Gen. 6.6, 11–12.
890. Gen. 6.9.
891–98. Gen. 9.8–17.
898–901. Gen. 8.22; 2 Pet. 3.12–13.
BOOK XII. 1–5. Added in second edition,
when book 10 of the first edition was divided
to make books 11 and 12; cf. 8.1–4 and note.
    1. bates: stops for refreshment of man and
horse (usually "baits," as in *S.A.* 1538).

"Thus thou hast seen one world begin and end,
And man as from a second stock proceed.
Much thou hast yet to see, but I perceive
Thy mortal sight to fail; objects divine
Must needs impair and weary human sense: 10
Henceforth what is to come I will relate;
Thou therefore give due audience, and attend.
      "This second source of men, while yet but few,
And while the dread of judgment past remains
Fresh in their minds, fearing the Deity,   15
With some regard to what is just and right
Shall lead their lives, and multiply apace,
Laboring the soil, and reaping plenteous crop,
Corn, wine and oil; and from the herd or flock
Oft sacrificing bullock, lamb, or kid,   20
With large wine-offerings poured, and sacred feast,
Shall spend their days in joy unblamed, and dwell
Long time in peace by families and tribes
Under paternal rule; till one shall rise
Of proud ambitious heart, who not content   25
With fair equality, fraternal state,
Will arrogate dominion undeserved
Over his brethren, and quite dispossess
Concord and law of Nature from the earth;
Hunting (and men, not beasts, shall be his game)   30
With war and hostile snare such as refuse
Subjection to his empire tyrannous.
A mighty hunter thence he shall be styled
Before the Lord, as in despite of Heav'n,
Or from Heav'n claiming second sovranty;   35
And from rebellion shall derive his name,
Though of rebellion others he accuse.
He with a crew whom like ambition joins
With him or under him to tyrannize,
Marching from Eden towards the west, shall find   40
The plain, wherein a black bituminous gurge
Boils out from under ground, the mouth of hell;
Of brick, and of that stuff, they cast to build
A city and tow'r, whose top may reach to heav'n;
And get themselves a name, lest far dispersed   45
In foreign lands their memory be lost,
Regardless whether good or evil fame.
But God, who oft descends to visit men
Unseen, and through their habitations walks
To mark their doings, them beholding soon,   50
Comes down to see their city, ere the tower

24. one: Nimrod (Gen. 10.8–10).
33–34. Gen. 10.9.
36. The name "Nimrod" was mistakenly linked with the Hebrew verb meaning "to rebel."

38–62. The tower of Babel (Gen. 10.10, 11.1–9).
41. gurge: whirlpool.

Obstruct heav'n tow'rs, and in derision sets
Upon their tongues a various spirit to raze
Quite out their native language, and instead
To sow a jangling noise of words unknown: 55
Forthwith a hideous gabble rises loud
Among the builders; each to other calls,
Not understood, till hoarse, and all in rage,
As mocked they storm; great laughter was in heav'n
And looking down, to see the hubbub strange   60
And hear the din; thus was the building left
Ridiculous, and the work Confusion named."
    Whereto thus Adam, fatherly displeased:
"O execrable son so to aspire
Above his brethren, to himself assuming   65
Authority usurped, from God not giv'n;
He gave us only over beast, fish, fowl
Dominion absolute; that right we hold
By his donation; but man over men
He made not lord; such title to himself   70
Reserving, human left from human free.
But this usurper his encroachment proud
Stays not on man; to God his tower intends
Siege and defiance. Wretched man! what food
Will he convey up thither to sustain   75
Himself and his rash army, where thin air
Above the clouds will pine his entrails gross,
And famish him of breath, if not of bread?"
    To whom thus Michael: "Justly thou abhorr'st
That son, who on the quiet state of men   80
Such trouble brought, affecting to subdue
Rational liberty; yet know withal,
Since thy original lapse, true liberty
Is lost, which always with right reason dwells
Twinned, and from her hath no dividual being;   85
Reason in man obscured, or not obeyed,
Immediately inordinate desires
And upstart passions catch the government
From reason, and to servitude reduce
Man till then free. Therefore since he permits   90
Within himself unworthy powers to reign
Over free reason, God in judgment just
Subjects him from without to violent lords;
Who oft as undeservedly enthrall

53. various: i.e. spirit of diversity, discord.
55. a jangling noise: in Sylvester, 2.2.2.202.
67–69. Gen. 9.2.
79–96. A central — and Platonic — article
of Milton's ethical and political creed (cf.
6.41–43, 9.1127–31). The linking of order in
the soul with order in the state is in the vein
of Plato's *Republic*.

84. right reason: glossary.
85. dividual: separable.
90–101. The idea that national corruption
invites conquest is recurrent in Milton's prose
and verse; cf. 11.797–801, *P.R.* 3.414–40,
4.131 f., *S.A.* 268 f.

His outward freedom: tyranny must be,   95
Though to the tyrant thereby no excuse.
Yet sometimes nations will decline so low
From virtue, which is reason, that no wrong,
But justice, and some fatal curse annexed,
Deprives them of their outward liberty,   100
Their inward lost: witness th' irreverent son
Of him who built the ark, who for the shame
Done to his father, heard this heavy curse,
Servant of servants, on his vicious race.
Thus will this latter, as the former world,   105
Still tend from bad to worse, till God at last,
Wearied with their iniquities, withdraw
His presence from among them, and avert
His holy eyes; resolving from thenceforth
To leave them to their own polluted ways,   110
And one peculiar nation to select
From all the rest, of whom to be invoked,
A nation from one faithful man to spring.
Him on this side Euphrates yet residing,
Bred up in idol-worship — O that men   115
(Canst thou believe?) should be so stupid grown,
While yet the patriarch lived who scaped the Flood,
As to forsake the living God, and fall
To worship their own work in wood and stone
For gods! — yet him God the Most High vouchsafes   120
To call by vision from his father's house,
His kindred and false gods, into a land
Which he will show him, and from him will raise
A mighty nation, and upon him show'r
His benediction so, that in his seed   125
All nations shall be blest; he straight obeys,
Not knowing to what land, yet firm believes.
I see him, but thou canst not, with what faith
He leaves his gods, his friends, and native soil,
Ur of Chaldaea, passing now the ford   130
To Haran, after him a cumbrous train
Of herds and flocks, and numerous servitude;
Not wand'ring poor, but trusting all his wealth
With God, who called him, in a land unknown.
Canaan he now attains; I see his tents   135
Pitched about Sechem, and the neighboring plain
Of Moreh; there by promise he receives
Gift to his progeny of all that land,

101–04. Gen. 9.21–25.
113–63. Abraham (Gen. 12–25).
114. on this side: i.e. east of.
115. idol-worship: Joshua 24.2; Milton, *C.D.* 1.17.
120–30. Gen. 12.1–2; Gal. 3.8; Acts 7.1–7; Heb. 11.8.

130. Ur: south of Babylon, on the Euphrates.
131. Haran: in northwest Mesopotamia (Gen. 11.31–32, 12.1–5).
132. servitude: servants.
136–37. Sechem (Shechem), Moreh: city and plain in central Palestine, north of Jerusalem (Gen. 12.6).

From Hamath northward to the Desert south
(Things by their names I call, though yet unnamed)   140
From Hermon east to the great western sea;
Mount Hermon, yonder sea, each place behold
In prospect, as I point them: on the shore
Mount Carmel; here the double-founted stream,
Jordan, true limit eastward; but his sons   145
Shall dwell to Senir, that long ridge of hills.
This ponder, that all nations of the earth
Shall in his seed be blessed; by that seed
Is meant thy great Deliverer, who shall bruise
The Serpent's head; whereof to thee anon   150
Plainlier shall be revealed. This patriarch blest,
Whom *faithful Abraham* due time shall call,
A son, and of his son a grandchild leaves,
Like him in faith, in wisdom, and renown.
The grandchild, with twelve sons increased, departs   155
From Canaan, to a land hereafter called
Egypt, divided by the river Nile;
See where it flows, disgorging at seven mouths
Into the sea. To sojourn in that land
He comes invited by a younger son   160
In time of dearth, a son whose worthy deeds
Raise him to be the second in that realm
Of Pharaoh. There he dies, and leaves his race
Growing into a nation, and now grown
Suspected to a sequent king, who seeks   165
To stop their overgrowth, as inmate guests
Too numerous; whence of guests he makes them slaves
Inhospitably, and kills their infant males:
Till by two brethren (those two brethren call
Moses and Aaron) sent from God to claim   170
His people from enthralment, they return
With glory and spoil back to their promised land.
But first the lawless tyrant, who denies
To know their God, or message to regard,
Must be compelled by signs and judgments dire;   175
To blood unshed the rivers must be turned,
Frogs, lice and flies must all his palace fill
With loathed intrusion, and fill all the land;
His cattle must of rot and murrain die,
Botches and blains must all his flesh emboss,   180

139. Hamath: in Syria on the Orontes.
141. Hermon: the highest peak in Palestine, in the north (Joshua 13.5–6).
141. east: i.e. in the east.   sea: Mediterranean.
144. Carmel: promontory near Haifa.
145. true limit: Num. 34.12.
146. Senir: 1 Chron. 5.23.
152. Gen. 17.5; Gal. 3.9.
153. son: Isaac (Gen. 21).   grandchild: Jacob (Gen. 25.26).

155–63. Gen. 39–50.
160–62. son: Joseph (Gen. 41.40–45).
163. dies . . . nation: Gen. 50.26; Exod. 1.6–7.
165. king: Pharaoh (Exod. 1.8 f.).
165–68. Exod. 1.9–22.
169–90. Exod. 3–12.
173. denies: refuses.
180. Botches: boils.   blains: blisters. emboss: cover with swellings.

And all his people; thunder mixed with hail,
Hail mixed with fire must rend th' Egyptian sky
And wheel on th' earth, devouring where it rolls;
What it devours not, herb or fruit, or grain,
A darksome cloud of locusts swarming down   185
Must eat, and on the ground leave nothing green;
Darkness must overshadow all his bounds,
Palpable darkness, and blot out three days;
Last with one midnight stroke all the first-born
Of Egypt must lie dead. Thus with ten wounds   190
The river-dragon tamed at length submits
To let his sojourners depart, and oft
Humbles his stubborn heart, but still as ice
More hardened after thaw, till in his rage
Pursuing whom he late dismissed, the sea   195
Swallows him with his host, but them lets pass
As on dry land between two crystal walls,
Awed by the rod of Moses so to stand
Divided, till his rescued gain their shore:
Such wondrous power God to his saint will lend,   200
Though present in his angel, who shall go
Before them in a cloud, and pillar of fire,
By day a cloud, by night a pillar of fire,
To guide them in their journey, and remove
Behind them, while th' obdúrate king pursues.   205
All night he will pursue, but his approach
Darkness defends between till morning watch;
Then through the fiery pillar and the cloud
God looking forth will trouble all his host
And craze their chariot wheels: when by command   210
Moses once more his potent rod extends
Over the sea; the sea his rod obeys;
On their embattled ranks the waves return,
And overwhelm their war. The race elect
Safe towards Canaan from the shore advance   215
Through the wild desert, not the readiest way,
Lest ent'ring on the Canaanite alarmed
War terrify them inexpert, and fear
Return them back to Egypt, choosing rather
Inglorious life with servitude; for life   220
To noble and ignoble is more sweet
Untrained in arms, where rashness leads not on.
This also shall they gain by their delay
In the wide wilderness: there they shall found

188. Palpable darkness: "darkness which may be felt" (Exod. 10.21).
191. The: ed. 1, This.   river-dragon: crocodile, i.e. Pharaoh (Ezek. 29.3).
194–214. Exod. 14.5–31.
197. crystal walls: cf. Milton, Ps. 136.49, "walls of glass"; Sylvester, 2.3.3.701, "walls of crystal."

200–04. Exod. 13.21–22.
207. defends: forbids, prevents.
210. craze: break (cf. 1.311 and Exod. 14).
211. Cf. 1.338.
214–20. Exod. 13.17–18.
215. shore: of the Red Sea.
217. alarmed: roused to arms.

Their government, and their great senate choose   225
Through the twelve tribes, to rule by laws ordained.
God from the mount of Sinai, whose gray top
Shall tremble, he descending, will himself
In thunder, lightning and loud trumpet's sound
Ordain them laws; part such as appertain   230
To civil justice, part religious rites
Of sacrifice, informing them, by types
And shadows, of that destined Seed to bruise
The Serpent, by what means he shall achieve
Mankind's deliverance. But the voice of God   235
To mortal ear is dreadful; they beseech
That Moses might report to them his will,
And terror cease; he grants what they besought,
Instructed that to God is no access
Without Mediator, whose high office now   240
Moses in figure bears, to introduce
One greater, of whose day he shall foretell,
And all the Prophets in their age the times
Of great Messiah shall sing. Thus laws and rites
Established, such delight hath God in men   245
Obedient to his will, that he vouchsafes
Among them to set up his tabernacle,
The Holy One with mortal men to dwell:
By his prescript a sanctuary is framed
Of cedar, overlaid with gold, therein   250
An Ark, and in the ark his testimony,
The records of his cov'nant; over these
A mercy-seat of gold between the wings
Of two bright Cherubim; before him burn
Seven lamps, as in a zodiac representing   255
The heav'nly fires; over the tent a cloud
Shall rest by day, a fiery gleam by night,
Save when they journey; and at length they come,
Conducted by his angel, to the land
Promised to Abraham and his seed. The rest   260
Were long to tell, how many battles fought,
How many kings destroyed, and kingdoms won,
Or how the sun shall in mid-heav'n stand still
A day entire, and night's due course adjourn,
Man's voice commanding, 'Sun, in Gibeon stand,   265
And thou, moon, in the vale of Aialon,
Till Israel overcome'; so call the third

225–26. Exod. 24.1–9; Num. 11.16–30.
227 f. Exod. 19.16–25.
232. See note below on 303.
235–38. Exod. 20.18–20.
238. what they besought: ed. 1, them their desire.
241–42. Deut. 18.15–19.
246–58. Exod. 25.
251–56. Exod. 25.17–37 and Exod. 37.

256–58. Exod. 40.34–38.
259. Exod. 23.23.
260. Gen. 22.17–18, 26.3, etc.
263–67. Joshua 10.12–13. Except for "vale" and "Aialon" in place of "valley" and "Ajalon," line 266 is the same as the phrase in Joshua 10.12 and is still closer to Sylvester, 2.3.4.551 (cf. note on 3.373).
267. Israel: Jacob (Gen. 32.28).

From Abraham, son of Isaac, and from him
His whole descent, who thus shall Canaan win."
    Here Adam interposed: "O sent from heav'n,   270
Enlight'ner of my darkness, gracious things
Thou hast revealed, those chiefly which concern
Just Abraham and his seed. Now first I find
Mine eyes true op'ning, and my heart much eased,
Erewhile perplexed with thoughts what would become   275
Of me and all mankind; but now I see
His day, in whom all nations shall be blest,
Favor unmerited by me, who sought
Forbidden knowledge by forbidden means.
This yet I apprehend not, why to those   280
Among whom God will deign to dwell on earth
So many and so various laws are giv'n;
So many laws argue so many sins
Among them; how can God with such reside?"
    To whom thus Michael: "Doubt not but that sin   285
Will reign among them, as of thee begot;
And therefore was law given them to evince
Their natural pravity, by stirring up
Sin against law to fight; that when they see
Law can discover sin, but not remove,   290
Save by those shadowy expiations weak,
The blood of bulls and goats, they may conclude
Some blood more precious must be paid for man,
Just for unjust, that in such righteousness
To them by faith imputed, they may find   295
Justification towards God, and peace
Of conscience, which the law by ceremonies
Cannot appease, nor man the moral part
Perform, and not performing cannot live.
So law appears imperfect, and but giv'n   300
With purpose to resign them in full time
Up to a better cov'nant, disciplined
From shadowy types to truth, from flesh to spirit,
From imposition of strict laws to free
Acceptance of large grace, from servile fear   305
To filial, works of law to works of faith.
And therefore shall not Moses, though of God
Highly beloved, being but the minister
Of law, his people into Canaan lead;
But Joshua whom the Gentiles Jesus call,   310

274. true op'ning: cf. 9.705–08, 865–66, 875, 985, 1070–71.

283–84. Cf. Tacitus, *Annales* 3.27.5.

285–306. Milton's grandest statement of the central doctrine of "Christian liberty," the individual freedom of the Christian as contrasted with the bondage of the Mosaic law; cf. Rom. 10.4 f.; Gal. 3–4; Heb. 9–10; etc.

287. evince: show.

288. pravity: wickedness.

303. shadowy types: persons and events in the Old Testament as prophetic or allegorical of their full realization in the New, e.g., Moses as a "Mediator" (above, 240 f.), Joshua (310–14). See Milton, *C.D.* 1.26–27.

307–09. Deut. 34; Milton, *C.D.* 1.26.

310. Joshua (in Greek form, "Jesus," "Saviour"): a type of Christ and leader of the Israelites into the promised land.

His name and office bearing, who shall quell
The adversary Serpent, and bring back
Through the world's wilderness long-wandered man
Safe to eternal Paradise of rest.
Meanwhile they in their earthly Canaan placed   315
Long time shall dwell and prosper, but when sins
National interrupt their public peace,
Provoking God to raise them enemies,
From whom as oft he saves them penitent,
By judges first, then under kings; of whom   320
The second, both for piety renowned
And puissant deeds, a promise shall receive
Irrevocable, that his regal throne
For ever shall endure; the like shall sing
All prophecy: that of the royal stock   325
Of David (so I name this king) shall rise
A Son, the Woman's Seed to thee foretold,
Foretold to Abraham, as in whom shall trust
All nations, and to kings foretold, of kings
The last, for of his reign shall be no end.   330
But first a long succession must ensue,
And his next son, for wealth and wisdom famed,
The clouded ark of God, till then in tents
Wand'ring, shall in a glorious temple enshrine.
Such follow him, as shall be registered   335
Part good, part bad, of bad the longer scroll,
Whose foul idolatries and other faults
Heaped to the popular sum, will so incense
God, as to leave them, and expose their land,
Their city, his temple, and his holy ark   340
With all his sacred things, a scorn and prey
To that proud city, whose high walls thou saw'st
Left in confusion, Babylon thence called.
There in captivity he lets them dwell
The space of seventy years, then brings them back,   345
Rememb'ring mercy, and his cov'nant sworn
To David, stablished as the days of Heav'n.
Returned from Babylon by leave of kings
Their lords, whom God disposed, the house of God
They first re-edify, and for a while   350
In mean estate live moderate, till grown
In wealth and multitude, factious they grow;
But first among the priests dissension springs,

311. who: Christ.
320. As recounted in Judges and Kings.
321. second: David (2 Sam. 7.16).
325. prophecy: e.g. Isa. 9.6–7, 11.10; Ps. 89.36–37; Dan. 7.13–14.
327. Son: Christ.
328. Foretold to Abraham: Gen. 15, etc.
332. next son: Solomon, son of David.

334. temple: 1 Kings 6; 2 Chron. 3–4.
344–45. The Babylon captivity, 606–536 B.C. (2 Kings 25; 2 Chron. 36; Jer. 39, 52).
347. Ps. 89.29.
348. kings: Cyrus, Darius, and Artaxerxes.
349–50. Ezra.
353–58. 2 Maccabees 3–4: etc.

Men who attend the altar, and should most
Endeavor peace; their strife pollution brings   355
Upon the temple itself; at last they seize
The scepter and regard not David's sons,
Then lose it to a stranger, that the true
Anointed King Messiah might be born
Barred of his right. Yet at his birth a star   360
Unseen before in heav'n proclaims him come,
And guides the eastern sages, who inquire
His place, to offer incense, myrrh, and gold;
His place of birth a solemn angel tells
To simple shepherds, keeping watch by night;   365
They gladly thither haste, and by a quire
Of squadroned angels hear his carol sung.
A virgin is his mother, but his sire
The Power of the Most High; he shall ascend
The throne hereditary, and bound his reign   370
With earth's wide bounds, his glory with the heav'ns."
     He ceased, discerning Adam with such joy
Surcharged, as had like grief been dewed in tears,
Without the vent of words, which these he breathed:
     "O prophet of glad tidings, finisher   375
Of utmost hope! now clear I understand
What oft my steadiest thoughts have searched in vain,
Why our great Expectation should be called
The Seed of Woman: Virgin Mother, hail,
High in the love of Heav'n, yet from my loins   380
Thou shalt proceed, and from thy womb the Son
Of God Most High; so God with man unites.
Needs must the Serpent now his capital bruise
Expect with mortal pain: say where and when
Their fight, what stroke shall bruise the victor's heel."   385
     To whom thus Michael: "Dream not of their fight
As of a duel, or the local wounds
Of head or heel: not therefore joins the Son
Manhood to Godhead, with more strength to foil
Thy enemy; nor so is overcome   390
Satan, whose fall from heav'n, a deadlier bruise,
Disabled not to give thee thy death's wound;
Which he who comes thy Saviour shall recure,
Not by destroying Satan, but his works
In thee and in thy seed. Nor can this be,   395
But by fulfilling that which thou didst want,
Obedience to the law of God, imposed

---

358. stranger: Antipater, made governor of Jerusalem by the Romans; father of King Herod.

360 f. Matt. 2, Luke 2. Cf. *Nativity* and *P.R.* 1.242–54.

363–64. place: Bethlehem.

367. squadroned: cf. *Nativity* 21.

370–71. Cf. Ps. 2.8; *Aen.* 1.278–79, 287.

379–80. Luke 1.28.

383. capital (a disyllable): "of the head" (10.181) and "fatal."

392. Disabled . . . give: did not disable from giving.

396. want: lack.

On penalty of death, and suffering death,
The penalty to thy transgression due,
And due to theirs which out of thine will grow: 400
So only can high justice rest appaid.
The law of God exact he shall fulfill
Both by obedience and by love, though love
Alone fulfill the law; thy punishment
He shall endure by coming in the flesh   405
To a reproachful life and cursèd death,
Proclaiming life to all who shall believe
In his redemption, and that his obedience
Imputed becomes theirs by faith, his merits
To save them, not their own, though legal works.   410
For this he shall live hated, be blasphemed,
Seized on by force, judged, and to death condemned
A shameful and accurst, nailed to the cross
By his own nation, slain for bringing life;
But to the cross he nails thy enemies,   415
The law that is against thee, and the sins
Of all mankind, with him there crucified,
Never to hurt them more who rightly trust
In this his satisfaction; so he dies,
But soon revives; Death over him no power   420
Shall long usurp; ere the third dawning light
Return, the stars of morn shall see him rise
Out of his grave, fresh as the dawning light,
Thy ransom paid, which man from Death redeems,
His death for man, as many as offered life   425
Neglect not, and the benefit embrace
By faith not void of works. This Godlike act
Annuls thy doom, the death thou shouldst have died,
In sin for ever lost from life; this act
Shall bruise the head of Satan, crush his strength,   430
Defeating Sin and Death, his two main arms,
And fix far deeper in his head their stings
Than temporal death shall bruise the victor's heel,
Or theirs whom he redeems, a death like sleep,
A gentle wafting to immortal life.   435
Nor after resurrection shall he stay
Longer on earth than certain times to appear
To his disciples, men who in his life
Still followed him; to them shall leave in charge
To teach all nations what of him they learned   440
And his salvation, them who shall believe
Baptizing in the profluent stream, the sign
Of washing them from guilt of sin to life

401. appaid: satisfied.
402–20. Cf. 3.227–41, 285 f.
415–17. Col. 2.14.
420–65. Cf. 3.245–65, 315–41.

436–41. Matt. 28.9–20; Mark 16; Luke 24;
John 20–21.
442. in . . . stream: cf. Milton, *C.D.* 1.28.

Pure, and in mind prepared, if so befall,
For death, like that which the Redeemer died.   445
All nations they shall teach; for from that day
Not only to the sons of Abraham's loins
Salvation shall be preached, but to the sons
Of Abraham's faith wherever through the world;
So in his seed all nations shall be blest.   450
Then to the heav'n of heav'ns he shall ascend
With victory, triumphing through the air
Over his foes and thine; there shall surprise
The Serpent, prince of air, and drag in chains
Through all his realm, and there confounded leave;   455
Then enter into glory, and resume
His seat at God's right hand, exalted high
Above all names in heav'n; and thence shall come,
When this world's dissolution shall be ripe,
With glory and power to judge both quick and dead,   460
To judge th' unfaithful dead, but to reward
His faithful, and receive them into bliss,
Whether in heav'n or earth, for then the earth
Shall all be Paradise, far happier place
Than this of Eden, and far happier days."   465
    So spake th' Archangel Michaël, then paused,
As at the world's great period; and our sire
Replete with joy and wonder thus replied:
    "O goodness infinite, goodness immense!
That all this good of evil shall produce,   470
And evil turn to good; more wonderful
Than that which by creation first brought forth
Light out of darkness! Full of doubt I stand,
Whether I should repent me now of sin
By me done and occasioned, or rejoice   475
Much more, that much more good thereof shall spring,
To God more glory, more good will to men
From God, and over wrath grace shall abound.
But say, if our Deliverer up to heav'n
Must reascend, what will betide the few   480
His faithful, left among th' unfaithful herd,
The enemies of truth; who then shall guide
His people, who defend? Will they not deal
Worse with his followers than with him they dealt?"
    "Be sure they will," said th' Angel; "but from heav'n   485
He to his own a Comforter will send,

445–50. Rom. 4.16; Gal. 3.7–9, 16; Eph. 4.11–12; etc.
451–65. Cf. 3.250–65, 315–41.
453–55. Rev. 11.18, 20.2–3.
460. *quick*: living (cf. the Apostles' Creed).
469–78. The traditional paradox of Adam's *felix culpa*, "the fortunate fall": Adam's sin, with all its evil consequences, provided the motive for Christ's incarnation and sacrifice, the working of divine love and grace, and hence man's reception into heavenly bliss.
470–71. Cf. 1.162–65, 217–20.
478. Rom. 5.20.
486. *Comforter*: the Holy Spirit (John 15.26).

The promise of the Father, who shall dwell,
His Spirit, within them, and the law of faith
Working through love, upon their hearts shall write,
To guide them in all truth, and also arm   490
With spiritual armor, able to resist
Satan's assaults, and quench his fiery darts,
What man can do against them, not afraid,
Though to the death, against such cruelties
With inward consolations recompensed,   495
And oft supported so as shall amaze
Their proudest persecutors. For the Spirit
Poured first on his Apostles, whom he sends
To evangelize the nations, then on all
Baptized, shall them with wondrous gifts endue   500
To speak all tongues, and do all miracles,
As did their Lord before them. Thus they win
Great numbers of each nation to receive
With joy the tidings brought from heav'n: at length
Their ministry performed, and race well run,   505
Their doctrine and their story written left,
They die; but in their room, as they forewarn,
Wolves shall succeed for teachers, grievous wolves,
Who all the sacred mysteries of heav'n
To their own vile advantages shall turn   510
Of lucre and ambition, and the truth
With superstitions and traditions taint,
Left only in those written records pure,
Though not but by the Spirit understood.
Then shall they seek to avail themselves of names,   515
Places and titles, and with these to join
Secular power, though feigning still to act
By spiritual, to themselves appropriating
The Spirit of God, promised alike and giv'n
To all believers; and from that pretense,   520
Spiritual laws by carnal power shall force
On every conscience; laws which none shall find
Left them enrolled, or what the Spirit within
Shall on the heart engrave. What will they then
But force the Spirit of Grace itself, and bind   525
His consort Liberty, what but unbuild
His living temples, built by faith to stand,
Their own faith, not another's; for on earth
Who against faith and conscience can be heard
Infallible? Yet many will presume: 530
Whence heavy persecution shall arise
On all who in the worship persevere

489. Gal. 5.6; Heb. 8.10.
491–92. Eph. 6.11–16.
493. Ps. 56.11.
497–502. Acts 2.
505. race: Heb. 12.1; 1 Cor. 9.24.
508 f. Milton's long-held view of the worldly

corruptions of the medieval church and the Anglican church of his age (cf. *Lycidas* 113 f., and the anti-episcopal tracts).
508. grievous wolves: in Acts 20.29.
525–26. 2 Cor. 3.17.
526–28. Cf. 1.17–18; 1 Cor. 3.17.

Of Spirit and Truth; the rest, far greater part,
Will deem in outward rites and specious forms
Religion satisfied; Truth shall retire   535
Bestuck with sland'rous darts, and works of faith
Rarely be found. So shall the world go on,
To good malignant, to bad men benign,
Under her own weight groaning, till the day
Appear of respiration to the just,   540
And vengeance to the wicked, at return
Of him so lately promised to thy aid,
The Woman's Seed, obscurely then foretold,
Now amplier known thy Saviour and thy Lord,
Last in the clouds from heav'n to be revealed   545
In glory of the Father, to dissolve
Satan with his perverted world; then raise
From the conflagrant mass, purged and refined,
New heav'ns, new earth, ages of endless date
Founded in righteousness and peace and love,   550
To bring forth fruits, joy and eternal bliss."
   He ended; and thus Adam last replied:
"How soon hath thy prediction, seer blest,
Measured this transient world, the race of time,
Till time stand fixed: beyond is all abyss,   555
Eternity, whose end no eye can reach.
Greatly instructed I shall hence depart,
Greatly in peace of thought, and have my fill
Of knowledge, what this vessel can contain;
Beyond which was my folly to aspire.   560
Henceforth I learn that to obey is best,
And love with fear the only God, to walk
As in his presence, ever to observe
His providence, and on him sole depend,
Merciful over all his works, with good   565
Still overcoming evil, and by small
Accomplishing great things, by things deemed weak
Subverting worldly strong, and worldly wise
By simply meek; that suffering for truth's sake
Is fortitude to highest victory,   570
And to the faithful death the gate of life;
Taught this by his example whom I now
Acknowledge my Redeemer ever blest."
   To whom thus also th' Angel last replied:

533. John 4.23–24.
539. Rom. 8.22.
540. respiration: refreshing (Acts 3.19), reward.
545–47. Matt. 24.30–31; 2 Thess. 1.7–8.
547–51. Cf. 3.333–35 (and note), 11.900–01, etc.
558 f. Here at the end of the poem the theme of intemperance in knowledge, of pride and presumption, is reinforced; cf. book 8 and the whole temptation of Eve.

559. this vessel: 1 Thess. 4.4.
561–82. Adam's new understanding of truly heroic knowledge is the opposite of Satan's creed; for one contrast, cf. 2.257–62.
565–68. Ps. 145.9; Rom. 12.21; 1 Cor. 1.27–28; 1 Pet. 2.21; Rev. 2.10.
573. In accepting, by faith, Michael's account of the means of redemption, Adam becomes a Christian, the first one.

"This having learnt, thou hast attained the sum   575
Of wisdom; hope no higher, though all the stars
Thou knew'st by name, and all th' ethereal powers,
All secrets of the deep, all Nature's works,
Or works of God in heav'n, air, earth, or sea,
And all the riches of this world enjoy'dst,   580
And all the rule, one empire; only add
Deeds to thy knowledge answerable, add faith,
Add virtue, patience, temperance, add love,
By name to come called charity, the soul
Of all the rest: then wilt thou not be loth   585
To leave this Paradise, but shalt possess
A paradise within thee, happier far.
Let us descend now therefore from this top
Of speculation; for the hour precise
Exacts our parting hence; and see the guards,   590
By me encamped on yonder hill, expect
Their motion, at whose front a flaming sword,
In signal of remove, waves fiercely round;
We may no longer stay: go, waken Eve;
Her also I with gentle dreams have calmed,   595
Portending good, and all her spirits composed
To meek submission: thou at season fit
Let her with thee partake what thou hast heard,
Chiefly what may concern her faith to know,
The great deliverance by her seed to come   600
(For by the Woman's Seed) on all mankind:
That ye may live, which will be many days,
Both in one faith unanimous though sad,
With cause for evils past, yet much more cheered
With meditation on the happy end."   605
    He ended, and they both descend the hill;
Descended, Adam to the bow'r where Eve
Lay sleeping ran before, but found her waked;
And thus with words not sad she him received:
    "Whence thou return'st, and whither went'st, I know;   610
For God is also in sleep, and dreams advise,
Which he hath sent propitious, some great good
Presaging, since with sorrow and heart's distress
Wearied I fell asleep. But now lead on;
In me is no delay; with thee to go,   615
Is to stay here; without thee here to stay,
Is to go hence unwilling; thou to me

575–76. sum Of wisdom: Ezek. 28.12.
581–84. 2 Pet. 1.5–7; 1 Cor. 13.
584. charity (*caritas*): the word used for "love" in most English versions of the Bible, as in 1 Cor. 13.
587. Cf. 4.75.
588–89. top Of speculation: high place of observation.

591–92. expect . . . motion: await the order to move.
611. Cf. *Iliad* 1.63.
614. lead on: cf. 9.631.
615. In . . . delay: cf. Virgil, *Ecl.* 3.52, *Aen.* 2.701, 12.11.
615–18. Cf. Ruth 1.16, *Iliad* 6.429–30, *P.L.* 11.290–92.

Art all things under heav'n, all places thou,
Who for my wilful crime art banished hence.
This further consolation yet secure   620
I carry hence; though all by me is lost,
Such favor I unworthy am vouchsafed,
By me the Promised Seed shall all restore."
    So spake our mother Eve, and Adam heard
Well pleased, but answered not; for now too nigh   625
Th' Archangel stood, and from the other hill
To their fixed station, all in bright array
The Cherubim descended; on the ground
Gliding metéorous, as ev'ning mist
Ris'n from a river o'er the marish glides,   630
And gathers ground fast at the laborer's heel
Homeward returning. High in front advanced,
The brandished sword of God before them blazed
Fierce as a comet; which with torrid heat,
And vapor as the Libyan air adust,   635
Began to parch that temperate clime; whereat
In either hand the hast'ning Angel caught
Our ling'ring parents, and to th' eastern gate
Led them direct, and down the cliff as fast
To the subjected plain; then disappeared.   640
They, looking back, all th' eastern side beheld
Of Paradise, so late their happy seat,
Waved over by that flaming brand, the gate
With dreadful faces thronged and fiery arms.
Some natural tears they dropped, but wiped them soon; 645
The world was all before them, where to choose
Their place of rest, and Providence their guide:
They hand in hand, with wand'ring steps and slow,
Through Eden took their solitary way.

                (1658?–1665?)

629. metéorous: like a meteor, above the ground; cf. 9.74–75, 158–59, 180–81.
630. marish: marsh.
631–32. An unobtrusive but poignant reminder of the judgment on Adam (10.201–08; cf. 1053 f.) and the everyday world of history. Cf. Gen. 3.19, 23.

633. Gen. 3.24.
635. vapor: waves of heat.
637–38. Cf. Gen. 19.15–16.
638. eastern gate: cf. 4.178, 11.190.
640. subjected: lying below (cf. Spenser, *F.Q.* 1.11.19.1).
648. hand in hand: see the note on 4.321.

PARADISE REGAINED

Paradise Regained and *Samson Agonistes* were published together in 1671 (or possibly 1670). *Paradise Regained* was a natural sequel to *Paradise Lost* and was presumably composed between 1665 and 1670. In the invocation of book 9 Milton had contrasted the martial pomp and heroism of traditional epic and romance with

> the better fortitude
> Of patience and heroic martyrdom,

and the long epic had partly borne out the contrast. But Adam, though his eyes had been opened by repentance and instruction, had barely set foot on the road of experience, and the earthly experience of God's Son lay far in the future. The title *Paradise Regained* might suggest the Crucifixion, but that story had been unapproachably told in the Gospels, and the preparatory trials in the wilderness showed the second Adam winning the moral and religious victory over Satan which the first Adam had lost, and exemplifying a kind of heroism within man's reach.

Especially in our day, when literature is largely committed to the anti-heroic, the mere idea of a perfect, sinless hero may seem to extinguish any possible interest before the poem is begun. On this point one general and one particular thing may be said. First, Milton the humanist had his full share — as his tract *Of Education* amply indicates — of the Renaissance faith in the inspiring power of great examples, a faith ardently attested by Sir Philip Sidney, Spenser, George Chapman, and many other English and foreign writers. Secondly, Milton follows two lines of dramatic suspense which come together and are resolved in the climactic temptation. On the one hand, Satan fears that the newly baptized teacher, sanctified by heaven, may be the divine being who, according to God's judgment after the fall, is to bruise the Serpent's head, to check the power Satan has been allowed in the world, and he is desperately anxious either to confirm or to dispel that fear by ascertaining Christ's identity. On the other hand, Christ himself in his human nature has only a limited knowledge of his own identity and mission; the prime essential of his character and situation is that — unlike the self-assertive and disobedient Eve and Adam — he waits in humble trust for God's progressive illumination and guidance.

In the personal passage in the *Reason of Church Government* (1642), when explaining why he felt obliged to postpone the writing of a major poem, Milton had referred to the book of Job as a model for a brief epic; and Job was evidently in his mind when he composed *Paradise Regained*. Though there is a slight epic framework, the poem is virtually a debate with elaborate stage directions; Christ is placed firmly in a historical setting created out of the familiar learning of a classicist. His immediate setting, the wilderness, becomes a symbol of his isolation from the world, and that isolation is heightened as the poem proceeds. Christ's early soliloquy summarizes his past life and his partial uncertainty about the future. Satan's first temptation, the demand that he perform the miracle of changing stones into bread, Christ rejects on the ground supplied by orthodox interpreters, that it would imply distrust of God's providence.

In the second book Christ's isolation is reinforced by the reactions of even those closest to him: his disciples, who expect him to set up an earthly kingdom, are dismayed by his strange disappearance, and his mother feels somewhat uneasy. Satan is much disturbed in reporting to his fellow demons the evident strength of the new adversary. Christ himself, after forty days of fasting, sleeps and dreams of the scanty food brought to Elijah by the ravens. In contrast to that temperate dream, Satan reappears to offer a magical and lavish banquet — a purple patch in a mainly bare poem, and an example of the worldly tempter's persistent inability to comprehend Christ's nature and mission. The banquet is the first of half a dozen stages, of ascending refinement and insidiousness, into which the temptation of "the kingdoms of the world" is divided. The successive offers — wealth, glory, the deliverance of Israel from Roman rule (a not ignoble aim, which Christ himself had earlier considered), alliance with either Parthia or Rome, the great powers of East and West, and even the imperial throne of Tiberius — are all vigorously rejected on moral or religious grounds or both; Christ's kingdom is not to be of this world. Christ's attitude belongs to the fable; but it may to taken to reflect Milton's own concern, in the Restoration period, with individual integrity rather than political action.

The climactic offer or counsel seems to have been Milton's original addition to traditional subdivisions of the second temptation. Many readers have been needlessly shocked by the whole passage — a beautiful evocation of Athens and its literature and philosophy, put into the mouth of Satan, and Christ's vehement dismissal of Greek culture and exaltation of the inspired truth of Zion. As both artist and champion of liberty, Milton had always been deeply attached to the classics, and he was still, as *Samson* and its preface and indeed parts of *Paradise Regained* testify, but he had often made the Christian humanist's distinction between the natural light of the best pagan minds and the supernatural light of revelation; and while Christian humanism had long accepted pagan wisdom as an ally, if one had to choose between self-sufficient reason and humble faith one could not hesitate. Moreover, things good in themselves may be tainted by the giver and his motives, in this case Satan and political power. Also, being what he is, and being likewise a Miltonic debater, Christ is forcefully one-sided; in earlier and less critical phases of the argument he had not been unwilling to display classical knowledge and he had ranked Socrates next to Job (3.96–99). For all its urgency, the condemnation of Greek culture is relative rather than absolute — as in book 8 of *Paradise Lost* Raphael had condemned astronomy and a husband's devotion to his wife not as bad in themselves but only if they came between man and God.

While Christ has been morally invulnerable, he is compassionately pictured as still more isolated and defenseless through a night of storm and torment brought on by Satan. The third temptation — Milton no doubt followed Luke's order for the sake of this climax — is Satan's challenge to Christ to lose his life or prove his divinity by a miracle, and both words and action are swift, dramatic, and ironic. Christ, in trusting himself utterly to God, for the first time realizes and affirms his divine identity, and stands; Satan realizes it at the same instant and falls.* Now — after two classical similes — Christ is given angelic food and hymned as the victor who has founded a fairer Paradise for man — or, as the opening of the poem had said, has raised Eden, a spiritual Eden, in the waste wilderness. The last four lines are one more of Milton's quietly paradoxical endings: "the Son of God, our Saviour meek"

unobserved

Home to his mother's house private returned.

In comparison with the spacious splendors of *Paradise Lost*, *Paradise Regained* has, ever since it was published, met with disparagement (which Milton himself did not relish), though a good many recent critics have recognized its distinctive character and power. Comparison with *Paradise Lost* is quite idle, since *Paradise Regained* was not an unsuccessful effort to provide an appendage in the same vein; it was a wholly different kind of poem, one of the last two of Milton's many experiments. The deliberate and consistent differences in conception, form, style, and rhythm are manifest, and need no elaboration here. If Milton's moral and religious passion and artistic control leave a reader unmoved, it should not be too readily assumed that the poet is at fault.

* See the note on 4.549 f.

PARADISE
REGAIN'D.
A
POEM.
In IV *BOOKS*.

To which is added

SAMSON AGONISTES.

The Author
JOHN MILTON.

LONDON,

Printed by *J. M* for *John Starkey* at the
Mitre in *Fleetstreet*, near *Temple-Bar.*
MDCLXXI.

Paradise Regained

The First Book

I WHO erewhile the happy garden sung,
By one man's disobedience lost, now sing
Recovered Paradise to all mankind,
By one man's firm obedience fully tried
Through all temptation, and the Tempter foiled   5
In all his wiles, defeated and repulsed,
And Eden raised in the waste wilderness.
    Thou, Spirit, who led'st this glorious Eremite
Into the desert, his victorious field
Against the spiritual foe, and brought'st him thence   10
By proof the undoubted Son of God, inspire,
As thou art wont, my prompted song, else mute,
And bear through highth or depth of nature's bounds
With prosperous wing full summed to tell of deeds
Above heroic, though in secret done,   15
And unrecorded left through many an age,
Worthy t' have not remained so long unsung.
    Now had the great Proclaimer, with a voice
More awful than the sound of trumpet, cried
Repentance, and Heaven's kingdom nigh at hand   20
To all baptized. To his great baptism flocked
With awe the regions round, and with them came
From Nazareth the son of Joseph deemed
To the flood Jordan, came as then obscure,
Unmarked, unknown; but him the Baptist soon   25
Descried, divinely warned, and witness bore
As to his worthier, and would have resigned
To him his heavenly office; nor was long
His witness unconfirmed: on him baptized
Heaven opened, and in likeness of a dove   30
The Spirit descended, while the Father's voice

BOOK I. 1–7. The retrospective proem recalls
the four lines that originally opened the *Aeneid*
(*Ille ego . . .*), lines imitated in the prelude to
book 1 of *The Faerie Queene*.
    2–4. Rom. 5.12, 19.
    7. A metaphorical Eden; cf. Isa. 51.3, *P.R.*
4.613–15, *P.L.* 12.587.
    8. Spirit: see the note on *P.L.* 1.17.
    14. summed: cf. *P.L.* 7.421 and note.

15. Above heroic: cf. *P.L.* 9.31–33.
    16. unrecorded: presumably as not told in
full.
    18. Proclaimer: John the Baptist (Matt.
3.1 f.; Mark 1.2 f.; Luke 3.2 f.; John 1.23).
    23. Nazareth: in Galilee.   Joseph: hus-
band of Mary, Jesus' mother.
    29–32. Matt. 3.16–17; Mark 1.10–11;
Luke 3.21–22; John 1.32.

From heav'n pronounced him his belovèd Son.
That heard the Adversary, who, roving still
About the world, at that assembly famed
Would not be last, and with the voice divine   35
Nigh thunder-struck, th' exalted man, to whom
Such high attest was giv'n, a while surveyed
With wonder; then with envy fraught and rage
Flies to his place, nor rests, but in mid-air
To council summons all his mighty peers,   40
Within thick clouds and dark tenfold involved,
A gloomy cónsistory; and them amidst
With looks aghast and sad he thus bespake:
    "O ancient Powers of air and this wide world
(For much more willingly I mention air,   45
This our old conquest, than remember hell,
Our hated habitation), well ye know
How many ages, as the years of men,
This universe we have possessed, and ruled
In manner at our will th' affairs of earth,   50
Since Adam and his facile consort Eve
Lost Paradise, deceived by me, though since
With dread attending when that fatal wound
Shall be inflicted by the seed of Eve
Upon my head. Long the decrees of Heav'n   55
Delay, for longest time to him is short;
And now too soon for us the circling hours
This dreaded time have compassed, wherein we
Must bide the stroke of that long-threatened wound,
At least if so we can, and by the head   60
Broken be not intended all our power
To be infringed, our freedom and our being
In this fair empire won of earth and air;
For this ill news I bring: the Woman's Seed,
Destined to this, is late of woman born.   65
His birth to our just fear gave no small cause;
But his growth now to youth's full flow'r, displaying
All virtue, grace and wisdom to achieve
Things highest, greatest, multiplies my fear.
Before him a great Prophet, to proclaim   70
His coming, is sent harbinger, who all
Invites, and in the consecrated stream
Pretends to wash off sin, and fit them so
Purified to receive him pure, or rather
To do him honor as their King. All come,   75
And he himself among them was baptized,

---

33. Adversary: cf. *P.L.* 1.81 and note.
39. mid-air: glossary (and *P.R.* 2.117).
42. gloomy consistory: cf. *Aen.* 3.679, *con-cilium horrendum,* and note on *P.L.* 1.795.
52–55. Gen. 3.15; cf. *P.L.* 10.179–81, etc.
56. Ps. 90.4.

57. circling hours: cf. *Odyssey* 1.16; *Aen.* 1.234, 6.748, etc.
62. infringed: broken.
66–69. Luke 2.40, 52.
70–85. See notes on 1.18 and 29–32.
74. 1 John 3.3.

Not thence to be more pure, but to receive
The testimony of Heaven, that who he is
Thenceforth the nations may not doubt. I saw
The Prophet do him reverence; on him rising   80
Out of the water, heav'n above the clouds
Unfold her crystal doors; thence on his head
A perfect dove descend, whate'er it meant,
And out of heav'n the Sov'reign Voice I heard,
'This is my Son beloved, in him am pleased.'   85
His mother then is mortal, but his Sire
He who obtains the monarchy of heav'n,
And what will he not do to advance his Son?
His first-begot we know, and sore have felt,
When his fierce thunder drove us to the deep;   90
Who this is we must learn, for man he seems
In all his lineaments, though in his face
The glimpses of his Father's glory shine.
Ye see our danger on the utmost edge
Of hazard, which admits no long debate,   95
But must with something sudden be opposed,
Not force, but well-couched fraud, well-woven snares,
Ere in the head of nations he appear
Their king, their leader, and supreme on earth.
I, when no other durst, sole undertook   100
The dismal expedition to find out
And ruin Adam, and the exploit performed
Successfully: a calmer voyage now
Will waft me; and the way found prosperous once
Induces best to hope of like success."   105
    He ended, and his words impression left
Of much amazement to th' infernal crew,
Distracted and surprised with deep dismay
At these sad tidings; but no time was then
For long indulgence to their fears or grief: 110
Unanimous they all commit the care
And management of this main enterprise
To him their great Dictator, whose attempt
At first against mankind so well had thrived
In Adam's overthrow, and led their march   115
From hell's deep-vaulted den to dwell in light,
Regents and potentates, and kings, yea gods,
Of many a pleasant realm and province wide.
So to the coast of Jordan he directs
His easy steps, girded with snaky wiles,   120
Where he might likeliest find this new-declared,

---

83. perfect: real, actual.
87. obtains: holds.
89–90. Cf. *P.L.* 6.746 f.
94–95. edge of hazard: cf. *All's Well That Ends Well* 3.3.6; *Iliad* 10.173.

97. well-couched: well framed and concealed.
117–18. Cf. *P.L.* 1.364 f.
120. Isa. 11.5.

This man of men, attested Son of God,
Temptation and all guile on him to try,
So to subvert whom he suspected raised
To end his reign on earth so long enjoyed;   125
But contrary unweeting he fulfilled
The purposed counsel preordained and fixed
Of the Most High, who in full frequence bright
Of angels, thus to Gabriel smiling spake:
    "Gabriel, this day by proof thou shalt behold,   130
Thou and all angels cónversant on earth
With man or men's affairs, how I begin
To verify that solemn message late,
On which I sent thee to the Virgin pure
In Galilee, that she should bear a son   135
Great in renown, and called the Son of God;
Then told'st her, doubting how these things could be
To her a virgin, that on her should come
The Holy Ghost, and the power of the Highest
O'ershadow her. This man, born and now upgrown,   140
To show him worthy of his birth divine
And high prediction, henceforth I expose
To Satan; let him tempt and now assay
His utmost subtlety, because he boasts
And vaunts of his great cunning to the throng   145
Of his apostasy; he might have learnt
Less overweening, since he failed in Job,
Whose constant perseverance overcame
Whate'er his cruel malice could invent.
He now shall know I can produce a man   150
Of female seed, far abler to resist
All his solicitations, and at length
All his vast force, and drive him back to hell,
Winning by conquest what the first man lost
By fallacy surprised. But first I mean   155
To exercise him in the wilderness;
There he shall first lay down the rudiments
Of his great warfare, ere I send him forth
To conquer Sin and Death, the two grand foes,
By humiliation and strong sufferance: 160
His weakness shall o'ercome Satanic strength
And all the world, and mass of sinful flesh;
That all the angels and ethereal powers,
They now, and men hereafter, may discern
From what consummate virtue I have chose   165
This perfect man, by merit called my Son,
To earn salvation for the sons of men."

133–40. Luke 1.26–28.
146. apostasy: fellow rebels or apostates
(cf. *P.L.* 1.125).

157–58. rudiments . . . warfare: cf. *Aen.*
11.156–57.
159. Cf. *P.L.* 2.721–22, 12.431.
161. 1 Cor. 1.27.

So spake the Eternal Father, and all heaven
Admiring stood a space, then into hymns
Burst forth, and in celestial measures moved,   170
Circling the throne and singing, while the hand
Sung with the voice, and this the argument:
"Victory and triumph to the Son of God
Now ent'ring his great duel, not of arms,
But to vanquish by wisdom hellish wiles.   175
The Father knows the Son; therefore secure
Ventures his filial virtue, though untried,
Against whate'er may tempt, whate'er seduce,
Allure, or terrify, or undermine.
Be frustrate, all ye stratagems of hell,   180
And devilish machinations, come to naught."
So they in heav'n their odes and vigils tuned.
Meanwhile the Son of God, who yet some days
Lodged in Bethabara where John baptized,
Musing and much revolving in his breast   185
How best the mighty work he might begin
Of Saviour to mankind, and which way first
Publish his godlike office now mature,
One day forth walked alone, the Spirit leading,
And his deep thoughts, the better to converse   190
With solitude, till far from track of men,
Thought following thought, and step by step led on,
He entered now the bordering desert wild,
And with dark shades and rocks environed round,
His holy meditations thus pursued: 195
"O what a multitude of thoughts at once
Awakened in me swarm, while I consider
What from within I feel myself, and hear
What from without comes often to my ears,
Ill sorting with my present state compared.   200
When I was yet a child, no childish play
To me was pleasing; all my mind was set
Serious to learn and know, and thence to do
What might be public good; myself I thought
Born to that end, born to promote all truth,   205
All righteous things. Therefore, above my years,
The Law of God I read, and found it sweet,
Made it my whole delight, and in it grew
To such perfection, that ere yet my age
Had measured twice six years, at our great Feast   210
I went into the Temple, there to hear
The teachers of our Law, and to propose

171–72. hand . . . voice: cf. Tibullus 3.4.41.
173. An echo of Giles Fletcher's title,
Christ's Victory and Triumph (1610)?
174–75. Cf. *P.L.* 12.386 f.
176. John 10.15.

182. vigils: nocturnal services.
184. Bethabara: on the Jordan (John 1.28).
204–06. John 18.37.
208. Made . . . delight: Ps. 1.2.
210–14. Luke 2.42–49.

What might improve my knowledge or their own,
And was admired by all; yet this not all
To which my spirit aspired. Victorious deeds   215
Flamed in my heart, heroic acts: one while
To rescue Israel from the Roman yoke,
Then to subdue and quell o'er all the earth
Brute violence and proud tyrannic pow'r,
Till truth were freed, and equity restored;   220
Yet held it more humane, more heavenly, first
By winning words to conquer willing hearts,
And make persuasion do the work of fear;
At least to try, and teach the erring soul
Not wilfully misdoing, but unware   225
Misled; the stubborn only to subdue.
These growing thoughts my mother soon perceiving,
By words at times cast forth, inly rejoiced,
And said to me apart: 'High are thy thoughts,
O Son, but nourish them and let them soar   230
To what highth sacred virtue and true worth
Can raise them, though above example high;
By matchless deeds express thy matchless Sire.
For know, thou art no son of mortal man;
Though men esteem thee low of parentage,   235
Thy Father is the Eternal King, who rules
All heaven and earth, angels and sons of men.
A messenger from God foretold thy birth
Conceived in me a virgin; he foretold
Thou shouldst be great and sit on David's throne,   240
And of thy kingdom there should be no end.
At thy nativity a glorious quire
Of angels in the fields of Bethlehem sung
To shepherds watching at their folds by night,
And told them the Messiah now was born,   245
Where they might see him; and to thee they came,
Directed to the manger where thou lay'st,
For in the inn was left no better room.
A star, not seen before, in heaven appearing
Guided the wise men thither from the East,   250
To honor thee with incense, myrrh, and gold,
By whose bright course led on they found the place,
Affirming it thy star new-grav'n in heaven,
By which they knew thee King of Israel born.
Just Simeon and prophetic Anna, warned   255
By vision, found thee in the Temple, and spake
Before the altar and the vested priest
Like things of thee to all that present stood.'
This having heard, straight I again revolved

218–19. Cf. *Aen.* 6.851–53.   242–48. Luke 2.7–16.
226. stubborn . . . subdue: *Aen.*, loc. cit.   249–54. Matt. 2.7–11.
239–41. Luke 1.32–33.   255–58. Luke 2.25–39.

The Law and Prophets, searching what was writ   260
Concerning the Messiah, to our scribes
Known partly, and soon found of whom they spake
I am; this chiefly, that my way must lie
Through many a hard assay even to the death,
Ere I the promised kingdom can attain,   265
Or work redemption for mankind, whose sins'
Full weight must be transferred upon my head.
Yet neither thus disheartened or dismayed,
The time prefixed I waited; when behold
The Baptist (of whose birth I oft had heard,   270
Not knew by sight) now come, who was to come
Before Messiah and his way prepare.
I as all others to his baptism came,
Which I believed was from above; but he
Straight knew me, and with loudest voice proclaimed   275
Me him (for it was shown him so from Heaven),
Me him whose harbinger he was; and first
Refused on me his baptism to confer,
As much his greater, and was hardly won.
But as I rose out of the laving stream,   280
Heaven opened her eternal doors, from whence
The Spirit descended on me like a dove,
And last, the sum of all, my Father's voice,
Audibly heard from heav'n, pronounced me his,
Me his belovèd Son, in whom alone   285
He was well pleased; by which I knew the time
Now full, that I no more should live obscure,
But openly begin, as best becomes
The authority which I derived from Heaven.
And now by some strong motion I am led   290
Into this wilderness, to what intent
I learn not yet, perhaps I need not know;
For what concerns my knowledge God reveals."
    So spake our Morning Star then in his rise,
And looking round on every side beheld   295
A pathless desert, dusk with horrid shades.
The way he came not having marked, return
Was difficult, by human steps untrod;
And he still on was led, but with such thoughts
Accompanied of things past and to come   300
Lodged in his breast, as well might recommend
Such solitude before choicest society.
Full forty days he passed — whether on hill

---

263. I am: John 8.58; Exod. 3.14.
267. Isa. 53.6; Heb. 9.28; 1 Pet. 2.24.
270–86. Matt. 3; Mark 1; Luke 3; John 1.
286–87. time Now full: Gal. 4.4.
292–93. Matt. 24.36; Mark 13.32.
294. Morning Star: Rev. 22.16.
296. Cf. *Aen.* 1.165.

296 f. Matt. 4.1–11; Mark 1.12–13; Luke
4.1–13.
301–02. Cf. Cicero, quoted in note on *P.L.*
8.427–28.
303 f. Milton follows Matthew (4.1 f.) in
having the temptations come after Christ's
forty-day fast.

Sometimes, anon in shady vale, each night
Under the covert of some ancient oak   305
Or cedar to defend him from the dew,
Or harbored in one cave, is not revealed;
Nor tasted human food, nor hunger felt
Till those days ended, hungered then at last
Among wild beasts; they at his sight grew mild,   310
Nor sleeping him nor waking harmed; his walk
The fiery serpent fled and noxious worm;
The lion and fierce tiger glared aloof.
But now an aged man in rural weeds,
Following, as seemed, the quest of some stray ewe,   315
Or withered sticks to gather, which might serve
Against a winter's day when winds blow keen
To warm him wet returned from field at eve,
He saw approach, who first with curious eye
Perused him, then with words thus uttered spake: 320
    "Sir, what ill chance hath brought thee to this place
So far from path or road of men, who pass
In troop or caravan, for single none
Durst ever, who returned, and dropped not here
His carcass, pined with hunger and with drouth?   325
I ask the rather, and the more admire,
For that to me thou seem'st the man whom late
Our new baptizing Prophet at the ford
Of Jordan honored so, and called thee Son
Of God. I saw and heard, for we sometimes   330
Who dwell this wild, constrained by want, come forth
To town or village nigh (nighest is far),
Where aught we hear, and curious are to hear,
What happens new; fame also finds us out."
    To whom the Son of God: "Who brought me hither   335
Will bring me hence; no other guide I seek."
    "By miracle he may," replied the swain,
"What other way I see not; for we here
Live on tough roots and stubs, to thirst inured
More than the camel, and to drink go far,   340
Men to much misery and hardship born.
But if thou be the Son of God, command
That out of these hard stones be made thee bread;
So shalt thou save thyself and us relieve
With food, whereof we wretched seldom taste."   345
    He ended, and the Son of God replied:
"Think'st thou such force in bread? Is it not written
(For I discern thee other than thou seem'st),

---

310. Among wild beasts: Mark 1.13 (elaborated by Giles Fletcher, *Christ's Victory on Earth* 1 f.); Isa. 65.25.

314–18. For Satan's disguise there were diverse precedents, e.g., the apparent hermits of Spenser (Archimago: *F.Q.* 1.1.29) and G. Fletcher (Satan: loc. cit., 15 f.).

327. For that: because.

342–44. Matt. 4.3; Luke 4.3, 23.39.

Man lives not by bread only, but each word
Proceeding from the mouth of God, who fed   350
Our fathers here with manna? In the Mount
Moses was forty days, nor eat nor drank,
And forty days Eliah without food
Wandered this barren waste; the same I now.
Why dost thou then suggest to me distrust,   355
Knowing who I am, as I know who thou art?"
    Whom thus answered th' Arch-Fiend now undisguised:
" 'Tis true, I am that Spirit unfortunate,
Who leagued with millions more in rash revolt
Kept not my happy station, but was driv'n   360
With them from bliss to the bottomless deep;
Yet to that hideous place not so confined
By rigor unconniving, but that oft
Leaving my dolorous prison I enjoy
Large liberty to round this globe of earth,   365
Or range in th' air, nor from the heav'n of heav'ns
Hath he excluded my resort sometimes.
I came among the Sons of God when he
Gave up into my hands Uzzean Job
To prove him, and illustrate his high worth;   370
And when to all his angels he proposed
To draw the proud king Ahab into fraud
That he might fall in Ramoth, they demurring,
I undertook that office, and the tongues
Of all his flattering prophets glibbed with lies   375
To his destruction, as I had in charge.
For what he bids I do; though I have lost
Much luster of my native brightness, lost
To be beloved of God, I have not lost
To love, at least contémplate and admire,   380
What I see excellent in good, or fair,
Or virtuous; I should so have lost all sense.
What can be then less in me than desire
To see thee and approach thee, whom I know
Declared the Son of God, to hear attent   385
Thy wisdom, and behold thy godlike deeds?
Men generally think me much a foe
To all mankind: why should I? They to me
Never did wrong or violence, by them
I lost not what I lost; rather by them   390
I gained what I have gained, and with them dwell

349–51. Deut. 8.3; Matt. 4.4; Luke 4.4;
Exod. 16.14–15.
  351–52. Exod. 24.18.
  352. eat: past tense (cf. *P.L.* 9.781).
  353–54. Eliah: Elijah (1 Kings 19.1–8).
  355. In Reformation theology the essence
of the first temptation was to inspire distrust of
God's providence (cf. G. Fletcher, *Christ's Vic-*

tory on Earth 20, marginal note).
  363. unconniving: watchful, not acquiescent.
  364–70. Job 1–2; 1 Pet. 5.8.
  369. Uzzean: of Uz, east of Palestine.
  371–76. Ahab: king of Israel seduced by
false prophets (1 Kings 22).
  375. glibbed: made glib.
  385. attent: attentively.

Copartner in these regions of the world,
If not disposer; lend them oft my aid,
Oft my advice by presages and signs,
And answers, oracles, portents and dreams,　　　　395
Whereby they may direct their future life.
Envy they say excites me, thus to gain
Companions of my misery and woe.
At first it may be; but long since with woe
Nearer acquainted, now I feel by proof　　　　400
That fellowship in pain divides not smart,
Nor lightens aught each man's peculiar load;
Small consolation then, were man adjoined.
This wounds me most (what can it less?) that man,
Man fall'n, shall be restored, I never more."　　　　405
　　To whom our Saviour sternly thus replied:
"Deservedly thou griev'st, composed of lies
From the beginning, and in lies wilt end,
Who boast'st release from hell, and leave to come
Into the heav'n of heavens. Thou com'st indeed,　　　　410
As a poor miserable captive thrall
Comes to the place where he before had sat
Among the prime in splendor, now deposed,
Ejected, emptied, gazed, unpitied, shunned,
A spectacle of ruin or of scorn　　　　415
To all the host of heaven; the happy place
Imparts to thee no happiness, no joy,
Rather inflames thy torment, representing
Lost bliss, to thee no more communicable;
So never more in hell than when in heaven.　　　　420
But thou art serviceable to heaven's King!
Wilt thou impute to obedience what thy fear
Extorts, or pleasure to do ill excites?
What but thy malice moved thee to misdeem
Of righteous Job, then cruelly to afflict him　　　　425
With all inflictions? But his patience won.
The other service was thy chosen task,
To be a liar in four hundred mouths;
For lying is thy sustenance, thy food.
Yet thou pretend'st to truth; all oracles　　　　430
By thee are giv'n, and what confessed more true
Among the nations? That hath been thy craft,
By mixing somewhat true to vent more lies.
But what have been thy answers, what but dark,

393–96. See below the note on 4.382–93.
399–402. Cf. *Aen.* 1.630.
401. A contradiction of a semi-proverbial sentiment, e.g., Marlowe, *Dr. Faustus* 474.
407–08. John 8.44.
427–28. other service; see note on 371–76 above.
430–59. Since tradition made the fallen angels the gods of the heathen religions (*P.L.* 1.364 f.), it followed that the Greek oracles were of diabolical inspiration. Cf. Lactantius, *Div. Inst.* 2.16; Augustine, *City of God, passim;* Milton, *Nativity* 173–80, *P.L.* 1.517–18; Sir Thomas Browne, *Religio Medici* 1.29. Cf. also Cicero, *De Divinatione* 2.56; Plutarch, "On the Cessation of Oracles."

Ambiguous, and with double sense deluding,   435
Which they who asked have seldom understood,
And not well understood, as good not known?
Who ever by consulting at thy shrine
Returned the wiser, or the more instruct
To fly or follow what concerned him most,   440
And run not sooner to his fatal snare?
For God hath justly giv'n the nations up
To thy delusions; justly, since they fell
Idolatrous; but when his purpose is
Among them to declare his providence,   445
To thee not known, whence hast thou then thy truth,
But from him or his angels president
In every province, who themselves disdaining
To approach thy temples, give thee in command
What to the smallest tittle thou shalt say   450
To thy adorers? Thou with trembling fear,
Or like a fawning parasite obey'st;
Then to thyself ascrib'st the truth foretold.
But this thy glory shall be soon retrenched;
No more shalt thou by oracling abuse   455
The Gentiles; henceforth oracles are ceased,
And thou no more with pomp and sacrifice
Shalt be inquired at Delphos or elsewhere,
At least in vain, for they shall find thee mute.
God hath now sent his living Oracle   460
Into the world, to teach his final will,
And sends his Spirit of Truth henceforth to dwell
In pious hearts, an inward oracle
To all truth requisite for men to know."
   So spake our Saviour; but the subtle Fiend,   465
Though inly stung with anger and disdain,
Dissembled, and this answer smooth returned:
   "Sharply thou hast insisted on rebuke,
And urged me hard with doings which not will
But misery hath wrested from me; where   470
Easily canst thou find one miserable,
And not enforced ofttimes to part from truth,
If it may stand him more in stead to lie,
Say and unsay, feign, flatter, or abjure?
But thou art placed above me, thou art Lord;   475
From thee I can and must submiss endure
Check or reproof, and glad to scape so quit.
Hard are the ways of truth, and rough to walk,
Smooth on the tongue discoursed, pleasing to th' ear,
And tunable as sylvan pipe or song;   480
What wonder then if I delight to hear

442–43. 2 Thess. 2.9–12.   462–64. John 16.13.
   460. Acts 7.38; Rom. 3.2; Heb. 5.12;
1 Pet. 4.11.

Her dictates from thy mouth? Most men admire
Virtue who follow not her lore. Permit me
To hear thee when I come (since no man comes),
And talk at least, though I despair to attain.   485
Thy Father, who is holy, wise and pure,
Suffers the hypocrite or atheous priest
To tread his sacred courts, and minister
About his altar, handling holy things,
Praying or vowing, and vouchsafed his voice   490
To Balaam reprobate, a prophet yet
Inspired; disdain not such access to me."
    To whom our Saviour, with unaltered brow:
"Thy coming hither, though I know thy scope,
I bid not or forbid; do as thou find'st   495
Permission from above; thou canst not more."
    He added not; and Satan, bowing low
His gray dissimulation, disappeared
Into thin air diffused: for now began
Night with her sullen wing to double-shade   500
The desert, fowls in their clay nests were couched;
And now wild beasts came forth the woods to roam.

The Second Book

Meanwhile the new-baptized, who yet remained
At Jordan with the Baptist, and had seen
Him whom they heard so late expressly called
Jesus Messiah, Son of God declared,
And on that high authority had believed,   5
And with him talked, and with him lodged, I mean
Andrew and Simon, famous after known
With others though in Holy Writ not named,
Now missing him, their joy so lately found,
So lately found, and so abruptly gone,   10
Began to doubt, and doubted many days,
And as the days increased, increased their doubt.
Sometimes they thought he might be only shown,
And for a time caught up to God, as once
Moses was in the Mount, and missing long,   15

482–83. Cf. *P.L.* 8.610–11 and note.
488. Isa. 1.12.
491. Balaam: a prophet who refused to obey the King of Moab's command to curse the Israelites (Num. 22–23).
492. disdain: refuse.
498. gray dissimulation. This effective abstraction occurs in John Ford's *The Broken Heart*, 4.2.99, but Milton's use of it is probably a coincidence.

499. Into . . . diffused. Cf. *The Tempest* 4.1.150; *In quintum Novembris* 161 and note.
500. Cf. *Comus* 335.
BOOK II. 4. Both the Hebrew "Messiah" and the Greek "Christ" mean "the anointed one."
7. Mark 1.16; John 1.37–41. The Gospels do not speak of disciples before the temptation, but their dramatic value is evident.
15. Moses: Exod. 19.

And the great Thisbite who on fiery wheels
Rode up to heaven, yet once again to come.
Therefore as those young prophets then with care
Sought lost Eliah, so in each place these
Nigh to Bethabara — in Jericho   20
The city of palms, Aenon, and Salem old,
Machaerus, and each town or city walled
On this side the broad lake Genezaret,
Or in Peraea — but returned in vain.
Then on the bank of Jordan, by a creek   25
Where winds with reeds, and osiers whisp'ring play,
Plain fishermen (no greater men them call),
Close in a cottage low together got,
Their unexpected loss and plaints outbreathed:
    "Alas, from what high hope to what relapse   30
Unlooked for are we fall'n! Our eyes beheld
Messiah certainly now come, so long
Expected of our fathers; we have heard
His words, his wisdom full of grace and truth.
'Now, now, for sure, deliverance is at hand,   35
The kingdom shall to Israel be restored:'
Thus we rejoiced, but soon our joy is turned
Into perplexity and new amaze;
For whither is he gone, what accident
Hath rapt him from us? Will he now retire   40
After appearance, and again prolong
Our expectation? God of Israel,
Send thy Messiah forth, the time is come;
Behold the kings of the earth, how they oppress
Thy chosen, to what highth their pow'r unjust   45
They have exalted, and behind them cast
All fear of thee; arise and vindicate
Thy glory, free thy people from their yoke!
But let us wait; thus far he hath performed,
Sent his Anointed, and to us revealed him,   50
By his great Prophet, pointed at and shown,
In public, and with him we have conversed.
Let us be glad of this, and all our fears
Lay on his providence; he will not fail,
Nor will withdraw him now, nor will recall,   55
Mock us with his blest sight, then snatch him hence;
Soon we shall see our hope, our joy, return."
    Thus they out of their plaints new hope resume

16–19. Thisbite: Elijah ("Eliah" in 19). Cf. 2 Kings 2.11–17 and Milton's first epigram on the Gunpowder Plot and his elegy on the bishop of Ely (lines 49–50).

17. yet . . . come: Mal. 4.5; Matt. 11.14, 17.11; Mark 9.11–13.

20–21. Jericho: north of the Dead Sea (Deut. 34.3).

21. Aenon, Salem: in Samaria (John 3.23).

22. Machaerus: a fortress east of the Dead Sea.

23. this side: the west.   Genezaret: Lake of Gennesaret or Sea of Galilee.

24. Peraea: region east of the Jordan and the Dead Sea.

34. John 1.14.

36. Acts 1.6.

To find whom at the first they found unsought.
But to his mother Mary, when she saw   60
Others returned from baptism, not her Son,
Nor left at Jordan, tidings of him none,
Within her breast though calm, her breast though pure,
Motherly cares and fears got head, and raised
Some troubled thoughts, which she in sighs thus clad: 65
    "O what avails me now that honor high
To have conceived of God, or that salute,
'Hail, highly favored, among women blest!'
While I to sorrows am no less advanced,
And fears as eminent, above the lot   70
Of other women, by the birth I bore,
In such a season born when scarce a shed
Could be obtained to shelter him or me
From the bleak air? A stable was our warmth,
A manger his; yet soon enforced to fly   75
Thence into Egypt, till the murd'rous king
Were dead, who sought his life, and missing filled
With infant blood the streets of Bethlehem;
From Egypt home returned, in Nazareth
Hath been our dwelling many years, his life   80
Private, unactive, calm, contemplative,
Little suspicious to any king. But now
Full grown to man, acknowledged, as I hear,
By John the Baptist, and in public shown,
Son owned from heaven by his Father's voice,   85
I looked for some great change. To honor? No,
But trouble, as old Simeon plain foretold,
That to the fall and rising he should be
Of many in Israel, and to a sign
Spoken against, that through my very soul   90
A sword shall pierce. This is my favored lot,
My exaltation to afflictions high;
Afflicted I may be, it seems, and blest;
I will not argue that, nor will repine.
But where delays he now? Some great intent   95
Conceals him. When twelve years he scarce had seen,
I lost him, but so found, as well I saw
He could not lose himself, but went about
His Father's business; what he meant I mused,
Since understand; much more his absence now   100
Thus long to some great purpose he obscures.
But I to wait with patience am inured;
My heart hath been a storehouse long of things
And sayings laid up, portending strange events."
    Thus Mary pondering oft, and oft to mind   105

66–82. Luke 1.26–35, 2.16–19; Matt.2.13–   87–91. Luke 2.34–35.
23.   96–99. Luke 2.43–50.
    76. king: Herod (Matt. 2.1–18).   102–08. Luke 2.19, 51.

Recalling what remarkably had passed
Since first her salutation heard, with thoughts
Meekly composed awaited the fulfilling;
The while her Son tracing the desert wild,
Sole but with holiest meditations fed,   110
Into himself descended, and at once
All his great work to come before him set:
How to begin, how to accomplish best
His end of being on earth, and mission high.
For Satan, with sly preface to return,   115
Had left him vacant, and with speed was gone
Up to the middle region of thick air,
Where all his Potentates in council sat;
There without sign of boast, or sign of joy,
Solicitous and blank he thus began: 120
    "Princes, heaven's ancient Sons, Ethereal Thrones,
Demonian Spirits now, from the element
Each of his reign allotted, rightlier called
Powers of fire, air, water, and earth beneath,
So may we hold our place and these mild seats   125
Without new trouble; such an enemy
Is ris'n to invade us, who no less
Threatens than our expulsion down to hell.
I, as I undertook, and with the vote
Consenting in full frequence was empow'red,   130
Have found him, viewed him, tasted him, but find
Far other labor to be undergone
Than when I dealt with Adam first of men,
Though Adam by his wife's allurement fell,
However to this man inferior far,   135
If he be man by mother's side at least,
With more than human gifts from Heaven adorned,
Perfections absolute, graces divine,
And amplitude of mind to greatest deeds.
Therefore I am returned, lest confidence   140
Of my success with Eve in Paradise
Deceive ye to persuasion over-sure
Of like succeeding here; I summon all
Rather to be in readiness, with hand
Or counsel to assist, lest I who erst   145
Thought none my equal, now be overmatched."
    So spake the old Serpent doubting, and from all
With clamor was assured their utmost aid
At his command; when from amidst them rose
Belial, the dissolutest Spirit that fell,   150

---

111. Into himself descended: cf. Persius, 4.23; Bacon, *Advancement of Learning* (ed. Spedding, London, 1870, 3, 315): "For the unlearned man knows not what it is to descend into himself. . . ."

122. element: glossary.
131. tasted: i.e., examined, tested (cf. Ps. 34.8).
150. Belial: glossary and *P.L.* 2.108 f.

The sensualest, and after Asmodai
The fleshliest incubus, and thus advised:
"Set women in his eye and in his walk,
Among daughters of men the fairest found;
Many are in each region passing fair   155
As the noon sky, more like to goddesses
Than mortal creatures, graceful and discreet,
Expert in amorous arts, enchanting tongues
Persuasive, virgin majesty with mild
And sweet allayed, yet terrible to approach,   160
Skilled to retire, and in retiring draw
Hearts after them tangled in amorous nets.
Such object hath the power to soft'n and tame
Severest temper, smooth the rugged'st brow,
Enerve, and with voluptuous hope dissolve,   165
Draw out with credulous desire, and lead
At will the manliest, resolutest breast,
As the magnetic hardest iron draws.
Women, when nothing else, beguiled the heart
Of wisest Solomon, and made him build,   170
And made him bow to the gods of his wives."
    To whom quick answer Satan thus returned:
"Belial, in much uneven scale thou weigh'st
All others by thyself; because of old
Thou thyself dot'st on womankind, admiring   175
Their shape, their color, and attractive grace,
None are, thou think'st, but taken with such toys.
Before the Flood thou with thy lusty crew,
False-titled Sons of God, roaming the earth
Cast wanton eyes on the daughters of men,   180
And coupled with them, and begot a race.
Have we not seen, or by relation heard,
In courts and regal chambers how thou lurk'st,
In wood or grove by mossy fountain-side,
In valley or green meadow, to waylay   185
Some beauty rare, Callisto, Clymene,
Daphne, or Semele, Antiopa,
Or Amymóne, Syrinx, many more
Too long, then lay'st thy scapes on names adored,
Apollo, Neptune, Jupiter, or Pan,   190
Satyr, or Faun, or Sylvan? But these haunts

---

151. Glossary, "Asmadai."
152. incubus: a demon visiting women in their sleep.
162. amorous nets: cf. *P.L.* 11.586.
165. Enerve: enervate.
166. Cf. Horace, Od. 1.5.9 (the ode Milton translated) and 4.1.30.
168. magnetic: magnet.
170. Solomon: cf. *P.L.* 1.400 f., 403, 444, and notes.
178–81. Milton is not contradicting Gen.

6.2–4 and *P.L.* 11.574–627 (see note), but ascribing similar acts to the fallen angels as pagan gods.
186–91. For some names see the glossary.
186. Clymene: mother of Phaethon by Apollo.
187. Antiopa: woman loved by Zeus.
188. Amymone: daughter of Danaus, loved by Poseidon.
189. scapes: escapades.

Delight not all; among the sons of men,
How many have with a smile made small account
Of beauty and her lures, easily scorned
All her assaults, on worthier things intent?   195
Remember that Pellean conqueror,
A youth, how all the beauties of the East
He slightly viewed, and slightly overpassed;
How he surnamed of Africa dismissed
In his prime youth the fair Iberian maid.   200
For Solomon, he lived at ease, and full
Of honor, wealth, high fare, aimed not beyond
Higher design than to enjoy his state;
Thence to the bait of women lay exposed.
But he whom we attempt is wiser far   205
Than Solomon, of more exalted mind,
Made and set wholly on the accomplishment
Of greatest things. What woman will you find,
Though of this age the wonder and the fame,
On whom his leisure will vouchsafe an eye   210
Of fond desire? Or should she confident,
As sitting queen adored on Beauty's throne,
Descend with all her winning charms begirt
To enamor, as the zone of Venus once
Wrought that effect on Jove (so fables tell),   215
How would one look from his majestic brow
Seated as on the top of Virtue's hill,
Discount'nance her despised, and put to rout
All her array, her female pride deject,
Or turn to reverent awe? For Beauty stands   220
In the admiration only of weak minds
Led captive; cease to admire, and all her plumes
Fall flat and shrink into a trivial toy,
At every sudden slighting quite abashed.
Therefore with manlier objects we must try   225
His constancy, with such as have more show
Of worth, of honor, glory, and popular praise,
Rocks whereon greatest men have oftest wrecked;
Or that which only seems to satisfy
Lawful desires of nature, not beyond.   230
And now I know he hungers where no food
Is to be found, in the wide wilderness;
The rest commit to me; I shall let pass
No advantage, and his strength as oft assay."
      He ceased, and heard their grant in loud acclaim;   235
Then forthwith to him takes a chosen band

196–200. The story of Alexander the Great (born at Pella in Macedon) is in Plutarch's *Alexander* 21–22; that of Scipio Africanus in Livy, 26.50, and Silius Italicus, 15.268–82.
201–04. Solomon. See note on 170 above.
214–15. *Iliad* 14.214–17.
216. his: Christ's.

217. Virtue's hill: a traditional image, e.g., Hesiod, *Works and Days* 289–92; Milton, Sonnet 9.4.
219. deject: dejected, cast down.
222–23. Cf. Ovid, *Ars Amatoria* 1.627–28.
236. Matt. 12.45.

Of Spirits likest to himself in guile
To be at hand, and at his beck appear,
If cause were to unfold some active scene
Of various persons, each to know his part;   240
Then to the desert takes with these his flight,
Where still from shade to shade the Son of God
After forty days' fasting had remained,
Now hung'ring first, and to himself thus said:
    "Where will this end? Four times ten days I have passed   245
Wand'ring this woody maze, and human food
Nor tasted, nor had appetite. That fast
To virtue I impute not, or count part
Of what I suffer here; if nature need not,
Or God support nature without repast   250
Though needing, what praise is it to endure?
But now I feel I hunger, which declares
Nature hath need of what she asks; yet God
Can satisfy that need some other way,
Though hunger still remain: so it remain   255
Without this body's wasting, I content me,
And from the sting of famine fear no harm,
Nor mind it, fed with better thoughts that feed
Me hung'ring more to do my Father's will."
    It was the hour of night, when thus the Son   260
Communed in silent walk, then laid him down
Under the hospitable covert nigh
Of trees thick interwoven; there he slept,
And dreamed, as appetite is wont to dream,
Of meats and drinks, nature's refreshment sweet.   265
Him thought he by the brook of Cherith stood
And saw the ravens with their horny beaks
Food to Elijah bringing even and morn,
Though ravenous, taught to abstain from what they brought.
He saw the Prophet also how he fled   270
Into the desert, and how there he slept
Under a juniper; then how, awaked,
He found his supper on the coals prepared,
And by the angel was bid rise and eat,
And eat the second time after repose,   275
The strength whereof sufficed him forty days;
Sometimes that with Elijah he partook,
Or as a guest with Daniel at his pulse.
Thus wore out night, and now the herald lark
Left his ground-nest, high tow'ring to descry   280
The morn's approach, and greet her with his song;
As lightly from his grassy couch up rose
Our Saviour, and found all was but a dream;
Fasting he went to sleep, and fasting waked.
Up to a hill anon his steps he reared,   285

258–59. John 4.34.   278. Dan. 1.8–19.
266–76. 1 Kings 17.3–6, 19.4–8.

From whose high top to ken the prospect round,
If cottage were in view, sheepcote or herd;
But cottage, herd or sheepcote none he saw,
Only in a bottom saw a pleasant grove,
With chant of tuneful birds resounding loud.   290
Thither he bent his way, determined there
To rest at noon, and entered soon the shade
High-roofed and walks beneath, and alleys brown
That opened in the midst a woody scene;
Nature's own work it seemed (nature taught art),   295
And to a superstitious eye the haunt
Of wood-gods and wood-nymphs. He viewed it round,
When suddenly a man before him stood,
Not rustic as before, but seemlier clad,
As one in city or court or palace bred,   300
And with fair speech these words to him addressed:
   "With granted leave officious I return,
But much more wonder that the Son of God
In this wild solitude so long should bide
Of all things destitute, and well I know,   305
Not without hunger. Others of some note,
As story tells, have trod this wilderness:
The fugitive bondwoman with her son,
Outcast Nebaioth, yet found he relief
By a providing angel; all the race   310
Of Israel here had famished, had not God
Rained from heaven manna; and that Prophet bold,
Native of Thebez, wand'ring here was fed
Twice by a voice inviting him to eat.
Of thee these forty days none hath regard,   315
Forty and more deserted here indeed."
   To whom thus Jesus: "What conclud'st thou hence?
They all had need, I as thou seest have none."
   "How hast thou hunger then?" Satan replied.
"Tell me, if food were now before thee set,   320
Wouldst thou not eat?" "Thereafter as I like
The giver," answered Jesus. "Why should that
Cause thy refusal?" said the subtle Fiend,
"Hast thou not right to all created things,
Owe not all creatures by just right to thee   325
Duty and service, nor to stay till bid,
But tender all their power? Nor mention I
Meats by the Law unclean, or offered first
To idols — those young Daniel could refuse;
Nor proffered by an enemy, though who   330

---

309. Nebaioth: the name of Ishmael's son
(Gen. 25.13), here used for Ishmael himself,
the son of the "bondwoman" Hagar (Gen. 21.
9–19).
  310–12. all . . . manna: Exod. 16.

313. Thebez: for Thisbe, the city of Elijah
in Gilead (cf. 266–76 above).
  321–22. Cf. *Comus* 702–03.
  324. Col. 1.16–18; Heb. 1.2.
  329. Cf. 2.278 and note, and 1 Cor. 10.28.

Would scruple that, with want oppressed? Behold
Nature ashamed, or better to express,
Troubled that thou shouldst hunger, hath purveyed
From all the elements her choicest store
To treat thee as beseems, and as her Lord   335
With honor; only deign to sit and eat."
    He spake no dream, for as his words had end,
Our Saviour lifting up his eyes beheld
In ample space under the broadest shade
A table richly spread, in regal mode,   340
With dishes piled, and meats of noblest sort
And savor, beasts of chase, or fowl of game,
In pastry built, or from the spit, or boiled,
Gris-amber-steamed; all fish from sea or shore,
Freshet, or purling brook, of shell or fin,   345
And exquisitest name, for which was drained
Pontus and Lucrine bay, and Afric coast.
Alas how simple, to these cates compared,
Was that crude apple that diverted Eve!
And at a stately sideboard by the wine   350
That fragrant smell diffused, in order stood
Tall stripling youths rich-clad, of fairer hue
Than Ganymede or Hylas; distant more
Under the trees now tripped, now solemn stood
Nymphs of Diana's train, and Naiades   355
With fruits and flowers from Amalthea's horn,
And ladies of th' Hesperides, that seemed
Fairer than feigned of old, or fabled since
Of fairy damsels met in forest wide
By knights of Logres, or of Lyonnesse,   360
Lancelot or Pelleas, or Pellenore;
And all the while harmonious airs were heard
Of chiming strings or charming pipes, and winds
Of gentlest gale Arabian odors fanned
From their soft wings, and Flora's earliest smells.   365
Such was the splendor, and the Tempter now
His invitation earnestly renewed:
    "What doubts the Son of God to sit and eat?
These are not fruits forbidden, no interdict
Defends the touching of these viands pure;   370

331 f. The banquet, which may be taken as the first stage of the second temptation, shows the gulf between Christ and Satan's view of him and is in contrast with Christ's own temperate dream of the ravens feeding Elijah. Cf. Spenser's Bower of Bliss (*F.Q.* 2.12) and G. Fletcher's *Christ's Victory on Earth* 39 f.

344. Gris-amber-steamed: glossary, "amber."

347. Lucrine bay: near Naples.

348. cates: delicacies.

349. diverted: led astray.

353. Ganymede: the Trojan youth Zeus took to heaven to be his cupbearer.

356. Amalthea was the nymph who nursed the infant Zeus with goat's milk, or the goat itself; Zeus made the goat's horn magically fruitful.

360. Logres: the middle region of Britain east of the Severn.   Lyonnesse: a mythical region west of Cornwall.

361. King Arthur's knights.

364. Cf. *P.L.* 4.162–63.

368. What doubts: why hesitates.

Their taste no knowledge works, at least of evil,
But life preserves, destroys life's enemy,
Hunger, with sweet restorative delight.
All these are Spirits of air, and woods, and springs,
Thy gentle ministers, who come to pay   375
Thee homage, and acknowledge thee their Lord.
What doubt'st thou, Son of God? Sit down and eat."
   To whom thus Jesus temperately replied:
"Said'st thou not that to all things I had right?
And who withholds my pow'r that right to use?   380
Shall I receive by gift what of my own,
When and where likes me best, I can command?
I can at will, doubt not, as soon as thou,
Command a table in this wilderness,
And call swift flights of angels ministrant,   385
Arrayed in glory, on my cup to attend.
Why shouldst thou then obtrude this diligence
In vain, where no acceptance it can find?
And with my hunger what hast thou to do?
Thy pompous delicacies I contemn,   390
And count thy specious gifts no gifts but guiles."
   To whom thus answered Satan malcontent:
"That I have also power to give thou seest;
If of that pow'r I bring thee voluntary
What I might have bestowed on whom I pleased,   395
And rather opportunely in this place
Chose to impart to thy apparent need,
Why shouldst thou not accept it? But I see
What I can do or offer is suspect;
Of these things others quickly will dispose   400
Whose pains have earned the far-fet spoil." With that
Both table and provision vanished quite
With sound of harpies' wings and talons heard;
Only the impórtune Tempter still remained,
And with these words his temptation pursued: 405
   "By hunger, that each other creature tames,
Thou art not to be harmed, therefore not moved;
Thy temperance invincible, besides,
For no allurement yields to appetite,
And all thy heart is set on high designs,   410
High actions: but wherewith to be achieved?
Great acts require great means of enterprise;
Thou art unknown, unfriended, low of birth,
A carpenter thy father known, thyself
Bred up in poverty and straits at home,   415

384. Ps. 78.19.
385. flights of angels: *Hamlet* 5.2.371.
391. Cf. Sophocles, *Ajax* 665; *Aen.* 2.49.
401. far-fet: far-fetched.
403. Cf. *The Tempest*, stage direction at
3.3.52; *Aen.* 3.225–28.
   411 f. Wealth, the second stage of the second temptation. Cf. Spenser's Cave of Mammon (*F.Q.* 2.7).

Lost in a desert here and hunger-bit.
Which way or from what hope dost thou aspire
To greatness? Whence authority deriv'st,
What followers, what retínue canst thou gain,
Or at thy heels the dizzy multitude,   420
Longer than thou canst feed them on thy cost?
Money brings honor, friends, conquest, and realms.
What raised Antipater the Edomite,
And his son Herod placed on Judah's throne
(Thy throne), but gold that got him puissant friends?   425
Therefore, if at great things thou wouldst arrive,
Get riches first, get wealth, and treasure heap,
Not difficult, if thou hearken to me;
Riches are mine, fortune is in my hand;
They whom I favor thrive in wealth amain,   430
While virtue, valor, wisdom, sit in want."
　　　To whom thus Jesus patiently replied:
"Yet wealth without these three is impotent
To gain dominion or to keep it gained.
Witness those ancient empires of the earth,   435
In highth of all their flowing wealth dissolved;
But men endued with these have oft attained
In lowest poverty to highest deeds:
Gideon and Jephtha, and the shepherd lad
Whose offspring on the throne of Judah sat   440
So many ages, and shall yet regain
That seat, and reign in Israel without end.
Among the heathen (for throughout the world
To me is not unknown what hath been done
Worthy of memorial) canst thou not remember   445
Quintius, Fabricius, Curius, Regulus?
For I esteem those names of men so poor
Who could do mighty things, and could contemn
Riches though offered from the hand of kings.
And what in me seems wanting, but that I   450
May also in this poverty as soon
Accomplish what they did, perhaps and more?
Extol not riches then, the toil of fools,
The wise man's cumbrance if not snare, more apt
To slacken virtue and abate her edge   455
Than prompt her to do aught may merit praise.
What if with like aversion I reject
Riches and realms? Yet not for that a crown,

---

423. Antipater: procurator of Judea and father of Herod. Edom was south of the Dead Sea.

427. Prov. 4.5; Matt. 6.33; Horace, *Epistles* 1.1.53–54.

439. Gideon: Judges 6–8. Jephtha: ibid., 11–12. shepherd lad: David. Cf. *P.L.* 12.325 f.; Ps. 78.70–71; Isa. 16.5; Ezek. 34.23–24; Luke 1.32–33.

445–49. Cf. Claudian, *De Quarto Consulatu Honorii Augusti* 410 f.

446. Examples of plain integrity among leaders of the Roman republic; for the heroic Regulus see Horace, *Od.* 3.5.

458. for that: because.

458 f. On the cares of kingship, cf. *2 Henry IV* 3.1 and *Henry V* 4.1 247 f.

Golden in show, is but a wreath of thorns,
Brings dangers, troubles, cares, and sleepless nights   460
To him who wears the regal diadem,
When on his shoulders each man's burden lies;
For therein stands the office of a king,
His honor, virtue, merit, and chief praise,
That for the public all this weight he bears.   465
Yet he who reigns within himself, and rules
Passions, desires, and fears, is more a king;
Which every wise and virtuous man attains:
And who attains not, ill aspires to rule
Cities of men, or headstrong multitudes,   470
Subject himself to anarchy within,
Or lawless passions in him which he serves.
But to guide nations in the way of truth
By saving doctrine, and from error lead
To know, and knowing worship God aright,   475
Is yet more kingly; this attracts the soul,
Governs the inner man, the nobler part,
That other o'er the body only reigns,
And oft by force, which to a generous mind
So reigning can be no sincere delight.   480
Besides, to give a kingdom hath been thought
Greater and nobler done, and to lay down
Far more magnanimous, than to assume.
Riches are needless then, both for themselves,
And for thy reason why they should be sought,   485
To gain a scepter, oftest better missed."

The Third Book

So spake the Son of God, and Satan stood
A while as mute, confounded what to say,
What to reply, confuted and convinced
Of his weak arguing and fallacious drift;
At length collecting all his serpent wiles,   5
With soothing words renewed, him thus accosts:
    "I see thou know'st what is of use to know,
What best to say canst say, to do canst do;
Thy actions to thy words accord, thy words
To thy large heart give utterance due, thy heart   10

467–80. A summary of the classical and Renaissance ideal of both ethical self-discipline and the philosopher-king.
481–83. E.g., the Roman emperor Diocletian (245–313 A.D.), the Emperor Charles V (1500–58), and Queen Christina of Sweden (1626–89), whom Milton eulogized in his *Second Defence* (*Works,* 8, 103–09) and who abdicated in 1654.

Contains of good, wise, just, the perfect shape.
Should kings and nations from thy mouth consult,
Thy counsel would be as the oracle
Urim and Thummim, those oraculous gems
On Aaron's breast, or tongue of seers old   15
Infallible; or wert thou sought to deeds
That might require th' array of war, thy skill
Of conduct would be such that all the world
Could not sustain thy prowess, or subsist
In battle, though against thy few in arms.   20
These godlike virtues wherefore dost thou hide?
Affecting private life, or more obscure
In savage wilderness, wherefore deprive
All earth her wonder at thy acts, thyself
The fame and glory, glory the reward   25
That sole excites to high attempts the flame
Of most erected spirits, most tempered pure
Ethereal, who all pleasures else despise,
All treasures and all gain esteem as dross,
And dignities and powers, all but the highest?   30
Thy years are ripe, and over-ripe; the son
Of Macedonian Philip had ere these
Won Asia and the throne of Cyrus held
At his dispose, young Scipio had brought down
The Carthaginian pride, young Pompey quelled   35
The Pontic king and in triumph had rode.
Yet years, and to ripe years judgment mature,
Quench not the thirst of glory, but augment.
Great Julius, whom now all the world admires,
The more he grew in years, the more inflamed   40
With glory, wept that he had lived so long
Inglorious. But thou yet art not too late."
     To whom our Saviour calmly thus replied:
"Thou neither dost persuade me to seek wealth
For empire's sake, nor empire to affect   45
For glory's sake, by all thy argument.
For what is glory but the blaze of fame,
The people's praise, if always praise unmixed?
And what the people but a herd confused,
A miscellaneous rabble, who extol   50
Things vulgar, and well weighed, scarce worth the praise?
They praise and they admire they know not what,

BOOK III. 14. Urim: glossary.

25 f. The third stage of the second temptation is the appeal to glory.

31 f. Alexander the Great was 25 when he overthrew the Persian kingdom (founded by Cyrus) at Arbela in 331 B.C.

34–35. Scipio drove the Carthaginians from Spain when he was 27–31.

35–36. Pompey at 25 received a triumph for his African victories; he did not conquer "the Pontic king" (Mithridates) until much later.

39–42. Plutarch, *Julius Caesar* 11.

47–59. This view of the rabble may suggest the disillusioned Milton — or Shakespeare — more than Christ; though Christ could at times be justly harsh, and here it is spurious fame that is being rejected.

47–48. Cf. Seneca, *Epistles* 102.17–18.

And know not whom, but as one leads the other;
And what delight to be by such extolled,
To live upon their tongues and be their talk,   55
Of whom to be dispraised were no small praise?
His lot who dares be singularly good.
Th' intelligent among them and the wise
Are few, and glory scarce of few is raised.
This is true glory and renown, when God   60
Looking on the earth, with approbation marks
The just man, and divulges him through heaven
To all his angels, who with true applause
Recount his praises; thus he did to Job,
When to extend his fame through heaven and earth,   65
As thou to thy reproach may'st well remember,
He asked thee, 'Hast thou seen my servant Job?'
Famous he was in heaven, on earth less known,
Where glory is false glory, attributed
To things not glorious, men not worthy of fame.   70
They err who count it glorious to subdue
By conquest far and wide, to overrun
Large countries, and in field great battles win,
Great cities by assault. What do these worthies
But rob and spoil, burn, slaughter, and enslave   75
Peaceable nations, neighboring or remote,
Made captive, yet deserving freedom more
Than those their conquerors, who leave behind
Nothing but ruin wheresoe'er they rove,
And all the flourishing works of peace destroy,   80
Then swell with pride, and must be titled gods,
Great benefactors of mankind, deliverers,
Worshiped with temple, priest, and sacrifice?
One is the son of Jove, of Mars the other,
Till conqueror Death discover them scarce men,   85
Rolling in brutish vices, and deformed,
Violent or shameful death their due reward.
But if there be in glory aught of good,
It may by means far different be attained
Without ambition, war, or violence;   90
By deeds of peace, by wisdom eminent,
By patience, temperance. I mention still
Him whom thy wrongs, with saintly patience borne,
Made famous in a land and times obscure:
Who names not now with honor patient Job?   95
Poor Socrates (who next more memorable?)
By what he taught and suffered for so doing,
For truth's sake suffering death unjust, lives now

60–64. Cf. *Lycidas* 76–84.
67. Job 2.3.
71–83. Cf. *P.L.* 11.688–99, 787–96.

84. E.g., Alexander (*P.L.* 9.508–10 and note) and Romulus (*Aen.* 1.273–74).
96–99. See, in particular, Plato's *Apology, Crito,* and *Phaedo.*

Equal in fame to proudest conquerors.
Yet if for fame and glory aught be done,   100
Aught suffered, if young African for fame
His wasted country freed from Punic rage,
The deed becomes unpraised, the man at least,
And loses, though but verbal, his reward.
Shall I seek glory then, as vain men seek,   105
Oft not deserved? I seek not mine, but his
Who sent me, and thereby witness whence I am."
    To whom the Tempter murmuring thus replied:
"Think not so slight of glory, therein least
Resembling thy great Father: he seeks glory,   110
And for his glory all things made, all things
Orders and governs; nor content in heaven
By all his angels glorified, requires
Glory from men, from all men good or bad,
Wise or unwise, no difference, no exemption;   115
Above all sacrifice or hallowed gift
Glory he requires, and glory he receives
Promiscuous from all nations, Jew, or Greek,
Or barbarous, nor exception hath declared;
From us, his foes pronounced, glory he exacts."   120
    To whom our Saviour fervently replied:
"And reason; since his word all things produced,
Though chiefly not for glory as prime end,
But to show forth his goodness, and impart
His good communicable to every soul   125
Freely; of whom what could he less expect
Than glory and benediction, that is thanks,
The slightest, easiest, readiest recompense
From them who could return him nothing else,
And not returning that, would likeliest render   130
Contempt instead, dishonor, obloquy?
Hard recompense, unsuitable return
For so much good, so much beneficence.
But why should man seek glory, who of his own
Hath nothing, and to whom nothing belongs   135
But condemnation, ignominy, and shame?
Who for so many benefits received
Turned recreant to God, ingrate and false,
And so of all true good himself despoiled,
Yet, sacrilegious, to himself would take   140
That which to God alone of right belongs;
Yet so much bounty is in God, such grace,
That who advance his glory, not their own,

---

101. young   African: Scipio   (3.34–35
above).
   106–07. John 8.50, 5.30–32.
   110–11. Cf. *P.L.* 3.164; Rev. 4.11.
   122. word. Presumably Milton would not
have Christ use "word" in the sense of John
1.1 and *P.L.* 7.163 f., but only in reference to
God's creative decree.
   126–31. Cf. *P.L.* 4.42–48.

Them he himself to glory will advance."
So spake the Son of God; and here again   145
Satan had not to answer, but stood struck
With guilt of his own sin, for he himself
Insatiable of glory had lost all:
Yet of another plea bethought him soon.
    "Of glory as thou wilt," said he, "so deem;   150
Worth or not worth the seeking, let it pass.
But to a kingdom thou art born, ordained
To sit upon thy father David's throne,
By mother's side thy father, though thy right
Be now in powerful hands, that will not part   155
Easily from possession won with arms;
Judea now and all the Promised Land,
Reduced a province under Roman yoke,
Obeys Tiberius, nor is always ruled
With temperate sway; oft have they violated   160
The Temple, oft the Law with foul affronts,
Abominations rather, as did once
Antiochus. And think'st thou to regain
Thy right by sitting still or thus retiring?
So did not Machabeus: he indeed   165
Retired unto the desert, but with arms,
And o'er a mighty king so oft prevailed
That by strong hand his family obtained,
Though priests, the crown, and David's throne usurped,
With Modin and her suburbs once content.   170
If kingdom move thee not, let move thee zeal
And duty; zeal and duty are not slow,
But on occasion's forelock watchful wait.
They themselves rather are occasion best —
Zeal of thy father's house, duty to free   175
Thy country from her heathen servitude;
So shalt thou best fulfill, best verify
The Prophets old, who sung thy endless reign,
The happier reign the sooner it begins.
Reign then; what canst thou better do the while?"   180
    To whom our Saviour answer thus returned:
"All things are best fulfilled in their due time,
And time there is for all things, Truth hath said.
If of my reign prophetic Writ hath told
That it shall never end, so when begin   185
The Father in his purpose hath decreed,

---

152 f. The fourth stage of the second temptation, the freeing of Israel from the Roman
yoke (cf. Christ's own early thoughts, 1.216–
17).
    153. Luke 1.32.
    159. Tiberius: emperor of Rome, 14–37 A.D.
    163. Antiochus Epiphanes, king of Syria
and oppressor of the Jews (1 Macc. 1.1.20 f.).

165–71. Machabeus (Judas Maccabeus)
born at Modin in Judea; Jewish leader against
Antiochus (1 Macc. 1.2 f.).
    173. occasion's forelock: proverbial (cf.
Spenser, *F.Q.* 2.4.4).
    175. Ps. 69.9; John 2.17.
    182. Rom. 5.6; 1 Tim. 2.6; Titus 1.3.
    183. Eccles. 3.1 f., 17.

He in whose hand all times and seasons roll.
What if he hath decreed that I shall first
Be tried in humble state, and things adverse,
By tribulations, injuries, insults,   190
Contempts, and scorns, and snares, and violence,
Suffering, abstaining, quietly expecting
Without distrust or doubt, that he may know
What I can suffer, how obey? Who best
Can suffer best can do; best reign who first   195
Well hath obeyed; just trial ere I merit
My exaltation without change or end.
But what concerns it thee when I begin
My everlasting kingdom? Why art thou
Solicitous, what moves thy inquisition?   200
Know'st thou not that my rising is thy fall,
And my promotion will be thy destruction?"
    To whom the Tempter, inly racked, replied:
"Let that come when it comes; all hope is lost
Of my reception into grace; what worse?   205
For where no hope is left, is left no fear.
If there be worse, the expectation more
Of worse torments me than the feeling can.
I would be at the worst; worst is my port,
My harbor and my ultimate repose,   210
The end I would attain, my final good.
My error was my error, and my crime
My crime, whatever for itself condemned,
And will alike be punished, whether thou
Reign or reign not; though to that gentle brow   215
Willingly I could fly, and hope thy reign,
From that placid aspéct and meek regard,
Rather than aggravate my evil state,
Would stand between me and thy Father's ire
(Whose ire I dread more than the fire of hell),   220
A shelter and a kind of shading cool
Interposition, as a summer's cloud.
If I then to the worst that can be haste,
Why move thy feet so slow to what is best,
Happiest both to thyself and all the world,   225
That thou who worthiest art shouldst be their king?
Perhaps thou linger'st in deep thoughts detained
Of the enterprise so hazardous and high;
No wonder, for though in thee be united
What of perfection can in man be found,   230
Or human nature can receive, consider
Thy life hath yet been private, most part spent
At home, scarce viewed the Galilean towns,

187. Acts 1.7.
194–96. A principle recurrent in Greek and
Roman writers and in Milton, e.g., Plato, *Laws*

6.715C–D, 762E; Cicero, *De Legibus* 3.2.5;
Seneca, *De Ira* 2.15.4.

And once a year Jerusalem, few days'
Short sojourn; and what thence couldst thou observe?   235
The world thou hast not seen, much less her glory,
Empires, and monarchs, and their radiant courts,
Best school of best experience, quickest insight
In all things that to greatest actions lead.
The wisest, unexperienced, will be ever   240
Timorous and loth, with novice modesty
(As he who seeking asses found a kingdom)
Irresolute, unhardy, unadvent'rous.
But I will bring thee where thou soon shalt quit
Those rudiments, and see before thine eyes   245
The monarchies of the earth, their pomp and state,
Sufficient introduction to inform
Thee, of thyself so apt, in regal arts,
And regal mysteries; that thou may'st know
How best their opposition to withstand."   250
        With that (such power was giv'n him then) he took
The Son of God up to a mountain high.
It was a mountain at whose verdant feet
A spacious plain outstretched in circuit wide
Lay pleasant; from his side two rivers flowed,   255
Th' one winding, the other straight, and left between
Fair champaign with less rivers interveined,
Then meeting joined their tribute to the sea:
Fertile of corn the glebe, of oil, and wine;
With herds the pastures thronged, with flocks the hills;   260
Huge cities and high-tow'red, that well might seem
The seats of mightiest monarchs; and so large
The prospect was that here and there was room
For barren desert fountainless and dry.
To this high mountain-top the Tempter brought   265
Our Saviour, and new train of words began:
        "Well have we speeded, and o'er hill and dale,
Forest and field, and flood, temples and towers,
Cut shorter many a league. Here thou behold'st
Assyria and her empire's ancient bounds,   270
Araxes and the Caspian lake, thence on
As far as Indus east, Euphrates west,
And oft beyond; to south the Persian bay,
And inaccessible the Arabian drouth:
Here Nineveh, of length within her wall   275
Several days' journey, built by Ninus old,
Of that first golden monarchy the seat,

235. Short sojourn: Luke 2.41.
242. he: Saul (1 Sam. 9.3. f., 10.1).
251–4.169. The fifth stage of the second
temptation, "the kingdoms of the world" — the
whole of the second in Luke (4.5–8). Cf. *P.L.*
11.377–84.

255. two rivers: Tigris and Euphrates.
259. glebe: soil.
271. Araxes: Armenian river flowing into
the Caspian Sea.
274. drouth: desert.

And seat of Salmanassar, whose success
Israel in long captivity still mourns;
There Babylon, the wonder of all tongues,   280
As ancient, but rebuilt by him who twice
Judah and all thy father David's house
Led captive and Jerusalem laid waste,
Till Cyrus set them free; Persepolis
His city there thou seest, and Bactra there;   285
Ecbatana her structure vast there shows,
And Hecatompylos her hundred gates;
There Susa by Choaspes, amber stream,
The drink of none but kings; of later fame,
Built by Emathian, or by Parthian hands,   290
The great Seleucia, Nisibis, and there
Artaxata, Teredon, Ctesiphon,
Turning with easy eye thou may'st behold.
All these the Parthian (now some ages past
By great Arsaces led, who founded first   295
That empire) under his dominion holds,
From the luxurious kings of Antioch won.
And just in time thou com'st to have a view
Of his great power; for now the Parthian king
In Ctesiphon hath gathered all his host   300
Against the Scythian, whose incursions wild
Have wasted Sogdiana; to her aid
He marches now in haste. See, though from far,
His thousands, in what martial equipage
They issue forth, steel bows and shafts their arms,   305
Of equal dread in flight or in pursuit,
All horsemen, in which fight they most excel;
See how in warlike muster they appear,
In rhombs and wedges, and half-moons, and wings."
    He looked and saw what numbers numberless   310
The city gates outpoured, light-armèd troops
In coats of mail and military pride;
In mail their horses clad, yet fleet and strong,
Prancing their riders bore, the flower and choice
Of many provinces from bound to bound,   315

278. Salmanassar. Shalmaneser V (d. 722 b.c.), king of Assyria (or his successor, Sargon), captured Samaria and deported many of its people (2 Kings 18.9–12, 17.3–6, 24).

281–83. Nebuchadnezzar twice captured Jerusalem (597, 586 b.c.) and carried off its king and many inhabitants (2 Kings 24–25; Dan. 1).

284. In 538 Cyrus, founder of the Persian empire, took Babylon and released the captive Jews (2 Chron. 36.22–23; Ezra 1 f.). Persepolis: in southern Persia.

285. Bactra: the ancient capital of Bactria (modern Balkh, in Afghanistan).

287. Hecatompylos: a Parthian city.

288. Choaspes: a river east of the Tigris famous for its pure water.

291. Nisibis: in northern Mesopotamia.

292. Artaxata: in Armenia, on the Araxes river.   Teredon: at northwest end of the Persian Gulf.   Ctesiphon: on the Tigris.

295. Arsaces: founder of the Parthian empire, c. 248 b.c.

297. Antioch: capital of Syria.

302. Sogdiana: region northeast of Parthia.

309. rhombs: diamond-shapèd formations. wedges: triangular formations.

From Arachosia, from Candaor east,
And Margiana to the Hyrcanian cliffs
Of Caucasus, and dark Iberian dales,
From Atropatia and the neighboring plains
Of Ádiabéne, Media, and the south   320
Of Susiana to Balsara's hav'n.
He saw them in their forms of battle ranged,
How quick they wheeled, and flying behind them shot
Sharp sleet of arrowy showers against the face
Of their pursuers, and overcame by flight;   325
The field all iron cast a gleaming brown;
Nor wanted clouds of foot, nor on each horn
Cuirassiers all in steel for standing fight,
Chariots or elephants indorsed with towers
Of archers, nor of laboring pioneers   330
A multitude, with spades and axes armed
To lay hills plain, fell woods, or valleys fill,
Or where plain was raise hill, or overlay
With bridges rivers proud, as with a yoke;
Mules after these, camels and dromedaries,   335
And wagons fraught with utensils of war.
Such forces met not, nor so wide a camp,
When Agrican with all his northern powers
Besieged Albracca, as romances tell,
The city of Gallaphrone, from thence to win   340
The fairest of her sex, Angelica
His daughter, sought by many prowest knights,
Both paynim and the peers of Charlemain.
Such and so numerous was their chivalry;
At sight whereof the Fiend yet more presumed,   345
And to our Saviour thus his words renewed:
    "That thou may'st know I seek not to engage
Thy virtue, and not every way secure
On no slight grounds thy safety, hear, and mark
To what end I have brought thee hither and shown   350
All this fair sight. Thy kingdom, though foretold
By prophet or by angel, unless thou
Endeavor, as thy father David did,
Thou never shalt obtain; prediction still
In all things, and all men, supposes means;   355
Without means used, what it predicts revokes.

316. Arachosia: region west of the Indus.
Candaor: Kandahar, in Afghanistan.
317. Margiana, Hyrcania: southeast of the
Caspian Sea.
318. Caucasus: mountains between the
Black Sea and the Caspian.   Iberian: of
Georgia, between the Black Sea and the Caspian.
319. Atropatia: northwest part of Media.
320. Adiabene: part of Assyria.   Media:
north of Persia and west of Parthia.

321. Susiana: between Media and the Persian Gulf.   Balsara: Basra, a city just north
of the Gulf.
322–24. The Roman poets often alluded to
this maneuver of the Parthian cavalry — shooting backward while retiring.
329. indorsed: loaded on the back.
338. Agrican: Tartar king (in Boiardo's
Orlando Innamorato) who attacked Gallaphrone, king of Cathay and father of Angelica.
342. prowest: bravest.

But say thou wert possessed of David's throne
By free consent of all, none opposite,
Samaritan or Jew; how couldst thou hope
Long to enjoy it quiet and secure,   360
Between two such enclosing enemies,
Roman and Parthian? Therefore one of these
Thou must make sure thy own; the Parthian first
By my advice, as nearer and of late
Found able by invasion to annoy   365
Thy country, and captive lead away her kings
Antigonus and old Hyrcanus bound,
Maugre the Roman. It shall be my task
To render thee the Parthian at dispose;
Choose which thou wilt, by conquest or by league.   370
By him thou shalt regain, without him not,
That which alone can truly reinstall thee
In David's royal seat, his true successor;
Deliverance of thy brethren, those ten tribes
Whose offspring in his territory yet serve   375
In Habor, and among the Medes dispersed;
Ten sons of Jacob, two of Joseph lost
Thus long from Israel, serving as of old
Their fathers in the land of Egypt served,
This offer sets before thee to deliver.   380
These if from servitude thou shalt restore
To their inheritance, then, nor till then,
Thou on the throne of David in full glory,
From Egypt to Euphrates and beyond
Shalt reign, and Rome or Caesar not need fear."   385
　　　To whom our Saviour answered thus, unmoved:
"Much ostentation vain of fleshly arm,
And fragile arms, much instrument of war,
Long in preparing, soon to nothing brought,
Before mine eyes thou hast set; and in my ear   390
Vented much policy, and projects deep
Of enemies, of aids, battles and leagues,
Plausible to the world, to me worth naught.
Means I must use, thou say'st, prediction else
Will unpredict and fail me of the throne: 395
My time, I told thee (and that time for thee
Were better farthest off), is not yet come.
When that comes, think not thou to find me slack
On my part aught endeavoring, or to need
Thy politic maxims, or that cumbersome   400
Luggage of war there shown me, argument

367. Antigonus, nephew of Hyrcanus, invaded Syria with Parthian help (40 B.C.).
374–76. See the notes on 278 f.
376. Habor: 2 Kings 17.6.
377. The ten tribes include the "two of
Joseph," those of Ephraim and Manasseh.

384. Gen. 15.18.
387. fleshly arm: Jer. 17.5.
393. plausible: worthy of applause.
395. fail: cause to miss.
396–97. John 7.6.

Of human weakness rather than of strength.
My brethren, as thou call'st them, those ten tribes,
I must deliver, if I mean to reign
David's true heir, and his full scepter sway   405
To just extent over all Israel's sons;
But whence to thee this zeal? Where was it then
For Israel, or for David, or his throne,
When thou stood'st up his tempter to the pride
Of numb'ring Israel, which cost the lives   410
Of threescore and ten thousand Israelites
By three days' pestilence? Such was thy zeal
To Israel then, the same that now to me.
As for those captive tribes, themselves were they
Who wrought their own captivity, fell off   415
From God to worship calves, the deities
Of Egypt, Baal next and Ashtaroth,
And all the idolatries of heathen round,
Besides their other worse than heathenish crimes;
Nor in the land of their captivity   420
Humbled themselves, or penitent besought
The God of their forefathers, but so died
Impenitent, and left a race behind
Like to themselves, distinguishable scarce
From Gentiles but by circumcision vain,   425
And God with idols in their worship joined.
Should I of these the liberty regard,
Who freed, as to their ancient patrimony,
Unhumbled, unrepentant, unreformed,
Headlong would follow, and to their gods perhaps   430
Of Bethel and of Dan? No, let them serve
Their enemies, who serve idols with God.
Yet he at length, time to himself best known,
Rememb'ring Abraham, by some wondrous call
May bring them back repentant and sincere,   435
And at their passing cleave the Assyrian flood,
While to their native land with joy they haste,
As the Red Sea and Jordan once he cleft,
When to the Promised Land their fathers passed;
To his due time and providence I leave them."   440
    So spake Israel's true King, and to the Fiend
Made answer meet, that made void all his wiles.
So fares it when with truth falsehood contends.

407–12. 1 Chron. 21.1–14.   431. Cf. *P.L.* 1.484–85 and note.
414–26. 2 Kings 17.7–20; etc.   434. Gen. 15.18.
416. Cf. *P.L.* 1.482–84 and notes.   436. Assyrian flood: Euphrates (Isa. 11.16).

The Fourth Book

Perplexed and troubled at his bad success
The Tempter stood, nor had what to reply,
Discovered in his fraud, thrown from his hope,
So oft, and the persuasive rhetoric
That sleeked his tongue, and won so much on Eve,   5
So little here, nay lost; but Eve was Eve,
This far his overmatch, who, self-deceived
And rash, beforehand had no better weighed
The strength he was to cope with, or his own.
But as a man who had been matchless held   10
In cunning, overreached where least he thought,
To salve his credit, and for very spite,
Still will be tempting him who foils him still,
And never cease, though to his shame the more;
Or as a swarm of flies in vintage time,   15
About the wine-press where sweet must is poured,
Beat off, returns as oft with humming sound;
Or surging waves against a solid rock,
Though all to shivers dashed, the assault renew,
Vain batt'ry, and in froth or bubbles end;   20
So Satan, whom repulse upon repulse
Met ever, and to shameful silence brought,
Yet gives not o'er though desperate of success,
And his vain importunity pursues.
He brought our Saviour to the western side   25
Of that high mountain, whence he might behold
Another plain, long but in breadth not wide;
Washed by the southern sea, and on the north
To equal length backed with a ridge of hills
That screened the fruits of the earth and seats of men   30
From cold Septentrion blasts; thence in the midst
Divided by a river, of whose banks
On each side an imperial city stood,
With towers and temples proudly elevate
On seven small hills, with palaces adorned,   35
Porches and theaters, baths, aqueducts,
Statues and trophies, and triumphal arcs,
Gardens and groves presented to his eyes,
Above the highth of mountains interposed:
By what strange parallax or optic skill   40
Of vision multiplied through air, or glass

BOOK IV. 15–17. Cf. Milton, *In quintum
Novembris* 178–80; *Iliad* 2.469–71, 16.641–
43.
16. must: new wine.
27. plain: of central Italy.
29. hills: Apennines.

31. Septentrion: northern.
32. river: Tiber.
36. Porches: colonnades.
40. parallax: the apparent displacement of
a star due to an observer's changing position.

Of telescope, were curious to inquire.
And now the Tempter thus his silence broke:
    "The city which thou seest no other deem
Than great and glorious Rome, queen of the earth   45
So far renowned, and with the spoils enriched
Of nations; there the Capitol thou seest
Above the rest lifting his stately head
On the Tarpeian rock, her citadel
Impregnable; and there Mount Palatine,   50
The imperial palace, compass huge, and high
The structure, skill of noblest architects,
With gilded battlements, conspicuous far,
Turrets and terraces, and glittering spires.
Many a fair edifice besides, more like   55
Houses of gods (so well I have disposed
My airy microscope), thou may'st behold
Outside and inside both, pillars and roofs,
Carved work, the hand of famed artificers
In cedar, marble, ivory or gold.   60
Thence to the gates cast round thine eye, and see
What conflux issuing forth, or ent'ring in:
Praetors, proconsuls to their provinces
Hasting or on return, in robes of state;
Lictors and rods, the ensigns of their power;   65
Legions and cohorts, turms of horse and wings;
Or embassies from regions far remote
In various habits on the Appian road,
Or on the Aemilian, some from farthest south,
Syene, and where the shadow both way falls,   70
Meroë, Nilotic isle, and more to west,
The realm of Bocchus to the Blackmoor sea;
From the Asian kings and Parthian among these,
From India and the golden Chersoness,
And utmost Indian isle Tapróbanè,   75
Dusk faces with white silken turbans wreathed;
From Gallia, Gades, and the British west,
Germans, and Scythians, and Sarmatians north
Beyond Danubius to the Tauric pool.

47–49. The temple of Jupiter Capitolinus on the Capitoline hill, of which the Tarpeian rock was a part.

50. Palatine: another of Rome's seven hills.

54. spires: towers?

63. Both consuls and praetors, inferior magistrates, might become provincial governors on leaving civic office.

65. Lictors: attendants of Roman magistrates who carried symbolic rods or *fasces*.

66. turms: troops of cavalry, parts of a "wing."

68. Appian road: from Rome to Brindisi.

69. Aemilian: the road northward from Rome.

70. Syene: Aswan in southern Egypt.

70–71. Meroë: a tract (supposed island) in the upper Nile; see Pliny, *Nat. Hist.* 2.75.104.

72. Bocchus: king of Mauretania (Morocco, etc.) *c.* 105 B.C.   Blackmoor: the Mediterranean off Morocco and Algeria.

74. The "golden Chersonese" (Milton's spelling avoided a rhyme with "these") was identified with Sumatra and Java or the Malay peninsula; it and Taprobane (Ceylon or Sumatra) were mentioned together in Ariosto, *O.F.* 15.17.

76. turbants: turbans.

77. Gallia: Gaul, France.   Gades: Cadiz.

78. Sarmatians: people east of Germany.

79. Tauric pool: Sea of Azof.

All nations now to Rome obedience pay,   80
To Rome's great Emperor, whose wide domain
In ample territory, wealth and power,
Civility of manners, arts, and arms,
And long renown thou justly may'st prefer
Before the Parthian. These two thrones except,   85
The rest are barbarous, and scarce worth the sight,
Shared among petty kings too far removed;
These having shown thee, I have shown thee all
The kingdoms of the world, and all their glory.
This Emperor hath no son, and now is old,   90
Old and lascivious, and from Rome retired
To Capreae, an island small but strong
On the Campanian shore, with purpose there
His horrid lusts in private to enjoy,
Committing to a wicked favorite   95
All public cares, and yet of him suspicious,
Hated of all, and hating. With what ease,
Endued with regal virtues as thou art,
Appearing, and beginning noble deeds,
Might'st thou expel this monster from his throne,   100
Now made a sty, and in his place ascending
A victor people free from servile yoke?
And with my help thou may'st; to me the power
Is given, and by that right I give it thee.
Aim therefore at no less than all the world,   105
Aim at the highest; without the highest attained
Will be for thee no sitting, or not long,
On David's throne, be prophesied what will."
      To whom the Son of God unmoved replied:
"Nor doth this grandeur and majestic show   110
Of luxury, though called magnificence,
More than of arms before, allure mine eye,
Much less my mind; though thou shouldst add to tell
Their sumptuous gluttonies, and gorgeous feasts
On citron tables or Atlantic stone   115
(For I have also heard, perhaps have read),
Their wines of Setia, Cales, and Falerne,
Chios and Crete, and how they quaff in gold,
Crystal and myrrhine cups embossed with gems
And studs of pearl — to me shouldst tell who thirst   120
And hunger still. Then embassies thou show'st
From nations far and nigh; what honor that,
But tedious waste of time to sit and hear
So many hollow compliments and lies,
Outlandish flatteries? Then proceed'st to talk   125

90. Emperor: Tiberius.
92. Capreae: Capri, south of Naples.
95. favorite: Sejanus.
115. citron: citrus wood.   Atlantic: from
the Atlas mountains in north Africa.

117. Districts south of Rome.
118. Chios: island off Asia Minor.
119. myrrhine: made of a rare stone,
murrha.

Of the Emperor, how easily subdued,
How gloriously; I shall, thou say'st, expel
A brutish monster: what if I withal
Expel a Devil who first made him such?
Let his tormentor Conscience find him out;   130
For him I was not sent, nor yet to free
That people, victor once, now vile and base,
Deservedly made vassal; who once just,
Frugal, and mild, and temperate, conquered well,
But govern ill the nations under yoke,   135
Peeling their provinces, exhausted all
By lust and rapine; first ambitious grown
Of triumph, that insulting vanity;
Then cruel, by their sports to blood inured
Of fighting beasts, and men to beasts exposed;   140
Luxurious by their wealth, and greedier still,
And from the daily scene effeminate.
What wise and valiant man would seek to free
These thus degenerate, by themselves enslaved,
Or could of inward slaves make outward free?   145
Know therefore when my season comes to sit
On David's throne, it shall be like a tree
Spreading and overshadowing all the earth,
Or as a stone that shall to pieces dash
All monarchies besides throughout the world,   150
And of my kingdom there shall be no end.
Means there shall be to this, but what the means
Is not for thee to know, nor me to tell."
   To whom the Tempter impudent replied:
"I see all offers made by me how slight   155
Thou valu'st, because offered, and reject'st.
Nothing will please the difficult and nice,
Or nothing more than still to contradict.
On the other side know also thou, that I
On what I offer set as high esteem,   160
Nor what I part with mean to give for naught.
All these which in a moment thou behold'st,
The kingdoms of the world, to thee I give;
For giv'n to me, I give to whom I please,
No trifle; yet with this reserve, not else,   165
On this condition, if thou wilt fall down,
And worship me as thy superior lord,
Easily done, and hold them all of me;
For what can less so great a gift deserve?"
   Whom thus our Saviour answered with disdain: 170
"I never liked thy talk, thy offers less;
Now both abhor, since thou hast dared to utter

136. Peeling: plundering.   147–49. Dan. 2.34–35, 4.11.
142. scene: theatre.   165–68. Luke 4.6–7; Matt. 4.9.
145. Cf. *P.L.* 12.82 f., etc.

The abominable terms, impious condition;
But I endure the time, till which expired,
Thou hast permission on me. It is written   175
The first of all commandments, 'Thou shalt worship
The Lord thy God, and only him shalt serve';
And dar'st thou to the Son of God propound
To worship thee accurst, now more accurst
For this attempt bolder than that on Eve,   180
And more blasphémous? Which expect to rue.
The kingdoms of the world to thee were giv'n?
Permitted rather, and by thee usurped;
Other donation none thou canst produce.
If given, by whom but by the King of kings,   185
God over all supreme? If giv'n to thee,
By thee how fairly is the Giver now
Repaid! But gratitude in thee is lost
Long since. Wert thou so void of fear or shame
As offer them to me the Son of God,   190
To me my own, on such abhorrèd pact,
That I fall down and worship thee as God?
Get thee behind me; plain thou now appear'st
That Evil One, Satan for ever damned."
    To whom the Fiend with fear abashed replied: 195
"Be not so sore offended, Son of God,
Though sons of God both angels are and men,
If I, to try whether in higher sort
Than these thou bear'st that title, have proposed
What both from men and angels I receive,   200
Tetrarchs of fire, air, flood, and on the earth
Nations besides from all the quartered winds,
God of this world invoked and world beneath;
Who then thou art, whose coming is foretold
To me so fatal, me it most concerns.   205
The trial hath endamaged thee no way,
Rather more honor left and more esteem;
Me naught advantaged, missing what I aimed.
Therefore let pass, as they are transitory,
The kingdoms of this world; I shall no more   210
Advise thee; gain them as thou canst, or not.
And thou thyself seem'st otherwise inclined
Than to a worldly crown, addicted more
To contemplation and profound dispute,
As by that early action may be judged,   215
When slipping from thy mother's eye thou went'st
Alone into the Temple; there wast found
Among the gravest Rabbis disputant

176–77. Exod. 20.3; Deut. 6.13; Matt. 4.10.
184. donation: warrant, authority.
185–86. 1 Tim. 6.15; Rev. 17.14, 19.16.
193. Get . . . me: Luke 4.8.

201. Tetrarchs: subordinate rulers (of a quarter of a country); cf. 2.124.
203. God . . . world: 2 Cor. 4.4.
215–20. Cf. 1.210–14.

On points and questions fitting Moses' chair,
Teaching, not taught; the childhood shows the man,   220
As morning shows the day. Be famous then
By wisdom; as thy empire must extend,
So let extend thy mind o'er all the world,
In knowledge, all things in it comprehend.
All knowledge is not couched in Moses' Law,   225
The Pentateuch or what the Prophets wrote;
The Gentiles also know, and write, and teach
To admiration, led by nature's light;
And with the Gentiles much thou must converse,
Ruling them by persuasion as thou mean'st;   230
Without their learning, how wilt thou with them,
Or they with thee hold conversation meet?
How wilt thou reason with them, how refute
Their idolisms, traditions, paradoxes?
Error by his own arms is best evinced.   235
Look once more, ere we leave this specular mount,
Westward, much nearer by southwest; behold
Where on the Aegean shore a city stands
Built nobly, pure the air, and light the soil,
Athens, the eye of Greece, mother of arts   240
And eloquence, native to famous wits
Or hospitable, in her sweet recess,
City or suburban, studious walks and shades;
See there the olive grove of Academe,
Plato's retirement, where the Attic bird   245
Trills her thick-warbled notes the summer long;
There flow'ry hill Hymettus with the sound
Of bees' industrious murmur oft invites
To studious musing; there Ilissus rolls
His whispering stream. Within the walls then view   250
The schools of ancient sages: his who bred
Great Alexander to subdue the world,
Lyceum there, and painted Stoa next.
There thou shalt hear and learn the secret power
Of harmony in tones and numbers hit   255
By voice or hand, and various-measured verse,
Aeolian charms and Dorian lyric odes,
And his who gave them breath, but higher sung,

---

219. Moses' chair: Matt. 23.2.

221–364. This passage is commented upon in the headnote.

226. Pentateuch: the first five books of the Old Testament.

225–35. Cf. *Areopagitica* (*Works*, 4, 302, 306–07).

236. specular mount: cf. *P.L.* 12.588–89 and note.

238–80. The history of Greek culture is here presented as if it were contemporary, like the picture of Rome.

241. wits: men of learning and genius.

245. Attic bird: nightingale (cf. Sophocles, *Oedipus at Colonus* 671 f.).

251. who: Aristotle, Alexander's tutor, who later taught in the Lyceum, an Athenian gymnasium.

253. Stoa: an Athenian colonnade (with frescoes), where Zeno taught "Stoic" philosophy.

257. charms: lyrics of Sappho et al. who wrote in the Aeolic dialect.   Doric lyric odes: Pindar's.

Blind Melesigenes, thence Homer called,
Whose poem Phoebus challenged for his own.   260
Thence what the lofty grave tragedians taught
In chorus or iambic, teachers best
Of moral prudence, with delight received
In brief sententious precepts, while they treat
Of fate, and chance, and change in human life,   265
High actions and high passions best describing.
Thence to the famous orators repair,
Those ancient, whose resistless eloquence
Wielded at will that fierce democraty,
Shook the Arsenal and fulmined over Greece,   270
To Macedon, and Artaxerxes' throne;
To sage philosophy next lend thine ear,
From heaven descended to the low-roofed house
Of Socrates — see there his tenement —
Whom well inspired the oracle pronounced   275
Wisest of men; from whose mouth issued forth
Mellifluous streams that watered all the schools
Of Academics old and new, with those
Surnamed Peripatetics, and the sect
Epicurean, and the Stoic severe;   280
These here revolve, or, as thou lik'st, at home,
Till time mature thee to a kingdom's weight;
These rules will render thee a king complete
Within thyself, much more with empire joined."

    To whom our Saviour sagely thus replied: 285
"Think not but that I know these things, or think
I know them not; not therefore am I short
Of knowing what I ought. He who receives
Light from above, from the Fountain of Light,
No other doctrine needs, though granted true;   290
But these are false, or little else but dreams,
Conjectures, fancies, built on nothing firm.

259. Melesigenes: one of Homer's reputed birthplaces was on the river Meles in Asia Minor.
260. Cf. *Greek Anthology* 9.455.
262. iambic: the meter of Greek tragic dialogue.
268. eloquence: especially Demosthenes' orations against Philip of Macedon.
270. Arsenal: a building at Piraeus, the Athenian harbor, on which work was suspended in 339 B.C. as a result of Demosthenes' influence. fulmined: thundered and lightened.
271. Both the first and the second Artaxerxes, kings of Persia, were involved with Greece in the 5th and 4th centuries.
273. Cicero spoke of Socrates' bringing philosophy down from cosmic to ethical questions (*Academica* 1.4.15; *Tusculan Disput.* 5.4.10); heavenly inspiration may be also suggested.
275–76. See Plato's *Apology* (which includes references to Socrates' poverty).

276–77. Cf. Milton's Epilogue to his Latin Elegies.
278. Academics . . . new: philosophic schools which made Platonism more syncretic, sceptical, and practical.
279. Peripatetics: Aristotelians.
282–84. Here, as in 221–23, Satan is thinking of learning as an adjunct to political power; cf. Christ's ideal king, 2.466 f.
286–364. This whole speech is commented upon in the headnote.
288–92. Cf. Donne, *Sermons*, ed. Potter and Simpson, 4, 124: "All knowledge is ignorance, except it conduce to the knowledge of the Scriptures, and all the Scriptures lead us to Christ." Milton's old antagonist, Joseph Hall, the devotee of Seneca, had in *Heaven upon Earth* (1606) contrasted the limited light of pagan reason with revelation: "Not Athens must teach this lesson, but Jerusalem."

The first and wisest of them all professed
To know this only, that he nothing knew;
The next to fabling fell and smooth conceits;   295
A third sort doubted all things, though plain sense;
Others in virtue placed felicity,
But virtue joined with riches and long life;
In corporal pleasure he, and careless ease;
The Stoic last in philosophic pride,   300
By him called virtue; and his virtuous man,
Wise, perfect in himself, and all possessing
Equal to God, oft shames not to prefer,
As fearing God nor man, contemning all
Wealth, pleasure, pain or torment, death and life,   305
Which when he lists, he leaves, or boasts he can,
For all his tedious talk is but vain boast,
Or subtle shifts conviction to evade.
Alas what can they teach, and not mislead,
Ignorant of themselves, of God much more,   310
And how the world began, and how man fell
Degraded by himself, on grace depending?
Much of the soul they talk, but all awry,
And in themselves seek virtue, and to themselves
All glory arrogate, to God give none;   315
Rather accuse him under usual names,
Fortune and fate, as one regardless quite
Of mortal things. Who therefore seeks in these
True wisdom, finds her not, or by delusion
Far worse, her false resemblance only meets,   320
An empty cloud. However, many books,
Wise men have said, are wearisome; who reads
Incessantly, and to his reading brings not
A spirit and judgment equal or superior
(And what he brings, what needs he elsewhere seek?),   325
Uncertain and unsettled still remains,
Deep versed in books and shallow in himself,
Crude or intoxicate, collecting toys
And trifles for choice matters, worth a sponge,
As children gathering pebbles on the shore.   330
Or if I would delight my private hours
With music or with poem, where so soon
As in our native language can I find

293–94. Socrates (*Apology* 21); but cf.
P.R. 3.96–99.
  295. Plato and his use of myths.
  296. The sceptical followers of Pyrrho.
  297–98. Peripatetics.
  299. he: Epicurus.
  309–21. Col. 2.1–9. Cf. *P.L.* 2.557–69.
  320–21. her . . . cloud. In spite of the
context, Milton's classical instincts prompt an
allusion to the myth of Ixion who, seeking to
embrace Hera, clasped a cloud instead.

  321–22. Eccles. 12.12.
  321–30. Cf. Seneca, *Epistles* 88.
  329. sponge: the Roman equivalent of an
eraser.
  330. Cf. Donne, *Sermons*, ed. Potter and
Simpson, 3, 360: "they [the merely rational]
have got no further than to have walked by a
tempestuous sea and to have gathered pebbles
and speckled cockle-shells." Newton's famous
use of the same image came long after Milton's.

That solace? All our law and story strewed
With hymns, our Psalms with artful terms inscribed,   335
Our Hebrew songs and harps in Babylon,
That pleased so well our victors' ear, declare
That rather Greece from us these arts derived;
Ill imitated, while they loudest sing
The vices of their deities, and their own,   340
In fable, hymn, or song, so personating
Their gods ridiculous, and themselves past shame.
Remove their swelling epithets, thick laid
As varnish on a harlot's cheek, the rest,
Thin sown with aught of profit or delight,   345
Will far be found unworthy to compare
With Sion's songs, to all true tastes excelling,
Where God is praised aright, and godlike men,
The Holiest of Holies, and his saints;
Such are from God inspired, not such from thee;   350
Unless where moral virtue is expressed
By light of nature not in all quite lost.
Their orators thou then extoll'st, as those
The top of eloquence, statists indeed,
And lovers of their country, as may seem;   355
But herein to our Prophets far beneath,
As men divinely taught, and better teaching
The solid rules of civil government
In their majestic unaffected style
Than all the oratory of Greece and Rome.   360
In them is plainest taught, and easiest learnt,
What makes a nation happy, and keeps it so,
What ruins kingdoms, and lays cities flat;
These only with our Law best form a king."
        So spake the Son of God; but Satan now   365
Quite at a loss, for all his darts were spent,
Thus to our Saviour with stern brow replied:
        "Since neither wealth, nor honor, arms nor arts,
Kingdom nor empire pleases thee, nor aught
By me proposed in life contemplative,   370
Or active, tended on by glory, or fame,
What dost thou in this world? The wilderness
For thee is fittest place; I found thee there,

---

334 f. Cf. Milton, *Reason of Church Government* (*Works*, 3, 1, 237–39); Donne, *Sermons*, 2, 170–71: "There are not so eloquent books in the world as the Scriptures: accept those names of tropes and figures which the grammarians and rhetoricians have put upon us, and we may be bold to say that in all their authors, Greek and Latin, we cannot find so high and so lively examples of those tropes and those figures as we may in the Scriptures."
336–37. Ps. 137.1–3.
343–44. Cf. *Hamlet* 3.1.51.

345. profit or delight: a byword in Renaissance criticism, thanks especially to Horace, *Ars Poetica* 333–34, 343; cf. Marlowe, *Dr. Faustus* 81: "O what a world of profit and delight."
347 f. Sion's songs: cf. *P.L.* 3.29–32.
351–52. As in Plato, Xenophon, Aristotle, Cicero, Seneca — what Milton in 1642 had called "the noblest philosophy" (*Works*, 3, 1, 305–06); cf. *Of Education* (ibid., 4, 284).
354. statists: statesmen.
366. darts: Eph. 6.16.

And thither will return thee. Yet remember
What I foretell thee; soon thou shalt have cause   375
To wish thou never hadst rejected thus
Nicely or cautiously my offered aid,
Which would have set thee in short time with ease
On David's throne, or throne of all the world,
Now at full age, fulness of time, thy season,   380
When prophecies of thee are best fulfilled.
Now contrary, if I read aught in heaven,
Or heav'n write aught of fate, by what the stars
Voluminous, or single characters
In their conjunction met, give me to spell,   385
Sorrows, and labors, opposition, hate,
Attends thee, scorns, reproaches, injuries,
Violence and stripes, and lastly cruel death;
A kingdom they portend thee, but what kingdom,
Real or allegoric, I discern not,   390
Nor when; eternal sure, as without end,
Without beginning; for no date prefixed
Directs me in the starry rubric set."
    So saying he took (for still he knew his power
Not yet expired) and to the wilderness   395
Brought back the Son of God, and left him there,
Feigning to disappear. Darkness now rose,
As daylight sunk, and brought in louring night,
Her shadowy offspring, unsubstantial both,
Privation mere of light and absent day.   400
Our Saviour meek and with untroubled mind
After his airy jaunt, though hurried sore,
Hungry and cold betook him to his rest,
Wherever, under some concourse of shades
Whose branching arms thick intertwined might shield   405
From dews and damps of night his sheltered head;
But sheltered slept in vain, for at his head
The Tempter watched, and soon with ugly dreams
Disturbed his sleep. And either tropic now
Gan thunder, and both ends of heav'n; the clouds   410
From many a horrid rift abortive poured
Fierce rain with lightning mixed, water with fire
In ruin reconciled; nor slept the winds
Within their stony caves, but rushed abroad
From the four hinges of the world, and fell   415

382–93. While Milton's poems, notably *P.L.*, have allusions which seem to imply the limited acceptance of astrology permissible in Christian tradition, here (as in 1.393–96) Satan is expounding judicial astrology, or forecasting, which was generally condemned as irreligious and unlawful. In England after as well as before 1660, and especially in regard to the year 1666 (cf. Rev. 13.18), there was much concern and debate over portents of disaster and the actual disasters of 1665–66. Cf. lines 481–91.

384. voluminous: collectively, as in a book.
409. either tropic: north and south parts of the sky.
413. ruin: fall.
413–15. Cf. *Aen.* 1.52–63.
415. hinges: cf. *Nativity* 122.

On the vexed wilderness, whose tallest pines,
Though rooted deep as high, and sturdiest oaks
Bowed their stiff necks, loaden with stormy blasts,
Or torn up sheer. Ill wast thou shrouded then,
O patient Son of God, yet only stood'st   420
Unshaken; nor yet stayed the terror there:
Infernal ghosts, and hellish furies, round
Environed thee; some howled, some yelled, some shrieked,
Some bent at thee their fiery darts, while thou
Sat'st unappalled in calm and sinless peace.   425
Thus passed the night so foul till Morning fair
Came forth with pilgrim steps in amice gray,
Who with her radiant finger stilled the roar
Of thunder, chased the clouds, and laid the winds
And grisly specters, which the Fiend had raised   430
To tempt the Son of God with terrors dire.
And now the sun with more effectual beams
Had cheered the face of earth, and dried the wet
From drooping plant, or dropping tree; the birds,
Who all things now behold more fresh and green,   435
After a night of storm so ruinous,
Cleared up their choicest notes in bush and spray
To gratulate the sweet return of morn.
Nor yet amidst this joy and brightest morn
Was absent, after all his mischief done,   440
The Prince of Darkness; glad would also seem
Of this fair change, and to our Saviour came,
Yet with no new device (they all were spent),
Rather by this his last affront resolved,
Desperate of better course, to vent his rage   445
And mad despite to be so oft repelled.
Him walking on a sunny hill he found,
Backed on the north and west by a thick wood;
Out of the wood he starts in wonted shape,
And in a careless mood thus to him said: 450
    "Fair morning yet betides thee, Son of God,
After a dismal night; I heard the wrack
As earth and sky would mingle, but myself
Was distant; and these flaws, though mortals fear them
As dangerous to the pillared frame of heaven,   455
Or to the earth's dark basis underneath,
Are to the main as inconsiderable,
And harmless, if not wholesome, as a sneeze
To man's less universe, and soon are gone.
Yet as being ofttimes noxious where they light   460

427. amice: religious hood with gray fur. Cf. *Lycidas* 187.

431. The night of torment is not merely a narrative interlude but a Satanic effort at "temptation" through terror, and also a symbolic anticipation of Christ's passion and resurrection (cf. 386 f., 477 f.).

453. As . . . mingle: cf. *Aen.* 1.133–34.

458–59. In medical tradition a sneeze was said to be a wholesome purgation of the brain.

459. man's less universe: the human body.

On man, beast, plant, wasteful and turbulent,
Like turbulencies in the affairs of men,
Over whose heads they roar, and seem to point,
They oft fore-signify and threaten ill:
This tempest at this desert most was bent;   465
Of men at thee, for only thou here dwell'st.
Did I not tell thee, if thou didst reject
The perfect season offered with my aid
To win thy destined seat, but wilt prolong
All to the push of fate, pursue thy way   470
Of gaining David's throne no man knows when,
For both the when and how is nowhere told,
Thou shalt be what thou art ordained, no doubt;
For angels have proclaimed it, but concealing
The time and means? Each act is rightliest done,   475
Not when it must, but when it may be best.
If thou observe not this, be sure to find,
What I foretold thee, many a hard assay
Of dangers, and adversities and pains,
Ere thou of Israel's scepter get fast hold;   480
Whereof this ominous night that closed thee round,
So many terrors, voices, prodigies,
May warn thee, as a sure foregoing sign."
    So talked he, while the Son of God went on
And stayed not, but in brief him answered thus: 485
    "Me worse than wet thou find'st not; other harm
Those terrors which thou speak'st of did me none.
I never feared they could, though noising loud
And threat'ning nigh; what they can do as signs
Betok'ning or ill-boding I contemn   490
As false portents, not sent from God, but thee;
Who knowing I shall reign past thy preventing,
Obtrud'st thy offered aid, that I accepting
At least might seem to hold all power of thee,
Ambitious Spirit, and wouldst be thought my God,   495
And storm'st, refused, thinking to terrify
Me to thy will; desist, thou art discerned
And toil'st in vain, nor me in vain molest."
    To whom the Fiend now swoll'n with rage replied:
"Then hear, O son of David, virgin-born,   500
For Son of God to me is yet in doubt;
Of the Messiah I have heard foretold
By all the Prophets; of thy birth, at length
Announced by Gabriel, with the first I knew,
And of the angelic song in Bethlehem field,   505
On thy birth-night, that sung thee Saviour born.
From that time seldom have I ceased to eye
Thy infancy, thy childhood, and thy youth,
Thy manhood last, though yet in private bred;
Till at the ford of Jordan whither all   510

Flocked to the Baptist, I among the rest,
Though not to be baptized, by voice from heav'n
Heard thee pronounced the Son of God beloved.
Thenceforth I thought thee worth my nearer view
And narrower scrutiny, that I might learn   515
In what degree or meaning thou art called
The Son of God, which bears no single sense;
The Son of God I also am, or was,
And if I was, I am; relation stands;
All men are sons of God; yet thee I thought   520
In some respect far higher so declared.
Therefore I watched thy footsteps from that hour,
And followed thee still on to this waste wild,
Where by all best conjectures I collect
Thou art to be my fatal enemy.   525
Good reason then, if I beforehand seek
To understand my adversary, who
And what he is; his wisdom, power, intent;
By parle, or composition, truce, or league
To win him, or win from him what I can.   530
And opportunity I here have had
To try thee, sift thee, and confess have found thee
Proof against all temptation as a rock
Of adamant, and as a center firm,
To the utmost of mere man both wise and good,   535
Not more; for honors, riches, kingdoms, glory
Have been before contemned, and may again;
Therefore to know what more thou art than man,
Worth naming Son of God by voice from heav'n,
Another method I must now begin."   540
    So saying he caught him up, and without wing
Of hippogrif bore through the air sublime
Over the wilderness and o'er the plain,
Till underneath them fair Jerusalem,
The Holy City, lifted high her towers,   545
And higher yet the glorious Temple reared
Her pile, far off appearing like a mount
Of alabaster, topped with golden spires:
There on the highest pinnacle he set
The Son of God, and added thus in scorn: 550

518–20. Ps. 82.6–7; John 10.34.
533. rock: 1 Cor. 10.4.
534. The original "center, firm To . . . good" does not make logical sense; the punctuation is accordingly changed.
542. hippogrif: winged beast in Ariosto, *O.F.* 4.18, etc.
549 f. What is in Luke (4.9–13) the third and last temptation becomes here a direct challenge to Christ to prove his divinity. It brings together and resolves the two lines of dramatic suspense. Christ trusts completely in God and stands: the event answers Satan's questioning of Christ's identity and Christ's own uncertainty; for the first time he declares that he is "the Lord thy God." Some critics reject this last idea and see Milton using what had been a more favored theological tradition, that Christ's words only repudiate a gratuitous and presumptuous appeal to God's power; but this interpretation would surely drain much of the significance out of Milton's climax, which would seem to require both miraculous proof of Christ's divinity and his own full recognition of it.

"There stand, if thou wilt stand; to stand upright
Will ask thee skill. I to thy Father's house
Have brought thee, and highest placed; highest is best.
Now show thy progeny; if not to stand,
Cast thyself down, safely if Son of God;   555
For it is written, 'He will give command
Concerning thee to his angels; in their hands
They shall uplift thee, lest at any time
Thou chance to dash thy foot against a stone.' "
   To whom thus Jesus: "Also it is written,   560
'Tempt not the Lord thy God.' " He said, and stood.
But Satan smitten with amazement fell,
As when Earth's son Antaeus (to compare
Small things with greatest) in Irassa strove
With Jove's Alcides, and oft foiled still rose,   565
Receiving from his mother Earth new strength,
Fresh from his fall, and fiercer grapple joined,
Throttled at length in the air, expired and fell;
So after many a foil the Tempter proud,
Renewing fresh assaults, amidst his pride   570
Fell whence he stood to see his Victor fall.
And as that Theban monster that proposed
Her riddle, and him who solved it not, devour'd,
That once found out and solved, for grief and spite
Cast herself headlong from th' Ismenian steep,   575
So strook with dread and anguish fell the Fiend,
And to his crew, that sat consulting, brought
Joyless triumphals of his hoped success,
Ruin, and desperation, and dismay,
Who durst so proudly tempt the son of God.   580
So Satan fell; and straight a fiery globe
Of angels on full sail of wing flew nigh,
Who on their plumy vans received him soft
From his uneasy station, and upbore
As on a floating couch through the blithe air;   585
Then in a flow'ry valley set him down
On a green bank, and set before him spread
A table of celestial food, divine,
Ambrosial, fruits fetched from the Tree of Life,
And from the Fount of Life ambrosial drink,   590

---

554. progeny: parentage.
556–59. Ps. 91.11–12.
560–61. Deut. 6.16.
563–68. These and lines 572–75, the only
elaborate classical similes in *P.R.*, are no less
apt than unexpected. The giant Antaeus, who
received fresh strength when he touched his
mother Earth, was overcome by Hercules' holding him aloft (Sandys, on *Met.* 9, saw an
allegorical conflict between body and soul).
  564. Irassa: in north Africa.

572–75. The Theban sphinx, when Oedipus
solved her riddle.
575. Ismenian: Theban (from the river
Ismenus).
581–93. Elaborated from Matt. 4.11, Luke
4.10–11, probably G. Fletcher's *Christ's Victory on Earth* (38 and 61) and *Christ's Triumph after Death* (13), and perhaps Apuleius'
tale of Psyche (*Metamorphoses,* end of book
4).
589–90. Gen. 2.9; Rev. 2.7, 21.6, 22.1–2.
Cf. *P.L.* 3.353–57.

That soon refreshed him wearied, and repaired
What hunger, if aught hunger had impaired,
Or thirst, and as he fed, angelic quires
Sung heavenly anthems of his victory
Over temptation and the Tempter proud: 595
　"True Image of the Father, whether throned
In the bosom of bliss, and light of light
Conceiving, or remote from heaven, enshrined
In fleshly tabernacle, and human form,
Wand'ring the wilderness, whatever place,   600
Habit, or state, or motion, still expressing
The Son of God, with God-like force endued
Against th' attempter of thy Father's throne,
And thief of Paradise; him long of old
Thou didst debel, and down from heav'n cast   605
With all his army; now thou hast avenged
Supplanted Adam, and by vanquishing
Temptation hast regained lost Paradise,
And frustrated the conquest fraudulent.
He never more henceforth will dare set foot   610
In Paradise to tempt; his snares are broke.
For though that seat of earthly bliss be failed,
A fairer Paradise is founded now
For Adam and his chosen sons, whom thou
A Saviour art come down to reinstall;   615
Where they shall dwell secure, when time shall be
Of tempter and temptation without fear.
But thou, Infernal Serpent, shalt not long
Rule in the clouds; like an autumnal star
Or lightning thou shalt fall from heav'n trod down   620
Under his feet. For proof, ere this thou feel'st
Thy wound, yet not thy last and deadliest wound,
By this repulse received, and hold'st in hell
No triumph; in all her gates Abaddon rues
Thy bold attempt. Hereafter learn with awe   625
To dread the Son of God: he all unarmed
Shall chase thee with the terror of his voice
From thy demoniac holds, possession foul,
Thee and thy legions; yelling they shall fly,
And beg to hide them in a herd of swine,   630
Lest he command them down into the deep,
Bound, and to torment sent before their time.
Hail, Son of the Most High, heir of both worlds,
Queller of Satan, on thy glorious work
Now enter, and begin to save mankind."   635

596–99. John 1.4–5, 9, 14, 18.
605. debel: wear down in war (cf. *Aen.*
6.853).
611. Ps. 124.7.
612. be failed: is gone (*P.L.* 11.829 f.).

613. A fairer Paradise: cf. 1.7 and *P.L.*
12.587.
619–21. Luke 10.18; Rom. 16.20; cf. *P.L.*
10.190.
624. Abaddon: hell.
630. Matt. 8.28–33.

> Thus they the Son of God, our Saviour meek,
> Sung Victor, and from heavenly feast refreshed
> Brought on his way with joy; he unobserved
> Home to his mother's house private returned.
>
> (1665?–1670)

636–39. A tissue of quiet contrasts between Christ's divinity and humanity.

SAMSON AGONISTES

Samson Agonistes was published along with *Paradise Regained* in 1671 (or possibly 1670). It may have been composed at any time between 1660 and 1670; some recent arguments for the 1640's or 1650's appear quite unconvincing. *Paradise Regained* reflects mainly the private moral and religious fortitude that became Milton's settled frame of mind after the prolonged shock of the Restoration, though much of its censure of timeless aims and evils could be applied to contemporary England. In *Samson* both private and public strains are likewise present, though antagonism to the restored monarchy may be nearer the surface; that has been one argument for dating the drama in 1660–61. Yet one may doubt if Milton would have stopped in the middle of *Paradise Lost* to compose *Samson*, and, moreover, one would expect the epic to have been followed directly by its sequel, *Paradise Regained*. On the whole, there is a good case for the traditional view that *Samson* was Milton's last work; in the years just before 1670 some external or internal stimulus might have strongly revived his sense of the heroic past and ignoble present.

But the public or topical background — to postpone the personal element — is a minor aspect of the tragedy, the only tragedy in English on the Greek model that can be ranked with the ancient originals. Milton's prefatory references to "Aeschylus, Sophocles, and Euripides, the three tragic poets unequalled yet by any," and to the unities — and to modern Italian practice — are what might be expected from a scholar-poet of the Renaissance tradition; and he was avowedly not writing for the stage. Elements of *Samson* remind us of all three of the Greek authors of tragedy: the "epic" predominance of the protagonist and the strongly religious conception of sin and righteousness are Aeschylean; the efforts of successive interlocutors to break down the protagonist's resolution, the pervasiveness of irony both general and particular, and the handling of the chorus are Sophoclean; the strain of ratiocination and the presence and self-exculpation of a masterful "bad" woman suggest Euripides. But a poet who had a lifelong familiarity with Greek drama did not need to study models and choose features for imitation; the resemblances are a matter of affinity in moral, religious, and artistic temper. The particular Greek plays nearest to *Samson* are *Prometheus Bound* and *Oedipus at Colonus;* and the Heracles of Hebrew story reminds us of Euripides' plays about his Greek counterpart.

The story, like everything else in the Bible, had long been in Milton's mind. He had included episodes from Samson's life in the list of dramatic subjects he compiled about 1640; at the end of the *Reason of Church Government* (1642) he had drawn a parallel between Samson and a king betrayed by prelatical wiles; in *Areopagitica* (1644) he had seen a new England "rousing herself like a strong man after sleep, and shaking her invincible locks"; and Adam and Eve had awakened after their sensual play like

> Herculean Samson from the harlot-lap
> Of Philistean Dalilah.

(In the drama Dalila has the status of a wife.) Milton changed Israel's champion from the brawny barbarian of Judges into a man of sensitive conscience, integrity, and piety. As in *Comus* and the epics, Milton's subject is temptation, fall (actual or possible), and recovery, and one ground for the drama's strong appeal to modern readers is that the hero, unlike Milton's other protagonists, is an ordinary sinful human being. Theological and literary tradition — however much or little he knew of it — contained elements of Milton's Samson, though his realistic conception was hardly compatible with one traditional idea, that of Samson as a "type" of Christ. *Paradise Regained* has a minimum of Christian theology, but *Samson*, while a Christian play, has none. Milton had spoken (in *Of Education*) of decorum as "the grand masterpiece to observe," and it is remarkable that so earnestly Christian a poet could so strictly maintain Hebraic decorum, avoiding overt reference to any specifically Christian belief or idea; there is not even the hope of immortality for Samson, and no flights of angels sing him to his rest. If there is any violation of Greek tragic decorum, it is in Samson's sense of responsibility to God, yet that is not felt as a violation.

Up to the reported catastrophe the action goes on in the mind of Samson. The germ of his regeneration appears in the middle of his opening speech, where he acknowledges his own responsibility for his lot; this admission, however, is preceded and followed by natural but self-centered complaints. As the drama develops and Samson reacts to the utterances of the chorus, Manoa, Dalila, and Harapha, self-centeredness, wounded pride, distrust of God's providence give way by degrees to selfless, penitent humility, renewed faith in God's favor and providential care, and, toward the end, untroubled exaltation of spirit. From this steady upward progression there is one prolonged lapse, in lines 558–651, reinforced by the ensuing chorus; such a lapse into despair, natural enough in itself, prevents the movement of recovery from appearing contrived. The different effects that the interlocutors have on Samson are alike in one thing, that all are contrary to their expectations. This large structural irony is supported by innumerable particular ironies and ambiguities, which begin with the title and the first line: the word "Agonistes" means something more than a contestant in public games, and "A little onward lend thy guiding hand" is something more than a request to a fellow slave.

Like the Christ of *Paradise Regained* — but, except at the end, without Christ's sustaining innocence and faith — Samson is more or less isolated from all those around him. The chorus are "Job's comforters," since, while sympathetic, they turn the knife in Samson's wound; so does his bustling, well-meaning father; and the treacherous and possessive Dalila and the simple-minded braggart Harapha are of course Philistines. As Samson moves from despair — his chief temptation — toward faith, hope, and courage, the reader comprehends the grounds and process of his recovery as even his sympathizers in the drama do not. And though at the last they pronounce heartfelt and noble eulogies, they appear to have seen only the outward proof of God's continued trust in his champion, not the way in which Samson had regained trust in God and in himself as God's agent. If an occasional reader recoils from a martyrdom involving mass-slaughter, the climax of the story could not have been altered even had Milton so desired; possibly he would not have grieved if Whitehall had suffered the fate of the theatre of Gaza, but we cannot take out of its dramatic context an act symbolic of the hero's rebirth.

More substantial parallels between Samson and Milton are obvious (and lines 692–704 seem to be a clear reference to the government's reprisals upon Commonwealth leaders and to Milton's own physical pains). The poet was eyeless in London and — if he still felt like the author of the *Ready and Easy Way* — he was, metaphorically, at the mill with slaves. He did not, certainly, have Samson's overwhelming sense of having betrayed God's cause (and it would surely be going too far to bring up his first marriage, a private disaster without public consequences), but he had known the despair of witnessing the wreck of his and other men's hopes and labors for the nation. We can say with confidence that Milton could not have re-created the story of Samson without thinking of his own share in the Revolution, and such heroic memories would do much to explain the impassioned energy of the drama. At the same time he was, as always, the impersonal artist, and his own feelings, whatever they may have been, were sublimated; there is nothing in the drama that does not logically belong to the fable. Also — now that political action is impossible — *Samson* links itself with the two epics as another characteristically Miltonic assertion of God's providence and the possibility of individual man's attaining or maintaining faith and fortitude.

It is sometimes said that a genuine Christian could not write a tragedy because the essence of tragedy is nullified by belief in a providential God or by the prospect of a heavenly reward for the protagonist. But, it may be repeated, no heavenly reward is held out for Samson, as it is for Hamlet, and belief in the workings of Providence does not nullify, in a limited human view of things, the fact and the mystery of good and evil, suffering and death. Milton himself, as his preface shows, had no thought of possible inconsistency; and many years earlier, remarking in his Commonplace Book on Lactantius' hostility to drama, he had asked: "For what in all philosophy is more important or more sacred or more exalted than a tragedy rightly produced, what more useful for seeing at a single view the events and changes of human life?" (*C.P.W.* 1, 491). A. S. P. Woodhouse sums up the case of *Samson* thus (to quote parts of his exegesis): Milton

> has made the way of repentance and restoration, the way back to God, also the way that leads inevitably to the catastrophe, and has thus achieved at a stroke the only kind of irony that is at once compatible with a Christian outlook and as potent as any to be found in tragedy anywhere. Moreover, he has shown the necessity which thus conjoins Samson's salvation and victory with his death to be no arbitrary imposition of the overruling Power, but the outcome of Samson's conduct — of his sin and of his subsequent repentance. That his repentance is achieved under the impulsion of divine grace does not alter the fact that it is Samson's own. . . .
>
> The conclusion . . . is directed wholly to reconciliation, mitigating the sense of disaster: first on the human level, and, when that is completed, by invoking the overruling Power, by showing the place of Samson's sacrifice, of his whole experience, in the providential order of God, who does not force men's wills but nevertheless controls the event. The emphasis of this comment is justified not

only on doctrinal but on artistic grounds. The very strength of the element of tragic irony in the action both permits and demands it. And the irony and the resolution of irony alike depend on the fact that this is a Christan tragedy: that is to say, a tragedy which, however scrupulously it adheres to classical conventions, is written unfalteringly from a Christian point of view.*

In style and versification *Samson* was Milton's most radical experiment. He necessarily abandoned the richness, the large sweep and rapid flow, and the syntactical complexities of *Paradise Lost*, and he went beyond the simplicity of *Paradise Regained*, to forge a more dramatic idiom. Blank verse of sinewy massiveness and frequent irregularity is mixed with choral and other passages of more or less short lines of no less muscular compression. It is not "free verse" in the modern sense; the rhythmic units can be scanned as traditional metrical feet, however boldly manipulated and combined. The total result is a new, semi-colloquial, "prosaic" ruggedness which follows the movement of thought and feeling more closely than epic blank verse normally could. The semi-colloquialism has of course varying degrees of naturalness and elevation. The texture, even — or perhaps one should say especially — in its stiffness, reproduces the manner of Greek tragedy (if the three Greek poets may be lumped together) more faithfully than any English translation of a Greek play. All these features are exemplified in Samson's first speech. To mention two memorable choric similes, we might compare the restrained but florid irony of the picture of Dalila in her ill-gotten finery (710–24) and the "metaphysical" density of the lines on the phoenix (1699–1707). In general, the style as well as the form of *Samson* is a new kind of Miltonic classicism.

* "Tragic Effect in *Samson Agonistes*," *University of Toronto Quarterly,* 28 (1958–59), 220–21.

Samson Agonistes[1]

A DRAMATIC POEM

Aristotle, *Poetics*, c. 6. Τραγῳδία μίμησις πράξεως σπουδαίας, &c.

Tragoedia est imitatio actionis seriae, &c., per misericordiam et metum perficiens talium affectuum lustrationem.[2]

OF THAT SORT OF DRAMATIC POEM WHICH IS CALLED TRAGEDY

Tragedy, as it was anciently composed, hath been ever held the gravest, moralest, and most profitable of all other poems: therefore said by Aristotle to be of power, by raising pity and fear, or terror, to purge the mind of those and suchlike passions, that is, to temper and reduce them to just measure with a kind of delight, stirred up by reading or seeing those passions well imitated. Nor is Nature wanting in her own effects to make good his assertion; for so in physic, things of melancholic hue and quality are used against melancholy, sour against sour, salt to remove salt humors. Hence philosophers and other gravest writers, as Cicero, Plutarch, and others, frequently cite out of tragic poets, both to adorn and illustrate their discourse. The Apostle Paul himself thought it not unworthy to insert a verse of Euripides into the text of Holy Scripture, I Cor. 15. 33;[3] and Pareus,[4] commenting on the Revelation, divides the whole book as a tragedy, into acts distinguished each by a chorus of heavenly harpings and song between. Heretofore men in highest dignity have labored not a little to be thought able to compose a tragedy. Of that honor Dionysius the elder was no less ambitious than before of his attaining to the tyranny.[5] Augustus Caesar also had begun his *Ajax*, but, unable to please his own judgment with what he had begun, left it unfinished.[6] Seneca the philosopher is by some thought the author of those tragedies (at least the best of them) that go under that name.[7] Gregory Nazianzen, a Father of the Church, thought it not unbeseeming the sanctity of his person to write a tragedy, which he entitled *Christ Suffering*.[8] This is mentioned to vindicate tragedy from the small esteem, or rather infamy, which in the account of many it undergoes at

[1] Agonistes. Along with the Greek meanings, "contestant" and "actor" — which in this context carry a special irony — there is the Miltonic overtone of "God's champion."

[2] The Latin sentence, a translation from Aristotle which includes the Greek phrase quoted, is paraphrased and amplified in the first sentence of Milton's preface. He interprets catharsis — in the tradition of Italian critics — as the pleasurable reduction of passions to a desirable mean, and invokes the medical analogy.

[3] Euripides. The proverbial phrase quoted by St. Paul is now assigned to Menander.

[4] Pareus: glossary.

[5] Dionysius (*c.* 430–367 B.C.), tyrant of Syracuse.

[6] Augustus Caesar: see Suetonius, *Lives of the Caesars* 2.85.

[7] Seneca (5–4 B.C.–65 A.D.) is now credited with the tragedies as well as the philosophic prose.

[8] Gregory Nazianzen (d. *c.* 389) is not now considered the author of *Christ Suffering*.

this day with other common interludes; happening through the poet's error of intermixing comic stuff with tragic sadness and gravity, or introducing trivial and vulgar persons, which by all judicious hath been counted absurd, and brought in without discretion, corruptly to gratify the people. And though ancient tragedy use no prologue,[9] yet using sometimes, in case of self-defense, or explanation, that which Martial calls an epistle;[10] in behalf of this tragedy, coming forth after the ancient manner, much different from what among us passes for best, thus much beforehand may be epistled: that chorus is here introduced after the Greek manner, not ancient only but modern, and still in use among the Italians.[11] In the modeling therefore of this poem, with good reason, the ancients and Italians are rather followed, as of much more authority and fame. The measure of verse used in the chorus is of all sorts, called by the Greeks *monostrophic*, or rather *apolelymenon*,[12] without regard had to strophe, antistrophe, or epode, which were a kind of stanzas framed only for the music, then used with the chorus that sung; not essential to the poem, and therefore not material; or, being divided into stanzas or pauses, they may be called *alloeostropha*.[13] Division into act and scene, referring chiefly to the stage (to which this work never was intended), is here omitted.

It suffices if the whole drama be found not produced beyond the fifth act. Of the style and uniformity, and that commonly called the plot, whether intricate or explicit[14] — which is nothing indeed but such economy, or disposition of the fable, as may stand best with verisimilitude and decorum — they only will best judge who are not unacquainted with Aeschylus, Sophocles, and Euripides, the three tragic poets unequaled yet by any, and the best rule to all who endeavor to write tragedy. The circumscription of time wherein the whole drama begins and ends is, according to ancient rule and best example, within the space of twenty-four hours.[15]

THE ARGUMENT

Samson, made captive, blind, and now in the prison at Gaza, there to labor as in a common workhouse, on a festival day, in the general cessation from labor, comes forth into the open air, to a place nigh, somewhat retired, there to sit a while and bemoan his condition. Where he happens at length to be visited by certain friends and equals[16] of his tribe, which make the chorus, who seek to comfort him what they can; then by his old father, Manoa, who endeavors the like, and withal tells him his purpose to procure his liberty by ransom; lastly, that this feast was proclaimed by the Philistines as a day of thanksgiving for their deliverance from the hands of Samson, which yet more troubles him. Manoa then departs to prosecute his endeavor with the Philistian lords for Samson's redemption; who in the meanwhile is visited by other persons; and lastly by a public officer to require his coming to the feast before the lords and people, to play or show his strength in their presence. He at first refuses, dismissing the public officer with absolute denial to come; at length persuaded inwardly that this was from God, he yields to go along with

9 prologue: an introductory speech, outside the play, as used by Plautus, Terence, Shakespeare (rarely), Jonson, et al.

10 epistle: a prefatory letter in a book, addressed to a patron or readers.

11 Italians: In *Of Education* and elsewhere Milton showed his knowledge of and respect for Italian criticism and poetry.

12 *apolelymenon:* "free" from stanzaic patterns.

13 *alloeostropha:* with strophes or paragraphs of varying form.

14 intricate or explicit: complex or simple (Aristotle, *Poetics* 10).

15 While "ancient rule" was not canonical, the continuous action of a Greek play commonly required a brief time-scheme; this became one of the three unities in neoclassical criticism.

16 equals: men of about the same age.

him, who came now the second time with great threatenings to fetch him. The chorus yet remaining on the place, Manoa returns full of joyful hope to procure ere long his son's deliverance; in the midst of which discourse an Hebrew comes in haste, confusedly at first, and afterward more distinctly, relating the catastrophe, what Samson had done to the Philistines, and by accident to himself; wherewith the tragedy ends.

THE PERSONS

Samson.
Manoa, the father of Samson.
Dálila, his wife.
Harapha of Gath.
Public officer.
Messenger.
Chorus of Danites.[17]

The Scene, before the Prison in Gaza[18]

Samson. A little onward lend thy guiding hand
To these dark steps, a little further on,
For yonder bank hath choice of sun or shade;
There I am wont to sit, when any chance
Relieves me from my task of servile toil,   5
Daily in the common prison else enjoined me,
Where I, a prisoner chained, scarcely freely draw
The air imprisoned also, close and damp,
Unwholesome draught. But here I feel amends,
The breath of heav'n fresh-blowing, pure and sweet,   10
With day-spring born; here leave me to respire.
This day a solemn feast the people hold
To Dagon their sea-idol, and forbid
Laborious works; unwillingly this rest
Their superstition yields me; hence with leave   15
Retiring from the popular noise, I seek
This unfrequented place to find some ease,
Ease to the body some, none to the mind
From restless thoughts, that like a deadly swarm
Of hornets armed, no sooner found alone,   20
But rush upon me thronging, and present
Times past, what once I was, and what am now.
O wherefore was my birth from Heaven foretold

17 Danites: the tribe and district of Dan, northwest of Judah, to which Manoa and Samson belonged (Judges 13.2).

18 Gaza: one of the chief Philistine cities, on the south coast of Palestine.

1 f. Cf. the opening of *Oedipus at Colonus*, where the old, blind Oedipus is led forward by Antigone; Euripides, *Phoenissae* 834–35; and Sir Philip Sidney's *Arcadia*, ed. Feuillerat, p. 210.

1–2. These lines (along with the title) inaugurate the dramatic irony and ambiguity that run through the drama.

10–11. Another phrase that adds to the literal sense a suggestion of divine help (cf. Luke 1.78).

13. Dagon: cf. *P.L.* 1.457–66 and note.

23–29. Judges 13.3–5, 10–20; cf. Elijah (2 Kings 2.11).

Twice by an angel, who at last in sight
Of both my parents all in flames ascended   25
From off the altar, where an off'ring burned,
As in a fiery column charioting
His godlike presence, and from some great act
Or benefit revealed to Abraham's race?
Why was my breeding ordered and prescribed   30
As of a person separate to God,
Designed for great exploits, if I must die
Betrayed, captíved, and both my eyes put out,
Made of my enemies the scorn and gaze;
To grind in brazen fetters under task   35
With this Heav'n-gifted strength? O glorious strength,
Put to the labor of a beast, debased
Lower than bondslave! Promise was that I
Should Israel from Philistian yoke deliver;
Ask for this great deliverer now, and find him   40
Eyeless in Gaza at the mill with slaves,
Himself in bonds under Philistian yoke;
Yet stay, let me not rashly call in doubt
Divine prediction; what if all foretold
Had been fulfilled but through mine own default?   45
Whom have I to complain of but myself?
Who this high gift of strength committed to me,
In what part lodged, how easily bereft me,
Under the seal of silence could not keep,
But weakly to a woman must reveal it,   50
O'ercome with importunity and tears.
O impotence of mind, in body strong!
But what is strength without a double share
Of wisdom? Vast, unwieldy, burdensome,
Proudly secure, yet liable to fall   55
By weakest subtleties; not made to rule,
But to subserve where wisdom bears command.
God, when he gave me strength, to show withal
How slight the gift was, hung it in my hair.
But peace! I must not quarrel with the will   60
Of highest dispensation, which herein
Haply had ends above my reach to know:
Suffices that to me strength is my bane,
And proves the source of all my miseries,
So many, and so huge, that each apart   65
Would ask a life to wail; but chief of all,
O loss of sight, of thee I most complain!
Blind among enemies, O worse than chains,
Dungeon, or beggary, or decrepit age!
Light, the prime work of God, to me is extinct,   70

30–33. See note on 318.
38–39. Judges 13.5.
53–56. A traditional commonplace, e.g.,

Sophocles, *Ajax* 1250–52, Horace, *Od.* 3.4.65,
Ovid, *Met.* 13.363.
61. highest dispensation: God's providence.

And all her various objects of delight
Annulled, which might in part my grief have eased,
Inferior to the vilest now become
Of man or worm; the vilest here excel me,
They creep, yet see; I, dark in light exposed   75
To daily fraud, contempt, abuse and wrong,
Within doors, or without, still as a fool,
In power of others, never in my own;
Scarce half I seem to live, dead more than half.
O dark, dark, dark, amid the blaze of noon,   80
Irrecoverably dark, total eclipse
Without all hope of day!
O first-created beam, and thou great Word,
"Let there be light, and light was over all";
Why am I thus bereaved thy prime decree?   85
The sun to me is dark
And silent as the moon,
When she deserts the night,
Hid in her vacant interlunar cave.
Since light so necessary is to life,   90
And almost life itself, if it be true
That light is in the soul,
She all in every part, why was the sight
To such a tender ball as th' eye confined?
So obvious and so easy to be quenched,   95
And not, as feeling, through all parts diffused,
That she might look at will through every pore?
Then had I not been thus exiled from light,
As in the land of darkness, yet in light,
To live a life half dead, a living death,   100
And buried; but O yet more miserable!
Myself my sepulchre, a moving grave,
Buried, not yet exempt
By privilege of death and burial
From worst of other evils, pains and wrongs,   105
But made hereby obnoxious more
To all the miseries of life,
Life in captivity
Among inhuman foes.
But who are these? For with joint pace I hear   110
The tread of many feet steering this way;
Perhaps my enemies who come to stare
At my affliction, and perhaps to insult,
Their daily practice to afflict me more.
  Chorus. This, this is he; softly a while;   115

1a.

83–85. Gen. 1.3; cf. *P.L.* 3.1. Samson's being cut off from light suggests his alienation from God.
87. silent: i.e. dark (cf. *Aen.* 2.255; Dante, *Inf.* 1.60 and 5.28).
89. vacant: not functioning as a light-giver.

cave: where the moon was in antiquity supposed to be when not visible.
93–94. The idea of the soul as "all in every part" was a Christian commonplace, e.g., Augustine, *De Trinitate* 6.6 (Migne, 42, 929); Milton, *C.D.* 1.7.

Let us not break in upon him.
O change beyond report, thought, or belief!
See how he lies at random, carelessly diffused,
With languished head unpropped,
As one past hope, abandoned,   120
And by himself given over;
In slavish habit, ill-fitted weeds
O'erworn and soiled;
Or do my eyes misrepresent? Can this be he,
That heroic, that renowned,   125
Irresistible Samson? Whom unarmed
No strength of man, or fiercest wild beast could withstand;
Who tore the lion, as the lion tears the kid,
Ran on embattled armies clad in iron,
And, weaponless himself,   130
Made arms ridiculous, useless the forgery
Of brazen shield and spear, the hammered cuirass,
Chalýbean-tempered steel, and frock of mail
Adamantean proof;
But safest he who stood aloof,   135
When insupportably his foot advanced,
In scorn of their proud arms and warlike tools,
Spurned them to death by troops. The bold Ascalonite
Fled from his lion ramp, old warriors turned
Their plated backs under his heel;   140
Or grov'ling soiled their crested helmets in the dust.
Then with what trivial weapon came to hand,
The jaw of a dead ass, his sword of bone,
A thousand foreskins fell, the flower of Palestine,
In Ramath-lechi, famous to this day;   145
Then by main force pulled up, and on his shoulders bore
The gates of Azza, post and massy bar,
Up to the hill by Hebron, seat of giants old,
No journey of a Sabbath day, and loaded so;
Like whom the Gentiles feign to bear up heav'n.   150
Which shall I first bewail,
Thy bondage or lost sight,
Prison within prison
Inseparably dark?
Thou art become (O worst imprisonment!)   155

118. diffused: "poured out," sprawled.
128. Judges 14.5–6.
131. forgery: (1) made of metal (2) an imposture.
133. The Chalybes, on the Black Sea, were noted for their metal work.
136. insupportably: irresistibly.
142–45. Judges 15.15–17.
142. trivial: including the literal sense, "picked up at the crossroads" (*trivium*).
144. foreskins: the uncircumcised Philistines.

144. Palestine: here Philistia.
146–49. Judges 16.3.
147. Azza: Gaza.
148. Hebron: a city south of Jerusalem, over 30 miles from Gaza.   seat . . . old: Num. 13.22, 33; Joshua 11.21–22, 15.13–14.
149. Mosaic law forbade all but the briefest journeys on the Sabbath.
150. An oblique allusion to Atlas (glossary), in keeping with Hebraic decorum.

The dungeon of thyself; thy soul
(Which men enjoying sight oft without cause complain)
Imprisoned now indeed,
In real darkness of the body dwells,
Shut up from outward light   160
To incorporate with gloomy night;
For inward light, alas,
Puts forth no visual beam.
O mirror of our fickle state.
Since man on earth unparalleled!   165
The rarer thy example stands,
By how much from the top of wondrous glory,
Strongest of mortal men,
To lowest pitch of abject fortune thou art fall'n.
For him I reckon not in high estate   170
Whom long descent of birth
Or the sphere of fortune raises;
But thee whose strength, while virtue was her mate,
Might have subdued the earth,
Universally crowned with highest praises.   175
    Sam. I hear the sound of words; their sense the air
Dissolves unjointed ere it reach my ear.
    Chor. He speaks; let us draw nigh. Matchless in might,
The glory late of Israel, now the grief!
We come thy friends and neighbors not unknown   180
From Eshtaol and Zora's fruitful vale
To visit or bewail thee, or if better,
Counsel or consolation we may bring,
Salve to thy sores; apt words have power to swage
The tumors of a troubled mind,   185
And are as balm to festered wounds.
    Sam. Your coming, friends, revives me, for I learn
Now of my own experience, not by talk,
How counterfeit a coin they are who "friends"
Bear in their superscription (of the most   190
I would be understood). In prosperous days
They swarm, but in adverse withdraw their head,
Not to be found, though sought. Ye see, O friends,
How many evils have enclosed me round;
Yet that which was the worst now least afflicts me,   195
Blindness, for had I sight, confused with shame,
How could I once look up, or heave the head,
Who like a foolish pilot have shipwracked
My vessel trusted to me from above,
Gloriously rigged; and for a word, a tear,   200
Fool, have divulged the secret gift of God

---

172. sphere: wheel.
180–85. Cf. Job's friends (Job 2.11–13).
181. Places west of Jerusalem. Manoa was a citizen of Zora (Judges 13.3, 16.31).

184–86. Cf. Aeschylus, *Prometheus Bound* 380.
191–93. Cf. Ovid, *Tristia* 1.9.5–6; etc.

To a deceitful woman? Tell me, friends,
Am I not sung and proverbed for a fool
In every street, do they not say, "How well
Are come upon him his deserts"? Yet why?   205
Immeasurable strength they might behold
In me, of wisdom nothing more than mean;
This with the other should, at least, have paired;
These two proportioned ill drove me transverse.
    Chor. Tax not divine disposal; wisest men   210
Have erred, and by bad women been deceived;
And shall again, pretend they ne'er so wise.
Deject not then so overmuch thyself,
Who hast of sorrow thy full load besides.
Yet truth to say, I oft have heard men wonder   215
Why thou shouldst wed Philistian women rather
Than of thine own tribe fairer, or as fair,
At least of thy own nation, and as noble.
    Sam. The first I saw at Timna, and she pleased
Me, not my parents, that I sought to wed,   220
The daughter of an infidel: they knew not
That what I motioned was of God; I knew
From intimate impulse, and therefore urged
The marriage on; that by occasion hence
I might begin Israel's deliverance,   225
The work to which I was divinely called.
She proving false, the next I took to wife
(O that I never had! fond wish too late!)
Was in the vale of Sorec, Dálila,
That specious monster, my accomplished snare.   230
I thought it lawful from my former act,
And the same end, still watching to oppress
Israel's oppressors. Of what now I suffer
She was not the prime cause, but I myself,
Who vanquished with a peal of words (O weakness!)   235
Gave up my fort of silence to a woman.
    Chor. In seeking just occasion to provoke
The Philistine, thy country's enemy,
Thou never wast remiss, I bear thee witness:
Yet Israel still serves with all his sons.   240
    Sam. That fault I take not on me, but transfer
On Israel's governors and heads of tribes,
Who, seeing those great acts which God had done
Singly by me against their conquerors,
Acknowledged not, or not at all considered,   245
Deliverance offered: I on th' other side

203–05. Cf. Ps. 69.11, Job 17.6, 30.9.
208. paired: been equal.
209. drove . . . transverse. The phrase carries on the metaphor of a ship from 198–200.
219–26. Judges 14.1–4.

219. Timna: Timnath, a Philistine city.
229. Judges 16.4.
235–36. Judges 16.16–17.
240. serves: is in servitude (to the Philistines).

Used no ambition to commend my deeds;
The deeds themselves, though mute, spoke loud the doer;
But they persisted deaf, and would not seem
To count them things worth notice, till at length   250
Their lords the Philistines with gathered powers
Entered Judea seeking me, who then
Safe to the rock of Etham was retired,
Not flying, but forecasting in what place
To set upon them, what advantaged best;   255
Meanwhile the men of Judah, to prevent
The harass of their land, beset me round;
I willingly on some conditions came
Into their hands, and they as gladly yield me
To the uncircumcised a welcome prey,   260
Bound with two cords; but cords to me were threads
Touched with the flame: on their whole host I flew
Unarmed, and with a trivial weapon felled
Their choicest youth; they only lived who fled.
Had Judah that day joined, or one whole tribe,   265
They had by this possessed the towers of Gath,
And lorded over them whom now they serve;
But what more oft in nations grown corrupt,
And by their vices brought to servitude,
Than to love bondage more than liberty,   270
Bondage with ease than strenuous liberty;
And to despise, or envy, or suspect
Whom God hath of his special favor raised
As their deliverer; if he aught begin,
How frequent to desert him, and at last   275
To heap ingratitude on worthiest deeds?
    Chor. Thy words to my remembrance bring
How Succoth and the fort of Penuel
Their great deliverer contemned,
The matchless Gideon in pursuit   280
Of Madian and her vanquished kings:
And how ingrateful Ephraim
Had dealt with Jephtha, who by argument,
Not worse than by his shield and spear,
Defended Israel from the Ammonite,   285
Had not his prowess quelled their pride
In that sore battle when so many died
Without reprieve adjudged to death,
For want of well pronouncing *Shibboleth.*
    Sam. Of such examples add me to the roll;   290

---

247. ambition: canvassing (Latin sense).
252–64. Judges 15.8–17.
263. trivial weapon: see 142–43.
266. Gath: one of the chief Philistine cities; here for the whole country.

268–71. A Miltonic doctrine often affirmed; cf. *P.L.* 12.82 f., *P.R.* 4.131–45; etc.
277–81. Judges 8.1–17.
282–89. Judges 11 and 12.1–6.
283–85. Judges 11.14–27.
289. Judges 12.5–6.

Me easily indeed mine may neglect,
But God's proposed deliverance not so.
    Chor. Just are the ways of God,
And justifiable to men;
Unless there be who think not God at all: 295
If any be, they walk obscure;
For of such doctrine never was there school,
But the heart of the fool,
And no man therein doctor but himself.
    Yet more there be who doubt his ways not just,   300
As to his own edícts, found contradicting,
Then give the reins to wand'ring thought,
Regardless of his glory's diminution;
Till by their own perplexities involved
They ravel more, still less resolved,   305
But never find self-satisfying solution.
    As if they would confine th' Interminable,
And tie him to his own prescript,
Who made our laws to bind us, not himself,
And hath full right to exempt   310
Whomso it pleases him by choice
From national obstriction, without taint
Of sin, or legal debt;
For with his own laws he can best dispense.
    He would not else, who never wanted means,   315
Nor in respect of the enemy just cause,
To set his people free,
Have prompted this heroic Nazarite,
Against his vow of strictest purity,
To seek in marriage that fallacious bride,   320
Unclean, unchaste.
    Down, Reason, then, at least vain reasonings down,
Though Reason here aver
That moral verdict quits her of unclean:
Unchaste was subsequent; her stain, not his.   325
    But see, here comes thy reverend sire
With careful step, locks white as down,
Old Manoa: advise
Forthwith how thou ought'st to receive him.
    Sam. Ay me, another inward grief awaked   330
With mention of that name renews th' assault.
    Manoa. Brethren and men of Dan, for such ye seem,

291. mine: my people.
293. Rev. 15.3.
295. think: believe in.
295, 298: Ps. 14.1, 53.1.
300. Job 8.3, 16.11.
305. ravel: become confused.
307. Interminable: infinite, i.e. God.
312. obstriction: obligation (here the law against marriage with Gentiles, Deut. 7.3).
318. Nazarite: one of an ascetic sect es-

pecially dedicated to God's service (Num. 6.1–21; Judges 13.5, 7).
320–25. Probably the woman of Timnath (Judges 14.15–20), since the words imply that it was Samson's first marriage (and the Bible does not mention marriage with Dalila).
321. Unclean: as a Gentile.   unchaste: Judges 14.20.
327. careful: full of care.
328. advise: consider.

Though in this uncouth place; if old respect,
As I suppose, towards your once gloried friend,
My son now captive, hither hath informed   335
Your younger feet, while mine cast back with age
Came lagging after; say if he be here.

   Chor. As signal now in low dejected state,
As erst in highest, behold him where he lies.

   Man. O miserable change! is this the man,   340
That invincible Samson, far renowned,
The dread of Israel's foes, who with a strength
Equivalent to angels' walked their streets,
None offering fight; who single combatant
Duelled their armies ranked in proud array,   345
Himself an army, now unequal match
To save himself against a coward armed
At one spear's length? O ever-failing trust
In mortal strength! and oh what not in man
Deceivable and vain! Nay, what thing good   350
Prayed for, but often proves our woe, our bane?
I prayed for children, and thought barrenness
In wedlock a reproach; I gained a son,
And such a son as all men hailed me happy:
Who would be now a father in my stead?   355
O wherefore did God grant me my request,
And as a blessing with such pomp adorned?
Why are his gifts desirable, to tempt
Our earnest prayers, then giv'n with solemn hand
As graces, draw a scorpion's tail behind?   360
For this did the angel twice descend? For this
Ordained thy nurture holy, as of a plant;
Select and sacred, glorious for a while,
The miracle of men; then in an hour
Ensnared, assaulted, overcome, led bound,   365
Thy foes' derision, captive, poor, and blind,
Into a dungeon thrust, to work with slaves?
Alas, methinks whom God hath chosen once
To worthiest deeds, if he through frailty err,
He should not so o'erwhelm, and as a thrall   370
Subject him to so foul indignities,
Be it but for honor's sake of former deeds.

   Sam. Appoint not heavenly disposition, father.
Nothing of all these evils hath befall'n me
But justly; I myself have brought them on,   375
Sole author I, sole cause: if aught seem vile,
As vile hath been my folly, who have profaned
The mystery of God giv'n me under pledge
Of vow, and have betrayed it to a woman,
A Canaanite, my faithless enemy.   380

338. signal: conspicuous.
345. Duelled: fought alone.
361. See 24 above and note.
380. Canaanite: Philistine.

This well I knew, nor was at all surprised,
But warned by oft experience: did not she
Of Timna first betray me, and reveal
The secret wrested from me in her highth
Of nuptial love professed, carrying it straight   385
To them who had corrupted her, my spies,
And rivals? In this other was there found
More faith? Who also in her prime of love,
Spousal embraces, vitiated with gold,
Though offered only, by the scent conceived   390
Her spurious first-born, treason against me.
Thrice she assayed with flattering prayer and sighs
And amorous reproaches to win from me
My capital secret, in what part my strength
Lay stored, in what part summed, that she might know: 395
Thrice I deluded her, and turned to sport
Her importunity, each time perceiving
How openly, and with what impudence,
She purposed to betray me, and (which was worse
Than undissembled hate) with what contempt   400
She sought to make me traitor to myself;
Yet the fourth time, when must'ring all her wiles,
With blandished parleys, feminine assaults,
Tongue-batteries, she surceased not day nor night
To storm me over-watched, and wearied out,   405
At times when men seek most repose and rest,
I yielded, and unlocked her all my heart,
Who with a grain of manhood well resolved
Might easily have shook off all her snares;
But foul effeminacy held me yoked   410
Her bondslave; O indignity, O blot
To honor and religion! servile mind
Rewarded well with servile punishment!
The base degree to which I now am fall'n,
These rags, this grinding, is not yet so base   415
As was my former servitude, ignoble,
Unmanly, ignominious, infamous,
True slavery, and that blindness worse than this,
That saw not how degenerately I served.
   Man. I cannot praise thy marriage choices, son,   420
Rather approved them not; but thou didst plead
Divine impulsion prompting how thou might'st
Find some occasion to infest our foes.
I state not that; this I am sure, our foes
Found soon occasion thereby to make thee   425
Their captive, and their triumph; thou the sooner

382–87. Judges 14.8–19.
386. my spies: spies on me.
387. other: Dalila.
387–407. Judges 16.5–20.

390. scent: the offer of money.
394. capital: cf. *P.L.* 12.383 and note.
423. infest: harass.
424. state: give opinion on.

Where thou may'st bring thy off'rings, to avert
His further ire, with prayers and vows renewed.   520
    Sam. His pardon I implore; but as for life,
To what end should I seek it? When in strength
All mortals I excelled, and great in hopes
With youthful courage and magnanimous thoughts
Of birth from Heav'n foretold and high exploits,   525
Full of divine instinct, after some proof
Of acts indeed heroic, far beyond
The sons of Anak, famous now and blazed,
Fearless of danger, like a petty god
I walked about admired of all and dreaded   530
On hostile ground, none daring my affront.
Then swoll'n with pride into the snare I fell
Of fair fallacious looks, venereal trains,
Softened with pleasure and voluptuous life;
At length to lay my head and hallowed pledge   535
Of all my strength in the lascivious lap
Of a deceitful concubine who shore me
Like a tame wether, all my precious fleece,
Then turned me out ridiculous, despoiled,
Shav'n, and disarmed among my enemies.   540
    Chor. Desire of wine and all delicious drinks,
Which many a famous warrior overturns,
Thou couldst repress, nor did the dancing ruby
Sparkling outpoured, the flavor, or the smell,
Or taste that cheers the heart of gods and men,   545
Allure thee from the cool crystálline stream.
    Sam. Wherever fountain or fresh current flowed
Against the eastern ray, translucent, pure
With touch ethereal of heav'n's fiery rod,
I drank, from the clear milky juice allaying   550
Thirst, and refreshed; nor envied them the grape
Whose heads that turbulent liquor fills with fumes.
    Chor. O madness, to think use of strongest wines
And strongest drinks our chief support of health,
When God with these forbidd'n made choice to rear   555
His mighty champion, strong above compare,
Whose drink was only from the liquid brook.
    Sam. But what availed this temperance, not complete
Against another object more enticing?
What boots it at one gate to make defense,   560
And at another to let in the foe,

---

528. sons of Anak: giants (Num. 13.22, 33; Deut. 9.2).

529–31. The terms suggest Greek *hybris*, arrogant self-sufficiency that forgets human limitations.

531. my affront: to meet me.

533. venereal trains: sensual allurements.

535–40. Judges 16.19–20.

538. wether: cf. *Merchant of Venice* 4.1.114.

541–52. See note on Nazarite, 318.

543. ruby: wine of ruby color (cf. *P.L.* 5.633; Prov. 23.31).

545. Judges 9.13.

549. fiery rod: sun's ray.

550. milky juice: cf. *P.L.* 5.306.

Effeminately vanquished? By which means,
Now blind, disheartened, shamed, dishonored, quelled,
To what can I be useful, wherein serve
My nation, and the work from Heav'n imposed,   565
But to sit idle on the household hearth,
A burdenous drone? To visitants a gaze,
Or pitied object; these redundant locks,
Robustious to no purpose, clust'ring down,
Vain monument of strength; till length of years   570
And sedentary numbness craze my limbs
To a contemptible old age obscure.
Here rather let me drudge and earn my bread,
Till vermin or the draff of servile food
Consume me, and oft-invocated death   575
Hasten the welcome end of all my pains.
    Man. Wilt thou then serve the Philistines with that gift
Which was expressly giv'n thee to annoy them?
Better at home lie bed-rid, not only idle,
Inglorious, unemployed, with age outworn.   580
But God, who caused a fountain at thy prayer
From the dry ground to spring, thy thirst to allay
After the brunt of battle, can as easy
Cause light again within thy eyes to spring,
Wherewith to serve him better than thou hast;   585
And I persuade me so; why else this strength
Miraculous yet remaining in those locks?
His might continues in thee not for naught,
Nor shall his wondrous gifts be frustrate thus.
    Sam. All otherwise to me my thoughts portend,   590
That these dark orbs no more shall treat with light,
Nor th' other light of life continue long,
But yield to double darkness nigh at hand:
So much I feel my genial spirits droop,
My hopes all flat; nature within me seems   595
In all her functions weary of herself;
My race of glory run, and race of shame,
And I shall shortly be with them that rest.
    Man. Believe not these suggestions, which proceed
From anguish of the mind and humors black,   600
That mingle with thy fancy. I however
Must not omit a father's timely care
To prosecute the means of thy deliverance
By ransom or how else: meanwhile be calm,
And healing words from these thy friends admit.   605
    Sam. O that torment should not be confined

---

568. redundant: flowing luxuriantly.
569. Robustious: strong, flourishing.
581–83. Judges 15.18–19.
590 f., 606 f. Manoa's hopes of a ransom
and of his son's recovery have the effect of reversing the early upward movement and plung-
ing Samson into still deeper despair.
   594. genial: innate, vital.
   600. humors: glossary, and the opening of
Milton's preface to *S.A.*

To the body's wounds and sores,
With maladies innumerable
In heart, head, breast, and reins;
But must secret passage find   610
To th' inmost mind,
There exercise all his fierce accidents,
And on her purest spirits prey,
As on entrails, joints, and limbs,
With answerable pains, but more intense,   615
Though void of corporal sense.
   My griefs not only pain me
As a ling'ring disease,
But finding no redress, ferment and rage,
Nor less than wounds immedicable   620
Rankle, and fester, and gangrene,
To black mortification.
Thoughts, my tormentors, armed with deadly stings
Mangle my apprehensive tenderest parts,
Exasperate, exulcerate, and raise   625
Dire inflammation which no cooling herb
Or med'cinal liquor can assuage,
Nor breath of vernal air from snowy Alp.
Sleep hath forsook and giv'n me o'er
To death's benumbing opium as my only cure.   630
Thence faintings, swoonings of despair,
And sense of Heav'n's desertion.
   I was his nursling once and choice delight,
His destined from the womb,
Promised by heavenly message twice descending.   635
Under his special eye
Abstemious I grew up and thrived amain;
He led me on to mightiest deeds
Above the nerve of mortal arm
Against the uncircumcised, our enemies.   640
But now hath cast me off as never known,
And to those cruel enemies,
Whom I by his appointment had provoked,
Left me all helpless with th' irreparable loss
Of sight, reserved alive to be repeated   645
The subject of their cruelty or scorn.
Nor am I in the list of them that hope;
Hopeless are all my evils, all remédiless;
This one prayer yet remains, might I be heard,
No long petition — speedy death,   650
The close of all my miseries, and the balm.
   Chor. Many are the sayings of the wise

[handwritten marginal note:] } does not curse God

---

612. his: its (i.e. torment's).   accidents:
qualities, properties.
   624. my . . . parts: mind, conscience, imagination.

635. Cf. 23–26 and note.
   652–59. The language suggests classical and
especially Stoic essays of consolation, like
Seneca's.

In ancient and in modern books enrolled,
Extolling patience as the truest fortitude;
And to the bearing well of all calamities,   655
All chances incident to man's frail life,
Consolatories writ
With studied argument, and much persuasion sought,
Lenient of grief and anxious thought;
But with th' afflicted in his pangs their sound   660
Little prevails, or rather seems a tune
Harsh, and of dissonant mood from his complaint,
Unless he feel within
Some source of consolation from above,
Secret refreshings that repair his strength,   665
And fainting spirits uphold.
    God of our fathers, what is man!
That thou towards him with hand so various —
Or might I say contrarious? —
Temper'st thy providence through his short course,   670
Not evenly, as thou rul'st
The angelic orders and inferior creatures mute,
Irrational and brute.
Nor do I name of men the common rout,
That wand'ring loose about   675
Grow up and perish, as the summer fly,
Heads without name no more remembered;
But such as thou hast solemnly elected,
With gifts and graces eminently adorned
To some great work, thy glory,   680
And people's safety, which in part they effect;
Yet toward these thus dignified, thou oft
Amidst their highth of noon
Changest thy countenance and thy hand, with no regard
Of highest favors past   685
From thee on them, or them to thee of service.
    Nor only dost degrade them, or remit
To life obscured, which were a fair dismission,
But throw'st them lower than thou didst exalt them high,
Unseemly falls in human eye,   690
Too grievous for the trespass or omission;
Oft leav'st them to the hostile sword
Of heathen and profane, their carcasses
To dogs and fowls a prey, or else captíved,
Or to the unjust tribunals, under change of times,   695

659. lenient: soothing.
662. mood: mood and musical mode (Greek).
667 f. Ps. 8.4, Heb. 2.6, Job 7.17; cf. Seneca, *Hippolytus* 1123 f., Boethius, *Consol. Philos.* 1, met. 5.
672. angelic orders: glossary, "angels."
678. elected: chosen for special favor and service (cf. *P.L.* 3.183–84).
692–96. An apparent reference to the Restoration government's reprisals upon Commonwealth leaders — imprisonments, executions, and the exhuming and beheading of the bodies of Cromwell, Henry Ireton, and John Bradshaw in 1661.

And condemnation of the ingrateful multitude.
If these they scape, perhaps in poverty
With sickness and disease thou bow'st them down,
Painful diseases and deformed,
In crude old age;   700
Though not disordinate, yet causeless suff'ring
The punishment of dissolute days; in fine,
Just or unjust, alike seem miserable,
For oft alike, both come to evil end.
   So deal not with this once thy glorious champion,   705
The image of thy strength, and mighty minister.
What do I beg? How hast thou dealt already?
Behold him in this state calamitous, and turn
His labors, for thou canst, to peaceful end.
   But who is this, what thing of sea or land?   710
Female of sex it seems,
That so bedecked, ornate, and gay,
Comes this way sailing
Like a stately ship
Of Tarsus, bound for th' isles   715
Of Javan or Gadire,
With all her bravery on, and tackle trim,
Sails filled, and streamers waving,
Courted by all the winds that hold them play,
An amber scent of odorous perfume   720
Her harbinger, a damsel train behind;
Some rich Philistian matron she may seem,
And now at nearer view, no other certain
Than Dálila thy wife.
    Sam. My wife, my traitress, let her not come near me.   725
    Chor. Yet on she moves, now stands and eyes thee fixed,
About t' have spoke; but now, with head declined
Like a fair flower surcharged with dew, she weeps,
And words addressed seem into tears dissolved,
Wetting the borders of her silken veil;   730
But now again she makes address to speak.
   Dal. With doubtful feet and wavering resolution
I came, still dreading thy displeasure, Samson,
Which to have merited, without excuse,
I cannot but acknowledge; yet if tears   735
May expiate (though the fact more evil drew

697–700. Milton lost a large part of his savings in the first years of the Restoration, and suffered increasingly from the pains of gout.

700. crude: premature.

701–02. Even those who are not intemperate ("disordinate") suffer the pains commonly caused by dissipation.

710–22. This purple patch registers the contrast between Samson in his rags and Dalila in the finery bought with the proceeds of her betrayal. Many parallels have been suggested for Milton's nautical metaphor, e.g., Vida's *Christiad* 1.304–34 and Giles Fletcher's *Christ's Victory on Earth* 35–36.

715. The biblical Tarshish (2 Chron. 9.21; etc.) was identified with both the Cilician Tarsus (cf. *P.L.* 1.200) and a Spanish port; Milton here uses the former idea.

715–16. isles Of Javan: Greek islands (see note on *P.L.* 1.508).

716. Gadire: Cadiz.

In the perverse event than I foresaw),
My penance hath not slackened, though my pardon
No way assured. But conjugal affection,
Prevailing over fear and timorous doubt,   740
Hath led me on, desirous to behold
Once more thy face, and know of thy estate;
If aught in my ability may serve
To lighten what thou suffer'st, and appease
Thy mind with what amends is in my power,   745
Though late, yet in some part to recompense
My rash but more unfortunate misdeed.
   Sam. Out, out, hyena! These are thy wonted arts,
And arts of every woman false like thee,
To break all faith, all vows, deceive, betray;   750
Then as repentant to submit, beseech,
And reconcilement move with feigned remorse,
Confess, and promise wonders in her change,
Not truly penitent, but chief to try
Her husband, how far urged his patience bears,   755
His virtue or weakness which way to assail;
Then with more cautious and instructed skill
Again transgresses, and again submits;
That wisest and best men, full oft beguiled,
With goodness principled not to reject   760
The penitent, but ever to forgive,
Are drawn to wear out miserable days,
Entangled with a poisonous bosom snake,
If not by quick destruction soon cut off,
As I by thee, to ages an example.   765
   Dal. Yet hear me, Samson; not that I endeavor
To lessen or extenuate my offense,
But that on th' other side if it be weighed
By itself, with aggravations not surcharged,
Or else with just allowance counterpoised,   770
I may, if possible, thy pardon find
The easier towards me, or thy hatred less.
First granting, as I do, it was a weakness
In me, but incident to all our sex,
Curiosity, inquisitive, importúne   775
Of secrets, then with like infirmity
To publish them, both common female faults;
Was it not weakness also to make known
For importunity, that is for naught,
Wherein consisted all thy strength and safety?   780
To what I did thou show'dst me first the way.
But I to enemies revealed, and should not?
Nor shouldst thou have trusted that to woman's frailty:
Ere I to thee, thou to thyself wast cruel.

739–42. Cf. Euripides, *Troades* 914 f.   men by imitating the human voice and then
748. hyena: traditionally a beast that lured   devoured them.

Let weakness then with weakness come to parle,   785
So near related, or the same of kind;
Thine forgive mine, that men may censure thine
The gentler, if severely thou exact not
More strength from me than in thyself was found.
And what if love, which thou interpret'st hate,   790
The jealousy of love, powerful of sway
In human hearts, nor less in mine towards thee,
Caused what I did? I saw thee mutable
Of fancy, feared lest one day thou wouldst leave me
As her at Timna, sought by all means therefore   795
How to endear, and hold thee to me firmest:
No better way I saw than by impórtuning
To learn thy secrets, get into my power
Thy key of strength and safety. Thou wilt say,
"Why then revealed?" I was assured by those   800
Who tempted me that nothing was designed
Against thee but safe custody and hold:
That made for me; I knew that liberty
Would draw thee forth to perilous enterprises,
While I at home sat full of cares and fears,   805
Wailing thy absence in my widowed bed;
Here I should still enjoy thee day and night,
Mine and love's prisoner, not the Philistines',
Whole to myself, unhazarded abroad,
Fearless at home of partners in my love.   810
These reasons in love's law have passed for good,
Though fond and reasonless to some perhaps;
And love hath oft, well meaning, wrought much woe,
Yet always pity or pardon hath obtained.
Be not unlike all others, not austere   815
As thou art strong, inflexible as steel.
If thou in strength all mortals dost exceed,
In uncompassionate anger do not so.
    Sam. How cunningly the sorceress displays
Her own transgressions, to upbraid me mine!   820
That malice, not repentance, brought thee hither,
By this appears: I gave, thou say'st, th' example,
I led the way — bitter reproach, but true;
I to myself was false ere thou to me;
Such pardon therefore as I give my folly,   825
Take to thy wicked deed; which when thou seest
Impartial, self-severe, inexorable,
Thou wilt renounce thy seeking, and much rather
Confess it feigned. Weakness is thy excuse,
And I believe it, weakness to resist   830
Philistian gold; if weakness may excuse,
What murtherer, what traitor, parricide,
Incestuous, sacrilegious, but may plead it?

826. which: i.e. pardon.

All wickedness is weakness: that plea therefore
With God or man will gain thee no remission.   835
But love constrained thee? Call it furious rage
To satisfy thy lust: love seeks to have love;
My love how couldst thou hope, who took'st the way
To raise in me inexpiable hate,
Knowing, as needs I must, by thee betrayed?   840
In vain thou striv'st to cover shame with shame,
Or by evasions thy crime uncover'st more.
   Dal. Since thou determin'st weakness for no plea
In man or woman, though to thy own condemning,
Hear what assaults I had, what snares besides,   845
What sieges girt me round, ere I consented;
Which might have awed the best-resolved of men,
The constantest, to have yielded without blame.
It was not gold, as to my charge thou lay'st,
That wrought with me: thou know'st the magistrates   850
And princes of my country came in person,
Solicited, commanded, threatened, urged,
Adjured by all the bonds of civil duty
And of religion, pressed how just it was,
How honorable, how glorious to entrap   855
A common enemy, who had destroyed
Such numbers of our nation: and the priest
Was not behind, but ever at my ear,
Preaching how meritorious with the gods
It would be to ensnare an irreligious   860
Dishonorer of Dagon. What had I
To oppose against such powerful arguments?
Only my love of thee held long debate;
And combated in silence all these reasons
With hard contést. At length that grounded maxim,   865
So rife and celebrated in the mouths
Of wisest men, that to the public good
Private respects must yield, with grave authority
Took full possession of me and prevailed;
Virtue, as I thought, truth, duty, so enjoining,   870
   Sam. I thought where all thy circling wiles would end,
In feigned religion, smooth hypocrisy.
But had thy love, still odiously pretended,
Been, as it ought, sincere, it would have taught thee
Far other reasonings, brought forth other deeds.   875
I before all the daughters of my tribe
And of my nation chose thee from among
My enemies, loved thee, as too well thou knew'st,
Too well; unbosomed all my secrets to thee,
Not out of levity, but overpow'red   880
By thy request, who could deny thee nothing;
Yet now am judged an enemy. Why then

     857–61. The priest is not in Judges.

Didst thou at first receive me for thy husband,
Then, as since then, thy country's foe professed?
Being once a wife, for me thou wast to leave   885
Parents and country; nor was I their subject,
Nor under their protection, but my own;
Thou mine, not theirs. If aught against my life
Thy country sought of thee, it sought unjustly,
Against the law of nature, law of nations;   890
No more thy country, but an impious crew
Of men conspiring to uphold their state
By worse than hostile deeds, violating the ends
For which our country is a name so dear;
Not therefore to be obeyed. But zeal moved thee;   895
To please thy gods thou didst it; gods unable
To acquit themselves and prosecute their foes
But by ungodly deeds, the contradiction
Of their own deity, gods cannot be:
Less therefore to be pleased, obeyed, or feared.   900
These false pretexts and varnished colors failing,
Bare in thy guilt how foul must thou appear!
    Dal. In argument with men a woman ever
Goes by the worse, whatever be her cause.
    Sam. For want of words, no doubt, or lack of breath; 905
Witness when I was worried with thy peals.
    Dal. I was a fool, too rash, and quite mistaken
In what I thought would have succeeded best.
Let me obtain forgiveness of thee, Samson;
Afford me place to show what recompense   910
Towards thee I intend for what I have misdone,
Misguided; only what remains past cure
Bear not too sensibly, nor still insist
To afflict thyself in vain. Though sight be lost,
Life yet hath many solaces, enjoyed   915
Where other senses want not their delights
At home in leisure and domestic ease,
Exempt from many a care and chance to which
Eyesight exposes daily men abroad.
I to the lords will intercede, not doubting   920
Their favorable ear, that I may fetch thee
From forth this loathsome prison-house, to abide
With me, where my redoubled love and care
With nursing diligence, to me glad office,
May ever tend about thee to old age   925
With all things grateful cheered, and so supplied,
That what by me thou hast lost thou least shall miss.
    Sam. No, no, of my condition take no care;
It fits not; thou and I long since are twain;
Nor think me so unwary or accurst   930
To bring my feet again into the snare

885–86. Gen. 2.24.   913. sensibly: grievously.

Where once I have been caught; I know thy trains,
Though dearly to my cost, thy gins, and toils;
Thy fair enchanted cup and warbling charms
No more on me have power, their force is nulled; 935
So much of adder's wisdom I have learnt
To fence my ear against thy sorceries.
If in my flower of youth and strength, when all men
Loved, honored, feared me, thou alone could hate me,
Thy husband, slight me, sell me, and forgo me, 940
How wouldst thou use me now, blind, and thereby
Deceivable, in most things as a child
Helpless, thence easily contemned, and scorned,
And last neglected? How wouldst thou insult
When I must live uxorious to thy will 945
In perfect thraldom, how again betray me,
Bearing my words and doings to the lords
To gloss upon, and censuring, frown or smile?
This jail I count the house of liberty
To thine whose doors my feet shall never enter. 950
   Dal. Let me approach at least, and touch thy hand.
   Sam. Not for thy life, lest fierce remembrance wake
My sudden rage to tear thee joint by joint.
At distance I forgive thee, go with that;
Bewail thy falsehood, and the pious works 955
It hath brought forth to make thee memorable
Among illustrious women, faithful wives;
Cherish thy hastened widowhood with the gold
Of matrimonial treason: so farewell.
   Dal. I see thou art implacable, more deaf 960
To prayers than winds and seas; yet winds to seas
Are reconciled at length, and sea to shore:
Thy anger, unappeasable, still rages,
Eternal tempest never to be calmed.
Why do I humble thus myself, and suing 965
For peace, reap nothing but repulse and hate?
Bid go with evil omen and the brand
Of infamy upon my name denounced?
To mix with thy concernments I desist
Henceforth, nor too much disapprove my own. 970
Fame, if not double-faced, is double-mouthed,
And with contráry blast proclaims most deeds;
On both his wings, one black, th' other white,
Bears greatest names in his wild airy flight.
My name perhaps among the circumcised 975

933. gins: snares.
934–35. A veiled reference to Circe (the last of Milton's many allusions), perhaps including the Sirens (cf. *Comus* 252–61).
935. nulled: annulled.
936. The adder was popularly supposed to be deaf or to stop its ears (Ps. 58.4–5).
948. censuring: judging.
950. To: compared to.

951. Dalila's last effort, a direct appeal to Samson's senses, arouses him to sudden ferocity.
953. tear . . . joint: cf. *Romeo and Juliet* 5.3.35.
967–68 Cf. 955–59.
971–74. Fame: cf. *In quintum Novembris* 205–16; Chaucer, *House of Fame* 3.1572–1688.

In Dan, in Judah, and the bordering tribes,
To all posterity may stand defamed,
With malediction mentioned, and the blot
Of falsehood most unconjugal traduced.
But in my country where I most desire,   980
In Ekron, Gaza, Asdod, and in Gath,
I shall be named among the famousest
Of women, sung at solemn festivals,
Living and dead recorded, who, to save
Her country from a fierce destroyer, chose   985
Above the faith of wedlock bands; my tomb
With odors visited and annual flowers:
Not less renowned than in Mount Ephraim
Jael, who with inhospitable guile
Smote Sisera sleeping, through the temples nailed.   990
Nor shall I count it heinous to enjoy
The public marks of honor and reward
Conferred upon me, for the piety
Which to my country I was judged to have shown.
At this whoever envies or repines,   995
I leave him to his lot, and like my own.
  Chor. She's gone, a manifest serpent by her sting
Discovered in the end, till now concealed.
  Sam. So let her go; God sent her to debase me,
And aggravate my folly who committed   1000
To such a viper his most sacred trust
Of secrecy, my safety, and my life.
  Chor. Yet beauty, though injurious, hath strange power,
After offense returning, to regain
Love once possessed, nor can be easily   1005
Repulsed, without much inward passion felt
And secret sting of amorous remorse.
  Sam. Love-quarrels oft in pleasing concord end,
Not wedlock-treachery endangering life.
  Chor. It is not virtue, wisdom, valor, wit,   1010
Strength, comeliness of shape, or amplest merit
That woman's love can win or long inherit;
But what it is, hard is to say,
Harder to hit,
(Which way soever men refer it),   1015
Much like thy riddle, Samson, in one day
Or seven, though one should musing sit;
  If any of these, or all, the Timnian bride
Had not so soon preferred
Thy paranymph, worthless to thee compared,   1020
Successor in thy bed,

---

981. Ekron: Accaron (*P.L.* 1.466). For the other names, cf. *P.L.* 1.464 and note.
989–90. Jael, Sisera: Judges 4.15–22 and 5.
993. piety: in sense of Latin *pietas*.
1000. aggravate: make heavier.
1006. passion: suffering.

1008. Cf. Terence, *Andria* 555.
1012. inherit: possess.
1016. riddle: see note on 382–87.
1020. paranymph: "best man" (Judges 14.20).

Nor both so loosely disallied
Their nuptials, nor this last so treacherously
Had shorn the fatal harvest of thy head.
Is it for that such outward ornament   1025
Was lavished on their sex, that inward gifts
Were left for haste unfinished, judgment scant,
Capacity not raised to apprehend
Or value what is best
In choice, but oftest to affect the wrong?   1030
Or was too much of self-love mixed,
Of constancy no root infixed,
That either they love nothing, or not long?
    Whate'er it be, to wisest men and best
Seeming at first all heavenly under virgin veil,   1035
Soft, modest, meek, demure,
Once joined, the contrary she proves, a thorn
Intestine, far within defensive arms
A cleaving mischief, in his way to virtue
Adverse and turbulent; or by her charms   1040
Draws him awry enslaved
With dotage, and his sense depraved
To folly and shameful deeds which ruin ends.
What pilot so expert but needs must wreck,
Embarked with such a steers-mate at the helm?   1045
    Favored of Heav'n who finds
One virtuous, rarely found,
That in domestic good combines:
Happy that house! his way to peace is smooth;
But virtue which breaks through all opposition,   1050
And all temptation can remove,
Most shines and most is ácceptáble above.
    Therefore God's universal law
Gave to the man despotic power
Over his female in due awe,   1055
Nor from that right to part an hour,
Smile she or lour:
So shall he least confusion draw
On his whole life, not swayed
By female usurpation, nor dismayed.   1060
    But had we best retire? I see a storm.
    Sam. Fair days have oft contracted wind and rain.
    Chor. But this another kind of tempest brings.
    Sam. Be less abstruse, my riddling days are past.
    Chor. Look now for no enchanting voice, nor fear   1065
The bait of honied words; a rougher tongue

1022. both: the Timnian bride and Dalila.
1025. for that: because.
1034 f. Cf. Milton, *Doctrine and Discipline of Divorce* 1.3 (*Works*, 3, 2, 394–95); Euripides, *Hippolytus* 616 f.
1046–49. Prov. 12.4, 31.10–28.

1053 f. 1 Cor. 11.9; 1 Tim. 2.12; Eph. 5.22–23. Cf. *P.L.* 4.295–99, 635–38, 9.1182–86, 10.145–56, 888–909.
1062. contracted: brought.
1064. riddling days: see note on 382–87.

Draws hitherward; I know him by his stride,
The giant Harapha of Gath, his look
Haughty as is his pile high-built and proud.
Comes he in peace? What wind hath blown him hither   1070
I less conjecture than when first I saw
The sumptuous Dálila floating this way;
His habit carries peace, his brow defiance.
    Sam. Or peace or not, alike to me he comes.
    Chor. His fraught we soon shall know, he now arrives.   1075
    Harapha. I come not, Samson, to condole thy chance,
As these perhaps, yet wish it had not been,
Though for no friendly intent. I am of Gath;
Men call me Harapha, of stock renowned
As Og or Anak and the Emims old   1080
That Kiriathaim held; thou know'st me now,
If thou at all art known. Much I have heard
Of thy prodigious might and feats performed
Incredible to me, in this displeased,
That I was never present on the place   1085
Of those encounters where we might have tried
Each other's force in camp or listed field:
And now am come to see of whom such noise
Hath walked about, and each limb to survey,
If thy appearance answer loud report.   1090
    Sam. The way to know were not to see but taste.
    Har. Dost thou already single me? I thought
Gyves and the mill had tamed thee. O that fortune
Had brought me to the field where thou art famed
To have wrought such wonders with an ass's jaw;   1095
I should have forced thee soon wish other arms,
Or left thy carcass where the ass lay thrown:
So had the glory of prowess been recovered
To Palestine, won by a Philistine
From the unforeskinned race, of whom thou bear'st   1100
The highest name for valiant acts; that honor,
Certain to have won by mortal duel from thee.
I lose, prevented by thy eyes put out.
    Sam. Boast not of what thou wouldst have done, but do
What then thou wouldst; thou seest it in thy hand.   1105
    Har. To combat with a blind man I disdain,
And thou hast need much washing to be touched.
    Sam. Such usage as your honorable lords

1068 f. Harapha (the name means "the giant") is apparently Milton's invention and addition to the story, but is based on the biblical Goliath (1 Sam. 17.23–51; 2 Sam. 21.16–22; 1 Chron. 20.4–8).
1075. fraught: freight, business.
1077. these: the chorus.
1080. Anak: see note on 528.   Emims: a giant people east of the Jordan (Gen. 14.5, Deut. 2.10–11).

1081–82. thou . . . known: cf. *P.L.* 4.830.
1087. camp: field (of battle).   listed: cf. 463 and note.
1092. single: challenge.
1096. The word "wish" of seventeenth-century editions was first changed to "with" in Tonson's 1720 edition; the emendation seems unwarranted.

Afford me, assassinated and betrayed;
Who durst not with their whole united powers   1110
In fight withstand me single and unarmed,
Nor in the house with chamber ambushes
Close-banded durst attack me, no, not sleeping,
Till they had hired a woman with their gold,
Breaking her marriage faith, to circumvent me.   1115
Therefore without feigned shifts let be assigned
Some narrow place enclosed, where sight may give thee,
Or rather flight, no great advantage on me;
Then put on all thy gorgeous arms, thy helmet
And brigandine of brass, thy broad habergeon,   1120
Vant-brace and greaves, and gauntlet; add thy spear,
A weaver's beam, and seven-times-folded shield;
I only with an oaken staff will meet thee,
And raise such outcries on thy clattered iron,
Which long shall not withhold me from thy head,   1125
That in a little time while breath remains thee,
Thou oft shalt wish thyself at Gath to boast
Again in safety what thou wouldst have done
To Samson, but shalt never see Gath more.
  Har. Thou durst not thus disparage glorious arms   1130
Which greatest heroes have in battle worn,
Their ornament and safety, had not spells
And black enchantments, some magician's art,
Armed thee or charmed thee strong, which thou from Heaven
Feign'dst at thy birth was giv'n thee in thy hair,   1135
Where strength can least abide, though all thy hairs
Were bristles ranged like those that ridge the back
Of chafed wild boars, or ruffled porcupines.
  Sam. I know no spells, use no forbidden arts;
My trust is in the living God who gave me   1140
At my nativity this strength, diffused
No less through all my sinews, joints and bones,
Than thine, while I preserved these locks unshorn,
The pledge of my unviolated vow.
For proof hereof, if Dagon be thy god,   1145
Go to his temple, invocate his aid
With solemnest devotion, spread before him
How highly it concerns his glory now
To frustrate and dissolve these magic spells,
Which I to be the power of Israel's God   1150
Avow, and challenge Dagon to the test,

1109. assassinated: treacherously attacked.
1120. brigandine: tunic covered with metal
plates.   habergeon: coat of mail for upper
part of body.
  1121. Vant-brace: armor for the forearm.
  1122. weaver's beam. This and some other
details come from the account of Goliath (1
Sam. 17.5–7).
  1122. The kind of shield especially asso-

ciated with Ajax (*Iliad* 7.220; Ovid, *Met.* 13.2,
347).
  1137–38. Cf. *Iliad* 13.473; *Hamlet* 1.5.19–
20.
  1139 f. Samson's grand affirmation transcends the oath taken before medieval combats
by contestants who swore that they used no
magic but trusted only in God.

Offering to combat thee, his champion bold,
With th' utmost of his godhead seconded:
Then thou shalt see, or rather to thy sorrow
Soon feel, whose God is strongest, thine or mine.   1155
   Har. Presume not on thy God, whate'er he be;
Thee he regards not, owns not, hath cut off
Quite from his people, and delivered up
Into thy enemies' hand; permitted them
To put out both thine eyes, and fettered send thee   1160
Into the common prison, there to grind
Among the slaves and asses, thy comrádes,
As good for nothing else, no better service
With those thy boist'rous locks; no worthy match
For valor to assail, nor by the sword   1165
Of noble warrior, so to stain his honor,
But by the barber's razor best subdued.
   Sam. All these indignities, for such they are
From thine, these evils I deserve and more,
Acknowledge them from God inflicted on me   1170
Justly, yet despair not of his final pardon
Whose ear is ever open, and his eye
Gracious to readmit the suppliant;
In confidence whereof I once again
Defy thee to the trial of mortal fight,   1175
By combat to decide whose god is God,
Thine or whom I with Israel's sons adore.
   Har. Fair honor that thou dost thy God, in trusting
He will accept thee to defend his cause,
A murtherer, a revolter, and a robber.   1180
   Sam. Tongue-doughty giant, how dost thou prove me these?
   Har. Is not thy nation subject to our lords?
Their magistrates confessed it, when they took thee
As a league-breaker and delivered bound
Into our hands: for hadst thou not committed   1185
Notorious murder on those thirty men
At Ascalon, who never did thee harm,
Then like a robber stripp'dst them of their robes?
The Philistines, when thou hadst broke the league,
Went up with armèd powers thee only seeking,   1190
To others did no violence nor spoil.
   Sam. Among the daughters of the Philistines
I chose a wife, which argued me no foe,
And in your city held my nuptial feast;
But your ill-meaning politician lords,   1195
Under pretense of bridal friends and guests,
Appointed to await me thirty spies,

1168 f. Perhaps the most impressive testimony to Samson's renewed faith is this humble
confession to a contemptuous enemy.
  1169. thine: thy people.

1185–1204. Judges 14.
  1192–93. See however 224–26, 231–33,
and Judges 14.4.

Who threat'ning cruel death constrained the bride
To wring from me and tell to them my secret,
That solved the riddle which I had proposed.   1200
When I perceived all set on enmity,
As on my enemies, wherever chanced,
I used hostility, and took their spoil
To pay my underminers in their coin.
My nation was subjected to your lords?   1205
It was the force of conquest; force with force
Is well ejected when the conquered can.
But I a private person, whom my country
As a league-breaker gave up bound, presumed
Single rebellion and did hostile acts?   1210
I was no private but a person raised
With strength sufficient and command from Heav'n
To free my country; if their servile minds
Me their deliverer sent would not receive,
But to their masters gave me up for naught,   1215
Th' unworthier they; whence to this day they serve.
I was to do my part from Heav'n assigned,
And had performed it if my known offense
Had not disabled me, not all your force.
These shifts refuted, answer thy appellant,   1220
Though by his blindness maimed for high attempts,
Who now defies thee thrice to single fight,
As a petty enterprise of small enforce.
  Har. With thee, a man condemned, a slave enrolled,
Due by the law to capital punishment?   1225
To fight with thee no man of arms will deign.
  Sam. Cam'st thou for this, vain boaster, to survey me,
To descant on my strength, and give thy verdict?
Come nearer, part not hence so slight informed;
But take good heed my hand survey not thee.   1230
  Har. O Baal-zebub! can my ears unused
Hear these dishonors, and not render death?
  Sam. No man withholds thee, nothing from thy hand
Fear I incurable; bring up thy van;
My heels are fettered, but my fist is free.   1235
  Har. This insolence other kind of answer fits.
  Sam. Go, baffled coward, lest I run upon thee,
Though in these chains, bulk without spirit vast,
And with one buffet lay thy structure low,
Or swing thee in the air, then dash thee down   1240
To the hazard of thy brains and shattered sides.
  Har. By Astaroth, ere long thou shalt lament

1208 f. A main question of Renaissance
political thought was that of resistance to civil
authority, the sovereign. Calvin, while enjoining general obedience, allowed for resistance by duly constituted magistrates.
  1218. offense: revealing his secret to Dalila.

1223. enforce: effort.
1228. descant: comment at length.
1231. Baal-zebub: the Fly-god (glossary,
"Baal").
1237. baffled: disgraced.

These braveries in irons loaden on thee.
    Chor. His giantship is gone somewhat crestfall'n,
Stalking with less unconscionable strides,   1245
And lower looks, but in a sultry chafe.
    Sam. I dread him not, nor all his giant brood,
Though fame divulge him father of five sons,
All of gigantic size, Goliah chief.
    Chor. He will directly to the lords, I fear,   1250
And with malicious counsel stir them up
Some way or other yet further to afflict thee.
    Sam. He must allege some cause, and offered fight
Will not dare mention, lest a question rise
Whether he durst accept the offer or not,   1255
And that he durst not plain enough appeared.
Much more affliction than already felt
They cannot well impose, nor I sustain,
If they intend advantage of my labors,
The work of many hands, which earns my keeping   1260
With no small profit daily to my owners.
But come what will, my deadliest foe will prove
My speediest friend, by death to rid me hence,
The worst that he can give, to me the best.
Yet so it may fall out, because their end   1265
Is hate, not help to me, it may with mine
Draw their own ruin who attempt the deed.
    Chor. Oh how comely it is and how reviving
To the spirits of just men long oppressed,
When God into the hands of their deliverer   1270
Puts invincible might
To quell the mighty of the earth, th' oppressor,
The brute and boist'rous force of violent men,
Hardy and industrious to support
Tyrannic power, but raging to pursue   1275
The righteous and all such as honor truth!
He all their ammunition
And feats of war defeats
With plain heroic magnitude of mind
And celestial vigor armed;   1280
Their armories and magazines contemns,
Renders them useless, while
With winged expedition
Swift as the lightning glance he executes
His errand on the wicked, who surprised   1285
Lose their defense, distracted and amazed.
    But patience is more oft the exercise
Of saints, the trial of their fortitude,

1245. unconscionable: excessive.
1249. Goliah: Goliath, the giant killed by David (1 Sam. 17.4 f.; 2 Sam. 21.20–22).
1279–80. The two sources of Samson's re-

newed strength. In Heb. 11.32 f. he is listed among Hebrew heroes "Who through faith subdued kingdoms," etc.

Making them each his own deliverer,   *(idea of eventual victory)*
And victor over all   1290
That tyranny or fortune can inflict;
Either of these is in thy lot,
Samson, with might endued
Above the sons of men; but sight bereaved
May chance to number thee with those   1295
Whom patience finally must crown.
 This Idol's day hath been to thee no day of rest,
Laboring thy mind
More than the working day thy hands;
And yet perhaps more trouble is behind.   1300
For I descry this way
Some other tending; in his hand
A scepter or quaint staff he bears,
Comes on amain, speed in his look.
By his habit I discern him now   1305
A public officer, and now at hand.
His message will be short and voluble.
 Off. Hebrews, the pris'ner Samson here I seek.   *(Officer)*
 Chor. His manacles remark him; there he sits.
 Off. Samson, to thee our lords thus bid me say: 1310
This day to Dagon is a solemn feast,
With sacrifices, triumph, pomp, and games;
Thy strength they know surpassing human rate,
And now some public proof thereof require
To honor this great feast, and great assembly;   1315
Rise therefore with all speed and come along,
Where I will see thee heartened and fresh clad
To appear as fits before th' illustrious lords.
11. *Sam.* Thou know'st I am an Hebrew, therefore tell them
Our Law forbids at their religious rites   1320
My presence; for that cause I cannot come.
 Off. This answer, be assured, will not content them.
 Sam. Have they not sword-players, and ev'ry sort
Of gymnic artists, wrestlers, riders, runners,
Jugglers and dancers, antics, mummers, mimics,   1325
But they must pick me out with shackles tired,
And over-labored at their public mill,
To make them sport with blind activity?
Do they not seek occasion of new quarrels,
On my refusal, to distress me more,   1330
Or make a game of my calamities?
Return the way thou cam'st; I will not come.
 Off. Regard thyself; this will offend them highly.
 Sam. Myself? My conscience and internal peace.
Can they think me so broken, so debased   1335

1307. voluble: rapid.   1325. antics: clowns.   mummers: actors
1309. remark him: mark him out.   in dumb shows, etc.

With corporal servitude, that my mind ever
Will condescend to such absurd commands?
Although their drudge, to be their fool or jester,
And in my midst of sorrow and heart-grief
To show them feats and play before their god,   1340
The worst of all indignities, yet on me
Joined with extreme contempt? I will not come.
    Off. My message was imposed on me with speed,
Brooks no delay; is this thy resolution?
    Sam. So take it with what speed thy message needs.   1345
    Off. I am sorry what this stoutness will produce.
    Sam. Perhaps thou shalt have cause to sorrow indeed.
    Chor. Consider, Samson; matters now are strained
Up to the highth, whether to hold or break;
He's gone, and who knows how he may report   1350
Thy words by adding fuel to the flame?
Expect another message more imperious,
More lordly thund'ring than thou well wilt bear.
    Sam. Shall I abuse this consecrated gift
Of strength, again returning with my hair   1355
After my great transgression, so requite
Favor renewed, and add a greater sin
By prostituting holy things to idols;
A Nazarite in place abominable
Vaunting my strength in honor to their Dagon?   1360
Besides, how vile, contemptible, ridiculous,
What act more execrably unclean, profane?
    Chor. Yet with this strength thou serv'st the Philistines,
Idolatrous, uncircumcised, unclean.
    Sam. Not in their idol-worship, but by labor   1365
Honest and lawful to deserve my food
Of those who have me in their civil power.
    Chor. Where the heart joins not, outward acts defile not.
    Sam. Where outward force constrains, the sentence holds;
But who constrains me to the temple of Dagon,   1370
Not dragging? The Philistian lords command.
Commands are no constraints. If I obey them,
I do it freely, venturing to displease
God for the fear of man, and man prefer,
Set God behind; which in his jealousy   1375
Shall never, unrepented, find forgiveness.
Yet that he may dispense with me or thee,
Present in temples at idolatrous rites
For some important cause, thou need'st not doubt.
    Chor. How thou wilt here come off surmounts my reach.   1380
    Sam. Be of good courage; I begin to feel
Some rousing motions in me which dispose
To something extraordinary my thoughts.

12

1342. joined: enjoined.   1377. dispense with: grant dispensation,
1355. Judges 16.22.   permission.

I with this messenger will go along,
Nothing to do, be sure, that may dishonor   1385
Our Law, or stain my vow of Nazarite.
If there be aught of presage in the mind,
This day will be remarkable in my life
By some great act, or of my days the last.
    Chor. In time thou hast resolved; the man returns.   1390
    Off. Samson, this second message from our lords
To thee I am bid say: art thou our slave,
Our captive, at the public mill our drudge,
And dar'st thou at our sending and command
Dispute thy coming? Come without delay;   1395
Or we shall find such engines to assail
And hamper thee, as thou shalt come of force,
Though thou wert firmlier fastened than a rock.
    Sam. I could be well content to try their art,
Which to no few of them would prove pernicious.   1400
Yet knowing their advantages too many,
Because they shall not trail me through their streets
Like a wild beast, I am content to go.
Masters' commands come with a power resistless
To such as owe them absolute subjection;   1405
And for a life who will not change his purpose?
(So mutable are all the ways of men.)
Yet this be sure, in nothing to comply
Scandalous or forbidden in our Law.
    Off. I praise thy resolution; doff these links.   1410
By this compliance thou wilt win the lords
To favor, and perhaps to set thee free.
    Sam. Brethren, farewell; your company along
I will not wish, lest it perhaps offend them
To see me girt with friends; and how the sight   1415
Of me as of a common enemy,
So dreaded once, may now exasperate them,
I know not. Lords are lordliest in their wine;
And the well-feasted priest then soonest fired
With zeal, if aught religion seem concerned;   1420
No less the people on their holy-days
Impetuous, insolent, unquenchable;
Happen what may, of me expect to hear
Nothing dishonorable, impure, unworthy
Our God, our Law, my nation, or myself;   1425
The last of me or no I cannot warrant.
    Chor. Go, and the Holy One
Of Israel be thy guide
To what may serve his glory best, and spread his name
Great among the heathen round;   1430
Send thee the angel of thy birth, to stand

1388–89. Cf. Sophocles, *Trachiniae* 79–81.
1399–1409. Samson professes plausible reasons for compliance; his real reasons are quite
different.

Fast by thy side, who from thy father's field
Rode up in flames after his message told
Of thy conception, and be now a shield
Of fire; that spirit that first rushed on thee   1435
In the camp of Dan,
Be efficacious in thee now at need.
For never was from Heaven imparted
Measure of strength so great to mortal seed,
As in thy wondrous actions hath been seen.   1440
But wherefore comes old Manoa in such haste
With youthful steps? Much livelier than erewhile
He seems: supposing here to find his son,
Or of him bringing to us some glad news?
   Man. Peace with you, brethren; my inducement hither   1445
Was not at present here to find my son,
By order of the lords new parted hence
To come and play before them at their feast.
I heard all as I came, the city rings,
And numbers thither flock; I had no will,   1450
Lest I should see him forced to things unseemly.
But that which moved my coming now was chiefly
To give ye part with me what hope I have
With good success to work his liberty.
   Chor. That hope would much rejoice us to partake   1455
With thee; say, reverend sire; we thirst to hear.
   Man. I have attempted one by one the lords,
Either at home, or through the high street passing,
With supplication prone and father's tears
To accept of ransom for my son their pris'ner.   1460
Some much averse I found and wondrous harsh,
Contemptuous, proud, set on revenge and spite;
That part most reverenced Dagon and his priests;
Others more moderate seeming, but their aim
Private reward, for which both God and State   1465
They easily would set to sale; a third
More generous far and civil, who confessed
They had enough revenged, having reduced
Their foe to misery beneath their fears;
The rest was magnanimity to remit,   1470
If some convenient ransom were proposed.
What noise or shout was that? It tore the sky.
   Chor. Doubtless the people shouting to behold
Their once great dread, captive and blind before them,
Or at some proof of strength before them shown.   1475
   Man. His ransom, if my whole inheritance
May compass it, shall willingly be paid

1435–36. Judges 13.25.
1452 f. See note on 481 f. Manoa's hope of success (1452 f., 1476 f., 1490 f.) is that "false dawn" which in some Greek tragedies precedes the catastrophe.

1461–71. Parallel attitudes were shown by Restoration leaders toward leaders of the Commonwealth, perhaps toward Milton himself; such attitudes of course have appeared after any revolution.

And numbered down; much rather I shall choose
To live the poorest in my tribe, than richest,
And he in that calamitous prison left.   1480
No, I am fixed not to part hence without him.
For his redemption all my patrimony,
If need be, I am ready to forgo
And quit; not wanting him, I shall want nothing.
   Chor. Fathers are wont to lay up for their sons,   1485
Thou for thy son art bent to lay out all;
Sons wont to nurse their parents in old age,
Thou in old age car'st how to nurse thy son,
Made older than thy age through eyesight lost.
   Man. It shall be my delight to tend his eyes,   1490
And view him sitting in the house, ennobled
With all those high exploits by him achieved,
And on his shoulders waving down those locks
That of a nation armed the strength contained.
And I persuade me God had not permitted   1495
His strength again to grow up with his hair
Garrisoned round about him like a camp
Of faithful soldiery, were not his purpose
To use him further yet in some great service,
Not to sit idle with so great a gift   1500
Useless, and thence ridiculous, about him.
And since his strength with eyesight was not lost,
God will restore him eyesight to his strength.
   Chor. Thy hopes are not ill-founded nor seem vain
Of his delivery, and thy joy thereon   1505
Conceived, agreeable to a father's love;
In both which we, as next, participate.
   Man. I know your friendly minds and — O what noise!
Mercy of Heav'n, what hideous noise was that!
Horribly loud, unlike the former shout.   1510
   Chor. Noise call you it, or universal groan,
As if the whole inhabitation perished?
Blood, death, and dreadful deeds are in that noise,
Ruin, destruction at the utmost point.
   Man. Of ruin indeed methought I heard the noise.   1515
Oh it continues, they have slain my son.
   Chor. Thy son is rather slaying them; that outcry
From slaughter of one foe could not ascend.
   Man. Some dismal accident it needs must be;
What shall we do, stay here or run and see?   1520
   Chor. Best keep together here, lest running thither
We unawares run into danger's mouth.
This evil on the Philistines is fall'n;
From whom could else a general cry be heard?
The sufferers then will scarce molest us here;   1525
From other hands we need not much to fear.

1503. to: in addition to.   1512. inhabitation: population.

What if his eyesight (for to Israel's God
Nothing is hard) by miracle restored,
He now be dealing dole among his foes,
And over heaps of slaughtered walk his way?　　　　　1530
　　Man. That were a joy presumptuous to be thought.
　　Chor. Yet God hath wrought things as incredible
For his people of old; what hinders now?
　　Man. He can, I know, but doubt to think he will;
Yet hope would fain subscribe, and tempts belief.　　　1535
A little stay will bring some notice hither.
　　Chor. Of good or bad so great, of bad the sooner;
For evil news rides post, while good news baits.
And to our wish I see one hither speeding,
An Hebrew, as I guess, and of our tribe.　　　　　　1540
　　Messenger. O whither shall I run, or which way fly
The sight of this so horrid spectacle
Which erst my eyes beheld and yet behold?
For dire imagination still pursues me.
But providence or instinct of nature seems,　　　　　1545
Or reason, though disturbed and scarce consulted,
To have guided me aright, I know not how,
To thee first, reverend Manoa, and to these
My countrymen, whom here I knew remaining,
As at some distance from the place of horror,　　　　1550
So in the sad event too much concerned.
　　Man. The accident was loud, and here before thee
With rueful cry, yet what it was we hear not;
No preface needs, thou seest we long to know.
　　Mess. It would burst forth; but I recover breath　　1555
And sense distract, to know well what I utter.
　　Man. Tell us the sum, the circumstance defer.
　　Mess. Gaza yet stands, but all her sons are fall'n,
All in a moment overwhelmed and fall'n.
　　Man. Sad, but thou know'st to Israelites not saddest　1560
The desolation of a hostile city.
　　Mess. Feed on that first, there may in grief be surfeit.
　　Man. Relate by whom.
　　Mess.　　　　　　　By Samson.
　　Man.　　　　　　　　　　　　That still lessens
The sorrow, and converts it nigh to joy.
　　Mess. Ah, Manoa, I refrain, too suddenly　　　　　1565
To utter what will come at last too soon;
Lest evil tidings, with too rude irruption
Hitting thy aged ear, should pierce too deep.
　　Man. Suspense in news is torture, speak them out.
　　Mess. Then take the worst in brief: Samson is dead.　1570
　　Man. The worst indeed! O all my hope's defeated
To free him hence! But Death who sets all free

　1529. dole: a "gift" or "portion" and　　　1538. baits: pauses (to feed a horse).
"pain."　　　　　　　　　　　　　　　　　　1570. Cf. Sophocles, *Electra* 673.

Hath paid his ransom now and full discharge.
With windy joy this day had I conceived,
Hopeful of his delivery, which now proves   1575
Abortive as the first-born bloom of spring
Nipped with the lagging rear of winter's frost.
Yet ere I give the reins to grief, say first,
How died he? Death to life is crown or shame.
All by him fell, thou say'st; by whom fell he,   1580
What glorious hand gave Samson his death's wound?
    Mess. Unwounded of his enemies he fell.
    Man. Wearied with slaughter then, or how? Explain.
    Mess. By his own hands.
    Man.   Self-violence? What cause
Brought him so soon at variance with himself   1585
Among his foes?
    Mess.   Inevitable cause
At once both to destroy and be destroyed;
The edifice where all were met to see him,
Upon their heads and on his own he pulled.
    Man. O lastly over-strong against thyself!   1590
A dreadful way thou took'st to thy revenge.
More than enough we know; but while things yet
Are in confusion, give us, if thou canst,
Eye-witness of what first or last was done,
Relation more particular and distinct.   1595
    Mess. Occasions drew me early to this city,
And as the gates I entered with sunrise,
The morning trumpets festival proclaimed
Through each high street. Little I had despatched
When all abroad was rumored that this day   1600
Samson should be brought forth to show the people
Proof of his mighty strength in feats and games;
I sorrowed at his captive state, but minded
Not to be absent at that spectacle.
The building was a spacious theater   1605
Half round on two main pillars vaulted high,
With seats where all the lords, and each degree
Of sort, might sit in order to behold;
The other side was open, where the throng
On banks and scaffolds under sky might stand;   1610
I among these aloof obscurely stood.
The feast and noon grew high, and sacrifice
Had filled their hearts with mirth, high cheer, and wine,
When to their sports they turned. Immediately
Was Samson as a public servant brought,   1615
In their state livery clad; before him pipes
And timbrels; on each side went armèd guards,
Both horse and foot before him and behind

1576–77 Cf. *Love's Labor's Lost*   1608. sort: rank.
1.1.100–01.   1610. banks: benches.

Archers, and slingers, cataphracts and spears.
At sight of him the people with a shout   1620
Rifted the air, clamoring their god with praise,
Who had made their dreadful enemy their thrall.
He, patient but undaunted, where they led him,
Came to the place; and what was set before him,
Which without help of eye might be assayed,   1625
To heave, pull, draw, or break, he still performed,
All with incredible, stupendious force,
None daring to appear antagonist.
At length for intermission sake they led him
Between the pillars; he his guide requested   1630
(For so from such as nearer stood we heard),
As over-tired, to let him lean a while
Wtih both his arms on those two massy pillars
That to the archèd roof gave main support.
He unsuspicious led him; which when Samson   1635
Felt in his arms, with head a while inclined,
And eyes fast fixed he stood, as one who prayed,
Or some great matter in his mind revolved.
At last with head erect thus cried aloud:
"Hitherto, Lords, what your commands imposed   1640
I have performed, as reason was, obeying,
Not without wonder or delight beheld.
Now of my own accord such other trial
I mean to show you of my strength, yet greater,
As with amaze shall strike all who behold."   1645
This uttered, straining all his nerves he bowed;
As with the force of winds and waters pent
When mountains tremble, those two massy pillars
Wtih horrible convulsion to and fro
He tugged, he shook, till down they came and drew   1650
The whole roof after them, with burst of thunder
Upon the heads of all who sat beneath,
Lords, ladies, captains, counselors, or priests,
Their choice nobility and flower, not only
Of this but each Philistian city round,   1655
Met from all parts to solemnize this feast.
Samson, with these inmixed, inevitably
Pulled down the same destruction on himself;
The vulgar only scaped who stood without.
  Chor. O dearly bought revenge, yet glorious!   1660
Living or dying thou hast fulfilled
The work for which thou wast foretold
To Israel, and now li'st victorious
Among thy slain self-killed,

1619. cataphracts: armored men on armored horses.
1637–38. Milton alters the account in
Judges 16.28 f.
1647–48. Cf. *P.L.* 1.230–32, 6.195–98.

1664–67. Samson is cleared of the sin of
suicide (cf. Augustine, *City of God* 1.20);
among those who held otherwise was Donne,
Biathanatos 3.5.4.

Not willingly, but tangled in the fold   1665
Of dire necessity, whose law in death conjoined
Thee with thy slaughtered foes, in number more
Than all thy life had slain before.
 Semichor. While their hearts were jocund and sublime,
Drunk with idolatry, drunk with wine,   1670
And fat regorged of bulls and goats,
Chanting their idol, and preferring
Before our living Dread who dwells
In Silo, his bright sanctuary,
Among them he a spirit of frenzy sent,   1675
Who hurt their minds,
And urged them on with mad desire
To call in haste for their destroyer;
They only set on sport and play
Unweetingly importuned   1680
Their own destruction to come speedy upon them.
So fond are mortal men
Fall'n into wrath divine,   *revenge*
As their own ruin on themselves to invite,
Insensate left, or to sense reprobate,   1685
And with blindness internal struck.
 Semichor. But he, though blind of sight,
Despised and thought extinguished quite,
With inward eyes illuminated,
His fiery virtue roused   1690
From under ashes into sudden flame,
And as an ev'ning dragon came,
Assailant on the perchèd roosts
And nests in order ranged
Of tame villatic fowl; but as an eagle   1695
His cloudless thunder bolted on their heads.
So virtue, giv'n for lost,
Depressed, and overthrown, as seemed,
Like that self-begotten bird
In the Arabian woods embost,   1700
That no second knows nor third,
And lay erewhile a holocaust,
From out her ashy womb now teemed,
Revives, reflourishes, then vigorous most
When most unactive deemed,   1705
And though her body die, her fame survives,

1667–68. Judges 16.30.
1671. regorged: greedily devoured.
1674. Silo: Shiloh, west of the Jordan, where the Israelites set up the Ark of the Covenant (Joshua 18.1).
1675–83. Cf. Milton, *C.D.* 1.4 (*Works*, 14, 172–75), where he quotes the *Odyssey* 1.32–34.
1676. hurt their minds: a phrase used of Zeus, e.g. *Iliad* 15.724.

1686. blindness internal: cf. 418.
1692. dragon: serpent.
1695. villatic: domestic, barnyard.
1699. bird: glossary, "phoenix." The image (carried on from 1691) is apparently not here a Christian symbol of resurrection but is limited to human regeneration and earthly fame.
1700. embost: hidden in the woods, "imbosked."
1702. holocaust: a sacrifice burnt whole.

A secular bird, ages of lives.
    Man. Come, come, no time for lamentation now,
Nor much more cause; Samson hath quit himself
Like Samson, and heroicly hath finished   1710
A life heroic, on his enemies
Fully revenged; hath left them years of mourning,
And lamentation to the sons of Caphtor
Through all Philistian bounds. To Israel
Honor hath left, and freedom — let but them   1715
Find courage to lay hold on this occasion;
To himself and father's house eternal fame;
And, which is best and happiest yet, all this
With God not parted from him, as was feared,
But favoring and assisting to the end.   1720
Nothing is here for tears, nothing to wail
Or knock the breast, no weakness, no contempt,
Dispraise, or blame; nothing but well and fair,
And what may quiet us in a death so noble.
Let us go find the body where it lies   1725
Soaked in his enemies' blood, and from the stream
With lavers pure and cleansing herbs wash off
The clotted gore. I with what speed the while
(Gaza is not in plight to say us nay)
Will send for all my kindred, all my friends,   1730
To fetch him hence and solemnly attend
With silent obsequy and funeral train
Home to his father's house: there will I build him
A monument, and plant it round with shade
Of laurel ever green, and branching palm,   1735
With all his trophies hung, and acts enrolled
In copious legend, or sweet lyric song.
Thither shall all the valiant youth resort,
And from his memory inflame their breasts
To matchless valor and adventures high;   1740
The virgins also shall on feastful days
Visit his tomb with flowers, only bewailing
His lot unfortunate in nuptial choice,
From whence captivity and loss of eyes.
    Chor. All is best, though we oft doubt,   1745
What th' unsearchable dispose
Of Highest Wisdom brings about,
And ever best found in the close.
Oft he seems to hide his face,
But unexpectedly returns   1750

1707. secular: lasting for ages (cf. Claudian, *Phoenix* 104–05: *te saecula teste/cuncta revolvuntur*).
    1709. quit: acquitted himself, acted (with suggestion of "ended").
    1713. Caphtor: the Philistines' original home (of uncertain location).
    1721–22. Cf. Tacitus on the dead Agricola's virtues, *quas neque lugeri neque plangi fas est* (*Agricola* 46).
    1730–33. Judges 16.31.
    1733 f. Cf. Dalila, 986 f.
    1745 f. Cf. the conclusion of Euripides' *Alcestis, Bacchae*, etc.
    1749. Ps. 27.9.

And to his faithful champion hath in place
Bore witness gloriously; whence Gaza mourns,
And all that band them to resist
His uncontrollable intent:
His servants he, with new acquist   1755
Of true experience from this great event,
With peace and consolation hath dismissed,
And calm of mind, all passion spent.

(1660?–1670)

1751. in place: at the right place and time.
1752. whence Gaza mourns. Cf. Aeschylus,
Persians 511–12.

1755. acquist: acquisition.
1756. Cf. *P.L.* 1.118.
1758. Cf. Milton's preface to *S.A.*

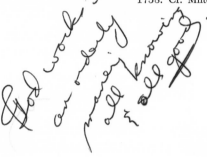

GLOSSARY

Aaron: Moses' brother, first high priest of the Israelites.

Abdiel. The name ("servant of God") is biblical (1 Chron. 5.15) but is not that of an angel.

abortive: unformed, monstrous, sterile.

Academe, Academy: Plato's Academy at Athens.

Acheron: a river in Hades; Hades itself.

admiration, admire: wonder.

Adonis: (1) a youth loved by Venus, who, when he was killed by a boar, caused the anemone to spring from his blood; his death and revival were celebrated in seasonal rites; (2) a river, rising in Lebanon, reddened by the earth in spring floods; (3) a legendary Garden of Adonis mentioned, along with that of Alcinous (q.v.), by Pliny, *Nat. Hist.* 19.49 (cf. Spenser, *F.Q.* 3.6).

adust(ed): dried, burnt by heat.

Aeolus: god of the winds, grandson of Hippotes.

Aeson: aged king restored to vigor when Medea boiled him in Thessalian herbs and juices.

afflicted: overthrown.

alablaster: alabaster.

alarmed: on guard, armed.

Albion: a son of Neptune and legendary king of Britain who gave the land his own name and who crossed over to Gaul to fight with Hercules. Cf. Milton, *Works,* 10, 4; Spenser, *F.Q.* 4.11.16.

Alcides: Hercules, grandson of Alceus.

Alcinous: king of Phaeacia who entertained Odysseus and whose gardens are described in the *Odyssey* 7.112 f.

Alp: any high mountain.

Alphéus: a river of Arcadia in Greece, a symbol of pastoral verse; the river god who loved Arethusa.

amain: with force or haste; greatly.

amarant(hus): an imaginary unfading flower; a crown of amaranthus was sometimes taken as symbolizing the heavenly reward of a righteous life (cf. 1 Pet. 1.4, 5.4).

amber: amber-colored; a metal alloy; of ambergris, used in perfumery and cooking.

amiable: lovely, lovable.

Ammon: Egyptian deity represented as a ram; identified with Jupiter.

Ammon, Ammonite: a nation east of the Jordan.

amuse: bewilder, daze.

angels. In medieval tradition there were nine orders: Seraphim, Cherubim, Thrones; Dominations, Virtues, Powers; Principalities, Archangels, Angels. Milton does not use the titles strictly; about two thirds of his angelic names are in the Bible and Apocrypha.

antic (antique): ornamented, old-fashioned, grotesque; a buffoon.

Aonia: part of Boeotia representing Mount Helicon and its fountains, associated with the Muses.

Apollo: born in Delos; god of the sun, of music, poetry, prophecy, and healing; slayer of the Python; lover of Daphne and of Hyacinthus; driver of the sun-chariot daily across the heavens from east to west.

Aquilo: the north or northeast wind.

Arcadia, Arcady: a region in southern Greece; the ideal pastoral world.

Arethusa: a nymph loved by Alpheus (q.v.) and changed into a Sicilian fountain; a symbol of pastoral verse.

argument: subject, theme; emblem.

Argus: the hundred-eyed son of Arestor set by Juno as a spy upon Io, whom she changed into a heifer after Io attracted the amorous Jove; he was charmed to sleep and killed by Hermes. Io was identified with the Egyptian goddess Isis.

Arion. To escape sailors' violence he leaped into the sea and was saved by dolphins he charmed with his music.

artful: artistic, skilful.

Ascalon: Philistine city.

Ashtoreth (*pl.* **Ashtaroth**): Astarte, a Semitic fertility goddess, the female counterpart of Baal; identified with Aphrodite and Venus and with Diana, goddess of the moon.

Asmadai, Asmodai, Asmodeus: the evil spirit (in the Apocryphal Book of Tobit) who loved the wife of Tobit's son and killed her successive husbands, and who, by Raphael's advice, was driven away by the smell of burning fish.

aspect: in astrology, the relative position and hence the good or bad influence of the planets.

asphodel: an immortal flower of the Elysian fields.

assay: try, trial.

Assyria: a kingdom between Armenia and Babylonia; the whole Assyrian empire.

astonish: dismay, stun.

Astraea: goddess of justice who left the earth after man grew corrupt and became Virgo in the zodiac.

Athene: *see* Pallas.

Atlas: the Titan who held up the sky; mountains in northwestern Africa.

attend: wait for.

Aurora: goddess of dawn, whose chariot preceded the sun; wife of the aged Tithonus; lover of Cephalus.

Ausonia: Italy.

Auster: the south or southwest wind.

Avernus: a lake near Naples, supposed to be an entrance to Hades; Hades itself.

awful: inspiring, or filled with, awe.

azurn: azure.

Baal (*pl.* **Baalim**): a fertility god of Asia Minor, worshiped under various local forms.

Babel: the tower (Gen. 11.1–9).

Babylon: the capital of Babylonia on the Euphrates; a Protestant name for papal Rome.

Bacchus: son of Jove and Amalthea (or Semele); god of wine; inaugurator of orgiastic rites.

Bactra: capital of Bactria (Afghanistan).

baleful: pernicious; full of pain.

balm: tree or shrub yielding aromatic juice; the juice itself.

Beelzebub: another name for Satan ("the prince of the devils," Matt. 12.24; cf. Luke 11.15–19); a Philistine god (2 Kings 1.2); in *P.L.*, Satan's lieutenant. *See* Baal.

Belial: a traditional personification of "worthlessness."

Belus: "Belus Priscus, reputed a god, and honored with temples; called Bel by the Assyrians, and Baal by the Hebrews" (G. Sandys, *Relation*, 1615, p. 207).

Bethel (**Luz**): a place north of Jerusalem where Jacob had his dream (Gen. 28.11–19) and the Israelites worshiped Jereboam's golden calf (1 Kings 12.20–33).

betimes: early, soon.

blank: pale, white; disconcert(ed); powerless.

blaze: proclaim.

blow: blossom; make blossom.

blue: livid.

bolt: sift, refine; discharge.

boon: bountiful; gay.

boot: be of use, profit.

Bootes: the northern constellation, "the Ploughman" or "Bear-keeper," which follows "the Wain" or Great Bear; ancient poets often referred to its slow movement.

Boreas: north wind.

bravery: finery; boasting.

Briareos: a hundred-armed Titan identified with Aegaeon.

brinded: brindled; tawny and streaked.

brown: dusky, dark.

buxom: lively, healthy; yielding.

Callisto: daughter of Arcadian king Lycaon, loved by Zeus, changed into the Great Bear; her son Arcas became the Lesser or Little Bear.

Canaan: the southern coastal region of Palestine; the promised land; Philistia.

carbuncle: gem of deep red color; deep red.

Castalia: a spring on Mount Parnassus, sacred to Apollo and the Muses: one also near Antioch in Syria, on the Orontes.

Cathaian: of Cathay (northern China), supposed to be the region north of China.

Celtic: French and/or British.

center: of the earth; the earth itself.

Cephalus: the hunter loved by Aurora.

Cerberus: the three-headed or many-headed watchdog of Hades; hence Cerberean.

Ceres: mother of Proserpine; goddess of agriculture; grain.

Chalcidian: Neapolitan (the region of Naples was settled by Greeks from Chalcis in Euboea).

champaign: open level country.

Chaos: the vast sea of unformed elements between hell and heaven in *P.L.;* the god of that abyss.

charm: song.

Charybdis: a monster identified with a whirlpool in the strait of Messina, across from Scylla.

Cherub, Cherubim: *see* angels.

Chimera: a fire-breathing monster of Greek myth.

Chiron: the centaur, son of Cronos and Philyra; tutor of Achilles and Aesculapius; wounded accidentally by one of Hercules' poisoned arrows.

Chloris: wife of Zephyr and goddess of flowers (Flora).

Cimmerian: belonging to a mythical land of darkness.

Circe: daughter of the Sun who lived on an island supposedly off the southwest coast of Italy and who bewitched Odysseus' men; by Milton made the mother of Comus.

Clio: properly the Muse of History, but, as she came first in Hesiod's list (*Theog.* 77), she often stood for poetry and literature in general.

close: cadence.

coast: district, side, border.

combustion: confusion, destruction.

concoct: digest, refine.

confine: district; border; border on.

connatural: innate; of the same nature.

conscience: consciousness.

consort: harmony; band of musicians; mate; wife; join.

converse: associate, live with.

convince: confute, convict.

couched: concealed, contained.

covenant. The covenant of grace, first adumbrated in Gen. 3.15 and fulfilled in redemption through Christ, superseded the Mosaic law of works (Milton, *C.D.* 1.26–27; *P.L.* 12.285 f.).

coy: reserved, shy.

craze: break, weaken.

crisped: curled, ruffled.

cross: oblique, malign, morose.

crude: unripe, undigested, coarse, chaotic.

Cupid: god of love, whose golden shafts kindled love and whose leaden ones repelled it; son of Venus; lover of Psyche.

Cybele: wife of Cronos, mother of the gods; "the great goddess," identified with Rhea and Ops; worshiped on Mount Ida and elsewhere; she wore a turreted headdress.

Cyllene: Arcadian mountain associated with Hermes.

Cynthia: Diana; the moon.

Cypris: Aphrodite or Venus, who rose from the sea near Cyprus.

Cytherea: Venus.

Dagon: Philistine god (1 Sam. 5.1–5).

Dan: a city that marked the northern limit of Palestine; one of the tribes of Israel.

dank: water, wet.

Daphne: daughter of the river-god Peneus who, loved and pursued by Apollo, was changed into a laurel; a grove, sacred to Apollo, on the Orontes river in Syria.

Dardanian: Trojan.

day-spring: daybreak.

decent: graceful, handsome.

Dee: the river that empties into the Irish Sea near Chester; its changes of flow were believed to be good or ill omens for England or Wales.

defend: forbid.

Delia: Diana (*see* Delos).

Delos: a floating island of the Cyclades created by Poseidon and anchored by Zeus for the birth of Apollo and Artemis (Diana).

Delphos: Delphi, the seat of Apollo's oracle on Mount Parnassus; hence Delphian, Delphic.

demure: modest, sober.

denounce: declare, proclaim.

derive: divert; pass on.

determine: end.

devote(d): doomed.

Dian(a): virgin huntress and goddess of the moon; a triform divinity representing the moon's three phases and the functions of Luna, Diana, and Hecate or Proserpine; twin sister of Apollo; lover of Endymion.

diffident: distrustful.

dight: dressed, adorned.

dip: cover with moisture; dye.

Dircean: Theban (from the fountain of Dirce at Thebes).

Dis: Pluto, god of the underworld, brother of Jove and Poseidon (Neptune).

discover: reveal.

dishonest: shameful, unchaste.

dismal: evil, fatal.

dole: pain, grief.

Dominations: *see* angels.

doom: judgment, decree; condemn.

Dorian, Doric: of southern Greece; strong and plain (of music and architecture); pastoral; Pindaric.

draff: refuse.

dragon: of dragons; a serpent; Satan (Rev. 12).

Druids: bardic priests of ancient Britain.

Earth-born: Giant sons of Earth (often confused with the also Earth-born Titans) who attacked the gods in heaven.

ebon: ebony, black.

Ecbatan(a): a city of Media, a summer residence of Persian kings.

eccentric: in Ptolemaic astronomy, a planetary orbit whose center is not the earth but on a line joining the earth and sun.

Eden: a tract between the Euphrates and the Tigris (the name means "pleasant").

elect: not those who, according to Calvin, were predestined to salvation, but all who believe in Christ: loyal; especially favored.

element: one of the four elements, earth, water, air, fire, with which Neoplatonism associated various orders of spirits; the sky; natural habitation.

Eliah, Elijah: the Hebrew prophet (1 Kings 17–21; 2 Kings 2).

Elysian: paradisal, heavenly.

Elysium: the classical abode of the blessed after death; perfect bliss.

Emathian: Macedonian, Thessalian.

emprise: daring.

empyreal: celestial, indestructible.

empyrean: heaven, the abode of God and the angels.

enameled: beautified with various colors.

engine: instrument, machine, cannon.

enow: enough.

entire: unimpaired, pure.

Ephraim: the tribe and hill country in central Palestine.

equal: impartial, just.

Erebus: son of Chaos, husband and brother of Night; darkness; the entrance to Hades; Hades itself.

eremite: hermit.

error: winding.

erst: lately, formerly.

ethereal: heavenly; composed of the indestructible fifth essence.

Etna: the Sicilian volcano under which Jove imprisoned rebellious Giants and Jove's thunderbolts were forged by Vulcan.

Eurus: the east or southeast wind.

event: result, outcome.

evince: show; overcome.

exhalation: a vapor that reached the highest and hot layer of air under the sphere of fire and hence might engender meteors, comets, and other ill omens.

extenuate: make less, weaken.

fact: act, feat.

fame: rumor.

fan: wing.

farder, fardest: Milton's preferred forms for "farther," "farthest."

Fates: the Greek Moirae, Roman Parcae (Clotho, Lachesis, and Atropos), who governed human lives.

Faunus, faun: goat-footed woodland divinity.

Favonius: the west wind, the Roman equivalent of the Greek Zephyr.

firmament: the eighth sphere of fixed stars; the whole atmosphere between the earth and the ninth sphere: the sky.

first moved: the *primum mobile,* the tenth and outermost sphere (within the hard outer shell of the universe) which kept the inner spheres in motion. See note on *P.L.* 3.418.

fixed, the: the fixed stars in the eighth sphere (cf. "firmament") which had one daily rotation from west to east.

fledge: fledged.

Flora: Roman goddess of flowers.

florid: flowery, bright, ruddy.

foil: defeat.

foment: warm, nourish.

fond: foolish.

force, of: perforce, of necessity.

frequence: assembly.

frequent: in crowds; fill.

front: forehead, face; vanguard.

Furies: Eumenides, Erinyes, the three infernal deities of vengeance.

Gabriel: in the Bible one of God's special ministers, as in the annunciation to Mary; in rabbinical tradition a warrior angel.

Galilee: a region of northern Palestine.

gay: bright, showy.

genial: creative; instinctive, natural; nuptial.

Genius: local divinity (*Nativity* 186; *Il Penseroso* 154; *Arcades*; *Lycidas* 183).

Gentiles: non-Jewish, especially Graeco-Roman, peoples; heathen.

gentle: of noble birth (and character).

Giants: sons of Earth who attacked the gods (*see* Titans).

Gideon: the champion of Israel against the Midianites (Judges 6 f.).

glister: glitter.

globe: sphere, ball; earth; moon; world; company.

globose: sphere, spherical.

gloze, glozing: flatter, flattering, specious.

god: angel; heathen god.

Gordian knot: a knot in the chariot of the Phrygian king Gordius which could be untied only by the conqueror of Asia; it was cut by Alexander.

Gorgons: three women-monsters (*see* Medusa).

Graces: Euphrosyne, Aglaia, and Thalia, who personified the refinements of life. See Spenser, *F.Q.* 6.10.21–24.

grain: color, dye.

grateful: pleasing.

habit: dress.

Haemonia: an old name for Thessaly, the land of witchcraft.

Hammon: *see* Ammon.

Harpies: ravenous bird-monsters (*Aen.* 3.211 f.).

hearse: bier.

heavenly Muse: *see* Urania.

Hebe: goddess of youth, cupbearer of the gods.

Hecate: underworld goddess of witchcraft; one aspect of the triune Diana.

Helicon: *see* Aonia.

Hercules: son of Zeus and Alcmena, the wife of Amphitryon; hero of the twelve labors.

Hermes (Mercury): son of Zeus and Maia, grandson of Atlas and Pleïone; messenger of the gods; marshal of the shades of the dead; giver of sleep.

Hermes Trismegistus ("thrice-great"): supposed author of Neoplatonic books written at Alexandria in the second and third centuries A.D., which, translated by the Florentine Platonist Marsilio Ficino, had much influence.

Hesperian: relating to the Hesperides; western; Italian; Spanish.

Hesperides: the daughters of Hesperus who guarded the golden apples; their gardens, off or in northwest Africa.

Hesperus: father of the Hesperides; the evening star.

highth: Milton's preferred form for "height."

hoar: gray, white, old.

horrid: rough, bristling, dreadful.

Hours: daughters of Zeus and Themis, goddesses of the seasons, especially the spring.

humor: the earth's moisture; one of the four humors of the body (blood, phlegm, choler, melancholy), the proportions of which determined a person's constitution and character.

hundred: Milton's preferred form was "hunderd."

Hyacinth: a Spartan prince loved by Apollo, whose quoit, deflected by the jealous Zephyr, killed him; from his blood came the flower, marked with the exclamation of woe, AI, AI.

Hydra: a many-headed serpent killed by Hercules.

Hylas: a young companion of Hercules, drawn down into the water by amorous nymphs (Theocritus, *Id.* 13).

Hymen: god of marriage.

Hymettus: hills near Athens famous for honey.

Hyperborean: northern.

Iapetus: a Titan, son of Heaven and Earth, father of Prometheus and Epimetheus; sometimes identified with Japhet, Noah's son.

Iberian: Spanish.

Ida: a mountain (1) in Crete where Jove was reared (2) near Troy, where Cybele was worshiped and where Paris judged the three goddesses.

Ilium: Troy.

impaled: surrounded.

impregn: impregnate.

impute: charge, attribute, transfer.

Ind: India.

Indus: river of northwest India.

infer: imply.

influence: of the stars (astrology).

instinct: impelled, inspired.

intend: consider, attend to.

Iris: goddess of the rainbow, daughter of Thaumas.

Isis: Egyptian goddess, sister and wife of Osiris, represented with a cow's horns; identified with Io.

Israel: Jewish nation; Jacob.

its: a word used only three times in Milton's verse: *Nativity* 106; *P.L.* 1.254 and 4.813; elsewhere he uses "his" or "her."

Ixion: a Greek king who, taken to heaven by Zeus, attempted to make love to Hera, but, through Zeus's contrivance, embraced a phantom and begot a centaur.

Jacob: son of Isaac; progenitor of the Israelites (Gen. 25–49).

Japhet: *see* Iapetus.

Jephthah: leader of the Gileadites against the Ammonites (Judges 11–12).

Jordan: the river forming the eastern boundary of Canaan, with two main sources at Dan and Paneas.

Joseph: son of Jacob and Rachel; father of Ephraim and Manasseh, for whom two tribes of Israel were named.

Jove: *see* Jupiter.

Judea: the southern division of Palestine, west of the Jordan and the Dead Sea.

Judah: the Jewish tribe west of the Dead Sea.

Juno (Hera): wife of Jupiter and queen of the gods.

Jupiter: Roman equivalent of Zeus; son of Cronos (Saturn) and chief of the Olympian gods.

Justice: *see* Astraea.

kind: nature, race, genus.

kindly: natural.

landscape: Milton's word was "lantskip."

Latona: mother of Apollo and Diana.

laver: bath, bowl.

lawns: open spaces in or between woods.

Lethe: the river of forgetfulness in Hades; Hades itself.

Leucothea: the name of Ino when she became a sea goddess; mother of Melicertes (Palaemon); identified with the Roman goddess of the dawn, Matuta.

Libya: the region between Egypt and Cyrenaica; Africa in general.

liquid: flowing, clear.

list: please, choose; listen.

living: brilliant, vivid; instinct with life.

longitude: from east to west; west.

Love: *see* Cupid.

Lucifer: "light-bringer," morning star (Venus); sun; Satan.

Luz: *see* Bethel.

main: expanse; universe; strong, important.

Mammon: "wealth" (Matt. 6.24), hence traditionally personified as a devil; cf. Spenser, *F.Q.* 2.7.

manna: Exod. 16.13–36.

mantling: spreading.

manure: cultivate.

massy: massive, strong, heavy.

maugre: in spite of.

Media: country south of the Caspian Sea.

Medusa: a Gorgon whose face turned beholders to stone and whose head was cut off by Perseus.

Memnon: a handsome Ethiopian prince who fought in the Trojan War; son of Tithonus, the mythical founder of Susa, and Aurora.

Memphian: Egyptian (from Memphis, the early capital).

Mercury: *see* Hermes.

Michael: the chief of angels (Milton, *C.D.* 1.9; Jude 9; Rev. 12.7).

mid-air, middle air: in tradition the middle layer of the threefold atmosphere surrounding the earth, a region cold, misty, stormy, and the special haunt of demons.

Moab: a nation east of the Dead Sea.

Moloch ("king"): a heathen god to whom human sacrifices were made (Lev. 18.21; 1 Kings 11.7; 2 Kings 23.10, etc.).

moment: force, weight.

mood: mode.

morning star: Lucifer, Venus.

mortal: subject to death; fatal; human, earthly.

murmurs: spells.

Muses: daughters of Zeus and Mnemosyne, inspiring goddesses of poetry, arts, and sciences; born in Pieria, near Mount Olympus; associated also with Mounts Parnassus and Helicon.

mysterious(ly): symbolical(ly).

mystic, mystical: mythical; symbolical.

Narcissus: the beautiful youth loved by the nymph Echo; enamored of his own image in a pool, he pined away and was changed into a flower.

nectared: heavenly, immortal.

Neptune (Poseidon): god of the sea.

Nereus: sea-god, father of the sea-nymphs; the sea itself.

nerves: sinews, strength.

nice: fastidious, refined, exact.

Night. Night and Erebus were children of Chaos and husband and wife; Night's chariot corresponded to that of Aurora or Phoebus.

Nineveh: the capital of Assyria on the Tigris, supposedly founded by Ninus (cf. Susa below).

Ninus: *see* Nineveh.

nitre, nitrous: in theory the air contained nitrous particles needed for combustion as well as for breathing, etc.

numbers: verses.

obdured: hardened.

obnoxious: liable, exposed to.

obsequious: obedient, following.

observe: honor, obey.

obvious: exposed, in the way.

Oceanus: a Titan, son of Heaven and Earth; god of the river encircling the earth.

odors: spices.

officious: dutifully serviceable.

Og: king of Bashan (Num. 21.33–35; Deut. 3.1–4, 11).

Olympus: the mountain range between Thessaly and Macedonia; the home of the gods; the Christian heaven.

opacous: dark, opaque.

Ops: *see* Cybele.

optic glass, tube: telescope.

orb: celestial sphere or body; the earth; circle; wheel.

orbicular: with circular motion; spherical.

Oreb: the mountain north of the Red Sea, including the peak of Sinai.

orient: eastern, rising, bright.

Orion: a giant hunter who had amatory vicissitudes; a constellation associated with storms.

Orontes: a Syrian river.

Orpheus: the archetypal poet: son of the Muse Calliope; his music charmed beasts, rivers, and trees and won his wife Eurydice

back from Pluto, though he lost her again by looking back; torn to pieces on the banks of the Hebrus by Thracian Bacchantes.

Orus (Horus): Egyptian god, son of Osiris and Isis, represented with a hawk's head.

Osiris: the chief Egyptian god, represented as a bull; brother and husband of Isis.

ounce: lynx.

Ouse. Milton's references are probably to the midland river that flows into the Wash; a Yorkshire Ouse joins the Humber.

Pales: a Roman goddess of sheep and shepherds.

Palladian: learned (from Pallas Athene).

Pallas Athene (Minerva): virgin goddess of wisdom and war, who sprang full-grown from the head of Zeus and whose shield bore the head of the Gorgon Medusa.

Pan: god of shepherds and of nature; a lover of music; in Renaissance poetry sometimes used for Christ, the good shepherd. See note on *P.L.* 2.266.

Paphos: the town in Cyprus which had the chief temple of Aphrodite (Venus); hence "Paphian."

pard: leopard.

Pareus, David (1548–1622): a German Protestant theologian often cited in Milton's prose works.

parle: parley, discussion.

Parnassus: a double-peaked mountain in central Greece which had Delphi and the Castalian spring on its slopes.

passing: exceedingly.

Pegasus: the winged horse associated with the Muses and with Bellerophon.

Pelops: progenitor of Atreus, Agamemnon, and other tragic figures. He was boiled by his father Tantalus as a feast for the gods; when he was restored to life by a second boiling, a missing part of a shoulder (which Demeter had eaten) was replaced by ivory.

Pelorus: a Sicilian promontory near Mount Etna.

Peneus: a river flowing through the Thessalian vale of Tempe; as a god, father of Daphne.

Peor: Baal-Peor, one of the many local Baals (Num. 25.3, 18, etc.).

pernicious: destructive, deadly.

Phaethon: son of Phoebus and ill-fated driver, for a day, of his father's sun-chariot.

Philistines: non-Semitic immigrants into Canaan, on the south coast of Palestine.

Philomel(a): the nightingale (see *Elegiac Verses*, note 7).

Phlegethon: a fiery river of Hades.

Phoebus: *see* Apollo.

phoenix: a mythical bird, unique of its kind, which died every 500 years, was reborn from its own ashes, and carried these to the temple of the sun at Heliopolis in Egypt (Ovid, *Met.* 15.391–407); Milton (*P.L.* 5.274) uses the nearby city of Thebes (the two names were traditionally interchangeable). The phoenix became a Christian symbol of resurrection.

Pieria: *see* Muses.

pioneers: sappers, engineers.

plat: plot of ground.

Ploughman: *see* Bootes.

Pluto: god of the underworld.

pole: the sky; North or South Pole; the imaginary axle of the universe, coinciding with the North Star.

Pomona: Roman goddess of fruit trees.

Pontus: region southeast of the Black Sea; the Sea itself.

port: bearing, demeanor.

pretense: claim.

prevent: anticipate.

Prometheus: son of the Titan Iapetus who stole fire from heaven to give to man (sometimes a metaphor for poetic inspiration).

proper: own.

Proserpin(e)(a): daughter of Ceres and Jove, abducted by Pluto from the vale of Enna in Sicily.

Proteus: old man of the sea, with the power of prophecy and of changing his shape; "shepherd" of seals.

pulse: beans, peas, etc.

Punic: Carthaginian, African.

Pythian: from Pytho, an early name for Delphi, where Apollo slew the Python and where the Pythian games he instituted were held.

Python: a huge serpent, born of the slime after Deucalion's flood, killed by Apollo.

quaint: elaborate, ingenious, dainty, odd.

quintessence: the fifth and ethereal substance, a sublimation of the four elements, of which the heavens and stars were made (*see* element).

quire: choir.

quit: be or set free from; acquit, resign; pay.

ramp: spring; rear up.

reck: concern, care.

recollect: summon up, rally.

reign: power, realm, rule.

reins: kidneys; seat of affections and emotions.

reluctance, reluctant: resistance, struggling.

remorse: remorse, pity.

represent: present to the mind.

reprobate: wicked, damned.

Rhea: daughter of Uranus and Ge (Heaven and Earth), wife of Cronos (Saturn); mother of the gods; identified with Cybele and Ops; also, in some myths, the wife of Ammon, the father (by Amalthea) of Bacchus.

right reason: the philosophic conscience, the power, implanted by God in all men, to apprehend truth and moral law (a Christian legacy from classical thought); cf. Milton, *C.D.* 1.2, 12, and 26, and the note on *P.L.* 6.176.

Romulus: the founder of Rome, called Quirinus after his deification.

round: make the rounds or circuit.

rout: band, crowd; defeat and flight.

rubied: ruby-colored.

ruin: fall, destruction (*ruina*); throw down, cause to fall.

ruth: pity.

sad: serious, sober, steadfast.

Samos: a large island near Asia Minor; the birthplace of Pythagoras.

Saturn (Cronos): son of Heaven and Earth; rebelled against Ophion, the ruler of Olympus, and reigned himself, creating a golden age; dethroned by his own son Jove (Zeus); in Roman myth, king of Italy in the golden age; in astrology, associated with contemplation and melancholy (cf. "saturnine"); in alchemy, with lead.

Satyrs: wanton sylvan divinities with some animal characteristics.

Scorpion: one of the signs in the zodiac.

Scylla: a destructive monster inhabiting a rock in the strait of Messina, opposite the whirlpool of Charybdis.

Scythians: barbarians north and northeast of the Black Sea.

secure: free from care or danger; confident.

seek to: be at a loss.

Seleucia: the capital of Alexander's general Seleucus, near Baghdad.

Semele: consumed by lightning when her lover Jove appeared to her in full splendor.

sentence: opinion, judgment.

Seon: Sihon, an Amorite king (Num. 21.21 f.; etc.).

Seraph, Seraphim: *see* angels.

shade: tree, bush, foliage.

shew: show.

shroud: shelter.

Sicanian: Sicilian.

Silvanus: an Italian wood-god; loved the boy Cyparissus, who died of grief for a deer Silvanus shot and was changed into a cypress tree.

Sinai: *see* Oreb.

Sion: Zion, the hill on which the temple of Jerusalem stood; the temple; the city; the people of Israel.

solemnity: rite, festivity.

sooth: truth, true.

sort: suit, agree.

sov'ran, sovran: Milton's preferred form for "sovereign."

spare: forbear, withhold.

speed (*p.p.* **sped**): fare well, prosper.

spell: consider, interpret.

sphere: in the old astronomy, one of the nine or ten non-solid spheres which revolved around the earth, each of the inner seven carrying a planet (moon, Mercury, Venus, sun, Mars, Jupiter, Saturn); the outer ones were the eighth (*see* fixed), the ninth or crystalline (*P.L.* 3.482), and the tenth or *primum mobile* (*see* first moved).

For the music of the spheres see the note on *Nativity* 125 f.

spirits: the fluids, natural, vital, and animal, which were associated respectively with the liver, heart, and brain, and were the agents of action and thought.

state: stately progress; majesty; throne; canopy; statesman.

still: always, continually.

strook: struck.

Stygian: relating to the Styx; infernal.

sublime: aloft, uplifted.

submiss: submissive.

subtle: refined, cunning, artful, discerning.

success: outcome, result.

summed: grown.

Susa: the winter capital of Persian kings (biblical Shushan), said to have been founded by Tithonus, father of Memnon.

suspense: suspended, in suspense.

swage: assuage.

Sylvan: *see* Silvanus.

Syrinx: a nymph pursued by Pan and changed into a reed.

Taenarus: the southernmost tip of Greece, which had a cave regarded as an entrance to Hades; Hades itself.

take: charm, affect.

Tarsus: the chief city and port of Cilicia in Asia Minor.

Tartar: of Tartary, in central Asia.

Tartarus: Hades, hell.

Tartessian: Atlantic (west of the Spanish Tartessus).

Taurus: the Bull in the zodiac.

teemed: born; bore.

Tethys: wife of Oceanus; the ocean.

Thammuz: the Babylonian prototype of Adonis.

Thebes: a city in Boeotia; a city on the Nile.

Themis: Greek goddess of justice.

Thetis: a sea-nymph; the sea.

Thrace: the country north of the Aegean Sea.

thwart: cross; transverse; injure.

Tiresias: the blind prophet of Thebes.

Titans: children of Heaven and Earth who were subdued by Zeus and hurled into Tartarus.

Tithonus: *see* Aurora.

toil: net, snare.

tower: soar up to; flight.

towered: furnished with towers.

toy: trifle.

train: anything drawn along, especially the hinder or lower part of a body; retinue.

trains: wiles, allurements.

trick: array, adorn.

Trinacrian: Sicilian.

tuft: clump of trees.

Tuscan: Florentine, Italian.

Typhoeus: a monster and rebel whom Jove imprisoned under Etna; sometimes identified with the Egyptian god Typhon who slew his brother Osiris.

Tyrian: of Tyre in Phoenicia.

Tyrrhene, Tyrrhenian: the part of the Mediterranean southwest of Italy.

unclean: morally or ceremonially impure.

uncouth: unknown, strange, fearsome.

unexpressive: inexpressible.

unkindly: unfavorable.

unreproved: not deserving reproof.

unweeting: unwitting, unaware.

Urania: the Muse of astronomy, associated in the Renaissance with exalted and religious inspiration; the Greek name means "heavenly."

Urim and **Thummim:** symbols in the breastplate of Aaron (Exod. 28.30) and later priests which were used in divination (Num. 27.21; 1 Sam. 28.6).

utter: outer (sometimes with modern sense also).

van: wing; vanguard.

Venus: goddess of love and beauty who rose from the sea near Cyprus or Cythera; lover of Adonis; mother of Aeneas; identified with Aphrodite; as a planet, the morning star (Lucifer) and the evening star (Hesperus).

viewless: invisible.

vicissitude: alternation.

virtue: potency, strength, merit.

Virtues: *see* angels.

virtuous: powerful.

Vulcan (**Mulciber, Hephaestus**): god of fire and metal work; in some myths the child of Juno (Hera) only; thrown from heaven by Jove, he fell on the island of Lemnos.

wain: wagon, chariot.

Wain: *see* Bootes.

wardrobe: Milton's word is "wardrope."

weeds: clothes.

ween: think, expect.

what: why.

whenas: when.

worm: snake.

Word: the Logos, the Son as the manifestation and agent of God's wisdom and power (John 1.1 f.; etc.).

wreck: wreak.

Zephyr: the west wind, husband of Chloris.

INDEX

569

A B C D E F G H I J – R – 7 3 2 1 0 / 6 9 8 7 6 5